LITERATURE
AND THE
ENVIRONMENT

A READER ON NATURE AND CULTURE

Lorraine Anderson

Scott Slovic
University of Nevada, Reno

John P. O'Grady
Boise State University

THE LONGMAN LITERATURE AND CULTURE SERIES

General Editor: Charles I. Schuster, University of Wisconsin—Milwaukee

Addison
Wesley
Longman

An imprint of Addison Wesley Longman, Inc.

New York · Reading, Massachusetts · Menlo Park, California · Harlow, England,
Don Mills, Ontario · Sydney · Mexico City · Madrid · Amsterdam

Editor-in-Chief: Patricia Rossi
Senior Editor: Lisa Moore
Development Editor: Katharine Glynn
Supplements Editor: Donna Campion
Marketing Manager: John Holdcroft
Project Manager: Bob Ginsberg
Design Manager: John Callahan
Cover Designer: Kay Petronio
Cover Illustration: Vincent Van Gogh, "Orchard," 1888/Planet Art
Prepress Services Supervisor: Valerie A. Vargas
Print Buyer: Hugh Crawford
Text Design: David Munger/DTC
Electronic Page Makeup: Karen Milholland/DTC
Printer and Binder: The Maple-Vail Book Manufacturing Group
Cover Printer: Coral Graphic Services, Inc.

For permission to use copyrighted material, grateful acknowledgment is made to the copyright holders on pages 530–535, which are hereby made part of this copyright page.

Library of Congress Cataloging-in-Publication Data

Literature and the environment : a reader on nature and culture /
  [compiled by] Lorraine Anderson, Scott Slovic, John P. O'Grady.
      p.   cm. -- (The Longman literature and culture series)
    Includes index.
    ISBN 0-321-01149-X
    1. Nature--Effect of human beings on--Literary collections.
  2. Culture--Environmental aspects--Literary collections. 3. Human
  ecology--Literary collections. 4. American literature.
  I. Anderson, Lorraine, 1952-   . II. Slovic, Scott, 1960-   .
  III. O'Grady, John P., 1958-   . IV. Series.
  PS509.N3L58   1998
  810.8'036--dc21   98-29877
                                                                    CIP

Please visit our website at http://longman.awl.com

ISBN 0-321-01149-X

7 8 9 10-MA-050403

CONTENTS

Part I
THE HUMAN ANIMAL   1

Our notions of nature start with how we see ourselves and other creatures.

1 OUR ANIMAL SELVES   3

What is wild and instinctual in our nature, and how do we respond to it? How does this response influence our relations with the outer world?

2 CLOSE ENCOUNTERS 63

How do we regard other creatures, and what do our encounters with them reveal about us?

3 HUNTING AND FISHING 115

Under what circumstances are we justified in taking the life of another creature? How do we handle the necessity to kill in order to live?

Part II

INHABITING PLACE   163

We work out our connections to nature in the particular place or places on earth where we spend our lives.

4 IMPRINT OF THE LAND   166

How does the experience of place affect our inner lives? How are we affected by natural versus artificial environments?

5 Visions of Home 222

What do we know about the place where we live, and what are our responsibilities—as individuals and communities—toward it?

6 POLITICS OF PLACE 297

What impact do politics and the power of one group over another have on particular places
and our experience of them?

Part III

ECONOMY AND ECOLOGY   353

Our economic ideas and values ultimately have consequences for the planetary ecosystem
of which we're a part.

7 GETTING AND SPENDING   355

How do our individual decisions about how to earn and spend money affect our own well-
being and that of the world?

8 LAND USE 402

What does our use of land say about who we are and what we value and believe?

9 PERIL AND RESPONSE 450

What are the prospects for the human enterprise given our current ways of thinking about the world?

CONTENTS BY GENRE

Essays: Personal Narrative

ESSAYS: SOCIAL ANALYSIS

BIOGRAPHY

CULTURAL COMMENTARY

FOREWORD

If an answer does not give rise
to a new question from itself,
it falls out of the dialogue.
—Mikhail Bakhtin

The volumes in the *Longman Literature and Culture Series* present thoughtful and diverse approaches to the teaching of literature. Each is devoted to a special topic and designed for classes ranging from composition courses with a literature emphasis to introductory courses in literature to literature courses that focus on special topics, American studies, and cultural studies courses. Although the selections in each volume can be considered in terms of their formal literary properties, the power of these works also derives from their ability to induce students to read, reread, think, sort out ideas, and connect personal views to the explicit and implicit values expressed in the literary works. In this way, the *Longman Literature and Culture Series* teaches critical analysis and critical thinking, abilities that will serve all students well, regardless of their majors.

Popular Fiction focuses on prose fiction through the exploration of many types of fiction not ordinarily studied in the college classroom. *Literature and the Environment, Literature, Culture, and Class, Literature, Race, and Ethnicity,* and *Literature and Gender* are all multigenre, with thematic clusters of readings exploring the central topic of the individual anthologies. These thematic clusters create series of links, allusions, and inflections among a wide variety of texts, and in this way, invite students to read actively and think critically. Meaningful contexts for the readings are provided by an introduction to each volume as well as chapter introductions and headnotes for every selection. An Instructor's Manual is also available for each anthology. These anthologies can be used in combination with each other, individually, and with other texts to suit the focus of the course.

- *Popular Fiction: An Anthology,* by Gary Hoppenstand (Michigan State University), is a collection of historical and contemporary works of prose fiction, including such authors as Edgar Allan Poe, Janet Dailey, Tony Hillerman, Walter Mosely, Stephen King, and Octavia Butler, and representing five popular genres: detective, romance, adventure, horror, and science fiction.

- *Literature and the Environment: A Reader on Nature and Culture*, by Lorraine Anderson, Scott Slovic (University of Nevada, Reno), and John P. O'Grady (Boise State University), is a thematic multigenre anthology that explores our relationship to nature and the role literature can play in shaping a culture responsive to environmental realities. It includes early writers such as John Muir, Henry David Thoreau, and Mary Austin, alongside contemporary voices such as Gary Snyder and Terry Tempest Williams.

- *Literature, Culture, and Class: A Thematic Anthology*, by Paul Lauter (Trinity College) and Ann Fitzgerald (American Museum of Natural History), is a consideration of class in "classless" America, including such authors as Edith Wharton, F. Scott Fitzgerald, Woody Guthrie, Alice Childress, Jimmy Santiago Baca, and Dorothy Allison. The selections allow students to better understand their own economic, political, and psychological contexts through learning about the ways in which social class and "class consciousness" have been experienced and changed over time in America.

- *Literature, Race, and Ethnicity: Contested American Identities*, by Joseph Skerrett (University of Massachusetts, Amherst), invites students to examine the history, depth, and persistence of the complex cultural attitudes toward race and ethnicity in America. The selections span from the late 1700s to the present, including a variety of genres from poems and letters to fiction and autobiography, essays, speeches, advertisements, and historical documents, with works by such writers as Thomas Jefferson, Frederick Douglass, Jacob Riis, Henry James, Langston Hughes, Maxine Hong Kingston, Constantine Panunzio, Lorna Dee Cervantes, Lawson Inada, and Louise Erdrich.

- *Literature and Gender: Thinking Critically Through Fiction, Poetry, and Drama*, by Robyn Wiegman (University of California, Irvine) and Elena Glasberg (California State University), assembles a provocative array of literary texts by such writers as Charlotte Perkins Gilman, Ernest Hemingway, Adrienne Rich, Tobias Wolf, Sherman Alexie, and Rita Dove, which explore the links between cultural beliefs, social institutions, sexual roles, and personal identity.

Although no single anthology, or series for that matter, can address the full complexity of literary expression, these anthologies do hope to engage students in the critical process of analysis by connecting literary texts to current social and cultural debates. In addition, these anthologies frame literature in pedagogically innovative ways, ways that will enable those students who find literature difficult to read, who think meaning is somehow locked inside a text, to critically engage with issues of interpretation, biography, and context. In this way, students begin to see that literature is a cultural expression that emerges from a complex consideration of and response to the world they share with the writers they read.

Very often, literary texts invite discussion on explosive issues in the classroom, provoking students to argue about the sexism of a short story or the racism expressed by a character. These anthologies, however, encourage students to take a step backward so that they can interrogate the cultural contexts of diverse works of literature. This shift away from the personal and toward the cultural should invite thoughtful and considered classroom discussion. Once students perceive this cultural frame, they will be better able to engage with texts, to see them as both profound expressions of the ordinary and eloquent achievements written by real people living in real time.

In addition, no set of anthologies can hope completely to resolve what is intended by the two central terms that anchor this discussion: "literature" and "culture." One of the most exciting contemporary discussions in English departments today centers on the very definition of literature: what it is, what it excludes, and what makes it work. If figuring out what we mean by "the literary" is difficult, determining the definition of "culture" is probably impossible. Like "nature," a term that John Stuart Mill analyzed over a hundred years ago, "culture" seems to designate everything or nothing at all. Is it something we make or does it make us? Is culture a neutral term designating human social activity, or something akin to class and status, a quality that marks you as either refined or vulgar, well-bred or common?

Not that we presume to have the correct answers or even all the appropriate questions. We realize that both the questions and the answers will be tentative and exploratory. Literature, it seems to all of us involved in this series, demands a willingness to maintain uncertainty, to probe multiple possibilities. It invites analysis and demands interpretation. It provokes conversations. This is the intention of the *Longman Literature and Culture Series:* to invite readings and rereadings of texts and contexts, of literature within the cultural and culture within the literary. Rather than answers, these anthologies pose questions and invitations.

Crafted to the vision of the individual editors, *Popular Fiction, Literature and the Environment, Literature, Culture, and Class, Literature, Race, and Ethnicity,* and *Literature and Gender* present an extraordinary range of material in such a way as to unsettle previous readings and provoke new ones. We hope the *Longman Literature and Culture Series* provides a welcoming invitation to all students to see that literature is deeply reflective of the fabric of everyday life.

CHARLES I. SCHUSTER
General Editor
University of Wisconsin, Milwaukee

ACKNOWLEDGMENTS

The authors of this volume would like to express their gratitude to the reviewers, who provided invaluable feedback and suggestions: Michael Branch, University of Nevada, Reno; Joanne Campbell, Indiana University; Sue Ellen Campbell, Colorado State University; Gregory Clark, Brigham Young University; Michel de Benedictis, Miami Dade Community College; Evelyn Funda, Utah State University, Logan; Cheryll Glotfelty, University of Nevada, Reno; Patrick Lawler, State University of New York, Syracuse; Thomas Lyon, Utah State University; Ian Marshall, Penn State Altoona; Michael McDowell, Portland Community College; Mike Meeker, Winona State University; David Robertson, University of California, Davis; Kent Ryden, University of Southern Maine; Don Scheese, Gustavus Adolphus College; Matthias Schubnell, University of the Incarnate Word; William Stephenson, Northland College; Lisa Stroud, Liberty University; David Teague, University of Delaware; Barbara Valdez, Boise State University; Lynn West, Spokane Community College.

TO THE STUDENT

American culture at the end of the twentieth century is in the throes of working out a new relationship with nature. We've all heard the warnings: human activity is changing the atmosphere, greatly accelerating the extinction of species, poisoning bodies of water and land, upsetting the crucial balance between food supplies and population, and using up nonrenewable resources at an alarming rate. Now we're faced with the task of deciding how—or whether—to respond. Ultimately this task faces each of us and comes down to the daily decisions we make about how we will live—what we will eat, what kind of dwelling and community we will live in, how we will get around, what we will spend our time and money on, what kind of work we will do, and how we will relate to places, other people, and other species.

Literature can help us think about these choices. It can act as both a mirror and a prod, showing us who we are and challenging us to imagine who we might be. By bringing together literature about the environment from a wide range of authors and from a variety of genres (short stories, poetry, and essays), we hope to help you explore both your relationship to nature and the role literature can play in shaping a culture responsive to environmental realities. We've also added to the mix writings that reflect the momentary concerns of our time and place and round out the cultural context, including journalism, letters, biography, memoir, and cultural commentary.

Fortunately, there is no lack of good writing on the environment. Some of the finest literature created in the last forty years addresses, implicitly or explicitly, the place of humans in the natural world. Indeed, the deepening of our environmental predicament has been accompanied by an unprecedented burgeoning of the number of humans putting pen to paper to celebrate connections with plants and animals, to muse on the farmer's relationship to the land, to report travels to distant frontiers where wilderness can still be found, to lament the loss of places and species dear to them, to ponder the cultural and philosophical and economic roots of the worsening crisis, and to praise some little corner of the earth where daily life still maintains contact with what is good, wild, and healthy. You'll meet many of these contemporary voices in the pages that follow. You'll also meet some of the forerunners of the current crop, such as Henry David Thoreau, Sarah Orne Jewett, John Muir, and Mary Austin. Although this book by no means encompasses a full roster of the historical antecedents of today's nature writers—which would need to include William Bartram, Nathaniel Hawthorne, James and Susan Fenimore Cooper, Ralph Waldo Emerson, Charles Darwin, Celia Laighton Thaxter, Herman Melville, Willa Cather, John Burroughs, Gene Stratton-Porter, Ernest Thompson Seton, Anna Botsford Comstock, Liberty Hyde Bailey, and Theodora Stanwell-Fletcher, among others—it nevertheless gives some indication of the long and rich tradition of nature writing in America.

We've organized the selections in this book into three parts. Part I, "The Human Animal," focuses attention on a salient fact: that to find nature we need look no farther than our own bodies, which are subject to the same irrevocable laws that govern all other living things, and our own minds and spirits, which feel a magnetic pull toward wildness and react against being overly domesticated. How do we choose to respond to what is wild and instinctual in ourselves? How do we see ourselves in relation to other creatures? How do we handle the necessity to kill in order to live? These questions are explored in the chapters "Our Animal Selves," "Close Encounters," and "Hunting and Fishing."

Part II, "Inhabiting Place," examines our relationship to those places on earth where we spend our lives. For better or for worse, the landscape of our childhood and youth makes an indelible imprint on our psyche. How can living in close contact with wild beauty nourish our souls, and what happens to us when wild places are paved over and we spend our days and nights in artificial environments? How much do we really know about the places where we live and the natural systems that support us there, and what are our responsibilities toward those places? What impact do politics and the power of one group over another have on particular places and our experience of them? The chapters "Imprint of the Land," "Visions of Home," and "Politics of Place" take up these questions.

Part III, "Economy and Ecology," considers the impact of our economic ideas and values on the planetary ecosystem of which we are a part. How do our individual decisions about how to earn and spend money affect both our own well-being and that of the larger world? What does our use of land say about what we value and believe? And what are the prospects for the human enterprise given our current ways of thinking about the world? These questions provide the impetus for the chapters "Getting and Spending," "Land Use," and "Peril and Response."

A culture is always in the process of creating itself. With our lives and our works we tell each other stories about what we believe and hope to be true. When we see the results of those stories we can make corrections based on our experience of what is desirable. If we see that our behavior is at odds with the increasingly urgent messages we are receiving from the biosphere, we can make changes. You are invited to read this book as a record of the stories that others have lived and are living, and then to live your own story. Work out a new relationship with nature, inner and outer, based on your own experience, not solely on the experiences of others. Trust yourself and know that the generations to come are counting on you to live the way you'd like the rest of the world to live. How well you succeed might just determine the fate of the earth.

*Our notions of nature
start with how we see ourselves and other creatures.*

THE HUMAN

ANIMAL

In our times, humans have walked on the moon and conceived life in a test tube. Although our scientific understanding and technological mastery of nature has enabled these marvelous achievements and increased our comfort and security, it has also exacted a price: our instinctual, emotional identification with nature has diminished. "Little we see in Nature that is ours," lamented the romantic poet William Wordsworth in an earlier era when the Industrial Revolution had begun to move masses of people off farms and into factories. In the face of this loss, some still-wild part of us searches for a way to reconnect with the natural world. Our long- ing inevitably returns us to our ancient ties with other animals.

Animal imagery has been created in all times and places in human culture. Think of the paintings found in prehistoric caves depicting horses, deer, and oxen; think of the biblical story of Noah's ark; think of the Chinese calendar, in which each year is symbolized by an animal; think of the totems crafted by native peoples repre- senting guardian or teacher animals such as ravens and bears. From our beginnings, our conception of other animals has dictated both how we value them and how we understand ourselves, and our art and literature have articulated these themes. This first part gives a sample of the literature that brings alive our connections to what the writer Henry Beston, in his classic memoir *The Outermost House* (1928), calls those "fellow prisoners of the splendour and travail of the earth."

The selections in "Our Animal Selves" explore what is still wild and instinctual in our nature. They do this by drawing comparisons between human and animal behavior. All find that at some basic level, most often the level of bodily experience, we are more like other animals than different from them. If this is the case, we have a choice about how to respond to our animal selves. Some of the writings in this section suggest we can only feel truly alive if we embrace our wild selves. This sentiment has been expressed by the poet Carl Sandburg thus: "The more civilized we become, the deeper is the fact that back in barbarism is something of the beauty and joy of life we have not brought with us." Other selections suggest that participating in our own wild nature is a prerequisite to responding caringly to nature around us, and conversely that if we deny the deeper part of the self beyond or below the conscious mind, we may act out our unlived lives in ways destructive to the environment. Admittedly, this topic of our own participation in the animal kingdom and of giving our wildness its due is a deeply complicated one only barely touched on here.

The biologist and author Edward O. Wilson points out in *The Diversity of Life* (1992) that in the United States and Canada, more people visit zoos and aquariums than attend all professional athletic events combined, citing this as evidence of what he calls biophilia, "the connections that human beings subconsciously seek with the rest of life." When we do "come into animal presence," as the poet Denise Levertov puts it, our reactions are telling. The selections in "Close Encounters" recount meetings between humans and other animals that reveal something of our attitudes toward those others and toward ourselves. Do we respond with wonder and awe, with fear, or with a callous disregard born of seeing too many flattened bodies of animals on our highways? "What happens to our hearts when we see them wounded or hurt?" wonders the psychologist James Hillman, who suggests that religion grew out of the human relationship to the animal. Do we see ourselves as superior to other animals or as fellow travelers? This latter question is crucial today, when the fate of countless species hinges on how we answer it (a truth highlighted by commentator Rush Limbaugh's remark, "If the spotted owl can't deal with man's superiority, screw it"). The readings in this chapter begin to suggest the moral dilemmas we confront regarding nonhuman animals. They also prompt us to consider how vastly lonely we would be without other creatures, upon whom we depend for so much.

In an age when few of us participate in killing the food we eat, we are insulated from the real implications of being part of the food chain. We must look to hunters and fishermen to articulate what it means to kill in order to live. Under what circumstances are we justified in taking the life of another creature? Many different answers to this question are possible, and thus the controversy begins. Vegetarians are often vociferous in their criticism of meat eaters; animal rights activists and other people of conscience are opposed to hunting under any circumstances. On the other hand, writers such as Richard Nelson and Paul Shepard suggest there may be no better way to feel our connectedness to nature than to kill our own food, provided we do it with a sacramental attitude. In "Hunting and Fishing," this part ends with readings that examine various facets of the issue of human predation on other animals.

1

*What is wild and instinctual in our nature,
and how do we respond to it? How does this response
influence our relations with the outer world?*

OUR ANIMAL SELVES

MARY OLIVER

B. 1935

*"To pay attention, this is our endless and proper work," writes Mary Oliver
in a prose poem entitled "Yes! No!" In ten published books of poetry, Oliver
conveys a sense of the grace and serenity that can be earned if we actively
work at noticing and honoring our connections to the natural world. Her
poetry has been noticed and honored as she has become what critic Stephen
Dobyns called "one of our very best poets." She won the 1984 Pulitzer Prize
for poetry for* American Primitive *(1983) and the 1992 National Book
Award for poetry for* New and Selected Poems *(1992).*

*Born in Cleveland and educated at Ohio State University and Vassar,
Oliver has lived in Provincetown, Massachusetts, for more than thirty years.
She explains in* Sierra *magazine (November/December 1991) that one of
the reasons she continues to live there is that "things are by now so familiar that I have no choice but to look deeper, and deeper, into the ordinary."
Her process in making a poem is to start with intense observation of "the
particulars of the world," accomplished on long walks with her dog on the
Cape Cod dunes, and then to let her mind "swing out slowly to great, exciting thoughts."*

In Sierra *she goes on to explain, "Before we move from recklessness into
responsibility, from selfishness to a decent happiness, we must want to save
our world. And in order to want to save the world, we must learn to love it
—and in order to love it we must become familiar with it again. That is
where my work begins, and why I keep walking, and looking." The following poem, from* American Primitive, *shows that for Oliver, learning to love
the world starts with learning to trust and love one's own body, its appetites
and its wildness. Because mortality is a frequent theme of hers, the poem
can also be read as an injunction to love life fiercely in its particulars while
we are alive.*

THE HONEY TREE

And so at last I climbed
the honey tree, ate
chunks of pure light, ate
the bodies of bees that could not
get out of my way, ate
the dark hair of the leaves,
the rippling bark,
the heartwood. Such
frenzy! But joy does that,
I'm told, in the beginning.
Later, maybe,
I'll come here only
sometimes and with a
middling hunger. But now
I climb like a snake,
I clamber like a bear to
the nuzzling place, to the light
salvaged by the thighs
of bees and racked up
in the body of the tree.
Oh, anyone can see
how I love myself at last!
how I love the world! climbing
by day or night
in the wind, in the leaves, kneeling
at the secret rip, the cords
of my body stretching
and singing in the
heaven of appetite.

—1983

ANNIE DILLARD

B. 1945

*Although the work of Annie Dillard often focuses on encounters with the
natural world, her underlying concern is the life of the mind, especially in
moments of intense awareness. She writes, "The mental landscape is as rich
and various as the human landscape on Main Street, and as the forest landscape on the hillsides. It is all a parade. It is all interesting. Dig anywhere."*

*Dillard was born and raised in Pittsburgh, Pennsylvania, the subject of
her memoir,* An American Childhood *(1987). She earned a B.A. and an M.A.
in creative writing at Hollins College in Virginia. After graduation, she lived
in a little cabin on Tinker Creek in the Blue Ridge Mountains near the col-*

lege. The journal she kept during that time, recording her quest for the truth about life and God, became Pilgrim at Tinker Creek (1974), her first published book of prose, which won the Pulitzer Prize in 1975. She has revealed that she wrote this book from hundreds of index cards, working fifteen- to sixteen-hour stints in a room with the shades drawn at the Hollins College Library. Since Pilgrim at Tinker Creek, she has published volumes of poetry, essays, criticism, and a novel. She now lives in Middletown, Connecticut, where she is writer-in-residence at Wesleyan University.

The following essay, "Living Like Weasels," appeared in the 1982 volume Teaching a Stone to Talk: Expeditions and Encounters. It demonstrates the characteristic flamboyance and outlandishness of Dillard's prose style, calculated to startle both writer and reader into alertness. Also characteristic is the use of an encounter with a strikingly alien nature as a way of understanding more profoundly her own mental habits. The long glance she exchanges with a weasel stuns her into contemplating "the purity of living in the physical senses and the dignity of living without bias or motive."

LIVING LIKE WEASELS

A weasel is wild. Who knows what he thinks? He sleeps in his underground den, his tail draped over his nose. Sometimes he lives in his den for two days without leaving. Outside, he stalks rabbits, mice, muskrats, and birds, killing more bodies than he can eat warm, and often dragging the carcasses home. Obedient to instinct, he bites his prey at the neck, either splitting the jugular vein at the throat or crunching the brain at the base of the skull, and he does not let go. One naturalist refused to kill a weasel who was socketed into his hand deeply as a rattlesnake. The man could in no way pry the tiny weasel off, and he had to walk half a mile to water, the weasel dangling from his palm, and soak him off like a stubborn label.

And once, says Ernest Thompson Seton—once, a man shot an eagle out of the sky. He examined the eagle and found the dry skull of a weasel fixed by the jaws to his throat. The supposition is that the eagle had pounced on the weasel and the weasel swiveled and bit as instinct taught him, tooth to neck, and nearly won. I would like to have seen that eagle from the air a few weeks or months before he was shot: was the whole weasel still attached to his feathered throat, a fur pendant? Or did the eagle eat what he could reach, gutting the living weasel with his talons before his breast, bending his beak, cleaning the beautiful airborne bones?

I have been reading about weasels because I saw one last week. I startled a weasel who startled me, and we exchanged a long glance.

Twenty minutes from my house, through the woods by the quarry and across the highway, is Hollins Pond, a remarkable piece of shallowness, where I like to go at sunset and sit on a tree trunk. Hollins Pond is also called Murray's Pond; it covers two acres of bottomland near Tinker Creek with six inches of water and six thousand lily pads. In winter, brown-and-white steers stand in the middle of it, merely dampening their hooves; from the distant shore they look like miracle itself, complete with miracle's nonchalance. Now, in summer, the steers are gone. The water lilies have blossomed and spread to a green horizontal plane that is terra firma to plodding blackbirds, and tremulous ceiling to black leeches, crayfish, and carp.

This is, mind you, suburbia. It is a five-minute walk in three directions to rows of houses, though none is visible here. There's a 55 mph highway at one end of the pond, and a nesting pair of wood ducks at the other. Under every bush is a muskrat hole or a beer can. The far end is an alternating series of fields and woods, fields and woods, threaded everywhere with motorcycle tracks—in whose bare clay wild turtles lay eggs.

So. I had crossed the highway, stepped over two low barbed-wire fences, and traced the motorcycle path in all gratitude through the wild rose and poison ivy of the pond's shoreline up into high grassy fields. Then I cut down through the woods to the mossy fallen tree where I sit. This tree is excellent. It makes a dry, uphol-stered bench at the upper, marshy end of the pond, a plush jetty raised from the thorny shore between a shallow blue body of water and a deep blue body of sky.

The sun had just set. I was relaxed on the tree trunk, ensconced in the lap of lichen, watching the lily pads at my feet tremble and part dreamily over the thrust-ing path of a carp. A yellow bird appeared to my right and flew behind me. It caught my eye; I swiveled around—and the next instant, inexplicably, I was looking down at a weasel, who was looking up at me.

Weasel! I'd never seen one wild before. He was ten inches long, thin as a curve, a muscled ribbon, brown as fruitwood, soft-furred, alert. His face was fierce, small and pointed as a lizard's; he would have made a good arrowhead. There was just a dot of chin, maybe two brown hairs' worth, and then the pure white fur began that spread down his underside. He had two black eyes I didn't see, any more than you see a window.

The weasel was stunned into stillness as he was emerging from beneath an enor-mous shaggy wild rose bush four feet away. I was stunned into stillness twisted backward on the tree trunk. Our eyes locked, and someone threw away the key.

Our look was as if two lovers, or deadly enemies, met unexpectedly on an over-grown path when each had been thinking of something else: a clearing blow to the gut. It was also a bright blow to the brain, or a sudden beating of brains, with all the charge and intimate grate of rubbed balloons. It emptied our lungs. It felled the for-est, moved the fields, and drained the pond; the world dismantled and tumbled into that black hole of eyes. If you and I looked at each other that way, our skulls would split and drop to our shoulders. But we don't. We keep our skulls. So.

He disappeared. This was only last week, and already I don't remember what shattered the enchantment. I think I blinked, I think I retrieved my brain from the weasel's brain, and tried to memorize what I was seeing, and the weasel felt the yank of separation, the careening splash-down into real life and the urgent current of instinct. He vanished under the wild rose. I waited motionless, my mind suddenly full of data and my spirit with pleadings, but he didn't return.

Please do not tell me about "approach-avoidance conflicts." I tell you I've been in that weasel's brain for sixty seconds, and he was in mine. Brains are private places, muttering through unique and secret tapes—but the weasel and I both plugged into another tape simultaneously, for a sweet and shocking time. Can I help it if it was a blank?

What goes on in his brain the rest of the time? What does a weasel think about? He won't say. His journal is tracks in clay, a spray of feathers, mouse blood and bone: uncollected, unconnected, loose-leaf, and blown.

I would like to learn, or remember, how to live. I come to Hollins Pond not so much to learn how to live as, frankly, to forget about it. That is, I don't think I can learn from a wild animal how to live in particular—shall I suck warm blood, hold my tail high, walk with my footprints precisely over the prints of my hands?—but I might learn something of mindlessness, something of the purity of living in the physical senses and the dignity of living without bias or motive. The weasel lives in necessity and we live in choice, hating necessity and dying at the last ignobly in its talons. I would like to live as I should, as the weasel lives as he should. And I suspect that for me the way is like the weasel's: open to time and death painlessly, noticing everything, remembering nothing, choosing the given with a fierce and pointed will.

I missed my chance. I should have gone for the throat. I should have lunged for that streak of white under the weasel's chin and held on, held on through mud and into the wild rose, held on for a dearer life. We could live under the wild rose wild as weasels, mute and uncomprehending. I could very calmly go wild. I could live two days in the den, curled, leaning on mouse fur, sniffing bird bones, blinking, licking, breathing musk, my hair tangled in the roots of grasses. Down is a good place to go, where the mind is single. Down is out, out of your ever-loving mind and back to your careless senses. I remember muteness as a prolonged and giddy fast, where every moment is a feast of utterance received. Time and events are merely poured, unremarked, and ingested directly, like blood pulsed into my gut through a jugular vein. Could two live that way? Could two live under the wild rose, and explore by the pond, so that the smooth mind of each is as everywhere present to the other, and as received and as unchallenged, as falling snow?

We could, you know. We can live any way we want. People take vows of poverty, chastity, and obedience—even of silence—by choice. The thing is to stalk your calling in a certain skilled and supple way, to locate the most tender and live spot and plug into that pulse. This is yielding, not fighting. A weasel doesn't "attack" anything; a weasel lives as he's meant to, yielding at every moment to the perfect freedom of single necessity.

I think it would be well, and proper, and obedient, and pure, to grasp your own necessity and not let it go, to dangle from it limp wherever it takes you. Then even death, where you're going no matter how you live, cannot you part. Seize it and let it seize you up aloft even, till your eyes burn out and drop; let your musky flesh fall off in shreds, and let your very bones unhinge and scatter, loosened over fields, over fields and woods, lightly, thoughtless, from any height at all, from as high as eagles.

—1982

KENT NELSON

B. 1943

Kent Nelson took only two English courses as an undergraduate at Yale University, where he was majoring in political science, but one of these was crucial to his eventual decision to make a career out of writing. In a class called "Daily Themes," the students had to write 300-word stories every day for eight weeks, and it was this process, he noted in a 1992 interview, that taught him some crucial things about writing: "It gradually dawned on me that to write fiction you had to know everything. You had to listen to the way people talked, you had to observe how they acted, you had to study the environment. That was a powerful revelation to me. Twenty-four hours a day, you're paying attention to everything you can pay attention to with the intention of learning from it. You have to train yourself."

Although he went on to earn a degree in environmental law from Harvard, Nelson has never practiced law. Instead, he has supported himself over the years with a series of part-time jobs as a tennis professional, city judge, travel agent, squash coach, bartender, and farmhand. More recently, Nelson has worked intermittently as a distinguished visiting professor at various universities, including Auburn University and the University of Alabama-Tuscaloosa. He has published three novels, Cold Wind River *(1981),* All Around Me Peaceful *(1989), and* Language in the Blood *(1991), the most recent of which received the Edward Abbey Ecofiction Award in 1992. His short story collections include* The Tennis Player *(1977) and* The Middle of Nowhere *(1991). Nelson has been honored with two grants from the National Endowment for the Arts, among other prizes and awards; two of his stories have been anthologized in* The Best American Short Stories.

Born in Cincinnati, Nelson began taking an interest in nature, especially birds, when he was growing up in Colorado Springs. An avid bird-watcher, he has recorded more than 670 species on his "life list." Much of Nelson's fiction is concerned with birds, either as a central narrative element or an incidental detail of place. The following story, "Irregular Flight" (1996), explores the passions of two lonely scientists whose shared love for birds draws them together in search of Cook's Petrel, an oceangoing bird rarely sighted inland. Nelson's characters, Claire and Slater, seeking to witness the irregular appearance of the petrel near California's Salton Sea, experience instead their own mysterious flights of fear and desire.

IRREGULAR FLIGHT

Claire had heard about the vagrant Thursday afternoon on the bird tape in L.A. and called me in Tucson. She couldn't get away from an early meeting at her lab, but met me at five at the post office in Indio. When I arrived she was sitting in the shade of her Land Rover, dressed in shorts and a loose khaki shirt and hiking boots. She'd cut her hair since I'd last seen her, and she looked slimmer, too, as if she'd been exercising. Yet my initial impression as she got up was not of her appearance so much as something else less tangible. The slow way she lifted her body, the way she tilted her head and shielded her eyes from the sun made her seem younger and patient and more threatening. "We'll take my car," she said. "The light's going fast, so we'd better hurry."

I got my binoculars and my scope and my overnight bag from the trunk of my Corolla. Claire opened the well of the Rover, and I threw my stuff in beside the cooler and her camping gear. "Who found the bird?" I asked.

"Strachen Donelly."

"You think the sighting is reliable?"

"One-hundred per cent."

"And you got directions?"

"They were on the tape. North shore, Salton Sea."

"A petrel could be anywhere."

"It could already be gone."

We got into the Rover and Claire started the engine, revved it, and we took off to the south. I rolled down the window and let the breeze blow in.

It was hard to pin down my history with Claire. When I knew her in Tucson she was married to a man I never met. She was a biologist, a little overweight, dark hair. For more than a year we shared a ride to the research institute where we worked—twenty minutes each way. We spoke mostly about the ongoing project which was to study the effects of radiation on flora and fauna in the zones of government nuclear testing in the Southwest. Our relationship was professional: she never asked me a personal question and never confessed anything about herself. At the same time, perhaps in the absence of anyone else, I thought she was my friend. I sensed things about her—how much more alert she was in the afternoons when we drove home, how on a particular day she was aware of the wind from the north; or sometimes I felt a distant anger from her, as if she knew she was not happy.

But she knew nothing about me. I lived alone. My father had died when I was a child, and my mother, who was slightly disturbed, lived back East in New England. I was not a social person. I had been to college, of course, and to graduate school in chemistry, and had simply never had the need to be with people. I had no expectations or desires. And yet I was perfectly at ease in this solitariness. I didn't want company. I liked my work, was enthralled by birds, and fascinated by what was happening in the wider world.

I had terrible insomnia, and often to appease the demons I stayed up all night and watched the international news. That I saw the slaughter in Rwanda, or a man walking on the moon, or watched as it was happening a bomb falling into a building in Iraq was thrilling to me, not for the occurrences themselves, but for their comprehension—that I could know all at once everything everywhere.

It was by accident that I discovered Claire's love for birds. One day on a group fact-finding excursion to a missile range—there were six of us; I was driving—I spotted a bird flying low over brush along a streambank. I had not seen it well—just a gray blur—but I knew it was a bird of prey. It was larger than a kestrel, smaller than a buteo. I slowed down and followed its flight, and from the backseat Claire said, "Mississippi Kite."

I pulled off the road and stopped. "Are you sure?"

"It's a kite, not hovering, and it has a black tail."

I trained my binoculars out the window and saw the long, pointed wings of a kite, the black, flared tail Claire had noticed. I was shocked at her precision, how she had seen so much in so brief a moment, how she had kept such a secret as bird-love from me all that time.

"Come on, Slater, keep driving," one of my colleagues said. "We want to get there some day and home again."

After that, we talked birds on our daily commute. Claire had traveled in quest of rarities—to Alaska, South Texas, the offshore islands of both coasts. Her knowledge was more extensive than mine. She knew biology and courtship rituals, field marks, food sources, habitat, and range overlaps. Compared to her, I was an amateur.

As the days went by, the commute seemed shorter. What I learned of birds, the places Claire had been, the details of her life startled me. I discovered, for example, that she had once spent a week on an island in the Bering Sea, alone, studying the nesting behavior of Arctic foxes and kittiwakes. The foxes had been introduced to kill rodents which plagued the Aleuts, but once the rodents were hard to find, the foxes preyed on birds. The birds had evolved a way to protect their young. When a fox appeared, the birds flew off their cliffside nests, and the fox finding the aban-doned fledglings, was lured down the steep terrain. When he had gone far enough, the birds swooped in and knocked him from the cliff into the water a hundred feet below. It was not so much the kittiwake behavior that interested me as that Claire had viewed it. She had the desire to be there, the patience and stamina to endure the cold sea breezes, the rugged terrain, and to still speak of the experience with wonder.

My life changed gradually. I slept better at night, and because of that, though I was still mesmerized by world events, I did not follow them so assiduously. On weekends I drove to the mountain canyons south of the city where the year-round streams made such perfect habitat for birds. I camped and woke early and listened to Sulphur-bellied Flycatchers and Grace's Warblers, and higher up, Hepatic Tanagers singing in the morning air.

Then one day in the spring on our way home, when we were stopped at a traffic light, she looked over at me behind the wheel. It was hot out, and neither of us liked air-conditioning, so the windows were open. My left arm hung loosely over the win-dow ledge. Her expression was soft in a way I had never seen before—forlorn.

"My husband got promoted," she said. "We're moving to Los Angeles."

I heard these words, but did not believe them. The light changed. I accelerated through the intersection. Colors bled in the air around me. I smelled exhaust. It was the first glimpse I had of her personal life, and I thought of questions to ask—what about your job? How can you leave the desert? Is this what you want? But I asked nothing.

The bird we were after was Cook's Petrel, a *Pterodroma* that nested on the islands off New Zealand. It was smallish—13 inches from head to tail—and had a black M pattern across its gray wings and back. Except for its breeding period, the Cook's, like other gadfly petrels, spent its life at sea. It fed on the wing, rarely alit on the water, wandered erratically throughout the Pacific. Its status off the California coast was uncertain. Several individuals had been photographed on pelagic trips over the years, but none had ever been seen inland, none ever before at the Salton Sea.

We drove the main road from Indio to Mecca, passed a dozen migrant workers in red and yellow and blue shirts and dresses hoeing lettuce, slid by groves of date palms and oranges. To the west, ten miles distant, were the treeless, sun-weary Santa Rosa Mountains, and southeastward, the Orocopias and the Chocolates which framed the valley with a jagged horizon. I didn't know what to say to Claire. Her abandoning me—that's how it felt—had made me afraid of her.

We slowed through Mecca, a few pastel buildings, mostly run-down—a general store, a gas station, a cafe. The houses and trailers had trellises covered with bougainvillea and in the dirt yards were empty fruit crates stacked high. At the south end of town, Claire turned onto an unmarked dirt road, and we crossed an irrigation canal. She handed me a piece of paper. "You navigate," she said.

I read the directions aloud. "We stay on this road to the next bridge," I said. "Then it's one mile to an adobe house. We turn left there toward the sea." I looked out through the windshield to the fading light over the mountains. There was no sea—just the absence of trees where the water must have been and the wide sky.

"How is work?" Claire asked.

"All right."

"No new discoveries?"

"We found contaminants on Cabeza Prieta," I said.

"You always knew they were there."

"But even with the evidence, there's no way the government will let us publish it. They pay for the research, then hide the results."

"You can't be so cynical," Claire said.

"Why not?"

We raised dust behind us on the dirt track, and ahead the small steel bridge appeared. We clanked across it, then ran along a broken fenceline. The smell of orange blossoms was thick on the breeze. We passed a broken-down Ford on the berm, then came to the adobe house where, on the left, a narrow lane opened up. Claire threaded the Land Rover through the mesquite brush on either side.

We proceeded past a nearly dry alkaline pond where four Black-necked Stilts dipped their long bills into the scum. A few peeps flew up and swerved over the canal, and as we neared the end of the pond, the stilts flew, too, and wheeled away to the west where the mountains were a dark blue haze. We climbed a low rise— maybe ten feet—and there before us was the sea, a great blue-gray sheen without wind or sunlight. High white cirrus above the mountains were reflected in the water.

When Claire left Tucson, I had been lonely in the lab. I retreated into my research with a vengeance, and yet I knew my work suffered. I was like a musician who, despite his talent, cannot bring himself to the emotional risk which lets the music live. Who cared whether the chromatic patterns of genes had been altered years before by A-tests in the desert? Or that groundwater was radioactive enough to make lizards sick?

On weekends I went to the desert instead of to the mountains. I camped on creosote flats or on the edge of a dry wash in the cover of palo verde. I sat in the sun as if to let the desert erode my whole body and mind. At night I listened to the high-pitched laughter of Elf Owls that derided my vanity and the soft calls of Poorwills that made me weep.

The Salton Sea lay in a sink created eons ago by the uplifting of the mountains. The Colorado River had silted in the south end of the basin at the Gulf of California, and then had changed its course eastward, leaving a valley without water. At the turn of the last century, the U.S. Army Corps of Engineers decided to construct a canal to irrigate the Imperial Valley, but typical of the government (as they had done in all those missile test sites), they miscalculated. During a spring run-off, the river cut a new channel into the canal before the canal was ready, and for eighteen months the whole river flooded into the Salton Basin. A sea was born.

"This is where the bird was seen," Claire said. "From the beach here."

She drove ahead to the collar of gray sand bordered on either side by thick saltillos. We got out and scanned the sea quickly with binoculars. Ducks and grebes floated on the near water, and a few gulls whirled in the air above us. A line of dark cormorants filed eastward toward the distant shore.

"What's farther out?" I asked.

"Terns, mostly. Common Terns. And a Black Skimmer. Let's look with the scopes."

We set up the tripods and scopes on the rise behind the beach. My scope was a Questar which gave good resolution to 40 power, and through it the indistinguishable birds far out over the water became what Claire said they were: Common Terns, two Black Skimmers, a flock of Cinnamon Teal. Three White-faced Ibises flew as silhouettes against the paling hills.

"I don't see anything unusual," Claire said. "Do you?"

"The problem is that now there are other birds farther out."

"But you could make out the bounding arcs of the way the petrel flies."

I saw no bounding arcs. The sun vanished from the high clouds, and without that refracted whiteness, the sea light diminished to a heavy gray. I gave up scanning and walked down to the shoreline where the smell of brine rose acrid to my nostrils. I kneeled and put my hand into the water. It was warm as the air. I took off my shoes and socks—I had on shorts already—and waded around the saltillo at the edge of the beach.

On the other side where the canal fed in was a brackish cove filled with drowned trees. It must have been a riparian woodland once, before the land had been converted to orange groves, before the canal brought wasted chemicals, before the inundation. The water was shallow, slick with algae, unmoving. The bare black branches of the trees spidered into the air, and on them herons and egrets perched like huge, grotesque, faintly-colored leaves. I felt as if I had stepped into a world already destroyed.

It was Claire who made me see this place in that way, though I blamed myself. I had created the person I was at that moment, the lonely soul. I had let myself be affected by the tenuous moments of conversation driving to and from work, by her knowledge of birds I wanted to make mine, by my foolishly thinking I knew something about her. And then to be so weak as to meet her here . . .

I thought for a moment of the earthquake that must be happening at that moment in Malaysia, or the train wreck in France, the children starving in Ethiopia. But all I knew was this world before me—the cove and the far shore, the dark beach, and beyond it, the date palms waving their spiky fronds against the barren hills.

"Slater?"

"I'm right here," I said. I turned, but I could not see her through the saltillos.

"Look west, flying low."

"Where?"

"About three o'clock."

I waded out into the shallows to be clear of the brush and lifted my glasses. Dark birds winged over the water.

"Do you see the bird I see?" Claire asked.

"I don't know."

I stepped around the brush to where she was, and she stood up from her scope. "It's a possible possible," she said. "But the light's not good enough to be positive of anything."

"But it might have been?"

"Anything might be," she said. She lifted her scope and collapsed the legs of the tripod and leaned it against the fender of the Land Rover. "Are you hungry?"

I was surprised by her tone, by the casual way she let the bird go.

She went around to the back of the Rover and lifted the gate. "I have ham-and-cheese sandwiches, potato salad, and beer."

It had not occurred to me to be hungry, but I was. I took a sandwich and a beer.

Claire went off to urinate up in the higher brush, and I climbed onto the hood of the Land Rover and rested my back against the windshield. The beer was cold. The pale sea, rising breeze, and the soft lapping of the waves made me lethargic, almost sleepy. I closed my eyes and listened to the drone of insects.

I must have dozed for a few minutes because when I opened my eyes it was night. I saw the red blinking light from an airplane far away among the stars. Claire was beside me, leaning into the fender, but I could not see her well in the darkness.

"Do you love me?" she asked.

Her voice surprised me. "You're married," I said.

"Is that an answer?"

"Isn't it?"

"After all that time together, you never called me."

"You never called me."

"Today I did. I tried to think of something that you would meet me for." She paused a moment. "What do you feel, Slater? Do you never feel anything?"

I did not know how to answer, and I looked away toward the sea where faraway lights of the small towns glimmered along the black shore.

"You don't have to turn away," she said.

She walked around to the front of the Land Rover and stood up on the bumper so I had to see her. She unbuttoned her shirt and held out the corners like wings. Her skin was pale in the warm air, luminous. I do not know what gave her the courage to risk herself in this way. She must have been tired from working all day, driving from L.A., delving through the heat to the beach where we were. And yet she was able to summon the kind of desire I had never imagined. She took off her shirt and knelt down on the hood near me.

"Can you see me?" she asked.

"Yes."

"And?"

I did not answer, and she bent forward and slid her hand under my shorts and touched me.

"Is this all right?" she asked.

Everything around me dissipated into one sensation. I was on the side of a cliff, petrified of falling and at the same time wanting to fall. I reached for her hand and pushed it away.

"Let me," she said.

She unsnapped my shorts and pulled them down. I did not resist. I felt the moist moving air, the touch of her hand again, and for the first time in my life, the eerie helplessness of desire. We spent the night on the hood of the Land Rover, the feathery air moving over us like water. In the morning at dawn, we dressed and heated water on the campstove for coffee and took up our vigil on the beach. We scanned through the scopes back and forth, back and forth, for the irregular flight of the petrel that may never have been there.

—1996

GARY SNYDER

B. 1930

In a short essay near the end of Turtle Island *(1974), the volume for which he won a Pulitzer Prize, Gary Snyder describes his role as a writer: "I wish to be a spokesman for a realm that is not usually represented either in intellectual chambers or in the chambers of government." Snyder's work, deeply informed by Buddhist practice, reminds us that human beings are indeed animals and that we share this realm we call "environment" with innumerable other beings, all of whom are deserving of our respect. In addition to being a highly successful poet and author of essays (he has published more than twenty books), Snyder has long demonstrated a commitment to political activism on behalf of the nonhuman world.*

Snyder grew up on a stump farm (land that was cleared of old-growth forest, with huge stumps remaining amid the fields) north of Seattle before moving to Portland, Oregon, where he went to high school and later graduated from Reed College. A formative influence during these years was the nearby Cascade Range; at fifteen he climbed Mount St. Helens, his first major peak. When he wasn't dreaming of or climbing in the mountains of the Pacific Northwest, he was studying the indigenous cultures of the region, absorbing the lessons of what he would later call "the old ways."

During the mid-1950s he lived in northern California and played an important role, along with fellow writers Kenneth Rexroth, Philip Whalen, and Jack Kerouac, in the literary movement that has come to be known as the San Francisco Renaissance. To pursue his deep interest in Buddhism, Snyder left for Japan in 1956, where he would remain—with occasional visits back to the United States—for more than a decade. When he returned to California in the late 1960s, he settled with his family in the foothills of the northern Sierra Nevada, where he continues to live, write, and work in the community. Much of his time today is spent working with the Yuba Watershed Institute, an association of his neighbors and friends that encourages government land management agencies to treat the surrounding forests with understanding and dignity.

In Snyder's view, what is often missing in our culture's "management decisions," whether in public land agencies or in business, is graceful conduct. The essay "The Etiquette of Freedom," collected in The Practice of the Wild *(1991), gently reminds readers of our ethical obligation, an obligation that becomes a joy once we recognize that we are indeed connected to everything else. The piece of that essay excerpted here explores what it means to say that a human is an animal. Snyder's poem "Song of the Taste" (from* Regarding Wave, *1970) celebrates the food web, which is perhaps the most visible sign that we humans are part of nature.*

FROM THE ETIQUETTE OF FREEDOM

Do you really believe you are an animal? We are now taught this in school. It is a wonderful piece of information: I have been enjoying it all my life and I come back to it over and over again, as something to investigate and test. I grew up on a small farm with cows and chickens, and with a second-growth forest right at the back fence, so I had the good fortune of seeing the human and animal as in the same realm. But many people who have been hearing this since childhood have not absorbed the implications of it, perhaps feel remote from the nonhuman world, are not *sure* they are animals. They would like to feel they might be something better than animals. That's understandable: other animals might feel they are something different than "just animals" too. But we must contemplate the shared ground of our common biological being before emphasizing the differences.

Our bodies are wild. The involuntary quick turn of the head at a shout, the vertigo at looking off a precipice, the heart-in-the-throat in a moment of danger, the catch of the breath, the quiet moments relaxing, staring, reflecting—all universal responses of this mammal body. They can be seen throughout the class. The body does not require the intercession of some conscious intellect to make it breathe, to keep the heart beating. It is to a great extent self-regulating, it is a life of its own. Sensation and perception do not exactly come from outside, and the unremitting thought and image flow are not exactly outside. The world is our consciousness, and it surrounds us. There are more things in mind, in the imagination, than "you" can keep track of—thoughts, memories, images, anger, delights, rise unbidden. The depths of mind, the unconscious, are our inner wilderness areas, and that is where a bobcat is *right now.* I do not mean personal bobcats in personal psyches, but the bobcat that roams from dream to dream. The conscious agenda-planning ego occupies every tiny territory, a little cubicle somewhere near the gate, keeping track of some of what goes in and out (and sometimes making expansionistic plots), and the rest takes care of itself. The body is, so to speak, in the mind. They are both wild.

Some will say, so far so good. "We are mammal primates. But we have language, and the animals don't." By some definitions perhaps they don't. But they do communicate extensively, and by call systems we are just beginning to grasp.

It would be a mistake to think that human beings got "smarter" at some point and invented first language and then society. Language and culture emerge from our biological-social natural existence, animals that we were/are. Language is a mind-body system that coevolved with our needs and nerves. Like imagination and the body, language rises unbidden. It is of a complexity that eludes our rational intellectual capacities. All attempts at scientific description of natural languages have fallen short of completeness, as the descriptive linguists readily confess, yet the child learns the mother tongue early and has virtually mastered it by six.

Language is learned in the house and in the fields, not at school. Without having ever been taught formal grammar we utter syntactically correct sentences, one after another, for all the waking hours of the years of our life. Without conscious device we constantly reach into the vast word-hoards in the depths of the wild unconscious. We cannot as individuals or even as a species take credit for this power. It came from someplace else: from the way clouds divide and mingle (and the arms of energy that coil first back and then forward), from the way the many flowerlets of a composite blossom divide and redivide, from the gleaming calligraphy of the ancient riverbeds under present riverbeds of the Yukon River streaming out the Yukon flats, from the wind in the pine needles, from the chuckles of grouse in the ceanothus bushes.

Language teaching in schools is a matter of corralling off a little of the language-behavior territory and cultivating a few favorite features—culturally defined elite forms that will help you apply for a job or give you social credibility at a party. One might even learn how to produce the byzantine artifact known as the professional paper. There are many excellent reasons to master these things, but the power, the *virtu*, remains on the side of the wild.

Social order is found throughout nature—long before the age of books and legal codes. It is inherently part of what we are, and its patterns follow the same foldings, checks and balances, as flesh or stone. What we call social organization and order in government is a set of forms that have been appropriated by the calculating mind from the operating principles in nature.

—1991

SONG OF THE TASTE

Eating the living germs of grasses
Eating the ova of large birds

the fleshy sweetness packed
around the sperm of swaying trees

The muscles of the flanks and thighs of
soft-voiced cows
the bounce in the lamb's leap
the swish in the ox's tail

Eating roots grown swoll
inside the soil

Drawing on life of living
clustered points of light spun
out of space
hidden in the grape.

Eating each other's seed
eating
ah, each other.

Kissing the lover in the mouth of bread:
lip to lip.

—1970

CLARISSA PINKOLA ESTÉS

Clarissa Pinkola Estés, Ph.D., a poet, Jungian psychoanalyst, and cantadora *(keeper of the old stories in the Latina tradition), saw in her clinical practice many women patients who were cut off from their own creativity. She found little in traditional psychology to help these women, so she began to use the stories, folktales, and legends told to her by her family elders and to write her own stories in order to delve more deeply into "the female underworld." She began following the tracks of what she calls the Wild Woman archetype, the innate instinctual self that enables women to revel in their intuitive, sexual, and creative energies. Over many years she wrote the body of work of which her best-selling book* Women Who Run with the Wolves: Myths and Stories of the Wild Woman Archetype *(1992) is just a portion.*

Born to Mexican parents and later adopted and raised by "a family of fiery Hungarians," Estés traces her love for the Wild Woman to her child-hood. She grew up in close contact with nature near the Great Lakes, pre-ferring the ground, trees, and caves to tables and chairs and wishing only to be "an ecstatic wanderer." Then, because she came of age in a time when women were "infantilized and treated as property," she learned to disguise her wildish nature. The way back to the Wild Woman for her was through the storytelling tradition she learned from her Hungarian and Latina fore-mothers and aunts, and through the study of analytical psychology and ethnology. She earned a doctorate from the Union Institute and served as executive director of the C. G. Jung Center for Education.

The following excerpt from Women Who Run with the Wolves *comes from the chapter entitled "Joyous Body: The Wild Flesh." In this chapter, as else-where in the book, Estés makes connections between what is done to women and what is done to the planet. She does not find it surprising that a culture that pressures women to carve up their bodies to conform to narrow stan-dards of beauty also feels no qualms about carving up a landscape. She sug-gests that by "not forsaking the joy of her natural body," a woman can begin to change cultural attitudes. For Estés, there is power in the body, which we can realize if we begin to see the body as "a series of doors and dreams and poems through which we can learn and know all manner of things."*

LA MARIPOSA, BUTTERFLY WOMAN

To tell you about the power of the body in another way, I have to tell you a story, a true, rather long story.

For years, tourists have thundered across the great American desert, hurrying through the "spiritual circuit": Monument Valley, Chaco Canyon, Mesa Verde, Kayenta, Keams Canyon, Painted Desert, and Canyon de Chelly. They peer up the pelvis of the Mother Grand Canyon, shake their heads, shrug their shoulders, and hurry home, only to again come charging across the desert the next summer, look-ing, looking some more, watching, watching some more.

Underneath it all is the same hunger for numinous experience that humans have had since the beginning of time. But sometimes this hunger is exacerbated, for many people have lost their ancestors. They often do not know the names of those beyond their grandparents. They have lost, in particular, the family stories. Spiritually, this situation causes sorrow . . . and hunger. So many are trying to re-create something important for soul sake.

For years tourists have come also to Puyé, a big dusty mesa in the middle of "nowhere," New Mexico. Here the *Anasazi,* the ancient ones, once called to each other across the mesas. A prehistoric sea, it is said, carved the thousands of grinning, leering, and moaning mouths and eyes into the rock walls there.

The Diné (Navajo), Jicarilla Apache, southern Ute, Hopi, Zuni, Santa Clara, Santa Domingo, Laguna, Picuris, Tesuque, all these desert tribes come together here. It is here that they dance themselves back into lodgepole pine trees, back into deer, back into eagles and *Katsinas,* powerful spirits.

And here too come visitors, some of whom are very starved of their geno-myths, detached from the spiritual placenta. They have forgotten their ancient Gods as well. They come to watch the ones who have *not* forgotten.

The road up to Puyé was built for horse hooves and moccasins. But over time automobiles became more powerful and now locals and visitors come in all manner of cars, trucks, convertibles, and vans. The vehicles all whine and smoke up the road in a slow, dusty parade.

Everyone parks *trochimochi,* willy-nilly, on the lumpy hillocks. By noon, the edge of the mesa looks like a thousand-car pileup. Some people park next to six-foot-tall hollyhocks thinking they will just knock over the plants to get out of their cars. But the hundred-year-old hollyhocks are like old iron women. Those who park next to them are trapped in their cars.

The sun turns into a fiery furnace by midday. Everyone trudges in hot shoes, burdened with an umbrella in case it rains (it will), an aluminum folding chair in case they tire (they will), and if they are visitors, perhaps a camera (if they're allowed), and pods of film cans hanging around their necks like garlic wreaths.

Visitors come with all manner of expectations, from the sacred to the profane. They come to see something that not everyone will be able to see, one of the wildest of the wild, a living numen, *La Mariposa,* the Butterfly Woman.

The last event of the day is the Butterfly Dance. Everyone anticipates with great delight this one-person dance. It is danced by a woman, and oh what a woman. As the sun begins to set, here comes an old man resplendent in forty pounds of formal-dress turquoise. With the loudspeakers squawking like a chicken espying a hawk, he whispers into the 1930s chrome microphone, "an' our nex' dance is gonna be th' Butterfly Dance." He limps away on the cuffs of his jeans.

Unlike a ballet recital, where the act is announced, the curtains part, and the dancers wobble out, here at Puyé, as at other tribal dances, the announcement of the dance may precede the dancer's appearance by anywhere from twenty minutes to forever. Where is the dancer? Tidying up the camper, perhaps. Air temperatures over 100 degrees are common, so last-minute repairs to sweat-streaked body paint are needed. If a dance belt, which belonged to the dancer's grandfather, breaks on the way to the arena, the dancer would not appear at all, for the spirit of the belt would need to rest. Dancers delay because a good song is playing on "Tony Lujan's Indian Hour" on radio Taos, KKIT (after Kit Carson).

Sometimes a dancer does not hear the loudspeaker and must be summoned by footrunner. And then always, of course, the dancer must speak to all relatives on the way to the arena, and most certainly stop to allow the little nephews and nieces a good look. How awed the little children are to see a towering *Katsina* spirit who looks suspiciously, a little at least, like Uncle Tomás, or a corn dancer who seems to strongly resemble Aunt Yazie. Lastly, there is the ubiquitous possibility that the dancer is still out on the Tesuque highway, legs dangling out the maw of a pickup truck while the muffler smudges the air black for a mile downwind.

While awaiting the Butterfly Dance in giddy anticipation, everyone chatters about butterfly maidens and the beauty of the Zuni girls who danced in ancient red-and-black garb with one shoulder bared, bright pink circles painted on their cheeks. They laud the young male deer-dancers who danced with pine boughs bound to their arms and legs.

Time passes.

And passes.

And passes.

People jingle coins in their pockets. They suck their teeth. The visitors are impatient to see this marvelous butterfly dancer.

Unexpectedly then, for everyone is bored to scowls, the drummer's arms begin drumming the sacred butterfly rhythm, and the chanters begin to cry to the Gods for all they are worth.

To the visitors, a butterfly is a delicate thing. "O fragile beauty," they dream. So they are necessarily shaken when out hops Maria Lujan. And she is big, really *big*, like the Venus of Willendorf, like the Mother of Days, like Diego Rivera's heroic-size woman who built Mexico City with a single curl of her wrist.

And Maria Lujan, oh, she is old, very, very old, like a woman come back from dust, old like old river, old like old pines at timberline. One of her shoulders is bare. Her red-and-black *manta*, blanket dress, hops up and down with her inside it. Her heavy body and her very skinny legs made her look like a hopping spider wrapped in a tamale.

She hops on one foot and then the other. She waves her feather fan to and fro. She is The Butterfly arrived to strengthen the weak. She is that which most think of as not strong: age, the butterfly, the feminine.

Butterfly Maiden's hair reaches to the ground. It is thick as ten maize sheaves and it is stone gray. And she wears butterfly wings—the kind you see on little children who are being angels in school plays. Her hips are like two bouncing bushel baskets and the fleshy shelf at the top of her buttocks is wide enough to ride two children.

She hops, hops, hops, not like a rabbit, but in footsteps that leave echoes.

"I am here, here, here . . .

"I am here, here, here . . .

"Awaken you, you, you!"

She sways her feather fan up and down, spreading the earth and the people of the earth with the pollinating spirit of the butterfly. Her shell bracelets rattle like snakes, her bell garters tinkle like rain. Her shadow with its big belly and little legs dances from one side of the dance circle to the other. Her feet leave little puffs of dust behind.

The tribes are reverent, involved. But some visitors look at each other and murmur "This is it? *This* is the Butterfly Maiden?" They are puzzled, some even disillusioned. They no longer seem to remember that the spirit world is a place where wolves are women, bears are husbands, and old women of lavish dimensions are butterflies.

Yes, it is fitting that Wild Woman/Butterfly Woman is old and substantial, for she carries the thunderworld in one breast, the underworld in the other. Her back is the curve of the planet Earth with all its crops and foods and animals. The back of her neck carries the sunrise and the sunset. Her left thigh holds all the lodgepoles, her right thigh all the she-wolves of the world. Her belly holds all the babies that will ever be born.

Butterfly Maiden is the female fertilizing force. Carrying the pollen from one place to another, she cross-fertilizes, just as the soul fertilizes mind with night-dreams, just as archetypes fertilize the mundane world. She is the center. She brings the opposites together by taking a little from here and putting it there. Transformation is no more complicated than that. This is what she teaches. This is how the butterfly does it. This is how the soul does it.

Butterfly Woman mends the erroneous idea that transformation is only for the tortured, the saintly, or only for the fabulously strong. The Self need not carry mountains to transform. A little is enough. A little goes a long way. A little changes much. The fertilizing force replaces the moving of mountains.

Butterfly Maiden pollinates the souls of the earth: It is easier than you think, she says. She is shaking her feather fan, and she's hopping, for she is spilling spiritual pollen all over the people who are there, Native Americans, little children, visitors, everyone. She is using her entire body as a blessing, her old, frail, big, short-legged, short-necked, spotted body. This is woman connected to her wild nature, the trans-lator of the instinctual, the fertilizing force, the mender, the rememberer of old ideas. She is *La voz mitológica*. She is Wild Woman personified.

The butterfly dancer must be old because she represents the soul that is old. She is wide of thigh and broad of rump because she carries much. Her gray hair certi-fies that she need no longer observe taboos about touching others. She is allowed to touch everyone: boys, babies, men, women, girl children, the old, the ill, and the dead. The Butterfly Woman can touch everyone. It is her privilege to touch all, at last. This is her power. Hers is the body of *La Mariposa*, the butterfly.

The body is like an earth. It is a land unto itself. It is as vulnerable to overbuilding, being carved into parcels, cut off, overmined, and shorn of its power as any land-scape. The wilder woman will not be easily swayed by redevelopment schemes. For her, the questions are not how to form but how to feel. The breast in all its shapes has the function of feeling and feeding. Does it feed? Does it feel? It is a good breast.

The hips, they are wide for a reason, inside them is a satiny ivory cradle for new life. A woman's hips are outriggers for the body above and below; they are portals, they are a lush cushion, the handholds for love, a place for children to hide behind. The legs, they are meant to take us, sometimes to propel us; they are the pulleys that help us lift, they are the *anillo*, the ring for encircling a lover. They cannot be too this or too that. They are what they are.

There is no "supposed to be" in bodies. The question is not size or shape or years of age, or even having two of everything, for some do not. But the wild issue is, does this body feel, does it have right connection to pleasure, to heart, to soul, to the wild? Does it have happiness, joy? Can it in its own way move, dance, jiggle, sway, thrust? Nothing else matters.

When I was a child, I was taken on a field trip to the Museum of Natural History in Chicago. There I saw the sculptures of Malvina Hoffman, dozens of life-size dark bronze sculptures in a great hall. She had sculpted the mostly naked bodies of people of the world and she had wild vision.

She lavished her love on the thin calf of the hunter, the long breasts of the mother with two grown children, the cones of flesh on the chest of the virgin, the old man's nuts hanging to mid thigh, the nose with nostrils bigger than the eyes, the nose hooked like a hawk's, the nose straight like a corner. She had fallen in love with ears like semaphores, and ears low near the chin and small as pecans. She had loved each hair coiled like a snake basket, or each hair wavy as a ribbon unfurling, or each hair straight as fever grass. She had the wild love *of* body. She understood the power *in* the body.

There is a line in Ntozake Shange's *for colored girls who have considered suicide/when the rainbow is enuf.* In the play, the woman in purple speaks after having struggled to deal with all the psychic and physical aspects of herself that the culture ignores or demeans. She sums herself up in these wise and peaceful words:

> *here is what i have . . . .*
> *poems*
> *big thighs*
> *lil tits*
> *&*
>
> *so much love*

This is the power of the body, our power, the power of the wildish woman. In mythos and fairy tales, deities and other great spirits test the hearts of humans by showing up in various forms that disguise their divinity. They show up in robes, rags, silver sashes, or with muddy feet. They show up with skin dark as old wood, or in scales made of rose petal, as a frail child, as a lime-yellow old woman, as a man who cannot speak, or as an animal who can. The great powers are testing to see if humans have yet learned to recognize the greatness of soul in all its varying forms.

Wild Woman shows up in many sizes, shapes, colors, and conditions. Stay awake so you can recognize the wild soul in all its many guises.

—1992

LESTER ROWNTREE
1879-1979

Horticulturalist, visionary, and writer, Lester Rowntree deserves attention outside of the small but devoted following she has long enjoyed among gardeners and students of California plant life. A prominent landscape architect once remarked that Rowntree's writing had the effect of making her readers want "to pack their rucksacks and head for the hills." Best known for her book Hardy Californians *(1936), she has been called the Zane Grey of the plant world, but a more apt comparison might be to say she is the floristic counterpart to Walt Whitman or Jack Kerouac. True to her Quaker heritage, Rowntree placed a tremendous emphasis on trusting firsthand* experience. Her job was to seek flowers—and to seek flowers was to seek herself.

Born Gertrude Ellen ("Nellie") Lester in 1879, Rowntree was raised in the Lake District of England. She attended an English public school, where tradition demanded that all students be addressed by their last names. Enjoying this tradition, she insisted upon being called Lester for the rest of her life, only later appending her husband's surname. Her family came to America in 1889 and settled on the Kansas prairie, and in 1891 they moved to southern California. She married in 1908 and gave birth to a son in 1911. When, in her early fifties, her marriage ended in divorce, she made a living by selling the seeds of California native plants that she herself collected in the wild. For the next three decades, her new vocation required that she take to the roads for nine months of each year, living out of her car, traveling all over the state in search of native wildflowers and shrubs. Her quest frequently took her far into the backcountry alone, a highly unusual activity for a woman in those days. Although the infirmities of age eventually brought an end to her solo excursions, her influence on gardeners, botanists, and even youthful spiritual seekers (especially during the late 1960s) remained powerful until the end. She died just a few days after her hundredth birthday.

"Collecting Myself" appeared in Nature Magazine (now long defunct) in 1950, when Rowntree was in the latter part of her halcyon years of wandering in the California wildlands in search of seeds. The essay's title can be taken symbolically, something akin to the Delphic Oracle's injunction, "Know Thyself." This philosophical view of life is best rendered by Rowntree herself in a letter she wrote when she was ninety-four: "How empty my present life would be without the memory of those glorious solo days in the field. They were the best ways of finding out the things I had to know. Books are essential but they are only springboards from which to jump into that much-to-be-desired world of getting knowledge for oneself."

COLLECTING MYSELF

Twenty-five years ago my gnawing curiosity to know more about plants in their native homes got out of hand. Loading the car carefully so as to keep the plant presses and seed bags away from the canteens; the camera things protected from the sharp tools; nesting the buckets so that they could not jibber, and laying the compulsory long-handled shovel with its mate the axe at a safe distance from the bedroll, I headed east. I crossed the California coast ranges and the central valley, crawled impatiently through the cities, hurried past the foothill summer-camp region with its Kumfy Kamps and DoDrop Inns, and reached mountain roads such as rejoice the heart of the vagabond, although they try the workings of a car. Finally I arrived, alone, on a mountain top from which I looked down on lakes, forests and far away toward still higher peaks.

Here, on my peak, the soil was born of rock fragments ground small by weather and water. The plants were small, but their flowers were large and bright. Rosy finches picked about on left-over snow drifts, and, until a short but rowdy tempest interfered, the air was pregnant with silence. At the end of this, my first lonely dash into the high, back-country of the West, I knew my feet were set on the wilderness path and the gypsy life was the normal one for me. I had turned seed-and-plant collector. Since then, as much time has been spent in the field as on my hillside overlooking the Pacific. The ground became my resting place, the sky my ceiling, and the sun my only clock.

The impedimenta of subsequent trips varied with the region invaded. More sweaters went to the mountains; more canteens to the desert. There was always a pile of gunny sacks to give traction when stuck in sand or mud. Books for mining friends now accompany me into the hills, fruit in season to the Indian territories, candy and trinkets for children in Mexico, and, wherever I go, a bundle of old magazines to supply highway tramps. There is a honk of the horn, a grin, flying paper, and the next minute the human pack rat is sitting beside the road forgetting his wanderlust in a story. Whether the journey is made entirely by car, or continued in areas where no car can go, on foot or with burro or pack horse, the seed-and-plant collector's procedure is pretty much the same. The work hours are long and engrossing, the physical activity arduous, the chores varying in character. Photographs must be taken, film holders emptied and refilled, drying specimens must be changed in the presses, seeds kept from molding, and the collected seedling plants, launched in cans on the first step of their careers as garden plants, must not be allowed to dry out. Above all, notebook and pencil must be kept busy, for field notes, on a botanizing jaunt, come second to the plants themselves. But these tasks and those connected with the mechanics of living are all accomplished in the quiet and beauty of the ultra-rural outdoors.

People and animals, as well as plants, share the collector's life. It was an Indian who led me to an half-acre swoop of the pretty little fringed pink, *Gilia dianthoides*. The driver of a road repair truck came to my rescue on a narrow mountain road, after I, a lone and unmechanical woman, locked myself out of my car. I fall in with miners, fishermen and hunters. They are as single-minded about their hobbies as I am about mine; fellow fanatics talking little else but ore, fishes and deer. The miners give me information, some of it true; the fishermen bestow on me their surplus catches; from the hunters I get a handout of venison or bear meat. We are a happy contented lot.

Anyone who, alone, makes his home in the open for any length of time is bound to strike up friendship with the wild creatures of his neighborhood. My feeling for the coyote is, I think, stronger and warmer than for any other wild animal. At night when he plays ball with sound, he speaks of vast expanses of land still unspoiled by man, and in his keening there is something akin to the glory of stars in a desert sky. When, on my way back after a year of field work in eastern and southern states, the carolling of coyotes came to me in my sleeping bag on the broad Texan floor, I lay and gloated, knowing that I was home at last. Early the next morning, as I left the dead embers of my breakfast fire and started off on a tour of inspection, I felt a presence. I could hear no sound but I knew I had company. Then I glimpsed a tan-colored fellow jogging along at a distance, just far enough away to prevent me from hearing his soft footfall. I broke into a trot. So did he. I walked again. So did he. After we had gone about a mile I turned back. My companion turned with me and together we trotted to the car. There, in plain sight, he stood watching while I got out a piece of bread. Putting it on the back-stone of my fireplace, I picked up my notebook and sat down a little way off while he ate it. For three days I worked that section, coming back each evening to my fireplace. Each morning I took an after-breakfast walk. Each morning I had company. Was it the same coyote? I have no way of proving it.

I question country folk unmercifully on the subject of coyotes, and glean all sorts of amazing "facts." Some of them are as hard to believe as the stories I am told about that antic bird, the roadrunner. I shall not soon forget the night when a coyote, evidently pursuing his customary path, got almost up to my cocoon-like sleeping bag before startling me out of a sound sleep with his enchanting, unearthly jabber. The wind must have been in the wrong direction for him, for it was I and not the coyote who showed surprise. I have seen a frightened coyote, however. The morning the San Francisquito Cañon dam, in Los Angeles County, broke I was in the hills nearby. I heard the sirens, thought that there must be a fire, an accident or a parade, and went on gathering wild lilac seed. By afternoon, although I knew there was no fire, I was sure there was serious trouble in the hills. Frightened animals passed close by me, paying not the slightest attention. There were rabbits and hares in large numbers, foxes and coyotes. I think I could have touched one coyote without any objection on his part. His tongue hung out, his whole body showed extreme exhaustion, and the look he gave me as he trotted wearily by plainly said: "Anything *you* could do to me is nothing to what I've just been through."

Khaki is a color that blends well with soil, tree-bark and foliage. A miner once told me that a phainopepla he had tamed would come to him only when he wore his khaki shirt. I have had hummingbirds light on the sleeve of a khaki shirt containing a motionless arm, and once, on the desert in Montana, when, at the end of the day, I was sitting on my khaki covered sleeping bag, writing up the day's notes, a rattlesnake on his way to a hole beneath a neighboring bush slowly passed across the bag within a foot of where I sat. The rattlesnake accepted my bedroll as a natural thing, and I accepted the rattlesnake as part of my setting. Before the war the wild animals on the Santa Barbara Channel Islands had seen so few people that they had not learned to be afraid. Foxes unflinchingly ate out of my hand, and parent cormorants raised no objection when I stroked their babies in the nest. Once, on the mainland, I found myself sitting next to a new-born deer. He was spotted and moist. We looked into one another's eyes with an understanding that I hope was mutual. He stayed where he had been placed, and I went on with my writing. I felt a particular kinship with the little creature for I too was spotted and I wanted to lie in the shade of bush and tree. My spots had been given me by hornets with misgivings about my khaki get-up being part of the scenery.

In their eagerness to find out what I am doing, country-folk sometimes insist that I need help when I do not. There was the time on the desert when I spread the moist blotters from my presses to dry on the hot sand, anchoring them with stones, wandered off to work and returned at evening to find my blotters carefully stacked and very moist. The stacker was probably the only person to pass by that day. And there was the morning a hunter had gone out of the Oregon mountains and at the nearest town reported that a woman was lost in the hills. That evening, just as I was finishing a wash beside a lily-fringed stream I was visited by two officers who were hard to convince that I was there from choice, that I was sane and that there was purpose in my work; that I was not lost and therefore could not be found. I usually hear visiting bears at night, and if my supplies are endangered, get up and see them safely slung to an outer bough of a tree. If I know that the bacon has been taken care of and the collection of manzanita berries out of harm's way, I pull the bedroll flap over my head and go to sleep again. But one night I slept so soundly that I never knew I was being robbed and woke to find my larder empty. My car was much lower down the mountain and I had only a burro with me. My work had not been accomplished and I did not want to break camp until it was. As I took the long walk to the nearest road I thought that this was a time I would really be glad of help, and remembered with contrition past proferred assistance that had gone, mentally at least, unthanked.

A new road was being made farther up the mountain and I planned to hitch a ride down to the nearest ranger station. Perhaps I would have to wait until the road trucks went down that evening. But then how was I to get back? I had not sat long beneath the tall sugar pine when along came my good Samaritan and I was perched beside the driver of a truck headed up-mountain to the latest road camp. I was led to the kitchen, where the cook took me under his wing and showed me his wares, an incredible sight to one who had been living on canned food, chocolate, carrots, raisins and an occasional slice of bacon. There was fresh bread, hot from the oven. There were pies and cookies. There were cakes en masse. It seemed strange to see all this newly baked food up there in the mountains. I shut my eyes and opened them quickly. The food was still there, and so was the smell of it, and the cook was saying benevolently: "Now what would you like?" There was nothing I did not like but I made an effort not to show it. The cook got a large basket. Into the basket went a pie, a cake, some cookies and bread. Out of the office came the boss, who flatly refused payment and told the driver of the truck to take me down the mountain to my sugar pine. As I remember it I did not get much botanical work done the rest of that day.

A certain amount of loneliness is necessary to us all, but after a long dose of it I find great joy in the companionship of others. Even the assurance that there are others is a comfort, and, although privacy is needed at night, it is comforting to hear the faraway murmur, like that of moving water, of the distant highway, or the remote rumble of a train. It is cheering to watch from the desert floor the hoisted air beacon's circling flash, and from a mountain meadow to raise the eyes to a fire lookout on its peak. Most field workers find lookouts irresistible. From them the surrounding country can easily be seen and the observer stationed there is usually well posted on the topography of his area. One summer, when I was working the mountains in Oregon, I spent an amusing and profitable six weeks being passed around from lookout to lookout. Each observer in his turn called up the nearest lookout, gave him some idea of the time of my arrival and told him in what I was interested. When I landed, all breathless, on the pinnacle we could go to work without the usual explanations.

The dunnage changes character as the collector moves along. Perishables yield space to gathered loot. Bags of aromatic seeds take the place of melons and grapes acquired on the way through fertile valleys. Cans of fruit juice are drunk so that the containers may serve as receptacles for small collected plants.

The pile of newspapers on top of the gunny sacks shrinks as the presses expand. I never have enough newspapers, and find myself estimating my friends by the bales of out-of-date newsprint they can produce for me. Besides being a vital necessity in the flower press, newspapers serve as table cloths, seats, covers, seed-bags, kindling, awnings, reinforcement in worn shoes, and even, sometimes, as reading matter.

My friends, the miners, are a never-ending source of information and entertainment, and I have profound respect for some of the miners' wives. In spite of the fact that they must work extremely hard, and have nothing of what is called social life—no movies, no bridge clubs, no beauty parlors—some of them cheerfully and happily turn a shack—often a crude one—into a home. Some wives live with their children at the nearest campground while the husband is building a cabin. Here the stoves, toilets and ready water facilitate the daily work. I know one woman who manages to keep her family healthy even though her only cooking utensils are a frying pan, a bucket and a kettle. Barefooted, summer and winter, her children walk four miles to school, sometimes bringing a rattlesnake home for the evening meal. They have few books and no toys, but find joy in the outdoor world and in sharing in the creation of a home.

Not all miners' wives are so contented and I came to know one of these dissatisfied ones very well. Her husband had stopped to comment on the contents of my open-mouthed pup tent crammed with assorted cargo such as film-changing bag, books and presses. "It's not for you but your stuff," he remarked, and I explained that I could stand a shower better than most of my dunnage. Before he left I had promised to call on his wife.

Two days later I picked my way between the chickens on the porch, and, thrusting aside a curtain of bedraggled hop vine, I knocked at the cabin door. Inside the living-dining-bed room a small brisk woman of about forty-five dusted a chair with her apron and asked me to sit down. During the next five minutes I learned, among other matters, that she had had thirteen children, five of whom were living, and then she unburdened herself on a matter close to her heart and said, "I want to read. Some folks say its wrong to read. Do you?" I assured her that I thought reading to be no wrong. Then she took two books from between the kerosene lamp and a mason jar of paper roses. One was a book on etiquette and the other a folder advertising a steamship line. With a generous impulse she thrust them into my hands with, "Read them. Sit and read them." I thanked her and said I had left my glasses in camp. "I'll loan you mine," she offered and rummaged in the table drawer. But the community glasses were out on duty, and as I rose to go I promised to keep her supplied with reading matter if she would make the time to use it.

The bitter of the collector's life, which is mingled with the sweet, is soon forgotten. I have to dig deep into my memory to recollect one burro that refused to be pulled or pushed over the fallen trees that span some of the smaller mountain rivers, refused also to walk across in the water and allow me to go dryshod over the log. The only way to get the stubborn beast across was to get down into the water with him, even though it came up to my neck, and, as buddies on equal terms, take our ducking together. I must stop and think back to recall that spring day on the distant desert when, on the first calm day, after waiting ten days for the wind to subside enough to let me make close-up exposures of flowers, I dropped and broke my ground glass.

In the mountains there are always plenty of lakes and rivers to bathe in. On the desert there is either a great deal of water or none at all. Where water is scarce it is always a nice gesture for a caller to be offered a bath. One day as I passed a miner's headquarters I was hailed by: "Want a bath?" Acceptance was made with gusto, and I was led to a palm-screened compartment partially enclosing a massive bathtub. At one end of the tub there was a huge hole and from the other protruded a pipe, which must have been nine inches across. I ran for my towel and soap and when I got back the miner was washing out the tub. As he went out of the bathroom's open side he said, "Yell when you're ready and I'll turn it on. It's an artesian well." Never have I enjoyed a bath so much. The pure water gushed in at one end and roared out at the other and I sat in between, soaping, scrubbing and blessing the miner.

The West coast is rapidly becoming cluttered up with people; the collector must go farther afield for freedom in which to carry on his activities, and trust to strong legs to take him to rewarding fastnesses. September usually finds the gleaner high in the mountains, for seeds of most alpines ripen just before the first snow covers the plant. By October the collector is driven down by snowstorms. He must leave the high granite and its seed-ribboned crevices. For the last time in the season he hears the echo of the lead horse's bell, the piercing whistle of the packer. He rides (or walks) out, leaving blue gentians flowering in the snow.

Packing out of the mountains is less joyful than packing in. I leave something behind me. I do not mean my comb or camera tripod, but a bit of myself. And I am vaguely unhappy at having done so. Back in the man-made world I am, for a time, filled with nostalgia for high places that I had made my own. I champ at the confines of walls and ceilings. I make adjustments, but I keep trying to recapture that fading fairy tale of the free life among rocks and plants and wild creatures. As I settle down, relearning how to live the well-rounded life, I begin to perceive that the tame, as well as the wild, has its place when it comes to collecting myself.

—1950

TERRY TEMPEST WILLIAMS

B. 1955

Terry Tempest Williams is a storyteller rooted in family, church, and place. A fifth-generation Mormon, she was born in Salt Lake City, Utah, and learned to love the natural world on family camping trips and on birding expeditions with her paternal grandmother. Spending time with the Navajo as a teacher while pursuing a master's degree in environmental education at the University of Utah, she found that through story she could integrate her passion for landscape and literature. She was hired in 1979 as curator of education at the Utah Museum of Natural History, where she still works as naturalist-in-residence.

In eight books published since 1984, Williams has evolved from a woman writing safely within the bounds of traditional gender roles to one risking more and more pointed challenges to the status quo. Two of her first three books were for children; her first book for adults, Pieces of White Shell *(1984), grew out of her work with Navajo children. But by the time her memoir* Refuge *was published in 1991, the "poetics of place" evident in her early work had given way to a "politics of place" growing out of an "erotics of place," which is further articulated in her recent creative nonfiction,* An Unspoken Hunger *(1994) and* Desert Quartet *(1995).*

Williams said in a 1994 interview, "One reason the erotic is so intriguing to me is because in the culture I was raised in eroticism is the ultimate taboo. It isn't your body that is valued; it's your soul. . . . Why is that? What are we afraid of? That's the question I keep asking myself." To Williams, what is erotic is that moment in a relationship when heart, mind, spirit, and flesh are fully engaged. An erotics of place, then, acknowledges our deep

*hunger for full engagement with the land. As the following essay (first pub-
lished in Northern Lights, Winter 1995) makes clear, Williams believes that
fear of the erotic keeps us disengaged from the natural world and makes
us capable of abusing each other and the land. True to her word, Williams
is committed to living an erotic life, in spiritual and physical dialogue with
landscape.*

THE EROTIC LANDSCAPE

A woman stands on her tiptoes, naked, holding draped fabric close to her body as
it cascades over her breasts, down her belly and legs, like water. A strand of pearls
hangs down her back; her eyes are closed. She is at peace within her own erotic landscape.

This photograph, taken at Studio d'Ora in Vienna in 1934, is the first image I see
in Det Erotiske Museum in Copenhagen, Denmarke. I take another step into the
foyer and find myself confronted with a six-foot golden phallus mounted on a
pedestal. I am tempted to touch it, as I recall the bronze statues of women in museums around the world whose breasts and buttocks have been polished perfectly by
the hands of men, but I refrain.

A visitor to this museum in Copenhagen can wander through four floors of
exhibits ranging from a solitary Greek vase, circa 530 B.C., depicting Pan chasing
Echo, to a wax tableau of Fanny Hill, 1749, to a prostitute's room reconstructed
from an 1839 Danish police report.

Spiraling up to the fourth floor (you may choose to descend at this point to the
Aphrodite Cafe for coffee and pastries), the visitor arrives at the Erotic Tabernacle,
the climax of this museum experience. Here, you are assaulted with twelve television
screens, four across and three down, which together create a montage of pornography from 1920 through 1990, complete with the music of Pink Floyd's *The Wall*.

As I watch these images of men and women simultaneously moving from one
position to the next, I wonder about our notion of the erotic—why it is so often
aligned with the pornographic, the limited view of the voyeur watching the act of
intercourse without any interest in the relationship itself.

I wonder what walls we have constructed to keep our true erotic nature tamed.
And I am curious why we continue to distance ourselves from natural sources.

What are we afraid of?

There is an image of a woman in the desert, her back arched as her hands lift
her body up from black rocks. Naked. She spreads her legs over a boulder etched by
the Ancient Ones; a line of white lightning zigzags from her mons pubis. She is perfectly in place, engaged, ecstatic, and wild. This is Judy Dater's photograph
Self-Portrait with Petroglyph.

To be in relation to everything around us, above us, below us, earth, sky, bones,
blood, flesh, is to see the world whole, even holy. But the world we frequently surrender to defies our participation and seduces us into believing that our only place
in nature is as spectator, onlooker. A society of individuals who only observe a landscape from behind the lens of a camera or the window of an automobile without
entering in is perhaps no different from the person who obtains sexual gratification
from looking at the sexual actions or organs of others.

The golden phallus I did not touch, in the end, did not touch me. It became a stump, a severance of the body I could not feel.

Eroticism, being in relation, calls the inner life into play. No longer numb, we feel the magnetic pull of our bodies toward something stronger, more vital than simply ourselves. Arousal becomes a dance with longing. We form a secret partnership with possibility.

I recall a day in the slickrock country of southern Utah where I was camped inside a small canyon. Before dawn, coyotes yipped, yapped, and sang. It was a chorus of young desert dogs.

The sun rose as did I. There is a silence to creation. I stood and faced east, stretched upward, stretched down, pressed my hands together.

I knelt on the sand still marked by the patter of rain and lit my stove, which purred like my cat at home. I boiled water for tea, slowly poured it into my earthen cup, then dipped the rose-hip tea bag in and out, in and out until the water turned pink. My morning ritual was complete as I wrapped my hands around the warmth of my cup and drank.

Not far, an old juniper stood in the clearing, deeply rooted and gnarled. I had never seen such a knowledgeable tree. Perhaps it was the silver sheen of its shredded bark that reminded me of my grandmother, her windblown hair in the desert, her weathered face, the way she held me as a child. I wanted to climb into the arms of this tree.

With both hands on one of its stronger boughs, I pulled myself up and lifted my right leg over the branch so I was straddling it, then leaned back into the body of the juniper and brought my knees up to my chest. I nestled in. I was hidden, perfectly shaded from the heat. I had forgotten what it felt like to really be held.

Hours passed, who knows how long; the angle of the sunlight shifted. I realized something had passed between us by the change in my countenance, the slowing of my pulse, and the softness of my eyes as though I were awakening from a desert trance. The lacelike evergreen canopy brushed my hair.

I finally inched my way down, wrapping my hands around the trunk. Feet on earth. I took out my water bottle and saturated the roots. I left the desert in a state of wetness.

The Erotic Museum in Copenhagen opened July 26, 1992. It closed on August 31, 1993 because of financial difficulties. More than 100,000 visitors from around the world had paid to see erotica on display.

"The erotic has often been misnamed by men and used against women," says Audre Lorde in *Uses of the Erotic.* "It has been made into the confused, the trivial, the psychotic, and plasticized sensation. For this reason, we have turned away from the exploration and consideration of the erotic as a source of power and information, confusing it with the pornographic. But pornography is a direct denial of the power of the erotic, for it represents the suppression of true feeling. Pornography emphasizes sensation without feeling."

Without Feeling. Perhaps these two words are the key, the only way we can begin to understand our abuse of each other and our abuse of the land. Could it be that what we fear most is our capacity to feel, and so we annihilate symbolically and physically that which is beautiful and tender, anything that dares us to consider our creative selves? The erotic world is silenced, reduced to a collection of objects we can curate and control, be it a vase, a woman, or wilderness. Our lives become a

piece in the puzzle of pornography as we go through the motions of daily intercourse without any engagement of the soul.

A group of friends gather in the desert—call it a pilgrimage—at the confluence of
the Little Colorado and the Colorado rivers in the Grand Canyon. It is high noon in
June, hot, very hot. They walk upstream, men and women, moving against the current of the turquoise water. Nothing but deep joy can be imagined. Their arms fan
the air as they teeter on unstable stones, white stones in the river. They are searching for mud with the consistency of chocolate mousse and find it, delicious pale
mud, perfect for bathing. They take off their clothes and sink to their waists, turn,
roll over, and wallow in pleasure. Their skins are slippery with clay. They rub each
other's bodies—arms, shoulders, backs, toes, even their faces are painted in mud,
and they become the animals they are. Blue eyes. Green eyes. Brown eyes behind
masks. In the heat, lying on ledges, they bake until they crack like terracotta. For
hours they dream the life of lizards.

In time, they submerge themselves into Little Colorado, diving deep and surfac-
ing freshly human, skins sparkling, glistening, cold and refreshed. Nothing can contain their exuberance but the river. They allow themselves to be swept away—floating on bellies, head first or backs, feet first—laughing, contemplating, an unspoken
hunger quelled.

D. H. Lawrence writes, "There exist two great modes of life—the religious and the
sexual." Eroticism is their badge.

Ole Ege is the man behind the Erotic Museum in Denmark. It was his vision of
eroticism that he wanted to institutionalize. It is his collection that now resides in
storage somewhere in Copenhagen.

Standing on the sidewalk next to the red banners that advertise the museum, I
watched each object, each exhibit, each wax figure, being carried out of the white
building and loaded into two Volvo moving vans on Vesterbrogade 31, minutes
away from Tivoli Gardens, where the harlequins danced.

That was Labor Day weekend 1993. Seven months later, the museum opened
once again. Ole Ege's vision of the erotic life is being celebrated, this time in a new
location and with a more solid base of support.

"Denmark has been liberated sexually for 25 years," he says. "But we are not yet
liberated in our minds. It is a matter of individual morality how one conceives this
subject. For me, eroticism relates to all the highest and finest things of life. Every
couple on earth participates in this confirmation of the creation, the urge we have
to share ourselves, to make each other whole."

The idea that governs an erotic museum and the ideal behind an erotic life may never
find a perfect resolution. Here lies our dilemma as human beings: Nothing exists in isolation. We need a context for eros, not a pedestal, not a video screen. The lightning we
witness crack and charge a night sky in the desert is the same electricity we feel in ourselves whenever we dare to touch flesh, rock, body, and earth. We must take our love
outdoors where reciprocity replaces voyeurism. We can choose to photograph a tree or
we can sit in its arms, where we are participating in wild nature, even our own.

The woman in the desert stands and extends her arms. Rumi speaks, "Let the
beauty of what we love be what we do. There are hundreds of ways to kneel and kiss
the ground."

—1995

Jack London

1876-1916

*Jack London was among the first prospectors to travel to the Yukon
Territory in northwest Canada after gold was discovered along the
Klondike River in 1897. Although he returned to San Francisco penniless
and in poor health a year later, his experiences would provide the material
for some of his best writing, beginning with his first book of stories,* The Son
of the Wolf: Tales of the Far North *(1900), and including his best-known
short novels,* The Call of the Wild *(1903) and* White Fang *(1906). The most
characteristic of the fifty books he published during his relatively brief
career deal with the human struggle for survival in the face of nature's brutal indifference. They seem to suggest that to survive in this contest, we
must recover the primal instincts that we have allowed to atrophy in the
name of reason.*

*Born in San Francisco and abandoned by his father, a roving astrologer,
London adopted the surname of his stepfather. Forced by his family's
poverty to quit school at fourteen, he worked for several years in a cannery
and as a longshoreman before going to Japan as a sailor and seeing the
United States as a hobo riding the freight trains. He educated himself by
reading works by such authors as Darwin, Marx, and Nietzsche, and completed his entire high school coursework in one year at the age of nineteen.
He attended the University of California at Berkeley for one year and
became a socialist before joining the gold rush to the Yukon. A cruise to the
South Pacific in 1907 stimulated a series of tales set there. In 1910, as a prolific but uneven novelist, short story writer, essayist, and journalist, London
settled on a ranch near Glen Ellen, California.*

"To Build a Fire," originally collected in Lost Face *(1910), is one of
London's most popular stories. It follows the thoughts of a man who chooses
to ignore the warnings of old-timers and to travel on a bitterly cold day in
the Yukon, contrasting his rational awareness with the instinctual awareness of his almost-wild dog that "it was not good to walk abroad in such
fearful cold." The man's attitude toward his dog, who seems to exhibit more
sense in the situation, is telling: there is "no keen intimacy" between them,
and the man regards the dog as his "toil slave." In the end his egotism and
lack of imagination are his undoing. Had the man been able to surrender
his belief in reason and fall back upon the instinctual animal wisdom carried in his own blood, the story might have ended differently.*

To Build a Fire

Day had broken cold and grey, exceedingly cold and grey, when the man turned
aside from the main Yukon trail and climbed the high earth-bank, where a dim and
little-travelled trail led eastward through the fat spruce timberland. It was a steep
bank, and he paused for breath at the top, excusing the act to himself by looking at
his watch. It was nine o'clock. There was no sun nor hint of sun, though there was
not a cloud in the sky. It was a clear day, and yet there seemed an intangible pall

over the face of things, a subtle gloom that made the day dark, and that was due to the absence of sun. This fact did not worry the man. He was used to the lack of sun. It had been days since he had seen the sun, and he knew that a few more days must pass before that cheerful orb, due south, would just peep above the skyline and dip immediately from view.

The man flung a look back along the way he had come. The Yukon lay a mile wide and hidden under three feet of ice. On top of this ice were as many feet of snow. It was all pure white, rolling in gentle undulations where the ice jams of the freeze-up had formed. North and south, as far as his eye could see, it was unbroken white, save for a dark hairline that curved and twisted from around the spruce-covered island to the south, and that curved and twisted away into the north, where it disappeared behind another spruce-covered island. This dark hairline was the trail—the main trail—that led south five hundred miles to the Chilcoot Pass, Dyea, and salt water; and that led north seventy miles to Dawson, and still on to the north a thousand miles to Nulato, and finally to St. Michael, on Bering Sea, a thousand miles and half a thousand more.

But all this—the mysterious, far-reaching hairline trail, the absence of sun from the sky, the tremendous cold, and the strangeness and weirdness of it all—made no impression on the man. It was not because he was long used to it. He was a newcomer in the land, a *chechaquo*, and this was his first winter. The trouble with him was that he was without imagination. He was quick and alert in the things of life, but only in the things, and not in the significances. Fifty degrees below zero meant eighty-odd degrees of frost. Such fact impressed him as being cold and uncomfortable, and that was all. It did not lead him to meditate upon his frailty as a creature of temperature, and upon man's frailty in general, able only to live within certain narrow limits of heat and cold; and from there on it did not lead him to the conjectural field of immortality and man's place in the universe. Fifty degrees below zero stood for a bite of frost that hurt and that must be guarded against by the use of mittens, ear flaps, warm moccasins, and thick socks. Fifty degrees below zero. That there should be anything more to it than that was a thought that never entered his head.

As he turned to go on, he spat speculatively. There was a sharp explosive crackle that startled him. He spat again. And again, in the air, before it could fall to the snow, the spittle crackled. He knew that at fifty below spittle crackled on the snow, but this spittle had crackled in the air. Undoubtedly it was colder than fifty below—how much colder he did not know. But the temperature did not matter. He was bound for the old claim on the left fork of Henderson Creek, where the boys were already. They had come over across the divide from the Indian Creek country, while he had come the roundabout way to take a look at the possibilities of getting out logs in the spring from the islands in the Yukon. He would be in to camp by six o'clock; a bit after dark, it was true, but the boys would be there, a fire would be going, and a hot supper would be ready. As for lunch, he pressed his hand against the protruding bundle under his jacket. It was also under his shirt, wrapped up in a handkerchief and lying against the naked skin. It was the only way to keep the biscuits from freezing. He smiled agreeably to himself as he thought of those biscuits, each cut open and sopped in bacon grease, and each enclosing a generous slice of fried bacon.

He plunged in among the big spruce trees. The trail was faint. A foot of snow had fallen since the last sled had passed over, and he was glad he was without a sled, travelling light. In fact, he carried nothing but the lunch wrapped in the handkerchief. He was surprised, however, at the cold. It certainly was cold, he concluded, as he rubbed his numb nose and cheekbones with his mittened hand. He was a warm-whiskered man, but the hair on his face did not protect the high cheekbones and the eager nose that thrust itself aggressively into the frosty air.

At the man's heels trotted a dog, a big native husky, the proper wolf-dog, grey-coated and without any visible or temperamental difference from its brother, the wild wolf. The animal was depressed by the tremendous cold. It knew that it was no time for travelling. Its instinct told it a truer tale than was told to the man by the man's judgment. In reality, it was not merely colder than fifty below zero; it was colder than sixty below, than seventy below. It was seventy-five below zero. Since the freezing point is thirty-two above zero, it meant that one hundred and seven degrees of frost obtained. The dog did not know anything about thermometers. Possibly in its brain there was no sharp consciousness of a condition of very cold such as was in the man's brain. But the brute had its instinct. It experienced a vague but menacing apprehension that subdued it and made it slink along at the man's heels, and that made it question eagerly every unwonted movement of the man as if expecting him to go into camp or to seek shelter somewhere and build a fire. The dog had learned fire, and it wanted fire, or else to burrow under the snow and cuddle its warmth away from the air.

The frozen moisture of its breathing had settled on its fur in a fine powder of frost, and especially were its jowls, muzzle, and eyelashes whitened by its crystal breath. The man's red beard and moustache were likewise frosted, but more solidly, the deposit taking the form of ice and increasing with every warm, moist breath he exhaled. Also, the man was chewing tobacco, and the muzzle of ice held his lips so rigidly that he was unable to clear his chin when he expelled the juice. The result was a crystal beard of the colour and solidity of amber was increasing its length on his chin. If he fell down it would shatter itself, like glass, into brittle fragments. But he did not mind the appendage. It was the penalty all tobacco chewers paid in that country, and he had been out before in two cold snaps. They had not been so cold as this, he knew, but by the spirit thermometer at Sixty Mile he knew they had been registered at fifty below and at fifty-five.

He held on through the level stretch of woods for several miles, crossed a wide flat of nigger heads, and dropped down a bank to the frozen bed of a small stream. This was Henderson Creek, and he knew he was ten miles from the forks. He looked at his watch. It was ten o'clock. He was making four miles an hour, and he calculated that he would arrive at the forks at half-past twelve. He decided to celebrate that event by eating his lunch there.

The dog dropped in again at his heels, with a tail drooping discouragement, as the man swung along the creek bed. The furrow of the old sled trail was plainly visible, but a dozen inches of snow covered up the marks of the last runners. In a month no man had come up or down that silent creek. The man held steadily on. He was not much given to thinking, and just then particularly he had nothing to think about save that he would eat lunch at the forks and that at six o'clock he would be in camp with the boys. There was nobody to talk to; and, had there been, speech would have been impossible because of the ice muzzle on his mouth. So he continued monotonously to chew tobacco and to increase the length of his amber beard.

Once in a while the thought reiterated itself that it was very cold and that he had never experienced such cold. As he walked along he rubbed his cheekbones and nose with the back of his mittened hand. He did this automatically, now and again changing hands. But, rub as he would, the instant he stopped his cheekbones went numb, and the following instant the end of his nose went numb. He was sure to frost his cheeks; he knew that, and experienced a pang of regret that he had not devised a nose strap of the sort Bud wore in cold snaps. Such a strap passed across the cheeks, as well, and saved them. But it didn't matter much, after all. What were frosted cheeks? A bit painful, that was all; they were never serious.

Empty as the man's mind was of thoughts, he was keenly observant, and he noticed the changes in the creeks, the curves and bends and timber jams, and always he sharply noted where he placed his feet. Once, coming round a bend, he shied abruptly, like a startled horse, curved away from the place where he had been walking, and retreated several paces back along the trail. The creek he knew was frozen clear to the bottom—no creek could contain water in that arctic winter—but he knew also that there were springs that bubbled out from the hillsides and ran along under the snow and on top of the ice of the creek. He knew that the coldest snaps never froze these springs, and he knew likewise their danger. They were traps. They hid pools of water under the snow that might be three inches deep, or three feet. Sometimes a skin of ice half an inch thick covered them, and in turn was covered by the snow. Sometimes there were alternate layers of water and ice skin, so that when one broke through he kept on breaking through for a while, sometimes wetting himself to the waist.

That was why he had shied in such a panic. He had felt the give under his feet and heard the crackle of a snow-hidden ice skin. And to get his feet wet in such a temperature meant trouble and danger. At the very least it meant delay, for he would be forced to stop and build a fire, and under its protection to bare his feet while he dried his socks and moccasins. He stood and studied the creek bed and its banks, and decided that the flow of water came from the right. He reflected awhile, rubbing his nose and cheeks, then skirted to the left, stepping gingerly and testing the footing for each step. Once clear of the danger, he took a fresh chew of tobacco and swung along at his four-mile gait.

In the course of the next two hours he came upon several similar traps. Usually the snow above the hidden pools had a sunken, candied appearance that advertised the danger. Once again, however, he compelled the dog to go on in front. The dog did not want to go. It hung back until the man shoved it forward, and then it went quickly across the white, unbroken surface. Suddenly it broke through, floundered to one side, and got away to firmer footing. It had wet its forefeet and legs, and almost immediately the water that clung to it turned to ice. It made quick efforts to lick the ice off its legs, then dropped down in the snow and began to bite out the ice that had formed between the toes. This was a matter of instinct. To permit the ice to remain would mean sore feet. It did not know this. It merely obeyed the mysterious prompting that arose from the deep crypts of its being. But the man knew, having achieved a judgment on the subject, and he removed the mitten from his right hand and helped to tear out the ice particles. He did not expose his fingers more than a minute, and was astonished at the swift numbness that smote them. It certainly was cold. He pulled on the mitten hastily, and beat the hand savagely across the chest.

At twelve o'clock the day was at its brightest. Yet the sun was too far south on its winter journey to clear the horizon. The bulge of the earth intervened between it and Henderson Creek, where the man walked under a clear sky at noon and cast no shadow. At half-past twelve, to the minute, he arrived at the forks of the creek. He was pleased at the speed he had made. If he kept it up, he would certainly be with the boys by six. He unbuttoned his jacket and shirt and drew forth his lunch. The action consumed no more than a quarter of a minute, yet in that brief moment the numbness laid hold of the exposed fingers. He did not put the mitten on, but, instead, struck the fingers a dozen sharp smashes against his leg. Then he sat down on a snow-covered log to eat. The sting that followed upon the striking of his fingers against his leg ceased so quickly that he was startled. He had had no chance to take a bite of biscuit. He struck the fingers repeatedly and returned them to the mitten, baring the other hand for the purpose of eating. He tried to take a mouthful, but the ice muzzle prevented. He had forgotten to build a fire and thaw out. He chuckled at his foolishness, and as he chuckled he noted the numbness creeping into the exposed fingers. Also, he noted that the stinging which had first come to his toes when he sat down was already passing away. He wondered whether the toes were warm or numb. He moved them inside the moccasins and decided that they were numb.

He pulled the mitten on hurriedly and stood up. He was a bit frightened. He stamped up and down until the stinging returned into the feet. It certainly was cold, was his thought. That man from Sulphur Creek had spoken the truth when telling how cold it sometimes got in the country. And he had laughed at him at the time! That showed one must not be too sure of things. There was no mistake about it, it *was* cold. He strode up and down, stamping his feet and threshing his arms, until reassured by the returning warmth. Then he got out matches and proceeded to make a fire. From the undergrowth, where high water of the previous spring had lodged a supply of seasoned twigs, he got his firewood. Working carefully from a small beginning, he soon had a roaring fire, over which he thawed the ice from his face and in the protection of which he ate his biscuits. For the moment the cold of space was outwitted. The dog took satisfaction in the fire, stretching out close enough for warmth and far enough away to escape being singed.

When the man had finished, he filled his pipe and took his comfortable time over a smoke. Then he pulled on his mittens, settled the ear-flaps of his cap firmly about his ears, and took the creek trail up the left fork. The dog was disappointed and yearned back towards the fire. This man did not know cold. Possibly all the generations of his ancestry had been ignorant of cold, of real cold, of cold one hundred and seven degrees below freezing point. But the dog knew; all its ancestry knew, and it had inherited the knowledge. And it knew that it was not good to walk abroad in such fearful cold. It was the time to lie snug in a hole in the snow and wait for a curtain of cloud to be drawn across the face of outer space whence this cold came. On the other hand, there was no keen intimacy between the dog and the man. The one was the toil slave of the other, and the only caresses it had ever received were the caresses of the whip lash and of harsh and menacing throat sounds that threatened the whip lash. So the dog made no effort to communicate its apprehension to the man. It was not concerned in the welfare of the man; it was for its own sake that it yearned back towards the fire. But the man whistled, and spoke to it with the sound of whip lashes, and the dog swung in at the man's heels and followed after.

The man took a chew of tobacco and proceeded to start a new amber beard. Also, his moist breath quickly powdered with white his moustache, eyebrows, and lashes. There did not seem to be so many springs on the left fork of the Henderson, and for half an hour the man saw no signs of any. And then it happened. At a place where there were no signs, where the soft, unbroken snow seemed to advertise solidity beneath, the man broke through. It was not deep. He wet himself half-way to the knees before he floundered out to the firm crust.

He was angry, and cursed his luck aloud. He had hoped to get into camp with the boys at six o'clock, and this would delay him an hour, for he would have to build a fire and dry out his footgear. This was imperative at that low temperature—he knew that much, and he turned aside to the bank, which he climbed. On top, tangled in the underbrush about the trunks of several small spruce trees, was a high-water deposit of dry firewood—sticks and twigs, principally, but also larger portions of seasoned branches and fine, dry, last year's grasses. He threw down several large pieces on top of the snow. This served for a foundation and prevented the young flame from drowning itself in the snow it otherwise would melt. The flame he got by touching a match to a small shred of birch bark that he took from his pocket. This burned even more readily than paper. Placing it on the foundation, he fed the young flame with wisps of dry grass and with the tiniest dry twigs.

He worked slowly and carefully, keenly aware of his danger. Gradually, as the flame grew stronger, he increased the size of the twigs with which he fed it. He squatted in the snow pulling the twigs out from their entanglement in the brush and feeding directly to the flame. He knew there must be no failure. When it is seventy-five below zero, a man must not fail in his first attempt to build a fire—that is, if his feet are wet. If his feet are dry, and he fails, he can run along the trail for half a mile and restore his circulation. But the circulation of wet and freezing feet cannot be restored by running when it is seventy-five below. No matter how fast he runs, the wet feet will freeze the harder.

All this the man knew. The old-timer on Sulphur Creek had told him about it the previous fall, and now he was appreciating the advice. Already all sensation had gone out of his feet. To build the fire he had been forced to remove his mittens, and the fingers had quickly gone numb. His pace of four miles an hour had kept his heart pumping blood to the surface of his body and to all the extremities. But the instant he stopped, the action of the pump eased down. The cold of space smote the unprotected tip of the planet, and he, being on that unprotected tip, received the full force of the blow. The blood of his body recoiled before it. The blood was alive, like the dog, and like the dog it wanted to hide away and cover itself up from the fearful cold. So long as he walked four miles an hour, he pumped that blood, willy-nilly, to the surface; but now it ebbed away and sank down into the recesses of his body. The extremities were the first to feel its absence. His wet feet froze the faster, and his exposed fingers numbed the faster, though they had not yet begun to freeze. Nose and cheeks were already freezing, while the skin of all his body chilled as it lost its blood.

But he was safe. Toes and nose and cheeks would be only touched by the frost, for the fire was beginning to burn with strength. He was feeding it with twigs the size of his finger. In another minute he would be able to feed it with branches the size of his wrist, and then he could remove his wet footgear, and, while it dried, he could keep his naked feet warm by the fire, rubbing them at first, of course, with snow. The fire was a success. He was safe. He remembered the advice of the old-timer on Sulphur Creek, and smiled. The old-timer had been very serious in laying down the law that no man must travel alone in the Klondike after fifty below. Well, here he was; he had had the accident; he was alone; and he had saved himself. Those old-timers were rather womanish, some of them, he thought. All a man had to do was to keep his head, and he was all right. Any man who was a man could travel alone. But it was surprising, the rapidity with which his cheeks and nose were freezing. And he had not thought his fingers could go lifeless in so short a time. Lifeless they were, for he could scarcely make them move together to grip a twig, and they seemed remote from his body and from him. When he touched a twig, he had to look and see whether or not he had hold of it. The wires were pretty well down between him and his finger ends.

All of which counted for little. There was the fire, snapping and crackling and promising life with every dancing flame. He started to untie his moccasins. They were coated with ice; the thick German socks were like sheaths of iron halfway to the knees; and the moccasin strings were like rods of steel all twisted and knotted as by some conflagration. For a moment he tugged with his numb fingers, then, realizing the folly of it, he drew his sheath knife.

But before he could cut the strings, it happened. It was his own fault or, rather, his mistake. He should not have built the fire under the spruce tree. He should have built it in the open. But it had been easier to pull the twigs from the brush and drop them directly on the fire. Now the tree under which he had done this carried a weight of snow on its boughs. No wind had blown for weeks, and each bough was fully freighted. Each time he had pulled a twig he had communicated a slight agitation to the tree—an imperceptible agitation, so far as he was concerned, but an agitation sufficient to bring about the disaster. High up in the tree one bough capsized its load of snow. This fell on the boughs beneath, capsizing them. This process continued, spreading out and involving the whole tree. It grew like an avalanche, and it descended without warning upon the man and the fire, and the fire was blotted out! Where it had burned was a mantle of fresh and disordered snow.

The man was shocked. It was as though he had just heard his own sentence of death. For a moment he sat and stared at the spot where the fire had been. Then he grew very calm. Perhaps the old-timer on Sulphur Creek was right. If he had only had a trail mate he would have been in no danger now. The trail mate could have built the fire. Well, it was up to him to build the fire over again, and this second time there must be no failure. Even if he succeeded, he would most likely lose some toes. His feet must be badly frozen by now, and there would be some time before the second fire was ready.

Such were his thoughts, but he did not sit and think them. He was busy all the time they were passing through his mind. He made a new foundation for a fire, this time in the open, where no treacherous tree could blot it out. Next he gathered dry grasses and tiny twigs from the high-water flotsam. He could not bring his fingers together to pull them out, but he was able to gather them by the handful. In this way he got many rotten twigs and bits of green moss that were undesirable, but it was the best he could do. He worked methodically, even collecting an armful of the larger branches to be used later when the fire gathered strength. And all the while the dog sat and watched him, a certain yearning wistfulness in its eyes, for it looked upon him as the fire provider, and the fire was slow in coming.

When all was ready, the man reached in his pocket for a second piece of birch bark. He knew the bark was there, and, though he could not feel it with his fingers, he could hear its crisp rustling as he fumbled for it. Try as he would, he could not clutch hold of it. And all the time, in his consciousness was the knowledge that each instant his feet were freezing. This thought tended to put him in a panic, but he fought against it and kept calm. He pulled on his mittens with his teeth, and threshed his arms back and forth, beating his hands with all his might against his sides. He did this sitting down, and he stood up to do it; and all the while the dog sat in the snow, its wolf brush of a tail curled around warmly over its forefront, its sharp wolf ears pricked forward intently as it watched the man. And the man, as he beat and threshed with his arms and hands, felt a great surge of envy as he regarded the creature that was warm and secure in its natural covering.

After a time he was aware of the first faraway signals of sensation in his beaten fingers. The faint tingling grew stronger till it evolved into a stinging ache that was excruciating, but which the man hailed with satisfaction. He stripped the mitten from his right hand and fetched forth the birch bark. The exposed fingers were quickly going numb again. Next he brought out his bunch of sulphur matches. But the tremendous cold had already driven the life out of his fingers. In his effort to separate one match from the others, the whole bunch fell in the snow. He tried to pick it out of the snow, but failed. The dead fingers could neither touch nor clutch. He was very careful. He drove the thought of his freezing feet, and nose and cheeks, out of his mind, devoting his whole soul to the matches. He watched, using the sense of vision in place of that touch, and when he saw his fingers on each side of the bunch, he closed them—that is, he willed to close them, for the wires were down, and the fingers did not obey. He pulled the mitten on the right hand, and beat it fiercely against his knee. Then with both mittened hands, he scooped the bunch of matches, along with much snow, into his lap. Yet he was no better off.

After some manipulation he managed to get the bunch between the heels of his mittened hands. In this fashion he carried it to his mouth. The ice crackled and snapped when by a violent effort he opened his mouth. He drew the lower jaw in, curled the upper lip out of the way, and scraped the bunch with his upper teeth in order to separate a match. He succeeded in getting one, which he dropped on his lap. He was no better off. He could not pick it up. Then he devised a way. He picked it up in his teeth and scratched it on his leg. Twenty times he scratched before he succeeded in lighting it. As it flamed he held it with his teeth to the birch bark. But the burning brimstone went up his nostrils and into his lungs, causing him to cough spasmodically. The match fell into the snow and went out.

The old-timer on Sulphur Creek was right, he thought in the moment of controlled despair that ensued: after fifty below, a man should travel with a partner. He beat his hands, but failed in exciting any sensation. Suddenly he bared both hands, removing the mittens with his teeth. He caught the whole bunch between the heels of his hands. His arm muscles not being frozen enabled him to press the hand heels tightly against the matches. Then he scratched the bunch along his leg. It flared into flame, seventy sulphur matches at once! There was no wind to blow them out. He kept his head to one side to escape the strangling fumes, and held the blazing bunch to the birch bark. As he so held it, he became aware of sensation in his hand. His flesh was burning. He could smell it. Deep down below the surface he could feel it. The sensation developed into pain that grew acute. And still he endured it, holding the flame of the matches clumsily to the bark that would not light readily because his own burning hands were in the way, absorbing most of the flame.

At last, when he could endure no more, he jerked his hands apart. The blazing matches fell sizzling into the snow, but the birch bark was alight. He began laying dry grasses and the tiniest twigs on the flame. He could not pick and choose, for he had to lift the fuel between the heels of his hands. Small pieces of rotten wood and green moss clung to the twigs, and he bit them off as well as he could with his teeth.

He cherished the flame carefully and awkwardly. It meant life, and it must not perish. The withdrawal of blood from the surface of his body now made him begin to shiver, and he grew more awkward. A large piece of green moss fell squarely on the little fire. He tried to poke it out with his fingers, but his shivering frame made him poke too far, and he disrupted the nucleus of the little fire, the burning grasses and tiny twigs separating and scattering. He tried to poke them together again, but in spite of the tenseness of the effort, his shivering got away with him, and the twigs were hopelessly scattered. Each twig gushed a puff of smoke and went out. The fire provider had failed. As he looked apathetically about him, his eyes chanced on the dog, sitting across the ruins of the fire from him, in the snow, making restless, hunching movements, slightly lifting one forefoot and then the other, shifting its weight back and forth on them with wistful eagerness.

The sight of the dog put a wild idea into his head. He remembered the tale of the man, caught in a blizzard, who killed a steer and crawled inside the carcass, and so was saved. He would kill the dog and bury his hands in the warm body until the numbness went out of them. Then he could build another fire. He spoke to the dog, calling it to him; but in his voice was a strange note of fear that frightened the animal, who had never known the man to speak in such a way before. Something was the matter, and its suspicious nature sensed danger—it knew not what danger, but somewhere, somehow, in its brain arose an apprehension of the man. It flattened its ears down at the sound of the man's voice, and its restless, hunching movements and the liftings and shiftings of its forefeet became more pronounced; but it would not come to the man. He got on his hands and knees and crawled towards the dog. This unusual posture again excited suspicion, and the animal sidled mincingly away.

The man sat up in the snow for a moment and struggled for calmness. Then he pulled on his mittens, by means of his teeth, and got upon his feet. He glanced down at first in order to assure himself that he was really standing up, for the absence of sensation in his feet left him unrelated to the earth. His erect position in itself started to drive the webs of suspicion from the dog's mind; and when he spoke peremptorily, with the sound of whip lashes in his voice, the dog rendered its customary allegiance and came to him. As it came within reaching distance, the man lost his control. His arms flashed out to the dog, and he experienced genuine surprise when he discovered that his hands could not clutch, that there was neither bend nor feeling in the fingers. He had forgotten for the moment that they were frozen and that they were freezing more and more. All this happened quickly, and before the animal could get away, he encircled its body with his arms. He sat down in the snow, and in this fashion held the dog, while it snarled and whined and struggled.

But it was all he could do, hold its body encircled in his arms and sit there. He realized he could not kill the dog. There was no way to do it. With his helpless hands he could neither draw nor hold his sheath knife nor throttle the animal. He released it, and it plunged wildly away, with tail between its legs, and still snarling. It halted forty feet away and surveyed him curiously, with ears sharply pricked forward.

The man looked down at his hands in order to locate them, and found them hanging on the ends of his arms. It struck him as curious that one should have to use his eyes in order to find out where his hands were. He began threshing his arms back and forth, beating the mittened hands against his sides. He did this for five minutes, violently, and his heart pumped enough blood up to the surface to put a stop to his shivering. But no sensation was aroused in the hands. He had an impression that they hung like weights on the ends of his arms, but when he tried to run the impression down, he could not find it.

A certain fear of death, dull and oppressive, came to him. This fear quickly became poignant as he realized that it was no longer a mere matter of freezing his fingers and toes, or of losing his hands and feet, but that it was a matter of life and death with the chances against him. This threw him into a panic, and he turned and ran up the creek bed along the old, dim trail. The dog joined in behind him and kept up with him. He ran blindly, without intention, in fear such as he had never known in his life. Slowly, as he ploughed and foundered through the snow, he began to see things again—the banks of the creek, the old timber jams, the leafless aspens, and the sky. The running made him feel better. He did not shiver. Maybe, if he ran on, his feet would thaw out; and, anyway, if he ran far enough, he would reach camp and the boys. Without doubt he would lose some fingers and toes and some of his face; but the boys would take care of him, and save the rest of him when he got there. And at the same time there was another thought in his mind that said he would never get to the camp and the boys; that it was too many miles away, that the freezing had too great a start on him, and that he would soon be stiff and dead. This thought he kept in the background and refused to consider. Sometimes it pushed itself forward and demanded to be heard but he thrust it back and strove to think of other things.

It struck him as curious that he could run at all on feet so frozen that he could not feel them when they struck the earth and took the weight of his body. He seemed to himself to skim along above the surface, and to have no connection with the earth. Somewhere he had once seen a winged Mercury, and he wondered if Mercury felt as he felt when skimming over the earth.

His theory of running until he reached camp and the boys had one flaw in it: he lacked the endurance. Several times he stumbled, and finally he tottered, crumpled up, and fell. When he tried to rise, he failed. He must sit and rest, he decided, and next time he would merely walk and keep on going. As he sat and regained his breath, he noted that he was feeling quite warm and comfortable. He was not shivering, and it even seemed that a warm glow had come to his chest and trunk. And yet, when he touched his nose or cheeks, there was no sensation. Running would not thaw them out. Nor would it thaw out his hands and feet. Then the thought came to him that the frozen portions of his body must be extending. He tried to keep this thought down, to forget it, to think of something else; he was aware of the panicky feeling that it caused, and he was afraid of the panic. But the thought asserted itself, and persisted, until it produced a vision of his body totally frozen. This was too much, and he made another wild run along the trail. Once he slowed down to a walk, but the thought of the freezing extending itself made him run again.

And all the time the dog ran with him, at his heels. When he fell down a second time, it curled its tail over its forefeet and sat in front of him, facing him, curiously eager and intent. The warmth and security of the animal angered him, and he cursed it till it flattened down its ears appealingly. This time the shivering came more quickly upon the man. He was losing in his battle with the frost. It was creeping into his body from all sides. The thought of it drove him on, but he ran no more than a hundred feet, when he staggered and pitched headlong. It was his last panic. When he had recovered his breath and control, he sat up and entertained in his mind the conception of meeting death with dignity. However, the conception did not come to him in such terms. His idea of it was that he had been making a fool of himself, running around like a chicken with its head cut off—such was the simile that occurred to him. Well, he was bound to freeze anyway, and he might as well take it decently. With this newfound peace of mind came the first glimmerings of drowsiness. A good idea, he thought, to sleep off to death. It was like taking an anaesthetic. Freezing was not so bad as people thought. There were lots worse ways to die.

He pictured the boys finding his body next day. Suddenly he found himself with them, coming along the trail looking for himself. And, still with them, he came around a turn in the trail and found himself lying in the snow. He did not belong with himself any more, for even then he was out of himself, standing with the boys and looking at himself in the snow. It certainly was cold, was his thought. When he got back to the States he could tell the folks what real cold was. He drifted on from this to a vision of the old-timer on Sulphur Creek. He could see him quite clearly, warm and comfortable, and smoking a pipe.

"You were right, old hoss; you were right," the man mumbled to the old-timer of Sulphur Creek.

Then the man drowsed off into what seemed to him the most comfortable and satisfying sleep he had ever known. The dog sat facing him and waiting. The brief day drew to a close in a long, slow twilight. There were no signs of a fire to be made, and, besides, never in the dog's experience had it known a man to sit like that in the snow and make no fire. As the twilight drew on, its eager yearning for the fire mastered it, and with a great lifting and shifting of forefeet, it whined softly, then flattened its ears down in anticipation of being chidden by the man. But the man remained silent. Later the dog whined loudly. And still later it crept close to the man and caught the scent of death. This made the animal bristle and back away. A little longer it delayed, howling under the stars that leaped and danced and shone brightly in the cold sky. Then it turned and trotted up the trail in the direction of the camp it knew, where were the other food providers and fire providers.

—1910

JON TEVLIN

B. 1958

In the late 1980s a men's movement began to take shape in the United States, based on the feeling that men have lost something since the advent of civilization and, more recently, women's liberation. Led by Minnesota poet Robert Bly, men began to gather together on weekend retreats "to get in touch with the wild man inside"—to become more in tune with their bodies, their inner boys, and nature. "We will become animals and heroes, honor our ancestors . . . drum, frolic, and play together," read the promotional brochure that piqued the interest of journalist Jon Tevlin and led him to attend a "mythopoetic" weekend retreat near Minneapolis.

Tevlin was born in Minneapolis and earned a B.A. in journalism and political science from the University of Minnesota before becoming a freelance writer. For eight years he specialized in writing first-person essays and profiles, often focused on male-female relationships, for a variety of publications. In 1995 he became the senior editor of the Twin Cities Reader, *an alternative weekly newspaper.*

Tevlin approached the mythopoetic weekend described in the following piece, which first appeared in Minneapolis's City Pages (June 28, 1989), with some skepticism. The weekend seems to have done nothing to dispel his feeling that if men need to participate in more honest and meaningful exchanges, to become more aware of their lives and their relationships, frolicking in the male wilderness may not be the best means to that end.

Of Hawks and Men: A Weekend in the Male Wilderness

A beautiful Friday afternoon, second weekend of walleye season, somewhere in the Western suburbs of the Twin Cities. I was following a roughly drawn map with the words "Mythopoetic Weekend—A Journey Into the Male Wilderness" scrawled across the top. As I came to a rise where a dirt road met the sun, it occurred to me that I was profoundly lost.

This may or may not have been an omen. Suffice to say I was eventually directed to Camp Kingswood by an old man in a bait shop who claimed he was "damned near blind." He probably thought I was just looking for *fish*. Actually, I was looking for the heart of the "new masculinity," where our fathers, brothers (literal and figurative), and ancestors lurk in the forested cul de sacs of the male soul. According to the doyens of the new maleness movement, it is a deep, dark place, where the "wild man" of our collective unconscious cries out—"Arooo!"—from some inner bog. Where our animal instincts speak in tongues and say things like, "We must learn to actualize our selves." Where women and liquor are absolutely prohibited. It is a hostile place.

Because I got lost, I arrived late to Camp Kingswood; mythopoesy was already running rampant. Most of the dozen participants had chosen their group, symbolized by an animal which would "transport us from the logical world to the illogical, animal world." At the bunkhouse where we would sleep, group leaders had tried to influence prospective members by constructing the habitat of either the wolf or the red-tailed hawk. When I saw the hawks' nest—a bunch of branches circled around some plastic lounge chairs—I knew I was home. For the remainder of the weekend, I would soar with the raptors, a decision that elicited from a fellow hawk a somewhat disturbing birdlike stare. "Caw! Caw!" he said, in an apparent attempt to welcome me.

"Howdy," I said.

One of the first to greet me was a man with a clipboard who asked for the remainder of the $225 tuition, "so we can do away with the material world and move on to the spiritual." The next man to greet me was our weekend "group facilitator," a small man in an Amish-style beard with the highly improbable name of Shepherd Bliss. Bliss, a professor of psychology at John F. Kennedy University in San Francisco and author of several books on men and mythology, is a well-known speaker and leader of men's retreats who has been featured on national news programs and in periodicals. According to a résumé I had received earlier, he has also been an Army officer and an ordained United Methodist minister. He had dropped his given first name—Walter—several years ago, but invited us to call him Shepherd. The symbolism of that name was not lost on this camper.

I met the rest of my fellow travelers during what Shepherd called "a naming exercise," in which each man moved to the center of our circle and said his name.

We followed that with short biographies of ourselves, each man in turn coaxed to "get beneath the superficial," and open ourselves to the group. We each got three minutes, the time dutifully logged by Shepherd.

It was during this time I was discovered to be the youngest participant. "Stand up," Shepherd said. "This is the youngest man here. I want you all to acknowledge that." They did. I don't know why.

There was really only one other man—a 60-year-old businessman—who didn't have a previous link with some type of men's group. Because he exhibited initial skepticism, he became my natural confidant. The rest ranged from a psychoanalyst-men's leader from Ohio to an assorted bag of refugees from bad marriages and ugly childhoods. Many were cultural vagabonds, expatriates from the various venues of self-help—yoga, Tai Chi, meditation, est.

Most of us were self-conscious, and all a bit anxious about being here. But while I expected them to be hesitant about sharing their ghosts and fears, many instead erupted over the merest inquiry about themselves, spilling over like boiling pots to a hostage, but sincerely interested, audience:

"When I was a kid, they called me 'handbags,'" confessed a large, amiable man. "It was very painful."

"I recently discovered I had a child inside me that was never allowed to play," said another. "And now that child is on fire."

Though we'd only met a few hours ago, some of the men wept openly—not as much over their own stories as over the stories of others.

"I feel the power in what you are saying" was a common response to each story. In fact, their words revealed a kind of gooeyness wrapped in clinical psych jargon. Other than that, they were decent, normal guys with fairly typical emotional landscapes—filled with divots, I mean.

Early that evening, I had the first of several basic philosophical differences with Shepherd. In the middle of a serious discussion, he lifted one leg and issued a loud, sudden emission. "When I was walking with [Gary] this afternoon he farted very loudly," said Shepherd, wisely. "I became immediately at ease. It's a natural behavior—a very *male* behavior. Farting is one of those typically *male* behaviors that has been suppressed by society."

Thus sanctioned by Shepherd, flatulence would become a major form of communication for the rest of the weekend. Though I didn't say so at the time, it occurred to me that some male rituals are suppressed for perfectly legitimate social reasons. Farting loudly in public is one taboo of which I personally approve.

The retreat, though independent of local and national men's groups, was patterned after dozens of others held around the country. They are popular particularly in California, specifically near San Francisco. But as men become increasingly confused about their role, these retreats are drawing larger and larger numbers; it has, in effect, become a part of the national self-awareness movement, which by now has become a huge national industry. The gatherings range from small ones like ours to massive men-ins drawing hundreds of participants. The biggest ones—the grand-daddies, if you will—are those hosted by Minnesota poet Robert Bly, the widely acknowledged guru and spiritual pioneer of a loose coalition of men's groups and men-advocates.

Although he was not physically in evidence at Camp Kingswood, Bly's presence cast a large shadow on the events, so much so that I began to think of the reverence shown him as "The Cult of Robert." His poetry was recited. His quotes were committed to memory. His philosophy was expounded. We heard about his wrestling prowess, his "barrel chest," and his affinity for water. Shepherd would tell me later that he envied Robert's ability to be "belligerent" to people he didn't like. "He's so honest," he said. I noticed that everyone referred to him as "Robert," regardless of whether they'd ever met him.

Robert's premise—the one that was underscored this weekend, anyway—is that men, in the face of the feminist movement of the past two decades, have lost their sense of the "deep masculine," not to mention the more temporal role models needed to bring the species into proper manhood. Gone are the gods of ancient mythology. Gone are the true warriors and true lovers, the kings and leaders, replaced by the pop culture heroes of television. According to Robert and his followers, men have also given away their "wild man," an ancient part of the male psyche which allows them a measure of playfulness, and connects men to their "father earth." The wild man, who appears in myths and fables, is not a creature of malice or brutality, they say, but one comfortable with his masculinity. (Despite what some women fear, we are assured that this is not a reaction to feminism, but rather a parallel sort of growth.)

The purpose of the seminar was to reunite the modern man with the wild man through mythology, poetry, mask-making, and drumming. Or, in the lexicon of the promotional material: "To form a weekend community of diverse individuals which can help restore the positive male community and facilitate the healing of each man and the context of humans, animals, and plants within which he dwells. . . . We will become animals and heroes, honor our ancestors . . . drum, frolic, and play together."

Forewarned though I was, I found myself totally unprepared for the frolicking.

As he spoke of recovering the "wild man within" that first night, Shepherd slowly dropped to his knees. "Some of you may want to temporarily leave the world of the two-leggeds, and join me in the world of the four-leggeds," he said. One by one, we slid from our orange Naugahyde chairs onto an orange shag carpet ripped straight out of the 1960s. "You may find yourself behaving like these four-leggeds; you may be scratching the earth, getting in contact with the dirt and world around you."

As he spoke, people began pawing at the ground. Some rolled on the carpet, tiny flecks of orange shag sticking to their hair and beards. "You may find yourself behaving like the most masculine of all animals—the ram," Shepherd said in a coaxing voice. "And you may find yourself butting heads."

I felt a slight nudge in my left side, and another on my right. Two men were in front of me, foreheads locked tightly.

"You may find unfamiliar noises emerging from your throats!" Shepherd suggested as he crawled around the carpet. There were gurgles and bleats, a few wolf calls, and the unmistakable shriek of a red-tailed hawk. Hesitant at first, I eventually began to snort. "Grau, pffft, grrr," I said. "Awk, awk," someone replied.

Out of the corner of my eye, I saw Shepherd coming toward me, head down, tufts of white hair ringing a bald spot. I pivoted, and met him squarely—perhaps a little too squarely, I think in retrospect. He recoiled, and sought another ram. Meanwhile, I felt a slight presence at my rear, and turned to see a man beginning to sniff my buttocks.

"Woof!" he said.

There are times in the life of each man when he comes to a precipice and is forced to look back and try to determine what odd spin of the earth, what misstep or wrong turn, has led him to a certain unfortunate and unexplainable spot. For me, this was that time. How did I get to this particular orange shag carpet at this particular Methodist bible camp in Mound, Minnesota, crawling around with a dozen middle-aged men with torn athletic socks and smelly feet, snorting and mooing and sniffing under the orders of a diminutive psychologist from San Francisco?

When each and every head had been fully butted, we regained our chairs and discussed our reactions. One man in the corner said he "felt resistance to being controlled," and for the first time I saw a glimmer of hope. Shepherd thanked "Doug" for the input, then moved straight into the sumo wrestling and the repetitive drumming.

By this time I noticed some quirks about our facilitator. Although he constantly urged us to be "playful," Shepherd himself seemed to be about as playful as . . . well, a psychology professor. His posture seemed unnaturally erect, as though he'd been a recent whiplash victim, and one-on-one he was decidedly impersonal. It was during the wrestling that I had a fantasy. In my fantasy, I imagined Shepherd choosing me to wrestle, and I imagined myself suddenly stepping beyond the boundaries of behavior I realized he had constructed. I saw myself letting loose of the control I observed in the other wrestlers, and throwing Shepherd suddenly to the ground—in effect, introducing real life to the group.

Saturday was to be a time for the "heavy cognitive material." Much of Shepherd's work with men derives from the theories of psychologist Carl Jung, who used archetypes—supposedly innate symbols or "archaic remnants" residing deep inside each person—to investigate the individual psyche.

Many little things took on added meaning here at Camp Kingswood. I noticed, in fact, that virtually everything that happened during the weekend was deemed somehow significant, particularly by Shepherd and the group leaders. When the hired cooks brought chicken, for example, Shepherd was "delighted in this meal. It very much speaks of the family that we will become. The fact that they brought it in whole, rather than in pieces, speaks of something." Whether it spoke of the laziness of the chef or something more primal, he never speculated.

We spent much of our time working on masks, alter egos which we would use in a "Brazilian-style Carnival" that night, and heard several poems by "Robert," as well as by Whitman and Yeats. We also rehearsed for our "animal display," which the hawk leader (the psychologist from Ohio) explained as a skit designed to let us "become our symbol animal; to remove ourselves from the logical world and be wild and spontaneous."

We practiced our display on the beach, in full view of a half-dozen fishermen floating in bass boats offshore. We decided we would represent our clan by linking arms in a V-formation, becoming one giant, swooping hawk. It was during this time I noticed another positive sign. The older businessman paused at one point, his red tail replaced by a red face. "This is ridiculous," he said.

"Sure it's ridiculous," said the hawk leader. "That's the point of the whole weekend, to be ridiculous—you have to let yourself get beyond the logical world. You *have* to be spontaneous." Eventually, we all complied, cavorting and cawing up and down the beach, flapping our wings in unity, a carefully orchestrated and emphatically mandated brand of spontaneous zaniness. Every so often, one of us would dip low and scream "Awk! Awk!" As we soared, young men passed slowly in their bass boats, drinking Schlitz, watching us cautiously, the old ideas of masculinity keeping a respectful distance from the new.

On Saturday, we also did "guided meditations," one to meet our father and one to encounter a personal animal tour leader to help us "commune with the wilderness." As we lay on the floor, Shepherd's voice directed us through the jungles of our subconscious. He told us to imagine meeting a wild animal, then to walk with this animal, talk with this animal, make friends with this animal. Try as I might, I could think only of The Wizard of Oz and Dorothy's scrawny dog, Toto. I was enjoying this walk immensely when it occurred to me that someone was snoring loudly. "It's okay to give yourself over to the sleep," Shepherd responded to the intrusion. "Sleeping does not mean you are bored. It is sometimes a natural reaction to a stimulus. And yawning may be a way for the spirits to enter the soul."

The father meditation was similar, with Shepherd leading the way. Spirits appeared to be entering open mouths at a breakneck pace. Afterwards, we broke into twos to share our experiences, and I got Shepherd. While I described my image—playing snooker and drinking Grain Belt with my dad at Lavardo's Pool Hall on Lake Street—Shepherd sucked in spirits like they were going out of style, continually gazing out the window. In the middle of a sentence, he glanced at his watch and said, "Sorry, time's up." His image was vague. He mumbled something about a father in a wheelchair, and thinking "there are probably some issues to resolve with him, but I don't know what." He yawned and said, "One of the things about being a facilitator is that you don't participate in all the activities."

It was then I realized that Shepherd was absent whenever we did something even slightly silly or embarrassing; he didn't make a mask or do an animal display. Ironically, Shepherd—the man who was to lead us into our more playful, more sensitive masculinity—was becoming an enigma, an ethereal figure who floated about the camp reciting odd bits of poetry, stopping now and again to observe a group activity, but never really participating.

That night we displayed our masks around the campfire, each of us—except Shepherd—taking turns running from the woods to the circle of men, who shouted "Devil," or "Hades," as if we were playing some Greek version of charades. Shepherd recited some poetry, and one man blew a conch "to see how the animals would respond." The response was immediate—a single pistol shot piercing the darkness. "That must be from the rifle range I passed on the way here," someone said.

I was quickly tiring of all this myth-making and role-playing, which I began to see as another way for a group of men to avoid any honest and meaningful exchange. The coarse jokes and superficial dialogue of the real world had simply been replaced by skits and psychologists' babble. When Shepherd ordered more drumming, I sneaked off to bed, the thumping of the bongos pulling me into a deep sleep.

By morning, I had decided the male wilderness was full of ticks, and that the gods of masculinity were calling elsewhere. I don't know quite what I'd expected from the weekend—perhaps discussion about our goals and fears, about how to get along better with ourselves and with women. Or maybe I just wanted a few laughs with some confident men. But what I found was that insecurity, insincerity, and manipulation still reigned; "beaver" jokes still went unchallenged. And though

Shepherd had constantly encouraged us to be "playful," he was one of the stiffest and most pedantic men I'd ever met. All this forced spontaneity was making me feel decidedly rigid and contrived.

If this was indeed a glimpse into the masculinity of the future, then the forest is deeper and darker than I'd imagined. Somewhere out there, I hope, are men willing to take chances, to become more aware of their lives and their relationships. But out there too, I fear, is a growing number of posers and "professionals" willing to make a business out of it.

So after breakfast, during a group meeting, I told Shepherd what I thought about the seminar. A couple others joined in, and after a terse discussion, Shepherd thanked us for our "input" and moved on to the scheduled mythological activities. I, however, did the first truly spontaneous and manly thing I'd done all weekend: I went to my room, packed my bags, and pulled Shepherd aside. "I don't think running around the woods in my mask will do anything more for me at this point," I said. "And, frankly, the best way I can think of to advance relations between women and men right now is to go home and spend the day talking with my wife."

As I said goodbye to the rest of the hawks and wolves I felt something unexpected: I liked these guys. For much of the weekend I had the queer sensation that I was in a high school sociology class in which the teacher put us into incompatible groups, and that I was waiting for the bell so I could get the hell out. What had been mixed feelings of disgust and pity toward many of them had somehow evolved into a sincere respect. At least they had the courage to try to improve their lot and understand themselves a little better; I was just fairly certain that butting heads in the woods was not the way to do it, Robert and his followers notwithstanding.

I said goodbye to the hawks; two of them hugged me. As I was leaving, one of the others touched my hand and said: "Nice connecting with you." Shepherd did not embrace me, nor even shake my hand. But he did hand me a computer printout listing upcoming men's conferences he would be conducting.

As I left the campground I felt a tension release inside me. I snapped on the radio, and heard a sweet but powerful feminine voice from within; Linda Ronstadt was singing "Poor, Poor, Pitiful Me." I turned it up as loud as it would go, stepping hard on the accelerator. I felt the power.

—1989

HENRY DAVID THOREAU
1817-1862

"I go and come with a strange liberty in Nature, a part of herself," wrote Henry David Thoreau. Writer, political activist, natural historian, and surveyor, Thoreau is one of the central figures in American cultural history, ironic indeed for an author so fiercely critical of American culture. He was born in Concord, Massachusetts, and though he made extensive travels in New England and once as far west as Minnesota, he was perfectly content to spend most of his life in his native town. Paradoxically, in his willful insistence upon staying at home he became one of the most cosmopolitan citizens the town of Concord has ever produced.

A graduate of Harvard University as well as a close friend and one-time disciple of Ralph Waldo Emerson, Thoreau is usually associated with the group of intellectuals and writers who called themselves the transcendentalists. Thoreau's life and writings, however, resist such easy categorization. He was very much engaged with the dominant political issue of his lifetime, the question of slavery. His eloquent denouncements of a government that would condone such immorality had influence in his own time but even more profoundly in the twentieth century, when his writings—in particular the essay "Resistance to Civil Government," now known more widely as "Civil Disobedience"—helped shape the philosophy of activists such as Mahatma Gandhi and Martin Luther King, Jr.

Thoreau is best remembered today for his retreat (he called it an "experiment") conducted in a small house he built for himself in the woods at Walden Pond from 1845 to 1847, the events of which provided him with the material for his masterpiece, Walden (1854). This book is frequently mistaken to be the account of a man who turned his back on society and fled to the woods as a sort of hermit, but in fact one of Thoreau's great themes is to urge his reader to participate fully in the world and to recognize the moral responsibilities inherent in being human. In "Solitude," the fifth chapter of Walden, he warns against the distraction of excessive contact with human society and reminds us of our essentially spiritual nature and our kinship with nonhuman nature. According to Thoreau, awareness of what we have in common with other animals and with all of nature can keep us from ever having to feel truly alone.

SOLITUDE

This is a delicious evening, when the whole body is one sense, and imbibes delight through every pore. I go and come with a strange liberty in Nature, a part of herself. As I walk along the stony shore of the pond in my shirt sleeves, though it is cool as well as cloudy and windy, and I see nothing special to attract me, all the elements are unusually congenial to me. The bullfrogs trump to usher in the night, and the note of the whippoorwill is borne on the rippling wind from over the water. Sympathy with the fluttering alder and poplar leaves almost takes away my breath; yet, like the lake, my serenity is rippled but not ruffled. These small waves raised by the evening wind are as remote from storm as the smooth reflecting surface. Though it is now dark, the wind still blows and roars in the wood, the waves still dash, and some creatures lull the rest with their notes. The repose is never complete. The wildest animals do not repose, but seek their prey now; the fox, and skunk, and rabbit, now roam the fields and woods without fear. They are Nature's watchmen—links which connect the days of animated life.

When I return to my house I find that visitors have been there and left their cards, either a bunch of flowers, or a wreath of evergreen, or a name in pencil on a yellow walnut leaf or a chip. They who come rarely to the woods take some little piece of the forest into their hands to play with by the way, which they leave, either intentionally or accidentally. One has peeled a willow wand, woven it into a ring, and dropped it on my table. I could always tell if visitors had called in my absence, either by the bended twigs or grass, or the print of their shoes, and generally of what sex or age or quality they were by some slight trace left, as a flower dropped, or a bunch of grass plucked and thrown away, even as far off as the railroad, half a mile distant, or by the lingering odor of a cigar or pipe. Nay, I was frequently notified of the passage of a traveler along the highway sixty rods off by the scent of his pipe.

There is commonly sufficient space about us. Our horizon is never quite at our elbows. The thick wood is not just at our door, nor the pond, but somewhat is always clearing, familiar and worn by us, appropriated and fenced in some way, and reclaimed from Nature. For what reason have I this vast range and circuit, some square miles of unfrequented forest, for my privacy, abandoned to me by men? My nearest neighbor is a mile distant, and no house is visible from any place but the hilltops within half a mile of my own. I have my horizon bounded by woods all to myself; a distant view of the railroad where it touches the pond on the one hand, and of the fence which skirts the woodland road on the other. But for the most part it is as solitary where I live as on the prairies. It is as much Asia or Africa as New England. I have, as it were, my own sun and moon and stars, and a little world all to myself. At night there was never a traveler passed my house, or knocked at my door, more than if I were the first or last man; unless it were in the spring, when at long intervals some came from the village to fish for pouts—they plainly fished much more in the Walden Pond of their own natures, and baited their hooks with darkness—but they soon retreated, usually with light baskets, and left "the world to darkness and to me," and the black kernel of the night was never profaned by any human neighborhood. I believe that men are generally still a little afraid of the dark, though the witches are all hung, and Christianity and candles have been introduced.

Yet I experienced sometimes that the most sweet and tender, the most innocent and encouraging society may be found in any natural object, even for the poor misanthrope and most melancholy man. There can be no very black melancholy to him who lives in the midst of Nature and has his senses still. There was never yet such a storm but it was Aeolian music to a healthy and innocent ear. Nothing can rightly compel a simple and brave man to a vulgar sadness. While I enjoy the friendship of the seasons I trust that nothing can make life a burden to me. The gentle rain which waters my beans and keeps me in the house today is not drear and melancholy, but good for me too. Though it prevents my hoeing them, it is of far more worth than my hoeing. If it should continue so long as to cause the seeds to rot in the ground and destroy the potatoes in the lowlands, it would still be good for the grass on the uplands, and, being good for the grass, it would be good for me. Sometimes, when I compare myself with other men, it seems as if I were more favored by the gods than they, beyond any deserts that I am conscious of; as if I had a warrant and surety at their hands which my fellows have not, and were especially guided and guarded. I do not flatter myself, but if it be possible they flatter me. I have never felt lonesome, or in the least oppressed by a sense of solitude, but once, and that was a few weeks after I came to the woods, when, for an hour, I doubted if the near neighborhood of man was not essential to a serene and healthy life. To be alone was something unpleasant. But I was at the same time conscious of a slight insanity in my mood, and seemed to foresee my recovery. In the midst of a gentle rain while these thoughts prevailed, I was suddenly sensible of such sweet and beneficent society in Nature, in the very pattering of the drops, and in every sound and sight around my house, an infinite and unaccountable friendliness all at once like an atmosphere sustaining me, as made the fancied advantages of human neighborhood insignificant, and I have never thought of them since. Every little pine needle expanded and swelled with sympathy and befriended me. I was so distinctly made aware of the presence of something kindred to me, even in scenes which we are accustomed to call wild and dreary, and also that the nearest of blood to me and humanest was not a person nor a villager, that I thought no place could ever be strange to me again.

> "Mourning untimely consumes the sad;
> Few are their days in the land of the living,
> Beautiful daughter of Toscar."

Some of my pleasantest hours were during the long rainstorms in the spring or fall, which confined me to the house for the afternoon as well as the forenoon, soothed by their ceaseless roar and pelting; when an early twilight ushered in a long evening in which many thoughts had time to take root and unfold themselves. In those driving northeast rains which tried the village houses so, when the maids stood ready with mop and pail in front entries to keep the deluge out, I sat behind my door in my little house, which was all entry, and thoroughly enjoyed its protection. In one heavy thundershower the lightning struck a large pitch pine across the pond, making a very conspicuous and perfectly regular spiral groove from top to bottom, an inch or more deep, and four or five inches wide, as you would groove a walking-stick. I passed it again the other day, and was struck with awe on looking up and beholding that mark, now more distinct than ever, where a terrific and resistless bolt came down out of the harmless sky eight years ago. Men frequently say to me, "I should think you would feel lonesome down there, and want to be nearer to folks, rainy and snowy days and nights especially." I am tempted to reply to such, This whole earth which we inhabit is but a point in space. How far apart, think you, dwell the two most distant inhabitants of yonder star, the breadth of whose disk cannot be appreciated by our instruments? Why should I feel lonely? is not our planet in the Milky Way? This which you put seems to me not to be the most important question. What sort of space is that which separates a man from his fellows and makes him solitary? I have found that no exertion of the legs can bring two minds much nearer to one another. What do we want most to dwell near to? Not to many men surely, the depot, the post-office, the barroom, the meeting-house, the school-house, the grocery, Beacon Hill, or the Five Points, where men most congregate, but to the perennial source of our life, whence in all our experience we have found that to issue, as the willow stands near the water and sends out its roots in that direction. This will vary with different natures, but this is the place where a wise man will dig his cellar. . . . I one evening overtook one of my townsmen, who has accumulated what is called "a handsome property"—though I never got a *fair* view of it—on the Walden road, driving a pair of cattle to market, who inquired of me how I could bring my mind to give up so many of the comforts of life. I answered that I was very sure I liked it passably well; I was not joking. And so I went home to my bed, and left him to pick his way through the darkness and the mud to Brighton—or Brighttown—which place he would reach some time in the morning.

Any prospect of awakening or coming to life to a dead man makes indifferent all times and places. The place where that may occur is always the same, and indescribably pleasant to all our senses. For the most part we allow only outlying and transient circumstances to make our occasions. They are, in fact, the cause of our distraction. Nearest to all things is that power which fashions their being. *Next* to us the grandest laws are continually being executed. *Next* to us is not the workman whom we have hired, with whom we love so well to talk, but the workman whose work we are.

"How vast and profound is the influence of the subtile powers of Heaven and of Earth!

"We seek to perceive them, and we do not see them; we seek to hear them, and we do not hear them; identified with the substance of things, they cannot be separated from them.

"They cause that in all the universe men purify and sanctify their hearts, and clothe themselves in their holiday garments to offer sacrifices and oblations to their ancestors. It is an ocean of subtile intelligences. They are everywhere, above us, on our left, on our right; they environ us on all sides."

We are the subjects of an experiment which is not a little interesting to me. Can we not do without the society of our gossips a little while under these circumstances, have our own thoughts to cheer us? Confucius says truly, "Virtue does not remain as an abandoned orphan; it must of necessity have neighbors."

With thinking we may be beside ourselves in a same sense. By a conscious effort of the mind we can stand aloof from actions and their consequences; and all things, good and bad, go by us like a torrent. We are not wholly involved in Nature. I may be either the driftwood in the stream, or Indra in the sky looking down on it. I *may* be affected by a theatrical exhibition; on the other hand, I *may not* be affected by an actual event which appears to concern me much more. I only know myself as a human entity; the scene, so to speak, of thoughts and affections; and am sensible of a certain doubleness by which I can stand as remote from myself as from another. However intense my experience, I am conscious of the presence and criticism of a part of me, which, as it were, is not a part of me, but spectator, sharing no experience, but taking note of it; and that is no more I than it is you. When the play, it may be the tragedy, of life is over, the spectator goes his way. It was a kind of fiction, a work of the imagination only, so far as he was concerned. This doubleness may easily make us poor neighbors and friends sometimes.

I find it wholesome to be alone the greater part of the time. To be in company, even with the best, is soon wearisome and dissipating. I love to be alone. I never found the companion that was so companionable as solitude. We are for the most part more lonely when we go abroad among men than when we stay in our chambers. A man thinking or working is always alone, let him be where he will. Solitude is not measured by the miles of space that intervene between a man and his fellows. The really diligent student in one of the crowded hives of Cambridge College is as solitary as a dervish in the desert. The farmer can work alone in the field or the woods all day, hoeing or chopping, and not feel lonesome, because he is employed; but when he comes home at night he cannot sit down in a room alone, at the mercy of his thoughts, but must be where he can "see the folks," and recreate, and as he thinks remunerate, himself for his day's solitude; and hence he wonders how the student can sit alone in the house all night and most of the day without ennui and "the blues"; but he does not realize that the student, though in the house, is still at work in *his* field, and chopping in *his* woods, as the farmer in his, and in turn seeks the same recreation and society that the latter does, though it may be a more condensed form of it.

Society is commonly too cheap. We meet at very short intervals, not having had time to acquire any new value for each other. We meet at meals three times a day, and give each other a new taste of that old musty cheese that we are. We have had to agree on a certain set of rules, called etiquette and politeness, to make this frequent meeting tolerable and that we need not come to open war. We meet at the post-office, and at the sociable, and about the fireside every night; we live thick and are in each other's way, and stumble over one another, and I think that we thus lose some respect for one another. Certainly less frequency would suffice for all important and hearty communications. Consider the girls in a factory—never alone, hardly in their dreams. It would be better if there were but one inhabitant to a square mile, as where I live. The value of a man is not in his skin, that we should touch him.

I have heard of a man lost in the woods and dying of famine and exhaustion at the foot of a tree, whose loneliness was relieved by the grotesque visions with which, owing to bodily weakness, his diseased imagination surrounded him, and which he believed to be real. So also, owing to bodily and mental health and strength, we may be continually cheered by a like but more normal and natural society, and come to know that we are never alone.

I have a great deal of company in my house; especially in the morning, when nobody calls. Let me suggest a few comparisons, that someone may convey an idea of my situation. I am no more lonely than the loon in the pond that laughs so loud, or than Walden Pond itself. What company has that lonely lake, I pray? And yet it has not the blue devils, but the blue angels in it, in the azure tint of its waters. The sun is alone, except in thick weather, when there sometimes appear to be two, but one is a mock sun. God is alone—but the devil, he is far from being alone, he sees a great deal of company, he is legion. I am no more lonely than a single mullein or dandelion in a pasture, or a bean leaf, or sorrel, or a horsefly, or a bumblebee. I am no more lonely than the Mill Brook, or a weather cock, or the North Star, or the south wind, or an April shower, or a January thaw, or the first spider in a new house.

I have occasional visits in the long winter evenings, when the snow falls fast and the wind howls in the wood, from an old settler and original proprietor, who is reported to have dug Walden Pond, and stoned it, and fringed it with pine woods; who tells me stories of old time and of new eternity; and between us we manage to pass a cheerful evening with social mirth and pleasant views of things, even without apples or cider—a most wise and humorous friend, whom I love much, who keeps himself more secret than ever did Goffe or Whalley; and though he is thought to be dead, none can show where he is buried. An elderly dame, too, dwells in my neighborhood, invisible to most persons, in whose odorous herb garden I love to stroll sometimes, gathering simples and listening to her fables; for she has a genius of unequaled fertility, and her memory runs back farther than mythology, and she can tell me the original of every fable, and on what fact every one is founded, for the incidents occurred when she was young. A ruddy and lusty old dame, who delights in all weathers and seasons, and is likely to outlive all her children yet.

The indescribable innocence and beneficence of Nature—of sun and wind and rain, of summer and winter—such health, such cheer, they afford forever! and such sympathy have they ever with our race, that all Nature would be affected, and the sun's brightness fade, and the winds would sigh humanely, and the clouds rain tears, and the woods shed their leaves and put on mourning in midsummer, if any man should ever for a just cause grieve. Shall I not have intelligence with the earth? Am I not partly leaves and vegetable mould myself?

What is the pill which will keep us well, serene, contented? Not my or thy great-grandfather's, but our great-grandmother Nature's universal, vegetable, botanic medicines, by which she has kept herself young always, outlived so many old Parrs in her day, and fed her health with their decaying fatness. For my panacea, instead of one of those quack vials of a mixture dipped from Acheron and the Dead Sea, which come out of those long shallow black-schooner-looking wagons which we sometimes see made to carry bottles, let me have a draught of undiluted morning air. Morning air! If men will not drink of this at the fountainhead of the day, why, then, we must even bottle up some and sell it in the shops, for the benefit of those who have lost their subscription ticket to morning time in this world. But remember, it will not keep quite till noonday even in the coolest cellar, but drive out the stopples long ere that and follow westward the steps of Aurora. I am no worshiper of Hygeia, who was the daughter of that old herb-doctor Aesculapius, and who is represented on monuments holding a serpent in one hand, and in the other a cup out of which the serpent sometimes drinks; but rather of Hebe, cupbearer to Jupiter, who was the daughter of Juno and wild lettuce, and who had the power of restoring gods and men to the vigor of youth. She was probably the only thoroughly sound-conditioned, healthy, and robust young lady that ever walked the globe, and wherever she came it was spring.

—1854

TOM WOLFE

B. 1931

Tom Wolfe is the originator of the literary style known as new journalism, also practiced by such prominent writers as Truman Capote, Norman Mailer, and Hunter S. Thompson. New journalism, in contrast to the traditional journalism that aims for accurate and dispassionate reporting of the bare facts, applies the techniques of fiction to the reporting of actual events and interjects the author's own personality and prejudices. Wolfe developed this approach in the 1960s while writing feature articles for Esquire *and other publications. He honed it in* The Electric Kool-Aid Acid Test *(1968), an investigation of the 1960s counterculture, and in* The Right Stuff *(1979), a portrayal of the first astronauts.*

Born in Richmond, Virginia, Wolfe earned a Ph.D. from Yale University in American studies. "Wolfe is essentially a satirist and a student of sociology who writes about people as if they were specimens under his microscope," comments one critical appraisal of his work. Wolfe branched out into novels with The Bonfire of the Vanities *(1987), a harshly realistic portrayal of New York as a dog-eat-dog city.*

Foreshadowing that portrayal is the following selection from Wolfe's 1968 book, The Pump House Gang. *In "O Rotten Gotham," Wolfe employs his characteristic colorful hyperbole to examine what happens when "humans' basic animal requirements for space" are not respected, a chronic situation in overcrowded cities. Like a good sociologist, he speculates that cultural differences in requirements for space account for the uneasiness different ethnic groups feel around one another.*

O ROTTEN GOTHAM

I just spent two days with Edward T. Hall, an anthropologist, watching thousands of my fellow New Yorkers short-circuiting themselves into hot little twitching death balls with jolts of their own adrenalin. Dr. Hall says it is overcrowding that does it. Overcrowding gets the adrenalin going, and the adrenalin gets them hyped up. And here they are, hyped up, turning bilious, nephritic, queer, autistic, sadistic, barren, batty, sloppy, hot-in-the-pants, chancred-on-the-flankers, leering, puling, numb— the usual in New York, in other words, and God knows what else. Dr. Hall has the theory that overcrowding has already thrown New York into a state of behavioral sink. Behavioral sink is a term from ethology, which is the study of how animals relate to their environment. Among animals, the sink winds up with a "population collapse" or "massive die-off." O rotten Gotham.

It got to be easy to look at New Yorkers as animals, especially looking down from some place like a balcony at Grand Central at the rush hour Friday afternoon. The floor was filled with the poor white humans, running around, dodging, blinking their eyes, making a sound like a pen full of starlings or rats or something.

"Listen to them skid," says Dr. Hall.

He was right. The poor old etiolate animals were out there skidding on their rubber soles. You could hear it once he pointed it out. They stop short to keep from hitting somebody or because they are disoriented and they suddenly stop and look around, and they skid on their rubber-sole shoes, and a screech goes up. They pour out onto the floor down the escalators from the Pan-Am Building, from 42nd Street, from Lexington Avenue, up out of subways, down into subways, railroad trains, up into helicopters—

"You can also hear the helicopters all the way down here," says Dr. Hall. The sound of the helicopters using the roof of the Pan-Am Building nearly fifty stories up beats right through. "It it weren't for this ceiling"—he is referring to the very high ceiling in Grand Central—"this place would be unbearable with this kind of crowding. And yet they'll probably never 'waste' space like this again."

They screech! And the adrenal glands in all those poor white animals enlarge, micrometer by micrometer, to the size of cantaloupes. Dr. Hall pulls a Minox camera out of a holster he has on his belt and starts shooting away at the human scurry. The Sink!

Dr. Hall has the Minox up to his eye—he is a slender man, calm, 52 years old, young-looking, an anthropologist who has worked with Navajos, Hopis, Spanish-Americans, Negroes, Trukese. He was the most important anthropologist in the government during the crucial years of the foreign aid program, the 1950's. He directed both the Point Four training program and the Human Relations Area Files. He wrote *The Silent Language* and *The Hidden Dimension*, two books that are picking up the kind of "underground" following his friend Marshall McLuhan started picking up about five years ago. He teaches at the Illinois Institute of Technology, lives with his wife, Mildred, in a high-ceilinged town house on one of the last great residential streets in downtown Chicago, Astor Street; has a grown son and daughter, loves good food, good wine, the relaxed, civilized life—but comes to New York with a Minox at his eye to record—perfect!—The Sink.

We really got down in there by walking down into the Lexington Avenue line subway stop under Grand Central. We inhaled those nice big fluffy fumes of human sweat, urine, effluvia, and sebaceous secretions. One old female human was already stroked out on the upper level, on a stretcher, with two policemen standing by. The other humans barely looked at her. They rushed into line. They bellied each other, haunch to paunch, down the stairs. Human heads shone through the gratings. The species North European tried to create bubbles of space around themselves, about a foot and a half in diameter

"See, he's reacting against the line," says Dr. Hall.

—but the species Mediterranean presses on in. The hell with bubbles of space. The species North European resents that, this male human behind him presses forward toward the booth . . . *breathing* on him, he's disgusted. He pulls out of the line entirely, the species Mediterranean resents him for resenting it, and neither of them realizes what the hell they are getting irritable about exactly. And in all of them the old adrenals grow another micrometer.

Dr. Hall whips out the Minox. Too perfect! The bottom of The Sink.

It is the sheer overcrowding, such as occurs in the business sections of Manhattan five days a week and in Harlem, Bedford-Stuyvesant, southeast Bronx every day—sheer overcrowding is converting New Yorkers into animals in a sink pen. Dr. Hall's argument runs as follows: all animals, including birds, seem to have a built-in, inherited requirement to have a certain amount of territory, space, to lead their lives in. Even if they have all the food they need, and there are no predatory animals threatening them, they cannot tolerate crowding beyond a certain point. No more than two hundred wild Norway rats can survive on a quarter acre of ground, for example, even when they are given all the food they can eat. They just die off.

But why? To find out, ethologists have run experiments on all sorts of animals, from stickleback crabs to Sika deer. In one major experiment, an ethologist named John Calhoun put some domesticated white Norway rats in a pen with four sections to it, connected by ramps. Calhoun knew from previous experiments that the rats tend to split up into groups of ten to twelve and that the pen, therefore, would hold forty to forty-eight rats comfortably, assuming they formed four equal groups. He allowed them to reproduce until there were eighty rats, balanced between male and female, but did not let it get any more crowded. He kept them supplied with plenty of food, water, and nesting materials. In other words, all their more obvious needs were taken care of. A less obvious need—space—was not. To the human eye, the pen did not even look especially crowded. But to the rats, it was crowded beyond endurance.

The entire colony was soon plunged into a profound behavioral sink. "The sink," said Calhoun, "is the outcome of any behavioral process that collects animals together in unusually great numbers. The unhealthy connotations of the term are not accidental: a behavioral sink does act to aggravate all forms of pathology that can be found within a group."

For a start, long before the rat population reached eighty, a status hierarchy had developed in the pen. Two dominant male rats took over the two end sections, acquired harems of eight to ten females each, and forced the rest of the rats into the two middle pens. All the overcrowding took place in the middle pens. That was where the "sink" hit. The aristocrat rats at the ends grew bigger, sleeker, healthier, and more secure the whole time.

In The Sink, meanwhile, nest building, courting, sex behavior, reproduction, social organization, health—all of it went to pieces. Normally, Norway rats have a mating ritual in which the male chases the female, the female ducks down into a burrow and sticks her head up to watch the male. He performs a little dance outside the burrow, then she comes out, and he mounts her, usually for a few seconds. When The Sink set in, however, no more than three males—the dominant males in the middle sections—kept up the old customs. The rest tried everything from satyrism to homosexuality or else gave up on sex altogether. Some of the subordinate males spent all their time chasing females. Three or four might chase one female at the same time, and instead of stopping at the burrow entrance for the ritual, they would charge right in. Once mounted, they would hold on for minutes instead of the usual seconds.

Homosexuality rose sharply. So did bisexuality. Some males would mount any-thing—males, females, babies, senescent rats, anything. Still other males dropped sexual activity altogether, wouldn't fight and, in fact, would hardly move except when the other rats slept. Occasionally a female from the aristocrat rats' harems would come over the ramps and into the middle sections to sample life in The Sink. When she had had enough, she would run back up the ramp. Sink males would give chase up to the top of the ramp, which is to say, to the very edge of the aristocratic preserve. But one glance from one of the king rats would stop them cold and they would return to The Sink.

The slumming females from the harems had their adventures and then returned to a placid, healthy life. Females in The Sink, however, were ravaged, physically and psychologically. Pregnant rats had trouble continuing pregnancy. The rate of mis-carriages increased significantly, and females started dying from tumors and other disorders of the mammary glands, sex organs, uterus, ovaries, and Fallopian tubes. Typically, their kidneys, livers, and adrenals were also enlarged or diseased or showed other signs associated with stress.

Child-rearing became totally disorganized. The females lost the interest or the stamina to build nests and did not keep them up if they did build them. In the gen-eral filth and confusion, they would not put themselves out to save offspring they were momentarily separated from. Frantic, even sadistic competition among the males was going on all around them and rendering their lives chaotic. The males began unprovoked and senseless assaults upon one another, often in the form of tail-biting. Ordinarily, rats will suppress this kind of behavior when it crops up. In The Sink, male rats gave up all policing and just looked out for themselves. The "pecking order" among males in The Sink was never stable. Normally, male rats set up a three-class structure. Under the pressure of overcrowding, however, they broke up into all sorts of unstable subclasses, cliques, packs—and constantly pushed, probed, explored, tested one another's power. Anyone was fair game, except for the aristocrats in the end pens.

Calhoun kept the population down to eighty, so that the next stage, "population collapse" or "massive die-off," did not occur. But the autopsies showed that the pat-tern—as in the diseases among the female rats—was already there.

The classic study of die-off was John J. Christian's study of Sika deer on James Island in the Chesapeake Bay, west of Cambridge, Maryland. Four or five of the deer had been released on the island, which was 280 acres and uninhabited, in 1916. By 1955 they had bred freely into a herd of 280 to 300. The population density was only about one deer per acre at this point, but Christian knew that this was already too high for the Sikas' inborn space requirements, and something would give before long. For two years the number of deer remained 280 to 300. But suddenly, in 1958, over half the deer died; 161 carcasses were recovered. In 1959 more deer died and the population steadied at about 80.

In two years, two-thirds of the herd had died. Why? It was not starvation. In fact, all the deer collected were in excellent condition, with well-developed muscles, shining coats, and fat deposits between the muscles. In practically all the deer, however, the adrenal glands had enlarged by 50 percent. Christian concluded that the die-off was due to "shock following severe metabolic disturbance, probably as a result of prolonged adrenocortical hyperactivity. . . . There was no evidence of infection, starvation, or other obvious cause to explain the mass mortality." In other words, the constant stress of overpopulation, plus the normal stress of the cold of the winter, had kept the adrenalin flowing so constantly in the deer that their systems were depleted of blood sugar and they died of shock.

Well, the white humans are still skidding and darting across the floor of Grand Central. Dr. Hall listens a moment longer to the skidding and the darting noises, and then says, "You know, I've been on commuter trains here after everyone has been through one of these rushes and I'll tell you, there is enough acid flowing in the stomachs in every car to dissolve the rails underneath."

Just a little invisible acid bath for the linings to round off the day. The ulcers the acids cause, of course, are the one disease people have already been taught to associate with the stress of city life. But overcrowding, as Dr. Hall sees it, raises a lot more hell with the body than just ulcers. In everyday life in New York—just the usual, getting to work, working in massively congested areas like 42nd Street between Fifth Avenue and Lexington, especially now that the Pan-Am Building is set in there, working in cubicles such as those in the editorial offices at Time-Life, Inc., which Dr. Hall cites as typical of New York's poor handling of space, working in cubicles with low ceilings and, often, no access to a window, while construction crews all over Manhattan drive everybody up the Masonite wall with air-pressure generators with noises up to the boil-a-brain decibel levels, then rushing to get home, piling into subways and trains, fighting for time and for space, the usual day in New York—the whole now-normal thing keeps shooting jolts of adrenalin into the body, breaking down the body's defenses and winding up with the work-a-daddy human animal stroked out at the breakfast table with his head apoplexed like a cauliflower out of his $6.95 semispread Pima-cotton shirt, and nosed over into a plate of No-Kolestro egg substitute, signing off with the black thrombosis, cancer, kidney, liver, or stomach failure, and the adrenals ooze to a halt, the size of eggplants in July.

One of the people whose work Dr. Hall is interested in on this score is Rene Dubos at the Rockefeller Institute. Dubos's work indicates that specific organisms, such as the tuberculosis bacillus or a pneumonia virus, can seldom be considered "the cause" of a disease. The germ or virus, apparently, has to work in combination with other things that have already broken the body down in some way—such as the old adrenal hyperactivity. Dr. Hall would like to see some autopsy studies made to record the size of adrenal glands in New York, especially of people crowded into slums and people who go through the full rush-hour-work-rush-hour cycle every day. He is afraid that until there is some clinical, statistical data on how overcrowding actually ravages the human body, no one will be willing to do anything about it. Even in so obvious a thing as air pollution, the pattern is familiar. Until people can actually see the smoke or smell the sulphur or feel the sting in their eyes, politicians will not get excited about it, even though it is well known that many of the lethal substances polluting the air are invisible and odorless. For one thing, most politicians are like the aristocrat rats. They are insulated from The Sink by practically sultanic buffers—limousines, chauffeurs, secretaries, aides-de-camp, doormen, shuttered houses, high-floor apartments. They almost never ride subways, fight rush hours, much less live in the slums or work in the Pan-Am Building.

We took a cab from Grand Central to go up to Harlem, and by 48th Street we were already socked into one of those great, total traffic jams on First Avenue on Friday afternoon. Dr. Hall motions for me to survey the scene, and there they all are, humans, male and female, behind the glass of their automobile windows, soundlessly going through the torture of their own adrenalin jolts. This male over here contracts his jaw muscles so hard that they bunch up into a great cheese Danish pattern. He twists his lips, he bleeds from the eyeballs, he shouts . . . soundlessly behind glass . . . the fat corrugates on the back of his neck, his whole body shakes as he pounds the heel of his hand into the steering wheel. The female human in the car ahead of him whips her head around, she bares her teeth, she screams . . . soundlessly behind glass . . . she throws her hands up in the air, Whaddya expect me—Yah, yuh stupid—and they all sit there, trapped in their own congestion, bleeding hate all over each other, shorting out the ganglia and—goddam it—

Dr. Hall sits back and watches it all. This is it! The Sink! And where is everybody's wandering boy?

Dr. Hall says, "We need a study in which drivers who go through these rush hours every day would wear GSR bands."

GSR?

"Galvanic skin response. It measures the electric potential of the skin, which is a function of sweating. If a person gets highly nervous, his palms begin to sweat. It is an index of tension. There are some other fairly simple devices that would record respiration and pulse. I think everybody who goes through this kind of experience all the time should take his own pulse—not literally—but just be aware of what's happening to him. You can usually tell when stress is beginning to get you physically."

In testing people crowded into New York's slums, Dr. Hall would like to take it one step further—gather information on the plasma hydrocortisone level in the blood or the corticosteroids in the urine. Both have been demonstrated to be reliable indicators of stress, and testing procedures are simple.

The slums—we finally made it up to East Harlem. We drove into 101st Street, and there was a new, avant-garde little church building, the Church of the Epiphany, which Dr. Hall liked—and, next to it, a pile of rubble where a row of buildings had been torn down, and from the back windows of the tenements beyond several people were busy "airmailing," throwing garbage out the window, into the rubble, beer cans, red shreds, the No-Money-Down Eames roller stand for a TV set, all flying through the air onto the scaggy sump. We drove around some more in Harlem, and a sequence was repeated, trash, buildings falling down, buildings torn down, rubble, scaggy sumps or, suddenly, a cluster of high-rise apartment projects, with fences around the grass.

"You know what this city looks like?" Dr. Hall said. "It looks bombed out. I used to live at Broadway and 124th Street back in 1946 when I was studying at Columbia. I can't tell you how much Harlem has changed in twenty years. It looks bombed out. It's broken down. People who live in New York get used to it and don't realize how filthy the city has become. The whole thing is typical of a behavioral sink. So is something like the Kitty Genovese case—a girl raped and murdered in the courtyard of an apartment complex and forty or fifty people look on from their apartments and nobody even calls the police. That kind of apathy and anomie is typical of the general psychological deterioration of The Sink."

He looked at the high-rise housing projects and found them mainly testimony to how little planners know about humans' basic animal requirements for space.

"Even on the simplest terms," he said, "it is pointless to build one of these blocks much over five stories high. Suppose a family lives on the fifteenth floor. The mother will be completely cut off from her children if they are playing down below, because the elevators are constantly broken in these projects, and it often takes half an hour, literally half an hour, to get the elevator if it is running. That's very common. A mother in that situation is just as much a victim of overcrowding as if she were back in the tenement block. Some Negro leaders have a bitter joke about how the white man is solving the slum problem by stacking Negroes up vertically, and there is a lot to that."

For one thing, says Dr. Hall, planners have no idea of the different space requirements of people from different cultures, such as Negroes and Puerto Ricans. They are all treated as if they were minute, compact middle-class whites. As with the Sika deer, who are overcrowded at one per acre, overcrowding is a relative thing for the human animal, as well. Each species has its own feeling for space. The feeling may be "subjective," but it is quite real.

Dr. Hall's theories on space and territory are based on the same information, gathered by biologists, ethologists, and anthropologists, chiefly, as Robert Ardrey's. Ardrey has written two well-publicized books, *African Genesis* and *The Territorial Imperative*. *Life* magazine ran big excerpts from *The Territorial Imperative*, all about how the drive to acquire territory and property and add to it and achieve status is built into all animals, including man, over thousands of centuries of genetic history, etc., and is a more powerful drive than sex. *Life's* big display prompted Marshall McLuhan to crack, "They see this as a great historic justification for free enterprise and Republicanism. If the birds do it and the stickle-back crabs do it, then it's right for man." To people like Hall and McLuhan, and Ardrey, for that matter, the right or wrong of it is irrelevant. The only thing they find inexcusable is the kind of thinking, by influential people, that isn't even aware of all this. Such as the thinking of most city planners.

"The planners always show you a bird's-eye view of what they are doing," he said. "You've seen those scale models. Everyone stands around the table and looks down and says that's great. It never occurs to anyone that they are taking a bird's-eye view. In the end, these projects do turn out fine, when viewed from an airplane."

As an anthropologist, Dr. Hall has to shake his head every time he hears planners talking about fully integrated housing projects for the year 1980 or 1990, as if by then all cultural groups will have the same feeling for space and will live placidly side by side, happy as the happy burghers who plan all the good clean bird's-eye views. According to his findings, the very fact that every cultural group does have its own peculiar, unspoken feeling for space is what is responsible for much of the uneasiness one group feels around the other.

It is like the North European and the Mediterranean in the subway line. The North European, without ever realizing it, tries to keep a bubble of space around himself, and the moment a stranger invades that sphere, he feels threatened. Mediterranean peoples tend to come from cultures where everyone is much more involved physically, publicly, with one another on a day-to-day basis and feels no uneasiness about mixing it up in public, but may have very different ideas about space inside the home. Even Negroes brought up in America have a different vocabulary of space and gesture from the North European Americans who, historically, have been their models, according to Dr. Hall. The failure of Negroes and whites to communicate well often boils down to things like this: some white will be interviewing a Negro for a job; the Negro's culture has taught him to show somebody you are interested by looking right at him and listening intently to what he has to say. But the species North European requires something more. He expects his listener to nod from time to time, as if to say, "Yes, keep going." If he doesn't get this nodding, he feels anxious, for fear the listener doesn't agree with him or has switched off. The Negro may learn that the white expects this sort of thing, but he isn't used to the precise kind of nodding that is customary, and so he may start overresponding, nodding like mad, and at this point the North European is liable to think he has some kind of stupid Uncle Tom on his hands, and the guy still doesn't get the job.

The whole handling of space in New York is so chaotic, says Dr. Hall, that even middle-class housing now seems to be based on the bird's-eye models for slum projects. He took a look at the big Park West Village development, set up originally to provide housing in Manhattan for families in the middle-income range, and found its handling of space very much like a slum project with slightly larger balconies. He felt the time has come to start subsidizing the middle class in New York on its own terms—namely, the kind of truly "human" spaces that still remain in brownstones.

"I think New York City should seriously consider a program of encouraging the middle-class development of an area like Chelsea, which is already starting to come up. People are beginning to renovate houses there on their own, and I think if the city would subsidize that sort of thing with tax reliefs and so forth, you would be amazed at what would result. What New York needs is a string of minor successes in the housing field, just to show everyone that it can be done, and I think the middle class can still do that for you. The alternative is to keep on doing what you're doing now, trying to lift a very large lower class up by main force almost and finding it a very slow and discouraging process.

"But before deciding how to redesign space in New York," he said, "people must first simply realize how severe the problem already is. And the handwriting is already on the wall."

"A study published in 1962," he said, "surveyed a representative sample of people living in New York slums and found only 18 percent of them free from emotional symptoms. Thirty-eight percent were in need of psychiatric help, and 23 percent were seriously disturbed or incapacitated. Now, this study was published in 1962, which means the work probably went on from 1955 to 1960. There is no telling how bad it is now. In a behavioral sink, crises can develop rapidly."

Dr. Hall would like to see a large-scale study similar to that undertaken by two sociopsychologists, Chombart de Lauwe and his wife, in a French working-class town. They found a direct relationship between crowding and general breakdown. In families where people were crowded into the apartment so that there was less than 86 to 108 square feet per person, social and physical disorders doubled. That would mean that for four people the smallest floor space they could tolerate would be an apartment, say, 12 by 30 feet.

What would one find in Harlem? "It is fairly obvious," Dr. Hall wrote in *The Hidden Dimension*, "that the American Negroes and people of Spanish culture who are flocking to our cities are being very seriously stressed. Not only are they in a setting that does not fit them, but they have passed the limits of their own tolerance of stress. The United States is faced with the fact that two of its creative and sensitive peoples are in the process of being destroyed and like Samson could bring down the structure that houses us all."

Dr. Hall goes out to the airport, to go back to Chicago, and I am coming back in a cab, along the East River Drive. It is four in the afternoon, but already the damned drive is clogging up. There is a 1959 Oldsmobile just to the right of me. There are about eight people in there, a lot of popeyed silhouettes against a leopard-skin dashboard, leopard-skin seats—and the driver is classic. He has a mustache, sideburns down to his jaw socket, and a tattoo on his forearm with a Rossetti painting of Jane Burden Morris with her hair long. All right; it is even touching, like a postcard photo of the main drag in San Pedro, California. But suddenly Sideburns guns it and cuts in front of my cab so that my driver has to hit the brakes, and then hardly 100 feet ahead Sideburns hits a wall of traffic himself and has to hit his brakes, and then it happens. A stuffed white Angora animal, a dog, no, it's a Pekingese cat, is mounted in his rear window—as soon as he hits the brakes its *eyes* light up, Nighttown pink. To keep from ramming him, my driver has to hit the brakes again, too, and so here I am, out in an insane, jammed-up expressway at four in the afternoon, shuddering to a stop while a stuffed Pekingese grows bigger and bigger and brighter in the eyeballs directly in front of me. Jolt! Nighttown pink! Hey—that's me the adrenalin is hitting, *I* am this white human sitting in a projectile heading amid a mass of clotted humans toward white Angora stuffed goddam leopard-dash Pekingese freaking cat—kill that damned Angora—Jolt!—got me— another micrometer on the old adrenals—

—1968

PATTIANN ROGERS

B. 1940

Pattiann Rogers writes lushly detailed poetry that describes the profusion and extravagance of nature and at the same time conveys a sense of the divinity that encompasses it all. In seven books of poems, she has strived to capture "that elusive divinity as it comes to us and recedes from us in its myriad and glorious manifestations." She takes delight in her own fully embodied participation in the natural world, as such poems as her noted "Rolling Naked in the Morning Dew" make clear.

Born in Joplin, Missouri, Rogers earned a B.A. at the University of Missouri and an M.A. at the University of Houston. She has taught as a visiting writer at several universities and won numerous prizes and grants for her poetry. Her most recent book is Eating Bread and Honey *(1997). The mother of two grown sons, she has also written essays about the importance of parenting, declaring in one entitled "Cradle," "I cannot think of anything more important for the future of the earth than that we have loving, diligent mothers and fathers caring for our children." She lives in Castle Rock, Colorado, with her husband.*

"Knot," from her 1989 volume Splitting and Binding, *points up the irony that the brain that observes and analyzes and classifies and separates cannot itself be separated from the web of nature. Though with our intellect we may feel above and in control of it all, in fact this is an illusion, and our animal bodies are securely woven into a larger reality.*

KNOT

Watching the close forest this afternoon
and the riverland beyond, I delineate
quail down from the dandelion's shiver
from the blowzy silver of the cobweb
in which both are tangled. I am skillful
at tracing the white egret within the white
branches of the dead willow where it roosts
and at separating the heron's graceful neck
from the leaning stems of the blue-green
lilies surrounding. I know how to unravel
sawgrasses knitted to iris leaves knitted
to sweet vernals. I can unwind sunlight
from the switches of the water in the slough
and divide the grey sumac's hazy hedge
from the hazy grey of the sky, the red vein
of the hibiscus from its red blossom.

All afternoon I part, I isolate, I untie,
I undo, while all the while the oak
shadows, easing forward, slowly ensnare me,
and the calls of the wood peewees catch
and latch in my gestures, and the spicebush
swallowtails weave their attachments
into my attitude, and the damp sedge
fragrances hook and secure, and the swaying
Spanish mosses loop my coming sleep,
and I am marsh-shackled, forest-twined,
even as the new stars, showing now
through the night-spaces of the sweet gum
and beech, squeeze into the dark
bone of my breast, take their perfectly
secured stitches up and down, pull
all of their thousand threads tight
and fasten, fasten.

—1989

2

How do we regard other creatures,
and what do our encounters
with them reveal about us?

CLOSE ENCOUNTERS

DENISE LEVERTOV

1923-1997

Denise Levertov was born and raised in England but became one of the most American of poets, notable for her political activism against the Vietnam War and later against nuclear proliferation and American intervention in El Salvador. Her subject matter has been described as "feminine without being feminist": many of her poems explore the complex truths of a woman's life and of intimate relationships, while others express a large concern for social justice and a love for the earth and its creatures. Always her work reflects her belief that a poem is a record of an inner song, a "sonic, sensuous event."

Levertov was educated mostly at home by her Welsh mother, BBC programs, and private tutors during a bucolic childhood in Ilford, Essex. She became a nurse during World War II, married the writer Mitchell Goodman (she was later divorced after bearing a son), and emigrated to the United States in 1948, becoming a naturalized citizen in 1955. She taught at a number of universities, including Tufts and Stanford, served as poetry editor of the liberal journal The Nation, and published more than a dozen volumes of poetry as well as collections of essays and reviews.

"Come into Animal Presence" (collected in Poems 1960-1967), takes up a recurring theme in Levertov's work: the world is infused with a holy radiance, if only we have eyes to see it. The poem suggests that although our sight has faltered, we can regain a sense of joy by once again seeing animals as they are, sacred presences complete and perfect in themselves, not dependent on our estimation for their value.

COME INTO ANIMAL PRESENCE

Come into animal presence.
No man is so guileless as
the serpent. The lonely white
rabbit on the roof is a star
twitching its ears at the rain.
The llama intricately
folding its hind legs to be seated
not disdains but mildly
disregards human approval.
What joy when the insouciant
armadillo glances at us and doesn't
quicken his trotting
across the track into the palm bush.
What is this joy? That no animal
falters, but knows what it must do?
That the snake has no blemish,
that the rabbit inspects his strange surroundings
in white star-silence? The llama
rests in dignity, the armadillo
has some intention to pursue in the palm forest.
Those who were sacred have remained so,
holiness does not dissolve, it is a presence
of bronze, only the sight that saw it
faltered and turned from it.
An old joy returns in holy presence.

—1966

JAMES WRIGHT
1927-1980

James Wright published nine books of poetry during his career and achieved prominence, together with William Stafford, Robert Bly, and Louis Simpson, as a poet of the "emotive imagination." Critics have referred to these poets as deep imagists, emphasizing their extension of the school of early-twentieth-century imagist poetry (exemplified by poets such as Ezra Pound, H. D., and William Carlos Williams) to highlight the emotional aspect of experience. Wright's work frequently explores specific instances of either human suffering or natural beauty, and sometimes the conjunction of the two. In a 1975 interview for the Paris Review, *Peter Stitt asked Wright if he viewed himself as a nature poet in the tradition of Robert Frost, and the poet replied: "Human beings are unhappily part of nature, perhaps nature become conscious of itself. Oh, how I would love to be a chickadee! But I can't be a chickadee, all I can be is what I am. I love the natural world and I'm conscious of the pain in it. So I'm a nature poet who writes about human beings in nature. I love Nietzsche, who called man 'the sick animal.'"*

Wright was born and raised in the steel mill town of Martins Ferry, Ohio. Following military service in Japan during World War II, he attended Kenyon College in Ohio, graduating in 1952. A Fulbright scholarship sent him to the University of Vienna for a year, and then he enrolled at the University of Washington, earning his M.A. in 1954 and his Ph.D. in 1959. A student of Theodore Roethke at Washington, Wright received several awards for his own poetry as a graduate student, and his first collection, The Green Wall, *was selected for the Yale Series of Younger Poets in 1957. He taught at the University of Minnesota and Macalester College in St. Paul until 1965; from 1966 until his death, he was on the faculty at Hunter College in New York City. Wright's books of poetry include* Saint Judas *(1959),* The Branch Will Not Break *(1963),* Shall We Gather at the River *(1968), and* To a Blossoming Pear Tree *(1977). In 1972, his* Collected Poems *won the Pulitzer Prize.*

"A Blessing," from The Branch Will Not Break, *is one of James Wright's best-known poems. It shows how contact with "nature" (the ponies, the landscape, the breeze) can inspire personal revelations for the human observer/participant. The narrator and his friend stop their car on a Minnesota highway and cross a barbed wire fence (thus leaving behind the human realm) to encounter two horses in an evening pasture. The "happiness" of the horses could be a projection of the narrator's happiness at making contact with nonhuman otherness, just as the horses' "loneliness" could actually be that of the human narrator prior to this moment of contact. The poem is full of images of desire—desire to make contact with otherness and to extend the boundaries of self. The final three lines are typical of Wright's style of concluding with a non sequitur; they imagine (and perhaps anticipate) transcendence of the isolated human self, transcendence of loneliness.*

A BLESSING

Just off the highway to Rochester, Minnesota,
Twilight bounds softly forth on the grass.
And the eyes of those two Indian ponies
Darken with kindness.
They have come gladly out of the willows
To welcome my friend and me.
We step over the barbed wire into the pasture
Where they have been grazing all day, alone.
They ripple tensely, they can hardly contain their happiness
That we have come.
They bow shyly as wet swans. They love each other.
There is no loneliness like theirs.
At home once more,
They begin munching the young tufts of spring in the darkness.
I would like to hold the slenderer one in my arms,
For she has walked over to me
And nuzzled my left hand.

She is black and white,
Her mane falls wild on her forehead,
And the light breeze moves me to caress her long ear
That is delicate as the skin over a girl's wrist.
Suddenly I realize
That if I stepped out of my body I would break
Into blossom.

—1963

WALT WHITMAN

1819-1892

Walt Whitman, one of America's most influential poets, is considered by some scholars to be the principal ancestor of modern poetry in this country. His only book of poetry, Leaves of Grass, *was published in nine ever-expanding editions between 1855 and 1892 and can be read as a single, long, complexly structured poem.* Leaves of Grass *explores the poet's life in relation to his native place, American culture, the natural world, and the greater cosmos. As such, the work belongs to the genre of the autobiographical epic poem; it echoes William Wordsworth's* The Prelude *(1795) and anticipates such personal epic poems of the twentieth century as William Carlos Williams's* Paterson *and Ezra Pound's* The Cantos.

For the nineteenth-century psychologist Richard Maurice Bucke, though, Whitman's significance went far beyond his influential literary experiments. Bucke wrote extensively about Whitman in his book Cosmic Consciousness *(1901), claiming that "Walt Whitman is the best, most perfect, example the world has so far had of the Cosmic Sense, first because he is the man in whom the new faculty has been, probably, most perfectly developed, and especially because he is, par excellence, the man who in modern times has written distinctly and at large from the point of view of Cosmic Consciousness." Bucke thus places Whitman as the exemplar of the exalted state of universal consciousness that, he explains, has been demonstrated to a lesser degree by such historical figures as Gautama Buddha, Jesus, Saint Paul, Dante, Francis Bacon, William Blake, and others.*

Whitman rose to this state from rather humble roots. Born in Huntington on Long Island, New York, he moved with his family to Brooklyn when he was four years old. His father was a carpenter and an unsuccessful real estate speculator. Whitman attended public schools for about six years in Brooklyn and ended his formal education when he was eleven. In 1831, at the age of twelve, he began working for a weekly newspaper called the Long Island Patriot; *for the next fifteen years, Whitman contributed to a variety of New York area newspapers before being named editor of the* Brooklyn Daily Eagle. *In the early 1850s, he began to devote himself to the craft of poetry; in 1855 two of his friends assisted him in setting the type for the first edition of* Leaves of Grass.

The following piece is Section 32 of "Song of Myself," the 52-section poem sequence that appeared in all nine editions of Leaves of Grass. *This poem anticipates James Wright's "A Blessing" with the basic scenario of a human being making contact with a horse, the sense of longing that results from such an encounter, and the desire somehow to exceed the human condition. "Walt Whitman, a cosmos, of Manhattan the son," he writes in Section 24 of "Song of Myself." The phrase "infinite and omnigenous" in the following selection similarly celebrates his expansive sense of self ("cosmic consciousness"), implying his feeling of connectedness to all biological genera.*

I THINK I COULD TURN
AND LIVE WITH ANIMALS

I think I could turn and live with animals, they're so placid and self-contain'd,
I stand and look at them long and long.

They do not sweat and whine about their condition,
They do not lie awake in the dark and weep for their sins,
They do not make me sick discussing their duty to God,
Not one is dissatisfied, not one is demented with the mania of owning things,
Not one kneels to another, nor to his kind that lived thousands of years ago,
Not one is respectable or unhappy over the whole earth.

So they show their relations to me and I accept them,
They bring me tokens of myself, they evince them plainly in their possession.
I wonder where they get those tokens,
Did I pass that way huge times ago and negligently drop them?

Myself moving forward then and now and forever,
Gathering and showing more always and with velocity,
Infinite and omnigenous, and the like of these among them,
Not too exclusive toward the reachers of my remembrancers,
Picking out here one that I love, and now go with him on brotherly terms.

A gigantic beauty of a stallion, fresh and responsive to my caresses,
Head high in the forehead, wide between the ears,
Limbs glossy and supple, tail dusting the ground,
Eyes full of sparkling wickedness, ears finely cut, flexibly moving.

His nostrils dilate as my heels embrace him,
His well-built limbs tremble with pleasure as we race around and return.
I but use you a minute, then I resign you, stallion,
Why do I need your paces when I myself out-gallop them?
Even as I stand or sit passing faster than you.

—1855

JOHN UPDIKE
B. 1932

John Updike, one of the most distinguished contemporary American writers, has published more than sixty books during his career, ranging from poetry to short fiction, to novels, to essay collections, to autobiography and children's books. He is probably best known for his series of Rabbit *novels—*Rabbit, Run *(1960),* Rabbit Redux *(1971),* Rabbit Is Rich *(1981), and* Rabbit at Rest *(1990)—describing the midlife angst of the middle-class American male. Many of his works are set in suburban communities much like his hometown of Shillington, Pennsylvania, and explore the lives of ordinary people; memory and perception are recurring themes.*

Updike earned his B.A. at Harvard University, then attended the Ruskin School of Drawing and Fine Art in Oxford, England, for a year. Many of his early works appeared in the New Yorker, *earning Updike a solid reputation while still in his thirties. Among many other awards, Updike received the National Book Award for fiction in 1963 for his novel* The Centaur; *in 1982, his novel* Rabbit Is Rich *won the Pulitzer Prize for fiction, the American Book Award, and the National Book Critics Circle Award. Massachusetts has been his home for many years.*

The following story was published in Updike's 1962 collection Pigeon Feathers and Other Stories. *The anonymous male protagonist in this story is encased and isolated from the natural world by layers of architecture, clothing, social inhibitions, and mind. Wandering through his still-dark house one winter's dawn, he sees "everything through three polished sheets of glass: the memory of his drunkenness, his present insufficiency of sleep, and the infiltrating brilliance of the circumambient snow," but we sense that the multiple filters obscuring his perception of "reality" include more than just these. What finally jars him, at least momentarily, into an awareness of the outside world is the sudden appearance of a large black crow, nearly crashing into a window. "Something happened," Updike tells us.*

This story is reminiscent of Wallace Stevens's poem "Not Ideas About the Thing But the Thing Itself," which similarly uses the perception of birds outside on a winter morning as the scenario for exploring the remoteness of physical reality: "[That scrawny cry] was part of the colossal sun / Surrounded by its choral rings, / Still far away. It was like / A new knowledge of reality."

THE CROW IN THE WOODS

All the warm night the secret snow fell so adhesively that every twig in the woods about their little rented house supported a tall slice of white, an upward projection which in the shadowless glow of early morning lifted depth from the scene, made it seem Chinese, calligraphic, a stiff tapestry hung from the gray sky, a shield of lace interwoven with black thread. Jack wondered if he had ever seen anything so beautiful before. The snow had stopped. As if it had been a function of his sleep.

He was standing in his bathrobe by the window at dawn because last evening, amid an intricate and antique luxury, he and his wife had dined with their landlords. Two wines, red and darker red, had come with the dinner. Candles on the long table. Two other couples, older, subtly ravaged. Dinner over, the men and women separated and then, the men's throats rasped by brandy and cigars, rejoined in a large room whose walls were, astoundingly, green silk. The mixed sexes chattered immersed in an incoherent brilliance like chandelier facets clashing. And at the end (the clock on the gray marble mantel stating the precipitate hour with golden hands whose threadlike fineness seemed itself a kind of pointed tact) in a final and desperate-feeling flight all swooped up the curving stairs and by invitation into the chamber where in daytime hours the white-haired hostess conducted her marvelous hobby of *cartonnage*. She had fashioned a pagoda of cut colored papers. On the walls there were paper bouquets of flowers framed. On the worktable the most immense, the most triumphantly glossy and nozzled bottle of Elmer's Glue Jack had ever seen; he had never dreamed such a size could exist. The blue bull impressed on the bottle jubilantly laughed. Servants came and wrapped their coats around them. On the front porch the departing guests discovered at midnight a world thinly disguised in snow. The universal descent of snow restricted the area of their vision; outdoors had a domed intimacy. The guests carolled praise; the host, a short and old man, arthritic, preened: his dinner, his wine, his wife's *cartonnage*, and now his snow. Looped, the young couple returned to the little rented house that even was his. They satisfied the sitter, dismissed her into the storm like a disgrace, and, late as it was, made love. So in a reflex of gratitude, when six hours later their child cried, the man arose instead of his wife, and administered comfort.

The soaked diaper released an invisible cloud of ammonia that washed tears into his eyes. The whiteness edging the windows made decisive and cutting the light of the sun, burning behind the sky like a bulb in a paper lampshade. The child's room had become incandescent; the wallpaper, flowered with pale violets, glowed evenly, so that even the fluff-cluttered corners brimmed with purity.

The wordless girl, stripped and puzzled, studied the usual figure of her father, out of season at this hour. The purple bathrobe's wool embrace and the cold pressure of the floor on his feet alike felt flattering; magnified him. His naked giant's thighs kept thrusting between the leaves of the bathrobe into the white air. He saw them, saw everything, through three polished sheets of glass: the memory of his drunkenness, his present insufficiency of sleep, and the infiltrating brilliance of the circumambient snow. As his impressions were sharp, so he was soft. The parallel floorcracks, the paint's salmon sheen, his daughter's sombre and intent gaze like the gaze of a chemically distended pupil—these things received through an instrument which fatigue had wiped clean of distractions, bit deeply into him and pressed, with an urgency not disagreeable, on his bowels.

Though the house was small, it had two bathrooms. He used the one attached to his daughter's room, where the square shower-curtain rod wobbled and tipped from the repeated weight of wet diapers. Around its bolted root the ceiling plaster had crumbled. He stood under a small shadow of amazement looking down at the oval of still water in which floated his several feces like short rotten sticks, strangely burnished.

The toilet flushed; the whole illuminated interior of the little house seemed purged into action. He dressed his daughter's tumblesome body deftly and carried her to the stairs. The top landing gave on the door to his bedroom; he looked in and saw that his wife had changed position in the broadened bed. Her naked arms were flung out of the covers and rested, crook'd, each to a pillow, like spotted ivory framing the cameo of her averted, maned skull. One breast, lifted by the twist of her shoulders, shallow in her sleep, was with its budded center exposed. The sun, probing the shredding sky, sent low through the woods and windowpanes a diluted filigree, finer than color, that spread across her and up the swarthy oak headboard a rhomboidal web. Like moths alighting on gauze, her blue eyes opened.

Discovered, he hid downstairs. The child absentmindedly patted the back of his neck as they descended the tricky narrow steps. These weak touches made his interior tremble as with tentative sunshine. Downstairs was darker. The reflection of the snow was absorbed by the dank and porous furniture. Rented. Good morning, Mr. Thermostat. The milkman would be late today: chains slogging a tune on his stout tires: glory be. The childbearing arm of him ached.

He was unable to find the box of child's cereal. The cupboards brimmed with fine sugar and plastic spoons sprawling in polychrome fans. The catch of the tray of the high chair snagged; the girl's legs were hinged the wrong way. Multiplying motions of uncertainty he set water to heating in a cold-handled pan. Winter. Warm cereal. Where? The ceiling rumbled; the plumbing sang.

Came the wife and mother, came, wrapped in a cocoon that made her body shapeless, her face white. She had not been able to go back to sleep after he had left the bed. Proud, relieved, soft, he sat at the small pine table burnished with linseed oil. Gerber's wheat-dust came to smoke in the child's tray. Orange juice, slender as a crayon, was conjured before him. Like her sister the earth, the woman puts forth easy flowers of abundance. As he lifted the glass to his lips he smelled her on his fingertips.

And now released to return to his companion through the window, he again stared. The woods at their distance across the frosted lawn were a Chinese screen in which an immense alphabet of twigs lay hushed: a black robe crusted with white braid standing of its own stiffness. Nothing in it stirred. There was no depth, the sky a pearl slab, the woods a fabric of vision in which vases, arches, and fountains were hushed.

His wife set before him a boiled egg smashed and running on a piece of toast on a pink plate chipped and gleaming on the oblique placemat of sunlight flecked with the windowpane's imperfections.

Something happened. Outdoors a huge black bird came flapping with a crow's laborious wingbeat. It banked and, tilted to fit its feet, fell toward the woods. His heart halted in alarm for the crow, with such recklessness assaulting an inviolable surface, seeking so blindly a niche for its strenuous bulk where there was no depth. It could not enter. Its black shape shattering like an instant of flak, the crow plopped into a high branch and sent snow showering from a quadrant of lace. Its wings spread and settled. The vision destroyed, his heart overflowed. "Clare!" he cried.

The woman's pragmatic blue eyes flicked from his face to the window where she saw only snow and rested on the forgotten food steaming between his hands. Her lips moved:

"Eat your egg."

—1962

MAXINE HONG KINGSTON

B. 1940

Declared a Living Treasure of Hawaii in 1980, Maxine Hong Kingston has in three major works brought the Chinese-American experience into American literature. Her first book, The Woman Warrior: Memoir of a Girlhood Among Ghosts *(1976), tells the story of growing up biculturally in California, and the second,* China Men *(1980), chronicles the immigration of her father, grandfather, and other male relatives to the West; both interweave legends, folklore, autobiography, and history. A novel,* Tripmaster Monkey *(1989), follows the life of a Chinese-American playwright in San Francisco in the 1960s. Kingston has also written poems, short stories, and articles for magazines and journals.*

Born the oldest of six children of educated Chinese immigrant parents, Maxine Hong worked in the laundry her parents operated in Stockton, California. She earned a B.A. from the University of California at Berkeley, where she majored in engineering before switching to English literature, and married the actor Earll Kingston in 1962. Kingston financed her writing through a series of teaching jobs in California and then Hawaii, where she and her husband moved in 1967 with their son. The success of The Woman Warrior, *which won the National Book Critics Circle Award for nonfiction, enabled Kingston to give up teaching as a steady occupation and devote herself to her writing. But after she and her husband moved back to California in 1984, she returned to the classroom; she now teaches creative writing at UC Berkeley.*

A concern that recurs in Kingston's work is the imagined versus the real. The following piece, originally published in the New York Times *(1978), shows her imagination at play as she encounters some sea creatures at the beach. Although her biologist friend can name the creatures, we get the feeling Kingston prefers her own expansive, delighted view of nature to his increasingly narrow expertise. She seems to value her ability to wonder over the extraordinary things she observes around her in nature.*

A CITY PERSON ENCOUNTERING NATURE

A city person encountering nature hardly recognizes it, has no patience for its cycles, and disregards animals and plants unless they roar and exfoliate in spectacular aberrations. Preferring the city myself, I can better discern natural phenomena when books point them out; I also need to verify what I think I've seen, even though charts of phyla and species are orderly whereas nature is wild, unruly.

Last summer, my friend and I spent three days together at a beach cottage. She got up early every morning to see what "critters" the ocean washed up. The only remarkable things I'd seen at that beach in years were Portuguese man-o-war and a flightless bird, big like a pelican; the closer I waded toward it, the farther out to sea the bird bobbed.

We found flecks of whitish gelatin, each about a quarter of an inch in diameter.

The wet sand was otherwise clean and flat. The crabs had not yet dug their holes. We picked up the blobs on our fingertips and put them in a saucer of sea water along with seaweeds and some branches of coral.

One of the things quivered, then it bulged, unfolded, and flipped over or inside out. It stretched and turned over like a human being getting out of bed. It opened and opened to twice its original size. Two arms and two legs flexed, and feathery wings flared, webbing the arms and legs to the body, which tapered to a graceful tail. Its ankles had tiny wings on them—like Mercury. Its back muscles were articulated like a comic book superhero's—blue and silver metallic leotards outlined with black racing stripes. It's a spaceman, I thought. A tiny spaceman in a spacesuit.

I felt my mind go wild. A little spaceship had dropped a spaceman onto our planet. The other blob went through its gyrations and also metamorphosed into a spaceman. I felt as if I were having the flying dream where I watch two perfect beings wheel in the sky.

The two critters glided about, touched the saucer's edges. Suddenly, the first one contorted itself, turned over, made a bulge like an octopus head, then flipped back, streamlined again. A hole in its side like a porthole or a vent opened and shut. The motions happened so fast, we were not certain we had seen them until both creatures had repeated them many times.

I had seen similar quickenings: dry strawberry vines and dead trout revive in water. Leaves and fins unfurl; colors return.

We went outside to catch more, and our eyes accustomed, found a baby critter. So there were more than a pair of these in the universe. So they grew. The baby had apparently been in the sun too long, though, and did not revive.

The next morning, bored that the critters were not performing more tricks, we blew on them to get them moving. By accident, their eyes or mouths faced, and suckled together. There was a churning. They wrapped their arms, legs, wings around one another.

Not knowing whether they were killing each other or mating, we tried unsuccessfully to part them. Guts, like two worms, came out of the portholes. Intestines, I thought; they're going to die. But the two excrescences braided together like DNA strands, then whipped apart, turned pale, and smokily receded into the holes. The critters parted, flipped, and floated away from each other.

After a long time, both of them fitted their armpits between the coral branches; we assumed that they were depositing eggs.

When we checked the clock, four hours had gone by. We'd both thought it had only been about twenty minutes.

That afternoon, the creatures seemed less distinct, their sharp lines blurring. I rubbed my eyes; the feathers were indeed melting. The beings were disintegrating in the water. I threw the coral as far out as I could into the ocean.

Later, back in town, we showed our biologist friend our sketches, I burbling about visitors from outer space, and he said they were nudibranchs. This was our friend who as a kid had vowed that he would study Nature, but in college, he specialized in marine biology, and in graduate school, he studied shrimps. He was now doing research on one species of shrimp that he had discovered on one reef off O'ahu.

A new climate helps me to see nature. Here are some sights upon moving to Hawai'i:

Seven black ants, led by an orange one, dismembered a fly.

I peeled sunburn off my nose, and later recognized it as the flake of something an ant was marching away with.

A mushroom grew in a damp corner of the living room.

Giant philodendrons tear apart the cars abandoned in the jungle. Tendrils crawl out of the hoods; they climb the shafts of the steam shovels that had dug the highway. Roofs and trunks break open, turn red, orange, brown, and sag into the dirt.

Needing to reach explanations of such strangeness, we bought an English magazine, The Countryman, which reports "The Wild Life and Tame" news.

"Stamped to death—A hitherto peaceful herd of about fifty cows, being fetched in from pasture, suddenly began to rush around, and bellow in a most alarming manner. The source of their interest was a crippled gull, which did its best to escape; but the cows, snorting and bellowing, trampled it to death. They then quieted down and left the field normally.

—Charles Brudett, Hants."

Also: "Big eye, Spring, 1967—When I was living in the Karoo, a man brought me a five-foot cobra which he had just killed. It had been unusually sluggish and the tail of another snake protruded from its mouth. This proved to be a boomslang, also poisonous but back-fanged; it was 1½ inches longer than the cobra and its head-end had been partly digested.

—J. S. Taylor, Fife."

I took some students to the zoo after reading Blake's "Tiger, Tiger, Burning Bright," Stevens's "Thirteen Ways of Looking at a Blackbird," and Lorenz's King Solomon's Ring. They saw the monkeys catch a pigeon and tear it apart. I kept reminding them that that was extraordinary. "Watch an animal going about its regular habits," I said, but then they saw an alligator shut its jaws on a low-flying pigeon. I remembered that I don't see ordinary stuff either.

I've watched ants make off with a used Band-Aid. I've watched a single termite bore through a book, a circle clean through. I saw a pigeon vomit milk, and didn't know whether it was sick, or whether its babies had died and the milk sacs in its throat were engorged. I have a friend who was pregnant at the same time as her mare, and, just exactly like the Chinese superstition that only one of the babies would live, the horse gave birth to a foal in two pieces.

When he was about four, we took our son crabbing for the "crabs with no eyes," as he called them. They did have eyes, but they were on stalks. The crabs fingered the bait as if with hands; very delicately they touched it, turned it, swung it. One grabbed hold of the line, and we pulled it up. But our son, a Cancer, said, "Let's name him Linda." We put Linda back in the river and went home.

—1978

RITA DOVE

B. 1952

When Rita Dove became the seventh poet laureate of the United States in 1993, she was the first African American and the youngest person to hold that position, which she occupied for two one-year terms. She is perhaps best known for her Pulitzer Prize–winning book Thomas and Beulah (1986), a collection of poems based loosely on family stories about her maternal grandmother and grandfather. That book exhibits her characteristic technique of focusing on life's everyday moments—"the smaller, crystallized details we all hinge our lives on"—and connecting them to larger historical currents. Dove has published five poetry collections, a book of short stories (Fifth Sunday, 1985), a novel (Through the Ivory Gate, 1992), and two plays (The Siberian Village, 1991; The Darker Face of the Earth, 1994).

At the time of Dove's birth in Akron, Ohio, her father, who held a master's degree in chemistry, was working as an elevator operator for the Goodyear Tire and Rubber Company because it did not hire blacks as research scientists. Eventually he broke the color barrier to become the company's first black chemist, providing a powerful role model for young Rita. She earned a B.A. in English from Miami University of Ohio before spending a year in Germany as a Fulbright scholar and receiving an M.F.A. from the University of Iowa. In 1979 she married the German writer Fred Viebahn; the two have a daughter and live outside Charlottesville, Virginia. Dove taught at Arizona State University for eight years and is now Commonwealth Professor of English at the University of Virginia.

"Crab-Boil," which is collected in Grace Notes (1989), was inspired by an experience Dove had in Florida in 1962, her first encounter with the reality of racism. In a 1993 interview in the Chicago Tribune, Dove recalled her inability to understand why her family was supposed to remain on the side reserved for blacks, when they were the only ones at the beach that day. The poem draws an effective parallel between the objectification of animals and of ethnic groups that allows others to treat them callously.

CRAB-BOIL

(Ft. Myers, 1962)

Why do I remember the sky
above the forbidden beach,
why only blue and the scratch,
shell on tin, of their distress?
The rest

imagination supplies:
bucket and angry pink beseeching
claws. Why does Aunt Helen
laugh before saying "Look at that—

a bunch of niggers, not
a-one get out 'fore the others pull him
back." I don't believe her—

just as I don't believe they won't come
and chase us back to the colored-only shore
crisp with litter and broken glass.

"When do we kill them?"
"Kill'em? Hell the water does *that*.
They don't feel a thing . . . no nervous system."

I decide to believe this: I'm hungry.
Dismantled, they're merely exotic.
A blushing meat. After all, she *has*
grown old in the South. If
we're kicked out now, I'm ready.

−1989

BARRY LOPEZ

B. 1945

One of the preeminent contemporary American nature writers, Barry Lopez was attracted as a college student to the monastic life. But after visiting the Kentucky monastery where Thomas Merton had lived, Lopez decided against it, commenting, "The work I wanted to do with my life—I didn't have anything specific in mind—I was going to do outside." His training in philosophy and theology at the University of Notre Dame left him with the belief that "you had to be responsible in your life for what you did. You had to be responsible as a human being, responsible as a writer." Lopez's writing clearly emerges from this attitude and is marked by a sense of the moral responsibility toward the planet incurred by the human presence in the world.

Barry Lopez was born in Port Chester, New York, but spent his childhood years in the San Fernando Valley of southern California before returning to New York to attend a Jesuit prep school. At Notre Dame he earned a B.A. in 1966 and an M.A. in teaching in 1968. After a brief stint in graduate school at the University of Oregon (first in creative writing, then in journalism), Lopez quit in 1970 to become a free-lance magazine writer. In addition to his numerous contributions to such magazines as the North American Review, Harper's, *and the* Georgia Review, *Lopez has published volumes of fiction and nonfiction as well as a collection of Native American coyote stories. Many of the short stories collected in* Desert Notes *(1976),* River Notes *(1979),* Winter Count *(1982), and* Field Notes *(1995) display affinities with Native American storytelling and rely upon the sort of uncanny occurrences associated with contemporary magical realism. Both his fiction and his essays gravitate toward the relation between human beings and animals, the subject of his 1978 book* Of Wolves and Men, *which received the John Burroughs Medal for outstanding natural history writing, and the focus of much of* Arctic Dreams: Imagination and Desire in a Northern Landscape, *winner of the 1986 American Book Award. Lopez has lived with his wife, Sandra, for more than twenty-five years in the rainy pine forests along the McKenzie River east of Eugene, Oregon.*

The following essay, from the anthology On Nature's Terms: Contemporary Voices *(1992), first appeared in slightly different form in a*

1989 issue of the journal Witness. *It tells the story of a drive Lopez made from Oregon to Indiana, stopping along the way to offer gestures of "respect" toward animals killed by automobiles. "Why do you bother?" someone asks along the way, to which Lopez responds, "You never know. . . . The ones you give some semblance of burial, to whom you offer an apology, may have been like seers in a parallel culture. It is an act of respect, a technique of awareness." "Apologia" disrupts our complacent attitude toward "road kill," stimulating both anger and compassion. It forces us to wonder what these dead animals represent.*

APOLOGIA

A few miles east of home in the Cascades I slow down and pull over for two raccoons, sprawled still as stones in the road. I carry them to the side and lay them in sun-shot, windblown grass in the barrow pit. In eastern Oregon, along U.S. 20, black-tailed jackrabbits lie like welts of sod—three, four, then a fifth. By the bridge over Jordan Creek, just shy of the Idaho border, in the drainage of the Owyhee River, a crumpled adolescent porcupine leers up almost maniacally over its blood-flecked teeth. I carry each one away from the tarmac into a cover of grass or brush out of decency, I think. And worry. Who are these animals, their lights gone out? What journeys have fallen apart here?

I do not stop to remove each dark blister from the road. I wince before the recently dead, feel my lips tighten, see something else, a fence post, in the spontaneous aversion of my eyes, and pull over. I imagine white silk threads of life still vibrating inside them, even if the body's husk is stretched out for yards, stuck like oiled muslin to the road. The energy that held them erect leaves like a bullet; but the memory of that energy fades slowly from the wrinkled cornea, the bloodless fur.

The raccoons and, later, a red fox carry like sacks of wet gravel and sand. Each animal is like a solitary child's shoe in the road.

Once a man asked, Why do you bother? You never know, I said. The ones you give some semblance of burial, to whom you offer an apology, may have been like seers in a parallel culture. It is an act of respect, a technique of awareness.

In Idaho I hit a young sage sparrow—*thwack* against the right fender in the very split second I see it. Its companion rises a foot higher from the same spot, slow as smoke, and sails off clean into the desert. I rest the walloped bird in my left hand, my right thumb pressed to its chest. I feel for the wail of the heart. Its eyes glisten like rain on crystal. Nothing but warmth. I shut the tiny eyelids and lay it beside a clump of bunchgrass. Beyond a barbed-wire fence the overgrazed range is littered with cow flops. The road curves away to the south. I nod before I go, a ridiculous gesture, out of simple grief.

I pass four spotted skunks. The swirling air is acrid with the rupture of each life.

Darkness rises in the valleys of Idaho. East of Grand View, south of the Snake River, nighthawks swoop the road for gnats, silent on the wing as owls. On a descending curve I see two of them lying soft as clouds in the road. I turn around and come back. The sudden slowing down and my K-turn at the bottom of the hill draw the attention of a man who steps away from a tractor, a dozen yards from where the birds lie. I can tell by his step, the suspicious tilt of his head, that he is wary, vaguely proprietary. Offended, or irritated, he may throw the birds back into the road when I leave. So I wait, subdued like a penitent, a body in each hand.

He speaks first, a low voice, a deep murmur weighted with awe. He has been watching these flocks feeding just above the road for several evenings. He calls them whippoorwills. He gestures for a carcass. How odd, yes, the way they concentrate their hunting right on the road, I say. He runs a finger down the smooth arc of the belly and remarks on the small whiskered bill. He pulls one long wing out straight, but not roughly. He marvels. He glances at my car, baffled by this out-of-state courtesy. Two dozen nighthawks career past, back and forth at arm's length, feeding at our height and lower. He asks if I would mind—as though I owned it—if he took the bird up to the house to show his wife. "She's never seen anything like this." He's fascinated. "Not close."

I trust, later, he will put it in the fields, not throw the body in the trash, a whirligig.

North of Pinedale in western Wyoming on U.S. 189, below the Gros Ventre Range, I see a big doe from a great distance, the low rays of first light gleaming in her tawny reddish hair. She rests askew, like a crushed tree. I drag her to the shoulder, then down a long slope by the petals of her ears. A gunnysack of plaster mud, ears cold as rain gutters. All of her doesn't come. I climb back up for the missing leg. The stain of her is darker than the black asphalt. The stains go north and off to the south as far as I can see.

On an afternoon trafficless, quiet as a cloister, headed across South Pass in the Wind River Range, I swerve violently but hit an animal, and then try to wrestle the gravel-spewing skid in a straight line along the lip of an embankment. I know even as I struggle for control the irony of this: I could pitch off here to my own death, easily. The bird is dead somewhere in the road behind me. Only a few seconds and I am safely back on the road, nauseated, light-headed.

It is hard to distinguish among younger gulls. I turn this one around slowly in my hands. It could be a western gull, a mew gull, a California gull. I do not remember well enough the bill markings, the color of the legs. I have no doubt about the vertebrae shattered beneath the seamless white of its ropy neck.

East of Lusk, Wyoming, in Nebraska, I stop for a badger. I squat on the macadam to admire the long claws, the perfect set of its teeth in the broken jaw, the ramulose shading of its fur—how it differs slightly, as does every badger's, from the drawings and pictures in the field guides. A car drifts toward us over the prairie, coming on in the other lane, a white 1962 Chevrolet station wagon. The driver slows to pass. In the bright sunlight I can't see his face, only an arm and the gesture of his thick left hand. It opens in a kind of shrug, hangs briefly in limp sadness, then extends itself in supplication. Gone past, it curls into itself against the car door and is still.

Farther on in western Nebraska I pick up the small bodies of mice and birds. While I wait to retrieve these creatures I do not meet the eyes of passing drivers. Whoever they are, I feel anger toward them, in spite of the sparrow and the gull I myself have killed. We treat the attrition of lives on the road like the attrition of lives in war: horrifying, unavoidable, justified. Accepting the slaughter leaves people momentarily fractious, embarrassed. South of Broken Bow, at dawn, I cannot avoid an immature barn swallow. It hangs by its head, motionless in the slats of the grill.

I stop for a rabbit on Nebraska 806 and find, only a few feet away, a garter snake. What else have I missed, too small, too narrow? What has gone under or past me while I stared at mountains, hay meadows, fencerows, the beryl surface of rivers? In Wyoming I could not help but see pronghorn antelope swollen big as barrels by the side of the road, their legs splayed rigidly aloft. For animals that large people will stop. But how many have this habit of clearing the road of smaller creatures, people who would remove the ones I miss? I do not imagine I am alone. As much sorrow as the man's hand conveyed in Nebraska, it meant gratitude too for burying the dead.

Still, I do not wish to meet anyone's eyes.

In southwestern Iowa, outside Clarinda, I haul a deer into high grass out of sight of the road and begin to examine it. It is still whole, but the destruction is breathtaking. The skull, I soon discover, is fractured in four places; the jaw, hanging by shreds of mandibular muscle, is broken at the symphysis, beneath the incisors. The pelvis is crushed, the left hind leg unsocketed. All but two ribs are dislocated along the vertebral column, which is complexly fractured. The intestines have been driven forward into the chest. The heart and lungs have ruptured the chest wall at the base of the neck. The signature of a tractor-trailer truck: 78,000 pounds at 65 mph.

In front of a motel room in Ottumwa I finger-scrape the dry stiff carcasses of bumblebees, wasps, and butterflies from the grill and headlight mountings, and I scrub with a wet cloth to soften and wipe away the nap of crumbles, the insects, the aerial plankton of spiders and mites. I am uneasy carrying so many of the dead. The carnage is so obvious.

In Illinois, west of Kankakee, two raccoons as young as the ones in Oregon. In Indiana another raccoon, a gray squirrel. When I make the left turn into the driveway at the house of a friend outside South Bend, it is evening, hot and muggy. I can hear cicadas in a lone elm. I'm glad to be here.

From the driveway entrance I look back down Indiana 23, toward Indiana 8, remembering the farm roads of Illinois and Iowa. I remember how beautiful it was in the limpid air to drive Nebraska 2 through the Sand Hills, to see how far at dusk the land was etched east and west of Wyoming 28. I remember the imposition of the Wind River Range in a hard, blue sky beneath white ranks of buttonhook clouds, windy hay fields on the Snake River Plain, the welcome of Russian olive trees and willows in creek bottoms. The transformation of the heart such beauty engenders is not enough tonight to let me shed the heavier memory, a catalog too morbid to write out, too vivid to ignore.

I stand in the driveway now, listening to the cicadas whirring in the dark tree. My hands grip the sill of the open window at the driver's side, and I lean down as if to speak to someone still sitting there. The weight I wish to fall I cannot fathom, a sorrow over the world's dark hunger.

A light comes on over the porch. I hear a dead bolt thrown, the shiver of a door pulled free. The words of atonement I pronounce are too inept to offer me release. Or forgiveness. My friend is floating across the tree-shadowed lawn. What is to be done with the desire for exculpation?

"Later than we thought you'd be," he says.

I do not want the lavabo. I wish to make amends.

"I made more stops than I thought I would," I answer.

"Well, bring this in. And whatever I can take," he says.

I anticipate, in the powerful antidote of our conversation, the reassurance of a human enterprise, the forgiving embrace of the rational. It waits within, beyond the slow tail-wagging of two dogs standing at the screen door.

—1989

WILLIAM STAFFORD

1914-1993

As a poet, William Stafford prided himself on experimenting with ideas and forms, on entering the writing of each poem in the spirit of open-minded inquiry. "I feel very exploratory when I write," he once stated. "I feel like Daniel Boone going into Kentucky." His work often seems to display didactic, even moralistic, intentions, yet he steadfastly resisted claims that he used his poetry to advance a particular ideology. Regarding his most famous poem, "Traveling Through the Dark," he said, "I would like to dissociate myself from taking any kind of stance that would imply that being a writer is assuming a power of guidance or insight or anything like that. I'm not that kind of writer."

Stafford was born in Hutchinson, Kansas, and later studied at the University of Kansas, where he earned his B.A. in 1937 and his M.A. in 1945; he received his Ph.D. from the University of Iowa in 1955. During World War II, he was a conscientious objector, working in civilian public service camps from 1942 to 1946. A memoir about this experience, Down in My Heart, *was published in 1947. Stafford spent nearly all of his academic career at Lewis and Clark College in Portland, Oregon, teaching there between 1948 and 1980, when he became professor emeritus. He published more than thirty books of poetry during his career, not to mention five volumes of nonfiction and various edited books. His collection* Traveling Through the Dark *won the National Book Award for poetry in 1963. He served as poetry consultant to the Library of Congress in 1970 and was named poet laureate of Oregon in 1975.*

It's hard to read "Traveling Through the Dark" without trying to interpret the meaning of the protagonist's decision about what to do with the dead deer he encounters on a dark canyon road. Is it possible, in light of Stafford's reluctance to force his audience into a particular moral stance, that what matters is not the actual decision but the very quandary of decision making? Robert Bly, introducing the posthumous selection of Stafford's poems called The Darkness Around Us Is Deep *(1993), reads "Traveling Through the Dark" as the artist's struggle to weigh his allegiance to the animal world and to the human world: "The artist owes language to the human community but owes his or her breathing body to the animal community. Every poem we write, every day we live, we think about what we owe to each." "I thought hard for us all," the narrator states, and perhaps this is the only thing we know for sure: our encounters with the animal world, when taken to heart, necessitate hard thinking and cannot be taken lightly.*

TRAVELING THROUGH THE DARK

Traveling through the dark I found a deer
dead on the edge of the Wilson River road.
It is usually best to roll them into the canyon:
that road is narrow; to swerve might make more dead.

By glow of the tail-light I stumbled back of the car
and stood by the heap, a doe, a recent killing;
she had stiffened already, almost cold.
I dragged her off; she was large in the belly.

My fingers touching her side brought me the reason—
her side was warm; her fawn lay there waiting,
alive still, never to be born.
Beside that mountain road I hesitated.

The car aimed ahead its lowered parking lights;
under the hood purred the steady engine.
I stood in the glare of the warm exhaust turning red;
around our group I could hear the wilderness listen.

I thought hard for us all—my only swerving—,
then pushed her over the edge into the river.

—1962

URSULA K. LE GUIN

B. 1929

Although Ursula K. Le Guin is often labeled a science fiction writer, much
of her work really defies categorization. What her sixteen novels, eight col-
lections of short stories, nine collections of poetry, ten children's books, and
two books of essays and criticism have in common is a questioning of the
ways we normally perceive the world. Le Guin particularly enjoys inventing
cultures as a way to suggest new possibilities for human society and per-
sonality. The mythologies, social customs, and languages she imagines for
the inhabitants of her fictional worlds are presented as the logical result of
social and ecological pressures.

The daughter of anthropologist Alfred L. Kroeber and writer-folklorist
Theodora Kroeber, Le Guin was born in Berkeley, California, and educated
at Radcliffe (B.A., French and Italian) and Columbia (M.A., French and
Italian Renaissance literature). On a Fulbright scholarship to Paris, she met
and married Charles Le Guin, a historian; the couple settled in Portland and
raised three children. Le Guin sent out stories for ten years with virtually no
success before finding a niche in the science fiction market. The Left Hand
of Darkness (1969), widely regarded as her most important novel, won the

Hugo and Nebula awards from the Science Fiction Writers of America. In all, her work has received five Hugos, four Nebulas, a National Book Award, and a Newbery Silver Medal.

In her later work, starting with the novel Always Coming Home *(1985), which imagines an earth-friendly culture in post-eco-disaster northern California, Le Guin has begun to explore the power of writing like a woman. For her, this means acknowledging "the continuity, interdependence, and community of all life, all forms of being on earth," as she writes in* Buffalo Gals and Other Animal Presences *(1987), rather than accepting a male-defined hierarchy that devalues women, children, and animals. Part of this project is simply focusing attention on the moral, ethical, and psychological ground where humans and nonhuman animals meet, as she does in the following series of brief sketches that first appeared in* Harper's *magazine (August 1990).*

THE CREATURES ON MY MIND

I. The Beetle

When I stayed for a week in New Orleans, out near Tulane, I had an apartment with a balcony. It wasn't one of those cast-iron-lace showpieces of the French Quarter, but a deep, wood-railed balcony made for sitting outside in privacy, just the kind of place I like. But when I first stepped out on it, the first thing I saw was a huge beetle. It lay on its back directly under the light fixture. I thought it was dead, then saw its legs twitch and twitch again. No doubt it had been attracted by the light the night before, and had flown into it, and damaged itself mortally.

Big insects horrify me. As a child I feared moths and spiders, but adolescence cured me, as if those fears evaporated in the stew of hormones. But I never got enough hormones to make me easy with the large, hard-shelled insects: wood roaches, June bugs, mantises, cicadas. This beetle was a couple of inches long; its abdomen was ribbed, its legs long and jointed; it was dull reddish brown; it was dying. I felt a little sick seeing it lie there twitching, enough to keep me from sitting out on the balcony that first day.

Next morning, ashamed of my queasiness, I went out with the broom to sweep it away. But it was still twitching its legs and antennae, still dying. With the end of the broom handle I pushed it very gently a little farther toward the corner of the balcony, and then I sat to read and make notes in the wicker chair in the other corner, turned away from the beetle because its movements drew my eyes. My intense consciousness of it seemed to have something to do with my strangeness in that strange city, New Orleans, and my sense of being on the edge of the tropics—a hot, damp, swarming, fetid, luxuriant existence—as if my unease took the beetle as its visible sign. Why else did I think of it so much? I weighed maybe two thousand times what it weighed, and lived in a perceptual world utterly alien from its world. My feelings were quite out of proportion.

And if I had any courage or common sense, I kept telling myself, I'd step on the poor damned creature and put it out of its misery. We don't know what a beetle may or may not suffer, but it was, in the proper sense of the word, in agony, and the agony had gone on two nights and two days now. I put on my leather-soled loafers. But then I couldn't do it. It would crunch, ooze, squirt under my shoe. Could I hit it with the broom handle? No, I couldn't. I have had a cat with leukemia put down, and have stayed with a cat while he died; I think that if I were hungry, if I had reason to, I could kill for food, wring a chicken's neck, as my grandmothers did, with no more guilt and no less fellow feeling than they. My inability to kill this creature had nothing ethical about it, and no kindness in it. It was mere squeamishness. It was a little rotten place in me, like the soft brown spots in fruit: a sympathy that came not from respect but from loathing. It was a responsibility that would not act. It was guilt itself.

On the third morning the beetle was motionless, shrunken, dead. I got the broom again and swept it into the gutter of the balcony among dry leaves. And there it still is in the gutter of my mind, among dry leaves, a tiny dry husk, a ghost.

II. The Sparrow

In the humid New England summer the small cooling plant ran all day, making a deep, loud noise. Around the throbbing machinery was a frame of coarse wire net. I thought the bird was outside that wire net, then I hoped it was, then I wished it was. It was moving back and forth with the regularity of the trapped: the zoo animal that paces twelve feet east and twelve feet west and twelve feet east and twelve feet west, hour after hour; the heartbeat of the prisoner in the cell before the torture; the unending recurrence; the silent, steady panic. Back and forth, steadily fluttering between two wooden uprights just above a beam that supported the wire screen: a sparrow, ordinary, dusty, scrappy. I've seen sparrows fighting over territory till the feathers fly, and fucking cheerfully on telephone wires, and in winter gathering in trees in crowds like dirty little Christmas ornaments and talking all together like noisy children, chirp, charp, chirp, charp! But this sparrow was alone, and back and forth it went in terrible silence, trapped in wire and fear. What could I do? There was a door to the wire cage, but it was padlocked. I went on. I tell you I felt that bird beat its wings right here, here under my breast-bone in the hollow of my heart. I said in my mind, Is it my fault? Did I build the cage? Just because I happened to see it, is it my sparrow? But my heart was low already, and I knew now that I would be down, down like a bird whose wings won't bear it up, a starving bird.

Then on the path I saw the man, one of the campus managers. The bird's fear gave me courage to speak. "I'm so sorry to bother you," I said. "I'm just visiting here at the librarians conference—we met the other day in the office. I didn't know what to do, because there's a bird that got into the cooling plant there, inside the screen, and it can't get out." That was enough, too much, but I had to go on. "The noise of the machinery, I think the noise confuses it, and I didn't know what to do. I'm sorry." Why did I apologize? For what?

"Have a look," he said, not smiling, not frowning.

He turned and came with me. He saw the bird beating back and forth, back and forth in silence. He unlocked the padlock. He had the key.

The bird didn't see the door open behind it. It kept beating back and forth along the screen. I found a little stick on the path and threw it against the outside of the screen to frighten the bird into breaking its pattern. It went the wrong way, deeper into the cage, toward the machinery. I threw another stick, hard, and the bird veered and then turned and flew out. I watched the open door, I saw it fly.

The man and I closed the door. He locked it. "Be getting on," he said, not smiling, not frowning, and went on his way, a man with a lot on his mind, a hardworking man. But did he have no joy in it? That's what I think about now. Did he have the key, the power to set free, the will to do it, but no joy in doing it? It is his soul I think about now, if that is the word for it, the spirit, that sparrow.

III. The Gull

They were winged, all the creatures on my mind.

This one is hard to tell about. It was a seagull. Gulls on Klatsand Beach, on any North Pacific shore, are all alike in their two kinds: white adults with black wingtips and yellow bills; and yearlings, adult-sized but with delicately figured brown features. They soar and cry, swoop, glide, live, squabble, and grab; they stand in their multitudes at evening in the sunset shallows of the creek mouth before they rise in silence to fly out to sea, where they will sleep the night afloat on waves far out beyond the breakers, like a fleet of small white ships with sails furled and no riding lights. Gulls eat anything, gulls clean the beach, gulls eat dead gulls. There are no individual gulls. They are magnificent flyers, big, clean, strong birds, rapacious, suspicious, fearless. Sometimes as they ride the wind I have seen them as part of the wind and the sea, exactly as the foam, the sand, the fog is part of it all, all one, and in such moments of vision I have truly seen the gulls.

But this was one gull, an individual, for it stood alone near the low-tide water's edge with a broken wing. I saw first that the left wing dragged, then saw the naked bone jutting like an ivory knife up from blood-rusted feathers. Something had attacked it, something that could half tear away a wing, maybe a shark when it dove to catch a fish. It stood there. As I came nearer, it saw me. It gave no sign. It did not sidle away, as gulls do when you walk toward them, and then fly if you keep coming on. I stopped. It stood, its flat red feet in the shallow water of a tidal lagoon above the breakers. The tide was on the turn, returning. It stood and waited for the sea.

The idea that worried me was that a dog might find it before the sea did. Dogs roam that long beach. A dog chases gulls, barking and rushing, excited; the gulls fly up in a rush of wings; the dog trots back, maybe a little hangdog, to its owner strolling far down the beach. But a gull that could not fly and the smell of blood would put a dog into a frenzy of barking, lunging, teasing, torturing. I imagined that. My imagination makes me human and makes me a fool; it gives me all the world and exiles me from it. The gull stood waiting for the dog, for the other gulls, for the tide, for what came, living its life completely until death. Its eye looked straight through me, seeing truly, seeing nothing but the sea, the sand, the wind.

—1990

HARPER'S FORUM

In 1867 John Muir wrote in a journal: "How narrow we selfish, conceited creatures are in our sympathies! How blind to the rights of all the rest of creation!" Just over a century later, a man named Peter Singer published an essay in the New York Review of Books *entitled "Animal Liberation," which in effect launched what today is known as the animal rights move-*

ment. Although questions about the proper human treatment of animals are nothing new (indeed, they are ancient in their origin), discussion of such questions has in recent years been attended by a passion and at times a militancy not witnessed before. As is frequently the case with ethical issues, the questions are far easier to frame than they are to answer. Such issues put us on the frontier of moral theory, where the tried-and-true codes of behavior—our everyday ability to distinguish right from wrong, good from evil—fail us utterly.

"Just Like Us?" is a transcription of a conversation/debate among five people on the subject of animal rights, published in Harper's magazine in August 1988. In considering the various viewpoints expressed in this piece, it is well worth pondering what each of the participants means by the word right. What is the nature of the idea expressed by this commonplace term in the American vocabulary? Does the word right signify an intrinsic value, some essential quality bestowed by some higher power upon an individual being? Are there different kinds of rights, and if so, how then do we distinguish between animal rights and those other kinds, such as the "right to vote," the "right to life," or "women's rights"?

JUST LIKE US?

The following forum is based on a discussion held at the Cooper Union for the Advancement of Science and Art, in New York City. Jack Hitt served as moderator.

JACK HITT is a senior editor at *Harper's Magazine*.

ARTHUR CAPLAN is director of the Center for Biomedical Ethics at the University of Minnesota.

GARY FRANCIONE is a professor at the University of Pennsylvania Law School. He frequently litigates animal rights cases.

ROGER GOLDMAN is a constitutional law scholar and professor at Saint Louis University School of Law.

INGRID NEWKIRK is the national director of People for the Ethical Treatment of Animals, in Washington.

The relationship of man to animal has long been one of sympathy, manifested in such welfare organizations as the kindly Bide-A-Wee or the avuncular ASPCA. In the last few years, the politics of that relationship have been questioned by a number of new and vociferous interest groups which hold to the credo that animals are endowed with certain inalienable rights.

Typically, when animal rights advocates are called upon by the media to defend their views, they are seated across the table from research scientists. The discussion turns on the treatment of laboratory animals or the illegal efforts of fanatics who smuggle animals out of research facilities via latter-day underground railroads to freedom.

Behind these easy headlines, however, stand serious philosophical questions: How should we treat animals? Why do humans have rights and other animals not? If animals had rights, what would they be? To address these questions, *Harper's*

Magazine asked two leading animal rights activists to sit down with a philosopher and a constitutional scholar to examine the logic of their opinions.

Bunnies and Sewer Rats

JACK HITT: Let me ask a question that many readers might ask: Gary, why have you—a former Supreme Court law clerk and now a professor of law at the University of Pennsylvania—devoted your life to animal rights?

GARY FRANCIONE: I believe that animals have *rights*. This is not to say that animals have the same rights that we do, but the reasons that lead us to accord certain rights to human beings are equally applicable to animals. The problem is that our value system doesn't permit the breadth of vision necessary to understand that. We currently use the category of "species" as the relevant criterion for determining membership in our moral community, just as we once used race and sex to determine that membership.

If you asked white men in 1810 whether blacks had rights, most of them would have laughed at you. What was necessary then is necessary now. We must change the *way* we think: a paradigm shift in the way we think about animals. Rights for blacks and women were *the* constitutional issues of the nineteenth and twentieth centuries. Animal rights, once more people understand the issue, will emerge as *the* civil rights movement of the twenty-first century.

JACK HITT: I want to see where the logic of your beliefs takes us. Suppose I am the head of a company that has invented a dynamite new shampoo. It gives your hair great body; everyone is going to look like Lisa Bonet. But my preliminary tests show that it may cause some irritation or mild damage to the eye. So I've purchased 2,000 rabbits to test this shampoo on their eyes first. Roger, do you find anything offensive about testing shampoo this way?

ROGER GOLDMAN: As someone new to the animal rights issue, I don't find it particularly offensive.

JACK HITT: What if the only thing new about my shampoo is that it is just a different color?

ROGER GOLDMAN: If everything else is equal, then I would say the testing is unnecessary.

INGRID NEWKIRK: I think Roger hit the nail on the head. The public has absolutely no idea what the tests involve or whether they're necessary. I think Roger might object if he knew that there were alternatives, that a human-skin patch test can be substituted for the rabbit-blinding test. If consumers were informed, then no compassionate consumer would abide such cruelty.

GARY FRANCIONE: The problem is that we can use animals in any way we like because they are *property*. The law currently regards animals as no different from that pad of paper in front of you, Roger. If you own that pad, you can rip it up or burn it. By and large we treat animals no differently than glasses, cups, or paper.

ARTHUR CAPLAN: I know you lawyers love to talk about the property status of these little creatures, but there are other factors. We treat animals as property because people don't believe that animals have any moral worth. People look at rabbits and say, "There are many rabbits. If there are a few less rabbits, who cares?"

INGRID NEWKIRK: Not true. Many people, who don't support animal rights, *would* care if you stuck a knife in their rabbit or dog. They're deeply offended by acts of *individual* cruelty.

ARTHUR CAPLAN: Yes, but I suspect that if in your test we substituted ugly sewer rats for button-nosed rabbits, people might applaud the suffering. There are some animals that just don't register in the human consciousness. Rats don't, rabbits might, dogs and horses definitely do.

INGRID NEWKIRK: Not always. If the test were done to a sewer rat in *front* of a person, the average person would say, "Don't do that" or "Kill him quickly."

JACK HITT: Why?

INGRID NEWKIRK: It's institutionalized cruelty, born of our hideous compartmentalized thinking. If the killing is done behind closed doors, if the government says it must be done, or if some man or woman in a white coat assures us that it's for our benefit, we ignore our own ethical good sense and allow it to happen.

JACK HITT: If the frivolity of the original test bothers us, what if we up the ante? What if the product to be tested might yield a cure for baldness?

GARY FRANCIONE: Jack, that is a "utilitarian" argument which suggests that the rightness or wrongness of an action is determined by the *consequences* of that action. In the case of animals, it implies that animal exploitation produces benefits that justify that exploitation. I don't believe in utilitarian moral thought. It's dangerous because it easily leads to atrocious conclusions, both in how we treat humans and how we treat animals. I don't believe it is morally permissible to exploit weaker beings even if we derive benefits.

ROGER GOLDMAN: So not even the cancer cure?

GARY FRANCIONE: No, absolutely not.

ARTHUR CAPLAN: But you miss the point about moral selfishness. By the time you get to the baldness cure, people start to say, "I don't *care* about animals. My interests are a hell of a lot more important than the animals' interests. So if keeping hair on my head means sacrificing those animals, painlessly or not, I want it." It's not utilitarian—it's selfish.

GARY FRANCIONE: But you certainly wouldn't put that forward as a justification, would you?

ARTHUR CAPLAN: No, it's just a description.

GARY FRANCIONE: I can't argue with your assertion that people are selfish. But aren't we morally obliged to assess the consequences of that selfishness? To begin that assessment, people must become aware of the ways in which we exploit animals.

Maybe I'm just a hopeless optimist, but I believe that once people are confronted with these facts, they will reassess. The backlash that we're seeing from the exploitation industries—the meat companies and the biomedical research laboratories—is a reaction of fear. They know that the more people learn, the more people will reject this painful exploitation.

JACK HITT: But won't your movement always be hampered by that mix of moral utilitarianism and moral egotism? People will say, "Yes, be kind to animals up to a point of utilitarianism (so I can have my cancer cure) and up to a point of moral egotism (so I can have my sirloin)." There may be some shift in the moral center, but it will move only so far.

ARTHUR CAPLAN: I agree. Gary can remain optimistic, but confronting people with the facts won't get him very far. Moral egotism extends even into human relations. Let's not forget that we are in a city where you have to step over people to enter this building. People don't say, "Feed, clothe, and house them, and then tax me; I'll pay." We have a limited moral imagination. It may be peculiarly American, but you can show people pictures of starving children or homeless people or animals in leg traps, and many will say, "That's too bad. Life is hard, but I still want my pleasures, my enjoyments."

INGRID NEWKIRK: There are two answers to that. First, people accept the myth. They were brought up with the illusion that they *must* eat animals to be healthy. Now we know that's not true. Second, because of humankind's lack of moral—or even just plain— imagination, we activists have to tell people exactly what they *should* do. Then we must make it easier for them to do it. If we put a moral stepladder in front of people, a lot of them will walk up it. But most people feel powerless as individuals and ask, "Who am I? I'm only one person. What can I do?" We must show them.

JACK HITT: Roger, I'm wondering whether your moral center has shifted since we began. Originally you weren't offended by my using 2,000 rabbits to test a new shampoo. Are you now?

ROGER GOLDMAN: I am still a utilitarian. But if the test is unnecessary or just repetitive, clearly, I'm persuaded that it should be stopped.

INGRID NEWKIRK: Precisely Gary's point. Armed with the facts, Roger opts not to hurt animals.

Enfranchising All Creatures

JACK HITT: Art, what makes human beings have rights and animals not have rights?

ARTHUR CAPLAN: Some would argue a biblical distinction. God created humans in his image and did not create animals that way. That's one special property. Another philosophical basis is natural law, which holds that inalienable rights accrue to being human—that is a distinguishing feature in and of itself.

Personally I reject both those arguments. I subscribe to an entitlement view, which finds these rights grounded in certain innate properties, such as the ability to reason, the ability to suffer—

GARY FRANCIONE: Let's take the ability to suffer and consider it more carefully. The ability to use language or to reason is irrelevant to the right to be free from suffering. Only the ability to feel pain is relevant. Logically, it doesn't follow that you should restrict those rights to humans. On this primary level, the question must be *who* can feel pain, *who* can suffer? Certainly animals must be included within the reach of this fundamental right.

If you don't, then you are basing the right not to suffer pain on "intelligence." Consider the grotesque results if you apply that idea exclusively to human beings. Would you say that a smart person has a right to suffer less pain than a stupid person? That is effectively just what we say with animals. Even though they can suffer, we conclude that their suffering is irrelevant because we think we are smarter than they are.

ARTHUR CAPLAN: The ability to suffer does count, but the level of thinking and consciousness also counts. What makes us human? What grants us the right to life? It is not just a single attribute that makes us human. Rather, there is a cluster of properties: a sense of place in the world, a sense of time, a sense of self-awareness, a sense that one is somebody, a sense that one is morally relevant. When you add up these features, you begin to get to the level of entitlement to rights.

GARY FRANCIONE: And I am going to push you to think specifically about rights again. What must you possess in order to have a right to life? I think the most obvious answer is simply a *life!*

But let's play this question out in your terms. To have a right to life, you must possess a sense of self, a recollection of the past, and an anticipation of the future, to name a few. By those standards, the chimpanzee—and I would argue, the entire class of Mammalia—would be enfranchised to enjoy a right to life.

INGRID NEWKIRK: The question is, do they have an interest in living? If they do, then one has an obligation to recognize their natural rights. The most fundamental of these is a desire to live. They *are* alive, therefore they want to *be* alive, and therefore we should *let* them live.

The more profound question, though, is what distinguishes humans from other animals. Most scientists, at first, thought that what separates us from the other animals is that human beings use tools. So ethnologists went out into the field and returned with innumerable examples of tool use in animals. The scientists then concluded that it's not tool use but the *making* of tools. Ethnologists, such as Geza Teleki, came back with lots of different examples, everything from chimpanzees making fishing poles to ants making boats to cross rivers. One might think they would then elevate the criterion to making tools in *union* workshops, but they switched to "language." Then there was a discussion about what *is* language. Linguists, among them Noam Chomsky and Herbert Terrace, said language possessed certain "components." But when various ethnologists were able to satisfy each of these components, the Cartesian scientists became desperate and kept adding more components, including some pretty complicated ones, such as the ability to recite events in the distant past and to create new words based on past experiences. Eventually the number of components was up to sixteen! The final component was teaching someone else the language. But when Roger Fouts gave the signing ape, Washoe, a son, she independently taught him some seventy American hand-language signs.

ARTHUR CAPLAN: One of the sad facts of the literature of both animal and human rights is that everyone is eager to identify the magic property that separates humans from animals. Is it the ability to suffer? The ability to say something? The ability to say something *interesting?* I think the philosophers are all looking in the right place but are missing something. We have rights because we are *social.*

INGRID NEWKIRK: Since all animals are social, then you *would* extend rights to non-humans?

ARTHUR CAPLAN: It's not just sociability. Of course, all animals interact, but there is something about the way humans need to interact.

Suppose we were little Ayn Rands who marched about, self-sufficient, proud, and arrogant. If we were able to chop our own wood, cook our own meals, and fend off those who would assault us, then we wouldn't need any rights. You wouldn't need to have a right to free speech if there was no one to talk to!

My point is that our fundamental rights are not exclusively intellectual properties. They are the natural result of the unique way humans have come together to form societies, *dependent* on each other for survival and therefore respectful of each other's rights.

INGRID NEWKIRK: None of this differentiates humans from the other animals. You cannot find a relevant attribute in human beings that doesn't exist in animals as well. Darwin said that the only difference between humans and other animals was a difference of degree, not kind. If you ground any concept of human rights in a particular attribute, then animals will have to be included. Animals have rights.

ARTHUR CAPLAN: That brings up another problem I have with your entire argument. Throughout this discussion, I have argued my position in terms of *ethics.* I have spoken about our moral imagination and animal *interests* and human decency. Why? Because I don't want our relationship with animals to be cast as a battle of rights. Only in America, with its obsession for attorneys, courts, judges, and lawsuits, is the entire realm of human relationships reduced to a clash of rights.

So I ask you: Is our relationship with animals best conceived of under the rubric of rights? I don't think so. When I am dispensing rights, I'm relatively chintzy about it. Do embryos have rights? In my opinion, no. Do irretrievably comatose people have rights? I doubt it. Do mentally retarded people below some level of intellectual functioning have rights? Probably not.

There is a wide range of creatures—some of them human—for whom our rights language is not the best way to deal with them. I want people to deal with them out of a sense of fairness or a sense of humanity or a sense of duty, but not out of a claim to rights.

INGRID NEWKIRK: I don't like your supremacist view of a custodial responsibility that grants you the luxury to be magnanimous to those beneath you. The rights of animals are not peripheral interests. In this case, we are talking about blood, guts, pain, and death.

GARY FRANCIONE: Art, when you start talking about obligations without rights, you can justify violations of those obligations or intrusions more easily by spinning airy notions of utility. The reason many of our battles are played out in rights language is because our culture has evolved this notion that a right is something that stands between me and an intrusion. A right doesn't yield automatically because a stronger party might benefit.

If a scientist could cure cancer—without fail—by subjecting me against my will to a painful experiment, it wouldn't matter. I have a right not to be used that way.

ARTHUR CAPLAN: Ironically, I agree with you. That's exactly the role that rights language plays. It defines the barriers or lines that can't be crossed. But if you hand out rights willy-nilly, you lose that function.

INGRID NEWKIRK: When should we stop?

ARTHUR CAPLAN: I'm not sure I know the answer, but if you cheapen the currency of rights language, you've got to worry that rights may not be taken seriously. Soon you will have people arguing that trees have rights and that embryos have rights. And the tendency would be to say, "Sure, they have rights, but they are not *important* rights."

INGRID NEWKIRK: Art, wouldn't you rather err on the side of giving out too many rights rather than too few?

ARTHUR CAPLAN: No.

INGRID NEWKIRK: So, according to your view, maybe we should take away some of the rights we've already granted. After all, granting rights to blacks and women has deprived society of very important things, such as cheap labor. That a society evolves and expands its protective shield should not daunt us. That's like saying, if I continue to be charitable, my God, where will it ever end?

ARTHUR CAPLAN: It may not be rights or bust. There may be other ways to get people to conduct themselves decently without hauling out the heavy artillery of rights language every time.

INGRID NEWKIRK: People have to be pushed; society has to be pushed. Those who care deeply about a particular wrong have to pressure the general population. Eventually a law is passed, and the adjustments are made to correct past injustices. You have to bring these matters to a head.

JACK HITT: Roger, from a constitutional perspective, do you think that rights are cheapened when they are broadened?

ROGER GOLDMAN: When you put it in a constitutional context, you invite conflict.

That's inevitable. If you have a free press, you're going to have fair trial problems. If you start expanding rights of liberty, you run up against rights of equality. I don't think expansion cheapens them, but by elevating animal rights to a constitutional issue, you certainly multiply the difficulties.

JACK HITT: You could argue that conflict strengthens rights. If you had no conflict over free speech, would we have the solid right to free speech that we have today?

ROGER GOLDMAN: It depends on who wins. What would happen if free speech lost?

GARY FRANCIONE: Roger, you will have conflict and difficulties whether you cast our relationship with animals as one of obligations or rights. The real question is, are those obligations enforceable by state authority? If they are, there will be clashes and we will turn to the courts for resolution.

ARTHUR CAPLAN: Gary, I would like those obligations enforced by the authority, if you like, of empathy, by the power of character. What matters is how people view animals, how their feelings are touched by those animals, what drives them to care about those animals, not what rights the animals have.

GARY FRANCIONE: I agree that you don't effect massive social change exclusively through law, but law can certainly help. That's a classic law school debate: Do moral perceptions shape law or does law shape moral perceptions? It probably goes both ways. I have no doubt that we could effect a great change if animals were included within our constitutional framework.

INGRID NEWKIRK: Great changes often begin with the law. Remember the 1760s case of the West Indian slave Jonathan Strong. Strong's master had abandoned him in England after beating him badly. The judge in that case feared the consequences of emancipating a slave. But the judge freed Strong and declared, "Let justice prevail, though the heavens may fall."

Mojo, the Talking Chimpanzee

JACK HITT: Meet Mojo, the signing chimpanzee. Mojo is female and has learned more words than any other chimpanzee. One day you're signing away with Mojo, and she signs back, "I want a baby." Roger, are we under any obligation to grant her wish?

ROGER GOLDMAN: Since I am not persuaded animals have any rights, I don't believe there is any obligation.

JACK HITT: Doesn't it follow that if this chimpanzee can articulate a desire to have a child—a primal desire and one that we would never forbid humans—we have some obligation to fulfill it?

ARTHUR CAPLAN: You are alluding to a foundation for rights that we haven't yet discussed. Is the requirement for possessing a right the ability to *claim* it? That is, in order to hold a right to life, one must be able to articulate a claim to life, to be able to say, "I want to live."

There may be animals that can get to that level, and Mojo may be one of them. Nevertheless, I don't buy into that argument. Simply being able to claim a right does not necessarily entail an obligation to fulfill it.

GARY FRANCIONE: But Mojo does have the right to be left alone to pursue her desires, the right not to be in that cage. Aren't we violating some right of Mojo's by confining her so that she cannot satisfy that primal desire?

JACK HITT: Is this a fair syllogism? Mojo wants to be free; a right to freedom exists if you can claim it; ergo, Mojo has a right to be free. Does the ability to lay claim to a right automatically translate into the *possession* of such a right?

ARTHUR CAPLAN: You don't always generate obligations and duties from a parallel set of rights, matching one with another.

Look at the relationship that exists between family members. Some people might argue that children have certain rights to claim from their parents. But there is something wrong with that assumption. Parents have many obligations to their children, but it seems morally weird to reduce this relationship to a contractual model. It's not a free-market arrangement where you put down a rights chit, I put down an obligation chit, and we match them up.

My kid might say to me, "Dad, you have an obligation to care for my needs, and my need today is a new car." I don't enter into a negotiation based on a balancing of his rights and my duties. That is not the proper relationship.

INGRID NEWKIRK: But having a car is not a fundamental right, whereas the right not to be abused is. For example, children have a right not to be used in factories. That right had to be fought for in exactly the same way we are fighting for animal rights now.

ARTHUR CAPLAN: Gary, I want to press you further. A baby needs a heart, and some scientist believes the miniature swine's heart will do it.

GARY FRANCIONE: Would I take a healthy pig, remove its heart, and put it into the child? No.

ARTHUR CAPLAN: I am stymied by your absolutist position that makes it impossible even to consider the pig as a donor.

GARY FRANCIONE: What if the donor were a severely retarded child instead of a pig?

ARTHUR CAPLAN: No, because I've got to worry about the impact not only on the donor but on society as well.

GARY FRANCIONE: Art, assume I have a three-year-old prodigy who is a mathematical wizard. The child has a bad heart. The only way to save this prodigy is to take the heart out of another child. Should we *consider* a child from a low socioeconomic background who has limited mental abilities?

ARTHUR CAPLAN: You're wandering around a world of slopes, and I want to wander around a world of steps. I have argued strongly in my writing that it is possible for a human being—specifically an infant born with anencephaly, that is, without most of its brain—to drop below the threshold of a right to life. I think it would be ethical to use such a baby as a source for organ transplants. I do not believe there is a slippery slope between the child born with most of its brain missing and the retarded. There are certain thresholds below which one can make these decisions. At some point along the spectrum of life—many people would say a pig, and I would go further to include the anencephalic baby—we are safely below that threshold.

GARY FRANCIONE: You can't equate the pig with the anencephalic infant. The anencephalic child is not the subject of a life in any meaningful sense. That is to say, it does not possess that constellation of attributes—sense of self-awareness, anticipation of the future, memory of the past—that we have been discussing. The pig is clearly the subject of a meaningful life.

ARTHUR CAPLAN: But if it's a matter of saving the life of the baby, then I want a surgeon to saw out the pig's heart and put it in the baby's chest.

INGRID NEWKIRK: The pig can wish to have life, liberty, and the pursuit of happiness, and the anencephalic baby cannot.

ARTHUR CAPLAN: But you must also consider the effect on others. I don't think it's going to matter very much what the pig's parents think about that pig. Whereas the child's parents care about the baby, and they don't care about the pig.

GARY FRANCIONE: Then you change their reaction.

ARTHUR CAPLAN: I don't want to change their reaction. I want human beings to care about babies.

INGRID NEWKIRK: Like racism or sexism, that remark is pure speciesism.

ARTHUR CAPLAN: Speciesism! Mine is a legitimate distinction. The impact of this transplant is going to be different on humans than on lower animals.

INGRID NEWKIRK: "Lower animals." There comes speciesism rearing its ugly head again. Look, Art, I associate with the child; I don't associate with the pig. But we can't establish why that matters *except* that you are human and I am human.

If a building were burning and a baby baboon, a baby rat, and a baby child were inside, I'm sure I would save the child. But if the baboon mother went into the building, I'm sure she would take out the infant baboon. It's just that there is an instinct to save yourself first, then your immediate family, your countrymen, and on to your species. But we have to recognize and reject the self-interest that erects these barriers and try to recognize the rights of others who happen not to be exactly like ourselves.

ARTHUR CAPLAN: I think you can teach humans to care about the pig. The morally relevant factor here is that you will never get the pig to care about *me*.

INGRID NEWKIRK: Not true, Art. Read John Robbins's new book, *Diet for a New America*, in which he lists incidents of altruism by animals outside their own species. Everybody knows about dolphins rescuing sailors. Recently a pig rescued a child from a frozen lake and won an award!

ARTHUR CAPLAN: To the extent to which you can make animals drop *their* speciesism, perhaps you will be persuasive on this point.

INGRID NEWKIRK: Art, if you don't recognize my rights, that's tough for me. But that doesn't mean my rights don't exist.

GARY FRANCIONE: If blacks, as a group, got together and said, "We're going to make a conscious decision to dislike non-blacks," would you say that black people no longer had rights?

ARTHUR CAPLAN: No, but I would hold them accountable for their racism. I could never hold a pig accountable for its speciesism. And I am never going to see a meeting of pigs having that kind of conversation.

INGRID NEWKIRK: That happens when the Ku Klux Klan meets, and the ACLU upholds their rights.

ARTHUR CAPLAN: The difference is that there are certain things I expect of blacks, whites, yellows—of all human beings and maybe a few animals. But I am not going to hold the vast majority of animals to those standards.

INGRID NEWKIRK: So the punishment for their perceived deficiencies—which, incidentally, is shared by the human baby—is to beat them to death.

ARTHUR CAPLAN: I didn't say that. I am trying to reach for something that isn't captured by the speciesist charge. The difference between people and animals is that I can persuade people. I can *stimulate* their moral imaginations. But I can't do that with most animals, and I want that difference to count.

A World With No Dancing Bears

JACK HITT: How would you envision a society that embraced animal rights? What would happen to pets?

INGRID NEWKIRK: I don't use the word "pet." I think it's speciesist language. I prefer "companion animal." For one thing, we would no longer allow breeding. People could not create different breeds. There would be no pet shops. If people had companion animals in their homes, those animals would have to be refugees from the animal shelters and the streets. You would have a protective relationship with them just as you would with an orphaned child. But as the surplus of cats and dogs (artificially engineered by centuries of forced breeding) declined, eventually companion animals would be phased out, and we would return to a more symbiotic relationship—enjoyment at a distance.

GARY FRANCIONE: Much more than that would be phased out. For example, there would be no animals used for food, no laboratory experiments, no fur coats, and no hunting.

ROGER GOLDMAN: Would there be zoos?

GARY FRANCIONE: No zoos.

JACK HITT: Circuses?

GARY FRANCIONE: Circuses would have to change. Look, right now we countenance the taking of an animal from the wild—a bear—dressing that bear in a skirt and parading it in front of thousands of people while it balances a ball on its nose. When you think about it, that is perverted.

JACK HITT: Let's say that your logic prevails. People are sickened by dancing bears and are demanding a constitutional amendment. What would be the language of a Bill of Rights for animals?

INGRID NEWKIRK: It already exists. It's "life, liberty, and the pursuit of happiness." We just haven't extended it far enough.

ROGER GOLDMAN: I am assuming your amendment would restrict not only government action but private action as well. Our Constitution restricts only government action. The single exception is the Thirteenth Amendment, which prohibits both the government and the individual from the practice of slavery.

JACK HITT: To whom would these rights apply? Would they apply among animals themselves? Does the lion have to recognize the gazelle's right to life?

INGRID NEWKIRK: That's not our business. The behavior of the lion and the gazelle is a "tribal" issue, if you will. Those are the actions of other nations, and we cannot interfere.

ROGER GOLDMAN: What if we knew the lion was going to kill the gazelle—would we have an obligation to stop it?

INGRID NEWKIRK: It's not our business. This amendment restricts only our code of behavior.

JACK HITT: But what Roger is asking is, should the amendment be so broad as to restrict both individual and government action?

GARY FRANCIONE: It should be that broad. Of course, it would create a lot of issues we would have to work out. First, to whom would we extend these rights? I have a sneaking suspicion that any moment someone in this room will say, "But what about cockroaches? Will they have these rights? Do they have the right to have credit cards?" Hard questions would have to be answered, and we would have to determine which animals would hold rights and how to translate these rights into concrete protections from interference.

INGRID NEWKIRK: The health pioneer W. K. Kellogg limited it to "all those with faces." If you can look into the eyes of another, and that other looks back, that's one measure.

So the amendment shouldn't be limited, as some animal rights advocates

think, to mammals, because we know that birds, reptiles, insects, and fishes all
feel pain. They are capable of wanting to be alive. As long as we know that they
have these primal interests, then I think we need to explore down the line—if we
think it is down.

ROGER GOLDMAN: Let me go up the line. What about humans?

INGRID NEWKIRK: They would be just another animal in the pack.

ROGER GOLDMAN: But your amendment would massively expand the reach of the
Constitution for humans. For example, the Constitution does not require states
to provide rights for victims of crime. Under your proposal, if a state decrimi-
nalized adultery, shoplifting, or even murder, the victim's *constitutional* rights
would be violated.

ARTHUR CAPLAN: And if we take the face test, how is that going to affect the way we
treat the unborn? Must we enfranchise our fetuses? That's going to be the end
of abortion.

GARY FRANCIONE: Not necessarily. I am fairly comfortable with the notion that a fetus
does not have a right to life. But that is not to say that a fetus doesn't have a
right to be free from suffering. Fetuses do feel pain and they *ought* to be free
from suffering. But it doesn't make sense to talk about a fetus having a sense of
the past, anticipation of the future, and a sense of interaction with others.

ARTHUR CAPLAN: But a mouse?

GARY FRANCIONE: Sure.

ARTHUR CAPLAN: I guess we can experiment on and eat all the animal fetuses we want.

GARY FRANCIONE: I didn't say you had a right to inflict pain on animal fetuses. I don't
think you have a right to inflict pain on human fetuses.

ARTHUR CAPLAN: Are you suggesting that we can't inflict pain, but we can kill them?

INGRID NEWKIRK: You are talking about the manner in which abortions are currently performed, not whether they should be performed. Our standard of lack of suffering
holds up if you apply it across the board, for human and non-human fetuses.

ROGER GOLDMAN: Let me see if I can bring together those who advocate animal welfare
with those who believe animals hold rights. What about a different amendment,
similar to the difference between the Thirteenth Amendment, which is an absolute
ban on slavery, and the Fourteenth Amendment, which bans discrimination, but
not absolutely. In fact, the Fourteenth allows us to take race into account sometimes, such as affirmative action. Do the animal rights activists see a role for a limited amendment similar to the Fourteenth? It would broadly protect animals from
unnecessary suffering, but allow for some medical experiments.

GARY FRANCIONE: Does your amendment simply expand the word "persons" in the
Fourteenth Amendment to include animals?

ROGER GOLDMAN: No, but it is modeled on Fourteenth Amendment jurisprudence. It
would not permit experimentation on animals unless necessary for a compelling
need.

GARY FRANCIONE: I would favor this approach if the experimenter had the burden to
show the compelling need. I would have only one problem with adjudication
under this compelling-need standard. My fear is that the balance would always
favor the biomedical research community. Everyone agrees that no one should
needlessly use animals in experimentation. Yet we all know that millions of animals are being used for frivolous purposes. That is because the biomedical
researchers have persuaded enough people that their experiments are so important they have become "compelling" by definition.

ROGER GOLDMAN: Of course the difference with this constitutional amendment is that it wouldn't pass unless two-thirds of Congress and three-fourths of the states backed it, so if we're projecting a hundred years from now, you won't have the problem of science experts always prevailing.

GARY FRANCIONE: Roger, I would retire tomorrow if I could get your amendment. The problem is that our society economically *benefits* from exploitation. The animal industries are so strong that they have shaped an entire *value* system that justifies and perpetuates exploitation. So I am not sure your compelling-need test would result in anything substantially different from what we have now. That's why I favor a hard rights notion, to protect the defenseless absolutely. As soon as you let in the "balancers," people such as Art Caplan, you've got trouble.

ARTHUR CAPLAN: The problem with your constitutional amendment is that, finally, it is irrelevant to human behavior. When the lawyers, the constitutional adjudicators, and the Supreme Court justices aren't there, when it's just me and my companion animal or my bug in the woods, where are the animal's rights then?

There was a time when I was a little boy running around in the woods in New England. It was just a bunch of Japanese beetles in a jar and me. The question was: How is little Art going to deal with those Japanese beetles? Pull their wings off? Never let them out of the jar? Step on them? What do I do with those bugs? What do I think of bugs? No Supreme Court justice is going to tell me what to do with them.

INGRID NEWKIRK: A lot of these conflicts of moral obligation result from the wide variety of *unnatural* relationships we have with animals in the first place—whether it's little Art with his jar of Japanese beetles, or the scientist in the lab with his chimpanzee, or any one of us at home with a cat. Just take the single issue of the sterilization of pets. We now have burdened ourselves with the custodial obligation to sterilize thousands of animals because we have screwed up their reproductive cycles so much through domestication and inbreeding that they have many more offspring than they normally would. What would happen if we just left animals alone, to possess their own dignity? You know, you mentioned earlier that there is something cruel in the lion chasing down and killing the gazelle. Well, nature *is* cruel, but man is crueler yet.

—1988

PAT MURPHY

B. 1955

Because Pat Murphy often uses elements of science fiction in her novels and short stories, she has become known as a science fiction writer. Not all of her work is so easily classified, though. She describes her second novel, The Falling Woman *(1987), as a psychological fantasy and notes that the book was rejected by several science fiction publishers because they didn't see it as science fiction, yet it ended up winning the Nebula Award from the Science Fiction Writers of America in 1987. What Murphy tries to do in all of her writing is to get at what's going on beneath the surface of reality.*

The daughter of a research chemist and a registered nurse, Murphy was born in Spokane, Washington, and raised in Connecticut and

California. She earned a B.A. from the University of California, Santa Cruz, in biology and general science. For thirteen years she edited the Exploratorium Quarterly, the magazine of the Exploratorium, an interactive museum of science and art in San Francisco. She is now director of publications there, as well as a visiting lecturer in science fiction writing at Stanford University. Her short fiction has been collected in two volumes and appears in many magazines and anthologies; her four novels include The City, Not Long After *(1989) and* Nadya: The Wolf Chronicles *(1996), a historical feminist werewolf novel.*

The idea of a beast that's half-human and half-nonhuman animal recurs throughout the world's folklore and illustrates our fascination with imagining the closest encounter possible between humans and nonhumans, or perhaps our yearning to fully embrace our animal nature. Murphy's story "Rachel in Love"—which won a Nebula the same year as The Falling Woman—*tells one such story, the story of a chimp imprinted with a human mind. "In the Abode of the Snows" (first published in* Isaac Asimov's Science Fiction Magazine, *December 1986) approaches the topic from a different angle, recounting the story of Xavier Clark's search in the Himalayas for the man-ape known as the yeti.*

IN THE ABODE OF THE SNOWS

In a hospital room with white walls, Xavier Clark held the hand of his dying mother. The chill breeze from the air conditioner made him think of the snow-covered peaks of the Himalayas: Annapurna, Machhapuchhare, Dhaulagiri, Nilgiri. Places he had never been. His mother's shallow breathing could have been the whispering of snow crystals, blown by mountain breezes across a patch of ice. The veins beneath her pale skin were faintly blue, the color of glacial ice.

His mother's eyes were closed, and he knew she was dying. With each passing year, she had grown more frail, becoming as brittle as the delicate teacups that she kept locked in the china cabinet. Her hair had grown paler, becoming so ethereal that her scalp showed through no matter how carefully she combed and arranged the white wisps.

His mother's breathing stopped, and he listened, for a moment, to the quick light sound of his own breathing and the pounding of his own heart. Closing his eyes, he clung to his mother's hand and savored a faint uneasy feeling of release, as if his last tie to earth had been cut and he could soar like a balloon, leaving the ordinary world behind.

Xavier returned from the hospital to his mother's house. Though he had lived in the house for all of his forty years, he still thought of it as his mother's house. Even when his father had been alive, the house had been his mother's. His father had always seemed like a visitor, stopping at the house to rest and write between expeditions to Nepal.

When Xavier was five, his father had died in a snowslide on the eastern slope of Dhaulagiri. When Xavier tried to remember his father, he could picture only the broad-shouldered man that he had seen in out-of-focus book-jacket photos, a lifeless black-and-white image.

More clearly than Xavier remembered his father, he remembered his father's possessions: an elaborately carved prayer wheel that reeked of incense, a small rug on which two dragons curled about one another in an intricate pattern, a brass bowl that sang when struck with a wooden rod, wooden masks with great empty eyes and grimacing mouths, round brass bells the size of his fist attached to a strip of brightly colored tapestry. Upon receiving word of his father's death, Xavier's mother had taken all these exotic treasures, wrapped them in newspaper, and packed them in a steamer trunk that she pushed into a corner of the attic. As a child, Xavier had yearned to look at his father's belongings, but the steamer trunk was locked and he had known better than to ask his mother for the key.

His mother had never talked of his father after his death. She never remarried, raising Xavier herself, living frugally on the proceeds of his father's insurance policies and on royalties from his books.

As a teenager, Xavier bought copies of his father's three books: *Adventures on the Roof of the World, Land of Yak and Yeti*, and *The Magic of Nepal*. He hid the books from his mother and read them in his room when he was supposed to be doing his homework. On the map in the flyleaf of one book, he traced his father's journeys in red pen. In his sleep, he muttered the names of mountains: Machhapuchhare, Annapurna, Dhaulagiri, Nilgiri. He remembered the names of Himalayan rivers, fed by monsoon rains and melting snows. He knew the names of his father's porters—the Sherpas who accompanied the mountaineering expeditions—better than he knew the names of his own schoolmates.

He was a shy teenager with few friends. After graduating from high school, he attended the local college and majored in biology. He had planned to base his thesis on observations of mountain sheep in the Rockies, but just before he was due to leave, his mother had taken ill. He canceled his trip and spent the summer observing waterfowl in a local pond, writing a thesis on the behavior of coots in an urban environment.

At college graduation, he was offered a job as wildlife biologist in the Idaho National Forest. Upon receiving the good news, his mother suffered the first in a series of heart attacks. He accepted a position as biology teacher at the local high school and stayed home to nurse her.

Living in his mother's house with the silent memories of his father's glorious past, he had become a secretive and solitary man. His clothes hung loosely on his body, like the skin of a reptile preparing to molt. His students joked about him, saying that he looked like one of the thin, dry lizards that he kept in the classroom's terrarium. He had grown prematurely old, never leaving town because his mother was never well enough to travel and never well enough to be left alone.

In the empty house, the evening of his mother's death, Xavier was truly alone for the first time in decades. He felt strangely hollow—not lonely, but empty. He felt light, insubstantial, as if the slightest breeze could carry him away. He could do anything. He could go anywhere. He thought about his father's trunk and went to the attic.

The trunk had been pushed to the farthest corner, tucked under the eaves—behind a broken lamp, a dressmaker's dummy stuck with pins, a box of Xavier's old toys, and an overstuffed armchair with torn upholstery in which generations of mice had nested. The trunk was locked and, for a moment, Xavier hesitated, considering retreat. Then he realized that the house and all its contents were his. With a screwdriver and hammer, he attacked the trunk's rusty hasp and tore it free of the lid.

On top of the newspaper-wrapped bundles in the trunk lay a package wrapped in brown paper and decorated with Nepali stamps. Xavier carefully unwrapped the package and found a leatherbound notebook filled with spidery handwriting that looked curiously like his own.

Xavier opened the book and read a page: "I have decided to leave the expedition and press on alone, following the Kali Gandaki to its source. In the bleak northern hills, I am certain I will find the man-ape that the Sherpa call the yeti. Winter is coming and many will call me foolish, but I cannot turn back. I miss my wife and son, but I like to think that my son, if he were here, would understand. I cannot turn back. The mountains will not let me."

Mingling with the dusty air of the attic, Xavier thought he smelled incense, a foreign smell that awakened unfamiliar urges. Kneeling beside the trunk, with his father's journal in his hands, he felt, in some strange way, that he had made a decision. He knew that he would not return to school for the fall term.

In a new backpack, purchased at the local sporting goods store, Xavier packed field notebooks, camera, and many rolls of film. He bought a kerosene stove and tested it in the backyard, boiling water for tea in a lightweight aluminum pot. He bought a plane ticket to Katmandu by way of Bangkok and converted $5,000 cash into traveler's checks. He studied a book titled *Nepali Made Simple*, memorizing simple phrases. He haunted the local college library, reading all the accounts of yeti sightings that he could find.

Mountaineers described the beast as inhumanly tall and covered with shaggy hair. Some said it was nocturnal, prowling the barren slopes between the treeline and the permanent snows. Some said it was like a monkey; others, like a bear. Tibetans and Nepalis credited the beast with supernatural powers: its bones and scalp were valued as objects of great power.

He read his father's journal, lingering over descriptions of the terrain, the mountains, the wildlife. His father's books had maintained a heroic tone: men battled the wilderness, always fought fair, and usually triumphed. The journal gave a more realistic account: describing stomach upsets and bouts with dysentery, complaining of lazy porters, recording bribes given minor officials for quicker service. The journal told of superstitions: Tibetans believed that shamans could transform themselves into birds, that finding a hat was unlucky, that dogs howling at dawn were an inauspicious omen. Xavier read all this with great enthusiasm.

At night, Xavier dreamed of cold slopes, scoured clean by endless winds. He was filled with a feverish longing for the high country, where the snows never melt. He would find the yeti, track its movements, study its biology. He would finish the task that his father had begun and return to his mother's house to write of his success.

On his first day in Katmandu, Xavier wandered the narrow streets of the alien city, marveling at how strange and yet how familiar it seemed. It matched his father's descriptions, yet somehow, on some level, it seemed quite different.

A shy Hindu boy with a red tika dot painted on his forehead stared at Xavier from a dark doorway. The child wore no pants and his dark skin reflected a little light from the street, a subtle sheen on thin legs, thin buttocks. In the shade provided by a shrine to Ganesh, the elephant-headed son of Vishnu, a street dog rested and licked her sores.

The market smelled of incense, strong spices, and cow manure. Xavier shooed away the vendors who tried to sell him tourist trinkets, the rickshaw drivers who asked in broken English where he was going, the black market money changers who offered him a good rate, a very good rate, for American dollars. He was caught by the feeling that something was about to happen, something sudden and strange, something exotic and unanticipated. He stared about him with impassioned hungry eyes, watching for a secret signal that the adventure began here.

In a small square, bedsheets and other laundry flapped from the second floors of the surrounding houses. The wooden frames of the windows had been ornately carved sometime in the last three centuries. The faces of Hindu deities and demons stared from a complex background of twisting human bodies, vines, and flowers. In the square below, heaps of yellow grain dried in the autumn sun. Small children kept guard, stopping noisy games to chase away cows and dogs and pigs.

In a small street stall frequented only by Nepalis, Xavier ate lunch, crouching uncomfortably on a wooden bench just barely out of the street. The high clear piping of flutes played by flute sellers mingled with the honking of rickshaw horns and the jingling of bicycle bells.

Though the Nepalis ate with their hands, the shopkeeper insisted on giving Xavier a tarnished and bent fork and on showing the American how to sprinkle hot peppers on his *daal baat,* the rice and lentil dish that served as the staple of the Nepali diet. The shopkeeper, a wizened man in a high-crowned brimless hat, sat beside Xavier on the bench and watched him eat.

"You come from England?" the shopkeeper asked Xavier.

"No, from America."

"You going trekking?"

"Well, yes," he said. "I plan to go up past a town called Jomsom. I . . ." He hesitated, then plunged on. "I have read that yeti have been seen in that area."

"Ah, you wish to find the yeti?"

"Very much."

The shopkeeper studied him. "Westerners do not have the patience to find the yeti. They hurry, hurry, and never find what they look for."

"I have all the time in the world," Xavier said.

The shopkeeper folded his hands in his lap, smiled, and said, "You will need a guide. My cousin, Tempa, can take you where you need to go."

Xavier ate and listened to the shopkeeper praise the virtues of his cousin Tempa. Sitting in the open stall, he looked up at the thin strip of sky visible between the houses. A single bird flew over, heading northwest. Xavier watched it vanish from sight and knew, with the same certainty that had caused him to quit his job and come to Nepal, that he would go northwest to the Himalayas, to the high country where anything could happen.

On the fourth day on the trail, Xavier and Tempa were caught in a violent hailstorm that transformed the path into a running stream that splashed merrily around Xavier's boots. The water quickly penetrated the waterproof oil that Xavier had applied to the boots in Katmandu. His socks were soon soaked and his feet ached with the cold.

In a low stone hut that served as teahouse and provided primitive accommodations, they found shelter. The group of ragged porters that huddled by the fire looked up when Xavier ducked through the low doorway. The teahouse was filled with woodsmoke and the scent of unwashed clothing. The small fire that burned in the center of the single room seemed to provide more smoke than warmth.

Xavier blinked as his eyes adjusted to the dark interior. Not elegant accommodations, but better than a tent and no worse than the teahouses that had sheltered them for the past three days. Xavier propped his pack against the wall and hung his rain parka on a nail that jutted from the wooden doorframe.

The proprietress, a Tibetan woman, offered him *rokshi,* locally distilled wine, and he accepted gratefully. The clear liquor smelled faintly of apples and tasted overwhelmingly of alcohol. The first mouthful seared his mouth and throat with a bright, almost painful warmth that spread slowly to his chest. He sat on a wooden bench by the door and slowly unlaced his wet boots.

Tempa was already deep in conversation with the porters who crouched by the fire. He looked up at Xavier, his eyes reflecting the firelight. "They say that snow has fallen in the pass to the north," Tempa said to Xavier. "And a big storm is coming."

Xavier shrugged, pulled off his boots, and gingerly wiggled his toes. Since the very first day, Tempa had been complaining about the weight of his pack, the length of each day's hike, the perils of bad weather. "Not much we can do about the weather," he said.

Tempa frowned. "Big storm," he said. "Too late in the season to go on. Tomorrow, we go back."

Xavier shook his head and frowned at Tempa, trying to assume an air of authority. "Go back? We've just started. If there's a storm, we'll wait it out."

"Too cold," Tempa said. "Winter is here."

"Tomorrow, we go on," Xavier said. His father had written of stubborn porters and of the need to show them who was boss. "Do you understand? I'm not ready to go back."

Tempa returned unhappily to his friends by the fire. Xavier relaxed, loosened the collar of his damp flannel shirt, and leaned back against the stone wall of the teahouse. The warmth of the *rokshi* spread throughout his body. Outside, the rain had stopped and a rooster was crowing. Xavier closed his eyes and listened to the soft whispering of water flowing down the trail, the gentle clucking of the chickens that searched for edible insects in the scrubby weeds that grew just outside the teahouse door. The breeze that blew through the door smelled of mountains that had been washed clean by the rain. He took a deep breath, but caught a whiff of another scent, something stronger than the woodsmoke or the *rokshi*—an animal scent. He looked up to see an old man standing in the hut's open doorway.

Though the afternoon breeze was cold, the old man wore no shirt or jacket, only a loose loincloth of an indeterminate color. The cloth may once have been white, but it had become an uncertain shade of gray: the color of dust, of woodsmoke, of ashes and grime. The man's long gray-streaked hair was wound in a topknot. The ancient face was stern—a high forehead, a nose like a beak. Around the man's neck hung a string of round beads, each one a different shade of off-white. Xavier stared at the beads, recognizing them from a description in his father's journal. Each of the 108 beads had been carved from the bone of a different human skull. At the man's belt dangled a carved ivory *phurba,* the ritual dagger carried by all shamans of Bon, the ancient animistic religion that had preceded Buddhism in the Himalayas.

In one hand, the man carried a metal bowl, which he held out to the Tibetan woman. She beckoned him in and he squatted beside the fire.

"*Namaste,*" Xavier said, the traditional Nepali greeting that meant "I salute you." His voice was suddenly unsteady. Here was adventure—a traveling shaman visiting the same teahouse.

The old shaman stared at Xavier, but did not return his greeting.

Xavier beckoned to Tempa. "Who is the old man?" he whispered.

Tempa's small vocabulary deserted him when he did not find it convenient to speak English. Now, occupied with a glass of *rokshi* and eager to return to his friends, Tempa shrugged. "*Ta chaina.*" I don't know.

"Where is he from?"

Tempa frowned, seemingly reluctant to say anything about the old man. "He lives alone." Tempa waved an arm toward the hills.

"A hermit," Xavier said.

Tempa shrugged and returned to his friends.

The Tibetan woman served dinner, scooping a serving of rice into the old man's bowl and moistening the grain with a spoonful of *daal.* The old man silently accepted the offering. The woman dished out a similar dinner for the others.

After his third glass of *rokshi* and a plate of *daal baat,* Xavier had relaxed. The old man, he noticed, ate alone, squatting in a corner of the hut. With *rokshi*-induced courage, Xavier went to the corner and endeavored to begin a conversation with the old man.

"*Rokshi?*" Xavier said to the old man, and then he signaled to the woman for another glass. The old man studied Xavier with impassive black eyes, then accepted the glass.

"*Timiko ghar ke ho?*" the old man asked Xavier. "*Timi kaha jane?*" Where are you from? Where are you going?

Xavier replied in halting Nepali. I come from America. Then he waved a hand to indicate his destination, pointing northward toward the high cold mountains that filled his dreams. "*Meh-teh hirne,*" he said. Which meant, more or less, I look for the yeti.

The old man took Xavier's hand in a strong grip and peered into the American's face with sudden intensity. He spoke rapidly in Nepali, but Xavier could not follow his words. When Xavier shrugged, looking bewildered, the old man called to Tempa, who sat with the other porters by the fire. Tempa responded in Nepali.

The old man broke into a grin, his stern face collapsing into wrinkles. He reached out a withered hand and cupped Xavier's chin, lifting the biology teacher's face as a doting grandmother might lift the face of a shy child. The old man threw back his head and laughed at something that he saw in Xavier's face. He released his hold on Xavier, and said something, but the only word Xavier could catch in the rapid string of Nepali was "*meh-teh.*" Something about yeti.

Xavier smiled uneasily, wondering how his father would have handled a situation like this. "What's all that about?" Xavier asked Tempa. Reluctantly, Tempa left his friends and came to squat beside Xavier and the old man.

"He wants to know where you are going," Tempa said. "I tell him you look for the yeti."

Xavier nodded and smiled at the old man.

The old man said something else in rapid Nepali. Xavier shook his head and asked him to speak more slowly.

Still grinning the old man repeated himself, pausing after each word and accompanying his words with gestures. Xavier couldn't follow everything that the old man said, but he thought he caught the gist of it: The old man had seen the yeti many times. He was a powerful shaman and he had hunted the yeti many times.

Xavier poured the old man another cup of *rokshi* and asked him to tell about the yeti. Beside the fire, three porters played a noisy game of cards. Outside the door, by candlelight, the Tibetan woman washed the dinner dishes. Inside the smoky tea-house, Xavier leaned close to the old man, ignoring his animal scent, and listened to tales of the yeti.

The yeti looked like men, only different, the old man explained slowly. They hunted at night, and they were very strong. With only his hands, a yeti could kill a yak, break the neck. (The old man brought his hands together like a man snapping a stick.) The yeti is fierce and cunning.

Xavier, with hand gestures and halting Nepali, asked the old man how he hunted such a fierce beast. With a dirty finger, the old man tapped his temple and nodded sagely. He called out to the woman, and she brought a stoneware crock and two tin cups. The old man filled the cups with a ladle and offered one to Xavier. "Yo chang ho," the old man said. This is chang.

Xavier had heard of chang, a thick beer brewed with rice and barley. Unwilling to offend the old man, he sipped the thick beverage. It tasted like a mixture of sour porridge and alcohol, but after the first few sips, it wasn't too bad.

The old man tapped the cup and told Xavier that he hunted the yeti with chang. He launched into a long explanation which Xavier followed with difficulty. To catch a yeti, it seems, the old man found a village where a yeti had been bothering people, stealing their crops and killing their goats. On a night when the moon was new, the old man left a pot of chang in the path where the yeti would find it. The yeti drank the chang and fell asleep, and in the morning, the old man captured it easily. Yeti, said the old man, like chang.

More chang, more labored discussion of the habits of the yeti. Xavier grew accustomed to the smoke that filled the room. At some point, the Tibetan woman lit a candle, and the flickering light cast enormous shadows that danced on the walls. The old man's face, illuminated by the candle, seemed filled with sly amusement. Sometimes, it seemed to Xavier that the old man was laughing at him beneath the words, teasing him with some private joke. But the room seemed small and cozy and Xavier's Nepali improved with each glass of chang. It was a good life, a good place to be. Xavier lost track of how many cups of chang he drank. The old man seemed like a good friend, a faithful companion.

Somehow, Xavier found himself telling the old man about his father and his search for the yeti. Groping for words in Nepali, he tried to explain that he needed to find the yeti, to finish what his father had started. He tried to explain how he felt about the mountains. In a mixture of Nepali and English, he tried to describe his dreams of mountains and snow.

The old man listened intently, nodded as if he understood. Then he spoke softly, slowly, laying a hand on Xavier's hand. I can help you find the yeti, he said to Xavier. Do you want to see the yeti?

Drowsy from chang, half-mesmerized by the candlelight, Xavier took the old man's hands in both of his. "I want to find the yeti," he said in English.

The old man fumbled for something in the pouch that dangled at his belt. He displayed his findings to Xavier on the palm of a withered hand: a small brown bone etched with spidery characters. The bone was attached to a leather thong. It was made of yeti bone, the old man explained. Very powerful, very magical.

Xavier reached out and touched the small dried object. It was warm to the touch, like a small sleeping animal. The old man smiled. His dark eyes were caught in a mesh of wrinkles, like gleaming river pebbles in a bed of drying mud.

The old man nodded, as if reaching some conclusion, then looped the leather thong around Xavier's neck. Startled, Xavier protested, but the old man just smiled. When Xavier lifted the pendant, as if to remove it, the old man scolded him in Nepali.

They had more *chang* to celebrate, and Xavier's memories were fuzzy after that. He remembered the old man reassuring him that he would see the yeti. He remembered lying down on a bamboo mat by the fire and pulling his still damp sleeping bag over himself.

In his dreams, he fingered the bone that hung around his neck. He dreamed of studying the mark of a bare foot on the side of a snowy mountain. In the dream, he squatted to measure the length, the width. Suddenly, without surprise, he realized that his own feet were bare. His feet ached from the cold of the snow, and he was hungry, very hungry.

He blinked awake in the pale morning light. He could hear the hollow clanging of metal bells: a mule train was passing on the trail. The wood smoke that drifted through the hut's open door reminded him of the cold mist that filled the mountain gorges of his dreams. His head and belly ached, and he remembered drinking too much *rokshi*, too much *chang*.

The other bamboo mats were empty. The Tibetan woman crouched by the hearth, poking the fire that burned beneath the blackened teakettle. The porters were gone; the old man was gone. Confused by lingering dream images, Xavier sat up and felt the leather thong around his neck. The bone was there. He ran a fingernail over the rough surface and felt more confident. His throat was sore and his voice was hoarse when he asked the woman where his porter, Tempa, had gone.

The woman shook her head. "*Ta chuinu,*" she said. I don't know.

Xavier struggled from his sleeping bag and stumbled out of the hut, making for the boulder strewn slope that served as a latrine. The wind numbed his face and the gray world outside the hut seemed less substantial than his dreams. The sky was overcast; the mountains, hidden by distant haze. The ground underfoot was composed of mottled gray and brown pebbles, swept clean by the steady wind from the north. The trail, a faint track marked by the dung of pack mules and the scuff marks of hikers' boots, led northward.

Xavier stopped beside a large boulder. He noticed a large raven, perched on a distant rock, watching with interest as he pissed. "What do you want?" he said crossly to the bird. The bird regarded the man with bright curious eyes, shrieked once, then took flight, leaving him alone, blinking at the gray sky.

Xavier made his way back to the hut. Tempa was gone. When he asked the Tibetan woman again, she shrugged and said something about Tempa leaving very early in the morning. The porter had taken some of Xavier's possessions along with his own: Xavier's wool gloves and hat, the wool socks that had been drying by the fire, and the rupee notes that Xavier kept in his jacket pocket.

Xavier contemplated the desertion with mixed feelings. He could pursue the thieving porter, but if he turned back, he would miss his chance to search for the yeti. He was seized by uncertainty. Perhaps the weather was turning bad and he should turn back. Could he find his way without a guide? Should he abandon his provisions and trust to local supplies for his food?

At the same time, he was glad at the thought of traveling on alone. The porter had seemed skeptical of Xavier's plans from the first day on the trail. Tempa had, Xavier felt, lacked the proper spirit of adventure.

In the end, it was Xavier's memory of the old man's words that decided him. "You will see the yeti," said the old man. How could Xavier turn his back on such a prophecy?

Taking a loss, Xavier sold most of his remaining supplies to the Tibetan woman. He added the rest to his own load. When he left, his pack was heavier by about twenty pounds. Though he knew that his shoulders would be aching by noon, he whistled as he walked, relishing the thought of being alone in the desolate reaches of the Himalayas.

North of Ghasa, past the village of Tukche, the valley broadened. No trees grew on the great gray slopes. On the lee side of large boulders grew stunted bushes and patchy grasses, tough plants with foliage as dusty as the rocky slopes. Shaggy goats, snatching a thorny lunch in one such patch, stared at Xavier as he passed, their golden eyes faintly hostile. The children who tended the herd, two ragged boys with unruly hair and snotty noses, silently watched the white man with indifferent curiosity.

Once, a flock of ravens took flight from the hillside beside him, wheeling above him to darken the sky like a flight of demons. One raven from the flock kept pace with him for a time: flying ahead to perch on a *mani* wall, a jumbled construction built of flat stones carved with Buddhist prayers. As Xavier approached, the bird called out in a croaking guttural voice, then flew to a boulder a few hundred yards down the trail. Each time Xavier drew near, the bird flew on a little farther, then stopped by the trail, as if waiting for the man to catch up.

The wind blew constantly, kicking up the dust and carrying along leaves and twigs. It blasted the boulders and scoured the *mani* stones, as if trying to wipe the carved letters away. It chapped his lips, dried his throat, and rubbed dust into his skin and hair.

The trail followed the Kali Gandaki, a chilly turbulent river with waters as gray as the rounded granite boulders that lined its bank. In the valley, the river widened, flowing in a network of channels that merged and separated like the veins and arteries of a living animal. The trail wandered beside one of the channels. Beside the water, sparse red-brown grass grew, gray soil showing between the blades.

Without his wool cap, Xavier's ears were unprotected and the rushing of the wind blended with the rushing of the river and the shrill cries of insects in the grass. As he traveled north, signs of passing travelers grew fewer: the marks of boots in the mud; a few hoofprints; ancient horse droppings, long since dried to dust. The trail sometimes disappeared altogether, leaving Xavier to wander by the stream, searching for another sign to show him the way.

A few trees had grown there, reached maturity, then died. Their skeletons reached for the sky, twisted by the nagging wind and crippled where peasants had chopped away branches for firewood. The landscape had a dreamlike quality, as if this were a place that Xavier had imagined for himself. Dry branches rattled in the dry breeze. He was not startled when a raven flew from a twisted tree, laughing when the wind lifted it aloft. It seemed right for the raven to be there, to laugh, to fly ahead as if showing him the way.

The village of Jomsom was an unwelcome intrusion on the landscape, a cluster of low-lying stone houses inhabited by people who had been blasted into passivity by the constant wind. The streets and houses were gray and lifeless, and he passed through as quickly as he could.

A few miles beyond Jomsom, the trail forked: one branch led to Muktinath, a destination popular with trekkers. Xavier took the other branch, the ill-marked track that led to the north. A few miles down the trail, he stopped by the Kali Gandaki, clambering down the steep bank to the rushing water. Though the air was still cold, hiking had warmed him. The wind had eased and the sun was out. He stripped to the waist, draping his shirt over a rock and putting his watch beside it. He splashed the river water on his face, his chest, and up over his back, gasping when the cold water struck his skin, shaking his head like a wet dog.

He was toweling dry when he heard the harsh cry of a raven. The black bird was perched on the boulder beside his shirt. Xavier saw the raven peck at something on the rock, and he shouted, waving at the bird. The raven took flight, and Xavier saw that it carried his watch in its beak. The bird circled, the watch glinting in its beak. Then the wind caught the bird and it soared away over the woods, vanishing from sight.

Xavier did not miss the watch as much as he expected to. As the day passed, he grew accustomed to a timeless existence. He stopped to eat lunch when he was hungry, rested when he was tired. He camped out that night, stopping between villages beside the Kali Gandaki and using his mountain tent for the first time. He dreamed bright crystalline dreams: he was on a steep ice slope, pursuing a dark shape that remained always just a few steps ahead. He chased the dark shape to the edge of a precipice and slipped on the ice, realizing as he fell that the fleeing darkness was his own shadow.

When he woke, the ground was white with frost, and his breath made clouds that the wind swept away. At dusk the next day, he reached the village of Samagaon. The villagers eyed him with great suspicion: strangers were a rare sight so far from the trekking route.

With Tempa's theft, Xavier's supply of rupees had dwindled. He found only one teahouse, and the proprietor, a Gurkha soldier who had returned to his home village, scoffed at the American's traveler's checks, puffing his cheeks out and saying that the checks might be no good, he couldn't tell.

Xavier considered the matter, then offered to trade some of his equipment for cash and food. The man did not want a wool sweater or down jacket, but he inspected the kerosene stove carefully. On the spur of the moment, Xavier decided he could do without a stove. He demonstrated it carefully, filling the fuel tank with kerosene and lighting the burner. It coughed once or twice, then roared with a steady blue flame that lit one corner of the dark smoky tea shop. In limited Nepali, Xavier praised the stove: *"Ramro cha. Dheri ramro."* It's good, very good. His voice was hoarse from days of silence.

While Xavier bargained, two ragged little girls watched from behind the skirts of the man's wife. They stared with wide round eyes, trying to absorb this curiosity, this white man far from the places that white men were found. The shopkeeper came from a long line of traders, and he drove a hard bargain. In the end, Xavier traded for rice, lentils, curry powder, and two hundred rupees cash—a fraction of the stove's value, but he could carry no more food and the shopkeeper claimed that he had no more cash. Xavier spent the night on the shopkeeper's floor, ate a hurried breakfast of corn porridge sweetened with honey, and headed north.

He sang as he walked, a tuneless melody that seamed to ebb and flow like the rushing of the river. His beard was growing in, and when he saw his reflection in a still pool, he laughed at himself; a rough-looking character with a dirty face and good crop of stubble.

Early in the morning, he could see the mountains. But as the day progressed, clouds obscured the view, forming what looked like a new uncharted range of snow-covered peaks, billowing masses of pale gray cloud mountains.

Early in what he supposed to be the afternoon, the overcast sky grew darker. He reached a river crossing: the Kahe Lungpa, a swollen stream that tumbled down from the high peaks to meet the Kali Gandaki. The bridge over the river was down. Water rushed past one shattered wooden support, causing the rotten boards to shiver in the current. Perhaps the bridge had washed out during the monsoon storms. The crossing was far from any village and no doubt the few travelers who passed this way did not have the resources or time to repair or replace the bridge, but simply forded the river.

For a moment, he stood on the bank, gazing at the roaring stream. In one book, his father told of fording snow-fed rivers barefoot, preferring, he wrote, "the momentary discomfort of crossing barefoot to the prolonged chafing of sodden boots." Xavier reluctantly removed his boots, shivering in the cold breeze. He tied the boots to the pack, slipped on a pair of rubber thongs, rolled up the legs of his jeans, and stepped down into the water, knowing that if he hesitated, he would turn back.

The first few steps were painful, but the cold water numbed his feet, making the pain more bearable. The river dragged at his legs, trying to shift the rounded stones beneath his feet. He took his time, making sure that each foot was planted before trusting his weight to it, taking one slow step after another. Time had no meaning: he could have been walking through the water for an hour or a minute, he would not have known the difference.

He was halfway across when the first snowflakes fell. The pain returned to his feet: a sharp hurt that seemed to extend deep into his bones. He tried to move more quickly, but his feet could no longer feel the rocks beneath him. He stumbled, caught himself, then slipped again and fell, twisting to one side and catching himself on his arm. The river snatched at the pack; the current yanked it to and fro. Xavier clung to the pack's straps, struggling to regain his footing and to hoist the water-logged pack from the river. He staggered forward, floundering, gasping from the shock of the cold water, almost losing his thongs, dragging himself onto the far bank and flinging his pack beside him.

From the scraggly bushes on the riverside, a raven laughed hysterically. Xavier ignored the bird, breathing in great gasps and clutching at the damp grass that grew on the bank. After a moment, he rolled over to check his pack. Only then did he realize that the river had snatched the boots from his pack, as well as soaking his food, and drenching his sleeping bag.

For a moment, he lay on the ground, unwilling to move. His feet ached from the cold, his hands trembled. Then he felt for the carved bone pendant around his neck. The old man had said he would see the yeti. The reassurance comforted him. He forced himself to sit up and figure out how to get warm.

A pair of damp wool socks provided some protection for his feet; his wool sweater blocked some of the wind. He warmed himself with exercise, searching for driftwood in the bushes that grew along the river. When he was moving, his arms and legs did not tremble as violently.

An hour's search yielded a small stack of sticks, none bigger around than a finger, and a few damp logs, driftwood cast on shore by the river. His teeth chattering, he searched for tinder, scraps of dry material small enough to catch quickly. But the snow had dampened the leaves and grasses, leaving nothing dry.

The wind grew stronger, slicing through his wet clothing and making him shiver uncontrollably. With his pocketknife he whittled a few thin splinters from a stick, heaping them together in the shelter of a bush. He built a small teepee of sticks over the tinder and hunched over it.

The first match went out immediately. The head of the second match—wretched Nepali matches—broke off without catching. The third match burned reluctantly. When he held the flame beside his heap of shavings, two slivers of wood smoldered for a moment, but the red glow faded as soon as the match went out.

Xavier's hands shook as he carefully arranged grass beside the wood shavings. The grass, like the wood, would not burn. Desperate for warmth, he patted his pockets, searching for a scrap of paper. In his wallet, he found his traveler's checks, bone dry and warm from his body heat. They were worthless in the woods, and he hesitated only for a moment before crumpling a $50 check. He arranged the splinters of wood over the dry paper.

The check burned well, but it was small and it burned out before the wood caught. He sacrificed two more, holding his hands out to protect the tiny flame from the wind. The checks whispered as they burned, tiny crackling voices that spoke of distant places and hidden secrets. When he added the fourth and fifth check, the wood caught, flames moving reluctantly from stick to stick. He propped a driftwood log near the fire where it would dry, and made himself as comfortable as he could, sitting with his back in the bushes to protect it from the wind. He draped his wet sleeping bag over his lap where the fire would warm it.

The night was long. Despite the cold, he dozed off now and then, waking only to cough, a hoarse grating sound in the darkness. When he woke, he found himself clutching the bone. He dreamed of chasing the yeti through the pale gray crevices of cloud mountains. He woke to feed the fire, then returned to dreams.

After a time, the darkness and the cold no longer seemed alien. They were threatening, but familiar. It seemed natural to wake in the darkness, struggling for warmth.

In the morning, he hiked in rubber thongs. He coughed constantly. Once, on the outskirts of a village, a little girl who was tending a herd of goats greeted him timidly. He tried to reply, but the sound that came from his mouth was only a rough croaking, noise with no meaning like the clatter of rocks in a rock slide. He tried to smile, wanting to show the child that he meant no harm, but she scampered up the slope with her goats.

He hiked on for three days. Some of his food spoiled and he knew that food would be scarce farther north. But somehow, for some inexplicable reason, he was happy. The wool socks grew tattered and encrusted with mud, but his feet grew used to being cold. His beard grew thicker and he washed less frequently, growing accustomed to the grime on his face and hands. He hurried through villages, avoiding people. When he was greeted, he nodded, but remained silent.

He passed through the village of Dhi in the early evening, walking quickly through the darkness. Rather than making him eager for human company, solitude left him wishing for more solitude. A dog barked wildly from inside a house, a near hysterical baying. Xavier grinned savagely and kept walking. He despised the laundry flapping from the lines and the heaps of dung beside the trail. He slipped through the village, nodding a greeting to a woman filling a metal jug at a stream. She dropped the jug and stared at him. Though she called out, he did not stop, but kept walking away into the darkness to seek the mountains.

As he hiked, he listened to the wind, to the river's voice, to the chatter of ravens.

The sound seemed to flow through him, bringing him peace. Though the weather grew colder, he did not worry.

He made camp a day's walk from Dhi by the confluence of the Mustang Khola and a smaller stream that was unnamed on his map. The wind was constant there, sweeping around the boulders and scouring the rocks. In a small hollow between two house-size boulders, he pitched his tent.

The first night, he heard the howling of wolves in the distance. At midnight, he woke when snow began to fall, a gentle flurry that drifted against the tent. In the morning, he found the tracks of wolves in the snowflakes that powdered the ground near his fire ring.

During the first few days, he explored his surroundings. He saw fat short-tailed mice scampering among the rocks. Wild sheep, the blue Himalayan *bharal*, grazed by the stream. Xavier climbed upstream, following sheep trails among the boulders.

Half a day's scramble up the stream, he found a small cave, tucked among the rocks. From the look of the cave, it had once been inhabited—by a hermit, a holy man, or a *sennin*, a mountain lunatic. Three fire-blackened rocks formed a triangular hearth; a mound of brush in the back provided a scratchy bed. Beneath the cave, the valley broadened into a small meadow: tough, red-brown grass poked through the light snow. The cave's entrance offered a view of the river valley better than any he had found elsewhere.

He moved his gear to the cave just before the second snowfall and made his bed in the brush heap in the back. He grew adept at cooking over a small fire: the smoke made his eyes itch, but he grew used to that. In the cave, his sleep schedule changed. Daylight reflecting from the snow hurt his eyes, and so he slept through the brightest part of the day, then woke at twilight to watch the wolves chase the blue sheep through the moonlit valleys. He dreamed during those long daylight sleeps. In his dreams, the old man came to him and told him that he would see the yeti.

Somehow, he was certain that his goal was near. This valley had the flavor of the fantastic: the wind muttered of secrets; the boulders watched him as he slept. Sometimes, he believed that he would soon understand the language of the raven that perched outside his cave each evening. He knew this place as a man knows the landscape of his own dreams, and he knew that the yeti was here.

He woke and slept, woke and slept, watching the valley for signs of the unusual. His hair and beard grew long and wild. He discarded his tattered wool socks and his feet grew tough and calloused. His skin chapped in the wind. In the sand by the river, he discovered the mark of a broad bare foot; on a thorny bush, he found a red-gold tuft of hair. A few signs and a feeling, nothing more, but that was enough.

His supplies ran low, but he was reluctant to leave the valley to find more. He ate wild greens and trapped short-tailed mice in an old food tin and roasted them over the fire. Once, he found a *bharal* that had been killed by wolves, and he used his pocketknife to hack meat from the carcass.

In his dreams, the valley was filled with moving shadows that walked on two legs, shambling like bears, shaggy and slope-browed. When he woke, his dreams did not fade, but remained as sharp and clear as the world around him. He dreamed of the raven, but somehow the bird was more than a raven. The black bird was the old man who had given him the bone. The old man wanted something in return.

Xavier never went out by day.

At last, his food ran out completely. He captured one last mouse, charred its body in the fire, and picked its bones clean. By moonlight, he walked to the village of Dhi. The trail made him nervous; it was too well trodden. The first smell of woodsmoke made him stop. He heard barking dogs in the distance.

On the edge of the village, he paused to drink in a still pool. He was startled by his own reflection. His eyes were wild and rimmed with red; his face was covered with thick red-brown hair. He crouched in the field near a house, unwilling to go closer. Stacked in racks by the house were ears of corn, dried by the wind and the sun.

Hunger drove him forward, but something held him back. He did not belong here. The sky was growing light when he moved at last. He stood below the racks and reached up to pull corn free—one ear, two ears, a dozen, two dozen. He was tying them up into a bundle when he heard a sound.

Ten feet away stood a ragged boy, barefoot in the chilly morning. His face was smudged with dirt and already his nose was running. His eyes were wide, and they grew wider when Xavier looked at him. *"Meh-teh,"* he whispered, backing away from Xavier, then turning to run. *"Meh-teh!"*

Xavier ran too, losing one of his thongs in the rocks by the trail, abandoning the other. The raven led him on, laughing overhead. He ran back to his cave.

He roasted an ear of corn in the fire. It was charred and tough, but he ate it with relish. He slept for a long time, dreaming of the old man and the raven, two who were one. He knew that he belonged in this place. Each night, he went to the village and stole food. When the dogs barked, people ran from their huts, carrying torches and knives and shouting *"Meh-teh! Meh-teh!"*

One day soon he knew he would find a pot of *chang* in the path. The raven told him so in a dream. When he found the *chang,* he would drink it and fall asleep. The villagers would capture him and the old man who was the raven would take his scalp. That was the way of things. He was happy.

—1986

LESLIE MARMON SILKO

B. 1948

The folklore of the Laguna Pueblo people informs the writing of Leslie Marmon Silko. Born of mixed ancestry—Laguna Pueblo, Mexican, and white—in Albuquerque, New Mexico, Silko grew up at Laguna Pueblo listening to her great-grandmother and great-aunts tell stories. In her much-reprinted essay "Landscape, History, and the Pueblo Imagination" (1986), Silko explains that it was through oral narrative that the ancient Pueblo people maintained and transmitted their worldview, "complete with proven strategies for survival." In Laguna Pueblo culture, she says, stories bond the individual to the family, clan, and to the landscape.

Silko has continued the stories of her people by working as a poet (Laguna Woman: Poems, 1974), novelist (Ceremony, 1977; Almanac of the Dead, 1991), and writer of short stories (Storyteller, 1981). She earned a B.A. from the University of New Mexico in 1969 and then entered law school, but in 1971 she decided to make writing her career and did graduate work in English. Divorced from John Silko, she is the mother of two sons and has taught at the University of New Mexico and the University of

Arizona. In 1983 she received a MacArthur fellowship, which enabled her
to take an extended leave from her teaching position at the University of
Arizona and write Almanac of the Dead. She lives in Tucson, Arizona.

Woven throughout Silko's work is a critique of the Cartesian dualism
that cuts off the human from the natural world. "In the end we all originate
from the depths of the earth. Perhaps this is how all beings share in the
spirit of the Creator," she writes. In "Story from Bear Country" she imagines another way in which humans might share in and embrace the spirit
of the Creator. This poem appears in a collection of correspondence
between Silko and the poet James Wright, entitled The Delicacy and
Strength of Lace (1986).

STORY FROM BEAR COUNTRY

You will know
when you walk
in bear country.
By the silence
flowing swiftly between juniper trees
by the sundown colors of sandrock
all around you.

You may smell damp earth
scratched away
from yucca roots.
You may hear snorts and growls
slow and massive sounds
from caves
in the cliffs high above you.

It is difficult to explain
how they call you.
All but a few who went to them
left behind families
          grandparents
            and sons
              a good life.

The problem is
you will never want to return.
Their beauty will overcome your memory
like winter sun
melting ice shadows from snow.
And you will remain with them
locked forever inside yourself
            your eyes will see you
              dark shaggy thick.

We can send bear priests
loping after you
their medicine bags
bouncing against their chests.
Naked legs painted black
bear claw necklaces
rattling against
their capes of blue spruce.

They will follow your trail
into the narrow canyon
through the blue-gray mountain sage
to the clearing
where you stopped to look back
and saw only bear tracks
behind you.

When they call
faint memories
will writhe around your heart
and startle you with their distance.
But the others will listen
because bear priests sing
beautiful songs.
They must
if they are ever to call you back.

They will try to bring you
step by step
back to the place you stopped
and found only bear prints in the sand
where your feet had been.

Whose voice is this?
You may wonder
hearing this story when
after all
you are alone
hiking in these canyons and hills
while your wife and sons are waiting
back at the car for you.

But you have been listening to me
for some time now
from the very beginning in fact
and you are alone in this canyon of stillness
not even cedar birds flutter.
See, the sun is going down now
the sandrock is washed in its colors.

Don't be afraid
     we love you
     we've been calling you
all this time.
Go ahead
turn around
see the shape
of your footprints
in the sand.

—1986

PETER COYOTE

B. 1942

Peter Coyote has described himself as a writer who makes his living as an actor. He came of age in the early 1960s, and for his "bible" he carried around a copy of Donald Allen's landmark anthology The New American Poetry *(1960). At this same time, Coyote lived with the Diggers, a group of young people seeking an alternative style of living based on the principles of philosophical anarchism, best summed up in the Fourfold Digger Vow: 1) Freak out. 2) Come back. 3) Bandage the wounded and feed however many you can. 4) Never cheat.*

After cavorting in the wilds of northern California for many years with friends who included the poets Gary Snyder and Lew Welch, Coyote made his screen debut in the 1980 film Die Laughing. *You can catch a glimpse of him at work in* The Pursuit of D. B. Cooper *(1981),* Cross Creek *(a 1983 film adaptation of nature writer Marjorie Kinnan Rawlings's memoir of the same name), and* Outrageous Fortune *(1987), but like the four-footed subject of the following essay, Coyote is a trickster, hard to get hold of. When asked for information about himself, he wrote: "Peter Coyote came from nowhere and is working his way back."*

Originally appearing in a special issue of Coyote's Journal *(1982), "Muddy Prints on Mohair" could be described as a piece of contemporary folklore. Coyote, the trickster figure, plays a central role in Native American stories, and as the following piece observes, seems to be making his way into contemporary American culture. Whether encountered in a folktale or in everyday life, Coyote serves to bring us back to "reality." When our head swells with pride, the trickster bursts our bubble. When we are collapsing under the weight of despair, the trickster comes to lighten the load. For each of us, the trickster is the hard-to-see but ever-present teacher who has the audacity to make us the butt of a joke that leads to wisdom.*

MUDDY PRINTS ON MOHAIR

Stand in a puddle of water long enough and even rubber boots will leak. It is not surprising then, that after two centuries of occupation, and despite conscientious efforts to the contrary on the part of most humans, awareness of the essential energies of this continent's plants and animals has begun to exert an effect on transplanted Europeans, Asians, and Africans; insinuating themselves into our psyches and infiltrating our cultures.

Rings, charms, embroidered pillows, cruets, lorgnettes, cookie jars, and clocks with eyes that move, announce the supremacy of Owl as a totem for millions of Americans. Ceramic plates, statuary of varying dimensions, breast pins, drinking mugs, ashtrays and rings honor Frog. Each State has a native flower and bird associated with its sovereignty; sports teams compete under the heraldry of Bluejay, Hawk, Cougar, Bear and Lion. Consciousness of Whale, Baby Seal, pure water, clean air, sanctity of wilderness, snail darter, minute butterflies and salamanders has been the vehicle of massive political organizing. Even the Citizens Band Airwaves are flooded with names of "Tarweed," "Porcupine," "Meadowlark," and "Stinkbug."

Some prostitutes, poets, Zen students and several varieties of libertine have re-discovered the wit and utility of the Coyote-Trickster archetype. They have joined with those Native Americans who continue to recognize the beauty and worth of their ancient traditions, in creating a small but vital host who find value in this half-mental/half-mammal being.

I count myself among the number whose spinal telephone is being tapped by Coyote. Having spent some time thinking about him, being addressed by his name, raising some Coyote pups, talking to those who know him and his traditions well, and as eager as any to see him gain his recognition in our physical and cultural environment, I am delighted to see hosts of contemporary references to him cropping up in re-discovered myths, journals of ethno-poesy, union organizing literature and Roadrunner cartoons. I cannot help noticing however, the singularity with which most of these references herd Coyote into a limited and already overfull pantheon of American iconoclastic personalities.

Coyote absorbs Chaplin, W. C. Fields, Bogart, Garbo, Dietrich, Mae West, Dillinger, Midler and Cagney as more dated symbols of allegiances to personal codes. His once extensive range of possibilities and adaptation is being reduced to the narrow spectrum of anti-sociability and personal excess. An example is Coyote's (recent) association with Zen eccentrics.

Although Zen training and traditions stress personal experience and understanding (thus the aptness of the lone, homeless, wanderer as a symbol), the three treasures of Buddhism are Buddha, Dharma (the teachings), *and Sangha* (the community of like believers and practitioners). The transmission of Buddhism owes at least as much if not more to those who chose to operate *within* the non-personal, non-eccentric framework of tradition, as it does to those who have remained without. Personal liberation and tight community structure are not mutually exclusive, but in contemporary usage, Coyote is usually invoked as the crazy, enlightened loner whose purity is somehow measured by the number of forms and conventions he abuses. He is never (except in Native traditions) pictured as householder and community man. The rush to overlook this is a Coyote tricking that bears some watching.

I thought that it might serve our burgeoning interest in Coyote to share something of my own experience of his range of habitats, terrains, and markings so that future students not diminish his potential by maladaption, or, make the too frequent error of designating wide varieties of adaptive possibilities within one species as hosts of sub-species. It is to this that I dedicate the following.

Coyote is the miss in your engine.
He steals your concentration in
the Zendo. Mates for life. A good
family man who helps raise the kids.

A good team player, but satisfied
to be alone. He's handsome and
well groomed: teeth, hair, and eyes
shine. He likes prosperity and goes
for it: a tough young banker bearing
down at a high stakes tennis game.

He is total effort. Any good afternoon nap. Best dancer in the house.
The dealer and the sucker in a
sidewalk Monte game. An acquaintance
that hunts your power. The hooker
whose boyfriend comes out of the
closet while your pants are down.
He's also the boyfriend.

He eats grasshoppers and Cockerspaniels.
Drinks out of Bel-Aire swimming pools,
rainwater basins and cut lead-crystal
tumblers. He brings luck in gambling.
Inspires others to write about him. He
is jealousy.

A diligent mother. Top fashion model
with a fearless laugh. Easily bored.
He forgets what he was knowing.
He pretends to forget. Usually
gets the joke. Rarely follows advice.
Acts out our fantasies for us.

Is in the Bible as Onan's hand.
He's the gnawed squash in your garden.
The critical missing wrench from
your toolbox. He is the one who
returns with a harpooned acorn.

He may be Sirius, the dog star,
who, like Coyote, wanders and dies
awhile then comes back: companion
to Orion, the hunter, who like the
rest of us hunting enduring value and
knowledge, never forgets the brightest
star in our heavens.

—1982

Under what circumstances are we justified in taking the life of another creature? How do we handle the necessity to kill in order to live?

HUNTING AND FISHING

JAMES DICKEY
1923-1997

James Dickey produced nearly thirty books of fiction, poetry, and essays during his distinguished career. In his 1970 volume of autobiographical essays, Self-Interviews, *Dickey calls the poet "the intensified man"; he himself displayed intensity not only in his literary work but also in his life, as a college football player and track star, a bow hunter, a bluegrass guitarist, and a World War II fighter-bomber pilot. His fame among the general public derives largely from the adaptation of his 1970 novel* Deliverance *into a 1972 Hollywood film (starring Burt Reynolds and featuring Dickey himself in a cameo role).* Deliverance *is the story of four Atlanta businessmen who take off for several days of canoeing down an endangered river in backwoods Georgia, seeking to escape the boredom of their suburban lives. What they find is fear, danger, brutality, depravity, and violence—yet this descent into the primitive seems to restore the sanity and stability of the novel's narrator. Interestingly, Dickey published a poem (entitled "By Canoe through the Fir Forest") about a similar trip down a doomed river in the same issue of the* New Yorker *(June 16, 1962) in which the first installment of Rachel Carson's* Silent Spring *appeared.*

Born in Atlanta, Dickey was educated at Clemson College and Vanderbilt University. He held teaching and writer-in-residence positions at numerous universities before joining in 1969 the faculty of the University of South Carolina, where he taught until his death. His numerous awards include a National Book Award for his 1966 volume of poetry Buckdancer's Choice. *Dickey served as poetry consultant to the Library of Congress from 1966 to 1968 and read his poem "The Strength of Fields" at the 1977 inauguration of President Jimmy Carter, a fellow Georgian.*

The following poem, collected in Poems 1957-1967, *explores the relation between the writer's imaginative life and the intense, physical life of worldly experience. In particular, the writer and his dog seem to share a tendency to dream about the beloved intensity of hunting, the alertness of the chase. "Marvelous is the pursuit," writes Dickey. As he recalls a hunt he once took part in, the writer leaves his human self behind. He must awaken from "the dream of an animal" at daylight—that is, he must throw off not only the dream about fox hunting but also the animal thoughts of his own not-quite-human self.*

A DOG SLEEPING ON MY FEET

Being his resting place,
I do not even tense
The muscles of a leg
Or I would seem to be changing.
Instead, I turn the page
Of the notebook, carefully not

Remembering what I have written,
For now, with my feet beneath him
Dying like embers,
The poem is beginning to move
Up through my pine-prickling legs
Out of the night wood,

Taking hold of the pen by my fingers.
Before me the fox floats lightly,
On fire with his holy scent.
All, all are running.
Marvelous is the pursuit,
Like a dazzle of nails through the ankles,

Like a twisting shout through the trees
Sent after the flying fox
Through the holes of logs, over streams
Stock-still with the pressure of moonlight.
My killed legs,
My legs of a dead thing, follow,

Quick as pins, through the forest,
And all rushes on into dark
And ends on the brightness of paper.
When my hand, which speaks in a daze
The hypnotized language of beasts,
Shall falter, and fail

Back into the human tongue,
And the dog gets up and goes out

To wander the dawning yard,
I shall crawl to my human bed
And lie there smiling at sunrise,
With the scent of the fox

Burning my brain like an incense,
Floating out of the night wood,
Coming home to my wife and my sons
From the dream of an animal,
Assembling the self I must wake to,
Sleeping to grow back my legs.

—1967

WINTU TRIBE

The Wintu (or "Wintun") people are a California tribe that has traditionally inhabited a territory between the Sacramento Valley and the Coast Ranges in the northern part of the state. Ethnographers estimate there were approximately 15,000 Wintu in the mid-nineteenth century at the time of first contact with Anglo and Mexican explorers, missionaries, and gold prospectors. Wintu shamans guided the tribe's religious practices, instructing the people to worship a supreme being to whom they referred as "the one who is above." Food was procured primarily by hunting deer, rabbits, and bears, fishing for trout and salmon, and gathering acorns, berries, pine nuts, greens, and roots. Epidemics began to decimate the Wintu after contact with outsiders; then white ranchers occupied their lands and destroyed traditional food sources by grazing livestock, and miners polluted the tribe's fishing streams. Many of the remaining Wintu were massacred or forced onto reservations. Dam construction in the 1930s led to the flooding of tribal lands. By the late 1970s, no more than 900 racially and culturally mixed Wintu remained.

The following discussion of traditional Wintu hunting practices and beliefs is from the 1992 book Wisdom of the Elders: Sacred Native Stories of Nature, *edited by David Suzuki and Peter Knudtson. Although the language here is, for the most part, that of modern scholars, the ideas reflect the Wintu people's traditional view of nature and the act of hunting. Of particular significance is the concept of combining skill and luck to hunt successfully; native hunters like the Wintu, unlike Anglo-European hunters, have normally downplayed the importance of individual experience. The overriding sensibility of the Wintu, as represented in this discussion, was one of humility, respect, and even awe. The goal was not to conquer and control the natural world or even a small part of it (an individual animal), but to participate in "the sacred contract between human beings and kindred animals." Even this crucial relationship was "dwarfed by the sheer size and grandeur of a larger, fluid, yet orderly universe."*

THE WILLINGNESS OF A DEER TO DIE

While pursuing a deer through the sun-scorched foothills to the south of the snowy slopes of Mount Shasta, the Wintu hunter knows that to be highly successful this day, he must somehow reconcile two crucial forces: his skill and his luck.

His *skill* as a hunter is a variable over which he has managed to exercise some control; it arose from his own concrete, hard-won daily experience in this world. It is reflected in his prowess at carving a bow from yew wood and meticulously shaping the jeweled point of his arrow from volcanic obsidian; at expertly tracking the deer's fresh spoor in the rust-red soil; and at releasing his shot at precisely the right instant so that it flies straight into the most vulnerable organs of the fleeing deer, killing it cleanly.

But his *luck* as a hunter—that inevitable serendipity at play in the timely intersection of his own life and a particular deer's—is, in Wintu thinking, an entirely different matter. This difference is evident in how Wintu speak about the world around them and about its natural features and life-forms, including deer.

At dawn, for example, before eating, traditional Wintu often greet the first yellow rays of sunlight and all that they promise for this day, with an elemental, yet eloquent, morning prayer. In it, hopes for a successful hunt represent only one thread.

> *Behold the sun south above.*
> *Look at me down to the north.*
> *Let me wash my face with water; let me eat; let me eat food.*
> *I have no pain.*
> *Let me wash my face with water.*
> *Today let me kill a deer and bring it home to eat.*
> *Look at me down to the north, grandfather sun, old man.*
> *To the south and north I am active.*
> *Today I shall be happy.*

To the traditional Wintu, human experience and skill are capable of affecting only a tiny fraction of nature's immensity. The natural world that lies beyond a person's frail bubble of personal experience is fundamentally *unbounded, undifferentiated, timeless.* So, while individuals may think that by the time they reach old age, they have genuinely altered the world as they interacted with it, this is simply an illusion.

In truth, what they have done is no more than grant fleeting expression to a boundless eternity of ancient, preexisting patterns, relationships, and materials that are all a part of the grand design of the natural world. The individual Wintu, during the course of his or her transient lifetime on earth, merely actualizes *a given design endowing it with temporality.* As a mortal human being, as for other species, his role in the sacred order of the natural world is necessarily constrained. He neither *creates nor changes; the design remains immutable.*

This notion of a vast, orderly, and unchangeable cosmos beyond feeble human sensory limitations has a profound effect upon the Wintu hunter's view of his prospects during a deer hunt. In the first place, while his carefully honed hunting skills are certainly likely to improve his chances somewhat, his luck—or lack of it—is thought to be deeply connected with patterns of nature that lie, dim and unseen but always acknowledged, beyond his personal grasp.

Thus, if he succeeds this day in killing a deer, the hunter can justifiably attribute his success to a mixture of personal skill and temporary good fortune. But if he fails and is forced to walk out of the forest without a freshly dressed carcass slung over his shoulder, it is immediately clear to him that greater forces in nature have favored the life of this deer.

The survival of an animal that his misguided arrow fails to hit can only reflect the enduring order of the vast nature of things, so the luckless Wintu hunter does not complain, *"I cannot kill deer anymore."* Instead, in his wisdom about the workings of the cosmos, he says of this day simply, *"Deer don't want to die for me."*

And, should luck shine upon him and a deer—in an expression of nature's grand design—willingly die for him, the hunter accepts this gift with humility, gratitude, and courtesy. He accepts the deer's sacrifice only because he and his people genuinely need it. And he *utilizes every part of it, hoofs and marrow and hide and sinew and flex. Waste is abhorrent to him, not because he believes in the intrinsic virtue of thrift, but because the deer had died for him.*

By accepting the warm, energy- and nutrient-laden carcass as a supreme gift, and by honoring its willing sacrifice by respectfully handling its physical remains, the hunter confirms and revitalizes the sacred contract between human beings and kindred animals. His empathy for the elegant creature and his sense of its place in the cosmos compels him to communicate with the deceased deer and its unborn descendants with the same reverence with which he addresses his own family members and ancestors.

The relationship between Wintu hunter and deer, between human and beast, is thus horizontal. It is an ancient and familiar negotiation, punctuated by moments of joy and grief, between affectionate equals. In the end, this minute interspecies bond is dwarfed by the sheer size and grandeur of a larger, fluid, yet orderly universe, in which the fates of countless other elements are destined daily to intersect.

—1992

RICHARD K. NELSON

B. 1941

Born and raised in Wisconsin, anthropologist and writer Richard K. Nelson has lived for extended periods in Athabaskan Indian and Alaskan Eskimo villages. A scientist by training and an essayist by temperament, Nelson has described himself as having developed from being "a person who never intended to write to one who never intends to stop writing." His attitude toward his subject matter is deferential; he seeks, he says, "to serve my subject rather than to serve myself."

After receiving a B.S. and an M.S. from the University of Wisconsin, Madison, Nelson went on to earn a Ph.D. at the University of California, Santa Barbara. Of his twelve published books, the earlier works—which include Hunters of the Northern Ice *(1969) and* Hunters of the Northern Forest *(1973)—are anthropological studies, strictly scientific in their approach. By the time he published* Make Prayers to the Raven: A Koyukon View of the Northern Forest *(1983), Nelson was making a transition as a writer. "I tried to express my own feelings about Koyukon people and their traditions, while also staying within the bounds of scientific description." With his 1989 book,* The Island Within, *Nelson completed his literary metamorphosis. "It was my first step into the creative nonfiction usually called 'nature writing,' and into work that focuses on my own life rather than the lives of others." His latest book,* Heart and Blood: Living with Deer in America *(1997), is a deeply personal appreciation of deer as well as a serious examination of both sides of the hunting question.*

In "The Gifts," which was first published in a 1986 special issue of the journal Antaeus *devoted to nature writing and appears in a slightly different version as a chapter in* The Island Within, *Nelson portrays hunting as a meditative practice. The attentiveness and spiritual discipline that he describes as being required of the hunter are in many ways the same qualities required in the practice of writing. As Nelson himself has said, "Writing is the most solitary work imaginable, and spending long days alone is sometimes very difficult." As in hunting, though, long hard work at writing has its rewards. Nelson has captured on paper a native view of the connectedness of people to the world that is traditionally transmitted only orally. He offers "The Gifts" as a challenge to a Western society that he fears may be "irreversibly committed to the illusion that humanity is separate from and dominant over the natural world."*

THE GIFTS

Cold, clear, and calm in the pale blue morning. Snow on the high peaks brightening to amber. The bay a sheet of gray glass beneath a faint haze of steam. A November sun rises with the same fierce, chill stare of an owl's eye.

I stand at the window watching the slow dawn, and my mind fixes on the island. Nita comes softly down the stairs as I pack gear and complain of having slept too late for these short days. A few minutes later, Ethan trudges out onto the cold kitchen floor, barefoot and half asleep. We do not speak directly about hunting, to avoid acting proud or giving offense to the animals. I say only that I will go to the island and look around; Ethan says only that he would rather stay at home with Nita. I wish he would come along so I could teach him things, but know it will be quieter in the woods with just the dog.

They both wave from the window as I ease the skiff away from shore, crunching through cakes of freshwater ice the tide has carried in from Salmon River. It is a quick run through Windy Channel and out onto the freedom of the Sound, where the slopes of Mt. Sarichef bite cleanly into the frozen sky. The air stings against my face, but the rest of me is warm inside thick layers of clothes. Shungnak whines, paces, and looks over the gunwale toward the still-distant island.

Broad swells looming off the Pacific alternately lift the boat and drop it between smooth-walled canyons of water. Midway across the Sound a dark line of wind descends swiftly from the north, and within minutes we are surrounded by whitecaps. There are two choices: either beat straight up into them or cut an easier angle across the waves and take the spray. I vacillate for a while, then choose the icy spray over the intense pounding. Although I know it is wrong to curse the wind, I do it anyway.

A kittiwake sweeps over the water in great, vaulting arcs, its wings flexed against the touch and billow of the air. As it tilts its head passing over the boat, I think how clumsy and foolish we must look. The island's shore lifts slowly in dark walls of rock and timber that loom above the apron of snow-covered beach. As I approach the shelter of Low Point, the chop fades and the swell is smaller. I turn up along the lee, running between the kelp beds and the surf, straining my eyes for deer that may be feeding at the tide's edge.

Near the end of the point is a narrow gut that opens to a small, shallow anchorage. I ease the boat between the rocks, with lines of surf breaking close on either side. The waves rise and darken, their sharp edges sparkle in the sun, then long manes of spray whirl back as they turn inside out and pitch onto the shallow reef. The anchor slips down through ten feet of crystal water to settle among the kelp fronds and urchin-covered rocks. On a strong ebb the boat would go dry here, but today's tide change is only six feet. Before launching the punt I meticulously glass the broad, rocky shore and the sprawls of brown grass along the timber's edge. A tight bunch of rock sandpipers flashes up from the shingle and an otter loops along the windrows of drift logs, but there is no sign of deer. I can't help feeling a little anxious, because the season is drawing short and our year's supply of meat is not yet in. Throughout the fall, deer have been unusually wary, haunting the dense underbrush and slipping away at the least disturbance. I've come near a few, but these were young ones that I stalked only for the luxury of seeing them from close range.

Watching deer is the same pleasure now that it was when I was younger, when I loved animals only with my eyes and judged hunting to be outside the bounds of morality. Later, I tried expressing this love through studies of zoology, but this only seemed to put another kind of barrier between humanity and nature—the detachment of science and abstraction. Then, through anthropology, I encountered the entirely different views of nature found in other cultures. The hunting peoples were most fascinating because they had achieved deepest intimacy with their wild surroundings and had made natural history the focus of their lives. At the age of twenty-two, I went to live with Eskimos on the arctic coast of Alaska. It was my first year away from home, I had scarcely held a rifle in my hands, and the Eskimos—who call themselves the Real People—taught me their hunter's way.

The experience of living with Eskimos made very clear the direct, physical connectedness between all humans and the environments they draw existence from. Some years later, living with Koyukon Indians in Alaska's interior, I encountered a rich new dimension of that connectedness, and it profoundly changed my view of the world. Traditional Koyukon people follow a code of moral and ethical behavior that keeps a hunter in right relationship to the animals. They teach that all of nature is spiritual and aware, that it must be treated with respect, and that humans should approach the living world with restraint and humility. Now I struggle to learn if these same principles can apply in my own life and culture. Can we borrow from an ancient wisdom to structure a new relationship between ourselves and the environment? Or is Western society irreversibly committed to the illusion that humanity is separate from and dominant over the natural world?

A young bald eagle watches nervously from the peak of a tall hemlock as we bob ashore in the punt. Finally the bird lurches out, scoops its wings full of dense, cold air, and soars away beyond the line of trees. While I trudge up the long tide flat with the punt, Shungnak prances excitedly back and forth hunting for smells. The upper reaches are layered and slabbed with ice; slick cobbles shine like steel in the sun; frozen grass crackles underfoot. I lean the punt on a snow-covered log, pick up my rifle and small pack, and slip through the leafless alders into the forest.

My eyes take a moment adjusting to the sudden darkness, the deep green of boughs, and the somber, shadowy trunks. I feel safe and hidden here. The entire forest floor is covered with deep moss that should sponge gently beneath my feet. But today the softness is gone: frozen moss crunches with each step and brittle twigs snap, ringing out in the crisp air like strangers' voices. It takes a while to get used to this harshness in a forest that is usually so velvety and wet and silent. I listen to the clicking of gusts in the high branches and think that winter has come upon us like a fist.

At the base of a large nearby tree is a familiar patch of white—a scatter of deer bones—ribs, legs, vertebrae, two pelvis bones, and two skulls with half-bleached antlers. I put them here last winter, saying they were for the other animals, to make clear that they were not being thoughtlessly wasted. The scavengers soon picked them clean, the deer mice have gnawed them, and eventually they will be absorbed into the forest again. Koyukon elders say it shows respect, putting animal bones back in a clean, wild place instead of throwing them away with trash or scattering them in a garbage dump. The same obligations of etiquette that bind us to our human community also bind us to the natural community we live within.

Shungnak follows closely as we work our way back through a maze of windfalls, across clear disks of frozen ponds, and around patches of snow beneath openings in the forest canopy. I step and wait, trying to make no sound, knowing we could see deer at any moment. Deep snow has driven them down off the slopes and they are sure to be distracted with the business of the mating season.

We pick our way up the face of a high, steep scarp, then clamber atop a fallen log for a better view ahead. I peer into the semi-open understory of twiggy bushes, probing each space with my eyes. A downy woodpecker's call sparks from a nearby tree. Several minutes pass. Then a huckleberry branch moves, barely twitches, without the slightest noise . . . not far ahead.

Amid the scramble of brush where my eyes saw nothing a few minutes ago, a dim shape materializes, as if its own motion had created it. A doe steps into an open space, deep brown in her winter coat, soft and striking and lovely, dwarfed among the great trees, lifting her nose, looking right toward me. For perhaps a minute we are motionless in each other's gaze; then her head jerks to the left, her ears twitch back and forth, her tail flicks up, and she turns away in the stylized gait deer always use when alarmed.

Quick as a breath, quiet as a whisper, the doe glides off into the forest. Sometimes when I see a deer this way I know it is real at the moment, but afterward it seems like a daydream.

As we work our way back into the woods, I keep hoping for another look at her and thinking that a buck might have been following nearby. Any deer is legal game and I could almost certainly have taken her, but I would rather wait for a larger buck and let the doe bring on next year's young. Shungnak savors the ghost of her scent that hangs in the still air, but she has vanished.

Farther on, the snow deepens to a continuous cover beneath smaller trees, and we cross several sets of deer tracks, including some big prints with long toe drags. The snow helps to muffle our steps, but it is hard to see very far because the bushes are heavily loaded with powder. The thicket becomes a latticed maze of white on black, every branch hung and spangled in a thick fur of jeweled snow. We move through it like eagles cleaving between tumbled columns of cloud. New siftings occasionally drift down when the treetops are touched by the breeze.

Slots between the trunks up ahead shiver with blue where a muskeg opens. I angle toward it, feeling no need to hurry, picking every footstep carefully, stopping often to stare into the dizzying crannies, listening for any splinter of sound, keeping my senses tight and concentrated. A raven calls from high above the forest, and as I catch a glimpse of it an old question runs through my mind: Is this only the bird we see, or does it have the power and awareness Koyukon elders speak of? It lifts and plays on the wind far aloft, then folds up and rolls halfway over, a strong sign of luck in hunting. Never mind the issue of knowing; we should assume that power is here and let ourselves be moved by it.

I turn to look at Shungnak, taking advantage of her sharper hearing and magical sense of smell. She lifts her nose to the fresh but nebulous scent of several deer that have moved through here this morning. I watch her little radar ears, waiting for her to focus in one direction and hold it, hoping to see her body tense as it does when something moves nearby. But so far she only hears the twitching of red squirrels on dry bark. Shungnak and I have very different opinions of the squirrels. They excite her more than any other animal because she believes she will catch one someday. But for the hunter they are deceptive spurts of movement and sound, and their sputtering alarm calls alert the deer.

We approach a low, abrupt rise, covered with obscuring brush and curtained with snow. A lift of wind hisses in the high trees, then drops away and leaves us in near-complete silence. I pause to choose a path through a scramble of blueberry bushes and little windfalls ahead, then glance back at Shungnak. She has her eyes and ears fixed off toward our left, almost directly across the current of breeze. She stands very stiff, quivering slightly, leaning forward as if she has already started to run but cannot release her muscles. I shake my finger at her as a warning to stay.

I listen as closely as possible, but hear nothing. I work my eyes into every dark crevice and slot among the snowy branches, but see nothing. I stand perfectly still and wait, then look again at Shungnak. Her head turns so slowly that I can barely detect the movement, until finally she is looking straight ahead. Perhaps it is just another squirrel. . . . I consider taking a few steps for a better view.

Then I see it.

A long, dark body appears among the bushes, moving deliberately upwind, so close I can scarcely believe I didn't see it earlier. Without looking away, I carefully slide the breech closed and lift the rifle to my shoulder, almost certain that a deer this size will be a buck. Shungnak, now forgotten behind me, must be contorted with the suppressed urge to give chase.

The deer walks easily, silently, along the little rise, never looking our way. Then he makes a sharp turn straight toward us. Thick tines of his antlers curve over the place where I have the rifle aimed. Koyukon elders teach that animals will come to those who have shown them respect, and will allow themselves to be taken in what is only a temporary death. At a moment like this, it is easy to sense that despite my abiding doubt there is a shared world beyond the one we know directly, a world the Koyukon people empower with spirits, a world that demands recognition and exacts a price from those who ignore it.

This is a very large buck. It comes so quickly that I have no chance to shoot, and then it is so close that I haven't the heart to do it. Fifty feet away, the deer lowers his head almost to the ground and lifts a slender branch that blocks his path. Snow shakes down onto his neck and clings to the fur of his shoulders as he slips underneath. Then he half-lifts his head and keeps coming. I ease the rifle down to watch, wondering how much closer he will get. Just now he makes a long, soft rutting call, like the bleating of a sheep except lower and more hollow. His hooves tick against dry twigs hidden by the snow.

In the middle of a step he raises his head all the way up, and he sees me standing there—a stain against the pure white of the forest. A sudden spasm runs through his entire body, his front legs jerk apart, and he freezes all akimbo, head high, nostrils flared, coiled and hard. I can only look at him and wait, my mind snarled with irreconcilable emotions. Here is a perfect buck deer. In the Koyukon way, he has come to me; but in my own he has come too close. I am as congealed and transfixed as he is, as devoid of conscious thought. It is as if my mind has ceased to function and I only have eyes.

But the buck has no choice. He suddenly unwinds in a burst of ignited energy, springs straight up from the snow, turns in mid-flight, stabs the frozen earth again, and makes four great bounds off to the left. His thick body seems to float, relieved of its own weight, as if a deer has the power to unbind itself from gravity.

The same deeper impulse that governs the flight of a deer governs the predator's impulse to pursue it. I watch the first leaps without moving a muscle. Then, not pausing for an instant of deliberation, I raise the rifle back to my shoulder, follow the movement of the deer's fleeing form, and wait until it stops to stare back. Almost at that instant, still moving without conscious thought, freed of the ambiguities that held me before, now no less animal than the animal I watch, my hands warm and steady and certain, acting from a more elemental sense than the ones that brought me to this meeting, I carefully align the sights and let go the sudden power. The gift of the deer falls like a feather in the snow. And the rifle's sound has rolled off through the timber before I hear it.

I walk to the deer, now shaking a bit with swelling emotion. Shungnak is beside it already, whining and smelling, racing from one side to the other, stuffing her nose down in snow full of scent. She looks off into the brush, searching back and forth, as if the deer that ran is somewhere else, still running. She tries to lick at the blood that trickles down, but I stop her out of respect for the animal. Then, I suppose to consummate her own frustrated predatory energy, she takes a hard nip at its shoulder, shuns quickly away, and looks back as if she expects it to leap to its feet again.

As always, I whisper thanks to the animal for giving itself to me. The words are my own, not something I have learned from the Koyukon. Their elders might say that the words we use in prayer to spirits of the natural world do not matter. Nor, perhaps, does it matter what form these spirits take in our own thoughts. What truly matters is only that prayer be made, to affirm our humility in the presence of nurturing power. Most of humanity throughout history has said prayers to the powers of surrounding nature, which they have recognized as their source of life. Surely it is not too late to recover this ancestral wisdom.

It takes a few minutes before I settle down inside and can begin the other work. Then I hang the deer with rope strung over a low branch and back twice through pulley-loops. I cut away the dark, pungent scent glands on its legs, and next make a careful incision along its belly, just large enough to reach the warm insides. The stomach and intestines come easily and cleanly; I cut through the diaphragm, and there is a hollow sound as the lungs pull free. Placing them on the soft snow, I whisper that these parts are left here for the other animals. Shungnak wants to take some for herself but I tell her to keep away. It is said that the life and awareness leaves an animal's remains slowly, and there are rules about what should be eaten by a dog. She will have her share of the scraps later on, when more of the life is gone.

After the blood has drained out, I sew the opening shut with a piece of line to keep the insides clean, and then toggle the deer's forelegs through a slit in the hind leg joint, so it can be carried like a pack. I am barely strong enough to get it up onto my back, but there is plenty of time to work slowly toward the beach, stopping often to rest and cool down. During one of these stops I hear two ravens in an agitated exchange of croaks and gurgles, and I wonder if those black eyes have already spotted the remnants. No pure philanthropist, the raven gives a hunter luck only as a way of creating luck for himself.

Finally, I push through the low boughs of the beachside trees and ease my burden down. Afternoon sun throbs off the water, but a chill north wind takes all warmth from it. Little gusts splay in dark patterns across the anchorage; the boat paces on its mooring line; the Sound is racing with whitecaps. I take a good rest, watching a fox sparrow flit among the drift logs and a bunch of crows hassling over some bit of food at the water's edge.

Though I feel utterly satisfied, grateful, and contented, there is much to do and the day will slope away quickly. We are allowed more than one deer, so I will stay on the island for another look around tomorrow. It takes two trips to get everything out to the skiff, then we head up the shore toward the little cabin and secure anchorage at Bear Creek. By the time the boat is unloaded and tied off, the wind has faded and a late afternoon chill sinks down in the pitched, hard shadow of Sarichef.

Half-dry wood hisses and sputters, giving way reluctantly to flames in the rusted stove. It is nearly dusk when I bring the deer inside and set to work on it. Better to do this now than to wait, in case tomorrow is another day of luck. The animal hangs from a low beam, dim-lit by the kerosene lamp. I feel strange in its presence, as if it still watches, still glows with something of its life, still demands that nothing be done or spoken carelessly. A hunter should never let himself be deluded by pride or a false sense of dominance. It is not through our own power that we take life in nature; it is through the power of nature that life is given to us.

The soft hide peels away slowly from shining muscles, and the inner perfection of the deer's body is revealed. Koyukon and Eskimo hunters teach a refined art of taking an animal into its component parts, easing blades through crisp cartilage where bone joins bone, following the body's own design until it is disarticulated. There is no ugliness in it, only hands moving in concert with the beauty of an animal's making. Perhaps we have been too removed from this to understand, and we have lost touch with the process of one life being passed on to another. As my hands work inside the deer, it is as if something has already begun to flow into me.

When the work is finished, I take two large slices from the hind quarter and put them in a pan atop the now-crackling stove. In a separate pot, I boil scraps of meat and fat for Shungnak, who has waited with as much patience as possible for a husky raised in a hunter's team up north. When the meat is finished cooking I sit on a sawed log and eat straight from the pan.

A meal could not be simpler, more satisfying, or more directly a part of the living process. I wish Ethan was here to share it, and I would explain to him again that when we eat the deer its flesh is then our flesh. The deer changes form and becomes us, and we in turn become creatures made of deer. Each time we eat the deer we should remember it and feel gratitude for what it has given us. And each time, we should carry a thought like a prayer inside: "Thanks to the animal and to all that made it—the island and the forest, the air, and the rain . . ." We should remember that in the course of things, we are all generations of deer and of the earth-life that feeds us.

Warm inside my sleeping bag, I let the fire ebb away to coals. The lamp is out. The cabin roof creaks in the growing cold. I drift toward sleep, feeling pleased that there is no moon, so the deer will wait until dawn to feed. On the floor beside me, Shungnak jerks and whimpers in her dog's dreams.

Next morning we are in the woods with the early light. We follow yesterday's tracks, and just beyond the place of the buck, a pair of does drifts at the edge of sight and disappears. For an hour we angle north, then come slowly back somewhat deeper in the woods, moving crosswise to a growing easterly breeze. In two separate places, deer snort and pound away, invisible beyond a shroud of brush. Otherwise there is nothing.

Sometime after noon we come to a narrow muskeg with scattered lodgepole pines and a ragged edge of bushy, low-growing cedar. I squint against the sharp glare of snow. It has that peculiar look of old powder, a bit settled and touched by wind, very lovely but without the airy magic of a fresh fall. I gaze up the muskeg's easy slope, and above the encroaching wall of timber, seamed against the deep blue sky, is the brilliant peak of Sarichef with a great plume of snow streaming off in what must be a shuddering gale. It has a contradictory look of absoluteness and unreality about it, like a Himalayan summit suspended in mid-air over the saddle of a low ridge.

I move very slowly up the muskeg's east side, away from the breeze and in the sun's full warmth. Deer tracks crisscross the opening, but none of the animals stopped here to feed. Next to the bordering trees, the tracks follow a single, hard-packed trail, showing the deers' preference for cover. Shungnak keeps her nose to the thickly scented snow. We come across a pine sapling that a buck has torn with his antlers, scattering twigs and flakes of bark all around. But his tracks are hardened, frosted, and lack sharpness, so they are at least a day old.

We slip through a narrow point of trees, then follow the open edge again, pausing long moments between each footstep. A mixed tinkle of crossbills and siskins moves through the high timber, and a squirrel rattles from deep in the woods, too far off to be scolding us. Shungnak begins to pick up a strong ribbon of scent, but she hears nothing. I stop for several minutes to study the muskeg's long, raveled fringe, the tangle of shade and thicket, the glaze of mantled boughs.

Then my eye barely catches a fleck of movement up ahead, near the ground and almost hidden behind the trunk of a leaning pine, perhaps a squirrel's tail or a bird. I lift my hand slowly to shade the sun, stand dead still, and wait to see if something is there. Finally it moves again.

At the very edge of the trees, almost out of sight in a little swale, small and furry and bright-tinged, turning one direction and then another, is the funnel of a single ear. Having seen this, I soon make out the other ear and the slope of a doe's forehead. Her neck is behind the leaning pine, but on the other side I can barely see the soft, dark curve of her back above the snow. She is comfortably bedded, gazing placidly into the distance, chewing her cud.

Shungnak has stopped twenty yards behind me in the point of trees and has no idea about the deer. I shake my finger at her until she lays her ears back and sits. Then I watch the doe again. She is fifty yards ahead of me, ten yards beyond the leaning tree, and still looking off at an angle. Her left eye is clearly visible and she refuses to turn her head away, so it might be impossible to get any closer. Perhaps I should just wait here, in case a buck is attending her nearby. But however improbable it might be under these circumstances, a thought is lodged in my mind: I can get near her.

My first step sinks down softly, but the second makes a loud budging sound. She snaps my way, stops chewing, and stares for several minutes. It seems hopeless, especially out here in an open field of crisp snow with only the narrow treetrunk for a screen. But she slowly turns away and starts to chew again. I move just enough so the tree blocks her eye and the rest of her head, but I can still see her ears. Every time she chews they shake just a bit, so I can watch them and step when her hearing is obscured by the sound of her own jaws.

Either this works or the deer has decided to ignore me, because after a short while I am near enough so the noise of my feet has to reach her easily. She should have jumped up and run long ago, but instead she lays there in serene repose. I deliberate on every step, try for the softest snow, wait long minutes before the next move, stalking like a cat toward ambush. I watch beyond her, into the surrounding shadows and across to the muskeg's farther edge, for the shape of a buck deer; but there is nothing. I feel ponderous, clumsy-footed, out-of-place, inimical. I should turn and run away, take fear on the deer's behalf, flee the mirrored image in my mind. But I clutch the cold rifle at my side and creep closer.

The wind refuses to blow and my footsteps seem like thunder in the still sunshine. But the doe only turns once to look my way, without even pointing her ears toward me, then stares off and begins to chew again.

I am ten feet from the leaning tree. My heart pounds so hard, I think those enchanted ears should hear the rush of blood in my temples. Yet a strange certainty has come into me, a quite unmystical confidence. Perhaps she has decided I am another deer, a buck attracted by her musk or a doe feeding gradually toward her. My slow pace and lapses of stillness would not seem human. For myself, I have lost awareness of elapsed time; I have no feeling of patience or impatience. It is as if the deer has moved slowly toward me on a cloud of snow, and I am adrift in the pure motion of experience.

I take the last step to the trunk of the leaning pine. It is bare of branches, scarcely wider than my hand, but perfectly placed to break my odd profile. There is no hope of getting any closer, so I slowly poke my head out to watch. She has an ideal spot: screened from the wind, warmed by the sun, and with a clear view of the muskeg. I can see muscles working beneath the close fur of her jaw, the rise and fall of her side each time she breathes, the shining edge of her ebony eye.

I hold absolutely still, but her body begins to stiffen, she lifts her head higher, and her ears twitch anxiously. Then instead of looking at me she turns her face to the woods, shifting her ears toward a sound I cannot hear. A few seconds later, the unmistakable voice of a buck drifts up, strangely disembodied, as if it comes from an animal somewhere underneath the snow. I huddle as close to the tree as I can, press against the hard, dry bark, and peek out around its edge.

There is a gentle rise behind the doe, scattered with sapling pines and clusters of juniper bushes. A rhythmic crunching of snow comes invisibly from the slope, then a bough shakes . . . and a buck walks easily into the open sunshine.

Focusing his attention completely on the doe, he comes straight toward her and never sees my intrusive shape just beyond. He slips through a patch of small trees, stops a few feet from where she lies, lowers his head and stretches it toward her, then holds this odd pose for a long moment. She reaches her muzzle out to one side, trying to find his scent. When he starts to move up behind her she stands quickly, bends her body into a strange sideways arc, and stares back at him. A moment later she walks off a bit, lifts her tail, and puts droppings in her tracks. The buck moves to the warm ground of her bed and lowers his nose to the place where her female scent is strongest.

Inching like a reptile on a cold rock, I have stepped out from the tree and let my whole menacing profile become visible. The deer are thirty feet away and stand well apart, so they can both see me easily. I am a hunter hovering near his prey and a watcher craving inhuman love, torn between the deepest impulses, hot and shallow-breathed and seething with unreconciled intent, hidden from opened eyes that look into the nimbus of sun and see nothing but the shadow they have chosen for themselves. In this shadow now, the hunter has vanished and only the watcher remains.

Drawn by the honey of the doe's scent, the buck steps quickly toward her. And now the most extraordinary thing happens. The doe turns away from him and walks straight for me. There is no hesitation, only a wild deer coming along the trail of hardened snow where the other deer have passed, the trail in which I stand at this moment. She raises her head, looks at me, and steps without hesitation.

My existence is reduced to a pair of eyes; a rush of unbearable heat flushes through my cheeks; and a sense of absolute certainty fuses in my mind.

The snow blazes so brightly that my head aches. The deer is a dark form growing larger. I look up at the buck, half embarrassed, as if to apologize that she has chosen me over him. He stares at her for a moment, turns to follow, then stops and watches anxiously. I am struck by how gently her narrow hooves touch the trail, how little sound they make as she steps, how thick the fur is on her flank and shoulder, how unfathomable her eyes look. I am consumed with a sense of her perfect elegance in the brilliant light. And then I am lost again in the whirling intensity of experience.

The doe is now ten feet from me. She never pauses or looks away. Her feet punch down mechanically into the snow, coming closer and closer, until they are less than a yard from my own. Then she stops, stretches her neck calmly toward me, and lifts her nose.

There is not the slightest question in my mind, as if this was certain to happen and I have known all along exactly what to do. I slowly raise my hand and reach out . . .

And my fingers touch the soft, dry, gently needling fur on top of the deer's head, and press down to the living warmth of flesh underneath.

She makes no move and shows no fear, but I can feel the flaming strength and tension that flow in her wild body as in no other animal I have ever touched. Time expands and I am suspended in the clear reality of that moment.

Then, by the flawed conditioning of a lifetime among fearless domesticated things, I instinctively drop my hand and let the deer smell it. Her dark nose, wet and shining, touches gently against my skin at the exact instant I realize the absoluteness of my error. And a jolt runs through her entire body as she realizes hers. Her muscles seize and harden; she seems to wrench her eyes away from me but her body remains, rigid and paralyzed. Having been deceived by her other senses, she keeps her nose tight against my hand for one more moment.

Then all the energy inside her triggers in a series of exquisite bounds. She flings out over the hummocks of snow-covered moss, suspended in effortless flight like fog blown over the muskeg in a gale. Her body leaps with such power that the muscles should twang aloud like a bowstring; the earth should shudder and drum; but I hear no sound. In the center of the muskeg she stops to look back, as if to confirm what must seem impossible. The buck follows in more earthbound undulations; they dance away together, and I am left in the meeting-place alone.

There is a blur of rushing feet behind me. No longer able to restrain herself, Shungnak dashes past, buries her nose in the soft tracks, and then looks back to ask if we can run after them. I had completely forgotten her, sitting near enough to watch the whole encounter, somehow resisting what must have been a prodigious urge to explode in chase. When I reach out to hug her, she smells the hand that touched the deer. And it seems as if it happened long ago.

For the past year I have kept a secret dream, that I would someday come close enough to touch a deer on this island. But since the idea came it seemed harder than ever to get near them. Now, totally unexpected and in a strange way, it has happened. Was the deer caught by some reckless twinge of curiosity? Had she never encountered a human on this wild island? Did she yield to some odd amorous confusion? I really do not care. I would rather accept this as pure experience and not give in to the notion that everything must be explained.

Nor do I care to think that I was chosen to see some manifestation of power, because I have little tolerance for such dreams of self-importance. I have never asked that nature open any doors to reveal the truth of spirit or mystery; I aspire to no shaman's path; I expect no visions, no miracles except the ones that fill every instant of ordinary life.

But there are vital lessons in the experience of moments such as these, if we live them in the light of wisdom taken from the earth and shaped by generations of elders. Two deer came and gave the choices to me. One deer I took and we will now share a single body. The other deer I touched and we will now share that moment. These events could be seen as opposites, but they are in fact identical. Both are founded in the same principles, the same relationship, the same reciprocity.

Move slowly, stay quiet, watch carefully . . . and be ever humble. Never show the slightest arrogance or disrespect. Koyukon elders would explain, in words quite different from my own, that I moved into two moments of grace, or what they would call luck. This is the source of success for a hunter or a watcher, not skill, not cleverness, not guile. Something is only given in nature, never taken.

I have heard the elders say that everything in nature has its own spirit and possesses a power beyond ours. There is no way to prove them right or wrong, though the beauty and interrelatedness of things should be evidence enough. We need not ask for shining visions as proof, or for a message from a golden deer glowing in the sky of our dreams. Above all else, we should assume that power moves in the world around us and act accordingly. If it is a myth, then spirit is within the myth and we should live by it. And if there is a commandment to follow, it is to approach all of earth-life, of which we are a part, with humility and respect.

Well soaked and shivering from a rough trip across the Sound, we pull into the dark waters of the bay. Sunset burns on Twin Peaks and the spindled ridge of Antler

Mountain. The little house is warm with lights that shimmer on the calm near shore. I see Nita looking from the window and Ethan dashes out to wait by the tide, pitching rocks at the mooring buoy. He strains to see inside the boat, knowing that a hunter who tells his news aloud may offend the animals by sounding boastful. But when he sees the deer his excited voice seems to roll up and down the mountainside.

He runs for the house with Shungnak, carrying a load of gear, and I know he will burst inside with the news. Ethan, joyous and alive, boy made of deer.

—1986

JOYCE CAROL OATES

B. 1938

One of the most prolific of all contemporary writers, Joyce Carol Oates employs her powerful and plutonic talent across all genres: novels, short stories, nonfiction, poetry, and plays. Since the mid-1960s, she has been producing two books per year, making it challenging for her readers and critics to keep up with her. At age thirty-one, she became one of the youngest recipients of the National Book Award for fiction, for her novel them. *With great imaginative fortitude, Oates reveals for her readers that darkest and most fearsome locale in all of nature, the human mind. As she explains it, in terms suggestive of the spiritual themes that course through her work: "The serious writer, after all, bears witness."*

Born and raised in Lockport, New York, Oates has lived in New Jersey for many years, teaching at Princeton University. When asked how a life spent in a comfortable suburb and behind the walls of one of the nation's most prestigious universities could feed an imagination as wild and far-ranging as her own, she responded by quoting the French writer Flaubert: "You should live like a bourgeois so that you can be wild and original in your writing." While much of her writing probes the theme of humans confronting nature, Oates nevertheless is one of the most formidable critics of the genre of nature writing. In her gadfly essay "Against Nature," which appeared in a 1986 special issue of the journal Antaeus *devoted to nature writing, she notes that nature "inspires a painfully limited set of responses in 'nature-writers'—REVERENCE, AWE, PIETY, MYSTICAL ONENESS," and confesses her own resistance to nature writing as a genre, "except when it is brilliantly fictionalized in the service of a writer's individual vision," citing Thoreau's books and journal as an example of the latter. Oates actually has a surprising number of affinities with Thoreau, not the least of which is that she is as cognizant as he was of nature's irresistible power. Her final "resistance" to nature is, ironically, the same conclusion that many a talented writer who seeks somehow to capture nature ultimately comes to: "It eludes us even as it prepares to swallow us up, books and all."*

"The Buck" originally appeared in Story *magazine (Winter 1991). Reminiscent of William Faulkner's fiction in its exploration of archetypal motifs, this piece, like so much in Oates's oeuvre, is thickly textured, mythic, and finally disturbing. It "bears witness" to the dark complexities of nature,*

and especially of human nature. The buck seems to mean something different to each of the two protagonists, yet both seem to be acting out some aspect of their unlived lives in relation to the creature. Is our interaction with outer nature, then, determined by the distortions in our inner nature that culture forces upon each of us? Oates's story invites the reader to consider this possibility.

THE BUCK

This is such a terrible story, it's a story I have told a dozen times never knowing why.

Why I can't forget it, I mean. Why it's lodged so deep in me . . . like an arrow through the neck.

Like that arrow I never saw—fifteen-inch, steel-tipped, razor-sharp—that penetrated the deer's neck, and killed him, though not immediately. How many hours, I wonder, till he bled to death, till his body turned cold and grew heavier, they say the weight of Death is always heavier than that of life, how many hours, terrible hours— I don't know.

I was not a witness. I know only what I have heard. The sole witness did not survive.

Each time I tell this story of the wounded buck, the hunter who pursued him and the elderly woman who rescued him, or tried to rescue him, I think that maybe *this* telling will make a difference. *This* time a secret meaning will be revealed, as if without my volition; and I will be released.

But each telling is a subtle repudiation of a previous telling. So each telling is a new telling. Each telling a forgetting.

That arrow lodged ever more firmly, cruelly. In living flesh.

I'd take comfort in saying all this happened years ago, in some remote part of the country. *Once upon a time* I'd begin, but in fact it happened within the past year, and no more than eight miles from where I live, in a small town called Bethany, New Jersey.

Which is in Saugatuck County, in the northwestern corner of the state, bordering the Delaware River.

A region that's mainly rural—farmland, hills, some of the hills large enough to be called mountains. There aren't many roads in this part of New Jersey and the big interstate highways just slice through, gouge through the countryside, north and south, east and west. Strangers in a rush to get somewhere else.

The incident happened on the Snyder farm. A lonely place, no neighbors close by.

The name "Snyder" was always known in Saugatuck County even though, when I was growing up, the Snyders had sold off most of their land. In the family's prime in the 1930s, they'd owned three hundred twenty acres, most of it rich farmland; in the 1950s they'd begun to sell, piecemeal, as if grudgingly, maybe with the idea of one day buying their land back. But they never did—they died out, instead. Three brothers, all unmarried; and Melanie Snyder, the last of the family. Eighty-two years old when she was found dead in a room of the old farmhouse, last January.

In deer-hunting season. The season that had always frightened and outraged her. She'd been vigilant, for years. She'd acquired a local reputation. Her six acres of land—all that remained of the property—was scrupulously posted against hunters ("with gun, bow and arrow, dog") and trespassers. Before hunting with firearms was banned in Saugatuck County, Melanie Snyder patrolled her property in hunting season, on foot, fearless about moving in the direction of gunfire—"You!—what are you doing here?" she would call out, to hunters, "—don't you know this land is posted?" She was a lanky woman with a strong-boned face, skin that looked permanently wind-burnt, close-cropped starkly white hair. Her eyes were unusually dark and prominent, everyone commented on Melanie Snyder's eyes, she wasn't a woman any man, no matter his age, felt comfortable confronting, especially out in the woods.

She sent trespassers home, threatened to call the sheriff if they didn't leave. She'd stride through the woods clapping her hands to frighten off deer, pheasants, small game, send them panicked to safety.

White-tailed deer, or, as older generations called them, Virginia deer, were her favorites. "The most beautiful animals in creation." She hated it that state conservationists argued in favor of controlled hunting for the "good" of the deer themselves: to reduce their alarmingly fertile numbers.

She hated the idea of hunting with bow and arrow—as if it made any difference to a deer, how it died.

She hated the stealth and silence of the bow. With guns, you can at least hear the enemy.

His name was Wayne Kunz, "Woody" Kunz, part-owner of a small auto parts store in Delaware Gap, New Jersey, known to his circle of male friends as a good guy. A good sport. You might say—a "character."

The way he dressed—his hunting gear, for instance.

A black simulated-leather jumpsuit, over it the regulation fluorescent-orange vest. A bright-red cap, with earflaps. Boots to the knee, like a Nazi storm trooper's; mirror sunglasses hiding his pale lashless eyes. He had a large, round, singed-looking face, a small damp mouth: this big-bellied, quick-grinning fellow, the kind who keeps up a constant chatting murmur with himself, as if terrified of silence, of being finally *alone*.

He hadn't been able to talk any of his friends into coming with him, deer-hunting with bows and arrows.

Even showing them his new Atlas bow, forty-eight inches, sleek blond fiberglass "wood," showing them the quiver of arrows, synthetic-feathered, lightweight steel and steel-tipped and razor-sharp like no Indian's arrows had ever been—he'd been disappointed, disgusted with them, none of his friends wanting to come along, waking in the pre-dawn dark, driving out into Saugatuck County to kill a few deer.

Woody Kunz. Forty years old, five feet ten inches, two hundred pounds. He'd been married, years ago, but the marriage hadn't worked out, and there were no children.

Crashing clumsily through the underbrush, in pursuit of deer.

Not wanting to think he was lost—*was* he lost?

Talking to himself, cursing and begging himself, "C'mon, Woody, for Christ sake, Woody, move your fat *ass*," half-sobbing as, another time, a herd of deer broke and scattered before he could get into shooting range. Running and leaping through the woods, taunting him with their uplifted white tails, erect snowy-white tails like targets so he couldn't help but fire off an arrow—to fly into space, disappear.

"Fuck it, Woody! Fuck you, asshole!"

Later. He's tired. Even with the sunglasses his eyes are seared from the bright winter sun reflecting on the snow.

Knowing he deserves better but—another time the deer are too quick and smart for him, must be they scented him downwind, breaking to run before he even saw them, only heard them, silent except for the sound of their crashing hooves. This time, he fires a shot knowing it won't strike any target, no warm living flesh—must be, he does it to make himself feel bad.

Playing the fool in the eyes of anybody watching and he can't help but think uneasily that somebody *is* watching—if only the unblinking eye of God.

And then: he sees the buck.

His buck, yes, suddenly. Oh, Jesus, his heart clenches, he *knows*.

He has surprised the beautiful dun-colored animal drinking from a fast-running stream, the stream is frozen except for a channel of black water at its center, the buck with its antlered head lowered, Woody Kunz stares, hardly able to believe his good luck, rapidly counting the points of the antlers—eight? ten?—as he fits an arrow into place with trembling fingers, lifts the bow and sights along the arrow aiming for that point of the anatomy where neck and chest converge, it's a heart shot he hopes for, drawing back the arrow, feeling the power of the bow, releasing it and seemingly in the same instant the buck leaps, the arrow has struck him in the neck, there's a shriek of animal terror and pain and Woody Kunz shouts in ecstatic triumph.

But the buck isn't killed outright. To Woody's astonishment, and something like hurt, the buck turns and runs—flees.

Later he'd say he hadn't seen the No Trespassing signs in the woods, he hadn't come by way of the road so he hadn't seen them there, the usual state-issued sign forbidding hunting, trapping, trespassing on private land but Woody Kunz would claim he hadn't known it was private land exactly, he'd have to confess he might have been lost, tracking deer for hours moving more or less in a circle not able to gauge where the center of the circle might be, and yes, he was so excited, his adrenaline rushing in his veins as he hadn't felt it in God knows how long, half a lifetime maybe, so he hadn't seen the signs posting the Snyder property or if he'd seen them they had not registered upon his consciousness or if they'd registered upon his consciousness he hadn't known what they were, so tattered and weatherworn.

That was Woody Kunz's defense against a charge, if there was to be a charge, of unlawful trespassing and hunting on posted property.

Jesus is the most important person in all our lives!

Jesus abides in our hearts, no need to see Him!

These joyful pronouncements, or are they commandments, Melanie Snyder sometimes hears, rising out of the silence of the old house. The wind in the eaves, a shrieking of crows in the orchard. And this disembodied voice, the voice of her long-dead fiancé—waking her suddenly from one of her reveries, so she doesn't remember where she is, what year this is, what has happened to her, to have aged her so.

She'd fallen in love with her brothers, one by one. Her tall strong indifferent brothers.

Much later, to everyone's surprise and certainly to her own, she'd fallen in love with a young Lutheran preacher, just her age.

Standing just her height. Smiling at her shyly, his wire-rimmed glasses winking as if shyly too. Shaking her gloved hand. Hello, Miss Snyder. Like a brother who would at last see *her*.

Twenty-eight years old!—she'd been fated to be a spinster, of course. That plain, stubborn, sharp-tongued girl, eyes too large and stark and intelligent in her face to be "feminine"; her body flat as a board.

In this place in which girls married as young as sixteen, began having their babies at seventeen, were valued and praised and loved for such qualities as they shared with broodmares and milking cows, you cultivated irony to save your soul— and your pride.

Except: she fell in love with the visiting preacher, introduced to him by family friends, the two "young people" urged together to speak stumblingly, clumsily to each other of—what? Decades later Melanie Snyder won't remember a syllable, but she remembers the young man's preaching voice, *Jesus! Jesus is our only salvation!* He'd gripped the edges of the pulpit of the Bethany church, God-love shining in his face, white teeth bared like piano keys.

How it happened, how they became officially engaged—whether by their own decision, or others', they might not have been able to say. But it was time to marry, for both.

Plain, earnest, upright young people. Firm-believing Christians, of that there could be no doubt.

Did Melanie doubt?—no, never!

She was prepared to be a Christian wife, and to have her babies one by one. As God ordained.

There were passionate-seeming squeezes of her hand, there were chaste kisses, fluttery and insubstantial as a butterfly's wings. There were Sunday walks, in the afternoon. Jesus is the most important person in my life, I feel Him close beside us—don't you, Melanie?

The emptiness of the country lane, the silence of the sky, except for the crows' raucous jeering cries. Slow-spiraling hawks high overhead.

Oh, yes certainly! Oh, yes.

Melanie Snyder's fiancé. The young just-graduated seminary student, with his hope to be a missionary. He was an energetic softball player, a pitcher of above-average ability; he led the Sunday school children on hikes, canoe trips. But he was most himself there in the pulpit of the Bethany church elevated a few inches above the rapt congregation where even his shy stammering rose to passion, a kind of sensual power. How strong the bones of his earnest, homely face!—the fair-brown wings of hair brushed back neatly from his forehead! *Jesus, our redeemer. Jesus, our only salvation.* As if the God-love shining in the young man's face were a beacon, a lighthouse beacon, flung out into the night; giving light yet unseeing, blind, in itself.

The engagement was never officially terminated. Always, there were sound reasons for postponing the wedding. Their families were disappointed but eager, on both sides, to comply. His letters came to her like clockwork, every two weeks, from North Carolina, where he was stationed as a chaplain in the U.S. Army. Dutiful letters, buoyant letters about his work, his "mission"—his conviction that he was at last where God meant him to be.

Then the letters ceased. And they told Melanie he'd had an "accident" of some kind—there'd been a "misunderstanding" of some kind. He was discharged from his army post and re-assigned to a Lutheran church in St. Louis, where he was to assist an older minister. But why, Melanie asked. Why, what has happened, Melanie demanded to know, but never was she told, never would a young woman be told such a thing, not for her ears, not for an ignorant virgin's ears, she'd wept and protested and mourned and lapsed finally into shame, not knowing what had happened to ruin her happiness but knowing it must constitute a rejection of her, a repudiation of the womanliness she'd tried so hard—ah, so shamefully hard!—to take on.

That feeling, that sense of unworthiness, she would retain for years. Studying her face in a mirror, plain, frank, unyielding, those eyes alit with irony, she realized she'd known all along—she was fated to be a spinster, never to be any man's "wife."

And didn't that realization bring with it, in truth, relief?

Now, fifty years later, if those words *Jesus! Jesus abides in our hearts, no need to see Him!* ring out faintly in the silence of the old house, she turns aside, unhearing. For she's an old woman who has outlived such lies. Such subterfuge. She has taken revenge on Jesus Christ by ceasing to believe in Him—or in God, or in the Lutheran faith, or in such pieties as meekness, charity, love of one's enemies. Casting off her long-dead fiancé (who had not the courage even to write Melanie Snyder, finally, to release her from their engagement) she'd cast off his religion, as, drifting off from a friend, we lose the friends with whom he or she connected us, there being no deeper bond.

What is it?

She sees, in the lower pasture, almost out of the range of her vision, a movement of some kind: a swaying dun-colored shape, blurred by the frost on the aged glass. Standing in her kitchen, alert, aroused.

An animal of some kind? A large dog? A deer?

A wounded deer?

Melanie hurries to pull her sheepskin jacket from a peg, she's jamming her feet into boots, already angry, half-knowing what she'll see.

The first day of deer-hunting season but the hunting in Saugatuck County isn't with guns any longer. Guns you could at least hear, now the slaughter is with bow and arrow. Grown men playing at being Indians. Playing at killing.

The excuse is, the "excess" deer population in the county has to be kept down. White-tailed deer overbreeding, causing crop damage, auto accidents. As if men, the species of men who prowl the woods seeking innocent creatures to kill, need any excuse.

Melanie Snyder, who has known hunters all her life, including her own brothers, understands: to the hunter, killing an animal is just a substitute for killing another human being. Male, female. That's the forbidden fantasy.

She has never been frightened of accosting them, though, and she isn't now. Running outside. Into the gusty January air. A scowling wild-eyed old woman, sexless leathery face, white hair rising from her head in stiff tufts. She is wearing a soiled sheepskin jacket several sizes too large for her, a relic once belonging to one of her brothers; her boots are rubberized fishing boots, the castoffs of another, long-deceased brother.

Melanie is prepared for an ugly sight but this sight stuns her, at first—she hears herself cry out, "Oh. Oh, God."

A buck, full-grown, beautiful, with handsome pointed antlers, is staggering in her direction, thrashing his head from side to side desperate to dislodge an arrow that has penetrated his neck. His eyes roll in his head, his mouth is opening and closing spasmodically, blood flows bright and glistening from the wound, in fact it is two wounds, in the lower part of his neck near his left shoulder. Behind him, in the lower pasture, running clumsily after him, is the hunter, bow uplifted—a bizarre sight in black jumpsuit, bright-orange vest, comical red hat. Like a robot or a space-man, Melanie thinks, staring. She has never seen any hunter so costumed. Is this a man she should know?—a face, a name? He's a hefty man with pale-flushed skin, damp mouth, eyes hidden behind sunglasses with opaque mirrored lenses. His breath is steaming in the cold, he's clearly excited, agitated—dangerous. Fitting an arrow crookedly to his bow as if preparing, at this range, to shoot.

Melanie cries, "You!—get out of here!"

The hunter yells, "Lady, stand aside!"

"This land is posted!—I'll call the sheriff!"

"Lady, you better gimme a clear shot!"

The buck is snorting, stamping his sharp-hooved feet in the snow. Deranged by terror and panic he thrashes his antlered head from side to side, bleeding freely, bright-glistening blood underfoot, splattered onto Melanie Snyder's clothes as, instinctively, recklessly, she positions herself between the wounded animal and the hunter. She's pleading, angry—"Get off my land, haven't you done enough evil? This poor creature! Let him alone!"

The hunter, panting, gaping at her, can't seem to believe what he sees—a white-haired woman, in men's clothes, must be eighty years old, trying to shield a buck with an arrow through his neck. He advances to within a few yards of her, tries to circle around her. Saying incredulously, "That's my arrow for Christ sake, lady! That buck's a goner and he's *mine!*"

"Brute! Murderer! I'm telling you to get off my land or I'll call the sheriff and have you arrested!"

"Lady, that buck is goddamned dangerous—you better stand aside."

"*You* stand aside—get off my property!"

"Lady, for Christ sake—"

"You heard me: *get off my property.*"

So, for some minutes, there's an impasse.

Forever afterward Woody Kunz will remember, to his chagrin, and shame: the beautiful white-tail, full-grown buck with the most amazing spread of antlers he'd ever seen, *his* buck, *his* kill, *his* arrow sticking through the animal's neck—the wounded buck snorting, thrashing his head, stamping the ground, blood every-where, blood-tinged saliva hanging from his mouth in threads, and the crazy old woman shielding the buck with her body, refusing to surrender him to his rightful owner. And Woody Kunz is certain *he* is the rightful owner, he's shouting in the old woman's face, he's pleading with her, practically begging finally, the fucking deer is *his,* he earned it, he's been out tramping in the cold since seven this morning, God damn it if he's going to give up, face blotched and hot, tears of rage and impotence stinging his eyes, oh, Jesus, he'd grab the old hag by the shoulders, lift her clear, and fire another arrow this time into the heart so there'd be no doubt—except, somehow, he doesn't do it: doesn't dare.

Instead, he backs off. Still with his bow upraised, his handsome brand-new Atlas bow from Sears, but the arrow drooping, drooping useless in his fingers.

In a voice heavy with disgust, sarcasm, he says, "Okay, okay, lady—you win."

The last glimpse Woody Kunz has of this spectacle, the old woman is trying clumsily to pull the arrow out of the buck's neck!—and the buck is naturally putting up a struggle, swiping at her with his antlers, but weakly, sinking to his knees in the snow then scrambling to his feet again, still the old woman persists, sure she *is* crazy and deserves whatever happens to her, the front of her sheepskin jacket soaked in blood by now, blood even on her face, in her hair.

It isn't until late afternoon, hours later, that Woody Kunz returns home.

Having gotten lost in the countryside, wandering in circles in the woods, couldn't locate the road he'd parked his goddamned car on, muttering to himself, sick and furious and shamed, in a state of such agitation his head feels close to bursting, guts like a nest of tangled snakes. Never *never* is Woody Kunz going to live down this humiliation in his own eyes.

So he's decided not to tell anyone. Not even to fashion it into an anecdote, to entertain his friends. Woody Kunz being cheated out of a twelve-point buck by an old lady—shit, he'd rather die than have it known.

Sure, it crosses his mind he should maybe report the incident to the sheriff. Not to reiterate his claim of the deer—though the deer *is* his—but to report the old woman in case she's really in danger. Out there, seemingly alone, so old, in the middle of nowhere. A mortally wounded full-grown white-tail buck, crazed with pain and terror, like a visitation of God, in her care.

She's begging, desperate, "*Let* me help you, oh—please! oh, please! Let me—"

Tugging at the terrible arrow, tugging forward, tugging back, her fingers slippery with blood. Woman and beast struggling, the one disdainful, even reckless, of her safety; the other dazed by trauma or loss of blood—not lashing out as ordinarily he would, to attack an enemy, with bared teeth, antlers, sharp hooves.

"—oh, please, you must not die, please—"

It's probable that Melanie Snyder has herself become deranged. All of the world having shrunk to the task at hand, to the forcible removal of this steel bar that has penetrated the buck's neck, fifteen-inch steely glinting, sharp-tipped arrow with white, synthetic quills—nothing matters but that *the arrow must be removed.*

The bulging eyes roll upward, there's bloody froth at the shuddering nostrils, she smells, tastes, the hot rank breath—then the antlers strike her on the chest, she's falling, crying out in surprise.

And the buck has pushed past her, fleeing on skidding hooves, on legs near buckling at the knees, so strangely—were she fully conscious she would realize, *so* strangely—into her father's house.

It won't be until three days later, at about this hour of the morning, that they'll discover her—or the body she has become. Melanie Snyder, and the buck with the arrow through his neck.

But Melanie Snyder has no sense of what's coming, no cautionary fear. As if, this damp-gusty January morning, such a visitation, such urgency pressed upon her, has blotted out all anticipation of the future; let alone of danger.

In blind panic, voiding his bowels, the buck has run crashing into the old farmhouse, into the kitchen, through to the parlor, as Melanie Snyder sits dazed on the frozen ground beneath her rear stoop he turns, furious, charges into a corner of the room, collides with an upright piano making a brief discordant startled music, an explosion of muted notes, turns again crashing into a table laden with family photographs, a lamp of stippled milk-glass with a fluted shade, a renewed rush of adrenaline empowers him, turning again, half-rearing, hooves skidding on the thin, loose-lying Oriental carpet faded to near-transparency, he charges his reflection in a mirror as, out back, Melanie Snyder sits trying to summon her strength, trying to comprehend what has happened and what she must do.

She doesn't remember the buck having knocked her down—thus can't believe he *has* attacked her.

She thinks, Without me—he is doomed.

She hears one of her brothers speaking harshly, scolding, what is she doing there sitting on the ground for the Lord's sake, Melanie! but she ignores him testing her right ankle, the joint is livid with pain but not broken—she can shift her weight to her other foot—a high-pitched ringing in her head as of church bells and where there should be terror there's determination for Melanie Snyder is an independent woman, a woman far too proud to accept, let alone solicit, her neighbors' proffered aid since the death of the last of her brothers, she wills herself not to succumb to weakness now, in this hour of her trial.

Managing to get to her feet, moving with calculating slowness. As if her bones are made of glass.

Overhead, an opaque January sky, yet beautiful. Like slightly tarnished mother-of-pearl.

Except for the crows in their gathering place beyond the barns, and the hoarse *Uh-uh-uh* of her breathing—silence.

She enters the house. By painful inches, yet eagerly. Leaning heavily against the doorframe.

She sees the fresh blood-trail, sees and smells the moist animal droppings, so shocking, there, on the kitchen floor she keeps clean with a pointless yet self-satisfying fanaticism, the aged linoleum worn nearly colorless, yes, but Melanie has a houseowner's pride, and pride is all. The buck in his frenzy to escape the very confines he has plunged into is turning, rearing, snorting, crashing in the other room, Melanie calls, "—I'm here! I will help you!"—blindly too entering the parlor with its etiolated light, tassled shades drawn to cover three-quarters of the windows, as, decades ago, Melanie Snyder's mother had so drawn them, to protect the furnishings against the sun, surely she's a bizarre sight herself, drunk-swaying, staggering, her wrinkled face, hands glistening with blood, white hair in tufts as if she hasn't taken a brush to it in weeks, Melanie Snyder in the oversized sheepskin jacket she wears in town, driving a rusted Plymouth pickup truck with a useless muffler, everybody in Bethany knows Melanie Snyder though she doesn't know them, carelessly confuses sons with fathers, granddaughters with mothers, her own remote blood relations with total strangers, she's awkward in these rubberized boots many sizes too large for her shrunken feet, yet reaching out—unhesitantly, boldly—to the maddened buck who crouches in a corner facing her, his breath frothing in blood, in erratic shuddering waves, she is speaking softly, half-begging, "—I want to help you!—oh—" as the heavy head dips, the antlers rush at her, how astonishing the elegance of such male beauty, and the burden of it, God's design both playful and deadly shrewd, the strangeness of bone growing out of flesh, bone calcified and many-branched as a young apple tree, clumsily he charges this woman who is his enemy even as, with a look of startled concern, she opens her arms to him, the sharp antlers now striking her a second time in the chest and this time breaking her fragile collarbone as easily as one might break a chicken wishbone set to dry on a window sill for days, the momentum of his charge carries him helplessly forward, he falls, the arrow's quill brushing against Melanie Snyder's face, as he scrambles in a frenzy to upright himself, his sharp hooves catch her in the chest, belly, pelvis, he has fallen heavily, as if from a great height, as if flung down upon her, breath in wheezing shudders and the blood-froth bubbling around his mouth and Melanie Snyder lies pinned beneath the animal body, legs gone, lower part of her body gone, a void of numbness, not even pain, distant from her as something seen through the wrong end of a telescope, rapidly retreating.

How did it happen, how strange, they were of the same height now, or nearly—Melanie Snyder and her tall strong indifferent brothers. Never married, none of them, d'you know why?—no woman was ever quite good enough for the Snyder boys, and the girl, Melanie—well, one look at her and you know: a born spinster.

It's more than thirty years after they informed her, guardedly, without much sympathy—for perhaps sympathy would have invited tears, and they were not a family comfortable with tears—that her fiancé had been discharged from the army, that Melanie dares to ask, shyly, without her customary aggressiveness, what had really happened—what the mysterious "accident" or was it a "misunderstanding," had been. And her brother, her elder by six years, an aged slope-shouldered man with a deeply creased face, sighs, and passes his hand over his chin, and says, in a tone of mild but unmistakable contempt, "Don't ask."

She lies there beneath the dying animal, then beneath the lifeless stiffening body, face no more than four inches from the great head, the empty eyes—how many hours she's conscious, she can't gauge.

At first calling, into the silence, "Help—help me! Help—"

There is a telephone in the kitchen, rarely does it ring and when it rings Melanie Snyder frequently ignores it, doesn't want people inquiring after her, well-intentioned neighbors, good Lutherans from the church she hasn't set foot in, except for funerals, in twenty-odd years.

The dying animal!—beautiful even in dying, bleeding to death, soaking Melanie Syder's clothes with his blood, and isn't she bleeding too, from wounds in her throat and face?—her hands?

And he's dead, she feels the life pass from him, "Oh no, oh no," sobbing and pushing at the body, warm sticky blood by degrees cooling and congealing, the woodfire stove in the kitchen has gone out and cold eases in from out of doors, in fact the kitchen door must be open, creaking and banging in the wind. A void rises from the loose-fitting floorboards as from the lower part of Melanie's body, she's sobbing as if her heart is broken, she's furious, trying to lift the heavy body from her, clawing at the body, raking her torn nails and bleeding fingers against the buck's thick winter coat, a coarse-haired furry coat, but the buck's body will not budge.

The weight of death, so much more powerful than life.

Later. She wakes moaning and delirious, a din as of sleet pellets against the windows and the cold has congealed the buck's blood and her own, the numbness has moved higher, obliterating much of what she has known as "body" these eighty-odd years, she understands that she is dying—consciousness like a fragile bubble, or a skein of bubbles—yet she is able still to wish to summon her old strength, the bitter joy of her stubborn strength, pushing at the heavy animal body, dead furry weight, eyes sightless as glass and the arrow, the terrible arrow, the obscene arrow—"Let me *go*. Let me *free*."

Fainting, and waking. Drifting in and out of consciousness.

Hearing that faint ringing voice in the eaves, as always subtly chiding, in righteous reproach of Melanie Snyder, mixed with the wind and that profound agelessness of wind as if blowing to us from the farthest reaches of time as well as space—*Jesus! Jesus is our only salvation!—Jesus abides in our hearts!*—but in pride she turns aside unhearing, never has she begged nor will she beg no, Oh, never.

And does she regret her gesture, trying to save an innocent beast?—she does not.

And would she consent, even now, to having made a mistake, acted improvidently?—she would not.

When after nearly seventy-two hours Woody Kunz overcomes his manly embarrassment and notifies the Saugatuck County sheriff's office of the "incident" on the Snyder farm, and they go out to investigate, they find eighty-two-year-old Melanie Snyder dead, pinned beneath the dead white-tail buck, in the parlor of the old farmhouse in which no one outside the Snyder family had stepped for many years. An astonishing sight: human and animal bodies virtually locked together in the rigor of death, their mingled blood so soaked into Melanie Snyder's clothes, so frozen, it is possible to separate them only by force.

—1991

PAUL SHEPARD
1925-1996

Paul Shepard was at the forefront of the disciplines of human ecology and environmental philosophy for more than thirty years. His work frequently explored the biological, psychological, and philosophical aspects of human relations with the nonhuman world, especially with animals. In particular, Shepard emphasized the wild nature, the "animalness," of human beings. At the Fifth International Wilderness Conference in Norway in 1993, he delivered a talk entitled "Wilderness Is Where My Genome Lives," concluding that "our concern over the increasing rate of extinctions and the worldwide diminishing of biodiversity is, in the end, not altruism, nor ethics, nor charity. Wild species are true others, the components of wilderness and at the same time are the external correlates of our inmost selves." For Shepard, in other words, wild animals are profoundly linked to us, almost as "alter egos."

Born in Kansas City, Missouri, Shepard earned a B.A. at the University of Missouri and later an M.S. and a Ph.D. at Yale University. After teaching biology and environmental perception at the college level, in 1973 he became Avery Professor of Natural Philosophy and Human Ecology at Pitzer College and the Claremont Graduate School in southern California, a position he held for more than twenty years before retiring. Shepard's influential books include Man in the Landscape *(1967),* The Tender Carnivore and the Sacred Game *(1973),* Thinking Animals: Animals and the Development of Human Intelligence *(1978),* Nature and Madness *(1982), and (with Barry Sanders)* The Sacred Paw *(1983). With Daniel McKinley, he edited* The Subversive Science: Essays towards an Ecology of Man *(1969) and* Environ/mental: Essays on the Planet as Home *(1971). Shepard lived with his wife, environmental education scholar Florence R. Krall, in Salt Lake City, Utah, and Bondurant, Wyoming, until his death.*

The following selection is from a chapter in Man in the Landscape *concerning humans' relation to domestic and wild animals. Much of the chapter is devoted to examining Albert Schweitzer's concept of "reverence for life," but Shepard moves from this into analyzing the phenomenon of hunting. Without taking a simple pro- or anti-hunting stance, he tries to explain why hunting tends to be such a volatile issue. On the one hand, he notes, "The taking of a life, so evanescent in a cosmic scheme, is nonetheless profoundly moving to us as individuals. Killing an animal probably obliterates an awareness somewhat similar to our own consciousness." On the other hand, hunting is a deeply rooted human activity: "For perhaps 95 percent of their history men and 'near-men' have been hunters." Relying upon mythological, anthropological, and literary sources, Shepard proceeds not to argue for either hunters or their opponents, but to explore the meaning of hunting as an aspect of humans' relation to nonhuman nature.*

FROM FELLOW CREATURES

Killing animals for the meat industry or for scientific research can be rationalized to the satisfaction of all but a few, but hunting for sport is frequently regarded as morally indefensible. Some of my acquaintances class hunting with war and murder. They are humane and humanist, with broad literary knowledge, articulate and very keen, as it were, in the slaughter of the advocates of hunting. In a debate in *The Saturday Review,* for instance, Joseph Wood Krutch carved up his hunter opponent and served him to the readers, steaming in his own juices.

Hunting has been defended by the fiction that sporting activity in the field somehow prepared a young man for a higher plane of conduct in human affairs. But whatever validity this idea had became obsolete with the end of aristocratic social structure. It has been held that the hunt promotes character, self-reliance, and initiative—an untenable Theodore Roosevelt belief. The development of leadership does not depend on killing. Assertions are sometimes made about instinctive needs and vague primitive satisfactions and psychological benefits, but the sharpest opponents of hunting appear simply not to have forgiven Darwin and Freud to begin with. To suggest that hunting has psychic or evolutionary values only infuriates. Others claim that the hunter is really attempting to escape the roar and friction of civilization, to squeeze out of society's trammels for a few hours of recuperation. The outraged response is, of course, that hunting with a camera is equally rewarding and more uplifting. According to the Faulkner and Hemingway interpretation, hunting is a manipulation of symbols for proving one's virility or otherwise coping with the erosion of the human personality and the decadence of civilization.

Opposition to hunting for sport has its accusing finger on the act of killing. Determinism gives no out. We cannot plead that we are bipedal carnivorous mammals and damned to kill. We must discover what it means to search for an equilibrium between the polarities of nature and God. We find that to share in life is to participate in a traffic of energy and materials, the ultimate origin of which is a mystery, but which has its immediate source in the bodies of plants and other animals. As a society, we may be in danger of losing sight of this fact, kept vividly before us in hunting.

The condemnation of killing wild animals assumes that death is the worst of natural events, that order in nature is epitomized by living objects rather than the complex flow patterns of which objects are temporary formations. The implication is that carnivorous predation as a whole is evil. The anti-hunters face a paradox of their own making. Dr. Schweitzer, who did not believe in hunting for sport, sprinkled his jungle writings with accounts of righteous killing of predators. Europeans and Americans in the same *Zeitgeist* have always destroyed predators, the big cats, eagles, wolves, bears, and pests such as rodents, insects, and birds.

Joseph Wood Krutch condemns the hunter for killing, claiming that the distinction between life and death is one of the most absolute boundaries which we know. But this is not so. Life has atomic as well as planetary dimensions. The most satisfactory definitions and descriptions of life are in physical and chemical terms of events and processes which, occurring in a certain harmony, produce what we call life. The organic and the inorganic are mingled inextricably in the living body.

The traditional insistence upon the overwhelmingly tragic and unequivocal nature of death ignores the adaptive role of early death in most animal populations. It presumes that the landscape is a collection of *things*. In this view the dissolution of body and personality are always tragic and disruptive, and do not contribute to the perfection of an intelligible world. But death, as transformation in a larger system, is an essential aspect of elegant patterns which are orderly as well as beautiful: without death growth could not occur, energy could not flow beyond plants, nutrient substances would be trapped forever. Without death the pond, the forest, the prairie, the city could not exist. The extremely complicated structure of living communities has yet to be fully explored, but constitutes a field pattern. Plants and animals participate in them without question in an attitude of acceptance which in human terms would be called faith.

The unfortunate social and economic misapplication of Darwin's theory in the late nineteenth century can still be seen in reluctance to accept evolution as a significant factor in man's highest as well as his more primitive activities. Evolutionary theory also had the curious effect on some people of making nature seem more chaotic instead of less. Evolution is unrelated to the fate of individuals. We have projected our notions of ethics and our terror of death into our perception of all life. Animals die before they have lived out their potential life span; that is characteristic of the natural world and essential to our understanding of it.

A moral criterion is sometimes offered for killing limited to the necessity for food and defense. This logically opposes the sportsman and approves of the slaughterhouse. Under primitive conditions killing meant something quite different than it does in the modern slaughterhouse or by the broadscale application of chemical pesticides. The events of daily life in a hunting society are permeated with universal significance immediate to every individual. No activity of life is regarded as "merely" physical, but always related to a whole, partly unseen. We cannot now adopt animistic superstition nor regain that kind of consciousness, but we admire the poignant sense of the interpenetration of man and nature which primitive life ritualizes and we may seek its results. Primitive ways are nearly gone but we acknowledge that such reverence for life is more reverent and is better ecology than a fanatic emphasis on fear of death and the attempt at godship by judging all instances and causes of death among animals. To our repugnance for soil (dirt), parasitism (disease), and decay (slime) we add predation. We condemn it as though it were murder, and extend "justice" into biotic realms where it is meaningless, incorporating democracy with its protection of the "weak" and containment of the "strong." Man dominates some parts of nature, but there is no process known by which this vindicates extending his social ethics, his democracy, or any other ideological or moral system into the adaptations of populations or the interrelations of species.

Does the hunter not interfere in natural patterns and upset nature's balance? Yes and no. Man is not a demigod operating above and outside nature. But nature is in him as well as he in it. Nature's balance is always slightly upset.

Individuals are important. The taking of a life, so evanescent in a cosmic scheme, is nonetheless profoundly moving to us as individuals. Killing an animal probably obliterates an awareness somewhat similar to our own consciousness. As sympathetic and vulnerable humans, we are confronted with mystery by the death of any creature. This is why the tension over killing is so incisive and urgent. Our sympathy for a fellow creature is felt intensely at the crucial moment of death. Yet that emotion fulfills a cultural and personal necessity for evidence of our connection to large-scale processes in a moment of profound intensity. If the death is so experienced our response may be regarded as a form of behavior which unites men with nature rather than alienating them.

Mental well-being is defined by a mode of cultural behavior. Culture is an interface between man and his environment. Collective dreams and myths, apprehended symbolically, change slowly with the healthy functioning of society and the psychic security of its members. There is in literary and pictorial arts an iconography of hunting. With its artistic heritage, hunting is much more than a wanton vestige of barbarism. It is intimately associated with social order and with love. "Venery" is an archaic term meaning both sexual pursuit and hunting game—the foundation of love. The origins of human compassion belong to the hunters of old.

Hunting may be an inherent behavior, but it is not *only* an instinct. It is a framework of organization which acknowledges an extra-human context. Killing is not justified simply as indigenous or venerable. But it is a historical part of the activity of a people. It has a place in the total fabric of what they have become, a mode of their relationship to nature. For perhaps 95 percent of their history men and "near-men" have been hunters. Primitive peoples ritualize hunting except where hunting societies and the technological world have collided, where cultural deterioration has reduced customary inhibition to wanton killing.

Probably the richest collection of the ceremonies of propitiation of wild spirits by hunters is Sir James G. Frazer's *The Golden Bough.* If anthropologically obsolete, Frazer's perspective and genius for collecting remain nonetheless monumental. To judge from *The Golden Bough,* hunting has been universally bound by ceremonial preparation and epilogue. When British Columbian Lillooet Indians dispose of the bones of their kill in a certain way, saying, "See! I treat you respectfully. Nothing shall defile you! May I be successful in hunting and trapping!" they are not only seeking to perpetuate their food supply. They do more than solicit success and spiritual acquiescence. Their ceremony makes less distinction between subject and object than we assume in the orthodox sense of magic. Even Frazer's view of ritual as coercive and petitionary was perhaps too restrictive. The ceremony is also an affirmation and participation, not only manipulative but attuning, assimilative, and confrontative. Imitative magic is prototechnological and prescientific, but that part emphasizing "we-hood" and the participating in a larger whole are religious.

Both magic and religion in primitive ritual reveal fundamental components of the hunter's attitude. The organized ceremony simultaneously serves a magic and a religious purpose, and ecological and social functions as well. The ceremony is aimed at maintaining equilibrium in the total situation. The whole of life, corporeal and spiritual, is affected. The prey, or parts of it, are killed ritually and eaten sacramentally. By following the prescribed style the hunters sacrifice the prey in evocation of events too profound for conscious understanding. By its own self-imposed limitations the ritual hunt renounces further killing in favor of a larger context of interrelationship. If the preliminary solicitation is effective and the traditional procedure is followed, the hunt is successful. Unlike farmers who must labor in the fields and who earn by their sweat a grudging security within nature, the primitive hunter gets "something for nothing." The kill is a gift. Its bestowal depends on the conduct of the hunters. Without this gift the hunter will die. As Malinowski says, "food is the main link between man and his surroundings" and "by receiving it he feels the forces of destiny and providence." Of all foods meat is the gift *par excellence* because shortage of protein, not shortage of food *per se*, is the essence of starvation. The elusiveness of the quarry explicitly symbolizes the continuing dependence of human life on powers beyond human control. Hunting provides the logical nucleus for the evolution of communal life with its celebrations of a biosocial participation mystique and the sharing of the kill.

What do the hunt and kill actually do for the hunter? They confirm his continuity with the dynamic life of animal populations, his role in the complicated cycles of elements, his sharing in the sweep of evolution, and his place in the patterns of the flow of energy and in the web of his own society.

It may at first seem irrelevant to seek present values for us in the strongly schematized hunting behavior of primitive man. But "our deepest experience, needs, and aspirations are the same, as surely as the crucial biological and psychic transitions occur in the life of every human being and force culture to take account of them in aesthetic forms," says Richard V. Chase. Many anthropologists report that there is widespread belief in the immortality of the spirits of all living things, a point of view which we may be too barbaric to share. Frazer wrote, about the time Schweitzer was conceiving of "Reverence for Life," "If I am right in thus interpreting the thought of primitive man, the savage view of the nature of life singularly resembles the modern scientific doctrine of the conservation of energy." The idea of organic interrelationship which ecologists explore may spring not from inductive science at all, but from a rather fundamental human attitude toward the landscape. In these terms, the hunt is a singular expression of our identity with natural processes and is carried on with veneration appropriate to the mystery of those events.

This concept transcends particular economic situations. Men in all sorts of societies—primitive, pastoral, agricultural, and technical—continue to hunt fervently. The hunt has ceased to be the main source of food, but remains the ritual symbol of a larger transaction. The prey represents all that is received, whether from a host of animal gods, an arbitrary god, or from the law of probability.

It is sometimes said that hunters are cruel, insensitive, and barbaric. In fact, however, the hunter may experience life and death deeply. In a poem called "Castles and Distances" Richard Wilbur writes:

> *Oh, it is hunters alone*
> *Regret the beastly pain, it is they who love the foe*
> *That quarries out their force, and every arrow*
> *Is feathered soft with wishes to atone;*
> *Even the surest sword in sorrow*
> *Bleeds for its spoiling blow.*
>
> *Sometimes, as one can see*
> *Carved at Amboise in a high relief, on the lintel stone*
> *Of the castle chapel, hunters have strangely come*
> *To a mild close of the chase, bending the knee*
> *Instead of the bow, struck sweetly dumb*
> *To see from the brow bone*
>
> *Of the hounded stag a cross*
> *Grown, and the eyes clear with grace. . . .*

In urban and technological situations hunting continues to put us in close touch with nature, to provoke the study of natural history, and to nourish the idea of conservation. Even royalty is subject to the uncertainty of the gift. From the Middle Ages we have numerous examples of the values of the hunt. Its forms coincided with social structure in complex royal households and its practice stimulated first-hand observation at a time when hearsay and past authority were the main sources of information. The unique work of Frederick II in thirteenth-century ornithology is an example, an advance in the understanding of birds gathered during hunting trips afield. A more recent example is the work of the late Aldo Leopold. A hunter and a forester, his career was a living documentation of the slow sensitizing of a man to his environment through the medium of gun and dog. In postulating a "split rail value" for hunting, Leopold observed that hunting is a reenactment of a historically important activity when contact with the natural environment and the virtues of this contact were less obscured by modern urban life.

Civilization extends the means of food and energy distribution and of storage against lean years. The ultimate origin of food in the soil is no longer apparent to the average person, as even agriculture is a closed industrial process. In this engineered and insulated atmosphere the natural world has become a peripheral relic, a strange, sometimes entertaining, sometimes frightening curiosity. What has become of the *gift*? It has receded from view except for those who seek it. They may be found in the open country trying their luck. By various arbitrary limitations, both behavioral and mechanical, the hunter curbs his technological advantage. This peculiar assemblage of legal, ethical, and physical restraints constitutes sportsmanship, a contemporary ritual. The hunt is arbitrarily limited. The hunter brings to focus his whole physical and spiritual attention on the moment of the kill. He expects to eat the quarry, even though economically it is dietetically irrelevant. Yet he will cook and eat it in a mood of thoughtful celebration known only to hunters.

It follows that hunting is not just an excuse to get out of doors. Killing and eating the prey are the most important things that hunters do. The successful hunt is a solemn and yet glad event. It places man for a moment in vital rapport with a universe from which civilization tends to separate him by its fostering of an illusion of superiority and independence. The natural environment will always be mysterious, evoking an awe to be shared among all men who take the trouble to see it. If modern sportsmanship is a shallow substitute for the complex mythology or unifying ceremony of other cultures, we must acknowledge that only a part of the society hunts, that ritual forms of this technological era are still young and poorly defined, and that we are part of an age which may be said to be living on the accumulated capital—cultural and biological—of a million years of hardship, death, effort, and invention. Given a hard-earned margin magnified by machines, human society may behave irresponsibly for a time and forget the ties that bind it to the world.

Regardless of technological advance, man remains part of and dependent upon nature. The necessity of signifying and recognizing this relationship remains, though it may not seem so. The hunter is our agent of awareness. He is not only an observer but a participant and receiver. He knows that man is a member of a natural community and that the processes of nature will never become so well understood or controlled that faith will cease to be important.

—1967

SUSAN GRIFFIN
B. 1943

The radical feminist writer Susan Griffin has since the early 1970s pursued a commitment to articulating a woman-centered view of everyday life that deeply challenges the status quo. She has done so through volumes of poetry, a play, and works of nonfiction. "I am a woman born in and shaped by this civilization, with the mind of this civilization, but also with the mind and body of a woman," she has written. "The singing in my body daily returns me to a love of this earth. I know that by a slow practice, if I am to survive, I must learn to listen to this song." For Griffin, who has suffered from chronic fatigue syndrome and who teaches a workshop entitled "Writing from the Body," the voice of female experience is an embodied voice, as contrasted with the emotionless and detached voice of male authority.

Born in Los Angeles, Griffin earned a B.A. and an M.A. from San Francisco State University. She has reflected that her upbringing and education in California were probably less traditional than they would have been elsewhere and gave her the freedom to explore feminist issues. Her poems have been collected in such volumes as Like the Iris of an Eye *(1976) and* Unremembered Country *(1987), and her nonfiction works include* Pornography and Silence: Culture's Revenge Against Nature *(1981), A* Chorus of Stones: The Private Life of War *(1992), and* The Eros of Everyday Life: Essays on Ecology, Gender, and Society *(1995). Griffin has a grown daughter and lives in Berkeley, California.*

Griffin's 1978 volume Woman and Nature: The Roaring Inside Her, *from which the following selection is taken, is one of the most widely read feminist books from the 1970s. The work is an extended prose poem that grew out of a lecture Griffin was asked to give on women and ecology. In thinking about the links between feminism and ecology, she noticed that men in Western civilization have tended to place themselves above nature, just as they have tended to consider women both inferior to them and closer to nature. "The Hunt," which comes from the chapter entitled "His Power (He Tames What Is Wild)," draws a parallel between human courtship and hunting. It describes the patriarchal mindset that sees woman as "without a soul," as a temptress who is responsible for exciting the male desire to capture and subdue her—the same mindset that shows a callous disregard for the suffering of other creatures and that can wipe out whole species without remorse.*

THE HUNT

Is it by its indefiniteness it shadows forth the heartless voids and immensities of the universe, and thus stabs us from behind with the thought of annihilation when beholding the milky way?

HERMAN MELVILLE, *Moby-Dick*

And at last she could bear the burden of herself no more. She was to be had for the taking. To be had for the taking.

D. H. LAWRENCE, *Lady Chatterley's Lover*

She has captured his heart. She has overcome him. He cannot tear his eyes away. He is burning with passion. He cannot live without her. He pursues her. She makes him pursue her. The faster she runs, the stronger his desire. He will overtake her. He will make her his own. He will have her. (The boy chases the doe and her yearling for nearly two hours. She keeps running despite her wounds. He pursues her through pastures, over fences, groves of trees, crossing the road, up hills, volleys of rifle shots sounding, until perhaps twenty bullets are embedded in her body.) She has no mercy. She has dressed to excite his desire. She has no scruples. She has painted herself for him. She makes supple movements to entice him. She is without a soul. Beneath her painted face is flesh, are bones. She reveals only part of herself to him. She is wild. She flees whenever he approaches. She is teasing him. (Finally, she is defeated and falls and he sees that half of her head has been blown off, that one leg is gone, her abdomen split from her tail to her head, and her organs hang outside her body. Then four men encircle the fawn and harvest her too.) He is an easy target, he says. He says he is pierced. Love has shot him through, he says. He is a familiar mark. Riddled. Stripped to the bone. He is conquered, he says. (The boys, fond of hunting hare, search in particular for pregnant females.) He is fighting for his life. He faces annihilation in her, he says. He is losing himself to her, he says. Now, he must conquer her wildness, he says, he must tame her before she drives him wild, he says. (Once catching their prey, they step on her back, breaking it, and they call this "dancing on the hare.") Thus he goes on his knees to her. Thus he wins her over, he tells her he wants her. He makes her his own. He encloses her. He encircles her. He puts her under lock and key. He protects her. (Approaching the great mammals, the hunters make little sounds which they know will make the elephants form a defensive circle.) And once she is his, he prizes his delight. He feasts his eyes on her. He adorns her luxuriantly. He gives her ivory. He gives her perfume. (The older matriarchs stand to the outside of the circle to protect the calves and younger mothers.) He covers her with the skins of mink, beaver, muskrat, seal, raccoon, otter, ermine, fox, the feathers of ostriches, osprey, egret, ibis. (The hunters then encircle that circle and fire first into the bodies of the matriarchs. When these older elephants fall, the younger panic, yet unwilling to leave the bodies of their dead mothers, they make easy targets.) And thus he makes her soft. He makes her calm. He makes her grateful to him. He has tamed her, he says. She is content to be his, he says. (In the winter, if a single wolf has leaped over the walls of the city and terrorized the streets, the hunters go out in a band to rid the forest of the whole pack.) Her voice is now soothing to him. Her eyes no longer blaze, but look on him serenely. When he calls to her, she gives herself to him. Her ferocity lies under him. (The body of the great whale is strapped with explosives.) Now nothing of the old beast remains in her. (Eastern Bison, extinct 1825; Spectacled Cormorant, extinct 1852; Cape Lion, extinct 1865; Bonin Night Heron, extinct 1889; Barbary Lion, extinct 1922; Great Auk, extinct 1944.) And he can trust her wholly with himself. So he is blazing when he enters her, and she is consumed. (Florida Key Deer, vanishing; Wild Indian Buffalo, vanishing; Great Sable Antelope, vanishing.) Because she is his, she offers no resistance. She is a place of rest for him. A place of his making. And when his flesh begins to yield and his skin melts into her, he becomes soft, and he is without fear; he does not lose himself; though something in him gives way, he is not lost in her, because she is his now: he has captured her.

—1978

ALDO LEOPOLD

1887-1948

One of the central figures of twentieth-century American conservation history, Aldo Leopold was a writer, naturalist, and conservationist. Leopold's 1949 book A Sand County Almanac *has become an established classic, comparable in stature to Thoreau's* Walden *and providing the foundation for modern conservation ethics. Leopold's gifts for narrative prose and natural description are apparent primarily in the first two parts of* A Sand County Almanac, *consisting of the "almanac" (calendar) portion and "Sketches Here and There," from which the following piece is taken; his philosophical comments about human-nature relations emerge chiefly in the book's third and final part, entitled "The Upshot."*

Leopold was born in Burlington, Iowa, and spent his boyhood hunting and fishing in his native state. He joined the U.S. Forest Service after graduating from the School of Forestry at Yale University in 1909, eventually becoming chief of operations for the Arizona–New Mexico district. Initially, Leopold supported forestry chief Gifford Pinchot's notion of controlling predators in order to support populations of game animals, but he eventually became critical of human efforts to micro-manage natural resources and advocated the establishment of large, undisturbed wilderness tracts. In 1924, Leopold was transferred to the U.S. Forest Products Laboratory in Madison, Wisconsin. He worked there until leaving the Forest Service in 1928 to take a job with the Sporting Arms and Ammunitions Manufacturers' Institute, where his role was to perform a national survey of game conditions (documented in his landmark 1931 Report on a Game Survey of the North Central States) and to supervise game management research projects. In 1933, his book Game Management appeared and the University of Wisconsin granted him an endowed professorship of game management, which he held until his death.

"Thinking Like a Mountain," one of the best-known and most reprinted pieces in A Sand County Almanac, is an eloquent critique of the hitherto commonplace practice of wiping out predator species to protect livestock and game animals. The profound subtext of this essay is that natural ecosystems have their own logic of population control, and that human interference with any element in such a system is likely to be disastrous. It is difficult, perhaps even impossible, for us to appreciate the consequences of our management decisions if we think merely of our own short-term needs; rather, Leopold implies, we must try to consider the "greater good" of a healthy, balanced ecosystem. This is what it means to "think like a mountain."

THINKING LIKE A MOUNTAIN

A deep chesty bawl echoes from rimrock to rimrock, rolls down the mountain, and fades into the far blackness of the night. It is an outburst of wild defiant sorrow, and of contempt for all the adversities of the world.

Every living thing (and perhaps many a dead one as well) pays heed to that call. To the deer it is a reminder of the way of all flesh, to the pine a forecast of midnight scuffles and of blood upon the snow, to the coyote a promise of gleanings to come, to the cowman a threat of red ink at the bank, to the hunter a challenge of fang against bullet. Yet behind these obvious and immediate hopes and fears there lies a deeper meaning, known only to the mountain itself. Only the mountain has lived long enough to listen objectively to the howl of a wolf.

Those unable to decipher the hidden meaning know nevertheless that it is there, for it is felt in all wolf country, and distinguishes that country from all other land. It tingles in the spine of all who hear wolves by night, or who scan their tracks by day. Even without sight or sound of wolf, it is implicit in a hundred small events: the midnight whinny of a pack horse, the rattle of rolling rocks, the bound of a fleeing deer, the way shadows lie under the spruces. Only the ineducable tyro can fail to sense the presence or absence of wolves, or the fact that mountains have a secret opinion about them.

My own conviction on this score dates from the day I saw a wolf die. We were eating lunch on a high rimrock, at the foot of which a turbulent river elbowed its way. We saw what we thought was a doe fording the torrent, her breast awash in white water. When she climbed the bank toward us and shook out her tail, we realized our error: it was a wolf. A half-dozen others, evidently grown pups, sprang from the willows and all joined in a welcoming melee of wagging tails and playful maulings. What was literally a pile of wolves writhed and tumbled in the center of an open flat at the foot of our rimrock.

In those days we had never heard of passing up a chance to kill a wolf. In a second we were pumping lead into the pack, but with more excitement than accuracy: how to aim a steep downhill shot is always confusing. When our rifles were empty, the old wolf was down, and a pup was dragging a leg into impassable slide-rocks.

We reached the old wolf in time to watch a fierce green fire dying in her eyes. I realized then, and have known ever since, that there was something new to me in those eyes—something known only to her and to the mountain. I was young then, and full of trigger-itch; I thought that because fewer wolves meant more deer, that no wolves would mean hunters' paradise. But after seeing the green fire die, I sensed that neither the wolf nor the mountain agreed with such a view.

Since then I have lived to see state after state extirpate its wolves. I have watched the face of many a newly wolfless mountain, and seen the south-facing slopes wrinkle with a maze of new deer trails. I have seen every edible bush and seedling browsed, first to anaemic desuetude, and then to death. I have seen every edible tree defoliated to the height of a saddlehorn. Such a mountain looks as if someone had given God a new pruning shears, and forbidden Him all other exercise. In the end the starved bones of the hoped-for deer herd, dead of its own too-much, bleach with the bones of the dead sage, or molder under the high-lined junipers.

I now suspect that just as a deer herd lives in mortal fear of its wolves, so does a mountain live in mortal fear of its deer. And perhaps with better cause, for while a buck pulled down by wolves can be replaced in two or three years, a range pulled down by too many deer may fail of replacement in as many decades.

So also with cows. The cowman who cleans his range of wolves does not realize that he is taking over the wolf's job of trimming the herd to fit the range. He has not learned to think like a mountain. Hence we have dustbowls, and rivers washing the future into the sea.

We all strive for safety, prosperity, comfort, long life, and dullness. The deer strives with his supple legs, the cowman with trap and poison, the statesman with pen, the most of us with machines, votes, and dollars, but it all comes to the same thing: peace in our time. A measure of success in this is all well enough, and perhaps is a requisite to objective thinking, but too much safety seems to yield only danger in the long run. Perhaps this is behind Thoreau's dictum: In wildness is the salvation of the world. Perhaps this is the hidden meaning in the howl of the wolf, long known among mountains, but seldom perceived among men.

—1949

SARAH ORNE JEWETT

1849-1909

Sarah Orne Jewett met with early success as a writer, publishing her first story when she was eighteen, and went on to earn a solid reputation as a regionalist with her novels and stories of rural New England life. Her own identification with the landscape of her birth is mirrored by her characters, resilient women who know their native terrain with its flora and fauna. Jewett was one of the few women writers pictured on the "Authors" card deck of the time, which is where the young Willa Cather supposedly learned of her. Jewett became an important mentor to Cather, who later commented that Jewett's writings "melt into the land and the life of the land until they are not stories at all, but life itself."

Jewett was raised, spent part of each year, and died in a pre-Revolutionary house in South Berwick, Maine, bought by her grandfather, a prosperous shipbuilder. (This house is today open to the public as a historical landmark.) As a child, she accompanied her father, a country doctor, on his rounds, learning an appreciation of the everyday lives of common people and of the region's landscape. Her first published book was Deephaven (1877), a collection of what she called "sketches" that had appeared previously in the Atlantic. It was followed by eighteen other volumes during her lifetime; two collections of letters and one of verse were published posthumously. The Country of the Pointed Firs (1896), a series of loosely connected stories about life in a declining Maine whaling town, is her best-known work, rated by Willa Cather as one of three enduring American literary masterpieces, along with The Scarlet Letter and Huckleberry Finn.

The following story, "A White Heron," came out in a collection by that name in 1886, the same year the Audubon Society was formed to protect wild birds and their eggs. Women were visibly active at that time in the cause of bird conservation, which was seen as an extension of their concern with the domestic sphere. In "A White Heron," a nine-year-old girl is forced to choose between her yearning to please a handsome young ornithologist and her loyalty to a magnificent white heron whose nest the ornithologist is seeking. In a larger sense, the choice is also one between the conventional female role of subservience to a male, on the one hand, and "the satisfactions of an existence heart to heart with nature and the dumb life of the forest," on the other. "She could not understand why he killed the very birds he seemed to like so much," wrote Jewett in a classic statement of the gender polarity so often evident in debates over hunting.

A WHITE HERON

I

The woods were already filled with shadows one June evening, just before eight o'clock, though a bright sunset still glimmered faintly among the trunks of the trees. A little girl was driving home her cow, a plodding, dilatory, provoking creature in her behavior, but a valued companion for all that. They were going away from whatever light there was, and striking deep into the woods, but their feet were familiar with the path, and it was no matter whether their eyes could see it or not.

There was hardly a night the summer through when the old cow could be found waiting at the pasture bars; on the contrary, it was her greatest pleasure to hide herself away among the huckleberry bushes, and though she wore a loud bell she had made the discovery that if one stood perfectly still it would not ring. So Sylvia had to hunt for her until she found her, and call Co'! Co'! with never an answering Moo, until her childish patience was quite spent. If the creature had not given good milk and plenty of it, the case would have seemed very different to her owners. Besides, Sylvia had all the time there was, and very little use to make of it. Sometimes in pleasant weather it was a consolation to look upon the cow's pranks as an intelligent attempt to play hide and seek, and as the child had no playmates she lent herself to this amusement with a good deal of zest. Though this chase had been so long that the wary animal herself had given an unusual signal of her whereabouts, Sylvia had only laughed when she came upon Mistress Moolly at the swampside, and urged her affectionately homeward with a twig of birch leaves. The old cow was not inclined to wander farther, she even turned in the right direction for once as they left the pasture, and stepped along the road at a good pace. She was quite ready to be milked now, and seldom stopped to browse. Sylvia wondered what her grandmother would say because they were so late. It was a great while since she had left home at half-past five o'clock, but everybody knew the difficulty of making this errand a short one. Mrs. Tilley had chased the horned torment too many summer evenings herself to blame any one else for lingering, and was only thankful as she waited that she had Sylvia, nowadays, to give such valuable assistance. The good woman suspected that Sylvia loitered occasionally on her own account; there never was such a child for straying about out-of-doors since the world was made! Everybody said that it was a good change for a little maid who had tried to grow for eight years in a crowded manufacturing town, but as for Sylvia herself, it seemed as if she never had been alive at all before she came to live at the farm. She thought often with wistful compassion of a wretched geranium that belonged to a town neighbor.

"'Afraid of folks,'" old Mrs. Tilley said to herself, with a smile, after she had made the unlikely choice of Sylvia from her daughter's houseful of children, and was returning to the farm. "'Afraid of folks,' they said! I guess she won't be troubled no great with 'em up to the old place!" When they reached the door of the lonely house and stopped to unlock it, and the cat came to purr loudly, and rub against them, a deserted pussy, indeed, but fat with young robins, Sylvia whispered that this was a beautiful place to live in, and she never should wish to go home.

The companions followed the shady woodroad, the cow taking slow steps and the child very fast ones. The cow stopped long at the brook to drink, as if the pasture were not half a swamp, and Sylvia stood still and waited, letting her bare feet cool themselves in the shoal water, while the great twilight moths struck softly against her. She waded on through the brook as the cow moved away, and listened to the thrushes with a heart that beat fast with pleasure. There was a stirring in the great boughs overhead. They were full of little birds and beasts that seemed to be wide awake, and going about their world or else saying goodnight to each other in sleepy twitters. Sylvia herself felt sleepy as she walked along. However, it was not much farther to the house, and the air was soft and sweet. She was not often in the woods so late as this, and it made her feel as if she were a part of the gray shadows and the moving leaves. She was just thinking how long it seemed since she first came to the farm a year ago, and wondering if everything went on in the noisy town just the same as when she was there; the thought of the great red-faced boy who used to chase and frighten her made her hurry along the path to escape from the shadow of the trees.

Suddenly this little woods-girl is horror-stricken to hear a clear whistle not very far away. Not a bird's-whistle, which would have a sort of friendliness, but a boy's whistle, determined, and somewhat aggressive. Sylvia left the cow to whatever sad fate might await her, and stepped discreetly aside into the bushes, but she was just too late. The enemy had discovered her, and called out in a very cheerful and persuasive tone, "Halloa, little girl, how far is it to the road?" and trembling Sylvia answered almost inaudibly, "A good ways."

She did not dare to look boldly at the tall young man, who carried a gun over his shoulder, but she came out of her bush and again followed the cow, while he walked alongside.

"I have been hunting for some birds," the stranger said kindly, "and I have lost my way, and need a friend very much. Don't be afraid," he added gallantly. "Speak up and tell me what your name is, and whether you think I can spend the night at your house, and go out gunning early in the morning."

Sylvia was more alarmed than before. Would not her grandmother consider her much to blame? But who could have foreseen such an accident as this? It did not seem to be her fault, and she hung her head as if the stem of it were broken, but managed to answer "Sylvy," with much effort when her companion again asked her name.

Mrs. Tilley was standing in the doorway when the trio came into view. The cow gave a loud moo by way of explanation.

"Yes, you'd better speak up for yourself, you old trial! Where'd she tucked herself away this time, Sylvy?" But Sylvia kept an awed silence; she knew by instinct that her grandmother did not comprehend the gravity of the situation. She must be mistaking the stranger for one of the farmer-lads of the region.

The young man stood his gun beside the door, and dropped a lumpy game-bag beside it; then he bade Mrs. Tilley good-evening, and repeated his wayfarer's story, and asked if he could have a night's lodging.

"Put me anywhere you like," he said. "I must be off early in the morning, before day; but I am very hungry, indeed. You can give me some milk at any rate, that's plain."

"Dear sakes, yes," responded the hostess, whose long slumbering hospitality seemed to be easily awakened. "You might fare better if you went out to the main road a mile or so, but you're welcome to what we've got. I'll milk right off, and you make yourself at home. You can sleep on husks or feathers," she proffered graciously. "I raised them all myself. There's good pasturing for geese just below here towards the ma'sh. Now step round and set a plate for the gentleman, Sylvy!" And Sylvia promptly stepped. She was glad to have something to do, and she was hungry herself.

It was a surprise to find so clean and comfortable a little dwelling in this New England wilderness. The young man had known the horrors of its most primitive housekeeping, and the dreary squalor of that level of society which does not rebel at the companionship of hens. This was the best thrift of an old-fashioned farmstead, though on such a small scale that it seemed like a hermitage. He listened eagerly to the old woman's quaint talk, he watched Sylvia's pale face and shining gray eyes with ever growing enthusiasm, and insisted that this was the best supper he had eaten for a month, and afterward the new-made friends sat down in the door-way together while the moon came up.

Soon it would be berry-time, and Sylvia was a great help at picking. The cow was a good milker, though a plaguy thing to keep track of, the hostess gossiped frankly, adding presently that she had buried four children, so Sylvia's mother, and a son (who might be dead) in California were all the children she had left. "Dan, my boy, was a great hand to go gunning," she explained sadly. "I never wanted for pa'tridges or gray squer'ls while he was to home. He's been a great wand'rer, I expect, and he's no hand to write letters. There, I don't blame him, I'd ha' seen the world myself if it had been so I could."

"Sylvy takes after him," the grandmother continued affectionately, after a minute's pause. "There ain't a foot o' ground she don't know her way over, and the wild creaturs counts her one o' themselves. Squer'ls she'll tame to come an' feed right out o' her hands, and all sorts o' birds. Last winter she got the jay-birds to bangeing here, and I believe she'd 'a' scanted herself of her own meals to have plenty to throw out amongst 'em, if I hadn't kep' watch. Anything but crows, I tell her, I'm willin' to help support—though Dan he had a tamed one o' them that did seem to have reason same as folks. It was round here a good spell after he went away. Dan an' his father they didn't hitch,—but he never held up his head ag'in after Dan had dared him an' gone off."

The guest did not notice this hint of family sorrows in his eager interest in something else.

"So Sylvy knows all about birds, does she?" he exclaimed, as he looked round at the little girl who sat, very demure but increasingly sleepy, in the moonlight. "I am making a collection of birds myself. I have been at it every since I was a boy." (Mrs. Tilley smiled.) "There are two or three very rare ones I have been hunting for these five years. I mean to get them on my own ground if they can be found."

"Do you cage 'em up?" asked Mrs. Tilley doubtfully, in response to this enthusiastic announcement.

"Oh no, they're stuffed and preserved, dozens and dozens of them," said the ornithologist, "and I have shot or snared every one myself. I caught a glimpse of a white heron a few miles from here on Saturday, and I have followed it in this direction. They have never been found in this district at all. The little white heron, it is," and he turned again to look at Sylvia with the hope of discovering that the rare bird was one of her acquaintances.

But Sylvia was watching a hop-toad in the narrow footpath.

"You would know the heron if you saw it," the stranger continued eagerly. "A queer tall white bird with soft feathers and long thin legs. And it would have a nest perhaps in the top of a high tree, made of sticks, something like a hawk's nest."

Sylvia's heart gave a wild beat; she knew that strange white bird, and had once stolen softly near where it stood in some bright green swamp grass, away over at the other side of the woods. There was an open place where the sunshine always seemed strangely yellow and hot, where tall nodding rushes grew, and her grandmother had warned her that she might sink in the soft black mud underneath and never be heard of more. Not far beyond were the salt marshes just this side the sea itself, which Sylvia wondered and dreamed much about, but never had seen, whose great voice could sometimes be heard above the noise of the woods on stormy nights.

"I can't think of anything I should like so much as to find that heron's nest," the handsome stranger was saying. "I would give ten dollars to anybody who could show it to me," he added desperately, "and I mean to spend my whole vacation hunting for it if need be. Perhaps it was only migrating, or had been chased out of its own region by some bird of prey."

Mrs. Tilley gave amazed attention to all this, but Sylvia still watched the toad, not divining, as she might have done at some calmer time, that the creature wished to get to its hole under the door-step, and was much hindered by the unusual spectators at that hour of the evening. No amount of thought, that night, could decide how many wished-for treasures the ten dollars, so lightly spoken of, would buy.

The next day the young sportsman hovered about the woods, and Sylvia kept him company, having lost her first fear of the friendly lad, who proved to be most kind and sympathetic. He told her many things about the birds and what they knew and where they lived and what they did with themselves. And he gave her a jack-knife, which she thought as great a treasure as if she were a desert-islander. All day long he did not once make her troubled or afraid except when he brought down some unsuspecting singing creature from its bough. Sylvia would have liked him vastly better without his gun; she could not understand why he killed the very birds he seemed to like so much. But as the day waned, Sylvia still watched the young man with loving admiration. She had never seen anybody so charming and delightful; the woman's heart, asleep in the child, was vaguely thrilled by a dream of love. Some premonition of that great power stirred and swayed these young creatures who traversed the solemn woodlands with soft-footed silent care. They stopped to listen to a bird's song; they pressed forward again eagerly, parting the branches—speaking to each other rarely and in whispers; the young man going first and Sylvia following, fascinated, a few steps behind, with her gray eyes dark with excitement.

She grieved because the longed-for white heron was elusive, but she did not lead the guest, she only followed, and there was no such thing as speaking first. The sound of her own unquestioned voice would have terrified her—it was hard enough to answer yes or no when there was need of that. At last evening began to fall, and they drove the cow home together, and Sylvia smiled with pleasure when they came to the place where she heard the whistle and was afraid only the night before.

II

Half a mile from home, at the farther edge of the woods, where the land was highest, a great pine-tree stood, the last of its generation. Whether it was left for a boundary mark, or for what reason, no one could say, the woodchoppers who had felled its mates were dead and gone long ago, and a whole forest of sturdy trees, pines and oaks and maples, had grown again. But the stately head of this old pine towered above them all and made a landmark for sea and shore miles and miles away. Sylvia knew it well. She had always believed that whoever climbed to the top of it could see the ocean; and the little girl had often laid her hand on the great rough trunk and looked up wistfully at those dark boughs that the wind always stirred, no matter how hot and still the air might be below. Now she thought of the tree with a new excitement, for why, if one climbed it at break of day could not one see all the world, and easily discover from whence the white heron flew, and mark the place, and find the hidden nest?

What a spirit of adventure, what wild ambition! What fancied triumph and delight and glory for the later morning when she could make known the secret! It was almost too real and too great for the childish heart to bear.

All night the door of the little house stood open and the whippoorwills came and sang upon the very step. The young sportsman and his old hostess were sound asleep, but Sylvia's great design kept her broad awake and watching. She forgot to think of sleep. The short summer night seemed as long as the winter darkness, and at last when the whippoorwills ceased, and she was afraid the morning would after all come too soon, she stole out of the house and followed the pasture path through the woods, hastening toward the open ground beyond, listening with a sense of comfort and companionship to the drowsy twitter of a half-awakened bird, whose perch she had jarred in passing. Alas, if the great wave of human interest which flooded for the first time this dull little life should sweep away the satisfactions of an existence heart to heart with nature and the dumb life of the forest!

There was the huge tree asleep yet in the paling moonlight, and small and silly Sylvia began with utmost bravery to mount to the top of it, with tingling, eager blood coursing the channels of her whole frame, with her bare feet and fingers, that pinched and held like bird's claws to the monstrous ladder reaching up, up, almost to the sky itself. First she must mount the white oak tree that grew alongside, where she was almost lost among the dark branches and the green leaves heavy and wet with dew; a bird fluttered off its nest, and a red squirrel ran to and fro and scolded pettishly at the harmless housebreaker. Sylvia felt her way easily. She had often climbed there, and knew that higher still one of the oak's upper branches chafed against the pine trunk, just where its lower boughs were set close together. There, when she made the dangerous pass from one tree to the other, the great enterprise would really begin.

She crept out along the swaying oak limb at last, and took the daring step across into the old pine-tree. The way was harder than she thought; she must reach far and hold fast, the sharp dry twigs caught and held her and scratched her like angry talons, the pitch made her thin little fingers clumsy and stiff as she went round and round the tree's great stem, higher and higher upward. The sparrows and robins in the woods below were beginning to wake and twitter to the dawn, yet it seemed much lighter there aloft in the pine-tree, and the child knew she must hurry if her project were to be of any use.

The tree seemed to lengthen itself out as she went up, and to reach farther and farther upward. It was like a great main-mast to the voyaging earth; it must truly have been amazed that morning through all its ponderous frame as it felt this determined spark of human spirit wending its way from higher branch to branch. Who knows how steadily the least twigs held themselves to advantage this light, weak creature on her way! The old pine must have loved his new dependent. More than all the hawks, and bats, and moths, and even the sweet voiced thrushes, was the brave, beating heart of the solitary gray-eyed child. And the tree stood still and frowned away the winds that June morning while the dawn grew bright in the east.

Sylvia's face was like a pale star, if one had seen it from the ground, when the last thorny bough was past, and she stood trembling and tired but wholly triumphant, high in the treetop. Yes, there was the sea with the dawning sun making a golden dazzle over it, and toward that glorious east flew two hawks with slow-moving pinions. How low they looked in the air from that height when one had only seen them before far up, and dark against the blue sky. Their gray feathers were as soft as moths; they seemed only a little way from the tree, and Sylvia felt as if she too could go flying away among the clouds. Westward, the woodlands and farms reached miles and miles into the distance; here and there were church steeples, and white villages, truly it was a vast and awesome world!

The birds sang louder and louder. At last the sun came up bewilderingly bright. Sylvia could see the white sails of ships out at sea, and the clouds that were purple and rose-colored and yellow at first began to fade away. Where was the white heron's nest in the sea of green branches, and was this wonderful sight and pageant of the world the only reward for having climbed to such a giddy height? Now look down again, Sylvia, where the green marsh is set among the shining birches and dark hemlocks; there where you saw the white heron once you will see him again; look, look! a white spot of him like a single floating feather comes up from the dead hemlock and grows larger, and rises, and comes close at last, and goes by the landmark pine with steady sweep of wing and outstretched slender neck and crested head. And wait! wait! do not move a foot or a finger, little girl, do not send an arrow of light and consciousness from your two eager eyes, for the heron has perched on a pine bough not far beyond yours, and cries back to his mate on the nest and plumes his feathers for the new day!

The child gives a long sigh a minute later when a company of shouting cat-birds comes also to the tree, and vexed by their fluttering and lawlessness the solemn heron goes away. She knows his secret now, the wild, light, slender bird that floats and wavers, and goes back like an arrow presently to his home in the green world beneath. Then Sylvia, well satisfied, makes her perilous way down again, not daring to look far below the branch she stands on, ready to cry sometimes because her fingers ache and her lamed feet slip. Wondering over and over again what the stranger would say to her, and what he would think when she told him how to find his way straight to the heron's nest.

"Sylvy, Sylvy!" called the busy old grandmother again and again, but nobody answered, and the small husk bed was empty and Sylvia had disappeared.

The guest waked from a dream, and remembering his day's pleasure hurried to dress himself that might it sooner begin. He was sure from the way the shy little girl looked once or twice yesterday that she had at least seen the white heron, and now she must really be made to tell. Here she comes now, paler than ever, and her worn old frock is torn and tattered, and smeared with pine pitch. The grandmother and the sportsman stand in the door together and question her, and the splendid moment has come to speak of the dead hemlock-tree by the green marsh.

But Sylvia does not speak after all, though the old grandmother fretfully rebukes her, and the young man's kind, appealing eyes are looking straight in her own. He can make them rich with money; he has promised it, and they are poor now. He is so well worth making happy, and he waits to hear the story she can tell.

No, she must keep silence! What is it that suddenly forbids her and makes her dumb? Has she been nine years growing and now, when the great world for the first time puts out a hand to her, must she thrust it aside for a bird's sake? The murmur of the pine's green branches is in her ears, she remembers how the white heron came flying through the golden air and how they watched the sea and the morning together, and Sylvia cannot speak; she cannot tell the heron's secret and give its life away.

Dear loyalty, that suffered a sharp pang as the guest went away disappointed later in the day, that could have served and followed him and loved him as a dog loves! Many a night Sylvia heard the echo of his whistle haunting the pasture path as she came home with the loitering cow. She forgot even her sorrow at the sharp report of his gun and the sight of thrushes and sparrows dropping silent to the ground, their songs hushed and their pretty faces stained and wet with blood. Were the birds better friends than their hunter might have been,—who can tell? Whatever treasures were lost to her, woodlands and summer-time, remember! Bring your gifts and graces and tell your secrets to this lonely country child!

—1886

ERNEST HEMINGWAY

1899-1961

Winner of the Nobel Prize in literature in 1954, Ernest Hemingway never lost the affection for hunting and fishing that he had developed as a boy on family vacations in northern Michigan, and many of his writings reflect this lifelong passion for the outdoors. He also wrote about blood sports (such as bullfighting), war, and sex, reflecting his experience as a wartime ambulance driver, war correspondent, and extravagant womanizer who married four times. Hemingway saw physical exertion and contact with wild nature as a restorative force in his life, and after being badly wounded driving an ambulance in northern Italy, he returned to outdoor life in northern Michigan to recuperate. In his story "Big Two-Hearted River," which appeared in the 1925 collection In Our Time, *his hero Nick Adams does the same after suffering some unnamed wartime trauma.*

Hemingway was educated in his hometown of Oak Park, Illinois, and never attended college. Following high school, he became a cub reporter for the Kansas City Star *and then went to Italy during World War I as a driver for the Red Cross Ambulance Corps. He returned to Europe in 1920, serving as a foreign correspondent for the* Toronto Star *until 1924 and working on his fiction and essays. Hemingway later recorded his experiences in Paris as a member of the "lost generation" of American expatriate writers (including F. Scott Fitzgerald, Gertrude Stein, and John Dos Passos) in* A Moveable Feast *(published posthumously in 1964). In 1937–38, he covered the Spanish Civil War for the North American Newspaper Alliance. Some of Hemingway's best novels, including* The Sun Also Rises *(1926),* A Farewell to Arms *(1929), and* For Whom the Bell Tolls *(1941), reflect his experiences in wartime Europe and in Europe's bohemian intellectual scene, while such works as* Green Hills of Africa *(1935) and* The Old Man and the Sea *(1952) reveal his passion for hunting and fishing. Many of Hemingway's early pieces about the outdoors, including the following article, appeared in the* Toronto Star *in the early 1920s.*

"Fight with a 20-Pound Trout" was published in the Toronto Star Weekly *on April 10, 1920. This small essay is not merely a conventional fishing story about "the big one that got away" (or rather two big ones that got away), but a piece about the pleasure of telling (and listening to) a good fishing story. Such storytelling takes place indoors, where the fishing "is cheaper and the fish run bigger." After telling a yarn of his own, Hemingway delights in retelling his friend Jock Pentecost's story. The point seems to be not to replace outdoor experiences with fanciful tales, but to sharpen the teller's and the listeners' desire to get outside. Notice how this piece concludes, like all good fishing stories, with a reminder that the giant fish is "still in the river."*

FIGHT WITH A 20-POUND TROUT

Now when the old fly rod is hanging by its tip in the garret, and the flies that remain of the bright legions that opened the season are tattered feathered veterans and the patched waders are put away in the closet and the new net is lost, it looks as though the fishing season is over.

But it isn't. It is just under way. No, this doesn't mean that they are fishing for trout in New Zealand, or the Andes or Lago di Garda. This yarn deals with the opening of the great indoor fishing season.

More fish are caught in clubs at this time of year than ever were taken from the Nipigon. Bigger trout are taken around the tables in King Street cafeterias than win the prizes offered by the sporting magazines. And more fish get away within the confines of Toronto than are lost in all the trout streams of Christendom.

That's where indoor fishing has it on outdoor fishing. It is cheaper and the fish run bigger.

It's a peculiar thing that no man likes to hear another man talk about his golf game. Of course, most men spend the majority of their working hours talking about their golf game to other men. But do the other men enjoy it? They do not. They loathe it. They are merely listening in the hope that that blithering idiot will stop and give them a chance to talk about their own game.

For a man's golf game is self-contained within him. Outside influences haven't much to do with it. He is really just talking about himself.

Fishing is different. One fisherman loves to hear another fisherman tell about his fishing. For the fishing is something altogether outside of the fisherman. And while the one fisherman is listening he is mentally taking notes. Where did this all happen? How far is it from Toronto? Could he find the place? Are there any more as big up there? And so on.

We were fishing for rainbow trout where a little river comes into a lake and cuts a channel alongside the bank. Into the mouth of this river and the bay it empties into big schools of rainbow trout come out of the big lake. They chase the shiners and young herring and you can see their back fins coming out of the water like porpoises with a shower of minnows shooting up into the air. Every once in a while a big trout will jump clear of the water with a noise like somebody throwing a bathtub into the lake.

These monster trout won't touch a fly and we fish for them by casting out from the bank with minnows and letting them lie on the bottom of the channel. We use an Aberdeen number four hook, a six-foot leader and sixty-five yards of twenty-pound test line, a quadruple multiplying reel and a fly rod.

You cast your minnow out into the channel and let it sink to the bottom and there it waits until the trout grabs it. In the meantime you set the click on the reel and put a slab under the rod butt.

None of these lake rainbows run under four pounds and when one hits the minnow the reel buzzes, the rod tip jerks down and you grab the rod and strike and the fight is on. The point of this is that we have caught trout in this way over nine pounds in weight. We have never had one run out all the line and while we have lost many leaders we had never had a fish big enough to break the line.

One day in September I had just cast out the minnow into the channel, the rod was pointing up into the air and the click was set on the reel. I was about twenty-five yards down the shore getting some driftwood for a fire when the reel gave a shriek that mounted to about high C. Not the familiar bzzzzzzzz but a steady shriek. The rod jerked down so hard that it was flattened straight out on the water.

I raced for the rod the instant I heard the reel start. Just as I reached it the shriek of the reel stopped. There was a big wallowing explosion out in the lake, the line broke at the reel and the rod, the butt had been under a log and resting on another, shot up into the air. I jumped into the water but the line had vanished out into the lake.

Don't ask me how big he was. But he was big enough to take out over forty yards of line in the time it takes me to cover sixty feet and he was big enough to break a brand new twenty-three-pound test line without an instant's strain. As soon as his weight hit the direct pull of the line it snapped.

The other one I didn't see. But one night Jock Pentecost came into camp wet to the skin, his rod broken at the second joint, his net gone and a story that made our eyes bug out.

It seems that he was fishing a particularly deep and difficult stretch of river when he hooked a trout that he claimed was as long as his arm. He went down river with him through a pretty sizable rapids where he lost his net. Sometimes the fish would sulk at the foot of a big boulder and Jock would have to throw pebbles at him to start him moving. He was afraid to pump him too much with his rod for fear of parting the leader.

At other times the fish would rush and jump until Jock's heart would be somewhere in his gullet with each jump. Jock said that when the trout jumped he made a noise like a beaver diving into the water.

Of course it was a hopeless battle without a net and no other fisherman within two or three miles. Jock might have had a chance of beaching him if there had been any shallow places or patches of shingle. But the river runs waist deep and as fast as a mill race.

Jock claims that he fought the trout for an hour and a half and then the big fellow started down stream and something had to smash.

The enormous size of the fish and the length of time of the fight seemed unbelievable to us as it does to you. But Jock had the look of truth in his eyes.

Two weeks after the fish commission man netted some trout out below a dam on the river and put them upstream. They were too big to use the fish ladder. One of them was a rainbow weighing twenty-one pounds.

And what's more no one has caught him and he's still in the river.

—1920

ELIZABETH BISHOP
1911-1979

A year before she graduated from Vassar, where she had helped found a literary magazine, Elizabeth Bishop met the poet Marianne Moore. Moore convinced her to abandon her plans to attend medical school and instead to pursue writing, and Bishop went on to win the Pulitzer Prize for poetry in 1956 and the National Book Award for poetry in 1969. Many of Bishop's poems—from the 1927 "To a Tree" to the 1976 "The Moose"—convey a delightful intimacy with the natural world, a response both fresh and imaginative.

Born in Worcester, Massachusetts, and raised by two sets of grandparents, one in Nova Scotia and the other in Massachusetts, Bishop was pre-

vented by frail health from attending school regularly until she was sixteen. That year her first two poems appeared in the school magazine. Bishop led a peripatetic life as an adult, reflected in the names of her volumes of poetry Questions of Travel (1965) and Geography III (1976). She lived and traveled in England, Europe, North Africa, and South America, though she did finally settle down in Brazil for fifteen years, producing a book about the country (Brazil, 1962) for the Life World Library series. After leaving Brazil, she taught at the University of Washington, and then at Harvard from 1969 until her retirement in 1977. The Complete Poems: 1927–1979 came out in 1983.

"The Fish" appeared in Bishop's first volume of poetry, North and South (1946). This richly descriptive poem offers a different viewpoint on "the one that got away." There is a sense in this and other of Bishop's poems that looking at something long enough—"I stared and stared"—can cause a transformation of ordinary perceptions into a more magical and perhaps more accurate vision of reality. Thus Bishop's encounter with a scarred veteran of the waters becomes in the end a profound imaginative experience.

THE FISH

I caught a tremendous fish
and held him beside the boat
half out of water, with my hook
fast in a corner of his mouth.
He didn't fight.
He hadn't fought at all.
He hung a grunting weight,
battered and venerable
and homely. Here and there
his brown skin hung in strips
like ancient wallpaper,
and its pattern of darker brown
was like wallpaper:
shapes like full-blown roses
stained and lost through age.
He was speckled with barnacles,
fine rosettes of lime,
and infested
with tiny white sea-lice,
and underneath two or three
rags of green weed hung down.
While his gills were breathing in
the terrible oxygen
—the frightening gills,
fresh and crisp with blood,
that can cut so badly—
I thought of the coarse white flesh
packed in like feathers,

the big bones and the little bones,
the dramatic reds and blacks
of his shiny entrails,
and the pink swim-bladder
like a big peony.
I looked into his eyes
which were far larger than mine
but shallower, and yellowed,
the irises backed and packed
with tarnished tinfoil
seen through the lenses
of old scratched isinglass.
They shifted a little, but not
to return my stare.
—It was more like the tipping
of an object toward the light.
I admired his sullen face,
the mechanism of his jaw,
and then I saw
that from his lower lip
—if you could call it a lip—
grim, wet, and weaponlike,
hung five old pieces of fish-line,
or four and a wire leader
with the swivel still attached,
with all their five big hooks
grown firmly in his mouth.
A green line, frayed at the end
where he broke it, two heavier lines,
and a fine black thread
still crimped from the strain and snap
when it broke and he got away.
Like medals with their ribbons
frayed and wavering,
a five-haired beard of wisdom
trailing from his aching jaw.
I stared and stared
and victory filled up
the little rented boat,
from the pool of bilge
where oil had spread a rainbow
around the rusted engine
to the bailer rusted orange,
the sun-cracked thwarts,
the oarlocks on their strings,
the gunnels—until everything
was rainbow, rainbow, rainbow!
And I let the fish go.

                                    —1946

*We work out our connections
to nature in the particular
place or places on earth where
we spend our lives.*

INHABITING
PLACE

Place. The word, at first glance, seems trite and vacuous—and the phenomenon to which the word refers too vague, too universal, to warrant our attention. *Place* means everything, everywhere. The entire world is a place, and so are the particular chair where you sit reading this and the uncountable locations of the rest of the earth's inhabitants. The key word in the title of this part is *inhabiting,* which comes from the Latin word *inhabitare,* literally "to dwell in." For human beings, the concept of place can only be understood when it is associated with the physical and psychological experience of being in a specific location. The geographer Yi-Fu Tuan has even defined *place* as "a center of meaning constructed by experience." In other words, for Tuan, place is not merely a physical phenomenon—a chair or a room or a plot of land—but a "center of meaning," a locus of the mind's ideas and emotions. And the meaning of place is created through lived experience.

Until we begin consciously to *inhabit* the physical locations where we exist, the places remain vague, devoid of meaning. But when we begin to pay attention, place has the potential to become one of the primary dimensions of our lives. Wallace Stegner begins a 1986 essay called "The Sense of Place" by quoting his former student, Wendell Berry: "If you don't know where you are, you don't know who you are." The very notion of the human self, for writers like Stegner and Berry, is inseparable from the imprints that the physical world presses upon our imagination. For Stegner, one of the tragedies of American society is our geographical mobility, our apparent restless haste to spend a short time in many places, always moving on when things don't work out or when we simply get the itch to try something new. It could be argued that such mobility derives from spiritual malaise, from a lack of commitment or connectedness to the world, to other people. Another of Stegner's disciples, John Daniel, points out that the average American family moves once every four years. "Fluent in mobility," he notes in his book *The Trail Home* (1992), "we try haltingly to learn the alphabet of place." This occurs when we start to pay attention, to "hold the land in mind." Perhaps this is what it means to dwell in, or inhabit, a place.

The first chapter in this part, "Imprint of the Land," explores the myriad ways in which place determines not only our external lives but also our inner selves, our patterns of thought. The selections gathered here range from demonstrations of place-conscious writing to articulations of the processes by which the human mind comes to receive the imprint of a place. Sometimes we are lucky enough to realize, at a given moment, the value and power of the place where we are or another place that has been described to us. Other times, the significance of a place occurs to us after the fact, through the process of memory. For some writers, attentiveness to place is fundamental to the act of telling stories—a placeless narrative seems empty and unconvincing. Eudora Welty, whose tales of life in the South are permeated with a strong sense of place, has written in "Some Notes on River Country" that "perhaps it is the sense of place that gives us the belief that passionate things, in some essence, endure." The scholar Kent Ryden, in his book *Mapping the Invisible Landscape: Folklore, Writing, and the Sense of Place* (1993), has coined the term "invisible landscape" to describe the impressions the physical world leaves upon our minds, and he argues that "when we allow ourselves to become estranged from physical landscapes or the invisible landscapes that they support, abuse and pain and loss are inevitable. The results of this estrangement are not difficult to find on the landscape and in human history and usually take the form of unconscionable irresponsibility."

In a similar vein, Barry Lopez, in a book called *The Rediscovery of North America* (1990), wrestles with the Spanish word *querencia*, which implies "a place on the ground where one feels secure, a place from which one's strength of character is drawn." For Lopez, the effort to achieve querencia is a crucial challenge for us, "both a response to threat and a desire to find out who we are." Many people think of finding a particular place to ground the self—in its physical and emotional and intellectual aspects—as the act of finding home. *Home,* unlike the more abstract word *place,* is loaded with emotional resonance. The chapter "Visions of Home" presents a variety of perspectives on the idea of having a special place in the world to belong to. Some of these authors remember former homes and write with bittersweet voices that reflect the distance of years and miles, intimating the pain of loss. Others write ironically about minds incapable of fathoming place as home, or about places that seem to defy deep attachment. Many of us cringe at the practical questions about natural resources and waste disposal that the "Where You At?" quiz asks about the places we call home. But in order to dwell anywhere deeply and conscientiously, we must make every effort to know that place. Literature, even if it addresses the nuances of places we've never visited and have no special desire to see, can offer models for our own way of thinking, and writing, about home. As Scott Russell Sanders states in "Buckeye," "For each home ground we need new maps, living maps, stories and poems, photographs and paintings, essays and songs. We need to know where we are, so that we may dwell in our place with a full heart."

Experiencing and appreciating place is not only important to the individual person, not only a means of enriching the individual's sense of self, but necessary to the management of places and resources with sensitivity to the people who live there or have other forms of attachment. The selections in the chapter "Politics of Place" illustrate how the use and preservation of places can result in complex confrontations between groups and individuals. Many of us take for granted the security of the world and our own security as residents of a particular city or landscape or country. What would it be like to be kept from living in one's homeland by the racist or homophobic hatred of other people? What would it be like to see one's homeland occupied and brutalized by an imperialistic power or abused by a callous government? Who should have the final say about how places are managed—individual property owners, governmental bodies, or, in the case of public lands, the citizenry? The selections in "Politics of Place" show that a "center of meaning constructed by experience," to reuse Tuan's phrase, is both a social construction and a private sensory and emotional phenomenon. The meaning of place is no simple matter—and literature offers important insights regarding what and how place signifies.

4

How does the experience of place affect our inner lives? How are we affected by natural versus artificial environments?

IMPRINT OF THE LAND

KENNETH REXROTH

1905-1982

Kenneth Rexroth, one of the most significant American poets of the twentieth century, drew his literary inspiration from an eclectic array of sources, including various mystical traditions and the classical poetry of China and Japan. Although born in Indiana, he lived most of his life in northern California, where he was easily able to pursue his lifelong passion for the natural world—a passion immediately apparent in his poetry. An autodidact and many-sided genius, he never completed high school yet spent the last fifteen years of his life on the faculty of the University of California, Santa Barbara.

Wide-ranging in his literary talents, Rexroth was the author of two dozen books of verse, eight volumes of essays, an autobiography, and thirteen volumes of translation from six languages. The bulk of his poetry remains available to readers in The Collected Shorter Poems *(1967) and* The Collected Longer Poems *(1968), while the profound effects of Buddhism on his artistic vision can be seen in* On Flower Wreath Hill *(1976). Rexroth, in fact, is one of the most important translators of Chinese and Japanese poetry into English: his* One Hundred Poems from the Japanese *(1955) and* One Hundred Poems from the Chinese *(1956) are classics, providing an excellent introduction for American readers interested in exploring these important poetic traditions. Rexroth was also a major influence on a younger generation of writers that included Gary Snyder, Lawrence Ferlinghetti, and Allen Ginsberg. Since Rexroth's death, his work has suffered critical neglect but nevertheless continues to inspire new generations of readers.*

As a poet, Rexroth—unlike most of his contemporaries—believed a poem should serve as a direct communication between writer and reader. In a 1969 interview, he remarked that "a poem is an efficient vehicle for focusing attention, for giving direct experience." His work, characterized by mystical perception infused with a heightened eroticism, is often set in the wilds of the Sierra Nevada or along the rugged coast of northern California. "Incarnation," from The Collected Shorter Poems, *is representative of Rexroth's efforts to reestablish the poem as "vision," a direct apprehension of reality without grasping.*

INCARNATION

Climbing alone all day long
In the blazing waste of spring snow,
I came down with the sunset's edge
To the highest meadow, green
In the cold mist of waterfalls,
To a cobweb of water
Woven with innumerable
Bright flowers of wild iris;
And saw far down our fire's smoke
Rising between the canyon walls,
A human thing in the empty mountains.
And as I stood on the stones
In the midst of whirling water,
The whirling iris perfume
Caught me in a vision of you
More real than reality:
Fire in the deep curves of your hair:
Your hips whirled in a tango,
Out and back in dim scented light;
Your cheeks snow-flushed, the zithers
Ringing, all the crowded ski lodge
Dancing and singing; your arms
White in the brown autumn water,
Swimming through the fallen leaves,
Making a fluctuant cobweb
Of light on the sycamores;
Your thigh's exact curve, the fine gauze
Slipping through my hands, and you
Tense on the verge of abandon;
Your breasts' very touch and smell;
The sweet secret odor of sex.
Forever the thought of you,
And the splendor of the iris,
The crinkled iris petal,
The gold hairs powdered with pollen,
And the obscure cantata
Of the tangled water, and the
Burning, impassive snow peaks,

Are knotted together here.
This moment of fact and vision
Seizes immortality,
Becomes the person of this place.
The responsibility
Of love realized and beauty
Seen burns in a burning angel
Real beyond flower or stone.

                                        —1966

LANGSTON HUGHES
1902-1967

*One of the most prolific and influential African-American writers of the
twentieth century, Langston Hughes published twelve books during his lifetime, an eclectic assortment of poetry, fiction, drama, autobiography, and
journalism, plus an edited collection,* The Langston Hughes Reader *(1958).
Hughes came of age as a writer during the Harlem Renaissance of the
1920s, associating with other writers in New York such as Countee Cullen,
Claude McKay, and Zora Neale Hurston. But unlike Cullen and McKay,
whose work tends to be more highly wrought and more reflective of earlier
British literature, Hughes derived his poetic voice, in the tradition of Walt
Whitman, from the common speech of America, and particularly from the
black vernacular. One critic has commented that his greatest technical
accomplishment as a poet was in his fusing of the rhythms of blues and jazz
with traditional poetry.*

*Born in Joplin, Missouri, Hughes lived with his mother in Lawrence,
Kansas, until the age of twelve. He spent a year with his father and step-
mother in Lincoln, Illinois, then rejoined his mother in Cleveland, Ohio,
where he attended high school. After high school, Hughes lived a varied,
wandering life before finding his vocation as a writer. He spent time with
his father in Mexico, studied for a year at Columbia University, shipped out
on steamers to Africa and Europe, and did menial work in Washington,
D.C., where his mother had moved. In 1926, Alfred A. Knopf published
Hughes's first book of poetry,* The Weary Blues. *His second book,* Fine
Clothes to the Jew, *appeared a year later. He graduated from mostly black
Lincoln University in Pennsylvania in 1929. Hughes traveled widely and
worked on an extraordinary range of literary and journalistic projects right
up to his death.*

"The Negro Speaks of Rivers," an early poem, first published in Crisis
*(June 1921), celebrates the beauty and dignity of African peoples. The
mythic narrator, spanning both human history and vast geographical
space, articulates a sense of identity associated in particular with the great
rivers of Africa and America, suggesting the powerful connection between
prominent features of the natural world and human experience. The
poem's two refrains—"I've known rivers" and "My soul has grown deep like
the rivers"—imply that a rich, confident sense of self is contingent upon*

acknowledging the "imprint of the land." The Mississippi is the river of
Hughes's own childhood, while the Euphrates, the Congo, and the Nile are
the ancestral rivers of his people.

THE NEGRO SPEAKS OF RIVERS

I've known rivers:
I've known rivers ancient as the world and older than the
    flow of human blood in human veins.

My soul has grown deep like the rivers.

I bathed in the Euphrates when dawns were young.
I built my hut near the Congo and it lulled me to sleep.
I looked upon the Nile and raised the pyramids above it.
I heard the singing of the Mississippi when Abe Lincoln
    went down to New Orleans, and I've seen its muddy
    bosom turn all golden in the sunset.

I've known rivers:
Ancient, dusky rivers.

My soul has grown deep like the rivers.

                       —1921

BELL HOOKS

B. 1952

bell hooks was born Gloria Jean Watkins, but when she began writing she
took the name of her great-grandmother, "a sharp-tongued woman, a
woman who spoke her mind, a woman who was not afraid to talk back," as
a way to challenge her own impulse to hold back words. "Paralyzed by the
fear that I will not be able to name or speak words that fully articulate my
experience or the collective reality of struggling black people, I am tempted
to be silent," she has written. Still, she has lectured widely on race, gender,
class, and personal empowerment and has authored nearly a dozen books.
    hooks was born and raised in rural Kentucky, an experience that
imprinted her with a love for the land. She was educated at Stanford
University and taught English and women's studies at Oberlin College before
moving to a teaching position at City College of New York. Her first book,
Ain't I a Woman: Black Women and Feminism (1981), was named by
Publishers Weekly as one of the "twenty most influential women's books of
the last twenty years." Her other books include Talking Back: Thinking
Feminist, Thinking Black *(1988),* Yearning: Race and Gender in the Cultural

Marketplace *(1990), and* Sisters of the Yam: Black Women and Self-Recovery *(1993), from which the following selection is taken. With Cornel West, she coauthored* Breaking Bread: Insurgent Black Intellectual Life *(1991).*

In "Touching the Earth," hooks suggests that connection with the land is the necessary foundation for black self-empowerment, as it was for earlier generations that lived a rural life. "It has been easy for folks to forget that black people were first and foremost a people of the land, farmers. . . . Growing food to sustain life and flowers to please the soul, they were able to make a connection with the earth that was ongoing and life-affirming," she writes. Speculating that the black psyche was wounded when blacks moved from the agrarian South to the industrial North, she points out that estrangement from the land and from the body makes it easier for blacks to internalize white racist assumptions. Thus, restoring a connection to the natural world goes hand in hand with the struggle to end racism.

TOUCHING THE EARTH

When we love the earth, we are able to love ourselves more fully. I believe this. The ancestors taught me it was so. As a child I loved playing in dirt, in that rich Kentucky soil, that was a source of life. Before I understood anything about the pain and exploitation of the southern system of sharecropping, I understood that grown-up black folks loved the land. I could stand with my grandfather Daddy Jerry and look out at fields of growing vegetables, tomatoes, corn, collards, and know that this was his handiwork. I could see the look of pride on his face as I expressed wonder and awe at the magic of growing things. I knew that my grandmother Baba's backyard garden would yield beans, sweet potatoes, cabbage, and yellow squash, that she too would walk with pride among the rows and rows of growing vegetables showing us what the earth will give when tended lovingly.

From the moment of their first meeting, Native American and African people shared with one another a respect for the life-giving forces of nature, of the earth. African settlers in Florida taught the Creek Nation runaways, the "Seminoles," methods for rice cultivation. Native peoples taught recently arrived black folks all about the many uses of corn. (The hotwater cornbread we grew up eating came to our black southern diet from the world of the Indian.) Sharing the reverence for the earth, black and red people helped one another remember that, despite the white man's ways, the land belonged to everyone. Listen to these words attributed to Chief Seattle in 1854:

> How can you buy or sell the sky, the warmth of the land? The idea is strange to us. If we do not own the freshness of the air and the sparkle of the water, how can you buy them? Every part of this earth is sacred to my people. Every shining pine needle, every sandy shore, every mist in the dark woods, every clearing and humming insect is holy in the memory and experience of my people. We are part of the earth and it is part of us. The perfumed flowers are our sisters; the deer, the horse, the great eagle, these are our brothers. The rocky crests, the juices in the meadows, the body heat of the pony, and man all belong to the same family.

The sense of union and harmony with nature expressed here is echoed in testimony by black people who found that even though life in the new world was "harsh, harsh," in relationship to the earth one could be at peace. In the oral autobiography of granny midwife Onnie Lee Logan, who lived all her life in Alabama, she talks about the richness of farm life growing vegetables, raising chickens, and smoking meat. She reports:

We lived a happy, comfortable life to be right outa slavery times. I didn't know nothin else but the farm so it was happy and we was happy. We couldn't do anything else but be happy. We accept the days as they come and as they were. Day by day until you couldn't say there was any great hard time. We overlooked it. We didn't think nothin about it. We just went along. We had what it takes to make a good livin and go about it.

Living in modern society, without a sense of history, it has been easy for folks to forget that black people were first and foremost a people of the land, farmers. It is easy for folks to forget that at the first part of the 20th century, the vast majority of black folks in the United States lived in the agrarian south.

Living close to nature, black folks were able to cultivate a spirit of wonder and reverence for life. Growing food to sustain life and flowers to please the soul, they were able to make a connection with the earth that was ongoing and life-affirming. They were witnesses to beauty. In Wendell Berry's important discussion of the relationship between agriculture and human spiritual well-being, *The Unsettling of America*, he reminds us that working the land provides a location where folks can experience a sense of personal power and well-being:

We are working well when we use ourselves as the fellow creature of the plants, animals, material, and other people we are working with. Such work is unifying, healing. It brings us home from pride and despair, and places us responsibly within the human estate. It defines us as we are: not too good to work without our bodies, but too good to work poorly or joylessly or selfishly or alone.

There has been little or no work done on the psychological impact of the "great migration" of black people from the agrarian south to the industrialized north. Toni Morrison's novel *The Bluest Eye* attempts to fictively document the way moving from the agrarian south to the industrialized north wounded the psyches of black folk. Estranged from a natural world, where there was time for silence and contemplation, one of the "displaced" black folks in Morrison's novel, Miss Pauline, loses her capacity to experience the sensual world around her when she leaves southern soil to live in a northern city. The south is associated in her mind with a world of sensual beauty most deeply expressed in the world of nature. Indeed, when she falls in love for the first time she can name that experience only by evoking images from nature, from an agrarian world and near wilderness of natural splendor:

When I first seed Cholly, I want you to know it was like all the bits of color from that time down home when all us chil'ren went berry picking after a funeral and I put some in the pocket of my Sunday dress, and they mashed up and stained my hips. My whole dress was messed with purple, and it never did wash out. Not the dress nor me. I could feel that purple deep inside me. And that lemonade Mama used to make when Pap came in out of the fields. It be cool and yellowish, with seeds floating near the bottom. And that streak of green them june bugs made on the trees that night we left from down home. All of them colors was in me. Just sitting there.

Certainly, it must have been a profound blow to the collective psyche of black people to find themselves struggling to make a living in the industrial north away from the land. Industrial capitalism was not simply changing the nature of black work life, it altered the communal practices that were so central to survival in the agrarian south. And it fundamentally altered black people's relationship to the body. It is the loss of any capacity to appreciate her body, despite its flaws, Miss Pauline suffers when she moves north.

The motivation for black folks to leave the south and move north was both material and psychological. Black folks wanted to be free of the overt racial harassment that was a constant in southern life and they wanted access to material goods, to a level of material well-being that was not available in the agrarian south where white folks limited access to the spheres of economic power. Of course, they found that life in the north had its own perverse hardships, that racism was just as virulent there, that it was much harder for black people to become landowners. Without the space to grow food, to commune with nature, or to mediate the starkness of poverty with the splendor of nature, black people experienced profound depression. Working in conditions where the body was regarded solely as a tool (as in slavery), a profound estrangement occurred between mind and body. The way the body was represented became more important than the body itself. It did not matter if the body was well, only that it appeared well.

Estrangement from nature and engagement in mind/body splits made it all the more possible for black people to internalize white-supremacist assumptions about black identity. Learning contempt for blackness, southerners transplanted in the north suffered both culture shock and soul loss. Contrasting the harshness of city life with an agrarian world, the poet Waring Cuney wrote this popular poem in the 1920's, testifying to lost connection:

She does not know her beauty
She thinks her brown body
has no glory.
If she could dance naked,
Under palm trees
And see her image in the river
She would know.
But there are no palm trees on the street,
And dishwater gives back no images.

For many years, and even now, generations of black folks who migrated north to escape life in the south, returned down home in search of a spiritual nourishment, a healing, that was fundamentally connected to reaffirming one's connection to nature, to a contemplative life where one could take time, sit on the porch, walk, fish, and catch lightning bugs. If we think of urban life as a location where black folks learned to accept a mind/body split that made it possible to abuse the body, we can better understand the growth of nihilism and despair in the black psyche. And we can know that when we talk about healing that psyche we must also speak about restoring our connection to the natural world.

Wherever black folks live we can restore our relationship to the natural world by taking the time to commune with nature, to appreciate the other creatures who share this planet with humans. Even in my small New York City apartment I can pause to listen to birds sing, find a tree and watch it. We can grow plants—herbs, flowers, vegetables. Those novels by African-American writers (women and men) that talk about black migration from the agrarian south to the industrialized north describe in detail the way folks created space to grow flowers and vegetables. Although I come from country people with serious green thumbs, I have always felt that I could not garden. In the past few years, I have found that I can do it—that many gardens will grow, that I feel connected to my ancestors when I can put a meal on the table of food I grew. I especially love to plant collard greens. They are hardy, and easy to grow.

In modern society, there is also a tendency to see no correlation between the struggle for collective black self-recovery and ecological movements that seek to restore balance to the planet by changing our relationship to nature and to natural resources. Unmindful of our history of living harmoniously on the land, many contemporary black folks see no value in supporting ecological movements, or see ecology and the struggle to end racism as competing concerns. Recalling the legacy of our ancestors who knew that the way we regard land and nature will determine the level of our self-regard, black people must reclaim a spiritual legacy where we connect our well-being to the well being of the earth. This is a necessary dimension of healing. As Berry reminds us:

> Only by restoring the broken connections can we be healed. Connection is health. And what our society does its best to disguise from us is how ordinary, how commonly attainable, health is. We lose our health and create profitable diseases and dependencies by failing to see the direct connections between living and eating, eating and working, working and loving. In gardening, for instance, one works with the body to feed the body. The work, if it is knowledgeable, makes for excellent food. And it makes one hungry. The work thus makes eating both nourishing and joyful, not consumptive, and keeps the eater from getting fat and weak. This health, wholeness, is a source of delight.

Collective black self-recovery takes place when we begin to renew our relationship to the earth, when we remember the way of our ancestors. When the earth is sacred to us, our bodies can also be sacred to us.

—1993

LINDA HOGAN

B. 1947

Linda Hogan says that her job as a poet, novelist, and essayist is to listen to the world and translate it into a human tongue. "The earth writes through me," she has proclaimed. Some of the other voices she hears when she is in the process of writing belong to her Chickasaw ancestors on her father's side, who gave her a background of oral literature. The fact that her mother is white, from an immigrant Nebraska family, creates a natural tension that she says surfaces in her work and strengthens it.

Hogan was born in Denver but reared in Oklahoma. She earned an M.A. in English and creative writing from the University of Colorado, where she now teaches American Indian literature and creative writing. She has published several volumes of poetry; Seeing Through the Sun (1985) won the American Book Award from the Before Columbus Foundation, and The Book of Medicines (1993) was a finalist for the National Book Critics Circle Award. She has also published two collections of short stories, That Horse (1985) and The Big Woman (1987). Her first novel, Mean Spirit (1990), a finalist for the Pulitzer Prize in 1991, explores how white greed threatened to destroy the Osage Indian tribe early in this century when oil was discovered under their Oklahoma homeland; her second novel, Solar Storms (1995), weaves together the lives of five generations of Native American women in the Boundary Waters between Minnesota and Canada. Hogan has worked as a peace activist and wildlife rehabilitator, seeking to heal "the severed trust we humans hold with earth."

"What Holds the Water, What Holds the Light" is from Hogan's first book of essays, entitled Dwellings: A Spiritual History of the Living World *(1995). It urges us to accept the imprint of the land, the gifts of earth and sky, with respect and gratitude, though in our culture we are commonly not taught to do so. "Most of us are taught, somehow, about giving and accepting human gifts, but not about opening ourselves and our bodies to welcome the sun, the land, the visions of sky and dreaming, not about standing in the rain ecstatic with what is offered," writes Hogan in her plea for a more balanced way of being.*

WHAT HOLDS THE WATER, WHAT HOLDS THE LIGHT

Walking up the damp hill in the hot sun, there were signs of the recent heavy rains. The land smelled fresh, shaded plants still held moisture in their green clustered leaves, and fresh deer tracks pointed uphill like arrows in the dark, moist soil.

Along our way, my friend and I stopped at a cluster of large boulders to drink fresh rain collected in a hollow bowl that had been worn into stone over slow centuries. Bending over the stone, smelling earth up close, we drank sky off the surface of water. Mosses and ancient lichens lived there. And swimming in another stone cup were slender orange newts, alive and vibrant with the rains.

Drinking the water, I thought how earth and sky are generous with their gifts, and how good it is to receive them. Most of us are taught, somehow, about giving and accepting human gifts, but not about opening ourselves and our bodies to welcome the sun, the land, the visions of sky and dreaming, not about standing in the rain ecstatic with what is offered.

One time, visiting friends, I found they had placed a Mexican water jar on the sink and filled it for me. It was a thin clay that smelled of dank earth, the unfired and unshaped land it had once been. In it was rain come from dark sky. A cool breeze lived inside the container, the way wind blows from a well that is held in the cupped hands of earth, fed with underground springs and rivers.

The jar was made in Mexico City, once called Iztapalapa, the place where Montezuma lived during the time Cortés and his Spanish soldiers were colonizing the indigenous people and the land. Writer Barry Lopez has written about the aviaries of Iztapalapa that were burned by the Spanish, fires that burned the green hummingbirds and nesting blue herons, burned even the sound of wings and the white songs of egrets. It was not only the birds that died in those fires, but also the people and their records, the stories of human lives.

De Soto also had this disregard for life. He once captured an indigenous woman because she carried a large pearl. His intention was, when they were far from her homeland, to kill the woman and steal the pearl, but one morning along their journey she managed to escape. De Soto's anger was enormous. It was as if the woman had taken something from him, and that fierce anger resulted in the killing of people and a relentless, ongoing war against land.

Humans colonizing and conquering others have a propensity for this, for burning behind them what they cannot possess or control, as if their conflicts are not with themselves and their own way of being, but with the land itself.

In the 1930s, looters found the Spiro burial mounds of Oklahoma and sold to collectors artifacts that they removed from the dead. When caught and forbidden to continue their thefts, the men dynamited two of the mounds the way a wolverine sprays food so that nothing else will take possession of it.

It seems, looking back, that those invasions amounted to a hatred of life itself, of fertility and generation. The conquerers and looters refused to participate in a reciprocal and balanced exchange with life. They were unable to receive the best gifts of land, not gold or pearls or ownership, but a welcome acceptance of what is offered. They did not understand that the earth is generous and that encounters with the land might have been sustaining, or that their meetings with other humans could have led to an enriched confluence of ways. But here is a smaller event, one we are more likely to witness as a daily, common occurrence. Last year, I was at the Colorado River with a friend when two men from the Department of Fish and Wildlife came to stock the water with rainbow trout. We wanted to watch the silver-sided fish find their way to freedom in the water, so we stood quietly by as the men climbed into the truck bed and opened the tank that held fish. To our dismay, the men did not use the nets they carried with them to unload the fish. Instead they poured the fish into the bed of their truck, kicked them out and down the hill, and then into water. The fish that survived were motionless, shocked, gill slits barely moving, skin hanging off the wounds. At most, it would have taken only a few minutes longer for the men to have removed the fish carefully with their nets, to have treated the lives they handled with dignity and respect, with caretakers' hands.

These actions, all of them, must be what Bushman people mean when they say a person is far-hearted. This far-hearted kind of thinking is one we are especially prone to now, with our lives moving so quickly ahead, and it is one that sees life, other lives, as containers for our own uses and not as containers in a greater, holier sense.

Even wilderness is seen as having value only as it enhances and serves our human lives, our human world. While most of us agree that wilderness is necessary to our spiritual and psychological well-being, it is a container of far more, of mystery, of a life apart from ours. It is not only where we go to escape who we have become and what we have done, but it is also part of the natural laws, the workings of a world of beauty and depth we do not yet understand. It is something beyond us, something that does not need our hand in it. As one of our Indian elders has said, there are laws beyond our human laws, and ways above ours. We have no words for this in our language, or even for our experience of being there. Ours is a language of commerce and trade, of laws that can be bent in order that treaties might be broken, land wounded beyond healing. It is a language that is limited, emotionally and spiritually, as if it can't accommodate such magical strength and power. The ears of this language do not often hear the songs of the white egrets, the rain falling into stone bowls. So we make our own songs to contain these things, make ceremonies and poems, searching for a new way to speak, to say we want a new way to live in the world, to say that wilderness and water, blue herons and orange newts are invaluable not just to us, but in themselves, in the workings of the natural world that rules us whether we acknowledge it or not.

That clay water jar my friends filled with water might have been made of the same earth that housed the birds of Iztapalapa. It might have contained water the stunned trout once lived in. It was not only a bridge between the elements of earth, air, water, and fire but was also a bridge between people, a reservoir of love and friendship, the kind of care we need to offer back every day to the world as we begin to learn the land and its creatures, to know the world is the container for our lives, sometimes wild and untouched, sometimes moved by a caretaker's hands. Until we learn this, and learn our place at the bountiful table, how to be a guest here, this land will not support us, will not be hospitable, will turn on us.

That water jar was a reminder of how water and earth love each other the way they do, meeting at night, at the shore, being friends together, dissolving in each other, in the give and take that is where grace comes from.

—1995

LUCILLE CLIFTON

B. 1936

Given a name by her mother that means "light," Lucille Clifton returns again and again in her poetry to images of light and illuminates in simple language the deeper truths of her experience as a black woman. Her early poems came out of the Black Arts movement of the late 1960s and early 1970s; animated by anger and pride, they deal with subjects such as the facts of poverty and the memory of slavery. But an optimistic impulse at once spiritual and earthy is also at work in Clifton's poems. Commented one critic, "She assumes connection where the dualisms of our culture assume separation—between self and other, humans and nature, male and female, public and private life, pleasure and pain—and what emanates from her mixings, like the wave of energy released when atoms fuse, is something like joy."

Born in Depew, New York, Clifton attended Howard University and Fredonia State Teachers' College. She met and was influenced by Leroi Jones, Ishmael Reed, and Gwendolyn Brooks; Reed showed some of her poems to Langston Hughes, who published them in an anthology. When her first book of poems, Good Times, came out in 1969, Clifton was thirty-three years old and had six children under the age of ten. She has written numerous books for children since then, while maintaining a steady output of poetry and teaching at several colleges and universities. A family memoir entitled Generations was published in 1976. Recent volumes of poetry include Quilting: Poems 1987–1990 (1991) and Book of Light (1993).

"sonora desert poem," from Two-Headed Woman (1980), is a meditation on what can be learned from a desert landscape if one comes to it with all the senses wide open. The poem illustrates what one critic has said about Clifton's work: that it weds the transcendental expansiveness of Walt Whitman and the verbal compression of Emily Dickinson. Clifton dedicates the poem to Lois and Richard Shelton; Richard Shelton is a poet and writer whose poem "Sonora for Sale" warns that the desert "is all we have left to destroy."

SONORA DESERT POEM

for lois and richard shelton

1.

the ones who live in the desert,
if you knew them
you would understand everything.
they see it all and
never judge any
just drink the water when
they get the chance.
if i could grow arms on my scars
like them,
if i could learn
the patience they know
i wouldn't apologize for my thorns either
just stand in the desert
and witness.

2.

directions for watching the sun set in the desert

come to the landscape that was hidden under the sea.
look in the opposite direction.

reach for the mountain.
the mountain will ignore your hand.
the sun will fall on your back.
the landscape will fade away.
you will think you're alone until a flash
of green incredible light.

3.
directions for leaving the desert

push the bones back
under your skin.
finish the water.
they will notice your thorns and
ask you to testify.
turn toward the shade.
smile.
say nothing at all.

—1980

JOHN MUIR
1838-1914

John Muir, amateur natural historian, writer, family man, and political activist, is a central figure in the history of the American conservation movement. He was guided by a single, uncompromising principle: Everything in nature is connected to everything else. "We all travel the milky way together," he wrote, "trees and men." As is the case with all who are passionate, contradictions abound in Muir. Although he was equally as fond of bears, water ouzels, and poison oak as he was of trees, Muir can at times in his writing seem harsh and intolerant toward his fellow human beings, especially when their presence disrupts what he perceives to be the true order of nature, which is to say the wild. For his tireless efforts in rousing the nation's environmental consciousness, he was eventually honored—more than half a century after his death—by having his birthday designated as Earth Day.

Born in Dunbar, Scotland, Muir came to Wisconsin when he was still a boy, his father having decided to try his hand at a pioneer farm not far from Madison. In his autobiography, Muir describes these years living under a severe and autocratic father as less than happy. After attending but never graduating from the University of Wisconsin, Muir embarked on a long period of itinerating that took him to Canada, the Deep South, and finally California, where he sojourned in the Yosemite Valley and began a prolonged study of the natural history of the Sierra Nevada, mountains he called "the Range of Light." Although at age forty Muir left the Sierra to

marry, raise a family, and become a successful fruit rancher in Martinez,
California, his heart remained among the granite domes and sparkling
waters of Yosemite. Later in his life, Muir became a strong advocate for the
creation of national parks. Through works such as The Mountains of
California *(1894),* Our National Parks *(1901),* My First Summer in the Sierra
(1911), and Travels in Alaska *(1915), he built a strong constituency for the*
political preservation of American wildlands.

Although he wrote numerous essays and newspaper articles during his
*early adulthood in the mountains, Muir did not publish his first book—*The
Mountains of California—*until he was fifty-six years old. His best books are*
in fact collections, often with significant revisions, of his earlier writings.
The selection that follows is drawn from The Mountains of California. *As*
the piece shows, Muir based his natural history speculations on close obser-
vation and personal experience; this was in marked contrast to the objec-
tive, authoritarian methods of formally trained natural historians of the
time. Suffusing the piece is the exuberant love of wild nature that motivated
Muir's conservation crusades.

A WIND-STORM IN THE FORESTS

The mountain winds, like the dew and rain, sunshine and snow, are measured and
bestowed with love on the forests to develop their strength and beauty. However
restricted the scope of other forest influences, that of the winds is universal. The
snow bends and trims the upper forests every winter, the lightning strikes a single
tree here and there, while avalanches mow down thousands at a swoop as a gardener trims out a bed of flowers. But the winds go to every tree, fingering every leaf
and branch and furrowed bole; not one is forgotten; the Mountain Pine towering
with outstretched arms on the rugged buttresses of the icy peaks, the lowliest and
most retiring tenant of the dells; they seek and find them all, caressing them ten-
derly, bending them in lusty exercise, stimulating their growth, plucking off a leaf
or limb as required, or removing an entire tree or grove, now whispering and coo-
ing through the branches like a sleepy child, now roaring like the ocean; the winds
blessing the forests, the forests the winds, with ineffable beauty and harmony as the
sure result.

After one has seen pines six feet in diameter bending like grasses before a
mountain gale, and ever and anon some giant falling with a crash that shakes the
hills, it seems astonishing that any, save the lowest thickset trees, could ever have
found a period sufficiently stormless to establish themselves; or, once established,
that they should not, sooner or later, have been blown down. But when the storm is
over, and we behold the same forests tranquil again, towering fresh and unscathed
in erect majesty, and consider what centuries of storms have fallen upon them since
they were first planted,—hail, to break the tender seedlings; lightning, to scorch and
shatter; snow, winds, and avalanches, to crush and overwhelm,—while the manifest
result of all this wild storm-culture is the glorious perfection we behold; then faith
in Nature's forestry is established, and we cease to deplore the violence of her most
destructive gales, or of any other storm-implement whatsoever.

There are two trees in the Sierra forests that are never blown down, so long as they continue in sound health. These are the Juniper and the Dwarf Pine of the summit peaks. Their stiff, crooked roots grip the storm-beaten ledges like eagles' claws, while their lithe, cord-like branches bend round compliantly, offering but slight holds for winds, however violent. The other alpine conifers—the Needle Pine, Mountain Pine, Two-leaved Pine, and Hemlock Spruce—are never thinned out by this agent to any destructive extent, on account of their admirable toughness and the closeness of their growth. In general the same is true of the giants of the lower zones. The kingly Sugar Pine, towering aloft to a height of more than 200 feet, offers a fine mark to storm-winds; but it is not densely foliaged, and its long, horizontal arms swing round compliantly in the blast, like tresses of green, fluent algae in a brook; while the Silver Firs in most places keep their ranks well together in united strength. The Yellow or Silver Pine is more frequently overturned than any other tree on the Sierra, because its leaves and branches form a larger mass in proportion to its height, while in many places it is planted sparsely, leaving open lanes through which storms may enter with full force. Furthermore, because it is distributed along the lower portion of the range, which was the first to be left bare on the breaking up of the ice-sheet at the close of the glacial winter, the soil it is growing upon has been longer exposed to post-glacial weathering, and consequently is in a more crumbling, decayed condition than the fresher soils farther up the range, and therefore offers a less secure anchorage for the roots.

While exploring the forest zones of Mount Shasta, I discovered the path of a hurricane strewn with thousands of pines of this species. Great and small had been uprooted or wrenched off by sheer force, making a clean gap, like that made by a snow avalanche. But hurricanes capable of doing this class of work are rare in the Sierra, and when we have explored the forests from one extremity of the range to the other, we are compelled to believe that they are the most beautiful on the face of the earth, however we may regard the agents that have made them so.

There is always something deeply exciting, not only in the sounds of winds in the woods, which exert more or less influence over every mind, but in their varied water-like flow as manifested by the movements of the trees, especially those of the conifers. By no other trees are they rendered so extensively and impressively visible, not even by the lordly tropic palms or tree-ferns responsive to the gentlest breeze. The waving of a forest of the giant Sequoias is indescribably impressive and sublime, but the pines seem to me the best interpreters of winds. They are mighty waving goldenrods, ever in tune, singing and writing wind-music all their long century lives. Little, however, of this noble tree-waving and tree-music will you see or hear in the strictly alpine portion of the forests. The burly Juniper, whose girth sometimes more than equals its height, is about as rigid as the rocks on which it grows. The slender lash-like sprays of the Dwarf Pine stream out in wavering ripples, but the tallest and slenderest are far too unyielding to wave even in the heaviest gales. They only shake in quick, short vibrations. The Hemlock Spruce, however, and the Mountain Pine, and some of the tallest thickets of the Two-leaved species bow in storms with considerable scope and gracefulness. But it is only in the lower and middle zones that the meeting of winds and woods is to be seen in all its grandeur.

One of the most beautiful and exhilarating storms I ever enjoyed in the Sierra occurred in December, 1874, when I happened to be exploring one of the tributary valleys of the Yuba River. The sky and the ground and the trees had been thoroughly rain-washed and were dry again. The day was intensely pure, one of those incomparable bits of California winter, warm and balmy and full of white sparkling sunshine, redolent of all the purest influences of the spring, and at the same time enlivened with one of the most bracing wind-storms conceivable. Instead of camping out, as I usually do, I then chanced to be stopping at the house of a friend. But when the storm began to sound, I lost no time in pushing out into the woods to enjoy it. For on such occasions Nature has always something rare to show us, and the danger to life and limb is hardly greater than one would experience crouching deprecatingly beneath a roof.

It was still early morning when I found myself fairly adrift. Delicious sunshine came pouring over the hills, lighting the tops of the pines, and setting free a steam of summery fragrance that contrasted strangely with the wild tones of the storm. The air was mottled with pine-tassels and bright green plumes, that went flashing past in the sunlight like birds pursued. But there was not the slightest dustiness, nothing less pure than leaves, and ripe pollen, and flecks of withered bracken and moss. I heard trees falling for hours at the rate of one every two or three minutes; some uprooted, partly on account of the loose, water-soaked condition of the ground; others broken straight across, where some weakness caused by fire had determined the spot. The gestures of the various trees made a delightful study. Young Sugar Pines, light and feathery as squirrel-tails, were bowing almost to the ground; while the grand old patriarchs, whose massive boles had been tried in a hundred storms, waved solemnly above them, their long, arching branches streaming fluently on the gale, and every needle thrilling and ringing and shedding off keen lances of light like a diamond. The Douglas Spruces, with long sprays drawn out in level tresses, and needles massed in a gray, shimmering glow, presented a most striking appearance as they stood in bold relief along the hilltops. The madroños in the dells, with their red bark and large glossy leaves tilted every way, reflected the sunshine in throbbing spangles like those one so often sees on the rippled surface of a glacier lake. But the Silver Pines were now the most impressively beautiful of all. Colossal spires 200 feet in height waved like supple goldenrods chanting and bowing low as if in worship, while the whole mass of their long, tremulous foliage was kindled into one continuous blaze of white sun-fire. The force of the gale was such that the most steadfast monarch of them all rocked down to its roots with a motion plainly perceptible when one leaned against it. Nature was holding high festival, and every fiber of the most rigid giants thrilled with glad excitement.

I drifted on through the midst of this passionate music and motion, across many a glen, from ridge to ridge; often halting in the lee of a rock for shelter, or to gaze and listen. Even when the grand anthem had swelled to its highest pitch, I could distinctly hear the varying tones of individual trees,—Spruce, and Fir, and Pine, and leafless Oak,—and even the infinitely gentle rustle of the withered grasses at my feet. Each was expressing itself in its own way,—singing its own song, and making its own peculiar gestures,—manifesting a richness of variety to be found in no other forest I have yet seen. The coniferous woods of Canada, and the Carolinas, and Florida, are made up of trees that resemble one another about as nearly as blades of grass, and grow close together in much the same way. Coniferous trees, in general, seldom possess individual character, such as is manifest among Oaks and Elms. But the California forests are made up of a greater number of distinct species than any other in the world. And in them we find, not only a marked differentiation into special groups, but also a marked individuality in almost every tree, giving rise to storm effects indescribably glorious.

Toward midday, after a long, tingling scramble through copses of hazel and ceanothus, I gained the summit of the highest ridge in the neighborhood; and then it occurred to me that it would be a fine thing to climb one of the trees to obtain a wider outlook and get my ear close to the Æolian music of its topmost needles. But under the circumstances the choice of a tree was a serious matter. One whose instep was not very strong seemed in danger of being blown down, or of being struck by others in case they should fall; another was branchless to a considerable height above the ground, and at the same time too large to be grasped with arms and legs in climbing; while others were not favorably situated for clear views. After cautiously casting about, I made choice of the tallest of a group of Douglas Spruces that were growing close together like a tuft of grass, no one of which seemed likely to fall unless all the rest fell with it. Though comparatively young, they were about 100 feet high, and their lithe, brushy tops were rocking and swirling in wild ecstasy. Being accustomed to climb trees in making botanical studies, I experienced no difficulty in reaching the top of this one, and never before did I enjoy so noble an exhilaration of motion. The slender tops fairly flapped and swished in the passionate torrent, bending and swirling backward and forward, round and round, tracing indescribable combinations of vertical and horizontal curves, while I clung with muscles firm braced, like a bobolink on a reed.

In its widest sweeps my tree-top described an arc of from twenty to thirty degrees, but I felt sure of its elastic temper, having seen others of the same species still more severely tried—bent almost to the ground indeed, in heavy snows—without breaking a fiber. I was therefore safe, and free to take the wind into my pulses and enjoy the excited forest from my superb outlook. The view from here must be extremely beautiful in any weather. Now my eye roved over the piny hills and dales as over fields of waving grain, and felt the light running in ripples and broad swelling undulations across the valleys from ridge to ridge, as the shining foliage was stirred by corresponding waves of air. Oftentimes these waves of reflected light would break up suddenly into a kind of beaten foam, and again, after chasing one another in regular order, they would seem to bend forward in concentric curves, and disappear on some hill-side, like sea-waves on a shelving shore. The quantity of light reflected from the bent needles was so great as to make whole groves appear as if covered with snow, while the black shadows beneath the trees greatly enhanced the effect of the silvery splendor.

Excepting only the shadows there was nothing somber in all this wild sea of pines. On the contrary, notwithstanding this was the winter season, the colors were remarkably beautiful. The shafts of the pine and libocedrus were brown and purple, and most of the foliage was well tinged with yellow; the laurel groves, with the pale undersides of their leaves turned upward, made masses of gray; and then there was many a dash of chocolate color from clumps of manzanita, and jet of vivid crimson from the bark of the madroños, while the ground on the hillsides, appearing here and there through openings between the groves, displayed masses of pale purple and brown.

The sounds of the storm corresponded gloriously with this wild exuberance of light and motion. The profound bass of the naked branches and boles booming like waterfalls; the quick, tense vibrations of the pine-needles, now rising to a shrill, whistling hiss, now falling to a silky murmur; the rustling of laurel groves in the dells, and the keen metallic click of leaf on leaf—all this was heard in easy analysis when the attention was calmly bent.

The varied gestures of the multitude were seen to fine advantage, so that one could recognize the different species at a distance of several miles by this means alone, as well as by their forms and colors, and the way they reflected the light. All seemed strong and comfortable, as if really enjoying the storm, while responding to its most enthusiastic greetings. We hear much nowadays concerning the universal struggle for existence, but no struggle in the common meaning of the word was manifest here; no recognition of danger by any tree; no deprecation; but rather an invincible gladness as remote from exultation as from fear.

I kept my lofty perch for hours, frequently closing my eyes to enjoy the music by itself, or to feast quietly on the delicious fragrance that was streaming past. The fragrance of the woods was less marked than that produced during warm rain, when so many balsamic buds and leaves are steeped like tea; but, from the chafing of resiny branches against each other, and the incessant attrition of myriads of needles, the gale was spiced to a very tonic degree. And besides the fragrance from these local sources there were traces of scents brought from afar. For this wind came first from the sea, rubbing against its fresh, briny waves, then distilled through the redwoods, threading rich ferny gulches, and spreading itself in broad undulating currents over many a flower-enameled ridge of the coast mountains, then across the golden plains, up the purple foot-hills, and into these piny woods with the varied incense gathered by the way.

Winds are advertisements of all they touch, however much or little we may be able to read them; telling their wanderings even by their scents alone. Mariners detect the flowery perfume of land-winds far at sea, and sea-winds carry the fragrance of dulse and tangle far inland, where it is quickly recognized, though mingled with the scents of a thousand land-flowers. As an illustration of this, I may tell here that I breathed sea-air on the Firth of Forth, in Scotland, while a boy; then was taken to Wisconsin where I remained nineteen years; then, without in all this time having breathed one breath of the sea, I walked quietly, alone, from the middle of the Mississippi Valley to the Gulf of Mexico, on a botanical excursion, and while in Florida, far from the coast, my attention wholly bent on the splendid tropical vegetation about me, I suddenly recognized a sea-breeze, as it came sifting through the palmettos and blooming vine-tangles, which at once awakened and set free a thousand dormant associations, and made me a boy again in Scotland, as if all the intervening years had been annihilated.

Most people like to look at mountain rivers, and bear them in mind; but few care to look at the winds, though far more beautiful and sublime, and though they become at times about as visible as flowing water. When the north winds in winter are making upward sweeps over the curving summits of the High Sierra, the fact is sometimes published with flying snow-banners a mile long. Those portions of the winds thus embodied can scarce be wholly invisible, even to the darkest imagination. And when we look around over an agitated forest, we may see something of the wind that stirs it, by its effects upon the trees. Yonder it descends in a rush of water-like ripples, and sweeps over the bending pines from hill to hill. Nearer, we see detached plumes and leaves, now speeding by on level currents, now whirling in eddies, or, escaping over the edges of the whirls, soaring aloft on grand, upswelling domes of air, or tossing on flame-like crests. Smooth, deep currents, cascades, falls, and swirling eddies, sing around every tree and leaf, and over all the varied topography of the region with telling changes of form, like mountain rivers conforming to the features of their channels.

After tracing the Sierra streams from their fountains to the plains, marking where they bloom white in falls, glide in crystal plumes, surge gray and foam-filled in boulder-choked gorges, and slip through the woods in long, tranquil reaches—after thus learning their language and forms in detail, we may at length hear them chanting all together in one grand anthem, and comprehend them all in clear inner vision, covering the range like lace. But even this spectacle is far less sublime and not a whit more substantial than what we may behold of these storm-streams of air in the mountain woods.

We all travel the milky way together, trees and men; but it never occurred to me until this storm-day, while swinging in the wind, that trees are travelers, in the ordinary sense. They make many journeys, not extensive ones, it is true; but our own little journeys, away and back again, are only little more than tree-wavings—many of them not so much.

When the storm began to abate, I dismounted and sauntered down through the calming woods. The storm-tones died away, and, turning toward the east, I beheld the countless hosts of the forests hushed and tranquil, towering above one another on the slopes of the hills like a devout audience. The setting sun filled them with amber light, and seemed to say, while they listened, "My peace I give unto you."

As I gazed on the impressive scene, all the so-called ruin of the storm was forgotten, and never before did these noble woods appear so fresh, so joyous, so immortal.

—1911

PAM HOUSTON

B. 1962

Pam Houston drew on her experience as a river and hunting guide in writing a best-selling book of short stories while she was still in graduate school. Cowboys Are My Weakness (1992) is a wry look at the war between the sexes as played out by female narrators and a variety of men with outdoor preoccupations. Houston herself is a self-confessed "love junkie" with a taste for outdoor adventure. She has been a first mate/cook on sailboats in the Caribbean and the Great Lakes, a hunting guide in Alaska, and a river guide on the Colorado and the Zambezi in Zimbabwe. Born and raised in New Jersey, Houston graduated from Denison University in Ohio and taught creative writing there before working on a Ph.D. in creative writing at the University of Utah. She has contributed articles to magazines such as Mirabella *and* Mademoiselle, *and edited a collection entitled* Women on Hunting: Essays, Fiction, and Poetry *(1994).*

"When everything in your life is uncertain, there's nothing quite like the clarity and precision of fresh snow and blue sky," proclaims the narrator of "A Blizzard Under Blue Sky." This story is the only one in Cowboys Are My Weakness *that doesn't center on a male-female relationship, although certain problems in her love life are hinted at by the narrator as part of her motivation for going winter camping alone. In its description of how invigorating contact with the natural world can heal psychological and emotional ailments, the story is reminiscent of some of Ernest Hemingway's work.*

A BLIZZARD UNDER BLUE SKY

The doctor said I was clinically depressed. It was February, the month in which depression runs rampant in the inversion-cloaked Salt Lake Valley and the city dwellers escape to Park City, where the snow is fresh and the sun is shining and everybody is happy, except me. In truth, my life was on the verge of more spectacular and satisfying discoveries than I had ever imagined, but of course I couldn't see that far ahead. What I saw was work that wasn't getting done, bills that weren't getting paid, and a man I'd given my heart to weekending in the desert with his ex.

The doctor said, "I can give you drugs."

I said, "No way."

She said, "The machine that drives you is broken. You need something to help you get it fixed."

I said, "Winter camping."

She said, "Whatever floats your boat."

One of the things I love the most about the natural world is the way it gives you what's good for you even if you don't know it at the time. I had never been winter camping before, at least not in the high country, and the weekend I chose to try and fix my machine was the same weekend the air mass they called the Alaska Clipper showed up. It was thirty-two degrees below zero in town on the night I spent in my snow cave. I don't know how cold it was out on Beaver Creek. I had listened to the weather forecast, and to the advice of my housemate, Alex, who was an experienced winter camper.

"I don't know what you think you're going to prove by freezing to death," Alex said, "but if you've got to go, take my bivvy sack; it's warmer than anything you have."

"Thanks," I said.

"If you mix Kool-Aid with your water it won't freeze up," he said, "and don't forget lighting paste for your stove."

"Okay," I said.

"I hope it turns out to be worth it," he said, "because you are going to freeze your butt."

When everything in your life is uncertain, there's nothing quite like the clarity and precision of fresh snow and blue sky. That was the first thought I had on Saturday morning as I stepped away from the warmth of my truck and let my skis slap the snow in front of me. There was no wind and no clouds that morning, just still air and cold sunshine. The hair in my nostrils froze almost immediately. When I took a deep breath, my lungs only filled up halfway.

I opened the tailgate to excited whines and whimpers. I never go skiing without Jackson and Hailey: my two best friends, my yin and yang of dogs. Some of you might know Jackson. He's the oversized sheepdog-and-something-else with the great big nose and the bark that will shatter glass. He gets out and about more than I do. People I've never seen before come by my house daily and call him by name. He's all grace, and he's tireless; he won't go skiing with me unless I let him lead. Hailey is not so graceful, and her body seems in constant indecision when she runs. When we ski she stays behind me, and on the downhills she tries to sneak rides on my skis.

The dogs ran circles in the chest-high snow while I inventoried my backpack one more time to make sure I had everything I needed. My sleeping bag, my Thermarest, my stove, Alex's bivvy sack, matches, lighting paste, flashlight, knife. I brought three pairs of long underwear—tops and bottoms—so I could change once before I went to bed, and once again in the morning, so I wouldn't get chilled by my own sweat. I brought paper and pen, and Kool-Aid to mix with my water. I brought Mountain House chicken stew and some freeze-dried green peas, some peanut butter and honey, lots of dried apricots, coffee and Carnation instant breakfast for morning.

Jackson stood very still while I adjusted his backpack. He carries the dog food and enough water for all of us. He takes himself very seriously when he's got his pack on. He won't step off the trail for any reason, not even to chase rabbits, and he gets nervous and angry if I do. That morning he was impatient with me. "Miles to go, Mom," he said over his shoulder. I snapped my boots into my skis and we were off.

There are not too many good things you can say about temperatures that dip past twenty below zero, except this: They turn the landscape into a crystal palace and they turn your vision into Superman's. In the cold thin morning air the trees and mountains, even the twigs and shadows, seemed to leap out of the background like a 3-D movie, only it was better than 3-D because I could feel the sharpness of the air.

I have a friend in Moab who swears that Utah is the center of the fourth dimension, and although I know he has in mind something much different and more complicated than subzero weather, it was there, on that ice-edged morning, that I felt on the verge of seeing something more than depth perception in the brutal clarity of the morning sun.

As I kicked along the first couple of miles, I noticed the sun crawling higher in the sky and yet the day wasn't really warming, and I wondered if I should have brought another vest, another layer to put between me and the cold night ahead.

It was utterly quiet out there, and what minimal noise we made intruded on the morning like a brass band: the squeaking of my bindings, the slosh of the water in Jackson's pack, the whoosh of nylon, the jangle of dog tags. It was the bass line and percussion to some primal song, and I kept wanting to sing to it, but I didn't know the words.

Jackson and I crested the top of a hill and stopped to wait for Hailey. The trail stretched out as far as we could see into the meadow below us and beyond, a double track and pole plants carving though softer trails of rabbit and deer.

"Nice place," I said to Jackson, and his tail thumped the snow underneath him without sound.

We stopped for lunch near something that looked like it could be a lake in its other life, or maybe just a womb-shaped meadow. I made peanut butter and honey sandwiches for all of us, and we opened the apricots.

"It's fabulous here," I told the dogs. "But so far it's not working."

There had never been anything wrong with my life that a few good days in the wilderness wouldn't cure, but there I sat in the middle of all those crystal-coated trees, all that diamond-studded sunshine, and I didn't feel any better. Apparently clinical depression was not like having a bad day, it wasn't even like having a lot of bad days, it was more like a house of mirrors, it was like being in a room full of one-way glass.

"Come on, Mom," Jackson said. "Ski harder, go faster, climb higher."

Hailey turned her belly to the sun and groaned.

"He's right," I told her. "It's all we can do."

After lunch the sun had moved behind our backs, throwing a whole different light on the path ahead of us. The snow we moved through stopped being simply white and became translucent, hinting at other colors, reflections of blues and purples and grays. I thought of Moby Dick, you know, the whiteness of the whale, where white is really the absence of all color, and whiteness equals truth, and Ahab's search is finally futile, as he finds nothing but his own reflection.

"Put your mind where your skis are," Jackson said, and we made considerably better time after that.

The sun was getting quite low in the sky when I asked Jackson if he thought we should stop to build the snow cave, and he said he'd look for the next good bank. About one hundred yards down the trail we found it, a gentle slope with eastern exposure that didn't look like it would cave in under any circumstances. Jackson started to dig first.

Let me make one thing clear. I knew only slightly more about building snow caves than Jackson, having never built one, and all my knowledge coming from disaster tales of winter camping fatalities. I knew several things *not* to do when building a snow cave, but I was having a hard time knowing what exactly to do. But Jackson helped, and Hailey supervised, and before too long we had a little cave built, just big enough for three. We ate dinner quite pleased with our accomplishments and set the bivvy sack up inside the cave just as the sun slipped away and dusk came over Beaver Creek.

The temperature, which hadn't exactly soared during the day, dropped twenty degrees in as many minutes, and suddenly it didn't seem like such a great idea to change my long underwear. The original plan was to sleep with the dogs inside the bivvy sack but outside the sleeping bag, which was okay with Jackson the super-metabolizer, but not so with Hailey, the couch potato. She whined and wriggled and managed to stuff her entire fat body down inside my mummy bag, and Jackson stretched out full-length on top.

One of the unfortunate things about winter camping is that it has to happen when the days are so short. Fourteen hours is a long time to lie in a snow cave under the most perfect of circumstances. And when it's thirty-two below, or forty, fourteen hours seems like weeks.

I wish I could tell you I dropped right off to sleep. In truth, fear crept into my spine with the cold and I never closed my eyes. Cuddled there, amid my dogs and water bottles, I spent half of the night chastising myself for thinking I was Wonder Woman, not only risking my own life but the lives of my dogs, and the other half trying to keep the numbness in my feet from crawling up to my knees. When I did doze off, which was actually more like blacking out than dozing off, I'd come back to my senses wondering if I had frozen to death, but the alternating pain and numbness that started in my extremities and worked its way into my bones convinced me I must still be alive.

It was a clear night, and every now and again I would poke my head out of its nest of down and nylon to watch the progress of the moon across the sky. There is no doubt that it was the longest and most uncomfortable night of my life.

But then the sky began to get gray, and then it began to get pink, and before too long the sun was on my bivvy sack, not warm, exactly, but holding the promise of warmth later in the day. And I ate apricots and drank Kool-Aid-flavored coffee and celebrated the rebirth of my fingers and toes, and the survival of many more important parts of my body. I sang "Rocky Mountain High" and "If I Had a Hammer," and yodeled and whistled, and even danced the two-step with Jackson and let him lick my face. And when Hailey finally emerged from the sleeping bag a full hour after I did, we shared a peanut butter and honey sandwich and she said nothing ever tasted so good.

We broke camp and packed up and kicked in the snow cave with something resembling glee.

I was five miles down the trail before I realized what had happened. Not once in that fourteen-hour night did I think about deadlines, or bills, or the man in the desert. For the first time in many months I was happy to see a day beginning. The morning sunshine was like a present from the gods. What really happened, of course, is that I remembered about joy.

I know that one night out at thirty-two below doesn't sound like much to those of you who have climbed Everest or run the Iditarod or kayaked to Antarctica, and I won't try to convince you that my life was like the movies where depression goes away in one weekend, and all of life's problems vanish with a moment's clear sight. The simple truth of the matter is this: On Sunday I had a glimpse outside of the house of mirrors, on Saturday I couldn't have seen my way out of a paper bag. And while I was skiing back toward the truck that morning, a wind came up behind us and swirled the snow around our bodies like a blizzard under blue sky. And I was struck by the simple perfection of the snowflakes, and startled by the hopefulness of sun on frozen trees.

—1992

WALLACE STEVENS
1879-1955

Long regarded as one of the most abstract and difficult of the high modernist poets, Wallace Stevens would seem to have little in common with his contemporary Robert Frost. As a lawyer at several different New York law firms and later as an insurance company vice-president in urban Hartford, Connecticut, Stevens lived a life far removed from the earthy reality of a New England farm. Yet his work, like Frost's, often employs nature imagery and reveals a deep familiarity with the wildlands of the human mind. Stevens's Collected Poems *(1954), for which he posthumously won the Pulitzer Prize for poetry in 1955, serves as a field guide to the nature of human perception.*

From outward appearances, Stevens led a rather ordinary life, even a dull one, albeit privileged. He was born in Reading, Pennsylvania, attended Harvard University, and, at the direction of his lawyer father, received his law degree from New York University Law School. He was married in 1909 and remained so for the rest of his life. He and his wife had one child, a daughter, who later became an editor of her father's work. Where then did the compelling intensity of his poetry come from? The impulse seems to be primarily religious, but not in the institutional sense of the word. Although Stevens was raised in a conservative Christian household, by the time he reached adulthood he placed his faith in a "Supreme Fiction"—his way of referring to the writing and reading of poetry. For sharing this insight, Stevens was accused by some readers of heresy and by others of atheism, but Stevens himself—in a letter composed near the end of his life—had this to say: "I am not an atheist, although I do not believe in the same God in whom I believed when I was a boy."

Thus, his poetry may represent Stevens's attempt to come to terms with his understanding of God. This quest often takes the form of an inquiry into human perception, in which the refinement of perception is regarded as a spiritual discipline or practice. In this widened vision, nature is recognized as being vastly greater than the self. The poem that follows is characteristic; it instructs the reader in how to cultivate a more ample perception of the natural world. Of this poem Stevens wrote, "I shall explain 'The Snow Man' as an example of the necessity of identifying oneself with reality in order to understand it and enjoy it."

THE SNOW MAN

One must have a mind of winter
To regard the frost and the boughs
Of the pine-trees crusted with snow;

And have been cold a long time
To behold the junipers shagged with ice,
The spruces rough in the distant glitter

Of the January sun; and not to think
Of any misery in the sound of the wind,
In the sound of a few leaves,

Which is the sound of the land
Full of the same wind
That is blowing in the same bare place

For the listener, who listens in the snow,
And, nothing himself, beholds
Nothing that is not there and the nothing that is.

—1954

SIMON J. ORTIZ

B. 1941

In the introduction to his 1992 poetry collection, Woven Stone, Simon J. Ortiz reflects that what he does as a writer, teacher, and storyteller is to demystify language. "Making language familiar and accessible to others, bringing it within their grasp and comprehension, is what a writer, teacher,

and storyteller does or tries to do. I've been trying for over thirty years."
Whether he is demystifying the American language in a talk before a group
of Laguna Pueblo children or demystifying the language of his own native
community of Acoma Pueblo in New Mexico for English-speaking readers,
Ortiz communicates in a voice akin to the Native American oral tradition.
His fiction and poetry illuminate the trials and solaces of everyday life,
including the relation between human beings and the natural world.

Ortiz was born in Albuquerque and has spent much of his life in the
Southwest; he currently lives in Tucson, Arizona. He attended Fort Lewis
College, the University of New Mexico, and the University of Iowa, although he
never completed a degree. The author and editor of more than fifteen books,
Ortiz is widely regarded as one of the finest contemporary Native American
writers. He launched his literary career with the publication of Naked in the
Wind, *a book of poetry, in 1971. Since then he has published such poetry col-*
lections as Going for the Rain *(1976),* A Good Journey *(1977), and* Fight Back:
For the Sake of the People, For the Sake of the Land *(1980). His books of fic-*
tion include Howbah Indians *(1978) and* Fightin': New and Collected Stories
(1983). Ortiz also edited the well-known anthology of Native American short
fiction Earth Power Coming *(1983). Although he has supported himself pri-*
marily as a writer, he has taught at numerous colleges and universities.

The following poem, "Forever," appeared in Ortiz's 1994 collection,
After and Before the Lightning, *a work devoted largely to his encounter*
with the Great Plains while teaching at Sinte Gleska College in South Dakota
during 1985 and 1986. But "Forever" is obviously a poem about memory
and place of origin—about the imprint of the land as the poet sits in South
Dakota and looks with his mind's eye at the mesa to the south of his home-
town in New Mexico. In a life fraught with struggle and transience—fre-
quent geographical moves, divorce, financial insecurity—the snow-covered
mesa serves as an image of stability. Ortiz directs himself, in the poem's
final line, to "look right now." Implicitly, he is instructing readers to seek
refuge in their own mesas, snowfields, stones, and junipers of memory.

FOREVER

At Deetseyaamah, I liked looking south
at the mesa above "the white bridge"
that was always about to fall down
when I was a boy but it never did.
In March, snow was still on the mesa
even when it had melted everywhere else
since the snow was on the north slope.
I don't know, I just liked looking at it
because I could see stones and junipers
and snow always there like forever.
Of course, snow lasted for only a while
but that was enough, enough to stay
in my mind forever, like it is right now.

Look right now. It is a view of snow.

—1994

JACK KEROUAC

1922-1969

Best known as avatar of the Beat Generation and author of such autobiographical novels as On the Road *(1957) and* The Dharma Bums *(1958), Jack Kerouac has never wanted for readers nor escaped the swirl of controversy. Yet, among the vast legions of Kerouac devotees and defamers, what has been all but ignored is the keen and sensitive eye this writer had for the natural world. His sensibility—perhaps best described as devotional, in the spiritual meaning of the word—did not express itself in the form of natural history and philosophy, as did Henry David Thoreau's. Rather, it expressed itself in autobiographical prose charged with an emotional lyricism as intense as that found in Emily Dickinson's poetry but far more personally revealing. Kerouac paid a high price for this emotional candor, succumbing to the pressures of fame and dying of alcoholism at the relatively young age of forty-six.*

Born Jean Louis Lebris de Kerouac in the mill town of Lowell, Massachusetts, he was of French-Canadian descent and spoke only French at home. One of the most linguistically facile and playful writers in American literature, Kerouac did not begin to learn English until he started attending school; he still had a noticeable accent in high school. A football scholarship sent him to Columbia University, where he befriended that other guiding light of the Beats, Allen Ginsberg. Although Kerouac was born, raised, and died a Roman Catholic, he was always a spiritual questor, and his spiritual journeying brought him for a time to intense study of Buddhism. In the mid-1950s, an important literary confluence occurred when Kerouac and Ginsberg migrated to the San Francisco Bay Area and there met fellow writers Kenneth Rexroth and Gary Snyder. Snyder—who was himself already embarked on a Buddhist path—awakened Kerouac to the spiritual potential of the West Coast with its wild and seemingly endless mountains and rivers. The effects of this influence can be gleaned in The Dharma Bums, *in many ways Kerouac's most joyful book.*

"Alone on a Mountaintop" recounts a key experience in Kerouac's life: his only extended withdrawal from people. Kerouac had a deeply divided personality: he was very much a social creature, but he was also a sort of hermit who constantly vacillated between gloom and glory in his heart. It was the hermit in him who declared, "I needed solitude . . . I just wanted to lie in the grass and look at the clouds." The two months he spent alone on top of 6,000-foot Desolation Peak in Washington's rugged North Cascades were clearly important to him, as he rendered this episode in three different versions: at the end of The Dharma Bums, *at the beginning of* Desolation Angels *(1965), and here in this travel essay, which originally appeared in* Holiday *magazine in 1958 and later in the book* Lonesome Traveler *(1960).*

ALONE ON A MOUNTAINTOP

After all this kind of fanfare, and even more, I came to a point where I needed solitude and just stop the machine of "thinking" and "enjoying" what they call "living," I just wanted to lie in the grass and look at the clouds—

They say, too, in ancient scripture:—"Wisdom can only be obtained from the viewpoint of solitude."

And anyway I was sick and tired of all the ships and railroads and Times Squares of all time—

I applied with the U.S. Agriculture Department for a job as a fire lookout in the Mount Baker National Forest in the High Cascades of the Great Northwest.

Just to look at these words made me shiver to think of cool pine trees by a morning lake.

I beat my way out to Seattle three thousand miles from the heat and dust of eastern cities in June.

Anybody who's been to Seattle and missed Alaskan Way, the old water front, has missed the point—here the totem-pole stores, the waters of Puget Sound washing under old piers, the dark gloomy look of ancient warehouses and pier sheds, and the most antique locomotives in America switching boxcars up and down the water front, give a hint, under the pure cloud-mopped sparkling skies of the Northwest, of great country to come. Driving north from Seattle on Highway 99 is an exciting experience because suddenly you see the Cascade Mountains rising on the northeast horizon, truly *Komo Kulshan* under their uncountable snows. —The great peaks covered with trackless white, worlds of huge rock twisted and heaped and sometimes almost spiraled into fantastic unbelievable shapes.

All this is seen far above the dreaming fields of the Stilaquamish and Skagit valleys, agricultural flats of peaceful green, the soil so rich and dark it is proudly referred to by inhabitants as second only to the Nile in fertility. At Milltown Washington your car rolls over the bridge across the Skagit River. —To the left—seaward, westward—the Skagit flows into Skagit Bay and the Pacific Ocean. —At Burlington you turn right and head for the heart of the mountains along a rural valley road through sleepy little towns and one bustling agricultural market center known as Sedro-Woolley with hundreds of cars parked aslant on a typical country-town Main Street of hardware stores, grain-and-feed stores and five-and-tens. —On deeper into the deepening valley, cliffs rich with timber appearing by the side of the road, the narrowing river rushing more swiftly now, a pure translucent green like the green of the ocean on a cloudy day but a saltless rush of melted snow from the High Cascades—almost good enough to drink north of Marblemount. —The road curves more and more till you reach Concrete, the last town in Skagit Valley with a bank and a five-and-ten—after that the mountains rising secretly behind foothills are so close that now you don't see them but begin to feel them more and more.

At Marblemount the river is a swift torrent, the work of the quiet mountains. —Fallen logs beside the water provide good seats to enjoy a river wonderland, leaves jiggling in the good clean northwest wind seem to rejoice, the topmost trees on nearby timbered peaks swept and dimmed by low-flying clouds seem contented. —The clouds assume the faces of hermits or of nuns, or sometimes look like sad dog acts hurrying off into the wings over the horizon. —Snags struggle and gurgle in the heaving bulk of the river. —Logs rush by at twenty miles an hour. The air smells of pine and sawdust and bark and mud and twigs—birds flash over the water looking for secret fish.

As you drive north across the bridge at Marblemount and on to Newhalem the road narrows and twists until finally the Skagit is seen pouring over rocks, frothing, and small creeks come tumbling from steep hillsides and pile right in. —The mountains rise on all sides, only their shoulders and ribs visible, their heads out of sight and now snowcapped.

At Newhalem extensive road construction raises a cloud of dust over shacks and cats and rigs, the dam there is the first in a series that create the Skagit watershed which provides all the power for Seattle.

The road ends at Diablo, a peaceful company settlement of neat cottages and green lawns surrounded by close packed peaks named Pyramid and Colonial and Davis. —Here a huge lift takes you one thousand feet up to the level of Diablo Lake and Diablo Dam. —Over the dam pours a jet roar of water through which a stray log could go shooting out like a toothpick in a one-thousand-foot arc. —Here for the first time you're high enough really to begin to see the Cascades. Dazzles of light to the north show where Ross Lake sweeps back all the way to Canada, opening a view of the Mt. Baker National Forest as spectacular as any vista in the Colorado Rockies.

The Seattle City Light and Power boat leaves on regular schedule from a little pier near Diablo Dam and heads north between steep timbered rocky cliffs toward Ross Dam, about half an hour's ride. The passengers are power employees, hunters and fishermen and forestry workers. Below Ross Dam the footwork begins—you must climb a rocky trail one thousand feet to the level of the dam. Here the vast lake opens out, disclosing small resort floats offering rooms and boats for vacationists, and just beyond, the floats of the U.S. Forestry Service. From this point on, if you're lucky enough to be a rich man or a forest-fire lookout, you can get packed into the North Cascade Primitive Area by horse and mule and spend a summer of complete solitude.

I was a fire lookout, and after two nights of trying to sleep in the boom and slap of the Forest Service floats, they came for me one rainy morning—a powerful tugboat lashed to a large corral float bearing four mules and three horses, my own groceries, feed, batteries and equipment. —The muleskinner's name was Andy and he wore the same old floppy cowboy hat he'd worn in Wyoming twenty years ago. "Well, boy, now we're gonna put you away where we cant reach ya—you better get ready."

"It's just what I want, Andy, be alone for three solid months nobody to bother me."

"It's what you're sayin' now but you'll change your tune after a week."

I didn't believe him. —I was looking forward to an experience men seldom earn in this modern world: complete and comfortable solitude in the wilderness, day and night, sixty-three days and nights to be exact. We had no idea how much snow had fallen on my mountain during the winter and Andy said: "If there didnt it means you gotta hike two miles down that hard trail every day or every other day with two buckets, boy. I aint envyin' you—I been back there. And one day it's gonna be hot and you're about ready to broil, and bugs you cant even count 'em, and next day a li'l' ole summer blizzard come hit you around the corner of Hozomeen which sits right there near Canada in your back yard and you wont be able to stick logs fast enough in that potbelly stove of yours." —But I had a full rucksack loaded with turtleneck sweaters and warm shirts and pants and long wool socks bought on the Seattle water front, and gloves and an earmuff cap, and lots of instant soup and coffee in my grub list.

"Shoulda brought yourself a quart of brandy, boy," says Andy shaking his head as the tug pushed our corral float up Ross Lake through the log gate and around to the left dead north underneath the immense rain shroud of Sourdough Mountain and Ruby Mountain.

"Where's Desolation Peak?" I asked, meaning my own mountain (*A mountain to be kept forever,* I'd dreamed all that spring) (O lonesome traveler!)

"You ain't gonna see it today till we're practically on top it and by that time you'll be so soakin' wet you wont care."

Assistant Ranger Marty Gohlke of Marblemount Ranger Station was with us too, also giving me tips and instructions. Nobody seemed to envy Desolation Peak except me. After two hours pushing through the storming waves of the long rainy lake with dreary misty timber rising steeply on both sides and the mules and horses chomping on their feedbags patient in the downpour, we arrived at the foot of Desolation Trail and the tugman (who'd been providing us with good hot coffee in the pilot cabin) eased her over and settled the float against a steep muddy slope full of bushes and fallen trees. —The mule-skinner whacked the first mule and she lurched ahead with her double-sided pack of batteries and canned goods, hit the mud with forehoofs, scrambled, slipped, almost fell back in the lake and finally gave one mighty heave and went skittering out of sight in the fog to wait on the trail for the other mules and her master. —We all got off, cut the barge loose, waved to the tugman, mounted our horses and started up a sad and dripping party in heavy rain.

At first the trail, always steeply rising, was so dense with shrubbery we kept getting shower after shower from overhead and against our out-saddled knees. —The trail was deep with round rocks that kept causing the animals to slip. —At one point a great fallen tree made it impossible to go on until Old Andy and Marty went ahead with axes and cleared a short cut around the tree, sweating and cursing and hacking as I watched the animals. —By-and-by they were ready but the mules were afraid of the rough steepness of the short cut and had to be prodded through with sticks. —Soon the trail reached alpine meadows powdered with blue lupine everywhere in the drenching mists, and with little red poppies, tiny-budded flowers as delicate as designs on a small Japanese teacup. —Now the trail zigzagged widely back and forth up the high meadow. —Soon we saw the vast foggy heap of a rock-cliff face above and Andy yelled "Soon's we get up high as that we're almost there but that's another two thousand feet though you think you could reach up and touch it!"

I unfolded my nylon poncho and draped it over my head, and, drying a little, or, rather, ceasing to drip, I walked alongside the horse to warm my blood and began to feel better. But the other boys just rode along with their heads bowed in the rain. As for altitude all I could tell was from some occasional frightening spots on the trail where we could look down on distant treetops.

The alpine meadow reached to timber line and suddenly a great wind blew shafts of sleet on us. —"Gettin' near the top now!" yelled Andy—and suddenly there was snow on the trail, the horses were clumping through a foot of slush and mud, and to the left and right everything was blinding white in the gray fog. —"About five and a half thousand feet right now" said Andy rolling a cigarette as he rode in the rain. — We went down, then up another spell, down again, a slow gradual climb, and then Andy yelled "There she is!" and up ahead in the mountaintop gloom I saw a little shadowy peaked shack standing alone on the top of the world and gulped with fear.

"This my home all summer? And *this* is summer?"

The inside of the shack was even more miserable, damp and dirty, leftover groceries and magazines torn to shreds by rats and mice, the floor muddy, the windows impenetrable. —But hardy Old Andy who'd been through this kind of thing all his life got a roaring fire crackling in the potbelly stove and had me lay out a pot of water with almost half a can of coffee in it saying "Coffee aint no good 'less it's *strong!*" and pretty soon the coffee was boiling a nice brown aromatic foam and we got our cups out and drank deep. —

Meanwhile I'd gone out on the roof with Marty and removed the bucket from the chimney and put up the weather pole with the anemometer and done a few other chores—when we came back in Andy was frying Spam and eggs in a huge pan and it was almost like a party. —Outside, the patient animals chomped on their supper bags and were glad to rest by the old corral fence built of logs by some Desolation lookout of the Thirties.

Darkness came, incomprehensible.

In the gray morning after they'd slept in sleeping bags on the floor and I on the only bunk in my mummy bag, Andy and Marty left, laughing, saying, "Well, whatayou think now hey? We been here twelve hours and you still aint been able to see more than twelve feet!"

"By gosh that's right, what am I going to do for watching fires?"

"Dont worry boy, these clouds'll roll away and you'll be able to see a hunnerd miles in every direction."

I didn't believe it and I felt miserable and spent the day trying to clean up the shack or pacing twenty careful feet each way in my "yard" (the ends of which appeared to be sheer drops into silent gorges), and I went to bed early. —About bedtime I saw my first star, briefly, then giant phantom clouds billowed all around me and the star was gone. —But in that instant I thought I'd seen a mile-down maw of grayblack lake where Andy and Marty were back in the Forest Service boat which had met them at noon.

In the middle of the night I woke up suddenly and my hair was standing on end—I saw a huge black shadow in my window. —Then I saw that it had a star above it, and realized that this was Mt. Hozomeen (8080 feet) looking in my window from miles away near Canada. —I got up from the forlorn bunk with the mice scattering underneath and went outside and gasped to see black mountain shapes gianting all around, and not only that but the billowing curtains of the northern lights shifting behind the clouds. —It was a little too much for a city boy—the fear that the Abominable Snowman might be breathing behind me in the dark sent me back to bed where I buried my head inside my sleeping bag. —

But in the morning—Sunday, July sixth—I was amazed and overjoyed to see a clear blue sunny sky and down below, like a radiant pure snow sea, the clouds making a marshmallow cover for all the world and all the lake while I abided in warm sunshine among hundreds of miles of snow-white peaks. —I brewed coffee and sang and drank a cup on my drowsy warm doorstep.

At noon the clouds vanished and the lake appeared below, beautiful beyond belief, a perfect blue pool twenty five miles long and more, and the creeks like toy creeks and the timber green and fresh everywhere below and even the joyous little unfolding liquid tracks of vacationists' fishingboats on the lake and in the lagoons. —A perfect afternoon of sun, and behind the shack I discovered a snowfield big enough to provide me with buckets of cold water till late September.

My job was to watch for fires. One night a terrific lightning storm made a dry run across the Mt. Baker National Forest without any rainfall. —When I saw that ominous black cloud flashing wrathfully toward me I shut off the radio and laid the aerial on the ground and waited for the worst. —Hiss! hiss! said the wind, bringing dust and lightning nearer. —Tick! said the lightning rod, receiving a strand of electricity from a strike on nearby Skagit Peak. —Hiss! tick! and in my bed I felt the earth move. —Fifteen miles to the south, just east of Ruby Peak and somewhere near Panther Creek, a large fire raged, a huge orange spot. —At ten o'clock lightning hit it again and it flared up dangerously.

I was supposed to note the general area of lightning strikes. —By midnight I'd been staring so intently out the dark window I got hallucinations of fires everywhere, three of them right in Lightning Creek, phosphorescent orange verticals of ghost fire that seemed to come and go.

In the morning, there at 177° 16' where I'd seen the big fire was a strange brown patch in the snowy rock showing where the fire had raged and sputtered out in the all-night rain that followed the lightning. But the result of this storm was disastrous fifteen miles away at McAllister Creek where a great blaze had outlasted the rain and exploded the following afternoon in a cloud that could be seen from Seattle. I felt sorry for the fellows who had to fight these fires, the smoke-jumpers who parachuted down on them out of planes and the trail crews who hiked to them, climbing and scrambling over slippery rocks and scree slopes, arriving sweaty and exhausted only to face the wall of heat when they got there. As a lookout I had it pretty easy and only had to concentrate on reporting the exact location (by instrument findings) of every blaze I detected.

Most days, though, it was the routine that occupied me. —Up at seven or so every day, a pot of coffee brought to a boil over a handful of burning twigs, I'd go out in the alpine yard with a cup of coffee hooked in my thumb and leisurely make my wind speed and wind direction and temperature and moisture readings—then, after chopping wood, I'd use the two-way radio and report to the relay station on Sourdough. —At 10 A.M. I usually got hungry for breakfast, and I'd make delicious pancakes, eating them at my little table that was decorated with bouquets of mountain lupine and sprigs of fir.

Early in the afternoon was the usual time for my kick of the day, instant chocolate pudding with hot coffee. —Around two or three I'd lie on my back on the meadowside and watch the clouds float by, or pick blueberries and eat them right there. The radio was on loud enough to hear any calls for Desolation.

Then at sunset I'd roust up my supper out of cans of yams and Spam and peas, or sometimes just pea soup with corn muffins baked on top of the wood stove in aluminum foil. —Then I'd go out to that precipitous snow slope and shovel my two pails of snow for the water tub and gather an armful of fallen firewood from the hillside like the proverbial Old Woman of Japan. —For the chipmunks and conies I put pans of leftovers under the shack, in the middle of the night I could hear them clanking around. The rat would scramble down from the attic and eat some too.

Sometimes I'd yell questions at the rocks and trees, and across gorges, or yodel—"What is the meaning of the void?" The answer was perfect silence, so I knew. —

Before bedtime I'd read by kerosene lamp whatever books were in the shack. —It's amazing how people in solitary hunger after books. —After poring over every word of a medical tome, and the synopsized versions of Shakespeare's plays by Charles and Mary Lamb, I climbed up in the little attic and put together torn cowboy pocket books and magazines the mice had ravaged—I also played stud poker with three imaginary players.

Around bedtime I'd bring a cup of milk almost to a boil with a tablespoon of honey in it, and drink that for my lamby nightcap, then I'd curl up in my sleeping bag.

No man should go through life without once experiencing healthy, even bored solitude in the wilderness, finding himself depending solely on himself and thereby learning his true and hidden strength. —Learning, for instance, to eat when he's hungry and sleep when he's sleepy.

Also around bedtime was my singing time. I'd pace up and down the well-worn path in the dust of my rock singing all the show tunes I could remember, at the top of my voice too, with nobody to hear except the deer and the bear.

In the red dusk, the mountains were symphonies in pink snow—Jack Mountain, Three Fools Peak, Freezeout Peak, Golden Horn, Mt. Terror, Mt. Fury, Mt. Despair, Crooked Thumb Peak, Mt. Challenger and the incomparable Mt. Baker bigger than the world in the distance—and my own little Jackass Ridge that completed the Ridge of Desolation. —Pink snow and the clouds all distant and frilly like ancient remote cities of Buddhaland splendor, and the wind working incessantly—whish, whish— booming, at times rattling my shack.

For supper I made chop suey and baked some biscuits and put the leftovers in a pan for deer that came in the moonlit night and nibbled like big strange cows of peace—long-antlered buck and does and babies too—as I meditated in the alpine grass facing the magic moon-laned lake. —And I could see firs reflected in the moonlit lake five thousand feet below, upside down, pointing to infinity. —

And all the insects ceased in honor of the moon.

Sixty-three sunsets I saw revolve on that perpendicular hill—mad raging sunsets pouring in sea foams of cloud through unimaginable crags like the crags you grayly drew in pencil as a child, with every rose-tint of hope beyond, making you feel just like them, brilliant and bleak beyond words. —

Cold mornings with clouds billowing out of Lightning Gorge like smoke from a giant fire but the lake cerulean as ever.

August comes in with a blast that shakes your house and augurs little Augusticity—then that snowy-air and woodsmoke feeling—then the snow comes sweeping your way from Canada, and the wind rises and dark low clouds rush up as out of a forge. Suddenly a green-rose rainbow appears right on your ridge with steamy clouds all around and an orange sun turmoiling . . .

> What is a rainbow,
> Lord? —a hoop
> For the lowly

. . . and you go out and suddenly your shadow is ringed by the rainbow as you walk on the hilltop, a lovely haloed mystery making you want to pray. —

A blade of grass jiggling in the winds of infinity, anchored to a rock, and for your own poor gentle flesh no answer.

Your oil lamp burning in infinity.

One morning I found bear stool and signs of where the monster had taken a can of frozen milk and squeezed it in his paws and bit into it with one sharp tooth trying to suck out the paste. —In the foggy dawn I looked down the mysterious Ridge of Starvation with its fog-lost firs and its hills humping into invisibility, and the wind blowing the fog by like a faint blizzard and I realized that somewhere in the fog stalked the bear.

And it seemed as I sat there that this was the Primordial Bear, and that he owned all the Northwest and all the snow and commanded all the mountains. —He was King Bear, who could crush my head in his paws and crack my spine like a stick and this was his house, his yard, his domain. —Though I looked all day, he would not show himself in the mystery of those silent foggy slopes—he prowled at night among unknown lakes, and in the early morning the pearl-pure light that shadowed mountainsides of fir made him blink with respect. —He had millenniums of prowling here behind him, he had seen the Indians and Redcoats come and go, and would see much more. —He continuously heard the reassuring rapturous rush of silence, except when near creeks, he was aware of the light material the world is made of, yet he never discoursed, nor communicated by signs, nor wasted a breath complaining—he just nibbled and pawed and lumbered along snags paying no attention to things inanimate or animate. —His big mouth chew-chewed in the night, I could hear it across the mountain in the starlight. —Soon he would come out of the fog, huge, and come and stare in my window with big burning eyes. —He was Avalokitesvara the Bear, and his sign was the gray wind of autumn. —

I was waiting for him. He never came.

Finally the autumn rains, all-night gales of soaking rain as I lie warm as toast in my sleeping bag and the mornings open cold wild fall days with high wind, racing fogs, racing clouds, sudden bright sun, pristine light on hill patches and my fire crackling as I exult and sing at the top of my voice. —Outside my window a wind-swept chipmunk sits up straight on a rock, hands clasped he nibbles an oat between his paws—the little nutty lord of all he surveys.

Thinking of the stars night after night I begin to realize "The stars are words" and all the innumerable worlds in the Milky Way are words, and so is this world too. And I realize that no matter where I am, whether in a little room full of thought, or in this endless universe of stars and mountains, it's all in my mind. There's no need for solitude. So love life for what it is, and form no preconceptions whatever in your mind.

What strange sweet thoughts come to you in the mountain solitudes! —One night I realized that when you give people understanding and encouragement a funny little meek childish look abashes their eyes, no matter what they've been doing they weren't sure it was right—lambies all over the world.

For when you realize that God is Everything you know that you've got to love everything no matter how bad it is, in the ultimate sense it was neither good nor bad (consider the dust), it was just *what was,* that is, what was made to appear. —Some kind of drama to teach something to something, some "despiséd substance of divinest show."

And I realized I didnt have to hide myself in desolation but could accept society for better or for worse, like a wife—I saw that if it wasnt for the six senses, of seeing, hearing, smelling, touching, tasting and thinking, the self of that, which is nonexistent, there would be no phenomena to perceive at all, in fact no six senses or self. —The fear of extinction is much worse than extinction (death) itself. —To chase after extinction in the old Nirvanic sense of Buddhism is ultimately silly, as the dead indicate in the silence of their blissful sleep in Mother Earth which is an Angel hanging in orbit in Heaven anyway. —

I just lay on the mountain meadowside in the moonlight, head to grass, and heard the silent recognition of my temporary woes. —Yes, so to try to *attain* to Nirvana when you're already there, to attain to the top of a mountain when you're already there and only have to stay—thus, to *stay* in the Nirvana Bliss, is all I have to do, you have to do, no effort, no path really, no discipline but just to know that all is empty and awake, a Vision and a Movie in God's Universal Mind *(Alaya-Vijnana)* and to stay more or less wisely in that. —Because silence itself is the sound of diamonds which can cut through anything, the sound of Holy Emptiness, the sound of extinction and bliss, that graveyard silence which is like the silence of an infant's smile, the sound of eternity, of the blessedness surely to be believed, the sound of nothing-ever-happened-except-God (which I'd soon hear in a noisy Atlantic tempest). —What exists is God in His Emanation, what does not exist is God in His peaceful Neutrality, what neither exists nor does not exist is God's immortal primordial dawn of Father Sky (this world this very minute). —So I said:—"Stay in that, no dimensions here to any of the mountains or mosquitos and whole milky ways of worlds—" Because sensation is emptiness, old age is emptiness. —'T's only the Golden Eternity of God's Mind so practise kindness and sympathy, remember that men are *not responsible in themselves as men* for their ignorance and unkindness, they should be pitied, God does pity it, because who says anything about anything since everything is just what it is, free of interpretations. —God is not the "attainer," he is the "farer" in that which everything is, the "abider"—one caterpillar, a thousand hairs of God. —So know constantly that this is only you, God, empty and awake and eternally free as the unnumerable atoms of emptiness everywhere. —

I decided that when I would go back to the world down there I'd try to keep my mind clear in the midst of murky human ideas smoking like factories on the horizon through which I would walk, forward . . .

When I came down in September a cool old golden look had come into the forest, auguring cold snaps and frost and the eventual howling blizzard that would cover my shack completely, unless those winds at the top of the world would keep her bald. As I reached the bend in the trail where the shack would disappear and I would plunge down to the lake to meet the boat that would take me out and home, I turned and blessed Desolation Peak and the little pagoda on top and thanked them for the shelter and the lesson I'd been taught.

—1968

BARBARA KINGSOLVER

B. 1955

The fiction, poems, and essays of Barbara Kingsolver grow out of her early social and environmental activism and reflect her stated desire to change the world. She has said that the central idea behind the themes in her writing is that of "seeing ourselves as part of something larger," and that the issues she explores "are all aberrations that stem from a central disease of failing to respect the world and our place in it." Her first nationally published writing was a journalistic account of a strike against the Phelps Dodge Copper Corporation in Arizona, which later grew into a book,

Holding the Line: Women in the Great Arizona Mine Strike of 1983 *(1989).*
The heroism of common people and everyday lives is at the center of her
novels Animal Dreams *(1990),* The Bean Trees *(1992), and* Pigs in Heaven
(1993).

The daughter of a doctor who would accept home-grown vegetables
from patients too poor to pay in cash, Kingsolver was born in Annapolis,
Maryland, and grew up in Nicholas County, Kentucky, a rural area where
most people earned a subsistence income by farming. She attended DePauw
University in Indiana on a music scholarship but changed her major to biol-
ogy when she decided it would be more likely to get her a job. After gradu-
ation she traveled in Europe before settling in Tucson, Arizona, where she
was eventually a neighbor to Edward Abbey. Kingsolver earned an M.S. in
biology and ecology at the University of Arizona before taking a job as a
technical writer at the university's Office of Arid Land Studies. She subse-
quently worked on free-lance writing assignments during the day and con-
centrated on her own fiction and nonfiction at night, including writing
materials to promote human rights and environmental causes, until her
success enabled her to pursue her own writing full-time.

"The Memory Place," from High Tide in Tucson: Essays from Now or
Never *(1995), recounts a visit to a Nature Conservancy preserve in Kentucky*
that reminds Kingsolver of the landscape that imprinted her in childhood.
"Much of what I know about life, and almost everything I believe about the
way I want to live, was formed in those woods," she muses. The essay
expresses dismay over the degradation—created by abandoned strip mines,
herbicide and pesticide use, and pickup trucks—of a creek that provides
habitat for endangered species of mussels. What accounts for the "failure of
love for the land" that Kingsolver sees at Horse Lick Creek? It could be that,
as Kingsolver asserts in a February 1996 interview in The Progressive,
"urban life is a big part of the problem. If people could just get out and look.
And just sit still and be."

THE MEMORY PLACE

This is the kind of April morning no other month can touch: a world tinted in
watercolor pastels of redbud, dogtooth violet, and gentle rain. The trees are beginning to shrug off winter; the dark, leggy maple woods are shot through with gleaming constellations of white dogwood blossoms. The road winds through deep forest
near Cumberland Falls, Kentucky, carrying us across the Cumberland Plateau
toward Horse Lick Creek. Camille is quiet beside me in the front seat, until at last
she sighs and says, with a child's poetic logic, "This reminds me of the place I always
like to think about."

Me too, I tell her. It's the exact truth. I grew up roaming wooded hollows like
these, though they were more hemmed-in, keeping their secrets between the
wide-open cattle pastures and tobacco fields of Nicholas County, Kentucky. My
brother and sister and I would hoist cane fishing poles over our shoulders, as if we
intended to make ourselves useful, and head out to spend a Saturday doing nothing
of the kind. We haunted places we called the Crawdad Creek, the Downy Woods (for
downy woodpeckers and also for milkweed fluff), and—thrillingly, because we'd once

found big bones there—Dead Horse Draw. We caught crawfish with nothing but patience and our hands, boiled them with wild onions over a campfire, and ate them and declared them the best food on earth. We collected banana-scented pawpaw fruits, and were tempted by fleshy, fawn-colored mushrooms but left those alone. We watched birds whose names we didn't know build nests in trees whose names we generally did. We witnessed the unfurling of hickory and oak and maple leaves in the springtime, so tender as to appear nearly edible; we collected them and pressed them with a hot iron under waxed paper when they blushed and dropped in the fall. Then we waited again for spring, even more impatiently than we waited for Christmas, because its gifts were more abundant, needed no batteries, and somehow seemed more exclusively *ours*. I can't imagine that any discovery I ever make, in the rest of my life, will give me the same electric thrill I felt when I first found little righteous Jack in his crimson-curtained pulpit poking up from the base of a rotted log.

These were the adventures of my childhood: tame, I guess, by the standards established by Mowgli the Jungle boy or even Laura Ingalls Wilder. Nevertheless, it was the experience of nature, with its powerful lessons in static change and pre-dictable surprise. Much of what I know about life, and almost everything I believe about the way I want to live, was formed in those woods. In times of acute worry or insomnia or physical pain, when I close my eyes and bring to mind the place I always like to think about, it looks like the woods in Kentucky.

Horse Lick Creek is a tributary to the Rockcastle River, which drains most of east-ern Kentucky and has won enough points for beauty and biological diversity to be named a "wild river." The Nature Conservancy has chosen Horse Lick as a place to cherish particularly, and protect. The creek itself is 16 miles long, with a watershed of 40,000 acres; of this valley, 8,000 acres belong to the Forest Service, about 1,500 to the Nature Conservancy, and the remainder to small farms, whose rich bottoms are given over to tobacco and hay and corn, and whose many steep, untillable slopes are given to forest. The people who reside here have few choices about how they will earn a living. If they are landless, they can work for the school system or county gov-ernment, they can commute to a distant city, or they can apply for food stamps. If they do have land, they are cursed and blessed with farming. It's rough country. The most lucrative crop that will grow around here is marijuana, and while few would say they approve, everybody knows it's the truth.

Sand Gap, the town at the upper end of the valley, is the straggling remains of an old mining camp. Gapites, as the people of Sand Gap call themselves, take note of us as we pass through. We've met up now with Jim Hays, the Nature Conservancy employee who oversees this holding and develops prospects for purchasing other land to improve the integrity of the preserve. I phoned him in advance and he has been kind enough, on a rainy morning, to show us the way into the preserve. Camille and I jos-tle in the cab of his pickup like pickled eggs in a jar as we take in the territory, bounc-ing around blind curves and potholes big enough to swallow at least a good laying hen. We pass a grocery store with a front porch, and the Pony Lot Holiness Church. JESUS LOVES YOU, BOND WELCOMES YOU, declares a sign in another small settlement.

Jim grew up here, and speaks with the same hill cadences and turns of phrase that shaped my own speech in childhood. Holding tight to the wheel, he declares, "This is the hatefulest road in about three states. Everybody that lives on it wrecks." By way of evidence we pass a rusted car, well off the road and headed down-hollow; its crumpled nose still rests against the tree that ended its life, though it's hard to picture how it got there exactly. Between patches of woods there are pastures, tobacco fields, and houses with mowed yards and flower gardens and folkloric lawn art. Many a home has a "pouting house" out back, a tarpaper shack where a person can occasionally seek refuge from the rest of the family.

Turner's General Merchandise is the local landmark, meeting place, and commercial hub. It's an honest-to-goodness general store, with a plank floor and a pot-bellied stove, where you can browse the offerings of canned goods, brooms, onion sets, and more specialized items like overalls and cemetery wreaths. A pair of hunters come in to register and tag the wild turkey they've killed—the fourth one brought in today. It's opening day of turkey season, which will last two and a half weeks or until the allotted number of carcasses trail in, whichever comes first. If the season was not strictly controlled, the local turkey population would likely be extinct before first snowfall.

Nobody, and everybody, around here would say that Horse Lick Creek is special. Its a great place to go shoot, drive off-road vehicles, and camp out. In addition to the wild turkeys, the valley holds less conspicuous riches: limestone cliffs and caves that shelter insectivorous bats, including the endangered Indiana bat; shoals in the clear, fast water where many species of rare mussels hold on for their lives. All of this habitat is threatened by abandoned strip mines, herbicide and pesticide use, and literally anything that muddies the water. So earthy and simple a thing as mud might not seem hazardous, but in fact it is; fine silt clogs the gills of filter-feeding mussels, asphyxiates them, and this in turn starves out the organisms that depend on the filter feeders. Habitat destruction can be more subtle than a clear-cut or a forest fire; sometimes it's nearly invisible. Nor is it necessarily ugly. Many would argue that the monoculture of an Iowa cornfield is more beautiful than the long-grass prairie that made way for it. But when human encroachment alters the quality of a place that has supported life in its particular way for millions of years, the result is death, sure and multifarious. The mussels of Horse Lick evolved in clear streams, not muddy ones, and so some of the worst offenders here are not giant mining conglomerates but cattle or local travelers who stir up daily mudstorms in hundreds of spots where the road crosses the creek. Saving this little slice of life on earth—like most—will take not just legislation, but change at the level of the pickup truck.

Poverty rarely brings out the most generous human impulses, especially when it comes to environmental matters. Ask a hungry West African about the evils of deforestation, or an unemployed Oregon logger about the endangered spotted owl, and you'll get just about the same answer: I can't afford to think about that right now. Environmentalists must make a case, again and again, for the possibility that we can't afford *not* to think about it. We point to our wildest lands—the Amazon rain forests, the Arctic tundra—to inspire humans with the mighty grace of what we haven't yet wrecked. Those places have a power that speaks for itself, that seems to throw its own grandeur as a curse on the defiler. Fell the giant trees, flood the majestic canyons, and you will have hell and posterity to pay.

But Jackson County, Kentucky, is nobody's idea of wilderness. I wonder, as we bounce along: Who will complain, besides the mute mussels and secretive bats, if we muddy Horse Lick Creek?

Polly and Tom Milt Lakes settled here a hundred years ago, in a deep hollow above the creek. Polly was the county's schoolteacher. Tom Milt liked her looks, so he saved up to buy a geography book, then went to school and asked her to marry him.

Both were in their late teens. They raised nine children on the banks of Horse Lick. We pass by their homestead, where feral jonquils mark the ghost-boundaries of a front porch long gone.

Their main visible legacy is the Lakes family cemetery, hidden in a little glade. Camille and I wander quietly, touching headstones where seventy or more seasons of rain have eroded the intentions of permanent remembrance. A lot of babies lie here: Gladys, Colon, and Ollie May Lakes all died the same day they were born. A pair of twins, Tomie and Tiny, lived one and two days, respectively. Life has changed almost unimaginably since the mothers of these children grieved and labored here.

But the place itself seems relatively unaltered—at least at first glance. It wasn't a true wilderness even then, but a landscape possessed by hunters and farmers. Only the contents of the wildcat dumps have changed: the one I stopped earlier to inventory contained a hot-water heater, the headboard of a wooden bed, an avocado-green toilet, a playpen, and a coffee maker.

We make our way on down the valley. The hillside drops steeply away from the road, so that we're looking up at stately maple trunks on the left, and down into their upper branches on the right. The forest is unearthly: filtered light through maple leaves gives a green glow to the creek below us. Mayapples grow in bright assemblies like crowds of rain-slick umbrellas; red trilliums and wild ginger nod from the moss-carpeted banks. Ginseng grows here too—according to Jim, many a young man makes his truck insurance payments by digging "sang."

Deep in the woods at the bottom of a hollow we find Cool Springs, a spot where the rocky ground yawns open to reveal a rushing underground stream. The freshet merely surfaces and then runs away again, noisily, under a deeply undercut limestone cliff. I walk back into the cave as far as I can, to where the water roars down and away, steep and fast. I can feel the cold slabs of stone through the soles of my shoes. Turning back to the light, I see sunlit spray in a bright, wide arc, and the cave's mouth framed by a fringe of backlit maidenhair ferns.

Farther down the road we find the "swirl hole"—a hidden place in a rhododendron slick where the underground stream bubbles up again from the deep. The water is nearly icy and incredibly blue as it gushes up from the bedrock. We sit and watch, surrounded by dark rhododendrons and hemlocks, mesmerized by the repetitious swirling of the water. Camille tosses in tiny hemlock cones; they follow one another in single file along a spiral path, around and around the swirl hole and finally away, downstream, to where this clear water joins the opaque stream of Horse Lick Creek itself.

The pollution here is noticeable. Upstream we passed wildcat strip mines, bulldozed flats, and many fords where the road passes through the creek. The traffic we've seen on this road is recreational vehicles. At one point we encountered two stranded young men whose Ford pickup was sunk up to its doors in what they called a "soup hole," an enormous pothole full of water that looked like more fun than it turned out to be. We helped pull them out, but their engine only choked and coughed muddy water out the tailpipe—not a good sign. When we left them, they were headed back to town on foot.

When Tom Milt and Polly Lakes farmed and hunted this land, their lives were ruled by an economy that included powerful obligations to the future. If the land eroded badly, or the turkeys were all killed in one season, they and their children would not survive. Rarely does any creature have the luxury of fouling its own nest beyond redemption.

But now this territory is nobody's nest, exactly. It's more of a playground. The farmers have mostly gone to the cities for work, and with their hard-earned wages and leisure time they return with off-road vehicles. Careless recreation, and a failure of love for the land, are extracting their pound of flesh from Horse Lick Creek.

A map of this watershed is a jigsaw puzzle of public and private property. The Conservancy's largest holding lies at the lower end of the valley. We pass through Forest Service land to get to it, and park just short of a creek crossing where several tiny tributaries come together. Some of the streams are stained with iron ore, a deep, clear orange. I lean against the truck eating my sandwich while Camille stalks the butterflies that tremble in congregations around the mud puddles—tiger swallowtails. She tries to catch them with her hands, raising a languid cloud of yellow and black. They settle, only mildly perturbed, behind us, as we turn toward the creek.

We make our way across a fallow pasture to the tree-lined bank. The water here is invisibly clear in the shallows, an inviting blue green in the deeper, stiller places. We are half a mile downstream from one of the largest mussel shoals. Camille, a seasoned beachcomber, stalks the shoreline with the delicate thoroughness of a sandpiper, collecting piles of shells. I'm less thrilled than she by her findings, because I know they're the remains of a rare and dying species. The Cumberland Plateau is one of the world's richest sites of mussel evolution, but mussels are the most threatened group in North America. Siltation is killing them here, rendering up a daily body count. Unless the Conservancy acquires some of the key lands where there is heavy creek crossing, these species will soon graduate from "endangered" to "extinct."

Along the creekbanks we spot crayfish holes and hear the deep, throaty clicking of frogs. The high bank across from us is a steep mud cliff carved with round holes and elongated hollows; it looks like a miniature version of the windswept sandstone canyons I've come to know in the West. But everything here is scaled down, small and humane, sized for child adventures like those I pursued with tireless enthusiasm three decades ago. The hay fields beyond these woods, the hawk circling against a mackerel sky, the voices of frogs, the smells of mud and leaf mold, these things place me square in the middle of all my childhood memories.

I recognize, exactly, Camille's wide-eyed thrill when we discover a trail of deer tracks in the soft mud among bird-foot violets. She kneels to examine a cluster of fern fiddleheads the size of her own fist, and is startled by a mourning cloak butterfly (which, until I learned to read field guides, I understood as "morning cloak"). Someone in my childhood gave me the impression that fiddleheads and mourning cloaks were rare and precious. Now I realize they are fairly ordinary members of eastern woodland fauna and flora, but I still feel lucky and even virtuous—a gifted observer—when I see them.

For that matter, they probably *are* rare, in the scope of human experience. A great many people will live out their days without ever seeing such sights, or if they do, never *gasping*. My parents taught me this—to gasp, and feel lucky. They gave me the gift of making mountains out of nature's exquisite molehills. The day I captured and brought home a giant, luminescent green luna moth, they carried on as if it were the Hope diamond I'd discovered hanging on a shred of hickory bark. I owned the moth as my captive for a night, and set it free the next, after receiving an amazing present: strands of tiny green pearls—luna moth eggs—laid in fastidious rows on a hickory leaf. In the heat of my bedroom they hatched almost immediately, and I proudly took my legion of tiny caterpillars to school. I was disappointed when my schoolmates didn't jump for joy.

I suppose no one ever taught them how to strike it rich in the forest. But I know. My heart stops for a second, even now, here, on Horse Lick Creek, as Camille and I wait for the butterfly to light and fold its purple, gold-bordered wings. "That's a mourning cloak," I tell her. "It's *very rare.*"

In her lifetime it may well be true; she won't see a lot of these butterflies, or fern fiddleheads, or banks of trillium. She's growing up in another place, the upper Sonoran desert. It has its own treasures, and I inflate their importance as my parents once did for me. She signals to me at the breakfast table and we both hold perfectly still, watching the roadrunner outside our window as he raises his cockade of feathers in concentration while stalking a lizard. We gasp over the young, golden coyotes who come down to our pond for a drink. The fragile desert becomes more precious to me as it becomes a family treasure, the place she will always like to think about, after she's grown into adult worries and the need for imaginary refuge.

A new question in the environmentalist's canon, it seems to me, is this one: who will love the *imperfect* lands, the fragments of backyard desert paradise, the creek that runs between farms? In our passion to protect the last remnants of virgin wilderness, shall we surrender everything else in exchange? One might argue that it's a waste of finite resources to preserve and try to repair a place as tame as Horse Lick Creek. I wouldn't. I would say that our love for our natural home has to go beyond finite, into the boundless—like the love of a mother for her children, whose devotion extends to both the gifted and the scarred among her brood.

Domesticated though they are, I want the desert boundary lands of southern Arizona to remain intact. I believe in their remnant wildness. I am holding constant vigil over my daughter's memory place, the land of impossible childhood discovery, in hopes that it may remain a place of real refuge. I hope in thirty years she may come back from wherever she has gone to find the roadrunner thickets living on quietly, exactly as she remembered them. And someone, I hope, will be keeping downy woods and crawdad creeks safe for me.

—1995

JERRY MANDER
B. 1936

Since his best-selling Four Arguments for the Elimination of Television *was published in 1978, Jerry Mander has been one of the fiercest critics of technology and its effect of estranging people from themselves and the natural world. He claims that most technology is neither morally nor politically neutral; rather, it is inherently exploitative and alienating. In the epilogue to his 1991 book* In the Absence of the Sacred, *Mander issues a stern prophecy: "Living as we do now, using the resources we do, following the inherent drives of a commodity-oriented technological society, we are doomed to fail."*

Mander came to his calling, ironically enough, after a very successful career in public relations and advertising, having served as the president of

his own firm from 1965 to 1972. He quit the firm to devote himself to public interest campaigns. In recent years he has been a senior fellow at the
country's only nonprofit ad agency, the Public Media Center in San Francisco,
and a director of an ecological think tank, the Elmwood Institute in Berkeley,
California.

Our perception of the world, Mander argues, is increasingly shaped by
the artificial environments we inhabit. "Living constantly inside an environment of our own invention, reacting solely to things we ourselves have
created, we are essentially living inside our own minds," he writes in the following selection, Chapter 3 of Four Arguments for the Elimination of
Television. Mander's point in this chapter is that the people who shape the
artificial environments in which we live hold the true power, and no instrument is more effective to their pernicious ends than television. When we no
longer trust our own experience, when we no longer have insight into natural processes because the land no longer has any opportunity to leave its
imprint on us, we become susceptible to control. This, then, is the great danger of the modern age, according to Mander.

THE WALLING OF AWARENESS

During a six-month period in 1973, The New York Times reported the following
scientific findings:

A major research institute spent more than $50,000 to discover that the best
bait for mice is cheese.

Another study found that mother's milk was better balanced nutritionally for
infants than commercial formulas. That study also proved that mother's milk was
better for human infants than cow's milk or goat's milk.

A third study established that a walk is considerably healthier for the human
respiratory and circulatory systems, in fact for overall health and vitality, than a
ride in a car. Bicycling was also found to be beneficial.

A fourth project demonstrated that the juice of fresh oranges has more nutri-
tional value than either canned or frozen orange juice.

A fifth study proved conclusively that infants who are touched a lot frequently
grow into adults with greater self-confidence and have a more integrated relationship with the world than those who are not touched. This study found that touching, not merely sexual touching, but any touching of one person by another, seemed
to aid general health and even mental development among adults as well as
children.

The remarkable thing about these five studies, of course, is that anyone should
have found it necessary to undertake them. That some people did find them necessary can only mean that they felt there was some uncertainty about how the answers
would turn out.

And yet, anyone who has seen a mouse eating cheese or who has been touched
by the hand of another person already knows a great deal about these things,
assuming he or she gives credence to personal observation.

Similarly, anyone who has ever considered the question of artificial milk versus
human milk is unlikely to assume that Nestle's or Similac will improve on a feeding

arrangement that accounted for the growth of every human infant before modern times.

That any people retain doubts on these questions is symptomatic of two unfortunate conditions of modern existence: Human beings no longer trust observation, even of the self-evident, until it is confirmed by scientific or technological institutions; human beings have lost insight into natural processes—how the world works, the human role as one of many interlocking parts of the worldwide ecosystem—because natural processes are now exceedingly difficult to observe.

These two conditions combine to limit our knowledge and understanding to what we are told. They also leave us unable to judge the reliability or unreliability of the information we go by.

The problem begins with the physical environment in which we live.

Mediated Environments

When he was about five years old, my son Kai asked me, "Daddy, who built Mt. Tamalpais?"

Kai's question shocked me. I said, "Nobody built Mt. Tamalpais; it grew up out of the Earth thousands of years ago. No person could build a mountain."

I don't think this satisfied him, but it did start me on a new train of thought.

I think that was the first moment that I really looked around at the urban world in which he and I and the rest of our family and the majority of the people in this country live. I wanted to know how he could have gotten the notion that human beings are responsible for the construction of mountains. I soon realized that his mistaken impression was easy to understand; it was one that we all share on a deeper level.

Most Americans spend their lives within environments created by human beings. This is less the case if you live in Montana than if you live in Manhattan, but it is true to some extent all over the country. Natural environments have largely given way to human-created environments.

What we see, hear, touch, taste, smell, feel and understand about the world has been processed for us. Our experiences of the world can no longer be called direct, or primary. They are secondary, mediated experiences.

When we are walking in a forest, we can see and feel what the planet produces directly. Forests grow on their own without human intervention. When we see a forest, or experience it in other ways, we can count on the experience being directly between us and the planet. It is not mediated, interpreted or altered.

On the other hand, when we live in cities, no experience is directly between us and the planet. Virtually all experience is mediated in some way. Concrete covers whatever would grow from the ground. Buildings block the natural vistas. The water we drink comes from a faucet, not from a stream or the sky. All foliage has been confined by human considerations and redesigned according to human tastes. There are no wild animals, there are no rocky terrains, there is no cycle of bloom and decline. There is not even night and day. No food grows anywhere.

Most of us give little importance to this change in human experience of the world, if we notice it at all. We are so surrounded by a reconstructed world that it is difficult to grasp how astonishingly different it is from the world of only one hundred years ago, and that it bears virtually no resemblance to the world in which human beings lived for four million years before that. That this might affect the way we think, including our understanding of how our lives are connected to any non-human system, is rarely considered.

In fact, most of us assume that human understanding is now more thorough than before, that we know more than we ever did. This is because we have such faith in our rational, intellectual processes and the institutions we have created that we fail to observe their limits.

I have heard small children ask whether apples and oranges grow in stores. "Of course not," we tell them. "Fruit grows from the ground somewhere out in the countryside, and then it's put into trucks and brought to the stores."

But is this true? Have you seen that? Do you have a sense that what you are eating was once alive, growing on its own?

We learn in schools that fruit grows from the ground. We see pictures of fruit growing. But when we live in cities, confined to the walls and floors of our concrete environments, we don't actually see the slow process of a blossom appearing on a tree, then becoming a bud that grows into an apple. We learn this, but we can't really "know" what it means, or that a whole cycle is operating: sky to ground to root through tree to bud ripening into fruit that we can eat. Nor do we see particular value in this knowledge. It remains an idea to us, an abstraction that is difficult to integrate into our consciousness without direct experience of the process. Therefore we don't develop a feeling about it, a caring. In the end how can our children or we really grasp that fruit growing from trees has anything to do with humans growing from eating the fruit?

We have learned that water does not really originate in the pipes where we get it. We are educated to understand that it comes from sky (we have seen that, it is true!), lands in some faraway mountains, flows into rivers, which flow into little reservoirs, and then somehow it all goes through pipes into the sinks in our homes and then back out to—where? The ocean.

We learn there is something called evaporation that takes the water we don't need up to the sky. But is this true? Is there a pattern to it? How does it collect in the sky? Is it okay to rearrange the cycle with cloud seeding? Is it okay to collect the water in dams? Does anyone else need water? Do plants drink it? How do they get it? Does water go into the ground? In cities it rolls around on concrete and then pours into sewers. Since we are unable to observe most of the cycle, we learn about it in knowledge museums: schools, textbooks. We study to know. What we know is what we have studied. We know what the books say. What the books say is what the authors of the books learned from "experts" who, from time to time, turn out to be wrong.

Everyone knows about night and day. Half the time it's dark, half the time it's light. However, it doesn't work that way in our homes or outside in the streets. There is always light, and it is always the same, controlled by an automatic switch downtown. The stars are obscured by the city glow. The moon is washed out by a filter of light. It becomes a semimoon and our awareness of it inevitably dims.

We say it is night, but darkness moods and feelings lie dormant in us. Faced with *real* darkness, we become frightened, overreact, like a child whose parents have always left the light on. In three generations since Edison, we have become creatures of light alone.

One evening during 1975, I went with my family to a small park in the middle of San

Francisco to watch a partial eclipse of the moon. We saw it rise above the buildings, but it had little power. Hundreds of street lamps, flashing signs, and lighted buildings intruded. The street lamps, those new mercury-vapor arcs that give off a harsh pinkish-white light, were the worst problem. It was difficult to feel anything for the moon seen through this pinkish filter. The children became bored. We went for an ice cream.

Later that same evening, I went alone to a different park on a high hill. I imagined the city lights gone dark. I turned them off in my mind. Without the buildings diverting me, I gained the briefest feeling for how the moon must have been experienced by human beings of earlier centuries, why whole cultures and religions were based upon it, how they could know every nuance of its cycle and those of the stars, and how they could understand its connection with planting times, tides, and human fertility.

Only recently has our own culture produced new studies confirming the moon's effect on our bodies and minds, as well as its effect on plants. Earlier cultures, living without filters, did not need to rediscover the effects. People remained personally sensitive to their connections with the natural world. For most of us, this sensitivity and knowledge, or science, of older cultures is gone. If there are such connections, we have little awareness of them. Our environment has intervened.

Not long after the eclipse I just described, my wife, Anica, was told by her ninety-year-old grandmother that we should not permit our children to sleep where the moonlight could bathe them. Born in preindustrial Yugoslavia and having spent most of her life without technology, the old woman said the moon had too much power. One night, our oldest son, Yari, who was eight at the time, spent an evening at a friend's house, high on a hill, sleeping near a curtainless south-facing window. He called us in the morning to tell us of a disturbing thing that had happened to him during the night. He had awakened to find himself standing flush against the window, facing the full moon. He had gotten out of bed while still asleep, walked over to the window, and stood facing the moon. Only then did he wake up. He was frightened, he said, more by the oddness of the experience than any sense of real danger. Actually, he thought it rather special but didn't like having an experience different from what is expected and accepted, which is *not* to experience the power of the moon. He had been taught that what he had just been through couldn't happen; he wished it hadn't and it hasn't since.

Yari, like most of the rest of us, does not wish to accept the validity of his personal experience. The people who define the moon are now the scientists, astronomers and geologists who tell us which interactions with the world are possible and which are not, ridiculing any evidence to the contrary. The moon's cycle affects the oceans, they say, but it doesn't affect the body. Does that sound right to you? It doesn't to me. And yet, removed from any personal awareness of the moon, unable even to see it very well, let alone experience it, how are we to know what is right and what is wrong? Most of us cannot say if, this very evening, the moon will be out at all.

Perhaps you are a jogger. I am not, but friends have told me how that experience has broken them out of technologically created notions of time and distance. I have one friend in San Francisco who runs from his Russian Hill apartment to Ocean Beach and then back again, every morning. This is a distance of about eight miles.

There was a time, he told me, when the idea of walking, or bicycling that distance seemed impossible to him. Now the distance seems manageable, even easy. Near, not far. He has recovered a personal sense of distance.

I have made similar discoveries myself. Some years ago I decided to walk to work every day instead of driving. It changed getting to work into a pleasurable experience—no traffic jams or parking hassles—and I would stop now and then for coffee and a chat with a friend. More important, it changed my conception of distance. My office was twenty blocks from my home, about a thirty-minute walk. I noticed that walking that distance was extremely easy. I hadn't known that my previous conception of twenty blocks was one which technology had created. My knowledge was car-knowledge. I had become mentally and physically a car-person. Now I was connecting distance and range to my body, making the conception personal rather than mechanical, outside myself.

On another occasion, while away on a camping trip with my two children, I learned something about internal versus institutional-technological rhythm.

The three of us were suffering an awful boredom at first. My children complained that there was nothing to *do*. We were all so attuned to events coming along at urban speed in large, prominent packages, that our bodies and minds could not attune to the smaller, more subtle events of a forest.

By the second day, however, the children began to throw rocks into a stream and I found myself hearing things that I hadn't heard the day before: wind, the crunch of leaves under foot. The air was somehow clearer and fresher than it seemed to have been the day before. I began to wander around, aimlessly but interestedly.

On the third day, the children began to notice tiny creatures. They watched them closely and learned more about their habits in that one day than I know even now. They were soon imitating squirrels, birds, snakes, and they began to invent some animals.

By the fourth day, our urban-rhythm memory had given way to the natural rhythms of the forest. We started to take in all kinds of things that a few days before we hadn't noticed were there. It was as if our awareness was a dried-out root system that had to be fed.

Returning to the city a few days later, we could feel the speedup take place. It was like running to catch up with a train.

Sensory-Deprivation Environments

The modern office building is the archetypal example of the mediated environment. It contains nothing that did not first exist as a design plan in a human mind. The spaces are square, flat and small, eliminating a sense of height, depth and irregularity. The decor is rigidly controlled to a bland uniformity from room to room and door to floor. The effect is to dampen all interest in the space one inhabits.

Most modern office buildings have hermetically sealed windows. The air is processed, the temperature regulated. It is always the same. The body's largest sense organ, the skin, feels no wind, no changes in temperature, and is dulled.

Muzak homogenizes the sound environment. Some buildings even use "white noise," a deliberate mix of electronic sounds that merge into a hum. Seemingly innocuous, it fills the ears with an even background tone, obscuring random noises or passing conversations which might arouse interest or create a diversion.

The light remains constant from morning through night, from room to room until our awareness of light is as dulled as our awareness of temperature, and we are not aware of the passage of time. We are told that a constant level of light is good for our eyes, that it relieves strain. Is this true? What about the loss of a range of focus and the many changes in direction and intensity of light that our flexible eyes are designed to accommodate?

Those who build artificial environments view the senses as single, monolithic things, rather than abilities that have a range of capacity for a reason. We know, for example, that our eyes can see from the extremely dark to the extremely bright, from far to near, from distinct to indistinct, from obvious to subtle. They perceive objects moving quickly and those that are still. The eye is a wonderfully flexible organ, able to adjust instantly to a dazzling array of information, constantly changing, multileveled, perceiving objects far and near moving at different speeds simultaneously. A fully functioning visual capacity is equal to everything the natural environment offers as visual information. This would have to be so, since the interaction between the senses and the natural environment *created* the ranges of abilities that we needed to have. Sight did not just arrive one day, like Adam's rib; it coevolved with the ingredients around it which it was designed to see. When our eyes are continually exercised, when flexibility and dynamism are encouraged, then they *are* equal to the variety of stimuli that night and day have to offer. It is probably not wise always to have "good light" or to be for very long at fixed distances from anything. The result will be lack of exercise and eventual atrophy of the eyes' abilities.

When we reduce an aspect of environment from varied and multidimensional to fixed, we also change the human being who lives within it. Humans give up the capacity to adjust, just as the person who only walks cannot so easily handle the experience of running. The lungs, the heart and other muscles have not been exercised. The human being then becomes a creature with a narrower range of abilities and fewer feelings about the loss. We become grosser, simpler, less varied, like the environment.

The common response to this is that if we lose wide-spectrum sensory experience, we gain a deeper mental experience. This is not true. We only have less nonmental experience so the mental life seems richer by comparison. In fact, mental life is more enriched by a fully functioning sensory life.

In recent years, researchers have discovered some amazing things about the connections between mental and physical life by doing sensory-deprivation experiments. In such experiments, a human subject is cut off from as much sensory information as possible. This can be accomplished, for example, by a totally blank environment—white walls, no furniture, no sounds, constant temperature, constant light, no food and no windows. A more thorough method is to put the blindfolded subject inside a temperature-controlled suit floating in a water tank with only tubes to provide air and water, which are also at body temperature. This sensory-deprivation tank eliminates the tactile sense as well as an awareness of up and down.

Researchers have found that when sensory stimuli are suppressed this way, the subject at first lives a mental life because mental images are the only stimulation. But after a while, these images become disoriented and can be frightening. Disconnected from the world outside the mind, the subject is rootless and ungrounded.

If the experience goes on long enough, a kind of madness develops which can be allayed only by reintroducing sensory stimuli, direct contact with the world outside the subject's mind.

Before total disorientation occurs, a second effect takes place. That is a dramatic increase in focus on any stimulus at all that is introduced. In such a deprived environment, one single stimulus acquires extraordinary power and importance. In the most literal sense, the subject loses perspective and cannot put the stimulus in context. Such experiments have proven to be effective in halting heavy smoking habits, for example, when the experimenter speaks instructions to stop smoking or describes to the subject through a microphone the harmful, unpleasant aspects of smoking.

These experiments have shown that volunteers can be programmed to believe and do things they would not have done in a fully functional condition. The technique could be called brainwashing.

It would be going too far to call our modern offices sensory-deprivation chambers, but they are most certainly sensory-reduction chambers. They may not brainwash, but the elimination of sensory stimuli definitely increases focus on the task at hand, the work to be done, to the exclusion of all else. Modern offices were designed for that very purpose by people who knew what they were doing.

If people's senses were stimulated to experience anything approaching their potential range, it would be highly unlikely that people would sit for eight long hours at desks, reading memoranda, typing documents, studying columns of figures or pondering sales strategies. If birds were flying through the room, and wind were blowing the papers about, if the sun were shining in there, or people were lolling about on chaise lounges or taking baths while listening to various musical presentations, this would certainly divert the office worker from the mental work he or she is there to do. In fact, if offices were so arranged, little business would get done. This is why they are not so arranged. Any awareness of the senses, aside from their singular uses in reading and sometimes talking and listening, would be disastrous for office environments that require people to stay focused within narrow and specific functional modes.

Feeling is also discouraged by these environments. Reducing sensual variations is one good way of reducing feeling since the one stimulates the other. But there is also a hierarchy of values which further the process. Objectivity is the highest value that can be exhibited by an executive in an office. Orderliness is the highest value for a subordinate office worker. Both of these are most easily achieved if the human is effectively disconnected from the distractions of her or his senses, feelings and intuitions.

With the field of experience so drastically reduced for office workers, the stimuli which remain—paper work, mental work, business—loom larger and obtain an importance they would not have in a wider, more varied, more stimulating environment. The worker gets interested in them largely because that is what is available to get interested in.

Curiously, however, while eschewing feeling and intuition, business people often cannot resist using them. They come out as aberrations—fierce competitive drive, rage at small inconveniences, decisions that do not fit the models of objectivity. Such behavior in business sometimes makes me think of blades of grass growing upward through the pavement.

A more poignant example, perhaps, is that modern offices have proven to be such hot sexual environments. Aside from the occasional potted plant, the only creatures in offices with which it is possible to experience anything are other humans. With all other organic life absent and with the senses deprived of most possibilities for human experience, the occasional body which passes the desk becomes an especially potent sensual event, the only way out of the condition of suspended experience, and the only way to experience oneself as alive. In fact, the confinement of human beings within artificial environments may be a partial explanation of our new culture-wide obsession with and focus on sex.

I have been speaking mainly of cities. This has only been because their effects are most obvious. I don't want to create the impression that suburbs, retirement communities, recreational communities and the like offer any greater access to a wider range of experience.

Those places do have large trees, for example, and more small animals. The sky is more visible, without giant buildings to alter the view. But in most ways, suburban-type environments reveal less of natural processes than cities do. Cities, at least, offer a critical ingredient of the natural world, diversity, albeit a diversity that is confined to only human life forms. It does not nearly approach the complexity of any acre of an ordinary forest.

In suburbs the totality of experience is plotted in advance and then marketed on the basis of the plan. "We will have everything to serve the recreational needs of your family: playgrounds, ball fields, golf course, tennis courts, bowling alleys and picnic grounds." This, plus a front lawn, a back lawn, two large trees, and an attentive police force makes up the total package. Human beings then live inside that package.

Places formerly as diverse as forest, desert, marsh, plain and mountain have been unified into suburban tracts. The human senses, seeking outward for knowledge and stimulation, find only what has been prearranged by other humans.

In many ways the same can be said of rural environments. Land which once supported hundreds of varieties of plant and animal life has been transformed by agribusinesses. Insect life has been largely eliminated by massive spraying. For hundreds of square miles, the only living things are artichokes or tomatoes laid out in straight rows. The child seeking to know how nature works finds only spray planes, automated threshers, and miles of rows of a single crop.

Rooms inside Rooms

There are differences of opinion about what the critical moments were that led human beings away from the primary forms of experience—between person and planet—into secondary, mediated environments. Some go back as far as the control of fire, the domestication of animals, the invention of agriculture or the imposition of monotheism and patriarchy.

In my opinion, however, the most significant recent moment came with the control of electricity for power, about four generations ago. This made it possible to begin moving nearly all human functions indoors, and made the outdoors more like indoors.

In less than four generations out of an estimated one hundred thousand, we have fundamentally changed the nature of our interaction with the planet.

Our environment no longer grows on its own, by its own design, in its own time. The environment in which *we* live has been totally reconstructed solely by human intention and creation.

We find ourselves living inside a kind of nationwide room. We look around it and see only our own creations.

We go through life believing we are experiencing the world when actually our experiences are confined within entirely human conceptions. Our world has been thought up.

Our environment itself is the manifestation of the mental processes of other humans. Of all the species of the planet, and all the cultures of the human species, we twentieth-century Americans have become the first in history to live predominantly inside projections of our own minds.

We live in a kind of maelstrom, going ever deeper into our own thought processes, into subterranean caverns, where nonhuman reality is up, up, away somewhere. We are within a system of ever smaller, ever deeper concentric circles, and we consider each new depth that we reach greater progress and greater knowledge.

Our environment itself becomes an editor, filter and medium between ourselves and an alternative nonhuman, unedited, organic planetary reality.

We ask the child to understand nature and care about it, to know the difference between what humans create and what the planet does, but how can the child know these things? The child lives with us in a room inside a room inside another room. The child sees an apple in a store and assumes that the apple and the store are organically connected. The child sees streets, buildings and a mountain and assumes it was all put there by humans. How can the child assume otherwise? That is the obvious conclusion in a world in which all reality *is* created by humans.

As adults, we assume we are not so vulnerable to this mistake, that we are educated and our minds can save us. We "know" the difference between natural and artificial. And yet, we have no greater contact with the wider world than the child has.

Most people still give little importance to any of this. Those who take note of these changes usually speak of them in esoteric, aesthetic or philosophical terms. It makes good discussion at parties and in philosophy classes.

As we go, however, I hope it will become apparent that the most compelling outcome of these sudden changes in the way we experience life is the inevitable political one.

Living within artificial, reconstructed, arbitrary environments that are strictly the products of human conception, we have no way to be sure that we know what is true and what is not. We have lost context and perspective. What we know is what other humans tell us.

Therefore, whoever controls the processes of re-creation, effectively redefines reality for everyone else, and creates the entire world of human experience, our field of knowledge. We become subject to them. The confinement of our experience becomes the basis of their control of us.

The role of the media in all this is to confirm the validity of the arbitrary world in which we live. The role of television is to project that world, via images, into our heads, all of us at the same time.

—1978

ALBERTO RÍOS

B. 1952

A lifelong resident of Arizona, Alberto Ríos is a noted contemporary American poet and writer of short stories. One critic has commented that "Ríos's poetry is a kind of magical storytelling, and his stories are a kind of

*magical poetry." Like other prominent Chicano authors such as Rudolfo
Anaya, Gary Soto, Ray Gonzalez, Denise Chavez, and Benjamin Alire
Sáenz, Ríos demonstrates a particular knack for developing childhood
memories into vivid images and narratives.*

*The son of a British mother and a Mexican father, Ríos was born in
Nogales, Arizona, just north of the Mexican border. He began writing
poetry during junior high school. At the University of Arizona, he earned a
B.A. in English and creative writing in 1974 and a second B.A. in psychology a year later, both with honors. After a year in law school at Arizona,
Ríos quit to enter the university's M.F.A. program in creative writing and
completed the program in 1979. He has taught for many years at Arizona
State University in Tempe, where he is currently a professor of English. His
many volumes of poetry and short stories include* Whispering to Fool the
Wind *(1982), which received the Academy of American Poets' Walt Whitman Award, and* The Iguana Killer: Twelve Stories of the Heart *(1984), winner of the Western States Book Award for fiction.*

"The Secret Lion," from The Iguana Killer, *is a short story about how
children experience place. The "lion" is a metaphor for the power, the intensity, the sudden surprises, of this experience. Place, Ríos suggests, is fundamental to the lives of children, the solid foundation of experience; and yet,
curiously, place is also prone to change, to become mysteriously something
other than itself. The junior high kids in "The Secret Lion" gradually extend
their contact with special places from a nearby arroyo or valley (in this
case, more of a ditch) to the beautiful green lawn they encounter en route
to distant mountains; in each place, though, they experience loss and confusion. The transient intensity of "place experiences," the refocusing of
attention from old secret place to new secret place and back to old secret
place, the loss and regeneration of enchantment—these are the themes of
the following story.*

THE SECRET LION

I was twelve and in junior high school and something happened that we didn't have
a name for, but it was there nonetheless like a lion, and roaring, roaring that way
the biggest things do. Everything changed. Just that. Like the rug, the one that gets
pulled—or better, like the tablecloth those magicians pull where the stuff on the
table stays the same but the gasp! from the audience makes the staying-the-same
part not matter. Like that.

What happened was there were teachers now, not just one teacher, teach-erz,
and we felt personally abandoned somehow. When a person had all these teachers
now, he didn't get taken care of the same way, even though six was more than one.
Arithmetic went out the door when we walked in. And we saw girls now, but they
weren't the same girls we used to know because we couldn't talk to them anymore,
not the same way we used to, certainly not to Sandy, even though she was my neighbor, too. Not even to her. She just played the piano all the time. And there were
words, oh there were words in junior high school, and we wanted to know what they
were, and how a person did them—that's what school was supposed to be for. Only,

in junior high school, school wasn't school, everything was backward-like. If you went up to a teacher and said the word to try and find out what it meant you got in trouble for saying it. So we didn't. And we figured it must have been that way about other stuff, too, so we never said anything about anything—we weren't stupid.

But my friend Sergio and I, we solved junior high school. We would come home from school on the bus, put our books away, change shoes, and go across the highway to the arroyo. It was the one place we were not supposed to go. So we did. This was, after all, what junior high had at least shown us. It was our river, though, our personal Mississippi, our friend from long back, and it was full of stories and all the branch forts we had built in it when we were still the Vikings of America, with our own symbol, which we had carved everywhere, even in the sand, which let the water take it. That was good, we had decided; whoever was at the end of this river would know about us.

At the very very top of our growing lungs, what we would do down there was shout every dirty word we could think of, in every combination we could come up with, and we would yell about girls, and all the things we wanted to do with them, as loud as we could—we didn't know what we wanted to do with them, just things— and we would yell about teachers, and how we loved some of them, like Miss Crevelone, and how we wanted to dissect some of them, making signs of the cross, like priests, and we would yell this stuff over and over because it felt good, we couldn't explain why, it just felt good and for the first time in our lives there was nobody to tell us we couldn't. So we did.

One Thursday we were walking along shouting this way, and the railroad, the Southern Pacific, which ran above and along the far side of the arroyo, had dropped a grinding ball down there, which was, we found out later, a cannonball thing used in mining. A bunch of them were put in a big vat which turned around and crushed the ore. One had been dropped, or thrown—what do caboose men do when they get bored—but it got down there regardless and as we were walking along yelling about one girl or another, a particular Claudia, we found it, one of these things, looked at it, picked it up, and got very very excited, and held it and passed it back and forth, and we were saying "Guythisis, this is, geeGuythis . . .": we had this perception about nature then, that nature is imperfect and that round things are perfect: we said "GuyGodthis is perfect, thisisthis is perfect, it's round, round and heavy, it'sit's the best thing we'veeverseen. Whatisit?" We didn't know. We just knew it was great. We just, whatever, we played with it, held it some more.

And then we had to decide what to do with it. We knew, because of a lot of things, that if we were going to take this and show it to anybody, this discovery, this best thing, was going to be taken away from us. That's the way it works with little kids, like all the polished quartz, the tons of it we had collected piece by piece over the years. Junior high kids too. If we took it home, my mother, we knew, was going to look at it and say "throw that dirty thing in the, get rid of it." Simple like, like that. "But ma it's the best thing I" "Getridofit." Simple.

So we didn't. Take it home. Instead, we came up with the answer. We dug a hole and we buried it. And we marked it secretly. Lots of secret signs. And came back the next week to dig it up and, we didn't know, pass it around some more or something, but we didn't find it. We dug up that whole bank, and we never found it again. We tried.

Sergio and I talked about that ball or whatever it was when we couldn't find it. All we used were small words, neat, good. Kid words. What we were really saying, but didn't know the words, was how much that ball was like that place, that whole arroyo: couldn't tell anybody about it, didn't understand what it was, didn't have a name for it. It just felt good. It was just perfect in the way it was that place, that whole going to that place, that whole junior high school lion. It was just iron-heavy, it had no name, it felt good or not, we couldn't take it home to show our mothers, and once we buried it, it was gone forever.

The ball was gone, like the first reasons we had come to that arroyo years earlier, like the first time we had seen the arroyo, it was gone like everything else that had been taken away. This was not our first lesson. We stopped going to the arroyo after not finding the thing, the same way we had stopped going there years earlier and headed for the mountains. Nature seemed to keep pushing us around one way or another, teaching us the same thing every place we ended up. Nature's gang was tough that way, teaching us stuff.

When we were young we moved away from town, me and my family. Sergio's was already out there. Out in the wilds. Or at least the new place seemed like the wilds since everything looks bigger the smaller a man is. I was five, I guess, and we had moved three miles north of Nogales where we had lived, three miles north of the Mexican border. We looked across the highway in one direction and there was the arroyo; hills stood up in the other direction. Mountains, for a small man.

When the first summer came the very first place we went to was of course the one place we weren't supposed to go, the arroyo. We went down in there and found water running, summer rain water mostly, and we went swimming. But every third or fourth or fifth day, the sewage treatment plant that was, we found out, upstream, would release whatever it was that it released, and we would never know exactly what day that was, and a person really couldn't tell right off by looking at the water, not every time, not so a person could get out in time. So, we went swimming that summer and some days we had a lot of fun. Some days we didn't. We found a thousand ways to explain what happened on those other days, constructing elaborate stories about the neighborhood dogs, and hadn't she, my mother, miscalculated her step before, too? But she knew something was up because we'd come running into the house those days, wanting to take a shower, even—if this can be imagined—in the middle of the day.

That was the first time we stopped going to the arroyo. It taught us to look the other way. We decided, as the second side of summer came, we wanted to go into the mountains. They were still mountains then. We went running in one summer Thursday morning, my friend Sergio and I, into my mother's kitchen, and said, well, what'zin, what'zin those hills over there—we used her word so she'd understand us—and she said nothingdon'tworryaboutit. So we went out, and we weren't dumb, we thought with our eyes to each other, ohhoshe'stryingtokeepsomethingfromus. We knew adult.

We had read the books, after all; we knew about bridges and castles and wildtreacherousraging alligatormouth rivers. We wanted them. So we were going to go out and get them. We went back that morning into that kitchen and we said, "We're going out there, we're going into the hills, we're going away for three days, don't worry." She said, "All right."

"You know," I said to Sergio, "if we're going to go away for three days, well, we ought to at least pack a lunch."

But we were two young boys with no patience for what we thought at the time was mom-stuff: making sa-and-wiches. My mother didn't offer. So we got our little kid knapsacks that my mother had sewn for us, and into them we put the jar of mustard. A loaf of bread. Knivesforksplates, bottles of Coke, a can opener. This was lunch for the two of us. And we were weighed down, humped over to be strong enough to carry this stuff. But we started walking, anyway, into the hills. We were going to eat berries and stuff otherwise. "Goodbye." My mom said that.

After the first hill we were dead. But we walked. My mother could still see us. And we kept walking. We walked until we got to where the sun is straight overhead, noon. That place. Where that is doesn't matter; it's time to eat. The truth is we weren't anywhere close to that place. We just agreed that the sun was overhead and that it was time to eat, and by tilting our heads a little we could make that the truth.

"We really ought to start looking for a place to eat."

"Yeah. Let's look for a good place to eat." We went back and forth saying that for fifteen minutes, making it lunchtime because that's what we always said back and forth before lunchtimes at home. "Yeah, I'm hungry all right." I nodded my head. "Yeah, I'm hungry all right too. I'm hungry." He nodded his head. I nodded my head back. After a good deal more nodding, we were ready, just as we came over a little hill. We hadn't found the mountains yet. This was a little hill.

And on the other side of this hill we found heaven.

It was just what we thought it would be.

Perfect. Heaven was green, like nothing else in Arizona. And it wasn't a cemetery or like that because we had seen cemeteries and they had gravestones and stuff and this didn't. This was perfect, had trees, lots of trees, had birds, like we had never seen before. It was like "The Wizard of Oz," like when they got to Oz and everything was so green, so emerald, they had to wear those glasses, and we ran just like them, laughing, laughing that way we did that moment, and we went running down to this clearing in it all, hitting each other that good way we did.

We got down there, we kept laughing, we kept hitting each other, we unpacked our stuff, and we started acting "rich." We knew all about how to do that, like blowing on our nails, then rubbing them on our chests for the shine. We made our sandwiches, opened our Cokes, got out the rest of the stuff, the salt and pepper shakers. I found this particular hole and I put my Coke right into it, a perfect fit, and I called it my Coke-holder. I got down next to it on my back, because everyone knows that rich people eat lying down, and I got my sandwich in one hand and put my other arm around the Coke in its holder. When I wanted a drink, I lifted my neck a little, put out my lips, and tipped my Coke a little with the crook of my elbow. Ah.

We were there, lying down, eating our sandwiches, laughing, throwing bread at each other and out for the birds. This was heaven. We were laughing and we couldn't believe it. My mother *was* keeping something from us, ah ha, but we had found her out. We even found water over at the side of the clearing to wash our plates with— we had brought plates. Sergio started washing his plates when he was done, and I was being rich with my Coke, and this day in summer was right.

When suddenly these two men came, from around a corner of trees and the tallest grass we had ever seen. They had bags on their backs, leather bags, bags and sticks.

We didn't know what clubs were, but I learned later, like I learned about the grinding balls. The two men yelled at us. Most specifically, one wanted me to take my Coke out of my Coke-holder so he could sink his golf ball into it.

Something got taken away from us that moment. Heaven. We grew up a little bit, and couldn't go backward. We learned. No one had ever told us about golf. They had told us about heaven. And it went away. We got golf in exchange.

We went back to the arroyo for the rest of that summer, and tried to have fun the best we could. We learned to be ready for finding the grinding ball. We loved it, and when we buried it we knew what would happen. The truth is, we didn't look so hard for it. We were two boys and twelve summers then, and not stupid. Things get taken away.

We buried it because it was perfect. We didn't tell my mother, but together it was all we talked about, till we forgot. It was the lion.

—1984

TINO VILLANUEVA

B. 1941

Tino Villanueva grew up speaking Spanish in a family of migrant workers in San Marcos, Texas. As a boy, he hoped that his prowess as a baseball player might save him from the grueling life of a migrant farm laborer, not expecting that poetry would be his actual salvation. Because his family traveled annually across the state of Texas to pick cotton (as described in the following poem), he never attended school regularly. He first became interested in language while working at a furniture factory in San Marcos; hoping to pass the civil service exam and get a job at the local post office, Villanueva spent his evenings watching television and recording the words he didn't know in a spiral notebook, so that he could later look them up. He got the post office job but three years later was drafted to serve as an Army supply clerk in the Panama Canal Zone.

Upon his return to the United States, Villanueva used the GI Bill to attend Southwest Texas State University in San Marcos; he received his B.A. in Spanish there in 1969, with a minor in English. As an undergraduate, he began experimenting with poetry, imitating the work of Dylan Thomas as he gradually developed his own distinctive voice. In 1971, Villanueva received an M.A. from the State University of New York at Buffalo; in 1981 he completed his Ph.D. in contemporary Spanish poetry at Boston University. He has taught at Wellesley College and MIT and is currently Preceptor in Spanish at Boston University. The founding editor of Imagine: International Journal of Chicano Poetry, *Villanueva has published several collections of his own poetry, including* Hay Otra Voz Poems *(1972),* Shaking Off the Dark *(1984), and* Crónica de mis años peores *(1987). In 1994, he won the American Book Award for his book of poetry* Scene from the Movie GIANT.

Impressions and memories of a place, and of one's life there, may not always be pleasant. After winning the American Book Award, Villanueva returned to San Marcos High School and told students about his unlikely ascendance from field worker to college professor and poet. "I come from a family of cotton pickers," he said. "I have vivid memories of it. I hated it. No child has any business working twelve hours a day in the hot sun. Children should be in the library, in school, getting an education and having fun." "Haciendo apenas la recolección" (which could be translated as "Barely Remembering") appeared in the volume Shaking Off the Dark *and is about remembering place and transcending that place (and the emotionally and physically brutal lifestyle it required) through education, particularly through the language of poetry. With its triumphant concluding lines— "Weep no more, my common hands; / you shall not again / pick cotton"— this poem works through the process of "shaking off the dark" of painful memory, memory of place.*

HACIENDO APENAS LA RECOLECCIÓN

For weeks now
I have not been able
to liberate me from my name.
Always I am history I must wake to.
In idiot defeat I trace my routes
across a half-forgotten map of Texas.
I smooth out the folds stubborn
as the memory.

Let me see: I would start from San Marcos,
moving northward,
bored beyond recognition
in the stale air of a '52 Chevy:
to my left, the youngest of uncles
steadies the car;
to my right, grandfather finds humor
in the same joke.
I am hauled among family
extended across the back seat,
as the towns bury themselves forever
in my eyes: Austin, Lampasas, Brownwood,
past Abilene, Sweetwater,
along
the Panhandle's alien tallness.
There it is: Lubbock sounding harsh as ever.
I press its dark letters,
and dust on my fingertips is so alive
it startles them
as once did sand.
Then west, 10,000 acres and a finger's breadth,
is Levelland
where a thin house once stood,
keeping watch over me and my baseball glove
when the wrath of winds cleared the earth
of stooping folk.
There's Ropesville, where in fifth grade
I didn't make a friend.
My arm is taut by now and terrified.

It slackens,
begins falling back into place,
while the years are gathering slowly
along still roads and hill country,
downward
to where it all began—500 McKie Street.
I am home, and although the stars
are at rest tonight,
my strength is flowing.

Weep no more, my common hands;
you shall not again
pick cotton.   —1984

5

VISIONS OF HOME

WENDELL BERRY

B. 1934

Wendell Berry is a native of rural Kentucky who after leaving his home for stints as a graduate student and professor in California and New York made a conscious decision to return to Kentucky and "stay home." For nearly thirty years, he has taught off and on at the University of Kentucky, worked a small farm, raised his children, and published volume after volume of poetry, fiction, and essays. As early as 1969, in his essay "The Long-Legged House," Berry articulated the importance of place in his life: "Whereas most American writers—and even most Americans—of my time are displaced persons, I am a placed person. . . . My connection with this place comes not only from intimate familiarity that began in babyhood, but also from the even more profound and mysterious knowledge that is inherited, handed down in memories and names and gestures and feelings, and in tones and inflections of voice."

Berry attended the University of Kentucky, where he received his B.A. in 1956 and his M.A. in 1957. He then spent two years at Stanford University, first as a Wallace Stegner fellow in creative writing and then as a lecturer in creative writing. Subsequently he received a Guggenheim fellowship and moved to Italy for a year, then taught at New York University for three years before returning to Kentucky. He has explored and elaborated upon his notion of connectedness to place in dozens of books. His works of literary nonfiction include The Long-Legged House *(1969),* The Unsettling of America *(1977),* Home Economics *(1987),* What Are People For? *(1990), and* Another Turn of the Crank *(1995). Perhaps his best-known work of fiction is the novel* The Memory of Old Jack *(1974); he has published numerous collections of short fiction and poetry as well.*

The poem "Stay Home" first appeared in the 1980 collection A Part. *Berry echoes Walt Whitman's "Song of Myself" here in both admonishing* and inviting the reader to pay attention to his or her own experience. Whitman, hooking one hand around the reader's waist and "pointing to landscapes of continents and the public road" with the other, urges the reader to investigate the expansive world: "Not I, not anyone else can travel that road for you, / You must travel it for yourself" (Section 46). Berry, on the other hand, compels the reader not to travel, but like the poet himself to mirror the placid "stillness of the trees." The first lesson in developing a "vision of home" is patience, watchfulness, and attentiveness to the simple details of one's most familiar place.

STAY HOME

I will wait here in the fields
to see how well the rain
brings on the grass.
In the labor of the fields
longer than a man's life
I am at home. Don't come with me.
You stay home too.

I will be standing in the woods
where the old trees
move only with the wind
and then with gravity.
In the stillness of the trees
I am at home. Don't come with me.
You stay home too.

—1980

CAROL POLSGROVE

B. 1945

Although born in Louisville, Kentucky, Carol Polsgrove was raised in Nigeria by her missionary parents. She returned to the United States for college and was an English major at Wake Forest University. In 1973, she completed a Ph.D. in English at the University of Louisville. She has taught at Maysville Community College in Kentucky, Eastern Kentucky University, San Jose State University, and California State University at Hayward; she is currently an associate professor of journalism at Indiana University, where she specializes in teaching courses on the history and practice of "literary journalism." A former editor at The Progressive *and* Mother Jones, *she has published articles in the* Atlantic Monthly, Oceans, Environment, *and* Sierra. *In 1995, Polsgrove published* It Wasn't Pretty, Folks, But Didn't We have Fun? Esquire *in the Sixties.*

The following article, published in the November/December 1990 issue of Sierra *magazine, reflects Polsgrove's long interest in Wendell Berry's writing and philosophy of community and rural living, as well as her own practice of literary journalism ("journalism that comes out of the writer's sensibility rather than a formula"). The article describes Polsgrove's experience of visiting Berry's home in rural Kentucky. In the course of writing the article, Polsgrove had several separate conversations with Berry, but she chose to frame the essay within an autobiographical narrative of one particular visit to Berry's farm. Although she does not mention it in the article, Polsgrove was accompanied on this visit by her friend and Indiana University colleague Scott Russell Sanders, and another version of the meeting, presented in straightforward question-and-answer format, appeared in the May 1990 issue of* The Progressive, *signed by both Polsgrove and Sanders. "On a Scrap of Land" summarizes Wendell Berry's thoughts about the value and present jeopardy of rural lifestyles in the United States, ideas that have been collected in his many books.*

On a Scrap of Land in Henry County

Wendell Berry lives in a part of Kentucky that does not appear to change. Narrow lanes wind through quiet valleys; hawks light on roadside trees. Cars seldom pass the white-gabled houses. To my casual eye, it all looked pretty much as it did 18 years ago when I last visited Lanes Landing Farm near the town of Port Royal.

Since that first visit, I have taught in half a dozen universities and lived in half a dozen places. Berry, steady as the land around him, has stayed on with his wife, Tanya, in his steep-roofed house overlooking the Kentucky River, farming, writing essays, fiction, and poetry, and making occasional forays elsewhere to teach, lecture, or read from his work.

He has remained there not by chance, or because he had nothing better to do, but because 25 years ago he made a deliberate choice. He wrote about that decision in one of his early essays, "The Long-Legged House," the first piece I ever read by him.

The long-legged house was a two-room cabin built by his grandmother's bachelor brother back in the 1920s. As a young man, Berry often visited the house by the river.

"Clumsy in body and mind, I knew no place I could go to and feel certain I ought to be there," he wrote. But at the long-legged house he came upon days when he was "at peace, and happy. And those days that gave me peace suggested to me the possibility of a greater, more substantial peace—a decent, open, generous relation between a man's life and the world—that I have never achieved; but it must have begun to be then, and it has come more and more consciously to be, the hope and the ruling idea of my life."

He and Tanya married in May 1957, and spent the summer at the long-legged house. "In the life we lived that summer we represented to ourselves what we wanted—and it was *not* the headlong pilgrimage after money and comfort and prestige. We were spared that stress from the beginning. And there at the Camp we had around us the elemental world of water and light and earth and air. We felt the presences of the wild creatures, the river, the trees, the stars. Though we had our troubles, we had them in a true perspective. The universe, as we could see any night, is unimaginably large, and mostly empty, and mostly dark. We knew we needed to be together more than we needed to be apart."

Still, they left the house on the river. Berry studied with author Wallace Stegner at Stanford, sojourned in Italy on a Guggenheim fellowship, and taught at New York University. Not until 1964, when he was 30 years old, did he and Tanya and their two children return to Kentucky with the idea, this time, of staying. Teaching at the University of Kentucky in Lexington, he spent four days every week writing at the long-legged house.

When the nearby Lanes Landing property was put up for sale, Wendell and Tanya bought it as a summer place. But as they visited the house on weekends and walked the land, they "began to see possibilities" they could not resist.

"Our life began to offer itself to us in a new way, in the terms of that place, and we could not escape it or satisfy it by anything partial or temporary. We made up our minds to live there."

That commitment to a scrap of land in Henry County changed Wendell Berry as a writer. He has recalled for me what happened. "I was assuming that I was going to lead a literary life when I got back here," he said. But he found that his relationship with the place he had chosen could not be merely literary.

"When you live in your subject," he explained to me, "you can no longer think of it as raw material unless you're a monster. You don't think of your place as your subject any more than you think of your wife or children as your subject."

His sense of obligation to the region led him to write essays, thoughtful explorations of the world around him. "I began not just to see, but to ask why some things were here that were here, and why some things were not here that I felt needed to be here."

Why, he asked himself, had so many small family farms disappeared from the rural scene? He thought the question out to its economic, cultural, intellectual, and moral roots. The result was *The Unsettling of America: Culture & Agriculture*, published in 1977 by Sierra Club Books. Wes Jackson, founder of The Land Institute, near Salina, Kansas, says the book "launched the modern movement for sustainable agriculture."

To agricultural specialists, the fact that one American farmer can feed 80 people may be a solution; to Wendell Berry it is a problem. We would be better off, he believes, if more than 3 percent of America's people farmed the land, using fewer chemicals and machines.

Why have we turned our land over to industrialists? Sheer arrogance, Berry replied in *The Unsettling of America*. Lured by "an almost occult yearning for the future," he wrote, we have given ourselves up to technological fantasy. "The great convenience of the future as a context of behavior is that nobody knows anything about it. No rational person can see how using up the topsoil or the fossil fuels as quickly as possible can provide greater security for the future, but if enough wealth and power can conjure up the audacity to say that it can, then sheer fantasy is given the force of truth."

Berry speaks in this book with the voice that has set him apart from most contemporary writers and intellectuals. He is no timid postmodernist offering long halls of mirrors, illusions and guesses, ironies and double meanings. Berry sounds as certain of the truth—the hardrock, basic truth—as if God had given it to him.

When I visited him this year, settling in for a morning's talk near the wood stove in his living room, I found Berry as fierce as ever. His manner was kind, as down-home and companionable as the chairs and book-laden tables around us, but his thoughts were unflinching.

Folding his tall frame into a worn living-room chair, his feet warmed by sock moccasins, he told me I was wrong to imagine that things hadn't changed in Henry County. Things *have* changed, he said: "I see a number of things that make me seriously afraid."

When he digs post holes, in some spots he can dig five feet down through topsoil the whole way; in others he's in subsoil from the beginning. Ill-use and careless ways have worn down the land, "so you have to conclude that the country we're living in now is literally not the country that our ancestors inhabited."

America has turned its countryside into a Third World colony, he said. "The larger economy, the national economy that is really run for the benefit of a very few people, is preying upon and slowly destroying local communities everywhere.

"Everything we produce in rural America makes more money for other people than it does for those who produce it. They want our products as cheaply as they can be bought. They want to sell us their products as expensively as we can bear to pay for them. And they want our young people. And all this is working amazingly well. We're destroying rural America."

I thought of my own family: Just about everyone in my grandparents' generation lived on Kentucky farms, and none of their descendants do now.

Berry himself might easily have broken his family's long rural residency (they've been in this part of Kentucky since 1803); instead, he committed himself to a way of life that most educated folk of his generation rejected. And that commitment involved more than just living in the country and writing about it: He *imagined* his way deep into local culture.

In his fiction, Berry spins a web of country life as intricate and lovely as a spider's on a barbed-wire fence. In *The Memory of Old Jack, The Wild Birds, Nathan Coulter,* and other novels and stories, generations intertwine as parts of a community Berry calls a "membership." They live in one another's minds, rely on one another, care for one another, learn from one another how they best can live.

There is in these books an affection for country life so intense it resembles romanticism. Driving up through the country, I had been flooded by memories of great-aunts and uncles who had lived country lives that, to my recollection, had been lonely and hard. They didn't seem anything like the lives in Berry's fiction.

"The fiction is imaginary, and it isn't a record," he said, reminding me that he'd straightened me out on this point once before. "When I talk about community I'm not talking about something I know out of the past. I know some things out of the past that seem to confirm the idea of community. But the idea of community was never comprehensive enough. It excluded certain people, such as blacks, or Indians, and it excluded the things of nature."

Berry has confronted those exclusions in his book *The Hidden Wound*, a meditation on his family's slave-holding past and his own boyhood experience with blacks on his grandfather's farm. Trying to come to personal terms with racism, the "hidden wound" that all American whites bear, he found a relationship between the exploitation of human beings and the exploitation of nature. By enslaving blacks, he observed, whites cut their own ties to the land. By assigning hard "hand labor" first to slaves, later to machines, whites avoided intimacy with nature.

Disconnected, whites no longer cared, and what they no longer cared for, they destroyed.

"The white race in America has marketed and destroyed more of the fertility of the earth in less time than any other race that ever lived," he wrote.

Our culture's destructive flight from the physical is still very much on his mind. When we talked Sunday morning, stew and apples simmering on the stove, Berry complained, "The roadsides are littered with trash because people are eating more fast food, because nobody's giving time to food preparation."

As he explains in "The Pleasures of Eating," an essay in his newest collection, *What Are People For?*, the most natural of processes has become so industrialized that people have little idea of just what they are putting on their tables. They don't know where their food comes from or what's been added to or taken away from it. The food industry "will grow, deliver, and cook your food for you and (just like your mother) beg you to eat it. That they do not yet offer to insert it, pre-chewed, into your mouth is only because they have found no profitable way to do so." Like industrial sex, Berry writes, industrial eating is "a degraded, poor, and paltry thing."

Certainly, dinner with the Berrys was just what you'd imagine an authentic country dinner would be: a variety of tastes, all seeming to come straight from the food itself, and the pleasure of company besides.

Tanya had come home from church by mealtime, bringing with her the Berrys' two granddaughters. We ate together at a big round table in the kitchen. The girls ate quietly, then climbed into Tanya's and Wendell's laps and listened to our conversation, occasionally trading places.

One of the remedies he offers for our current cultural mess is a shift to more regional economies—cities buying food and dealing with their garbage within their region.

"We've got to scale our economy down," he said. "We've got to have a more decentralized, locally adapted kind of economy." In "The Pleasures of Eating" he suggests things city-dwellers could do to help halt the decline of rural life: grow and prepare their own food so they know what it's all about, buy close to home, buy directly from farmers.

Is this enough? Of course not, and Berry knows it. "The capacity of people in the cities to do things directly for themselves is extremely limited," he told me. "They can't produce food. They can't produce building materials or the materials needed for clothing. They're so cut off from the natural sources of their livelihood and so far cut off from fundamental skills, most of them, that they can't directly do much of anything."

If rural America is to be saved, it will have to be saved by those who live there, Berry believes. "People who are left in the country are going to have to start helping each other again in practical and economic ways," he said. In his own community, he has been trying to start a small-loan program, and has been to the state capital to protest other states' dumping their garbage in Kentucky.

In his work, Berry says again and again that we cannot save the land without saving the community that holds the knowledge of how we should care for the land, and why. In "The Work of Local Culture" (from *What Are People For?*), Berry discusses an old galvanized bucket that for 50 years has hung from a post on what was once his grandfather's farm. Every time he goes by that bucket, he looks in at the black humus forming from fallen leaves, animal droppings, and other natural debris. A good human community would be like that bucket, he says—it "holds local soil and local memory in place."

To some readers, Berry's preoccupation with the country renders him simply an ignorant Luddite, out of tune with his times. He stirred up a hornet's nest when *Harper's Magazine* reprinted a brief essay in which he explained why he does not use and will not buy a computer.

According to my reading of the essay, Berry uses pen and paper because he regards computer manufacturers as a conniving bunch who try to get people who don't need computers—like farmers and students—to spend significant sums of money on them. Moreover, computers depend on electricity, and he tries to use as little of that as he can. Finally, he likes his working relationship with Tanya, who types his work on an old Royal Standard and makes editorial suggestions in the margins.

Reader response was sharp-tongued. Reading Berry, said one letter-writer, was like "reading about the belief systems of unfamiliar tribal cultures." He suggested Berry try a quill pen.

Another (as Berry should have expected) took exception to his use of his wife as a typist: "Drop a pile of handwritten notes on Wife and you get back a finished manuscript . . . what computer can do that?"

The storm raged again earlier this year when *Utne Reader* reprinted the piece. Again, readers attacked Berry for maligning both computers and women. A friend who knew I was going to see him called me up and said, "You've got to tell Wendell to quit letting people reprint that article. It's going to ruin his reputation."

I was surprised, though, by the emotion in his own response to his critics. The intensity of readers' reactions, Berry wrote back in *Harper's*, suggested that he had obviously "scratched the skin of a technological fundamentalism that . . . cannot tolerate the smallest difference of opinion."

Two of the letter-writers, he wrote, had stereotyped and insulted his wife, "a woman they do not know," implying that she is "subservient, characterless, and stupid." Berry returned an insult of his own: these letter-writers "are audacious and irresponsible gossips." (I understood the strength of Berry's response a little better when Tanya told me there had been such an outpouring of anger that for a while they hated to get their mail.)

Berry is not accustomed to a negative response. His readers are usually respectful, even reverential. That reverence disturbs him, according to his friend Gene Logsdon, a writer-editor with a small farm in Ohio. Berry doesn't like being referred to as a prophet or put on a pedestal. "Wendell's got too much humor" for that. Besides, Logsdon told me, "Prophets usually tell you something you don't want to hear, but Wendell spoke my innermost thoughts."

Logsdon was working at *Farm Journal* when he read "The Long-Legged House." He interviewed Berry and found his example so powerful that he wound up quitting his job and going back to his homeland to farm and write.

Berry's old friend Ed McClanahan remembers mailing him the manuscript of a novella set in farm country. McClanahan had grown up in a small Kentucky town, but he didn't know much about farming, and he'd made a lot of mistakes. "Wendell went through the 120-page manuscript and made a conscientious list of all those errors," said McClanahan. "It was a great kindness."

McClanahan, Logsdon, Wes Jackson, and several others are part of a network of writers Berry talks to or corresponds with regularly. They seemed to me to make up a community of people trying to preserve small-scale farming and farm communities. But Berry was quick to correct me. The group, mostly separated by many miles, can only be a "network," he said, not a community. "The people in your *network* are not going to put your livestock in when they get out in the road."

The members of this network do, however, send each other manuscripts and books, which they sometimes dedicate to each other. Fellow writers, friends, and family are, Berry says, "constant sources of help, instruction, and inspiration to me. As a writer, I'm a sort of assembly or committee."

Others in the network are quick to credit Berry for his contributions. Wes Jackson calls him "our most profound spokesman. He's a constant source for me. We talk probably every week. I'm writing a speech right now, and I was thinking that much of what I have to say had its origins with Wendell."

Logsdon says, "He's clearly the beacon, the lighthouse, to whom everybody turns for the real, pure idealism of the movement." But to Logsdon, as to others, Berry is also a friend, "a really good companion, a man to ride the river with who thinks the way I do. Everyone who gets to know him realizes he's not just air. He really lives and believes what he says he lives and believes. That's to me a surpassing marvel."

Berry's front window looks straight out across the river valley to a ridge of hills. Before I said goodbye, we studied the tranquil scene together.

In the center of the frame, in the valley on the other side of the river, stood an abandoned tenant house. I wondered why people didn't tear down those tattered, empty buildings; Berry wondered why people didn't still live in them.

For Berry, a commitment to a place is like marriage. "When you talk about marriage to a place," he said, "you're talking about final commitment. You're not going to leave. You're going to give up that other so-lucrative motive of the industrial world: the idea that you'd be better off somewhere else or with somebody else.

"If you live in the presence of your history, it's harder to be arrogant. If you are not living in the presence of what you've done, which will always include some damage, it's too easy to be arrogant or silly. That's why some kind of social stability is necessary so that people aren't, all the time, escaping from their own history and the damage they've done.

"I live in this commitment all the time, knowing very well how attractive mobility is. I'd really like to be loved by somebody who doesn't know me, who would be susceptible to my charm." His eyes twinkled, as they often do; at 56 he is an attractive man, capable of taking pleasure in his own delightfulness. "I appreciate, exquisitely, how fine that would be. But I know it wouldn't last, and that I couldn't disguise myself for more than, oh, maybe 48 hours." His big laugh poured out.

"And I know it would be really nice, as I've said to Tanya, to go and get on the fifth floor of some damn apartment house and quit this getting up at night with the sheep."

That reminded him his ewes needed seeing to, so he went off for a while. Not long after, I drove down the wandering road, imagining what it would be like to pick a place on Earth and stay there, and take care of it.

—1990

JIM DODGE

B. 1945

Queried as to his politics, Jim Dodge once responded: "Reborn again Taoist dirt pagan." As to his religion, he wrote: "See politics." Dodge is passionate about the northern California landscape in which he was born and raised, and he is uncompromising in his commitment to protecting it from the ravages of short-sighted developers and a contemporary American culture that seems unable to "just say no" to consumerism. Over the course of his life he has worked variously as a sheepherder, woodcutter, apple picker, tree planter, and "environmental consultant" (which seems to be a polite way of saying "troublemaker"). For all of his activism on behalf of the natural world, however, Dodge is no tiresome wide-eyed zealot; he brings to his writing a clear-eyed skepticism always tempered with humor. "If we're going to align ourselves with nature," he once told an interviewer, "do we understand nature enough to even know what we're aligning ourselves with? It just turns into a tremendous thrashing confusion, which is how most things end up anyway."

In 1983 Dodge brought out his first novel, Fup, *a short and delightful story about a mallard that is too big to fly. The book was originally published by a small press in the San Francisco Bay Area, but rapid sales caught the attention of a major New York publisher—and suddenly Dodge had a best-seller on his hands. Two novels have followed, as well as a trove of accomplished poems. "Poetry is the most important thing in my life," he confessed to* People *magazine. "Fiction is my business and poetry my passion." Dodge brings a poet's sensibility to perceiving the landscape, which he sees as inseparable from the people who live in it.*

In his essay "Living by Life: Some Bioregional Theory and Practice" from the book Home! A Bioregional Reader *(edited by Van Andruss, Christopher Plant, Judith Plant, and Eleanor Wright, 1990), Dodge explores the elements of the bioregional movement, a loose affiliation of people and groups dedicated to participating fully in the lives of the places they inhabit. The movement has become more self-conscious in recent years with the advent of such gatherings as the North American Bioregional Congress, but participants remain committed first and foremost to their own particular home places. When asked how he came to philosophize about bioregionalism, Dodge replied: "I think the real reason bioregionalism appealed to me was that it was the best scale of perception to operate on, so I didn't have to think about the whole planet. I could think about my neighbors."*

LIVING BY LIFE: SOME BIOREGIONAL THEORY AND PRACTICE

I want to make it clear from the outset that I'm not all that sure what bioregionalism is. To my understanding, bioregionalism is an idea still in loose and amorphous formulation, and presently is more hopeful declaration than actual practice. In fact, "ideal" may be too generous: bioregionalism is more properly a notion, which is variously defined as a general idea, a belief, an opinion, an intuition, an inclination, an urge. Furthermore, as I think will prove apparent, bioregionalism is hardly a new notion; it has been the animating cultural principle through 99 percent of human history, and is at least as old as consciousness. Thus, no doubt, the urge.

My purpose here is not really to define bioregionalism—that will take care of itself in the course of things—but to mention some of the elements that I see composing the notion, and some possibilities for practice. I speak with no special privilege on the matter other than my longstanding and fairly studious regard for the subject, a regard enriched by my teachers and numerous bioregional friends. My only true qualification is that I'm fool enough to try.

"Bioregionalism" is from the Greek *bios* (life) and the French *region* (region), itself from the Latin *regia* (territory), and earlier, *regere* (to rule or govern). Etymologically, then, bioregionalism means life territory, place of life, or perhaps by reckless extension, government by life. If you can't imagine that government by life would be at least 40 billion times better than government by the Reagan administration, or Mobil Oil, or any other distant powerful monolith, then your heart is probably no bigger than a prune pit and you won't have much sympathy for what follows.

A central element of bioregionalism—and one that distinguishes it from similar politics of place—is the importance given to natural systems, both as the source of physical nutrition and as the body of metaphors from which our spirits draw sustenance. A natural system is a community of interdependent life, a mutual biological integration on the order of an ecosystem, for example. What constitutes this community is uncertain beyond the obvious—that it includes all interacting life forms, from the tiniest fleck of algae to human beings, as well as their biological processes. To this bare minimum, already impenetrably complex, bioregionalism adds the influences of cultural behavior, such as subsistence techniques and ceremonies. Many people further insist—sensibly, I think—that this community/ecosystem must also include the planetary processes and the larger figures of regulation: solar income, magnetism, gravity, and so forth. Bioregionalism is simply biological realism; in natural systems we find the physical truth of our being, the real obvious stuff like the need for oxygen as well as the more subtle need for moonlight, and perhaps other truths beyond those. Not surprisingly, then, bioregionalism holds that the health of natural systems is directly connected to our own physical/psychic health as individuals and as a species, and for that reason natural systems and their informing integrations deserve, if not utter veneration, at least our clearest attention and deepest respect. No matter how great our laws, technologies, or armies, we can't make the sun rise every morning nor the rain dance on the golden-back ferns.

To understand natural systems is to begin an understanding of the self, its common and particular essences—literal self-interest in its barest terms. "As above, so below," according to the old-tradition alchemists; natural systems as models of consciousness. When we destroy a river, we increase our thirst, ruin the beauty of free-flowing water, forsake the meat and spirit of the salmon, and lose a little bit of our souls.

Unfortunately, human society has also developed technologies that make it possible to lose big chunks all at once. If we make just one serious mistake with nuclear energy, for instance, our grandchildren may be born with bones like over-cooked spaghetti, or torn apart by mutant rats. Global nuclear war is suicide: the "losers" die instantly; the "winners" inherit slow radiation death and twisted chromosomes. By any sensible measure of self-interest, by any regard for life, nuclear war is abhorrent, unthinkable, and loathsomely stupid, and yet the United States and other nations spend billions to provide that possibility. It is the same mentality that pooh-poohs the growing concentration of poisons in the biosphere. It's like the farmer who was showing off his prize mule to a stranger one day when the mule suddenly fell over sideways and died. The farmer looked at the body in bewildered disbelief: "Damn," he said, "I've had this mule for 27 years and it's the first time he's ever done this." To which the stranger, being a biological realist, undoubtedly replied, "No shit."

While I find an amazing depth of agreement among bioregionalists on what constitutes bios, and on what general responsibilities attend our place in the skein of things, there is some disagreement—friendly but passionate—on what actually constitutes a distinct biological region (as opposed to arbitrary entities, like states and counties, where boundaries are established without the dimmest ecological perception, and therefore make for cultural incoherence and piecemeal environmental management). Since the very gut of bioregional thought is the integrity of natural systems and culture, with the function of culture being the mediation of the self and the ecosystem, one might think "bioregion" would be fairly tightly defined. But I think it must be kept in mind that, to paraphrase Poe and Jack Spicer, we're dealing with the grand concord of what does not stoop to definition. There are, however, a number of ideas floating around regarding the biological criteria for a region. I'll mention some of them below, limiting the examples to Northern California.

One criterion for determining a biological region is biotic shift, a percentage change in plant/animal species composition from one place to another—that is, if 15 to 25 percent of the species where I live are different from those where you live, we occupy different biological regions. We probably also experience different climates and walk on different soils, since those differences are reflected in species composition. Nearly everyone I've talked with agrees that biotic shift is a fairly slick and accurate way to make bioregional distinctions; the argument is over the percentage, which invariably seems arbitrary. Since the change in biotic composition is usually gradual, the biotic shift criterion permits vague and permeable boundaries between regions, which I personally favor. The idea, after all, is not to replace one set of lines with another, but simply to recognize inherent biological integrities for the purpose of sensible planning and management.

Another way to biologically consider regions is by watershed. This method is generally straightforward, since drainages are clearly apparent on topographical maps. Watershed is usually taken to mean river drainage, so if you live on Cottonwood Creek you are part of the Sacramento River drainage. The problem with "watersheds as bioregional criteria is that if you live in San Francisco you are also part of the Sacramento (and San Joaquin) River drainage, and that's a long way from Cottonwood Creek. Since any long drainage presents similar problems, most people who advance the watershed criterion make intradrainage distinctions (in the case of the Sacramento: headwaters, Central Valley, west slope Sierra, east slope Coast Range, and delta/bay). The west slope of the Coast Range, with its short-running rivers and strong Pacific influence, is often considered as a whole biological area, at least from the Gualala River to the Mattole River or, depending on who you're talking to, from the Russian River to the Eel River, though they aren't strictly west slope Coast Range rivers. The Klamath, Smith and Trinity drainages are often considered a single drainage system with the arguable inclusion of the Chetco and the Rogue.

A similar method of bioregional distinction is based upon land form. Roughly, Northern California breaks down into the Sierra, the Coast Range, the Central Valley, the Klamath Range, the southern part of the Cascade Range, and the Modoc Plateau. Considering the relationship between topography and water, it is not surprising that land form distinctions closely follow watersheds.

A different criterion for making bioregional distinctions is, awkwardly put, cultural/phenomenological: you are where you perceive you are; your turf is what you think it is, individually and collectively. Although the human sense of territory is deeply evolved and cultural/perceptual behavior certainly influences the sense of place, this view seems to me a bit anthropocentric. And though it is difficult *not* to view things in terms of human experience and values, it does seem wise to remember that human perception is notoriously prey to distortion and the strange delights of perversity. Our species hasn't done too well lately working essentially from this view; because we're ecological dominants doesn't necessarily mean we're ecological determinants. (In fairness, I should note that many friends think I'm unduly cranky on this subject.)

One of the more provocative ideas to delineate bioregions is in terms of "spirit places" or psyche-tuning power-presences, such as Mount Shasta and the Pacific Ocean. By this criterion, a bioregion is defined by the predominant psychophysical influence where you live. You have to live in its presence long enough to truly feel its force within you and that it's not mere descriptive geography.

Also provocative is the notion that bioregion is a vertical phenomenon having more to do with elevation than horizontal deployment—thus a distinction between hill people and flatlanders, which in Northern California also tends to mean country and city. A person living at 2000 feet in the Coast Range would have more in cultural common with a Sierra dweller at a similar altitude than with someone at sea level 20 miles away.

To briefly recapitulate, the criteria most often advanced for making bioregional distinctions are biotic shift, watershed, land form, cultural/phenomenological, spirit presence, and elevation. Taken together, as I think they should be, they give us a strong sense of where we're at and the life that enmeshes our own. Nobody I know is pushing for a quick definition anyway. Bioregionalism, what it is, occupies that point in development (more properly, renewal) where definition is unnecessary and perhaps dangerous. Better now to let definitions emerge from practice than impose them dogmatically from the git-go.

A second element of bioregionalism is anarchy. I hesitate using that fine word because it's been so distorted by reactionary shitheads to scare people that its connotative associations have become bloody chaos and fiends amok, rather than political decentralization, self-determination, and a commitment to social equity. Anarchy doesn't mean out of control; it means out of *their* control. Anarchy is based upon a sense of interdependent self-reliance, the conviction that we as a community, or a tight, small-scale federation of communities, can mind our own business, and can make decisions regarding our individual and communal lives and gladly accept the responsibilities and consequences of those decisions. Further, by consolidating decision making at a local, face-to-face level without having to constantly push information through insane bureaucratic hierarchies, we can act more quickly in relation to natural systems and, since we live there, hopefully with more knowledge and care.

The United States is simply too large and complex to be responsibly governed by a decision-making body of perhaps 1000 people representing 220,000,000 Americans and a large chunk of the biosphere, especially when those 1000 decision makers can only survive by compromise and generally are forced to front for heavy economic interests (media campaigns for national office are expensive). A government where one person represents the interests of 220,000 others is absurd, considering that not all the people voted for the winning representative (or even voted) and especially considering that most of those 220,000 people are capable of representing themselves. I think people do much better, express their deeper qualities, when their actions matter. Obviously one way to make government more meaningful and responsible is to involve people directly day by day, in the processes of decision, which only seems possible if we reduce the scale of government. A bioregion seems about the right size: say close to a small state, or along the lines of the Swiss canton system or American Indian tribes.

If nothing else, bioregional government—which theoretically would express the biological and cultural realities of people-in-place—would promote the diversity of biosocial experimentation; and in diversity is stability. The present system of national government seems about to collapse under the weight of its own emptiness. Our economy is dissolving like wet sugar. Violence is epidemic. The quality of our workmanship—always the hallmark of a proud people—has deteriorated so badly that we're ashamed to classify our products as durable goods. Our minds have been homogenized by television, which keeps our egos in perpetual infancy while substituting them for a sense of self. Our information comes from progressively fewer sources, none of them notably reliable. We spend more time posturing than we do getting it on. In short, American culture has become increasingly gutless and barren in our lifetimes, and the political system little more than a cover for an economics that ravages the planet and its people for the financial gain of very few. It seems almost a social obligation to explore alternatives. Our much-heralded standard of living hasn't done much for the quality of our daily lives; the glut of commodities, endlessly hurled at us out of the vast commodity spectacle, is just more shit on the windshield.

I don't want to imply that bioregionalism is the latest sectarian addition to the American Left, which historically has been more concerned with doctrinal purity and shafting each other than with effective practice. It's not a question of working within the system or outside the system, but simply of working, *somewhere*, to pull it off. And as I mentioned at the beginning, I'm not so sure bioregionalism even has a doctrine to be pure about—it's more a sense of direction (uphill, it seems) than the usual leftist highway to Utopia . . . or Ecotopia for that matter.

Just for the record, and to give some credence to the diversity of thought informing bioregionalism, I want to note some of the spirits I see at work in the early formulation of the notion: pantheists, Wobs, Reformed Marxists (that is, those who see the sun as the means of production), Diggers, liberterreans, Kropotkinites (mutual aid and coevolution), animists, alchemists (especially the old school), lefty Buddhists, Situationists (consummate analysts of the commodity spectacle), syndicalists, Provos, born-again Taoists, general outlaws, and others drawn to the decentralist banner by raw empathy.

A third element composing the bioregional notion is spirit. Since I can't claim any spiritual wisdom, and must admit to being virtually ignorant on the subject, I'm reluctant to offer more than the most tentative perceptions. What I think most bioregionalists hold in spiritual common is a profound regard for life—all life, not just white Americans, or humankind entire, but frogs, roses, mayflies, coyotes, lichens: all of it: the gopher snake and the gopher. For instance, we don't want to save the whales for the sweetsie-poo, lily-romantic reasons attributed to us by those who profit from their slaughter; we don't want them saved merely because they are magnificent creatures, so awesome that when you see one close from an open boat your heart roars; we want to save them for the most selfish of reasons: without them we are diminished.

In the bioregional spirit view we're all one creation, and it may seem almost simple-minded to add that there is a connection—even a necessary unity—between the natural world and the human mind (which may be just a fancy way of saying there is a connection between life and existence). Different people and groups have their own paths and practices and may describe this connection differently—profound, amusing, ineluctable, mysterious—but they all acknowledge the importance of the connection. The connection is archaic, primitive, and so obvious that it hasn't received much attention since the rise of Christian dominion and fossil-fuel industrialism. If it is a quality of archaic thought to dispute the culturally enforced dichotomy between the spiritual and the practical, I decidedly prefer the archaic view. What could possibly be of more *practical* concern than our spiritual well-being as individuals, as a species, and as members of a larger community of life? The Moral Majority certainly isn't going to take us in that direction; they're interested in business as usual, as their golden boy, James Watt, has demonstrated. We need fewer sermons and more prayers.

This sense of bioregional spirit isn't fixed to a single religious form or practice. Generally it isn't Christian-based or noticeably monotheistic, though such views aren't excluded. I think the main influences are the primitive animist/Great Spirit tradition of various Eastern and esoteric religious practices, and plain ol' paying attention. I may be stretching the accord, but I also see a shared awareness that the map is not the journey, and for that reason it is best to be alert and to respond to the opportunities presented rather than waste away wishing life would offer some worthy spiritual challenge (which it does, constantly, anyway). Call it whatever seems appropriate—enlightenment, fulfillment, spiritual maturity, happiness, self-realization—it has to be earned, and to be earned it has to be lived, and that means bringing it into our daily lives and working on it. Instant gratifications are not the deepest gratifications, I suspect, though Lord knows they certainly have their charms. The emphasis is definitely on the practice, not the doctrine, and especially on practicing what you preach; there is a general recognition that there are many paths, and that they are a further manifestation of crucial natural diversity. I might also note for serious backsliders that the play is as serious as the work, and there is a great willingness to celebrate; nobody is interested in a spirit whose holiness is constantly announced with sour piety and narrow self-righteousness.

Combining the three elements gives a loose idea of what I take to be bioregionalism: a decentralized, self-determined mode of social organization; a culture predicated upon biological integrities and acting in respectful accord; and a society which honors and abets the spiritual development of its members. Or so the theory goes.

However, it's not mere theory, for there have been many cultures founded essentially upon those principles; for example, it has been the dominant cultural mode of inhabitation on this continent. The point is not to go back, but to take the best forward. Renewal, not some misty retreat into what was.

Theories, ideas, notions—they have their generative and reclamative values, and certainly a loveliness, but without the palpable intelligence of practice they remain hovering in the nether regions of nifty entertainments or degrade into more flamboyant fads and diversions like literary movements and hula-hoops. Practice is what puts the heart to work. If theory establishes the game, practice is the gamble, and the first rule of all gambling games has it like this: you can play bad and win; you can play good and lose; but if you play good over the long haul you're gonna come out alright.

Bioregional practice (or applied strategy) can take as many forms as the imagination and nerves, but for purpose of example I've hacked it into two broad categories, resistance and renewal. Resistance involves a struggle between the bioregional forces (who represent intelligence, excellence, and care) and the forces of heartlessness (who represent a greed so lifeless and forsaken it can't even pass as ignorance). In a way, I think it really is that simple, that there is, always, a choice about how we will live our lives, that there is a state of constant opportunity for both spiritual succor and carnal delight, and that the way we choose to live is the deepest expression of who we truly are. If we consistently choose against the richest possibilities of life, against kindness, against beauty, against love and sweet regard, then we aren't much. Our only claim to dignity is trying our best to do what we think is right, to put some heart in it, some soul, flower and root. We're going to fall on our asses a lot, founder on our pettiness and covetousness and sloth, but at least there is the effort, and that's surely better than being just another quivering piece of the national cultural jello. Or so it seems to me.

However, the primary focus of resistance is not the homogeneous American supraculture—that can be resisted for the most part simply by refusing to participate, while at the same time trying to live our lives the way we think we should (knowing we'll get no encouragement whatsoever from the colonial overstructure). Rather, the focus of resistance is against the continuing destruction of natural systems. We can survive the ruthless homogeneity of national culture because there are many holes we can slip through, but we cannot survive if the natural systems that sustain us are destroyed. That has to be stopped if we want to continue living on this planet. That's not "environmentalism"; it's ecology with a vengeance. Personally, I think we should develop a Sophoclean appreciation for the laws of nature, and submit. Only within the fractional time frame of fossil-fuel industrialization have we begun to seriously insult the environment and impudently violate the conditions of life. We've done a great deal of damage in a very short time, and only because of the amazing flexibility of natural systems have we gotten away with it so far. But I don't think we'll destroy the planet; she will destroy us first, which is perhaps only to say we'll destroy ourselves. The most crucial point of resistance is choosing not to.

And then we must try to prevent others from doing it for us all, since by allowing monopoly-capital centralized government (which, like monotheism, is not so much putting all your eggs in one basket as dropping your one egg in a blender), we have given them the power to make such remote-control decisions. The way to prevent it is five-fold: by being a model for an alternative; by knowing more than they do; by being politically astute; by protecting what we value; and by any means necessary. (I think it's important to note that there is nearly complete agreement that nonviolence is the best means available, and that the use of violence is always a sad admission of desperation. Besides, they have all the money, guns, and lawyers. People advocating violent means are probably not very interested in living much longer.)

I think political smarts are best applied in the local community and county. Most crucial land use decisions, for instance, are made at the county level by boards of supervisors. The representative-to-constituent ratio is obviously much better in a county than in a country, and therefore informed and spirited constituents have a far greater influence on decisions and policies. Work to elect sympathetic representatives. Put some money where your heart is. Go to your share of the generally boring meetings and hearings. Challenge faulty information (thus the importance of knowing more than they do). Create alternatives. Stand your ground.

Buying land is also a strong political move; "ownership" is the best protection against gross environmental abuse, just as living on the land is the best defense against mass-media gelatin culture, assuming the quality of information influences the quality of thought. Owning land also affords increased political leverage within the present system. Besides, bioregionalism without a tangible land base would be like love without sex; the circuits of association wouldn't be complete. (Of course, it isn't necessary to own land to either appreciate it or resist its destruction, and I hope nobody infers that bioregionalism is for land aristocracy.)

The growth and strength of the "environmental movement" in the 1970s has encouraged awareness about the destruction of natural systems and the consequences of such callous disregard. This is all to the good, and we should continue to stay in their faces on critical issues. But it's going to be continual crisis ecology unless we come up with a persuasive economic alternative; otherwise, most people will go on choosing progress over maturity, for progress is deeply equated with payroll, and money, to most people, means life. It's that cold. It's also basically true, and many friends share my chagrin that it took us so long to grasp that truism. It now seems painfully obvious that the economic system must be transformed if we hope to protect natural systems from destruction in the name of Mammon. Economics seems to baffle everyone, especially me. I have no prescriptions to offer, except to note that it doesn't have to be one economic system, and that any economics should include a fair measure of value. What's needed is an economy that takes into true account the cost of biospheric destruction and at the same time feeds the family. People must be convinced that it's in their best economic interest to maintain healthy biological systems. The best place to meet this challenge is where you live— that is, personally and within the community.

It's probably also fairly plain that changing the economic system will involve changing our conception of what constitutes a fulfilled life and cracking the cultural mania for mindless consumption and its attendant waste. To realize what is alive within us, the who of who we are, we have to know what we truly need, and what is enough. As Marshall Sahlins has pointed out, affluence can be attained either through increasing production or reducing needs. Since increased production usually means ravaged natural systems, the best strategy seems the reduction of needs, and hopefully the consequent recognition that enough is plenty. A truly affluent society is one of material sufficiency and spiritual riches.

While we're keeping up this resistance in our daily lives—and I think it is in the quality of daily life rather than momentary thrills that the heart is proven—we can begin repairing the natural systems that have been damaged. Logged and mined watersheds need to be repaired. Streams have to be cleared. Trees planted. Check dams built to stop gully erosion. Long-term management strategies developed. Tough campaigns waged to secure funding for the work. There's a strong effort in this direction happening in Northern California now, much of it through worker co-ops and citizens' groups, with increasingly cooperative help from local and state agencies. This work has really just begun, and the field is wide open. So far it seems to satisfy the two feelings that prompted it: the sense that we have a responsibility to renew what we've wasted, and the need to practice "right livelihood," or work that provides a living while promoting the spirit.

Natural system renewal (or rehabilitation, or enhancement, or whatever other names it goes by) could well be our first environmental art. It requires a thorough knowledge of how natural systems work, delicate perceptions of specific sites, the development of appropriate techniques, and hard physical work of the kind that puts you to bed after dinner. What finer work than healing the Earth, where the rewards are both in the doing and the results? It deserves our participation and support. For the irrefutable fact of the matter is that if we want to explore the bioregional possibility, we've got to work, got to get dirty—either by sitting on our asses at environmental hearings or by busting them planting trees in the rain. Sniveling don't make it.

The chances of bioregionalism succeeding, like the chances of survival itself, are beside the point. If one person, or a few, or a community of people, live more fulfilling lives from bioregional practice, then it's successful. This country has a twisted idea of success: it is almost always a quantitative judgment—salary, wins, the number of rooms in the house, the number of people you command. Since bioregionalism by temperament is qualitative, the basis of judgment should be shifted accordingly. What they call a subculture, we call friends.

Most of the people I talk with feel we have a fighting chance to stop environmental destruction within 50 years and to turn the culture around within 800 to 1000 years. "Fighting chance" translates as long odds but good company, and bioregionalism is obviously directed at people whose hearts put a little gamble in their blood. Since we won't live to see the results of this hoped-for transformation, we might as well live to start it right, with the finest expressions of spirit and style we can muster, keeping in mind that there's only a functional difference between the flower and the root, that essentially they are part of the same abiding faith.

The Sun still rises every morning. Dig in.

—1990

Leonard Charles, Jim Dodge, Lynn Milliman, and Victoria Stockley

The following quiz, from the book Home! A Bioregional Reader, *was formulated by Jim Dodge and his friends. Charles, Dodge, Milliman, and Stockley lived together for seventeen years at Root Hog Ranch in the "Alta Pacific Bioregion" (the California coast north of San Francisco) and were the founding partners of an environmental consulting company. The purpose of the quiz is to raise people's awareness of how much they really know, or don't know, about the place they call home. Take the quiz. You may be surprised at what you learn about yourself—and about your bioregion.*

Where You At? A Bioregional Quiz

What follows is a self-scoring test on basic environmental perception of place. Scoring is done on the honor system, so if you fudge, cheat, or elude, you also get an idea of where you're at. The quiz is culture-bound, favoring those people who live in the country over city dwellers, and scores can be adjusted accordingly. Most of the questions, however, are of such a basic nature that undue allowances are not necessary.

1. Trace the water you drink from precipitation to tap.
2. How many days till the moon is full? (Slack of two days allowed.)
3. What soil series are you standing on?
4. What was the total rainfall in your area last year (July–June)? (Slack 1 inch for every 20 inches.)
5. When was the last time a fire burned your area?
6. What were the primary subsistence techniques of the culture that lived in your area before you?
7. Name five native edible plants in your region and their season(s) of availability.
8. From what direction do winter storms generally come in your region?
9. Where does your garbage go?
10. How long is the growing season where you live?
11. On what day of the year are the shadows the shortest where you live?
12. When do the deer rut in your region, and when are the young born?
13. Name five grasses in your area. Are any of them native?
14. Name five resident and five migratory birds in your area.
15. What is the land use history of where you live?
16. What primary ecological event/process influenced the land form where you live? (Bonus special: what's the evidence?)
17. What species have become extinct in your area?
18. What are the major plant associations in your region?
19. From where you're reading this, point north.
20. What spring wildflower is consistently among the first to bloom where you live?

Scoring:

0-3   You have your head up your ass.
4-7   It's hard to be in two places at once when you're not anywhere at all.
8-12   A fairly firm grasp of the obvious.
13-16 You're paying attention.
17-19 You know where you're at.
20   You not only know where you're at, you know where it's at.

—1990

ELLEN MELOY

Ellen Meloy met her husband, Mark, at a Halloween party. "He was Inappropriate Technology, I was Forest Detritus," she explains. Now the two are professional vagrants from March through October of each year: Mark is employed as a river ranger by the U.S. Bureau of Land Management and Ellen accompanies him as a volunteer on his regular float trips through Desolation Canyon on Utah's Green River. "River Life was wholly unplanned, though I loped toward it with certainty, if not intent, shedding silly careers and cruel boyfriends to fulfill, at last, an innately feral nature and an extraordinary obsession to experience weather," she writes in Raven's Exile: A Season on the Green River *(1994).*

Raven's Exile is Meloy's answer to the question she asks herself: "Why have we chosen downstream motion over ambition, scorpions over brief-cases, toad concerts over creeping nihilism?" Describing the geology and history (both human and natural) of Desolation Canyon, the book also portrays her attempt to learn how to practice "river citizenship" and thus to deserve the place as a home. Part of the price of this citizenship is the mandatory pilgrimage to Las Vegas described in the following essay. We cannot know the Colorado River, into which the Green flows, until we know Las Vegas and the uses it makes of the river's water, asserts Meloy.

No stranger to the politics of water in the West, Meloy grew up a fifth generation Californian whose family ranch now "lies beneath a reservoir with ranchettes, marinas, minimarts, and a drought problem." She has written for periodicals and anthologies as well as doing technical illustration and radio commentary on natural history. At work on a second book, she spends winters with her husband in Montana.

THE FLORA AND FAUNA OF LAS VEGAS

Human domination over nature is quite simply an illusion, a passing dream by a naïve species. It is an illusion that has cost us much, ensnared us in our own designs, given us a few boasts to make about our courage and genius, but all the same it is an illusion. Do what we will, the Colorado will one day find an unimpeded way to the sea.

—DONALD WORSTER, *Under Western Skies*

Ascent. Summit. Descent. The interstate highway, the asphalt river, slips off the Colorado Plateau, rises and falls over the Great Basin's rhythmic contours of basin and range, and flows southwest toward the Mojave Desert. In basin, the highway crosses the Sevier River, which the 1776 Domínguez-Escalante expedition, ever hoping to find a Pacific passage, erroneously linked with the Green River in the Uinta Basin. Through range, the meticulously graveled and graded highway slopes bury Fremont village sites, their remains relocated to museums to make way for the four-lane. A few petroglyph panels are visible from the road. We cannot study them. We cannot get off the highway. No exit. The panels pass in a blur, ancient peeps drowned by billboard shouts: IT'S THE REAL THING.

The flanks of the Tushar and Pavant ranges tip us into the Parowan Valley, where we nose the truck south into the current of traffic through Mormon farm towns, each with identical, master design brick churches surrounded by weekday-empty aprons of tarmac. Only Kmart has more parking lot. Solid and impervious, the churches may be rocket ships in disguise. When the Rapture comes, the Saints will simply hop in and blast off, smothering the apron in the dense vapor of afterburners without singeing a leaf on God's flora. Near Cedar City I glimpse a road kill that may or may not be a poodle flung from a recreational vehicle. At a rest stop a teenager lifts his muscle shirt and stares at his navel. We're closer, I think. We have entered the gravitational field.

Most of the billboards in St. George advertise Nevada casinos, luring Utahans over the nearby state line to Mesquite or Las Vegas, the pull on their retirement dollar stronger than the pull of their faith. Flanked by the Beaver Dam Mountains and Hurricane Cliffs, St. George hemorrhages subdivisions and factory outlet malls and a lunatic compulsion to have the most golf courses in the universe, irrigated by the Virgin River, soon to be dammed, IMAXed, and deflowered of rare desert tortoises. Perhaps St. Georgians deserve all the golf they can muster. Many are Downwinders, human receptacles of nuclear fallout that scars their lives with seemingly endless tragedy.

During the atmospheric nuclear testing in the Nevada desert west of St. George from 1951 to 1962, it was the Atomic Energy Commission's practice to wait until the wind blew toward Utah before detonating its "shots" in order to avoid contaminating populous Las Vegas or Los Angeles. An AEC memo declassified two decades after the test era described the people living in the fallout's path as "a low-use segment of the population." Loyal to a government they believed to be divinely inspired, taught by their church never to challenge authority, assured by that authority that the radiation was harmless, Utah's patriotic Mormons endured the toxic showers with little objection.

When Utahans and Nevadans reported their symptoms and fears, public health officials told them that only their "neurosis" about the bombs would make them ill. When women reported burns, peeling skin, nausea, and diarrhea—all symptoms of radiation sickness—when they said their hair, fingernails, and toenails fell out after a cloud of fallout passed over them, their doctors wrote "change of life" or "housewife's syndrome" or "recent hysterectomy" on their charts. The dangers of radiation were known but suppressed, a "noble lie" deemed a necessary cost of national security and the fight against communism. Bomb after bomb exploded, some of them, like Shot Harry in 1953, extremely "dirty" and lethal, showering fallout throughout the West. Each nuclear test released radiation in amounts comparable to the radiation released at Chernobyl in 1986. In at least two ways the Nevada tests were nothing like Chernobyl: There were 126 detonations. None was an accident.

At the Nevada state line we cast aside Utah's wholesome aura for its nemesis. Behind: Leave it to Beaver. Ahead: Sodom and Gomorrah. In dusk that sizzles at 103 degrees, the land sprawls in bowls of creosote bush cupped by serrated ribs of rock. Over a long rise, past a convoy of trucks afloat in mirages of diesel and heat, we top the crest of the final ridge and behold the valley below, an island of neon capped in sludgy brown smog, ringed by a rabid housing boom. Las Vegas. The meadows.

We grind down the freeway past warehouses and a cinder block wall over which a life-size white plaster elephant, rogue prop from a theme park, curls its trunk, flares its ears, and rests ivory tusks on the barrier that separates its lunging charge from the highway's shoulder. Oleander bushes, carbon monoxide-tolerant but poisonous in their own right—they once offed a few Boy Scouts who peeled their thin branches, impaled hot dogs on their tips, and roasted a lethal meal—line the freeway then surrender to a chute of concrete, where we fly without air-conditioning in the gridlock of an exit bottleneck, surrounded by chilled limousines and Porsches. No one leaps out to save our lives. The ambient light is pale yellow, like the inside of a banana peel.

Why this pilgrimage from Desolation Canyon, our home on Utah's Green River, to Glitter Gulch, from cougar-blessed red-rock wilderness to the apex of engineered fantasy, from mesmerization to masochism? Why have we ventured so far from the river? Because our river is here beneath our smoldering, heat-frayed, about-to-explode radials. Only in Egypt are more people dependent on the flow of one river than the people of Clark County, Nevada. By controlling the Colorado River through the state's southern tip, Nevadans freed themselves from the constraints posed by puny, ill-timed rainfall that otherwise barely sustained darkling beetles, chockwallas, and creosote bushes. In this century no place has been too remote or too parched to reach with a lifeline, and the Colorado River, by this point carrying water from the Green, San Juan, Virgin, and other tributaries, is Las Vegas's intravenous feeding, its umbilical to prosperity, the force that pulsates the neon through the tubes. Here the River immolates its wild treasures on the altar of entrepreneurial spirit. We have chosen to devote much of the West's greatest waterway to this city. Las Vegas is the twentieth century's ultimate perversion of the River and the site of a twenty-first-century water war.

For every river rat this visit is mandatory. We cannot know the River until we know this place. Our pilgrimage also carries corollary missions. I hope to learn what Las Vegans know about their water. There is field research to be done. And I want everyone in the Excalibur Hotel and Casino, a massive, pseudomedieval, castellated grotesquerie with jousting matches, banquets, and 4,032 hotel rooms—*4,032 toilets*—to flush their toilets at precisely the same moment.

I wait in the truck while my husband, Mark, registers at the hotel, the only vehicle-enclosed human in Nevada without a veneer of tinted safety glass between her and the rude assault of Real Air. I cannot go into the hotel because Real Air has fused my skin to the Naugahyde panel inside the truck door. My earrings, a Hopi man-in-the-maze design inlaid in silver, conduct so much heat, they sear man-in-the-maze-shaped burns on my neck.

The second thing Mark says to the waitress as we pump freon through our organs inside an air-conditioned restaurant: "Are you real?" She has a practiced tolerance for stupid questions and a tattoo on her left breast. The menu offers an entree called Heavy Trim Beef Primals. "I'd like a cheeseburger, please, hold the onions," Mark says, Green River sand spilling from his cuffs as he passes her the menu. "Are you real?"

The restaurant seethes with slick-baited bloodsuckers in shark-skin suits on cappuccino breaks from their drug harems and sieges of women wearing very short skirts who should not, Vegas being the one place where they can get away with this. The bun-grazing skirt on the cigarette girl remains immobile as she vigorously diversifies her cigarette-shy market by peddling illuminated Yo-Yos. The diners' sunburns, freshly acquired while powerboating on nearby Lake Mead, radiate sufficient heat to melt the ice in our water glasses. While we played Lost Tribe of the Oligocene on the river, male strippers became passé and musical revues with full-figured dancers became the rage: SENSATIONAL. TALENTED. PUDGY, proclaims one flashing Strip marquee.

"What are you in the mood for?" Mark asks about the evening's casino crawl. "Knights? Rome? The circus? The tropics? Urban South American festivities?" We settle on the Tropicana, an island-theme concoction whose grand entry sprouts the huge plaster heads of tiki gods from tidy plots of stale-smelling hothouse petunias, ferns, fountains, and sprinkler heads pumping liquid no faster than the desert air can evaporate it. The fountains, a bartender informs us, use wastewater recycled from guests' rooms. Despite his admonitions and fervent offers of bottled designer water, we down tap water by the gallons, never slaking our thirst. The bartender knows where his water comes from: Lake Mead, he says. We slug it down. Chlorine Lite with a bouquet of Evinrude.

In Las Vegas, the best survival strategy is a wholesale reduction of Self to imbecilic dipstick, easily managed in these clockless, windowless mazes of flashing lights and blaring gaming devices with nary a molecule of The Environment allowed across the transom. The idea is complete disconnection from Earth, a realignment of the senses through a techno-collage of myths and fantasies conjured by corporate hacks. At the Tropicana, I inspect each potted palm for signs of life. Then we transfer to the Río, Where It Is Always Carnival and not much different from the other casinos save for the Brazilian motif and the tiny televisions mounted above each video poker machine. I peer into the foliage of potted banana trees, expecting at least a cricket. No palm, no leaf, no pot is real, only the cigarette butts.

Mark disappears, mumbling about the anthropology of dentalfloss bikinis and a stripper named Bunny Fajitas. Before I'm trampled to death by a shriek of Rotarians from Pocatello, I duck away to rest on an outskirt, unused stair step. From there I watch a terrified woman in bright native African dress clutch the rail of a descending escalator in a death grip. At the escalator's foot, her family nurses her down in their melodic native tongue—from Senegal, perhaps, evidently an escalatorless nation. She survives. Everyone hugs. Hoover Dam's turbines juice the guitars and keyboards of a live band in the lobby. Smurf Intellect, Los Deli Meats, Heavy Trim Beef Primals, I didn't catch the name but the lyrics concern whips. A man in a crisp white shirt and dark slacks (waiter? missionary?) tells me I cannot sit on this step. I cannot sit anywhere, he asserts officiously, except on the stools at bars, poker and slot machines, and blackjack tables. He stares down his nose at me as if I had dripped cobra spit on his shoes and barks, "You must leave." Where's the river? Take me to the river. Take me to Senegal. At the Excalibur no one can be persuaded to induce hydro-gridlock by a simultaneous political flush of their toilets. Water simply seems too bountiful; it fills hoses, sprinklers, fountains, waterfalls, water slides, swimming pools, wishing wells, moats, fish tanks, and artificial lakes; it greens an epidemic of golf courses and chills a million cocktails.

A grown man in scarlet doublet and mustard yellow panty hose plops a tinsel wreath on my head and recites a sonnet in bad high-school Chaucer, prologue to a halfhearted sell on tickets to a jousting tournament. Somehow he knows I'm not the jousting type, but he lets me keep the wreath. A woman standing next to a video poker machine catches my eye: Liv Ullmann face, shorts, running shoes, a thick blond braid down her back, a dippy smile across a tanned face. She is singing from *The Sound of Music*. In strikingly muscular arms she clutches a grocery bag filled with folded newspapers. She rivets her gaze on the video machine as if it were Christopher Plummer or an Alp and hefts out, "The hills are alive . . ."

Daft with the sheer profusion of man-made matter, Mark and I return to our hotel room and fling ourselves onto the bed, hot, weighty sheets draped over our fantasy-stuffed bodies, our feet protruding like Jesus' under the shroud in Mantegna's painting *The Lamentation Over the Dead Christ*. Sometime in the fitful night, a voice crackles over the intercom box above the bathroom doorway. "Please do not panic," the voice urges us. "The fire alarms mean nothing. Please stay in your rooms."

The river of traffic streaming down the Strip will kill me if I back up three feet off the boulevard curb, where I'm in the bushes risking my life to study nature in Vegas's endangered vacant lots, its postage-stamp plots of unpaved Mojave. The inventory so far: crickets, ants, pigeons, wind-strewn "escort girl" flyers as numerous as scutes on a pit viper, and a playing card (the king of spades). Cowbirds (those toxic parents!) chase kazooing cicadas through muffler-sizzled oleander bushes too spindly in foliage to hide the random upturned shopping cart or shade me from sunlight intensified by its infinite reflection off chrome and windshields. I observe one stunted specimen of Aleppo pine, *Pinus halepensis*, a drought-tolerant Mediterranean import largely relegated to freeways and residential areas. I find few bugs in the bush and plenty in the yellow pages under "Pests": termites, earwigs, roaches, pill bugs, silverfish, scorpions, plus rodents and a category called "olive control." Physiographically the Mojave Desert is a transitional province between the Great Basin to the north and the Sonoran Desert to the south. Biological boundaries of all three deserts mix here, so one would expect creosote bush, catclaw, mesquite, yucca, geckos, horned lizards, and the like. But hardly a particle of native flora or fauna lives in Strip habitat. I crawl out of the bushes and hike to safety. Off to find the meadows, *las vegas*.

Negligible rainfall, barely four inches annually, comes to the austere bowl of desert in which Las Vegas spreads. Over a century and a half ago, a carpet of spring-fed grasslands grew in this basin, an oasis in a sea of thorns, alkali, and dust. Except for an occasional flash flood through the washes, the nearby mountains flushed little moisture from their peaks. The basin's water came from an underground aquifer created during the Pleistocene, when rainfall was abundant. Big Springs surfaced in a mad gurgle to form the headwaters of Las Vegas Creek, which flowed easterly along the valley floor, then disappeared into the sand. An exploration party in 1844 recorded the creek's temperature at 115 degrees. Eleven years later a Mormon mission watered travelers between Salt Lake City and California settlements. The missionaries also mined lead from an ore vein along the nearby Colorado River and shipped it north to be made into bullets by the church's public works unit. The missionaries took it upon themselves—these were busy people—to teach the Indians, mostly Paiute, "farming and hygiene," although no one bothered to ask the Indians if they cared to farm or needed help in attending to their bodies. Nineteenth-century zealotry seemed obsessed with putting natives behind plows, in pants. "Discontent with the teepee and the Indian camp," claimed Merrill Gates of the U.S. Board of Indian Commissioners in the 1880s, "is needed to get the Indian out of the blanket and into trousers—and trousers with a pocket in them, and with a pocket that aches to be filled with dollars!"

By 1907 wells tapped much of the groundwater. Their strength—good water at constant pressure—and cheap land lured more settlers, who drained the meadows for crops and pasture. For nearly fifty years water flowed into farm, pipe, and oblivion; no one capped the wells until 1955. Las Vegas Creek had dried up five years before. Big Springs, now under pavement and the lock and key of the municipal water district, surfaced no more, and parts of the Las Vegas Valley had subsided as much as five feet, so much water had been mined. The meadows disappeared but for a trace, I was told, at Lions Club and Fantasy Park near downtown Las Vegas.

I drive to Fantasy Park on a boulevard that parallels a brief stretch of creek straitjacketed by concrete riprap. The creek begins and ends in enormous culverts; it merely belches aboveground for a few blocks so people can throw their litter into it. Fantasy Park grows limp-leafed trees in even rows, and despite a posting that the park is for children twelve and under, a few prostrate bodies of napping transients drop bombs of drool into a rather seedy lawn. Casino blitz envelops the park, buffered by mortuaries. Downtown Las Vegas, once heartland of the economy of sin, is now an outlier to the upscale Strip. Unless razed, it has no space for the entertainment mall, the computer-programmed volcano, artificial rain forest, concourse of Roman statuary, circus, castle, or thirty-story pyramid.

However outstripped by the illusion vendors of the nineties, surely downtown Las Vegas scores highest for the Stupidity of Man exhibit's best archival photograph. The 1951 photograph shows Vegas Vic, a landmark, sixty-foot-high neon cowboy on the cornice of the Pioneer Club, beckoning the pilgrims to girls, gambling, and glitz. His thumb is up, his cigarette dangles from his lips. Behind Vegas Vic and the cityscape rises a white-hot cloud on a slender stem, one of the atom wranglers' earliest nuclear bombs, popped off on ground zero less than a hundred miles away.

In Fantasy Park the homeless nappers awaken and roll off what would be the meadows' last stand had a lawn not replaced them. One of the men zombie-walks across the turf to the Binary Plasma Center. Two others approach me for spare change, grass clippings stuck to their sweaty T-shirts. I donate my Fun Book, a collection of courtesy coupons for drinks, playing chips, and discounts at beauty parlors. Casually I ask them where Las Vegas water comes from. The answer is unanimous: the faucet.

Las Vegas's faucets feed one of the highest per-capita water consumption rates in the nation, serving over 800,000 residents, twenty million visitors a year, and a monthly influx of several thousand new residents, most of them quality-of-life refugees from California. To feed the housing boom and the gaming industry's insatiable quest for the next great attraction, Las Vegas will likely be using every last drop of its legal share of Colorado River by the year 2002. It has considered buying water from a desalination plant in Santa Barbara, California, to trade with Los Angeles for rights to more Colorado River water. Las Vegas secured the last of the unappropriated groundwater in its own valley and seeks unclaimed water from the nearby Virgin River. It has also applied to import water from aquifers beneath the "empty" basins in Nevada's outback—fossil water, the ancient rain stored since the Pleistocene and rationed to the surface in spring creeks and seeps that give life to bighorn sheep, fish, lizards, plants, birds, and ranchers. The controversy pits rural Nevada against Las Vegas, sparking memories of a water grab by another lifestyle-obsessed megalopolis: the plumbing of eastern Sierra Nevada runoff by the city of Los Angeles during the early century, an exportation that drained the Owens Valley nearly dry. Sierra water, stored in snowpack, renews itself. Nevada's aquifers would be mined.

While everyone tries to predict the nature of a twenty-first century water war, thousands more newcomers unpack and scream for faucets. Unless a tarantula leaps up and bites off their lips, few seem to notice they live in a desert. At the Las Vegas Natural History Museum, my next research stop, the feature exhibit is a three-hundred-gallon tank swarming with those fascinating Mojave Desert endemics: live sharks.

What does it take to make this emphatically arid place livable? Shade and water: The endless ripple of malls, warehouses, manufacturing plants, minicasinos, restaurants, car dealers, trailer parks, and spanking new residential estates beyond Strip and city speak of a desert culture carried leagues beyond those amenities by a titanic appetite. America's deserts became habitable by virtue of artifice, the replacement of natural flora, a rearrangement of contours, and most significant, the realignment of water: tap the springs and creeks, recontour the basin and flats, harness massive quantities of power and water from a river that flows through the chocolate brown andesite breccia walls of a primeval canyon that in the process is obliterated. We are on our way to Hoover Dam.

The basin cants away from the city toward the rough jumble of peaks above the Colorado River and Hoover's reservoir, Lake Mead. Someone has unpacked platter after platter of hundred-acre subdivisions, repeated motifs of flamingo pink and turquoise stucco with red, Spanish-style tile roofs. Concrete lining reroutes washes and arroyos to take the summer's flash floods somewhere, elsewhere. Hefty stucco walls enclose each community, deterring entry by thieves, perverts, Gila monsters, and lawn-spoiling Russian olive trees. The self-contained suburbs boast names like Legacy Legends and Verde Viejo. Who could lure real-estate dollars to places with names like Hell's Skillet, Arsenic Springs, Donkey Butt Wash, Limp Dick Crick?

The morning sizzles at ninety-six degrees before eight o'clock. Close to the dam, cars creep bumper to bumper beneath the giant towers and webs of transmission lines that carry rivers of energy to Nevada, California, and Arizona. We park short of the dam and join the queue under a skimpy aluminum ramada to await a shuttle bus that takes tourists the last few miles to the dam's crest. A sign reads WATCH FOR BIGHORN SHEEP, but everyone watches for the shuttle, deep-roasted outside their air-conditioned vehicles, red ants gnawing their ankles. Desolation Canyon has accustomed Mark and me to such discomfort, although we cannot assume a relaxed Fremont squat on the ground because it is covered in broken glass. For an hour we stand like stoic Kalahari hosts among rather testy Eskimo guests.

Several years ago I shed mud-caked river shoes and rude shorts, dressed respectably, and walked into the visitor center of another Colorado River megadam. Politely I asked the receptionist, "What would this river look like without the dam?" (Should I have flung my participles about so carelessly? Used *did* instead of *would*?

Was Dr. Freud in the room?) The receptionist looked at me as if I had just stuffed angry sharks into his pants. "Excuse me for a moment," he rasped, and disappeared behind an office door. The floor vibrated quietly as turbines somewhere in the dam's bowels mangled their requisite five hundred cats a minute. These dams unnerve me, they push encephalitic fluids against my skull, they hair up my tongue as though I had been licking lightbulb filaments. I felt the River's pressure, the lurking power of the outlaw. Before the receptionist returned I had to leave.

Today, at Hoover Dam, I have promised Mark I shall be on my best behavior. Alas, as the humming voltaics lop three years off our life spans, the courage I conjured to haul myself into the innards of Hoover suddenly fails, research be damned. We flee back to the truck and drive across the dam.

The angular rock of Black Canyon tilts, coils, and juts in colors that range from dark brown to purplish black. A construction road cut exposes a bright pink interior, a rock version of a yawning hippopotamus. No one spoke up for a wild Black Canyon, no moss-backed biocentric heretics suggested that humanity view nature as a mother rather than a pet or slave. In the thirties everyone was speaking up for jobs and relief from the Depression.

Gridlock stalls us on the dam's crest, where shuttles disgorge tourists who line up to buy tickets to make the descent into the powerhouse. "People still come here, drawn by the spirit of the Colorado," a tour brochure proclaims. I desperately seek river spirit to the left of the dam crest—a hundred miles upcanyon across Lake Mead, amidst Jet Skis, Wave Runners, houseboats, fluorescent jet boats, and a fifty-foot bathtub ring—and to its right—the undrowned canyon squirting a limpid stream from the dam's foot. Nearly a quarter mile below the rims of Black Canyon, the Río Colorado runs cold and clear, bereft of its red-brown complexion, its silt and peculiar native fish. It is neither *río* nor *colorado* but a thin, blue-green lake slackened by Lake Mohave, the reservoir behind the next dam sixty-seven miles downstream, another stair step in the plumbing that extends the remainder of the Colorado's course to the dry sands of Mexico.

We U-turn on the Arizona flank of the dam and cross back over the crest, ensnared in a second gridlock. My father, who watched Los Angeles boom and bloom on Colorado River water and hydropower as he grew up in the twenties and thirties, remembers that Boulder Dam, as Hoover Dam was first named, put men to work, four thousand Depression-starved men who desperately needed work, and food on the table of hungry families. Between 1931 and 1935, dam workers poured three and a quarter million cubic yards of concrete into this chasm with hardly a sandbar or ledge for footing and the indefatigable river roaring through the bypass tunnels, exposing the Mesozoic bedrock and ooze of a watercourse 13 million years in the making. I peer over Hoover's lip and think of the workers who fell to their deaths during construction. Legend says they still lie buried in the dam they built, limbs outstretched in descent now ossified in concrete. The dam was not poured in a solid mass. Solid, it would have dried 125 years later. Workers constructed a 726.4-foot-high stack of house-sized forms, two hundred hollow wooden boxes filled with concrete cooled by refrigerant piped through copper tubing, forms now hidden under the smooth, arching sheath of concrete athwart the dark walls of Black Canyon. Under construction, Hoover Dam looked like Swiss cheese.

We drive by the transmission towers for a final dose of electromagnetic radiation. Lake Mead spreads to the northeast, saved from suffocation by Glen Canyon Dam upstream. Glen trapped the millions of tons of sediment that were filling Lake

Mead at an alarming rate soon after Hoover Dam was built, threatening to render Hoover useless in about a hundred years. Lake Powell and its arms up Cataract Canyon and the Dirty Devil, San Juan, and other tributary rivers now hold the sediment behind Glen Canyon Dam. With Glen, the Colorado River's delta has moved from the Gulf of California to Nevada and Utah.

Hoover Dam rid the "natural menace," as the Bureau of Reclamation calls the virgin Colorado River, of its mud and its fury. During our tenure in the West, before the dam and since, we have loved neither mud nor fury. We have never loved this river. We have made war on it as if it were a pack of proud, unruly, elusive Apaches. Chase them down, catch them, tame them. Put pants on them. Hoover, Glen, and the others, triumphs in the reduction of wild river to tool, stand as secular cathedrals to environmental mastery, the monolithic beads in the necklace of river from Wyoming to Mexico, monuments to our species' uncanny ability to know how to do things and our failure to ask whether the environmental consequences might simply be too great.

Las Vegas makes no bones about its premier commodity—honest fraud—but I don't care much for the place. The exceptions, however, are the pink tongues on the pudgy white tigers in their all-white new-Babylonian habitat box on the entry concourse of the Mirage Hotel and Casino. Each time I visit the tigers, they sleep behind their plate-glass shield, their languid, potbellied bodies sprawled across elevated benches, the sweet tongues drowsily lolling below exquisitely whiskered cheeks. The Mirage sucks a river of people off the Strip onto its moving sidewalks, channels them past the narcoleptic cats and a wall-sized aquarium of parrot fish, wrasses, angelfish, sharks, and other tropical prisoners, and spills them into the tributaries that flow to gaming rooms, bars, shops, and restaurants. Earlier I had seen the Sound of Music woman sleeping on a patch of Strip lawn, a bag lady with one grocery bag and the body of a marathon runner. Now she is here, singing to the poker machines, and I would gleefully join her had I not the singing voice of gargled bats. Like mobile tide pools, a shoal of Frenchmen in bright aloha shirts riffles noisily forward with the stream. Perched on bar stools like herons on a riverbank are Vegas's sunset women, hard-fleshed, sinewy women in crayon makeup, pink stilettos, and gazes to convince the most egocentric lout that they know far more than he does. These women should be allowed to run Las Vegas. They probably do.

In the bar beneath the Mirage's artificial rain forest, Mark sips a herbivore's daiquiri afloat with Chinese parasols, fruit, carrots, celery, and other verdure. He scouts for naysaying casino personnel while I dive under the table and crawl around the rain forest in search of wildlife. The thicket grows bromeliads, ferns, philodendrons, cricket noises, and roof-raking palm trees that thrust fat boles up through the epoxied floor. The philodendrons are real. I emerge, harvest the crop from my daiquiri, and study the couple across from us, whose furtive looks reveal that some outlaw love may soon be consummated.

Our cocktail server, who thinks her water comes from California but is not sure, enlightens us about the construction crews that were furiously ingesting the Strip's remnant open spaces. We had seen the activity earlier in the day, and we wondered about the new building in the parking lot behind the Circus Circus Casino.

"What are they building at Circus Circus?" Mark asks.

"That's the Grand Slam Canyon," she tells us, clearing the table of peach pits, orange rinds, celery leaves, kelp.

Grand Slam Canyon promises the Grand Canyon without the Grand Canyon's pesky discomforts—its infernal heat, wind, roadlessness, and size that defies the three-day vacation, its cacti, lizards, snakes, biting insects, burro poop, boulders, rapids, the possibility of death. Amidst hundred-foot peaks, swimming pools, water slides, pueblos, and a replica of the Grand Canyon's Havasu Falls, inside a climate-controlled, vented, pink womb of a dome, Grand Slam Canyon visitors will fly through rapids and waterfalls in a roller coaster. The River made better than itself.

By midnight my tongue is furry and dry, as if I had swallowed a mouthful of casino carpet. We walk outside the Mirage, where a hundred or more spectators watch a volcano erupt in the palm garden, upstaging a rising moon, spewing fire from propane burners and sloshing wastewater down its tiered slopes. Out from nowhere a single, frantic female mallard duck, her underside lit to molten gold by the tongues of flame, tries desperately to land in the volcano's moat. Mark and I stare incredulously at the duck, two faces pointed skyward among hundreds pointed volcano-ward. Unable to land in this perilous jungle of people, lights, and fire, the duck veers down the block toward Caesars Palace. With a sudden *ffzzt* and a shower of sparks barely distinguishable from the ambient neon, the duck incinerates in the web of transmission lines slicing through a seventy-foot gap in the Strip high-rises, a skein of wire and cable that surges with the power of the River.

—1994

RICK BASS

B. 1958

Rick Bass began his writing career by penning stories about hunting and fishing during lunch breaks from his job as a petroleum geologist, while sitting on a park bench near his office in Jackson, Mississippi. Born in Houston, he first experienced the lure of nature and the power of storytelling during visits to his family's deer lease in the Texas hill country, west of Austin. When he attended college at Utah State University, Bass's goal was not to become a writer but to study anything that would enable him to spend time in the woods. He ended up majoring in petroleum geology, but along the way he took a workshop on writing nature essays. Bass worked as a petroleum geologist for several years after college. In 1987, he and Elizabeth Hughes moved to the remote Yaak Valley in northwestern Montana, where they live with their young daughters in a mountainous area without paved roads or telephone lines.

The Deer Pasture, a series of nostalgic essays about hunting with his family in central Texas, was published in 1985. Two years later, Bass published Wild to the Heart, *a collection of essays about wilderness experiences. Two more books appeared in 1989:* Oil Notes, *a description of his work as a geologist, and* The Watch, *his first collection of short fiction.* Winter: Notes from Montana, *a journal from his first year in the Yaak Valley, came out in 1991. A year later, Bass published* The Ninemile Wolves, *a book about the reintroduction of wild wolves in Montana that marks his increasing involvement with wilderness politics. His more recent works,* Platte River *(1994) and* In the Loyal Mountains *(1995), are collections of short stories;* The Lost Grizzlies: A Search for Survivors in the Wilderness of Colorado *(1995) recounts his efforts to find grizzly bears in the San Juan Mountains of southern Colorado;* The Book of Yaak *(1996) chronicles his efforts to protect the Yaak Valley from roads and logging.*

Much of Bass's writing celebrates his sense of attachment to his adopted landscape in Montana. He wrote of the Yaak Valley in Orion *magazine (Spring 1995) that "the people who live here—who stay here—have fallen in love with the shape of the land—the cycle of the days, in this deep, dark, wet forest, these steep mountains." But the following essay, first published in the* Los Angeles Times Magazine *(November 28, 1993), shows the author's continuing love for the wild places he knew as a child, the swamps on the west side of Houston and the rugged, rocky fields and creeks of the hill country. Bass's writing often combines storytelling and political advocacy, and we see this in "On Willow Creek" when he argues for the preservation of the hill country, writing, "When we run out of country, we will run out of stories. When we run out of stories, we will run out of sanity."*

On Willow Creek

I don't know how to start, but perhaps that's no matter. I am only 35 years old, and the land is more than a billion; how can I be expected to know what to say beyond "Please" and "Thank you" and "Ma'am"? The language of the hill country of Texas, or of any sacred place, is not the language of pen on paper or even of the human voice. It is the language of water cutting down through the country's humped chest of granite, cutting down to the heart and soul of the earth, down to a thing that lies far below and beyond our memory.

Being frail and human, however, memory is all we have to work with. I have to believe that somewhere out there is a point where my language—memory—will intersect with the hill country's language: the scent of cedar, the feel of morning mist, the blood of deer, glint of moon, shimmer of heat, crackle of ice, mountain lions, scorpions, centipedes, rattlesnakes and cacti. The cool, dark oaks and gold-leaved hickories along the creeks; the language of the hill country seems always to return to water. Along the creeks is where most of the wildlife is found. It is along a creek that the men in my family built a hunting cabin 60 years ago. We have lived in Texas for 120 years, and the men in my family have always hunted deer—hunting them in Tennessee before that, and Mississippi, and perhaps all the way back to the dawn of man, to the first hunter. Perhaps that link across the generations is completely unbroken, one of the few unfragmented systems remaining in this century: The Basses hunt deer—a small thing, but still whole and intact.

On this thousand acres deep in the hill country, though, it is only for the last 60 years that we've hunted deer—once a year, in November.

Sixty years. The land changes so much more slowly than we do. We race across it, gathering it all in—the scents, the sounds, the feel of that thousand acres. Granddaddy's gone now; Uncle Horace, John Dallas, Howard, gone too. Already I have lived long enough to see these men in my family cross that intersection where they finally learn and embrace the real language of the earth—the language of granite and history—leaving us, the survivors, behind, still speaking of them in terms of "memory. . . ."

We have not yet quite caught up with the billion-year-old land we love, that harbors us, but as we get older, we're beginning to learn a word or two and beginning to see (especially as we have children) how our own lives start to cut knifelike down through all that granite, the stone hump of the hill country, until we are like rivers and creeks ourselves, and we reach the end and the bottom, and then we understand.

Water. The cities and towns to the south and east of the hill country—Austin, San Antonio, Houston, La Grange, Uvalde, Goliad—I could chart them all, thousands of them, for they are all my home. These towns, these cities and these people drink from the heart of the hill country. The water in their bodies is the water that has come from beneath the hills, from the mystical 175-mile-long underground river called the Edwards Aquifer. The water is gathered in the hill country by the forces of nature, percolates down through the hills and mountains, and flows south, underground, toward the ocean.

That water we don't drink or pump onto our crops or give to our livestock—that tiny part that eludes us—continues on to the Gulf Coast, into the bays and estuaries, where delicate salinities are maintained for the birds, shrimp and other coastal inhabitants that at first glance seem to be far away from and unrelated to the inland mountains.

A scientist will tell you that it's all connected—that if you live in Texas, you must protect the honor and integrity of that country's core, for you are tied to it. It is as much a part of you as family—but if you are a child and given to daydreaming and wondering, I believe that you'll understand this by instinct. You don't need proof that the water moving through those shady creeks up in the wild hills and mountains is the same that later moves through your body. You can instead stand outside—even in the city, even in such a place as Houston—and look north with the wind in your face (or with a salt breeze at your back, carrying your essence back to the hill country like an offering), and you can feel the tremble and shimmer of that magic underground river, the yearning and timelessness of it, just beneath your 7-year-old feet. You can know of the allegiance you owe it, can sense this in a way that not even the scientists know. It is more like the way, when you are in your mother's arms, or your grandmother's, that you know it's all tied together, and that someday you are going to understand it all.

Of course that's the point of this story—that I was one of those children—and that I am here to say thank you to the country in which I was birthed and to ask, please, that the last good part of it not be divided into halves and then quarters and then eighths, and on, then further divided into the invisibility of neglect or dishonor.

The men would go north in the fall—my father and his brother Jimmy, driving up to the hill country from Houston, while Granddaddy came down from Ft. Worth. They would meet up in the high hills and low mountains, in the center of the state. I'd stand there on the back porch in Houston with my mother and watch them drive off—it would often be raining, and I'd step out into the rain to feel it on my face—and I'd know that they were going to a place of wildness, a place where they came from. I'd know it was an act of honor, of ritual, of integrity. I was that boy, and knew these things, but did not seriously believe that I would be old enough to go in the fall myself.

Instead, I sought out those woods I could reach. We lived out near the west edge of Houston, near what is now the Beltway, a few hundred yards from the slow curls of Buffalo Bayou. While the men in my family went up into the hill country (and at all other times of the year), I would spend my time in the tiny de facto wilderness between outlying subdivisions. Back in those still-undeveloped woods was a stagnating swamp, an old oxbow cut off from the rest of the bayou; you almost had to get lost to find it. I called it "Hidden Lake," and I would wade out into the swamp and seine for minnows, crawdads, mud puppies and polliwogs with a soup strainer. In those woods, not a mile from the Houston city limits, I saw turtles, bats, skunks, snakes, raccoons, deer, flying squirrels, rabbits and armadillos. There were bamboo thickets too, and of course the bayou itself, with giant alligator gars floating in patches of sunlit chocolate water, and Spanish moss hanging back in the old forest and wild violets growing along the banks. A lot of wildness can exist in a small place, if it is the right kind of country: a good country.

That country was, of course, too rich to last. The thick oaks fell to the saws, as did the dense giant hickories and the sun-towering, wind-murmuring pines. It's all concrete now; even the banks of the bayou have been channeled with cement. I remember my shock at finding the first survey stakes out in the grasslands (where once there had been buffalo) leading into those big woods along the bayou's rich edge. I remember asking my mother if the survey stakes meant someone was going to build a house out there—a cabin, perhaps. When told that a road was coming, I pulled the stakes up, but the road came anyway, and then the office buildings, and the highway, and the subdivisions.

The men would come back from the woods after a week. They would have bounty with them—a deer, heavy with antlers, strapped to the hood of the car (in those days people in the city did not have trucks), or a wild turkey. A pocket of black acorns; a piece of granite. An old rusting wolf trap found while out walking; an arrowhead. A piece of iron ore, red as rubies. A quartz boulder for my mother's garden. And always, they brought back stories: more stories, it seemed, than you could ever tell.

Sometimes my father or uncle would have something new about him—something that I had not seen when he'd left. A cut in the webbing of his hand cleaning the deer. Or a light in his eyes, a kind of easiness. Beard stubble, sometimes. These were men who had moved to the city and taken city jobs, who drove to work every morning wearing a suit, but they came back from the hill country with the beginnings of beards. There was always something different about them. The woods had marked them.

Because my parents could see that I had an instinctive draw to the animal world—to be more frank, because they could see that I was aflame with the wild—they did their best to keep me nourished, there in the city. My mother took me to the zoo every week, where I'd spend hours looking at the animals with a joy and an excitement, looking at exhibits that would now crush me with sadness. We went to the Museum of Natural History every Saturday. I heard lectures on jumping spiders and wolf spiders. I breathed fog against the aquarium panes, my face pressed to the glass as I watched the giant soft-shell turtles paddle slowly through their underwater, eerie green light. I bought a little rock sample of magnetite from the gift shop. The placard that came with the magnetite said it had come from Llano County, Texas. That was one of the two counties my father and uncle and grandfather hunted (the thousand acres straddled Llano and Gillespie counties).

This only fueled the fire of my love for a country I had not even seen—a country I could feel in my heart, however, and could feel in my hands, all the way to the tips of my fingers: a country whose energy, whose shimmering life force resonated all the way out into the plains, down into the flatlands.

All that sweet water, just beneath our feet. But only so much of it. It was not inexhaustible. We couldn't, or weren't supposed to, take more than was given to us. That was one of the rules of the system. My father, and the other men who hunted it, understood about this system, and other such systems; for them, the land, like our family itself, was a continuum. Each year, each step hiked across those steep slick-rock hills cut down deeper into the rocks, deeper into memory, gave them more stories, more knowledge, and at the same time, took them ever closer to the mystery that lay at the base of it.

I'd grip that rough, glittering magnetite like a talisman, would put my fingers to it and try to feel how it was different from other rocks—would try to feel the pull, the affinity it had for things made of iron. I'd hold it up to my arms and try to feel if it stirred my blood, and I believed that I could feel it.

I'd fall asleep listening to the murmur of the baseball game on the radio with the rock stuck magically to the iron frame of my bed. In the morning, I would sometimes take the rock and place it against my father's compass. I'd watch as the needle always followed the magnetite, and I felt my heart, and everything else inside me, swing with that compass needle, too.

When we run out of country, we will run out of stories.

When we run out of stories, we will run out of sanity.

We will not be able to depend on each other for anything—not for friendship or mercy, and certainly not for love or understanding.

Of course, we shouldn't protect a wild core such as the Texas hill country because it is a system still intact with the logic and sanity that these days too often eludes our lives in the cities. We should instead protect the hill country simply for its own sake, to show that we are still capable of understanding (and practicing) the concept of honor, loving a thing the way it is, and trying, for once, to not change it.

I like to think that in the 60 years we've been hunting and camping on that rough, hidden, thousand acres—through which Willow Creek cuts, flows, forks and twists, with murmuring little waterfalls over one- and two-foot ledges, the water sparkling—that we have not changed the humped land one bit.

I know that it has changed us. My grandfather hunted that country, as have his sons, and now we, my brothers and cousins, hunt it with them, and in the spring, we now bring our young children into the country to show them the part, the huge part, that is not hunting (and yet that for us is all inseparable from the hunting): the fields of bluebonnets and crimson paintbrushes, the baby raccoons, the quail, the zone-tailed hawks and buzzards circling Hudson Mountain, the pink capitol domes of granite rising all through the land as if once there lived a civilization even more ancient than our parents, grandparents and great-grandparents. . . .

A continuous thing is rare these days, when fragmentation seems more than ever to be the rule. I remember the first time I walked with my daughter on the thousand acres, on the land our family calls the "deer pasture." The loose, disintegrating granite chat crunched under her tiny tennis shoes, and she gripped my finger tight to keep from falling. The sound of that gravel underfoot (the pink mountains being worn away, along with our bodies) was a sound I'd heard all my life at the deer pasture, but this time, this first time with my daughter gripping my finger and look-ing down at the loose pink gravel that was making that sound, it affected me so strongly that I felt faint, felt so light that I thought I might take flight. . . .

A country, a landscape, can be sacred in an infinite number of ways. The quartz boulders in my mother's garden—my father brought her one each year, and I thought, and still think, it was one of the most romantic things I'd seen, that even while he was in the midst of wildness that one week each year, he was still thinking of her.

Other families had store-bought Douglas fir or blue spruce trees for Christmas; we had the spindly, strange mountain juniper ("cedar") from the deer pasture. Even though we lived to the south, we were still connected to that wild core, and these rituals and traditions were important to us, so fiercely felt and believed in that one might even call them a form of worship. We were raised Protestants, but in our hearts' and bodies' innocence were cutting a very fine line, tightroping along the mystical edge of pantheism. When Granddaddy was dying and we went to see him in the hospital room in Ft. Worth, I took a handful of arrowhead fragments from the deer pasture and put them under his bed. It seemed inconceivable to me that he not die as he had lived—always in some kind of contact with that wildness and the specificity of that thousand acres.

When Mom was sick—small, young and beautiful, the strongest and best patient the doctors had ever had, they all said—and she was sick a long time, living for years solely on the fire and passion within, long after the marrow had left her bones and the doctors could not bring it back, when she still never had anything other than a smile for each day; when my mother was sick, my father and brothers and I would take turns bringing her flowers from the deer pasture.

One of us would walk in through the door with that vase from the wild. There would be store-bought flowers, too, but those splashes of reds, yellows and blues, from lands she'd walked, lands she knew, are what lit up her face the most. The specificity of our lives together, and of our love: Those colors said it as well as the land can say anything—which is to say, perfectly. Indian paintbrushes. Bluebonnets. Liatris. Shooting stars. I'm certain those flowers helped her as much as did our platelets, the very blood and iron of ourselves, which we also shared with her. She really loved wildflowers, and she really loved the hill and brush country of Texas, and she really loved us.

My mother loved to drink iced tea. Sometimes she and my father and brothers and I would go up to the deer pasture in the dead, sullen heat of summer, in the shim-mering brightness. We'd ride around in the jeep wearing straw hats. We'd get out and walk down the creek, to the rock slide: a polished half-dome of pink granite with a sheet of water trickling over it, a 20-foot slide into the plunge pool below, with cool, clear water six feet deep, and a mud turtle (his face striped yellow, as if with war paint) and two big Midland soft shell turtles living there. An osprey nest, huge branches and sticks, rested in the dead cottonwood at the pool's edge.

My brothers and I would slide down that half-dome and into the pool again and again. A hundred degrees in the summer, and we'd go up and down that algae-slick rock like otters. We'd chase the turtles, would hold our breath and swim after them, paddling underwater in that lucid water while our parents sat in the rocks above and watched. What a gift it is, to see one's children happy, and engaged in the world, loving it.

We'd walk farther down the creek, then: a family. Fuller. My mother would finish her tea, would rattle ice cubes in her plastic cup. She'd crunch the ice cubes in that heat. She always drank her tea with a sprig of mint in it. At some point on one of our walks, she must have tossed her ice cubes and mint sprig out, because now there are two little mint fields along the creek: one by the camp house and one down at the water gap. I like to sit in the rocks above those little mint patches and look, and listen, and smell, and think. I feel the sun dappling on my arms, and watch the small birds flying around in the old oak and cedar along the creek. Goshawks courting in April, and wild turkeys gobbling. I like to sit there above the mint fields and feel my soul cutting down through that bedrock. It's happening fast. I, too, am becoming the earth.

What happens to us when all the sacred, all the whole, is gone—when there is no more whole? There will be only fragments of stories, fragments of culture, fragments of integrity. Even a child standing on the porch in Houston with the rain in his face can look north and know that it is all tied together, that we are the warblers, we are the zone-tailed hawks, we are the underground river: that it is all holy, and that some of it should not be allowed to disappear, as has so much, and so many of us, already.

Sycamores grow by running water, cottonwoods grow by still water. If we know the simple mysteries, then think of all the complex mysteries that lie just beneath us, buried in the bedrock, the bedrock we have been entrusted with protecting.

Stories. On my Uncle Jimmy's left calf, there is a scar where the wild pigs caught him one night. He and my father were coming back to camp after dark when they got between a sow and boar and their piglets. The piglets squealed in fright, which ignited the rage of the sow and boar. My father went up one tree and Uncle Jimmy up another, but the boar caught Jimmy with his tusk, cut the muscle clean to the bone.

Back in camp, Granddaddy and John Dallas and Howard and old Mr. Brooks (there for dominoes that night) heard all the yelling, as did their dogs. The men came running with hounds and lanterns, globes of light swinging crazily through the woods. They stumbled into the middle of the pigs, too. My father and Uncle Jimmy were up in the tops of small trees like raccoons. There were pigs everywhere, pigs and dogs fighting, men dropping their lanterns and climbing trees.... That sow and boar could have held an entire town at bay. They ran the dogs off and kept the men treed there in the darkness for over an hour, Uncle Jimmy's pants leg wet with blood, and fireflies blinking down on the creek below, and the boar's angry grunts, the sow's furious snufflings below, and the frightened murmurs and squeals of the little pigs.... The logic of that system was inescapable: Don't get between a sow and boar and their young.

The land, and our stories, have marked us.

My father and I are geologists. Uncle Jimmy and his two youngest sons manufacture steel pipe and sell it for use in drilling down through bedrock in search of oil, gas and water. Our hunting cabin is made of stone. We have a penchant for building stone walls. Our very lives are a metaphor for embracing the earth: for gripping boulders and lifting them to our chest and stacking them and building a life in and around the country's heart. I've sat on those same boulders and watched a mother bobcat and her two kittens come down to the creek to drink. There used to be an occasional jaguar in this part of the world, traveling up from Mexico, but that was almost 100 years ago.

Granddaddy would've been 90 in October. He and the old guy we leased from, Howard, were born in the same year, 1903, which was the number we used for the lock combination on the last gate leading into the property. It's one of the last places in the world that still makes sense to me. It is the place of my family, but it is more: It is a place that still abides by its own rules. The creeks have not yet been channeled with concrete. There is still a wildness beating beneath the rocks, and in the atoms of everything.

Each year, we grow closer to the land. Each year, it marks us more deeply. When the lightning strike burned the top of what is now called the Burned-Off Hill, we saw firsthand how for 20 years the wildlife preferred that area, but finally the protein content had been lowered again, and it was time for another fire.

My cousin Rick and I found a dead rattlesnake out on the highway two years ago. We put it in the back of the truck along with the wood for that night's campfire, put it down there in the middle of all that wood. That night Russell and Randy unloaded the wood, gathering great big armloads of it. Rick and I shined the flashlights in Russell's face then, and he realized he'd gathered up a great big armload of rattlesnake. We yelled at him to drop that snake, but he couldn't, it was all tangled up everywhere, all around his arms.

The land and its stories, and our stories: The time Randy and I were picking up one of what would be the new cabin's four cornerstones, to load into the truck. August. Randy dropped his end of the sandstone slab (about the size of a coffin) but didn't get his hand free in time. It might have been my fault. No more tea-sipping for cousin Randy. He sat down, stunned in the heat, and stared at the crushed pulpy end of that little finger. I thought strangely how some small part of it was already mashed in between the atoms of the rock, and how his blood was already dripping back into the iron-rich soil. Randy tried to shake off the pain, tried to stand and resume work, but the second he did his eyes rolled heavenward and he turned ghost-white in that awful heat and fell to the ground, began rolling down the steep hill to the bottom of the gulch.

On that hot day, all the little birds and other animals back in the cool shade of the oaks and cedars were resting, waiting for night to cool things off. What an odd creature man is, they had to be thinking. But we couldn't wait for night or its coolness. We were aflame with a love for that wild land, and our long, rock-sure history on it: our loving place on it.

Granddaddy knew the old Texan's trick of luring an armadillo in close by tossing pebbles in the dry leaves. The armadillo, with its radar-dish ears, believes the sound is that of jumping insects, and will follow the sound of your tossed pebbles right up to your feet before it understands the image of your boot or tennis shoe and leaps straight up, sneezes, then flees in wild alarm.

There is a startling assemblage of what I think of as "tender" life up there, seemingly a paradox for such a harsh, rocky, hot country. Cattails along the creeks tucked in between those folds of granite, those narrow canyons with names like Fat Man's Misery and boulder-strewn cataclysms such as Hell's Half Acre. Newts, polliwogs, bullfrogs, leopard frogs, mud turtles, pipits and wagtails, luna moths and viceroys, ferns and mosses. . . .

The old rock, the beautiful outcrops, holds the power of the hill country, but the mystery is the water; that's what brings the rock to life.

I remember one winter night, camped down at the deer pasture, when a rimy ice-fog had moved in, blanketing the hill country. I was just a teen-ager. I had stepped outside for a moment for the fresh, cold air; everyone else was still in the cabin, playing dominoes. (Granddaddy smoked like a chimney.) I couldn't see a thing in all that cold fog. There was just the sound of the creek running past camp; as it always has, as I hope it always will.

Then I heard the sound of a goose honking—approaching from the north. There is no sound more beautiful, especially at night, and I stood there and listened. Another goose joined in—that wild, magnificent honking—and then another.

It seemed, standing there in the dark, with the cabin's light behind me—the snap! snap! snap! sound of Granddaddy the domino king playing his ivories against the linoleum table—that I could barely stand the hugeness, the unlimited future of life. I could feel my youth, could feel my heart beating, and it seemed those geese were coming straight for me, as if they, too, could feel that barely controlled wildness and were attracted to it.

When they were directly above me, they began to fly in circles, more geese joining them. They came lower and lower, until I could hear the underlying readiness of those resonant honks; I could hear their grunts, their intake of air before each honk.

My father came out to see what was going on.

"They must be lost," he said. "This fog must be all over the hill country. Our light may be the only one they can see for miles," he said. "They're probably looking for a place to land, to rest for the night, but can't find their way down through the fog."

The geese were still honking and flying in circles, not a hundred feet over our heads. I'm sure they could hear the gurgle of the creek below. I stared up into the fog, expecting to see the first brave goose come slipping down through that fog, wings set in a glide of faith for the water it knew was just below. They were so close to it.

But they did not come. They circled our camp all night, keeping us awake; trying, it seemed, to pray that fog away with their honking, their sweet music; and in the morning, both the fog and the geese were gone, and it seemed that some part of me was gone with them, some tame or civilized part, and they had left behind a boy, a young man, who was now thoroughly wild and who thoroughly loved wild things. And I often still have the dream I had that night, that I was up with the geese, up in the cold night, peering down at the fuzzy glow of the cabin lights in the fog, that dim beacon of hope and mystery, safety and longing. . . .

The first longing years of my life that were spent exploring the small and doomed hemmed-in woods around Houston sometimes seem like days of the imagination, compared to my later days in the hill country. It seemed, when I went to Hidden Lake, or to the zoo, or the arboretum, or the museum, that I was only treading water.

I fell asleep each night with my aquariums bubbling, the postgame baseball show murmuring. That magic rock from Llano County, the magnetite, stuck to the side of my bed like a remora, or a guardian, seeing me through the night and perhaps filling me with a strange energy, a strange allegiance for a place I had not yet seen.

Finally the day came when I was old enough for my first hunting trip up to the deer pasture. My father took me there for "the second hunt," in late December. I would not go on the first hunt, the November hunt, until after I was out of college and a hunter. The "second hunt" was a euphemism for just camping, for hiking around, and for maybe occasionally carrying a rifle.

My father and I drove through the night in his old green-and-white 1956 Ford, through country I'd never seen, beneath stars I'd never seen. My father poured black coffee from an old thermos to stay awake. The trip took a long time in those days—more than six hours, with gravel clattering beneath the car for the last couple of hours.

I put my hand against the car window. It was colder, up in the hills. The stars were brighter. When I couldn't stay awake any longer, overwhelmed by the senses, I climbed into the back seat and wrapped up in an old Hudson's Bay blanket and lay down on the seat and slept. The land's rough murmur and jostling beneath me was a lullaby.

When I awoke, we had stopped for gas in Llano. We were the only car at the service station. We were surrounded by a pool of light. I could see the dark woods at the edge of the gravel parking lot, could smell the cedar. My father was talking to the gas station attendant. Before I was all the way awake, I grabbed a flashlight and got out and hurried out toward the woods. I went into the cedars, got down on my hands and knees, and with the flashlight began searching for the magnetite that I was sure was all over the place. I picked up small red rocks and held them against the metal flashlight to see if they'd stick.

When my father and the attendant came and got me out of the woods and asked where I had been going and what I'd been doing, I told them, "Looking for magnetite." How hard it must be, to be an adult, I thought then.

We drove on: an improbable series of twists and turns down washed-out canyons and up ridges, following thin caliche roads that shone ghostly white in the moonlight. I did not know then that I would come to learn every bend in those roads, every dip and rise, by heart. We clattered across a high-centered narrow cattle guard, and then another, and were on the property that we'd been leasing for 30 years—the thousand acres, our heart.

It was so cold. We were on our land. We did not own it, but it was ours because we loved it, belonged to it, and because we were engaged in its system. It dictated our movements as surely as it did those of any winter-range deer herd, any migrating warbler. It was ours because we loved it.

We descended toward the creek, and our cabin. The country came into view, brilliant in the headlights. Nighthawks flittered and flipped in the road before us, danced eerie acrobatic flights that looked as if they were trying to smother the dust in the road with their soft wings. Their eyes were glittering red in the headlights. It was as if we had stumbled into a witches' coven, but I wasn't frightened. They weren't bad witches; they were just wild.

Giant jack rabbits, with ears as tall again as they were, raced back and forth before us—leaped six feet into the air and reversed direction mid-leap, hit the ground running: a sea of jack rabbits before us, flowing, the high side of their seven-year cycle. A coyote darted into our headlights' beams, grabbed a jack rabbit and raced away. One jack rabbit sailed over the hood of our car, coming so close to the windshield that I could see his wide, manic eyes, looking so human. A buck deer loped across the road, just ahead. It was an explosion of life, all around us. Moths swarmed our headlights.

We had arrived at the wild place.

JOHN DANIEL

B. 1948

*The question of belonging is a major preoccupation in the writing of John
Daniel. The son of an itinerant labor organizer, Daniel had lived in twenty-
nine different dwellings by the time he was forty. One of those dwellings
was a cottage on the property of Wallace and Mary Stegner near Palo Alto,
California. Stegner was a major influence on Daniel, both as a writer and
as a role model of someone rooted in place. In the title essay from his book*
The Trail Home *(1992), Daniel admires and envies the Stegners' "engagement with their surroundings," cultivated over the course of forty years of
living on the same piece of land. "They know where they are in a way I
probably never will," he reflects. Daniel is also concerned with belonging to
the larger family of living things and is sharply critical of the failings of his
society in this regard, characterizing Americans as "sure of what belongs
to us but not at all sure of what we belong to."*

*Daniel was born in Spartanburg, South Carolina, and moved with his
family to Charlotte, North Carolina, then to Denver, and later to the suburbs
of Washington, D.C. When he was twelve, his parents bought a weekend cabin
on the Blue Ridge of northern Virginia, a landscape that fed his love of
nature. In 1966 Daniel migrated to Oregon to attend Reed College but
dropped out after four semesters and spent the next decade working first as
a choker-setter for a timber company and then as a railroad freight inspec-
tor. When he was thirty he moved to a ranch in eastern Oregon to write full-
time, and four years later was chosen for a Wallace Stegner fellowship in
poetry at Stanford University. He stayed on as a lecturer and simultaneously
earned an M.A. in English and creative writing, shortly thereafter becoming
poetry editor for* Wilderness *magazine. Besides his essay collection* The Trail
Home, *Daniel has published two books of poetry,* Common Ground *(1988)
and* All Things Touched by Wind *(1994), and* Looking After: A Son's Memoir
*(1996). Six new essays by Daniel accompany photographs by Larry Olson in
the 1997 book* Oregon Rivers. *Daniel lives with his wife near Eugene, Oregon.*

*"When human beings settle in a place for the long run, good things occur
overall, but there are dangers," warns Daniel in the following essay, first published in* Orion *magazine (Autumn 1995). "Marriage to place is something our
land and society need, but not all of us are the marrying kind," he writes, citing
the example of Edward Abbey as someone who came to his place from far off
and took hold, and of John Muir as the lifelong wanderer. Adopting the role of
devil's advocate in praising the potential benefits of rootlessness, Daniel offers
a corrective to those committed dwellers-in-place who might become self-
righteous or take themselves too seriously.*

A WORD IN FAVOR OF ROOTLESSNESS

I am one of the converted when it comes to the cultural and economic necessity of
finding place. Our rootlessness, our inability or refusal to accept the discipline of
living as responsive and responsible members of neighborhoods, communities,

landscapes, and ecosystems, is one of our most serious and widespread diseases. The history of our country, and especially of the American West, is in great part a record of damage done by generations of boomers, both individual and corporate, who have wrested from the land all that a place could give and continually moved on to take from another place. Boomers like Wallace Stegner's father, who, as we see him in *The Big Rock Candy Mountain*, "wanted to make a killing and end up on Easy Street." Like so many Americans, he was obsessed by the fruit of Tantalus: "Why remain in one dull plot of Earth when Heaven was reachable, was touchable, was just over there?"

We don't stand much chance of perpetuating ourselves as a culture, or restoring and sustaining the health of our land, unless we can outgrow our boomer adolescence and mature into stickers, or nesters—human beings willing to take on the responsibilities of living in communities rooted in place, conserving nature as we conserve ourselves. And maybe, slowly, we are headed in that direction. The joys and virtues of place are celebrated in a growing body of literature and discussed in conferences across the country. Bioregionalism, small-scale organic farming, urban food coops, and other manifestations of placedness seem to be burgeoning, or at least coming along.

That is all to the good. But as we all settle into our home places and local communities and bioregional niches, as we become the responsible economic and ecologic citizens we ought to be, I worry a little. I worry, for one thing, that we might become so pervasively settled in place that no unsettled places will remain. But I worry about us settlers, too. I feel at least a tinge of concern that we might allow our shared beliefs and practices to harden into orthodoxy, and I fret that the bath water of irresponsibility we are ready to toss out the door might contain a lively baby or two. These fears may turn out to be groundless, like most of my insomniac broodings. But they are on my mind, so indulge me, if you will, as I address some of the less salutary aspects of living in place and some of the joys and perhaps necessary virtues of rootlessness.

No power of place is more elemental or influential than climate, and I feel compelled to report that we who live in the wet regions of the Northwest suffer immensely from our climate. Melville's Ishmael experienced a damp, drizzly November in his soul, but only now and again. For us it is eternally so—or at least it feels like eternity. From October until June we slouch in our mossy-roofed houses listening to the incessant patter of rain, dark thoughts slowly forming themselves in the dull cloud chambers of our minds. It's been days, weeks, *years*, we believe, since a neighbor knocked or a letter arrived from friend or agent or editor. Those who live where sun and breezes play, engaged in their smiling businesses, have long forgotten us, if they ever cared for us at all. Rain drips from the eaves like poison into our souls. We sit. We sleep. We check the mail.

What but climate could it be that so rots the fiber of the Northwestern psyche? Or if not climate itself, then an epiphenomenon of climate—perhaps the spores of an undiscovered fungus floating around from all those decadent forests we environmentalists are so bent on preserving. We try to improve ourselves. We join support groups and twelve-step programs, we drink gallons of cappucino and caffe latte, we bathe our pallid bodies in the radiance of full-spectrum light machines. These measures keep us from dissolving outright into the sodden air, and when spring arrives we bestir ourselves outdoors, blinking against the occasional cruel sun and the lurid displays of rhododendrons. By summer we have cured sufficiently to sally forth to the mountains and the coast, where we linger in sunglasses and try to pass for normal.

But it is place we're talking about. The powers of place. As I write this my thoughts are perhaps unduly influenced by the fact that my right ear has swollen to the size and complexion of a rutabaga. I was working behind the cabin this afternoon, cutting up madrone and Douglas fir slash with the chain saw, when I apparently stepped too close to a yellowjacket nest. I injured none of their tribe, to my knowledge, but one of them sorely injured me. Those good and industrious citizens take place pretty seriously. I started to get out the .22 and shoot every one of them, but thought better of it and drank a tumbler of bourbon instead.

And now, a bit later, a spectacle outside my window only confirms my bitter state of mind. The place in question is the hummingbird feeder, and the chief influence of that place is to inspire in hummingbirds a fiercely intense desire to impale one another on their needlelike beaks. Surely they're expending more energy blustering in their buzzy way than they possibly can be deriving from the feeder. This behavior is not simply a consequence of feeding Kool-Aid to already over-amped birds—they try to kill each other over natural flower patches too. Nor can it be explained as the typically mindless and violent behavior of the male gender in general. Both sexes are represented in the fray, and females predominate. It is simply a demonstration of over-identification with place. Humans do it too. Look at Yosemite Valley on the Fourth of July. Look at any empty parking space in San Francisco. Look at Jerusalem.

When human beings settle in a place for the long run, good things occur overall, but there are dangers. Stickers run the severe risk of becoming sticks in the mud. Consider my state of Oregon, which was settled by nester-farmers who had one epic move in them, across the Oregon Trail, and having found paradise resolved not to stir again until the millennium. The more volatile and scintillating sorts—writers, murderers, prostitutes, lawyers, and other riffraff—tended toward California or Seattle. And so it happens that Oregonians are a complacent and conformist populace, excessively concerned with standards of behavior, bland and pasty on the outside, spiteful and poisonous within. It is we who originated the present nationwide spate of legal attacks on gay and lesbian rights. And it is we who consistently rank among the top five states in annual citizen challenges to morally subversive library books, books such as *Huckleberry Finn, The Catcher in the Rye,* and *The Color Purple.*

This pernicious pressure toward conformity is strongest in those places where communities are strongest and people live closest to the land—in the small towns. When my girlfriend and I lived in Klamath Falls in the early 1970s, we were frequently accosted by Mrs. Grandquist, our neighbor across the street. She was pointedly eager to lend us a lawn mower, and when she offered it she had the unnerving habit of looking at my hair. Our phone was just inside the front door, and sometimes as we arrived home it would ring before we were entirely *through* the door. "You left your lights on," Mrs. Grandquist would say. Or, "You ought to shut your windows when you leave. We've got burglars, you know." Not in that block of Denver Avenue, we didn't. Mrs. Grandquist and other watchful citizens with time on their hands kept insurance rates down, but the pressure of all those eyes and inquiring minds was at times intensely uncomfortable. Small towns are hard places in which to be different. Those yellowjackets are wary, and they can sting.

Customs of land use can be as ossified and difficult to budge as social customs.

The Amish, among other long-established rural communities, practice a good and responsible farming economy. But long-term association with a place no more *guarantees* good stewardship than a long-term marriage guarantees a loving and responsible relationship. As Aldo Leopold noted with pain, there are farmers who habitually abuse their land and cannot easily be induced to do otherwise. Thoreau saw the same thing in Concord—landspeople who in many ways must have known their places intimately, mistreated them continually. They whipped the dog every day because the dog was no good, and that's the way dogs had always been handled.

As for us of the green persuasions, we too are prone—perhaps more prone than most people—to orthodoxy and intolerance. It's not a good sign that we tend to lack a sense of humor about our values and work. We are too easily offended, a bit too holy in our beliefs. In Oregon, timber workers and Wise Use people are often more fun to be around than organizers and functionaries of the various green groups. Just compare bumper stickers. Ours say, "Stumps Don't Lie" or "Love Your Mother." Theirs say, "Earth First! (We'll Log the Other Planets Later)."

I don't mean to minimize the clear truth that ecological stupidity is epidemic in our land. I only mean to suggest that ecological correctness may not be the most helpful treatment. All of us, in any place or community or movement, tend to become insiders; we all need the stranger, the outsider, to shake up our perspective and keep us honest. Prominent among Edward Abbey's many virtues was his way of puncturing environmentalist pieties (and every other kind of piety). What's more, the outsider can see landscape with a certain clarity unavailable to the long-term resident. It was as a relative newcomer to the Southwest that Abbey took the notes that would become his best book, in which he imagined the canyon country more deeply than anyone had imagined it before. His eyes were sharpened by the passion of his outsider's love. He couldn't have written *Desert Solitaire* if he had been raised in Moab or Bluff.

Unlike Thoreau, who was born to his place, or Wendell Berry, who returned to the place he was born to, Edward Abbey came to his place from afar and took hold. More of a lifelong wanderer was John Muir, who we chiefly identify with the Sierra Nevada but who explored and sojourned in and wrote of a multitude of places, from the Gulf of Mexico to the Gulf of Alaska. I think Muir needed continually to see new landscapes and life forms in order to keep his passionate mind ignited. Some people have to be in motion, and their motion is not necessarily a pathology. For Muir it was an essential joy, a devotion, a continuous discovery of place and self. Marriage to place is something our land and society need, but not all of us are the marrying kind. Some of us are more given to the exhilarated attention and ardent exploration of *wooing*—less given to extended fidelity and more to rapture. "Rapture" is related to "rape" etymologically, but unlike the boomer, who ravages a place, the authentic wooer allows the place to ravish him.

Wooing often leads to marriage, of course, but not always. Is a life of wooing place after place less responsible than a life of settled marriage? It may be less sustainable, but the degree of its responsibility depends on the quality of the wooing. John Muir subjected himself utterly to the places he sought out. He walked from Wisconsin to the Gulf Coast, climbed a tree in a Sierra wind storm, survived a sub-zero night on the summit of Mount Shasta by scalding himself in a sulphurous volcanic vent. Nothing macho about it—he loved where he happened to be and refused to miss a lick of it. In his wandering, day to day and minute to minute, he was more placed than most of us will ever be, in a lifetime at home or a life on the move. Rootedness was not his genius and not his need.

Muir's devoted adventuring, of course, was something very different from the random restlessness of many in our culture today. Recently I sat through a dinner party during which the guests, most of them thirty-something, compared notes all evening about their travels through Asia. They were experts in border crossings, train transport, currency exchange, and even local art objects, but nothing I heard that evening indicated an influence of land or native peoples upon the traveler's soul. They were travel technicians. Many backpackers are the same, passing through wilderness places encapsulated in maps and objectives and high-tech gear. There *is* a pathology there, a serious one. It infects all of us to one degree or another. We have not yet arrived where we believe—and our color slides show—we have already been.

But if shifting around disconnected from land and community is our national disease, I would argue, perversely perhaps, or perhaps just homeopathically, that it is also an element of our national health. Hank Williams and others in our folk and country traditions stir something in many of us when they sing the delights of the open road, of rambling on the loose by foot or thumb or boxcar through the American countryside. Williams's "Ramblin' Man" believes that God intended him for a life of discovery beyond the horizons. Is this mere immaturity? Irresponsibility? An inability to relate to people or place? Maybe. But maybe also renewal, vitality, a growing of the soul. I know I'm never happier than when driving the highways and back roads of the West, pulling off somewhere, anywhere, to sleep in the truck and wake to a place I've never seen before. I can't defend the cost of that kind of travel in fossil fuel consumption and air befoulment—Williams's rambler at least took the fuel-efficient train—but I do know that it soothes and nurtures me as a man and a writer.

And if being rootless or even placeless is essential to some individuals, it may be essential in some way to the health of the culture. In Native American stories of the Northwest, I notice that Coyote doesn't seem to have a home. Either that, or he's sure on the road a lot. "Coyote was traveling upriver," the stories begin. "Coyote came over Neahkanie Mountain," "Coyote was going there. . . ." The stories take place in the early time when the order of the world was still in flux. Coyote, the placeless one, helps people and animals find their places. You wouldn't want to base a code of ethics on his character, which is unreliable and frequently ignoble, but he is the agent who introduces human beings to their roles and responsibilities in life. Coyote is the necessary inseminator. (Sometimes literally.) He is the shifty and shiftless traveler who fertilizes the locally rooted bloomings of the world.

Maybe Coyote moves among us as the stranger, often odd or even disagreeable, who brings reports from far places. Maybe that stranger is one of the carriers of our wildness, one of the mutant genes that keep our evolution fresh and thriving. It's for that stranger, says Elie Weisel, that an extra place is set at the Seder table. The voyager might arrive, the one who finds his home in the homes of others. He might tell a story, a story no one in the family is capable of telling, and children might hear that story and begin to imagine what they want their lives to be.

It could be Hank Williams who stops in, and he'll sing you a song (and maybe yours will be just the family he needs, and he won't have to die of whiskey and barbiturates in the back seat of a car). Or Huck Finn might be your stranger, on the run from civilisation, dressed as a girl and telling stupendous lies. It could be Dean

Moriarty, pausing on the road, and he never will stop talking. It might be Gerry Nanapush, the Chippewa power man Louise Erdrich has given us, escaped from jail still again to slip through the mists and snows with his old knowing. Or it might be Billy Parham or John Grady Cole, Cormac McCarthy's boy drifters—they'll want water for their horses, they'll be ready to eat, and if you're wise you'll feed them. They won't hardly talk themselves, but you may find yourself telling them the crucial story of your life.

Or yours may be the house where Odysseus calls, a still youngish man returning from war, passionate for his family and the flocks and vineyards of home. On the other hand, he could be an old man when he stands in your door. No one's quite sure what became of Odysseus. Homer tells us that he made it to Ithaca and set things in order, but the story leaves off there. Some say he resumed his settled life, living out his days as a placed and prosperous landsman. But others say that after all his adventures he couldn't live his old life again. Alfred, Lord Tennyson writes that he shipped out from Ithaca with his trusted crew. Maybe so, or maybe the poet got it only half right. Maybe Penelope, island bound for all those years, was stir crazy herself. Maybe they left the ranch to Telemachus and set out westward across the sea, two gray spirits yearning in desire

> To follow knowledge like a sinking star,
> Beyond the utmost bound of human thought.

—1995

RAYMOND CARVER

1938-1988

Raymond Carver, born into a working-class family in the logging community of Clatskanie, Oregon, became one of the most distinguished American fiction writers and poets of the twentieth century. Carver pumped gas, cleaned toilets, and managed an apartment complex before attending Humboldt State College (now California State University, Humboldt), Stanford University (on a Wallace Stegner fellowship), and the University of Iowa Writer's Workshop. Many of his short stories explore the struggles and private worries of common people; his characters, often poor and alcoholic, contemplate unemployment or bankruptcy or marital infidelity.

Carver published more than twenty books during his career, beginning with the poetry collection Near Klamath (1968). His collections of short fiction include Will You Please Be Quiet, Please? (1976), What We Talk About When We Talk About Love (1981), and Where I'm Calling From: New and Selected Stories (1988), and have been nominated at various times for the National Book Award, the Pulitzer Prize, and the National Book Critics Circle Award. Carver taught creative writing at the University of California at Santa Cruz and Berkeley; Syracuse University; the University of Iowa; Goddard College; and the University of Texas, El Paso. He died of lung cancer in 1988, having spent the last years of his life in Port Angeles, Washington.

"What's in Alaska?" first appeared in Will You Please Be Quiet, Please? *and was reprinted in* Where I'm Calling From. *It's a striking statement about disconnection and alienation, about indifference to place. We never learn where the characters are currently living, but Mary has received a vague job offer that may take her and Jack to Alaska. "I've always wanted to go to Alaska," says Jack, but he doesn't say why and the plan remains completely abstract within the narrative. Mary and Jack join their friends Helen and Carl for an evening of junk food and pot smoking, and Carl initiates the refrain: "What's in Alaska?" The characters' junk food diet and vagueness of speech mirror their indifference to the specifics of place. Carver tells this story not simply as an indictment of American culture, but as a revelation of the drabness of unrooted lives.*

WHAT'S IN ALASKA?

Jack got off work at three. He left the station and drove to a shoe store near his apartment. He put his foot up on the stool and let the clerk unlace his work boot.

"Something comfortable," Jack said. "For casual wear."

"I have something," the clerk said.

The clerk brought out three pairs of shoes and Jack said he would take the soft beige-colored shoes that made his feet feel free and springy. He paid the clerk and put the box with his boots under his arm. He looked down at his new shoes as he walked. Driving home, he felt that his foot moved freely from pedal to pedal.

"You bought some new shoes," Mary said. "Let me see."

"Do you like them?" Jack said.

"I don't like the color, but I'll bet they're comfortable. You needed new shoes."

He looked at the shoes again. "I've got to take a bath," he said.

"We'll have an early dinner," she said. "Helen and Carl asked us over tonight. Helen got Carl a water pipe for his birthday and they're anxious to try it out." Mary looked at him. "Is it all right with you?"

"What time?"

"Around seven."

"It's all right," he said.

She looked at his shoes again and sucked her cheeks. "Take your bath," she said.

Jack ran the water and took off his shoes and clothes. He lay in the tub for a while and then used a brush to get at the lube grease under his nails. He dropped his hands and then raised them to his eyes.

She opened the bathroom door. "I brought you a beer," she said. Steam drifted around her and out into the living room.

"I'll be out in a minute," he said. He drank some of the beer.

She sat on the edge of the tub and put her hand on his thigh. "Home from the wars," she said.

"Home from the wars," he said.

She moved her hand through the wet hair on his thigh. Then she clapped her hands. "Hey, I have something to tell you! I had an interview today, and I think they're going to offer me a job—in *Fairbanks*."

"Alaska?" he said.

She nodded. "What do you think of that?"

"I've always wanted to go to Alaska. Does it look pretty definite?"

She nodded again. "They liked me. They said I'd hear next week."

"That's great. Hand me a towel, will you? I'm getting out."

"I'll go and set the table," she said.

His fingertips and toes were pale and wrinkled. He dried slowly and put on clean clothes and the new shoes. He combed his hair and went out to the kitchen. He drank another beer while she put dinner on the table.

"We're supposed to bring some cream soda and something to munch on," she said. "We'll have to go by the store."

"Cream soda and munchies. Okay," he said.

When they had eaten, he helped her clear the table. Then they drove to the market and bought cream soda and potato chips and corn chips and onion-flavored snack crackers. At the checkout counter he added a handful of U-No bars to the order.

"Hey, yeah," she said when she saw them.

They drove home again and parked, and then they walked the block to Helen and Carl's.

Helen opened the door. Jack put the sack on the dining-room table. Mary sat down in the rocking chair and sniffed.

"We're late," she said. "They started without us, Jack." Helen laughed. "We had one when Carl came in. We haven't lighted the water pipe yet. We were waiting until you got here." She stood in the middle of the room, looking at them and grinning. "Let's see what's in the sack," she said. "Oh, wow! Say, I think I'll have one of these corn chips right now. You guys want some?"

"We just ate dinner," Jack said. "We'll have some pretty soon." Water had stopped running and Jack could hear Carl whistling in the bathroom.

"We have some Popsicles and some M&M's," Helen said. She stood beside the table and dug into the potato-chip bag. "If Carl ever gets out of the shower, he'll get the water pipe going." She opened the box of snack crackers and put one in her mouth. "Say, these are really good," she said.

"I don't know what Emily Post would say about you," Mary said.

Helen laughed. She shook her head.

Carl came out of the bathroom. "Hi, everybody. Hi, Jack. What's so funny?" he said, grinning. "I could hear you laughing."

"We were laughing at Helen," Mary said.

"Helen was just laughing," Jack said.

"She's funny." Carl said. "Look at the goodies! Hey, you guys ready for a glass of cream soda? I'll get the pipe going."

"I'll have a glass," Mary said. "What about you, Jack?"

"I'll have some," Jack said.

"Jack's on a little bummer tonight," Mary said.

"Why do you say that?" Jack asked. He looked at her. "That's a good way to put me on one."

"I was just teasing," Mary said. She came over and sat beside him on the sofa. "I was just teasing, honey."

"Hey, Jack, don't get on a bummer," Carl said. "Let me show you what I got for my birthday. Helen, open one of those bottles of cream soda while I get the pipe going. I'm real dry."

Helen carried the chips and crackers to the coffee table. Then she produced a bottle of cream soda and four glasses.

"Looks like we're going to have a party," Mary said.

"If I didn't starve myself all day, I'd put on ten pounds a week," Helen said.

"I know what you mean," Mary said.

Carl came out of the bedroom with the water pipe. "What do you think of this?" he said to Jack. He put the water pipe on the coffee table.

"That's really something," Jack said. He picked it up and looked at it.

"It's called a hookah," Helen said. "That's what they called it where I bought it. It's just a little one, but it does the job." She laughed.

"Where did you get it?" Mary said.

"What? That little place on Fourth Street. You know," Helen said.

"Sure. I know," Mary said. "I'll have to go in there some day," Mary said. She folded her hands and watched Carl.

"How does it work?" Jack said.

"You put the stuff here," Carl said. "And you light this. Then you inhale through this here and the smoke is filtered through the water. It has a good taste to it and it really hits you."

"I'd like to get Jack one for Christmas," Mary said. She looked at Jack and grinned and touched his arm.

"I'd like to have one," Jack said. He stretched his legs and looked at his shoes under the light.

"Here, try this," Carl said, letting out a thin stream of smoke and passing the tube to Jack. "See if this isn't okay."

Jack drew on the tube, held the smoke, and passed the tube to Helen.

"Mary first," Helen said. "I'll go after Mary. You guys have to catch up."

"I won't argue," Mary said. She slipped the tube in her mouth and drew rapidly, twice, and Jack watched the bubbles she made.

"That's really okay," Mary said. She passed the tube to Helen.

"We broke it in last night," Helen said, and laughed loudly.

"She was still stoned when she got up with the kids this morning," Carl said, and he laughed. He watched Helen pull on the tube.

"How are the kids?" Mary asked.

"They're fine," Carl said and put the tube in his mouth. Jack sipped the cream soda and watched the bubbles in the pipe. They reminded him of bubbles rising from a diving helmet. He imagined a lagoon and schools of remarkable fish.

Carl passed the tube.

Jack stood up and stretched.

"Where are you going, honey?" Mary asked.

"No place," Jack said. He sat down and shook his head and grinned. "Jesus."

Helen laughed.

"What's funny?" Jack said after a long time.

"God, I don't know," Helen said. She wiped her eyes and laughed again, and Mary and Carl laughed.

After a time Carl unscrewed the top of the water pipe and blew through one of the tubes. "It gets plugged sometimes."

"What did you mean when you said I was on a bummer?" Jack said to Mary.

"What?" Mary said.

Jack stared at her and blinked. "You said something about me being on a bummer. What made you say that?"

"I don't remember now, but I can tell when you are," she said. "But please don't bring up anything negative, okay?"

"Okay," Jack said. "All I'm saying is I don't know why you said that. If I wasn't on a bummer before you said it, it's enough when you say it to put me on one."

"If the shoe fits," Mary said. She leaned on the arm of the sofa and laughed until tears came.

"What was that?" Carl said. He looked at Jack and then at Mary. "I missed that one," Carl said.

"I should have made some dip for these chips," Helen said.

"Wasn't there another bottle of that cream soda?" Carl said.

"We bought two bottles," Jack said.

"Did we drink them both?" Carl said.

"Did we drink any?" Helen said and laughed. "No, I only opened one. I think I only opened one. I don't remember opening more than one," Helen said and laughed.

Jack passed the tube to Mary. She took his hand and guided the tube into her mouth. He watched the smoke flow over her lips a long time later.

"What about some cream soda?" Carl said.

Mary and Helen laughed.

"What about it?" Mary said.

"Well, I thought we were going to have us a glass," Carl said. He looked at Mary and grinned.

Mary and Helen laughed.

"What's funny?" Carl said. He looked at Helen and then at Mary. He shook his head. "I don't know about you guys," he said.

"We might go to Alaska," Jack said.

"Alaska?" Carl said. "What's in Alaska? What would you do up there?"

"I wish we could go someplace," Helen said.

"What's wrong with here?" Carl said. "What would you guys do in Alaska? I'm serious. I'd like to know."

Jack put a potato chip in his mouth and sipped his cream soda. "I don't know. What did you say?"

After a while Carl said, "What's in Alaska?"

"I don't know," Jack said. "Ask Mary. Mary knows. Mary, what am I going to do up there? Maybe I'll grow those giant cabbages you read about."

"Or pumpkins," Helen said. "Grow pumpkins."

"You'd clean up," Carl said. "Ship the pumpkins down here for Halloween. I'll be your distributor."

"Carl will be your distributor," Helen said.

"That's right," Carl said. "We'll clean up."

"Get rich," Mary said.

In a while Carl stood up. "I know what would taste good and that's some cream soda," Carl said.

Mary and Helen laughed.

"Go ahead and laugh," Carl said, grinning. "Who wants some?"

"Some what?" Mary said.

"Some cream soda," Carl said.

"You stood up like you were going to make a speech," Mary said.

"I hadn't thought of that," Carl said. He shook his head and laughed. He sat down. "That's good stuff," he said.

"We should have got more," Helen said.

"More what?" Mary said.

"More money," Carl said.

"No money," Jack said.

"Did I see some U-No bars in that sack?" Helen said.

"I bought some," Jack said. "I spotted them the last minute."

"U-No bars are good," Carl said.

"They're creamy," Mary said. "They melt in your mouth."

"We have some M&M's and Popsicles if anybody wants any," Carl said.

Mary said, "I'll have a Popsicle. Are you going to the kitchen?"

"Yeah, and I'm going to get the cream soda, too," Carl said. "I just remembered. You guys want a glass?"

"Just bring it all in and we'll decide," Helen said. "The M&M's too."

"Might be easier to move the kitchen out here," Carl said.

"When we lived in the city," Mary said, "people said you could see who'd turned on the night before by looking at their kitchen in the morning. We had a tiny kitchen when we lived in the city," she said.

"We had a tiny kitchen too," Jack said.

"I'm going out to see what I can find," Carl said.

"I'll come with you," Mary said.

Jack watched them walk to the kitchen. He settled back against the cushion and watched them walk. Then he leaned forward very slowly. He squinted. He saw Carl reach up to a shelf in the cupboard. He saw Mary move against Carl from behind and put her arms around his waist.

"Are you guys serious?" Helen said.

"Very serious," Jack said.

"About Alaska," Helen said.

He stared at her.

"I thought you said something," Helen said.

Carl and Mary came back. Carl carried a large bag of M&M's and a bottle of cream soda. Mary sucked on an orange Popsicle.

"Anybody want a sandwich?" Helen said. "We have sandwich stuff."

"Isn't it funny," Mary said. "You start with the desserts first and then you move on to the main course."

"It's funny," Jack said.

"Are you being sarcastic, honey?" Mary said.

"Who wants cream soda?" Carl said. "A round of cream soda coming up."

Jack held his glass out and Carl poured it full. Jack set the glass on the coffee table, but in reaching for it he knocked over the glass and the soda poured onto his shoe.

"Goddamn it," Jack said. "How do you like that? I spilled it on my shoe."

"Helen, do we have a towel? Get Jack a towel," Carl said.

"Those were new shoes," Mary said. "He just got them."

"They look comfortable," Helen said a long time later and handed Jack a towel.

"That's what I told him," Mary said.

Jack took the shoe off and rubbed the leather with the towel.

"It's done for," he said. "That cream soda will never come out."

Mary and Carl and Helen laughed.

"That reminds me, I read something in the paper," Helen said. She pushed on the tip of her nose with a finger and narrowed her eyes. "I can't remember what it was now," she said.

Jack worked the shoe back on. He put both feet under the lamp and looked at the shoes together.

"What did you read?" Carl said.

"What?" Helen said.

"You said you read something in the paper," Carl said.

Helen laughed. "I was just thinking about Alaska, and I remembered them finding a prehistoric man in a block of ice. Something reminded me."

"That wasn't in Alaska," Carl said.

"Maybe it wasn't, but it reminded me of it," Helen said.

"What *about* Alaska, you guys?" Carl said.

"There's nothing in Alaska," Jack said.

"He's on a bummer," Mary said.

"What'll you guys *do* in Alaska?" Carl said.

"There's nothing to do in Alaska," Jack said. He put his feet under the coffee table. Then he moved them out under the light once more. "Who wants a new pair of shoes?" Jack said.

"What's that noise?" Helen said.

They listened. Something scratched at the door.

"It sounds like Cindy," Carl said. "I'd better let her in."

"While you're up, get me a Popsicle," Helen said. She put her head back and laughed.

"I'll have another one too, honey," Mary said. "What did I say? I mean *Carl*," Mary said. "Excuse me. I thought I was talking to Jack."

"Popsicles all around," Carl said. "You want a Popsicle, Jack?"

"What?"

"You want an orange Popsicle?"

"An orange one," Jack said.

"Four Popsicles coming up," Carl said.

In a while he came back with the Popsicles and handed them around. He sat down and they heard the scratching again.

"I knew I was forgetting something," Carl said. He got up and opened the front door.

"Good Christ," he said, "if this isn't something. I guess Cindy went out for dinner tonight. Hey, you guys, look at this."

The cat carried a mouse into the living room, stopped to look at them, then carried the mouse down the hall.

"Did you see what I just saw?" Mary said. "Talk about a bummer."

Carl turned the hall light on. The cat carried the mouse out of the hall and into the bathroom.

"She's eating this mouse," Carl said.

"I don't think I want her eating a mouse in my bathroom," Helen said. "Make her get out of there. Some of the children's things are in there."

"She's not going to get out of here," Carl said.

"What about the mouse?" Mary said.

"What the hell," Carl said. "Cindy's got to learn to hunt if we're going to Alaska."

"Alaska?" Helen said. "What's all this about Alaska?"

"Don't ask me," Carl said. He stood near the bathroom door and watched the cat. "Mary and Jack said they're going to Alaska. Cindy's got to learn to hunt."

Mary put her chin in her hands and stared into the hall.

"She's eating the mouse," Carl said.

Helen finished the last of the corn chips. "I told him I didn't want Cindy eating a mouse in the bathroom. Carl?" Helen said.

"What?"

"Make her get out of the bathroom, I said," Helen said.

"For Christ's sake," Carl said.

"Look," Mary said. "Ugh. The goddamn cat is coming in here," Mary said.

"What's she doing?" Jack said.

The cat dragged the mouse under the coffee table. She lay down under the table and licked the mouse. She held the mouse in her paws and licked slowly, from head to tail.

"The cat's high," Carl said.

"It gives you the shivers," Mary said.

"It's just nature," Carl said.

"Look at her eyes," Mary said. "Look at the way she looks at us. She's high, all right."

Carl came over to the sofa and sat beside Mary. Mary inched toward Jack to give Carl room. She rested her hand on Jack's knee.

They watched the cat eat the mouse.

"Don't you ever feed that cat?" Mary said to Helen.

Helen laughed.

"You guys ready for another smoke?" Carl said.

"We have to go," Jack said.

"What's your hurry?" Carl said.

"Stay a little longer," Helen said. "You don't have to go yet."

Jack stared at Mary, who was staring at Carl. Carl stared at something on the rug near his feet.

Helen picked through the M&M's in her hand.

"I like the green ones best," Helen said.

"I have to work in the morning," Jack said.

"What a bummer he's on," Mary said. "You want to hear a bummer, folks? *There's* a bummer."

"Are you coming?" Jack said.

"Anybody want a glass of milk?" Carl said. "We've got some milk out there."

"I'm too full of cream soda," Mary said.

"There's no more cream soda," Carl said.

Helen laughed. She closed her eyes and then opened them and then laughed again.

"We have to go home," Jack said. In a while he stood up and said, "Did we have coats? I don't think we had coats."

"What? I don't think we had coats," Mary said. She stayed seated.

"We'd better go," Jack said.

"They have to go," Helen said.

Jack put his hands under Mary's shoulders and pulled her up.

"Good-bye, you guys," Mary said. She embraced Jack. "I'm so full I can hardly move," Mary said.

Helen laughed.

"Helen's always finding something to laugh at," Carl said, and Carl grinned. "What are you laughing at, Helen?"

"I don't know. Something Mary said," Helen said.

"What did I say?" Mary said.

"I can't remember," Helen said.

"We have to go," Jack said.

"So long," Carl said. "Take it easy."

Mary tried to laugh.

"Let's go," Jack said.

"Night, everybody," Carl said. "Night, Jack," Jack heard Carl say very, very slowly.

Outside, Mary held Jack's arm and walked with her head down. They moved slowly on the sidewalk. He listened to the scuffing sounds her shoes made. He heard the sharp and separate sound of a dog barking and above that a murmuring of very distant traffic.

She raised her head. "When we get home, Jack, I want to be fucked, talked to, diverted. Divert me, Jack. I need to be diverted tonight." She tightened her hold on his arm.

He could feel the dampness in that shoe. He unlocked the door and flipped the light.

"Come to bed," she said.

"I'm coming," he said.

He went to the kitchen and drank two glasses of water. He turned off the living-room light and felt his way along the wall into the bedroom.

"Jack!" she yelled. "Jack!"

"Jesus Christ, it's me!" he said. "I'm trying to get the light on."

He found the lamp, and she sat up in bed. Her eyes were bright. He pulled the stem on the alarm and began taking off his clothes. His knees trembled.

"Is there anything else to smoke?" she said.

"We don't have anything," he said.

"Then fix me a drink. We have something to drink. Don't tell me we don't have something to drink," she said.

"Just some beer."

They stared at each other.

"I'll have a beer," she said.

"You really want a beer?"

She nodded slowly and chewed her lip.

He came back with the beer. She was sitting with his pillow on her lap. He gave her the can of beer and then crawled into bed and pulled the covers up.

"I forgot to take my pill," she said.

"What?"

"I forgot my pill."

He got out of bed and brought her the pill. She opened her eyes and he dropped the pill onto her outstretched tongue. She swallowed some beer with the pill and he got back in bed.

"Take this. I can't keep my eyes open," she said.

He set the can on the floor and then stayed on his side and stared into the dark hallway. She put her arm over his ribs and her fingers crept across his chest.

"What's in Alaska?" she said.

He turned on his stomach and eased all the way to his side of the bed. In a moment she was snoring.

Just as he started to turn off the lamp, he thought he saw something in the hall. He kept staring and thought he saw it again, a pair of small eyes. His heart turned. He blinked and kept staring. He leaned over to look for something to throw. He picked up one of his shoes. He sat up straight and held the shoe with both hands. He heard her snoring and set his teeth. He waited. He waited for it to move once more, to make the slightest noise.

—1976

LUTHER STANDING BEAR

c. 1868-1939

Among the prominent writers of Native American literature, Luther Standing Bear is in many ways the most paradoxical—a Hollywood Indian who was also one of the most strident defenders of traditional Native ways of life. Less well known than two of his Sioux contemporaries, Dr. Charles A. Eastman and Gertrude Simmons Bonnin (a.k.a. Zitkala-Sa), Standing Bear sharply critiqued the American culture that during his lifetime obliterated the last of the old Native ways. In a 1931 article for H. L. Mencken's American Mercury *magazine, he wrote that by attempting to live on the reservation, he had tried to adapt himself and "make readjustments to fit the white man's mode of existence." This, he found, did not work. "I developed into a chronic disturber. I was a bad Indian, and the [U.S. government] agent and I never got on. I remained a hostile, even a savage, if you please. And I still am. I am incurable."*

Luther Standing Bear was probably born in what is now South Dakota. At age twelve he attended a school the U.S. government set up for Indian children in Pennsylvania. In his midteens he returned to his native land, only to find his people subjected to reservation life at Rosebud and Pine Ridge. In 1890 the massacre at Wounded Knee occurred, representing the final subjugation of Native peoples to the U.S. government. Around the turn of the century, Standing Bear worked for Buffalo Bill Cody's Wild West Show and traveled with them to perform in England. After returning home, he was chosen chief of the Oglala Sioux, but seven years later left the reservation because of repeated conflicts with the U.S. government Indian agents. He then made a career as a film actor in Hollywood. It was not until the 1920s that he began his literary career, publishing an autobiography, My People the Sioux *(1928), and an ethnographic study and cultural critique,* Land of the Spotted Eagle *(1933).*

"Nature" is taken from "Indian Wisdom," the seventh chapter in Land of the Spotted Eagle. *In both subject matter and tone, this piece compares to other Native American works with a strong political message, especially the popular but authentically suspect text of Chief Seattle's "the earth does not belong to man, man belongs to the earth" letter. Standing Bear, in portraying the now lost world of his Sioux ancestors, directs his readers' attention to the bankrupt moral core of mainstream America. Near the end of this book, in a section entitled "What the Indian Means to America," he writes: "The white man does not understand the Indian for the reason that he does not understand America. He is too far removed from its formative processes." In Standing Bear's day, a growing number of non-Indian readers were sympathetic to these words. There are significantly more such readers today.*

NATURE

The Lakota was a true naturist—a lover of Nature. He loved the earth and all things of the earth, the attachment growing with age. The old people came literally to love the soil and they sat or reclined on the ground with a feeling of being close to a mothering power. It was good for the skin to touch the earth and the old people liked to remove their moccasins and walk with bare feet on the sacred earth. Their tipis were built upon the earth and their altars were made of earth. The birds that flew in the air came to rest upon the earth and it was the final abiding place of all things that lived and grew. The soil was soothing, strengthening, cleansing, and healing.

This is why the old Indian still sits upon the earth instead of propping himself up and away from its life-giving forces. For him, to sit or lie upon the ground is to be able to think more deeply and to feel more keenly; he can see more clearly into the mysteries of life and come closer in kinship to other lives about him.

The earth was full of sounds which the old-time Indian could hear, sometimes putting his ear to it so as to hear more clearly. The forefathers of the Lakotas had done this for long ages until there had come to them real understanding of earth ways. It was almost as if the man were still a part of the earth as he was in the beginning, according to the legend of the tribe. This beautiful story of the genesis of the Lakota people furnished the foundation for the love they bore for earth and all things of the earth. Wherever the Lakota went, he was with Mother Earth. No matter where he roamed by day or slept by night, he was safe with her. This thought comforted and sustained the Lakota and he was eternally filled with gratitude.

From Wakan Tanka there came a great unifying life force that flowed in and through all things—the flowers of the plains, blowing winds, rocks, trees, birds, animals—and was the same force that had been breathed into the first man. Thus all things were kindred and brought together by the same Great Mystery.

Kinship with all creatures of the earth, sky, and water was a real and active principle. For the animal and bird world there existed a brotherly feeling that kept the Lakota safe among them. And so close did some of the Lakotas come to their feathered and furred friends that in true brotherhood they spoke a common tongue.

The animal had rights—the right of man's protection, the right to live, the right to multiply, the right to freedom, and the right to man's indebtedness—and in recognition of these rights the Lakota never enslaved the animal, and spared all life that was not needed for food and clothing.

This concept of life and its relations was humanizing and gave to the Lakota an abiding love. It filled his being with the joy and mystery of living; it gave him reverence for all life; it made a place for all things in the scheme of existence with equal importance to all. The Lakota could despise no creature, for all were of one blood, made by the same hand, and filled with the essence of the Great Mystery. In spirit the Lakota was humble and meek. 'Blessed are the meek: for they shall inherit the earth,' was true for the Lakota, and from the earth he inherited secrets long since forgotten. His religion was sane, normal, and human.

Reflection upon life and its meaning, consideration of its wonders, and observation of the world of creatures, began with childhood. The earth, which was called *Maka,* and the sun, called *Anpetuwi,* represented two functions somewhat analogous to those of male and female. The earth brought forth life, but the warming, enticing rays of the sun coaxed it into being. The earth yielded, the sun engendered.

In talking to children, the old Lakota would place a hand on the ground and explain: 'We sit in the lap of our Mother. From her we, and all other living things, come. We shall soon pass, but the place where we now rest will last forever.' So we, too, learned to sit or lie on the ground and become conscious of life about us in its multitude of forms. Sometimes we boys would sit motionless and watch the swallow, the tiny ants, or perhaps some small animal at its work and ponder on its industry and ingenuity; or we lay on our backs and looked long at the sky and when the stars came out made shapes from the various groups. The morning and evening star always attracted attention, and the Milky Way was a path which was traveled by the ghosts. The old people told us to heed *wa maka skan,* which were the 'moving things of earth.' This meant, of course, the animals that lived and moved about, and the stories they told of *wa maka skan* increased our interest and delight. The wolf, duck, eagle, hawk, spider, bear, and other creatures, had marvelous powers, and each one was useful and helpful to us. Then there were the warriors who lived in the sky and dashed about on their spirited horses during a thunder storm, their lances clashing with the thunder and glittering with the lightning. There was *wiwila,* the living spirit of the spring, and the stones that flew like a bird and talked like a man. Everything was possessed of personality, only differing with us in form. Knowledge was inherent in all things. The world was a library and its books were the stones, leaves, grass, brooks, and the birds and animals that shared, alike with us, the storms and blessings of earth. We learned to do what only the student of nature ever learns, and that was to feel beauty. We never railed at the storms, the furious winds, and the biting frosts and snows. To do so intensified human futility, so whatever came we adjusted ourselves, by more effort and energy if necessary, but without complaint. Even the lightning did us no harm, for whenever it came too close, mothers and grandmothers in every tipi put cedar leaves on the coals and their magic kept danger away. Bright days and dark days were both expressions of the Great Mystery, and the Indian reveled in being close to the Big Holy. His worship was unalloyed, free from the fears of civilization.

I have come to know that the white mind does not feel toward nature as does the Indian mind, and it is because, I believe, of the difference in childhood instruction. I have often noticed white boys gathered in a city by-street or alley jostling and pushing one another in a foolish manner. They spend much time in this aimless fashion, their natural faculties neither seeing, hearing, nor feeling the varied life that surrounds them. There is about them no awareness, no acuteness, and it is this dullness that gives ugly mannerisms full play; it takes from them natural poise and stimulation. In contrast, Indian boys, who are naturally reared, are alert to their surroundings; their senses are not narrowed to observing only one another, and they cannot spend hours seeing nothing, hearing nothing, and thinking nothing in particular. Observation was certain in its rewards; interest, wonder, admiration grew, and the fact was appreciated that life was more than mere human manifestation; that it was expressed in a multitude of forms. This appreciation enriched Lakota existence. Life was vivid and pulsing; nothing was casual and commonplace. The Indian lived—lived in every sense of the word—from his first to his last breath.

The character of the Indian's emotion left little room in his heart for antagonism toward his fellow creatures, this attitude giving him what is sometimes referred to as 'the Indian point of view.' Every true student, every lover of nature has 'the Indian point of view,' but there are few such students, for few white men approach nature in the Indian manner. The Indian and the white man sense things differently because the white man has put distance between himself and nature; and assuming a lofty place in the scheme of order of things has lost for him both reverence and understanding. Consequently the white man finds Indian philosophy obscure—wrapped, as he says, in a maze of ideas and symbols which he does not understand. A writer friend, a white man whose knowledge of 'Injuns' is far more profound and sympathetic than the average, once said that he had been privileged, on two occasions, to see the contents of an Indian medicine-man's bag in which were bits of earth, feathers, stones, and various other articles of symbolic nature; that a 'collector' showed him one and laughed, but a great and world-famous archeologist showed him the other with admiration and wonder. Many times the Indian is embarrassed and baffled by the white man's allusions to nature in such terms as crude, primitive, wild, rude, untamed, and savage. For the Lakota, mountains, lakes, rivers, springs, valleys, and woods were all finished beauty; winds, rain, snow, sunshine, day, night, and change of seasons brought interest; birds, insects, and animals filled the world with knowledge that defied the discernment of man.

But nothing the Great Mystery placed in the land of the Indian pleased the white man, and nothing escaped his transforming hand. Wherever forests have not been mowed down; wherever the animal is recessed in their quiet protection; wherever the earth is not bereft of four-footed life—that to him is an 'unbroken wilderness.' But since for the Lakota there was no wilderness; since nature was not dangerous but hospitable; not forbidding but friendly, Lakota philosophy was healthy—free from fear and dogmatism. And here I find the great distinction between the faith of the Indian and the white man. Indian faith sought the harmony of man with his surroundings; the other sought the dominance of surroundings. In sharing, in loving all and everything, one people naturally found a measure of the thing they sought; while, in fearing, the other found need of conquest. For one man the world was full of beauty; for the other it was a place of sin and ugliness to be endured until he went to another world, there to become a creature of wings, half-man and half-bird. Forever one man directed his Mystery to change the world He had made; forever this man pleaded with Him to chastise His wicked ones; and forever he implored his Wakan Tanka to send His light to earth. Small wonder this man could not understand the other.

But the old Lakota was wise. He knew that man's heart, away from nature, becomes hard; he knew that lack of respect for growing, living things soon led to lack of respect for humans too. So he kept his youth close to its softening influence.

—1933

JEANNE WAKATSUKI HOUSTON

B. 1934

Shortly after the bombing of Pearl Harbor by the Japanese, when Jeanne (Toyo) Wakatsuki was seven years old, the U.S. government forced her family to relocate from Long Beach (on the coast near Los Angeles) to an internment camp called Manzanar in the austere desert landscape of the Owens Valley in eastern California. As a result of President Roosevelt's signing of Executive Order 9066, which gave the War Department authority to define critical military zones and to remove from those zones anyone deemed a risk to the war effort, the same fate befell 110,000 other people of Japanese ancestry living on the West Coast, most of whom were American citizens. In 1973, Jeanne Wakatsuki Houston published an evocative memoir of her life in the internment camp and after. Entitled Farewell to Manzanar, *it is co-authored with her husband, the novelist James D. Houston. As a result of this book, she has become, in the words of the* Los Angeles Times, *"quite unintentionally, a voice for a heretofore silent segment of society."*

Manzanar, located just a few miles from where the writer Mary Austin had lived half a century earlier, was but one of several internment camps spread out across the remote areas of the interior West. With its blocks of wooden barracks, armed guards, and searchlight towers, it gave all the appearances of a concentration camp, yet the 10,000 people who suddenly found themselves resident there managed to establish a community not all that different from those they had left behind. Ansel Adams's book Born Free and Equal *(1944) provides a photographic record of life at Manzanar. In late 1944, the Supreme Court ruled that loyal U.S. citizens could not be held against their will in detention camps, but by then the war was nearly over and the humiliation suffered by a large segment of the American population could not be undone.*

"Rock Garden," like Farewell to Manzanar, *is drawn from Houston's childhood memories of the camp. It was first presented as a broadcast on National Public Radio's* Sounds of Writing *series during the summer of 1990 and later collected in the anthology* Dreamers and Desperadoes: Contemporary Short Fiction of the American West *(1993). The story gives a taste of how those interned at Manzanar went about making this foreign landscape their home. In particular, the old man named Morita has through meditation tuned into the spirits of the previous residents of the place and has discerned a link between his tribe and the earlier one that gives him a sense of belonging. His cultivation of a Zen garden, where rocks stand for mountains and tiny white pebbles raked in precise swirls approximate the look of a pool of water, is a devotional ritual that creates a sacred space in the midst of the camp. Thus by small daily acts he honors and binds himself to this place where he is held captive.*

ROCK GARDEN

Early morning was Reiko's favorite time. Above white-peaked Mount Whitney, the cloudless sky sparkled and crisp air cooled the desert flatland. Alone, she could sit on the tree stump outside the barracks door and watch people begin their day.

Her family's cubicle faced the latrines, giving her a grandstand view of neighbors clattering past in homemade wooden/*geta* slippers as they formed lines outside the two buildings—one for men, another for women. Like colored rags of a kite's tail, the queue of robes and kimonos snaked through the block's center. Yawning and clutching tin basins that held their toiletries, the neighbors seemed not to notice the lone spectator.

Since coming to the internment camp a year earlier, Reiko had learned to entertain herself. The elders had talked about starting a school, but so far, the only classes were those run by Miss Honda and Myrtle Fujino, old maids from Block 22. Shy and soft-spoken, the thirtyish spinsters volunteered their services, which actually amounted to caretaking, since neither was a teacher. They taught the girls sewing. Not knowing what to do with boys, they made them saw wood, or sent them out to the firebreaks, which were open, sandy acres between the barrack block compounds. For hours boys roamed in the sand, looking for arrowheads left from the days when Paiute Indians flourished in these high desert valleys.

Reiko hated sewing. She never had handled needles and thread, and kept pricking her fingers while stitching rag dolls made out of old clothes. What was supposed to be Raggedy Ann's white shirt face looked more like a mangled fist, lumps and bloody smears disfiguring it.

People-watching in the morning was much more interesting than sewing. It was Reiko's new game. She imagined herself a queen seated on a throne while the throngs passed in review. A wise and dignified queen. When Potato ran by in his Boy Scout uniform, twirling a dead rattlesnake like a lasso, she remained unruffled. Nor did she flinch when he came back and dangled the limp snake in front of her face.

Potato was the block idiot. Fat and tall, he always wore his Boy Scout uniform, swollen torso and haunches bursting at the khaki seams. He was twenty but had the mind of someone Reiko's age. She was ten. He was her court jester, and when she grew tired of the sinewy rope swaying in her face, she waved him away imperiously. With a final flick of the snake, he stuck his tongue at her and lumbered out of sight.

One morning someone joined her. Old man Morita, who lived two barracks away, was sitting outside his door, whittling wood. She figured he was people-watching, too. In the year they had been neighbors she never had spoken with him. Morita-san was deaf. The block people said the din of his wife's nagging had caused him to lose his hearing. Reiko believed it. She had heard Lady Morita's high-pitched rumbling while waiting in line at the mess hall. It was no wonder they called her Thunder-mouth. Her loud words crashed and gushed like white water storming over river rocks.

After a week of sitting, Reiko finally caught Morita-san looking her way. She waved. He smiled, creasing his walnut-brown face into tiny folds. Even from a distance, she could see his eyes were merry, and those eyes filled her with sadness. Both grandfathers were dead, and she hadn't seen her father for more than a year, ever since the FBI took him away to prison in North Dakota. The only male in the family was Ivan, who was fourteen. Seeing Morita-san's smiling eyes reminded Reiko how much she missed her father.

The next morning she waved at the old man and called cheerfully, "Good morning, Morita-san." Showing off she knew some Japanese, she added, "*O-hai-yo-gozai-mas.* Good morning." Then she remembered he probably couldn't read lips from a distance.

Morita-san beckoned. She scampered over to his perching place, which was a large square boulder, probably retrieved from one of the creeks. Sitting on the rock and framed by closed double wooden doors, he looked like pictures she had seen of her ancestors in Japan. He wore a dark blue kimono belted low on his belly and was barefoot.

"You like meditate in morning?"

It was the first time Reiko heard his voice. She had wondered if deaf people could speak, and it surprised her he spoke pidgin English, just like Ba-chan, her grandmother.

"What's meditate?" She spoke the new word slowly.

"Like pray," he said. His warm eyes crinkled. He dropped the long limb he was carving and bowed his forehead against his clasped hands. She'd seen Ba-chan doing the same thing before the Buddha statue in their room.

"Oh, to Buddha, you mean?"

"So, so," he answered. "I pray Indian spirit, too."

This fascinated Reiko. People said the internment camp was built over old Indian burial grounds. That's why there were so many arrowheads. The countless stories of Indian ghost sightings terrified her and she never walked in the firebreaks alone or went to the latrine at night except with Mama. In a way, she wished she weren't afraid, because she would like to see a ghost.

"Have you ever seen an Indian spirit?" she asked.

"All time. I see many. They talk me."

"Really? What do they say?" She wondered if he read their lips.

"They happy Japanese people here in desert. Say we come from same tribe across ocean."

He stood up, leaning on the cane he was whittling, and motioned for her to follow. Standing next to him, she was startled to see he was her height. They rounded the barrack corner past tall bamboo plants that extended in a row to the next barrack, screening from view the space between. She had often wondered what was behind that feathery wall.

Reiko knew she was entering a special place, maybe even a holy place. In her view, Morita-san already had changed from a deaf old henpecked man to a wizard.

Hidden behind the bamboo was a brilliant white lake of tiny pebbles. Kidney-shaped and smoothly raked, it was about four feet wide and seven long. At one end, five huge stones formed an altarlike platform. One flat stone held dried bones, rocks, feathers, and gnarled driftwood. Two covered urns stood in the middle.

She watched while the old man knelt before the altar, eyes closed, lips moving. He stood up and shuffled over to a moss-covered rock. With a tin cup, he drew water from a bucket and ladled it over the green velvet mound, chanting strange sounds.

"I teach you meditate," he said.

"*Arigato.* Thank you." She spoke another one of the few Japanese words she knew. She still didn't know what "meditate" was, but if it meant getting to know Morita-san, she would try it.

"Tomorrow morning. Same time," he said and patted the top of her head.

For some reason she decided not to tell anyone. Not that anyone would be interested. Since coming to camp, her brother and sister went their own way, making friends and eating in another block mess hall away from the family. Ba-chan was suspicious of everything and probably would claim that Morita-san's deafness was a punishment from the gods.

"Bad karma," she could hear her grandmother say. "He do something bad in past life."

The first few days he never spoke a word. He sat cross-legged, ignoring her. But she guessed that was the way he began things, remembering how he didn't acknowledge her when they people-watched earlier.

On the sixth morning, just as she was about to decide not to come anymore, things changed. He had set up a low table, a smooth, flat slab of driftwood, and motioned for her to sit down across from him.

"Close eyes," he said.

She obeyed. Her eyelids quivered, eager to lift so she could see what he was doing, but she kept them closed. A breeze blew above her head, like someone had waved a fan.

"Namu-amida-butsu . . . Crazee Horse-su . . . Geroneee-mo. Namu-amida-butsu . . . Crazee Horse-su . . . Geroneee-mo," he chanted. Over and over he singsonged the Buddhist mantra and Indian names until Reiko was lulled into a dreamy state.

She imagined braves on horses galloping across the open firebreak. She heard drumming—sharp, staccato beats that cracked like firecrackers. Racing back and forth across the desert, the horses' manes fluttered like torn flags, and orange smoke trailed from dilated nostrils. They flew to the desert's edge but stopped suddenly, rearing up and neighing. Something prevented them from passing over to green pastureland. It was barbed wire!

Her eyes snapped open. The old man was beating two smooth stones together. Clack-clack-clack.

"So, so. You see something?"

"Am I supposed to?"

"What you see?"

Reiko liked this game. "I saw Indians. They were riding horses with smoke coming out of their noses. They were trying to get out of camp."

"Hah! Hah!" Morita-san laughed loudly. "Very good. You good meditate."

"Is that all I do? Just imagine things?" It wasn't much different from making up stories about people, except she had never seen these Indians before.

He brought one of the urns to the table and from it retrieved a large obsidian arrowhead. It was glittering, black, and perfectly shaped.

"For you," he said.

She gasped, too pleased to speak.

"This magic. Make wish come true."

"Thank you, Morita-san. Arigato." She couldn't wait to show it to Ivan.

From that day on, Reiko practically lived at the old man's sanctuary. After breakfast, instead of going to recreation classes, she sat with him before the shrine, "meditating," and helped garden his rocks. She learned to chant while pouring water over the moss stone, which looked to her like a turtle, asleep with head drawn inside its shell. Once she thought she saw it move.

He taught her to rake the white pebbles with rusty prongs, to carve flowing lines that undulated through the frozen sea.

"Rock, water, plant, wood all same. You, me, rock same." He pointed at Reiko and then some stones. "Everything same, same."

It amazed Reiko how his garden reflected this. He had watered a boulder until it became alive with moss. It wouldn't surprise her if it did turn into a turtle someday and crawl away. And the lake of pebbles seemed to surge and roll, making her seasick if she stared too long.

Sometimes he performed rituals. After burning orange peels in a tin can, he sprinkled ashes on the altar and drew symbols . . . circles, diamonds, squares, calligraphy. They rarely talked, mostly meditating, which she saw as another form of people-watching, except she made up the people, too. When she told him what she saw in her mind, he would cackle and laugh very hard, slapping a hand against his sinewy thigh.

One day he took her outside the camp. People had begun to venture beyond the barbed-wire fence since the soldiers in the guard towers had left. Reiko was glad they were gone. She was afraid of guns. One of the soldiers had shot Daryl Izumi, who was only fifteen and just looking for arrowheads. She stayed far away from the high wooden towers, thinking of them as castle turrets bordering a wide desert moat.

About a half mile out, a clump of elder trees rose from the barren landscape. Inside the oasis, a creek gurgled over shiny white pebbles, the same as Morita-san's rock lake.

"We walk on path," he said, and splashed into the creek.

Reiko was baffled, but followed anyway, having learned to accept his strange way of seeing things.

As they waded in the creek/path, he picked up pebbles and driftwood, depositing them in a sack tied around his waist. It was almost as if he were plucking fruit from a watery garden.

Then one morning she found Morita-san dressed in shirt and baggy trousers and boots. He was tinkering with a bamboo fishing pole. She wondered if he planned on fishing in the pebbled lake, not doubting for one moment he could pull up a wriggling trout from its raked depths.

"I go fishing up mountain." He pointed west to the sheer wall of the high Sierra Nevada.

"But that's so far away. Are we allowed to go that far?"

Reiko knew it was at least ten miles to the base of the mountain.

"Me old man. I go fishing."

Just then, Lady Morita flung open the door and began jabbering. Morita-san continued working on his pole, as if she weren't there. Thunder rolled from her mouth. Finally she stomped back into the cubicle.

Reiko walked with him to the edge of camp.

"Can I go with you, Morita-san?" She felt nervous about his going alone.

"No," he said bluntly, then patted the top of her head, smiling. "I come back tonight."

He shuffled past the barbed wire. "I catch many fish!" he shouted, waving to her as he trudged through the sagebrush. She watched him weave around tumbleweed and boulders until he became a small spider, the bamboo pole an antenna scanning the desert. She imagined his path turning into a creek glittering with brilliant stones that led up to Mount Whitney.

He didn't return that night or the next day. By the third day, Mr. Kato, the block manager, called a meeting, and the men voted to form a search party. Lady Morita was screaming and hysterical, afraid the administration would find out her husband had violated the boundary. It was a mess . . . with neighbors arguing about ways to keep her from having a nervous breakdown.

Reiko wasn't worried. She knew Morita-san could take care of himself. The gossip made her angry, though. Someone said he had committed suicide, driven to it by his thunder-mouth wife. Someone else said he drove himself crazy meditating. She even heard he had hiked over the mountains to Fresno, where he was passing as Chinese.

After a week, she, too, became anxious. Very early in the morning, when the sky was gray and still sprinkled with stars, she stole over to the sanctuary. She sat in front of the shrine, cross-legged, the large arrowhead in her hand, and began to chant. She tried to emulate Morita-san.

"Namu-amida-butsu . . . Crazee Horse-su . . . Geroneee-mo. Namu-amida-butsu . . . Crazee Horse-su . . . Geroneee-mo." She made her voice quiver, sucking in her belly, surprising herself with strange guttural sounds. She lost track of time.

The urgent swishing of leaves . . . and then a horse's neigh broke her reverie. Across the rock lake, several warriors approached leading horses. When they arrived at the pool's edge, the pebbles turned to water. As the horses drank, their frothy flanks heaved. They had been riding hard. Suddenly a figure materialized. It was Morita-san! Standing with the braves as if he belonged there! Her heart raced. She wanted to open her eyes, to shout and swim across the pool!

But a whirlwind suddenly spun up from out of the center. It grew wider and wider, churning waves and shaking leaves, whirling through the garden. Encircling Morita-san and the Indians, it lifted them high over the barracks. Morita-san was smiling, waving to her with his bamboo pole. She stood up to wave back, and was just about to open her eyes when the figures became iridescent, enveloped in golden light.

"Morita-san!" she cried.

The search for the old man continued. After another week, it was called off. By then, Reiko had resigned herself to his permanent disappearance, even to the thought of death.

She returned to people-watching, no longer caring to meditate. And soon the much-talked-about school finally began, a real school like the one she had attended in Santa Monica before the war. Her life became full—with studies and new friends. Ivan began lessons at the judo pavilion, where Reiko spent many warm hours at dusk watching him flip and fall, grunting unintelligible commands.

Years later, in the last month before the camp closed, some Caucasian hunters hiking in the mountains reported sighting human bones at the bottom of a narrow ravine. It was assumed the remains were those of Morita-san. Reiko didn't feel too sad. Her old mentor had taught all things were one—flesh, rocks, plants, water. "Same, same," he had said. And so his bones, strewn about in the deep crevice, were resting comfortably, slowly returning to mountain granite and later, desert sand, while his ghost would roam the barbed-wire firebreaks forever with the Indians, his tribesmen, chanting and laughing as they galloped in the clear black night.

—1990

PAT MORA

B. 1942

Pat Mora is what she calls a "Texican," born in El Paso, Texas, of Mexican ancestry. Reflected in her work as a poet, essayist, and writer of children's stories is a commitment to retrieving her Mexican past as well as exploring the imprint of the Chihuahuan desert, in whose magical presence she has spent most of her life. Like many Chicana writers, Mora was motivated to write "because I felt our voices were absent from what is labeled American literature, but is U.S. Eurocentric literature seasoned sparingly with a bit of color." Comparing her work to that of a curandera, or traditional Mexican healer, she writes, "The Chicana writer seeks to heal cultural wounds of historical neglect by providing opportunities to remember the past, to share and ease bitterness, to describe what has been viewed as unworthy of description, to cure by incantations and rhythms, by listening with her entire being and responding."

Mora was educated at Texas Western College (B.A.) and the University of Texas at El Paso (M.A.). She taught English at the high school, community college, and university level before working as an administrator at the University of Texas at El Paso for most of the 1980s while she was honing her writing. The mother of three children, she has written many children's books, as well as four collections of poetry—Chants (1984), Borders (1986), Communion (1991), and Agua Santa: Holy Water (1995)—plus a book entitled Nepantla: Essays from the Land in the Middle (1993) and a family memoir, The House of Houses (1997). Although Mora moved to Cincinnati with her husband, an archaeologist and university professor, in 1989, her writing has continued to be influenced by the desert landscape she considers her home.

"Curandera" is from Chants. Mora has written, "The desert, mi madre, is my stern teacher." It is the teacher of the indigenous healer in the poem as well, who incorporates her knowledge of herbal lore, learned no doubt through the oral tradition of her people, with attention to the most subtle of changes in the natural world. "Curandera" documents and dignifies a way of life so attuned to the land and its rhythms that the woman and the desert seem almost to be a single organism.

CURANDERA

They think she lives alone
on the edge of town in a two-room house
where she moved when her husband died
at thirty-five of a gunshot wound
in the bed of another woman. The *curandera*
and house have aged together to the rhythm
of the desert.

She wakes early, lights candles before
her sacred statues, brews tea of *yerbabuena*.
She moves down her porch steps, rubs
cool morning sand into her hands, into her arms.
Like a large black bird, she feeds on
the desert, gathering herbs for her basket.

Her days are slow, days of grinding
dried snake into powder, of crushing
wild bees to mix with white wine.
And the townspeople come, hoping
to be touched by her ointments,
her hands, her prayers, her eyes.
She listens to their stories, and she listens
to the desert, always, to the desert.

By sunset she is tired. The wind
strokes the strands of long gray hair,
the smell of drying plants drifts
into her blood, the sun seeps
into her bones. She dozes
on her back porch. Rocking, rocking.

At night she cooks chopped cactus
and brews more tea. She brushes a layer
of sand from her bed, sand which covers
the table, stove, floor. She blows
the statues clean, the candles out.
Before sleeping, she listens to the message
of the owl and the *coyote*. She closes her eyes
and breathes with the mice and snakes
and wind.

—1984

WILLIAM KITTREDGE

B. 1932

A writer of fiction and essays, William Kittredge has made a name for himself in recent decades by crafting narratives of rustic life in the American West and articulating some of the most scathing critiques of the region's legacy of conquest. In "Owning It All," the title piece of his 1987 essay collection, he suggests that people in the West today are struggling to revise the "mythology" of the region, so rooted in violence toward nature and other people, and to find a new way to live—"a new story to inhabit," as he writes. Much of Kittredge's writing aims to dismantle the old story of the West and reimagine the region in a more wholesome and sustainable way.

Born and raised on his family's cattle ranch in southeastern Oregon,

Kittredge has spent most of his life in the West. He earned a B.S. in agriculture from Oregon State University, along the way studying with novelist Bernard Malamud. After an Air Force stint in Guam, he returned to the MC Ranch in Oregon's Warner Valley in 1958 and stayed until his family sold the ranch in 1967. Kittredge then spent a year at the University of Oregon before transferring to the M.F.A. program at the University of Iowa, from which he graduated in 1969. Aside from a year as a Wallace Stegner fellow at Stanford University, Kittredge has taught since then in the English department at the University of Montana. His publications include a volume of stories called We Are Not in This Together *(1988), the above-mentioned essay collection* Owning It All *(1987), the memoir* Hole in the Sky *(1992), and the essay collection* Who Owns the West? *(1996). Sharing the pseudonym Owen Rountree, Kittredge and S. M. Krauzer published a series of "action stories" in the early 1980s. He and his wife, Annick Smith, coedited* The Last Best Place: A Montana Anthology *(1988).*

In the following essay, published in the May-June 1994 issue of Audubon *magazine, Kittredge extends the reflections of* Owning It All *and* Hole in the Sky, *expressing not only criticism of the past but also hope for the future of Warner Valley and similar places in America. "We did great damage to the valley as we pursued our sweet impulse to create an agribusiness paradise," he acknowledges. An expression of interest by the Nature Conservancy in buying land in the valley prompts Kittredge to hope for "a second chance at paradise in my true heartland, an actual shot at reimagining desire." He envisions a process of reimagining that involves everyone—"ranchers, townspeople, conservationists"—and helps them notice the ways they all want so many of the same things, "like companionship in a community of people we respect and meaningful work." Through cooperation and an inclusive sense of community, he suggests, we have our best chance at restoring paradise.*

SECOND CHANCE AT PARADISE

A scab-handed, wandering child who rode off on old horses named Snip and Moon, I grew up with the constant, thronging presence of animals. Herds of feral hogs inhabited the swampland tule beds where the waterbirds nested. Those hogs would eat the downy young of the Canada geese if they could, but never caught them so far as I knew.

Sandhill cranes danced their courtship dances in our meadows. The haying and feeding and cowherding work couldn't have been done without the help of horses. We could only live the life we had with the help of horses.

All day Sunday sometimes in the summer my family would spread blankets by Deep Creek or Twenty-Mile Creek, and even we kids would catch all the rainbow trout we could stand.

Warner Valley, tucked against an enormous reach of Great Basin sagebrush and lava-rock desert in southeastern Oregon and northern Nevada, was a hidden world. The landlocked waters flowed down from the snowy mountains to the west but didn't find a way out to sea. They accumulated and evaporated in shallow lakes named Pelican, Crump, Hart, Stone Corral, and Bluejoint.

The late 1930s, when I was a child in that valley, were like the last years of the 19th century. What I want to get at is our isolation. We were 36 gravel-road miles over the Warner Mountains from the little lumbering and ranching town of Lakeview (maybe 2,500 souls). Warner Valley was not on the route to anywhere.

The way in was the way out. The deserts to the east were traced with wagon-track roads over the salt grass playas and around rimrocks from spring to spring, water hole to water hole, but nobody ever headed in that direction with the idea of going toward the future.

To the east lay deserts and more deserts. From a ridge above our buckaroo camp beside the desert spring at South Corral, we could see the long, notched, snowy ridge of Steens Mountain off in the eastern distances, high country where whores from Burns went in summer to camp with the sheepherders amid aspen trees at a place called Whorehouse Meadows, where nobody but wandering men ever went, men who would never be around when you needed them. And beyond, toward Idaho, there was more desert.

By the end of the Second World War my grandfather had got control of huge acreages in Warner, and my father was making serious progress at draining the swamplands. In the spring of 1946 my grandfather traded off close to 200 work teams for chicken feed. He replaced those horses with a fleet of John Deere tractors. Harness rotted in the barns until the barns were torn down.

I wonder if my father and his friends understood how irrevocably they were giving up what they seemed to care about more than anything when they talked of happiness—their lives in conjunction with the animals they worked with and hunted. I wonder why they acted like they didn't care.

Maybe they thought the animals were immortal. I recall those great teams of workhorses running the hayfields in summer before daybreak, their hooves echoing on the sod as we herded them toward the willow corral at some hay camp, the morning mists, and how the boy I was knew at least enough to know he loved them and that this love was enough reason to revere everything in sight for another morning. Those massive horses were like mirrors in which I could see my emotions reflected. If they loved this world, and they seemed to, with such satisfaction on those mornings when our breaths fogged before us, so did I.

Soon after World War II, electricity came to Warner, and telephones that sort of functioned. The road over the mountains and down along Deep Creek was paved. Our work in the fields had in so many ways gone mechanical. Eventually we had television. Our isolation was dissolving.

About the time I watched the first Beatles telecast, in the early 1960s, chamber-of-commerce gentlemen in Winnemucca, Nevada, got together with like-minded gentlemen from Lakeview and decided it made great economic sense to punch a highway across the deserts between those two little cities. Think of the tourists.

The two-lane asphalt ran north from Winnemucca to Denio, Oregon, then turned west to cross the million or so acres of rangeland we leased from the Bureau of Land Management (we saw those acreages as ours, like we owned them; in those days we virtually did), over the escarpment called the Doherty Slide, across Guano Valley and down Greaser Canyon, and through our meadowlands in Warner Valley.

I recall going out to watch the highway building as it proceeded, the self-important recklessness of those men at their work, the roaring of the D-8 Caterpillars and the clouds of dust rising behind the huge careening of the scrapers, and being excited, sort of full up with pride because the great world was at last coming to us in Warner Valley. Not that it ever did. The flow of tourism across those deserts never amounted to much. But maybe it will, one of these days.

Enormous changes were sweeping the world. We didn't want to encounter hippies or free love or revolutionaries on the streets in Lakeview. Or so we said. But like anybody, we yearned to be in on the action.

We were delighted, one Fourth of July, to hear that the Hell's Angels motorcycle gang from Oakland had headed across the deserts north to Winnemucca on their way to a weekend of kicking ass in Lakeview, and that they had been turned back by a single deputy sheriff.

There had been the long string of low riders coming on the two-lane blacktop across one of the great desert swales, and the deputy, all by himself, standing there by his Chevrolet. The deputy, a slight, balding man, had flagged down the leaders, and they'd had a talk. "Nothing I can do about it," the deputy had said, "but they're sighting in their deer rifles. These boys, they mean to sit back there three hundred yards and shoot you off them motorcycles. They won't apologize or anything. You fellows are way too far out in the country."

According to legend, the leaders of the Hell's Angels decided the deputy was right: They knew they were way too far out in the country, and they turned back. I never talked to anybody who knew if that story was true, but we loved it.

It was a story that told us we were not incapable of defending ourselves or powerless in a nation we understood to be going on without us. We never doubted some of our southeastern Oregon boys would have shot those Hell's Angels off their bikes. Some places were still big and open enough to be safe from outsiders.

During the great flood in December of 1964, when the Winnemucca-to-the-Sea highway acted like a dam across the valley, backing up water over 4,000 or 5,000 acres, my brother Pat walked a D-7 Caterpillar out along the asphalt and cut the highway three or four times, deep cuts so the floodwaters could pour through and drain away north. What he liked best, Pat said, was socking that bulldozer blade down and ripping up that asphalt with the yellow lines painted on it. We were still our own people.

But even as huge and open to anything as southeastern Oregon may have seemed in those old days, it was also inhabited by spooks. In autumn of the same year the Winnemucca-to-the-Sea highway came across our meadowlands, I had our heavy equipment, our Carry-All scrapers and D-7 bulldozers, at work on a great diversion canal we were cutting through 300 yards of sage-covered sand hills at the south end of Warner, rerouting Twenty-Mile Creek.

Soon we were turning up bones—human bones, lots of them. I recall a clear October afternoon and all those white bones scattered in the gravel, and my cat skinners standing there beside their great idling machines, perplexed and unwilling to continue. Ah, hell, never mind, I said. Crank 'em up. There was nothing to do but keep rolling. Maybe bones from an ancient Indian burial ground were sacred, but so was our work—more so, as I saw it. My cat skinners threatened to quit. I told them I'd give them a ride to town, where I'd find plenty of men who would welcome the work. My cat skinners didn't quit. I ducked my head so I couldn't see and drove away.

If you are going to bake a cake, you must break some eggs. That was a theory we knew about. We thought we were doing God's work. We were cultivating, creating order and what we liked to think of as a version of paradise.

What a pleasure that work was, like art, always there, always in need of improving, doing. It's reassuring, so long as the work is not boring, to wake up and find your work is still there, your tools still in the tunnel. You can lose a life in the work. People do.

But we left, we quit, in a run of family trouble. I have been gone from farming and Warner for 25 years. People ask if I don't feel a great sense of loss, cut off from the valley and the methods of my childhood. The answer is no.

Nothing much looks to have changed when I go back. The rimrock above the west side of the valley lies as black against the sunset light as it did when I was a child. The topography of my dreams, I like to think, is still intact.

But that's nonsense. We did great damage to the valley as we pursued our sweet impulse to create an agribusiness paradise. The rich peat ground began to go saline; the top layer just blew away. We drilled chemical fertilizers along with our barley seed and sprayed with 2, 4-D Ethyl and Parathion (which killed even the songbirds). Where did the waterbirds go? Waterbirds can be thought of as part of the charismatic megafauna. Everybody worries about waterbirds. But forms of life we didn't even know about were equally threatened.

Catostomus warnerensis, the Warner sucker, is now threatened. So are three other fish species in the region (three more are endangered, as are two plant species) and riparian tree communities of black cottonwood, red-osier dogwood, and willow. As a child I loved to duck down and wander animal trails through dense brush by the creeksides, where ring-necked pheasants and egg-eating raccoons and stalking lynx traveled. I wonder about colonies of red-osier dogwood and black cottonwood. Maybe I was often among them, curled in the dry grass and sleeping in the sun as I shared in their defenselessness and didn't know it.

The way we built canals in our efforts to contain the wildness of the valley and regulate the ways of water to our own uses must have been close to absolutely destructive to the Warner sucker, a creature we would not have valued at all, slippery and useless, thus valueless. It's likely I sent my gang of four D-7 Caterpillar bulldozers to clean out the brush along stretches of creekside thick with red-osier dogwood and black cottonwood.

Let in some light, let the grass grow, feed for the livestock—that was the theory. Maybe we didn't abandon those creatures in that valley; maybe we mostly destroyed them before we left. We did enormous damage to that valley in the 30-some years we were there. Countrysides like the Dordogne and Tuscany, which have been farmed thousands of years, look to be less damaged. But maybe that's because the serious kill-off took place so long ago.

I love Warner as a child loves its homeland, and some sense of responsibility for what's there stays with me. Or maybe I'm just trying to feel good about myself.

But that's what we all want to do, isn't it? It's my theory that everyone yearns—as we did in Warner, plowing those swamps, with all that bulldozing—to make a positive effect in the world. But how? How to keep from doing harm? Sometimes that seems to be the only question. We have to act. But to do so responsibly, we must first examine our desires. What do we really want?

A few years ago I went to Warner with filmmakers from NBC. Some footage ran on *The Today Show.* Sitting in an antique GMC pickup truck alongside a great reef of chemically contaminated cowshit that had been piled up outside the feedlot pens where fattening cattle existed like creatures in a machine, I found it in myself to say the valley should be given back to the birds and turned into a wildlife refuge.

It was a way of saying goodbye. I was saying the biological health of the valley was more important to me than the well-being of the community of ranchers who lived there. I had gone to grade school with some of them. It was an act people living in Warner mostly understood as betrayal.

Some eggs were broken, but I had at last gotten myself to say what I believed. Around 1991, when I heard that our ranch in Warner, along with two others out in the deserts to the east, was for sale and that the Nature Conservancy was interested, I was surprised by the degree to which I was moved and excited.

A huge expanse of territory was involved—1,114,005 acres in an intricate run of private, BLM, and state lands. It included wetlands in the Warner Valley (380,000 ducks, 19,000 geese, and 6,000 lesser sandhill cranes migrate through Warner), the Hart Mountain National Antelope Refuge, the Sheldon National Wildlife Refuge, and alpine habitats on Steens Mountain, the largest fault-block mountain in North America, with alpine aspen groves and great glacial cirques 3,000 feet deep and 20 miles in length (an area often mentioned as a possible national park).

Maybe, I thought, this would be a second chance at paradise in my true heartland, an actual shot at reimagining desire. What did I really want? A process, I think, with everybody involved—ranchers, townspeople, conservationists—all taking part in that reimagining. I wanted them to each try defining the so-called land of their heart's desiring the way they would have things if they were running the world. I wanted them to compare their versions of paradise and notice again the ways we all want so many of the same things—like companionship in a community of people we respect and meaningful work.

Then I wanted them to get started on the painstaking work of developing a practical plan for making their visions of the right life become actual, a plan for using, restoring, and preserving the world I grew up in. I liked to imagine that some of the pumps and dikes and headgates would be torn out in Warner and that some of the swamps would go back to tules. That's part of my idea of progress—re-create habitat for the waterbirds and the tiny, less charismatic creatures. But nothing like that has happened.

The Nature Conservancy did not end up buying the land. The MC Ranch, our old property in Warner Valley, was stripped of livestock and machinery and sold to what I understand to be a consortium of local ranchers. I have no idea of their plans—they don't confide in me, the turncoat.

But the world is inevitably coming to Warner Valley. The Bureau of Land Management recently purchased several thousand acres of prime hay land in north Warner and included it in a special management unit in which almost no grazing is allowed. The idea of the federal government buying land and taking it out of production (out of the tax base) was unthinkable when I lived in Warner.

Other unthinkable ideas are blowing in the wind. In May 1991 a consortium of environmental groups led by the Oregon Natural Resources Council announced its plan for southeastern Oregon. It included establishing a national park on Steens Mountain, three new national monuments, and 47 wilderness areas totaling more than 5 million acres; expanding the Hart Mountain refuge to include the wetlands in Warner Valley; creating a new national wildlife refuge at Lake Albert; attaining wild-and-scenic-river status for 54 streams totaling 835 miles; and phasing out, over a 10-year period, all livestock grazing on about 6.5 million acres of federal lands designated national park, preserve, wildlife refuge, wilderness, or wild and scenic river.

There's no use sighting in the scopes on the deer rifles, not anymore. This invasion will not be frightened away. There is not a thing for the people in my old homeland to do now but work out some accommodation with the thronging invading world.

So many of our people, in the old days of the American West, came seeking a fold in time, a hideaway place where they and generations after them could be at home. Think of *familia*, place and hearth and home fire, the fishing creek where it falls out of the mountains into the valley, and the Lombardy poplar beside the white house, and the orchard where children run in deep, sweet clover under the blossoming apple trees. But that's my paradise, at least as I remember it, not yours.

We have taken the West for about all it has to give, have lived like children, taking and taking for generations, and now that childhood is over.

It's time we gave something back to the natural systems of order that have supported us, some care and tenderness. That is the most operative notion, I think—tenderness. Our isolations are gone, in the West and everywhere. We need to give some time to the arts of cherishing the things we adore before they simply vanish. Maybe it will be like learning a skill: how to live in paradise.

—1994

SCOTT RUSSELL SANDERS

B. 1945

A 1995 collection of essays by Scott Russell Sanders entitled Writing from the Center *begins with this epigraph from William Carlos Williams: "Nothing can grow unless it taps into the soil." Tapping into the soil, exploring the roots of the self in a particular landscape, in a family and a larger community—this is the goal of much of Sanders's writing, particularly in his many volumes of personal essays. Typically, Sanders's work expresses a mood of wonderment, celebration, and exploration. Yet there is also an element of activism in his literary voice, a sense that certain places, kinds of people, and points of view are endangered and require outspoken defense. In the Autumn 1995 issue of* Orion *magazine, Sanders joined fellow writers Richard K. Nelson and Alison Hawthorne Deming in calling for a new "manifesto on behalf of the earth" that will help to launch a "shift in consciousness" to counteract the diminishment of the natural world.*

Sanders was born in Memphis, Tennessee, to a father who loved tools and a mother who loved plants. He traces his own love of physical labor (including the labor of writing) to one parent, his passion for nature to the other. Sanders grew up in Tennessee and Ohio before attending Brown University, where he majored in both English and physics. A Marshall scholarship to Cambridge University enabled him to pursue a Ph.D. in English. Since 1971, Sanders has taught in the English department at Indiana University, back in the Ohio River Valley that he regards as his home region. His nineteen books include novels, collections of short stories, a vol-

ume of literary criticism, and many books of personal essays, among them
The Paradise of Bombs (1987), Secrets of the Universe (1991), and Staying
Put: Making a Home in a Restless World *(1993).*

The following essay, which combines the rhapsodic and defensive
strands of Sanders's voice, appears in Writing from the Center. *"Buckeye"*
is about knowing, loving, and defending place. Inseparable from his sense
of connection to the Ohio farm where he grew up is Sanders's relationship
with his father, a relationship symbolized by a handmade wooden box with
two seeds ("buckeyes") inside that he inherited after his father's death.
When the government decided years ago to build a dam on the Mahoning
River and Sanders's family and their neighbors were forced by eminent
domain to sell their land, no one resisted. But he realized later that "if
enough people had believed that our scarred country was worth defending,
we might have dug in our heels and fought. Our attachments to the land
were all private. We had no shared lore, no literature, no art to root us
there, to give us courage, to help us stand our ground." "Buckeye," like
much of Sanders's work, is meant to be exactly this sort of literature.

BUCKEYE

Years after my father's heart quit, I keep in a wooden box on my desk the two buckeyes that were in his pocket when he died. Once the size of plums, the brown seeds
are shriveled now, hollow, hard as pebbles, yet they still gleam from the polish of
his hands. He used to reach for them in his overalls or suit pants and click them
together, or he would draw them out, cupped in his palm, and twirl them with his
blunt carpenter's fingers, all the while humming snatches of old tunes.

"Do you really believe buckeyes keep off arthritis?" I asked him more than once.
He would flex his hands and say, "I do so far."

My father never paid much heed to pain. Near the end, when his worn knee often
slipped out of joint, he would pound it back in place with a rubber mallet. If a splinter worked into his flesh beyond the reach of tweezers, he would heat the blade of
his knife over a cigarette lighter and slice through the skin. He sought to ward off
arthritis not because he feared pain but because he lived through his hands, and he
dreaded the swelling of knuckles, the stiffening of fingers. What use would he be if
he could no longer hold a hammer or guide a plow? When he was a boy he had
known farmers not yet forty years old whose hands had curled into claws, men so
crippled up they could not tie their own shoes, could not sign their names.

"I mean to tickle my grandchildren when they come along," he told me, "and I
mean to build doll houses and turn spindles for tiny chairs on my lathe."

So he fondled those buckeyes as if they were charms, carrying them with him
when our family moved from Ohio at the end of my childhood, bearing them to new
homes in Louisiana, then Oklahoma, Ontario, and Mississippi, carrying them still on
his final day when pain a thousand times fiercer than arthritis gripped his heart.

The box where I keep the buckeyes also comes from Ohio, made by my father
from a walnut plank he bought at a farm auction. I remember the auction, remember the sagging face of the widow whose home was being sold, remember my father
telling her he would prize that walnut as if he had watched the tree grow from a

sapling on his own land. He did not care for pewter or silver or gold, but he cherished wood. On the rare occasions when my mother coaxed him into a museum, he ignored the paintings or porcelain and studied the exhibit cases, the banisters, the moldings, the parquet floors.

I remember him planing that walnut board, sawing it, sanding it, joining piece to piece to make foot stools, picture frames, jewelry boxes. My own box, a bit larger than a soap dish, lined with red corduroy, was meant to hold earrings and pins, not buckeyes. The top is inlaid with pieces fitted so as to bring out the grain, four diagonal joints converging from the corners toward the center. If I stare long enough at those converging lines, they float free of the box and point to a center deeper than wood.

I learned to recognize buckeyes and beeches, sugar maples and shagbark hickories, wild cherries, walnuts, and dozens of other trees while tramping through the Ohio woods with my father. To his eyes, their shapes, their leaves, their bark, their winter buds were as distinctive as the set of a friend's shoulders. As with friends, he was partial to some, craving their company, so he would go out of his way to visit particular trees, walking in a circle around the splayed roots of a sycamore, laying his hand against the trunk of a white oak, ruffling the feathery green boughs of a cedar. "Trees breathe," he told me. "Listen."

I listened, and heard the stir of breath.

He was no botanist; the names and uses he taught me were those he had learned from country folks, not from books. Latin never crossed his lips. Only much later would I discover that the tree he called ironwood, its branches like muscular arms, good for ax handles, is known in books as hop hornbeam; what he called tuliptree or canoewood, ideal for log cabins, is officially the yellow poplar; what he called hoop ash, good for barrels and fence posts, appears in books as hackberry.

When he introduced me to the buckeye, he broke off a chunk of the gray bark and held it to my nose. I gagged.

"That's why the old-timers called it stinking buckeye," he told me. "They used it for cradles and feed troughs and peg legs.

"Why for peg legs?" I asked.

"Because it's light and hard to split, so it won't shatter when you're clumping around."

He showed me this tree in late summer, when the fruits had fallen and the ground was littered with prickly brown pods. He picked up one, as fat as a lemon, and peeled away the husk to reveal the shiny seed. He laid it in my palm and closed my fist around it so the seed peeped out from the circle formed by my index finger and thumb. "You see where it got the name?" he asked.

I saw: what gleamed in my hand was the bright eye of a deer. "It's beautiful," I said.

"It's beautiful," my father agreed, "but also poisonous. Nobody eats buckeyes, except maybe a fool squirrel."

I knew the gaze of deer from living in the Ravenna Arsenal, in Portage County, up in the northeastern corner of Ohio. After supper we often drove the Arsenal's gravel roads, past the munitions bunkers, past acres of rusting tanks and wrecked bombers, into the far fields where we counted deer. One June evening, while mist rose from the ponds, we counted 311, our family record. We found deer in herds, in bunches, in amorous pairs. We came upon lone bucks, their antlers lifted against the sky like the bare branches of dogwood. If you were quiet, if your hands were empty, if you moved slowly, you could leave the car and steal to within a few paces of a grazing deer, close enough to see the delicate lips, the twitching nostrils, the glossy, fathomless eyes.

The wooden box on my desk holds these grazing deer, as it holds the buckeyes and the walnut plank and the farm auction and the munitions bunkers and the breathing forests and my father's hands. I could lose the box, I could lose the polished seeds, but if I were to lose the memories I would become a bush without roots, and every new breeze would toss me about.

All those memories lead back to the northeastern corner of Ohio, where I learned to connect feelings with words. Much of the land I knew in that place as a child had been ravaged. The ponds in the Arsenal teemed with bluegill and beaver, but they were also laced with TNT from the making of bombs. Because the wolves and coyotes had long since been killed, some of the deer, so plump in the June grass, collapsed on the January snow, whittled by hunger to racks of bones. Outside the Arsenal's high barbed fences, many of the farms had failed, their barns caving in, their topsoil gone. Ravines were choked with swollen couches and junked washing machines and cars. Crossing fields, you had to be careful not to slice your feet on tin cans or shards of glass. Most of the rivers had been dammed, turning fertile valleys into scummy playgrounds for boats.

One free-flowing river, the Mahoning, ran past the small farm near the Arsenal where our family lived during my later years in Ohio. We owned just enough land to pasture three ponies and to grow vegetables for our table, but those few acres opened onto miles of woods and creeks and secret meadows. I walked that land in every season, every weather, following animal trails. But then the Mahoning, too, was doomed by a government decision; we were forced to sell our land, and a dam began to rise across the river.

If enough people had spoken for the river, we might have saved it. If enough people had believed that our scarred country was worth defending, we might have dug in our heels and fought. Our attachments to the land were all private. We had no shared lore, no literature, no art to root us there, to give us courage, to help us stand our ground. The only maps we had were those issued by the state, showing a maze of numbered lines stretched over emptiness. The Ohio landscape never showed up on postcards or posters, never unfurled like tapestry in films, rarely filled even a paragraph in books. There were no mountains in that place, no waterfalls, no rocky gorges, no vistas. It was a country of low hills, cut over woods, scoured fields, villages that had lost their purpose, roads that had lost their way.

"Let us love the country of here below," Simone Weil urged. "It is real; it offers resistance to love. It is this country that God has given us to love. He has willed that it should be difficult yet possible to love it." Which is the deeper truth about buckeyes, their poison or their beauty? I hold with the beauty; or rather, I am held by the beauty, without forgetting the poison. In my corner of Ohio the gullies were choked with trash, yet cedars flickered up like green flames from cracks in stone; in the evening bombs exploded at the ammunition dump, yet from the darkness came the mating cries of owls. I was saved from despair by knowing a few men and women who cared enough about the land to clean up trash, who planted walnuts and oaks that would long outlive them, who imagined a world that would have no call for bombs.

How could our hearts be large enough for heaven if they are not large enough for earth? The only country I am certain of is the one here below. The only paradise I know is the one lit by our everyday sun, this land of difficult love, shot through with shadow. The place where we learn this love, if we learn it at all, shimmers behind every new place we inhabit.

A family move carried me away from Ohio thirty years ago; my schooling and marriage and job have kept me away ever since, except for occasional visits. I returned to the site of our farm one cold November day, when the trees were skeletons and the ground shone with the yellow of fallen leaves. From a previous trip I knew that our house had been bulldozed, our yard and pasture had grown up in thickets, and the reservoir had flooded the woods. On my earlier visit I had merely gazed from the car, too numb with loss to climb out. But on this November day, I parked the car, drew on my hat and gloves, opened the door, and walked.

I was looking for some sign that we had lived there, some token of our affection for the place. All that I recognized, aside from the contours of the land, were two weeping willows that my father and I had planted near the road. They had been slips the length of my forearm when we set them out, and now their crowns rose higher than the telephone poles. When I touched them last, their trunks had been smooth and supple, as thin as my wrist, and now they were furrowed and stout. I took off my gloves and laid my hands against the rough bark. Immediately I felt the wince of tears. "Hello, Father," I said, quietly at first, then louder and louder, as if only shouts could reach him through the bark and miles and years.

Surprised by sobs, I turned from the willows and stumbled away toward the drowned woods, calling to my father. I sensed that he was nearby. Even as I called, I was wary of grief's deceptions. I had never seen his body after he died. By the time I reached the place of his death, a furnace had reduced him to ashes. The need to see him, to let go of him, to let go of this land and time, was powerful enough to summon mirages; I knew that. But I also knew, stumbling toward the woods, that my father was here.

At the bottom of a slope where the creek used to run, I came to an expanse of gray stumps and withered grass. It was a bay of the reservoir from which the water had retreated, the level drawn down by engineers or drought. I stood at the edge of this desolate ground, willing it back to life, trying to recall the woods where my father had taught me the names of trees. No green shoots rose. I walked out among the stumps. The grass crackled under my boots, breath rasped in my throat, but otherwise the world was silent.

Then a cry broke overhead and I looked up to see a red-tailed hawk launching out from the top of an oak—a band of dark feathers across the creamy breast and the tail splayed like rosy fingers against the sun. It was a red-tailed hawk for sure; and it was also my father. Not a symbol of my father, not a reminder, not a ghost, but the man himself, right there, circling in the air above me. I knew this as clearly as I knew the sun burned in the sky. A calm poured though me. My chest quit heaving. My eyes dried.

Hawk and father wheeled above me, circle upon circle, wings barely moving, head still. My own head was still, looking up, knowing and being known. Time scattered like fog. At length, father and hawk stroked the air with those powerful wings, three beats, then vanished over a ridge.

The voice of my education told me then and tells me now that I did not meet my father, that I merely projected my longing onto a bird. My education may well be right; yet nothing I heard in school, nothing I've ever read, no lesson reached by logic has ever convinced me as utterly or stirred me as deeply as did that red-tailed hawk. Nothing in my education prepared me to love a piece of the earth, least of all a humble, battered country like northeastern Ohio; I learned from the land itself.

Before leaving the drowned woods, I looked around at the ashen stumps, the wilted grass, and for the first time since moving from this place I was able to let it go. This ground was lost; the flood would reclaim it. But other ground could be saved, must be saved, in every watershed, every neighborhood. For each home ground we need new maps, living maps, stories and poems, photographs and paintings, essays and songs. We need to know where we are, so that we may dwell in our place with a full heart.

—1995

ROBERT FROST

1874-1963

By the time of his death, Robert Frost had become one of the most celebrated American poets of all time. Along with many other awards, he received an unprecedented four Pulitzer Prizes, for New Hampshire *(1924),* Collected Poems *(1931),* A Further Range *(1937), and* A Witness Tree *(1943). He was named the poet laureate of Vermont and had honorary degrees bestowed upon him by more than forty colleges and universities, including Oxford, Cambridge, and Michigan. On his seventy-fifth birthday, the U.S. Senate passed a resolution in his honor, stating that "his poems have helped to guide American thought and humor and wisdom, setting forth to our minds a reliable representation of ourselves and of all men." But perhaps the highlight of Frost's public life as the unofficial poet laureate of the United States came in 1961 when he read two poems at President Kennedy's inauguration, "Dedication" and "The Gift Outright," the latter written expressly for the occasion.*

Robert Frost's name is virtually synonymous with New England, and especially with the towns and pastures and mountains "north of Boston," as he put it in the title of his second collection of poetry in 1914. Frost wanted to be identified as a New Englander and consciously cultivated his connection with this region in more than thirty volumes of poetry, but he was actually born in San Francisco and lived there until he was eleven. After the death of his father, a newspaper reporter and editor, in 1885, the family moved to the mill town of Lawrence, Massachusetts, where his paternal grandparents lived. Frost began writing poetry at Lawrence High School and launched his career as a professional poet by selling a poem called "My Butterfly" to the New York Independent *for fifteen dollars in 1894. He started college at Dartmouth in 1892 but left after a year to help support his family by teaching; he later spent two years at Harvard before leaving without a degree. But despite the fact that he never completed college, Frost's achievements as a writer enabled him to teach at many distinguished universities, including Harvard, Yale, and Dartmouth.*

"The Gift Outright" is a departure from the typical Frost poem that explores in the first person such topics as mending fences, picking apples, chopping wood, and climbing trees. Instead, this poem seeks to encompass, in a mere sixteen lines, the entire history of contact between the European imagination and the North American landscape. It presents a vision of home that distinguishes between mere physical inhabitation and a deeper surrender to the land that sustains us. The poem seems to advocate the process of becoming native to a new place by giving ourselves, our imaginations, and eventually our stories and our art, to the actualities of the place.

THE GIFT OUTRIGHT

The land was ours before we were the land's.
She was our land more than a hundred years
Before we were her people. She was ours
In Massachusetts, in Virginia,
But we were England's, still colonials,
Possessing what we still were unpossessed by,
Possessed by what we now no more possessed.
Something we were withholding made us weak
Until we found out that it was ourselves
We were withholding from our land of living,
And forthwith found salvation in surrender.
Such as we were we gave ourselves outright
(The deed of gift was many deeds of war)
To the land vaguely realizing westward,
But still unstoried, artless, unenhanced,
Such as she was, such as she would become.

—1961

6

What impact do politics and the power of
one group over another have on particular
places and our experience of them?

POLITICS OF PLACE

WENDY ROSE

B. 1948

*Wendy Rose has attempted through political involvement and poetry to
resolve the dilemma of being a mixed-blood Indian who was raised in the
city as a Roman Catholic, completely estranged from her tribal traditions.
Underlying many of her poems is a sense of outrage at how Native
American culture has been devalued and stolen by outsiders and then given
back piecemeal in forms acceptable to the colonizers, such as museum
exhibits and circus acts. This outrage, along with her training as an anthropologist, has also motivated her to work with the American Indian Movement in protecting Indian burial grounds from destruction by culturally
insensitive developers.*

*Born in Oakland, California, of a Hopi father and a Miwok mixed-blood
mother, Rose earned a Ph.D. in anthropology at the University of California
at Berkeley, although her primary interest was in literature. She has
explained that the only academic department at UC Berkeley that would
deal with her dissertation on Indian literature was the anthropology department; the English department told her that American Indian literature was
not part of American literature. Rose has taught in Native American studies at UC Berkeley and California State University, Fresno, and currently
teaches at Fresno City College. A painter as well as a poet, one of her
favorite subjects is the centaur, reflecting "my hybrid status . . . like the centaur, I have always felt misunderstood and isolated—whether with Indians
or with non-Indians." Her hybrid status is also reflected in the titles of several of her volumes of poetry:* Academic Squaw *(1977),* What Happened
When the Hopi Hit New York *(1982), and* The Halfbreed Chronicles and
Other Poems *(1985).*

*"Long Division: A Tribal History" is the title poem of a collection pub-
lished in 1976; it was also collected in* Lost Copper *(1980), which was nominated for the American Book Award. It is a lamentation at the disposses-*

sion of native peoples, who are "bought and divided into clay pots," and an angry protest at the way that, as Rose once said in an interview, "Indians are deliberately made invisible . . . people can grow up in an area surrounded by Indian people who have maintained their culture, who still practice their religion, who live on federally administered reservation land, and the non-Indians do not know it."

LONG DIVISION: A TRIBAL HISTORY

Our skin loosely lies
across grass borders;
stones loading up
are loaded down with placement sticks,
a great tearing
and appearance of holes.
We are bought and divided
into clay pots; we die
on granite scaffolding
on the shape of the Sierras
and lie down with lips open
thrusting songs on the world.
Who are we and do we
still live? The doctor,
asleep, says no.
So outside of eternity
we struggle until our blood
has spread off our bodies
and frayed the sunset edges.
It's our blood that gives you
those southwestern skies.
Year after year we give,
harpooned with hope, only to fall
bouncing through the canyons,
our sings decreasing
with distance.
I suckle coyotes
and grieve.

—1976

BETH BRANT
B. 1941

"I write what I know, in language that is familiar. I tell the stories for those who cannot," says poet and short-story writer Beth Brant. A Mohawk of the Turtle Clan, Brant was born in Detroit and has lived there ever since. Her

Mohawk father was an assembly line worker for the Ford Motor Company; her white mother made quilts and made do, while her Mohawk grandparents told her stories from the native tradition. Brant's own stories and poems have appeared in magazines and anthologies of Native American literature; she edited A Gathering of Spirit: A Collection by North American Indian Women *(1984) and cofounded Turtle Grandmother, a library on North American Indian women. Her first collection of poems and stories, entitled* Mohawk Trail, *appeared in 1985.*

Brant's 1991 story collection Food and Spirits *focuses on modern Mohawk Indians who are trying to return to traditional values. "This Place" is the story of a gay man with AIDS who returns to his mother's house on the reservation to die. He feels he has been doubly persecuted—forced to leave his homeland and family and live in the city because his people "don't want queers, faggots living among them," but not welcome in the city because he is an Indian. Clearly, though, the native ways still hold power for him, and he has missed his connection to the place where he grew up. "You're just a rez boy," says the medicine man who is summoned to help him face death.*

THIS PLACE

"Mother, I am gay. I have AIDS." The telephone call that it almost killed him to make.

The silence. Then, "Come home to us."

David came home because he was dying. He expected to see his place of birth in a new way, as if he were a photographer capturing scenes through diverse lenses. *Scene one: through a living man's eyes. Scene two: through a dying man's eyes.* But the beauty remembered was the beauty that still existed. Nothing had changed in ten years. The water of the Bay just as blue and smooth. The white pines just as tall and green. The dirt roads as brown and rutted as the day he had left. His mother as small and beautiful, her dark hair with even more grey streaks running through the braid she wrapped around her head.

Had nothing changed but him?

He had left this place and gone to the city to look for other men like himself. He found them. He found a new life, a different life. He found so much. Even the virus that now ate at him. David came home and was afraid of death.

David could feel the virus changing his body, making marks on his insides. Outside, too, his body was marked: by the tumors growing on his face and the paleness of his skin. He worried that the virus was somehow taking away his color, bleaching the melanin that turned him polished copper in the summer and left him light terra cotta in winter. He could feel the virus at war with the melanin and he could not check the battle. He couldn't hold this virus in his fist and squeeze the death out of it. He could only wait and look in the mirror to see the casualty of this war. David was afraid.

"Mother, am I turning white?"

"No, my baby son. You are dark and beautiful. Your hair is black and shiny as ever. Your eyes are tired, but still as brown and strong as the day you left this place."

He knew she lied to him. Mothers lie about their children's pain. *It will go away,* they say. *I'll make it better,* they say. *Oh, Mother, make it better, make it go away. I'm afraid of death.*

He felt the virus eating his hair. It fell out in clumps as he combed it. His forehead got broader and receded further. The blackness of the strands had dulled to some nondescript color. His braid was thin and lifeless, not as it used to be, snapping like a whip across his back, or gliding down his back like a snake.

David's sister brought her children to see him. They crawled on his lap and kissed him. He was afraid for them. Afraid the virus would reach out of his body and grab these babies and eat at them until they, too, disappeared in its grip. The virus put a fear in him—a fear that he could wipe out his people by breathing, by talking, by living. David saw, in his dreams, the virus eating away at this place until it was gone.

His dreams were also about a place called death. Death seemed to be a gaping hole in the world where David looked and there was nothing. He would wake from these dreams sweating, his limbs filled with pain. He had lived his life so well, so hard, clutching it to him like food, swallowing and being nourished. He wanted to greet death like that, opening his arms to it, laughing and embracing that other world. But he was afraid.

"Mother, I am afraid of death."

"Joseph is coming to visit."

On a day when David was seated in his chair before the window, looking out at the way the bright sun had turned everything in the yard golden, he heard the pickup truck making its way down the dirt road to the house. He also heard a voice singing. David laughed out loud. The song being sung was "All My Exes Live in Texas," and he knew that Joseph was on his way to him.

The truck came to a screeching, convulsive stop. David's mother went out to greet the man who jumped from the truck laughing, "Where's the patient?" As David watched, Joseph extracted a brown paper bag and an orange-striped cat from the truck. "Meet my friend, the Prophet. You can call her Prophet." David's mother reached for the cat who nudged at her breast and looked into her face. Joseph kissed Grace on the cheek. Prophet licked Grace's face. David wondered at the fact that Joseph looked the same as he had when David was a child. Dressed in faded jeans and a flannel shirt, Joseph's face was lean and unlined. His nose was sharp and slightly curved at the end, like a bird's beak. His eyes were black and round, reminding David again of a bird, perhaps a kestrel or a falcon. Joseph wore long, beaded earrings that draped across the front of his shirt. His hair, black and coarse, was tied back with a leather string. His fingers were covered with silver-and-garnet-studded rings, his hands delicate but used. Joseph looked at the young man in the window and lifted his hand in a greeting. Then he smiled and his face took on the unfinished look of a child. David waved back, feeling excitement—the way he used to feel before going to a party.

"This ain't goin' to be like any party you ever went to," Joseph remarked as he stepped through the doorway. "Here, have a Prophet," and he lifted the orange cat from Grace's arms onto David's lap.

Prophet looked intently at David's face, then kneaded his lap and settled herself on it, where she purred. David stroked the orange fur and scratched the cat's head. She burrowed deeper in his lap. "I would get up to greet you, but I think Prophet's got something else in mind."

Joseph laughed. "We wouldn't want to disturb her highness. David, we have not seen each other in many years." He bent down to kiss the young man on his forehead. "You don't look so good." Joseph eyed him critically.

"Thanks. But you look the same as ever."

"You in a lot of pain," Joseph said in a statement, not a question.

"Yeah, a lot of pain. I take about fifty pills a day. They don't seem to make that much of a difference." David continued to stroke Prophet.

"You think I can cure you?"

"No."

"Good, because I can't. All of us are afraid of death, though. We don't know what to expect, what to take with us." He looked in his paper sack. "Maybe I got the right things here."

Grace went into the kitchen, and Joseph pulled up a chair and sat beside David. Looking at Prophet asleep on David's lap, Joseph remarked, "Cats is smart. This one had a brother looked just like her. I called him Tecumseh. One morning I woke up and he was gone. I asked the Prophet if she knew where her brother went. She looked at me and blinked, then turned her head away like I'd said somethin' rude. I went outside to look for Tecumseh and I found him, layin' dead under a rose bush. It was a good year for the roses, they was bloomin' to beat the band. He had chosen the red roses to die under. That was a good choice, don't you think? I buried him under that red rose bush. The old man knew what *he* wanted, but he had to let me know, me not bein' as smart as a cat. Prophet came out and sat on the grave. She sat there for three days and nights. Cats are different from us. We worry about fittin' things to our own purpose. Cats don't worry about them things. They live, they die. They get buried under a red rose bush. Smart, huh?"

"You got any spare rose bushes? Only make mine flaming pink!" David laughed, then began coughing, blood spattering the kleenex he held to his mouth.

The Prophet jumped from David's lap and sat on the floor, her back to him.

"Now I've done it," David gasped. "Come back. Here kitty, kitty, kitty."

The Prophet turned and gave him a look of contempt, her back twitching, her tail moving back and forth on the floor.

"Huh," Joseph said. "She ain't comin' back for a while. Don't like the name Kitty."

Grace came in to announce dinner. David grabbed his cane and shuffled to the table. He sat down, gasping for breath. "Takes longer every time. I think I'm losing feeling in my right leg, but what the hell, I'd crawl to the table for Mother's beef stew." He half-heartedly lifted the spoon to his mouth. "My appetite's still pretty good, isn't it, Mother?"

Grace smiled at her son. "The day your appetite goes is the day I go."

She had made fresh bread to eat with the stew and set dishes of pickles and cheese on the table. Joseph rubbed his hands together in glee. "This looks good!" They ate, talking local gossip, the Prophet sitting daintily beside Joseph's chair. David's hands shook as he barely fed himself, spilling stew on his blue shirt. Grace fussed and tied a napkin around his neck. David smiled, "Next, she'll be feeding me or giving me a bottle." He winked at his mother and blew a kiss across the table to her. She caught it and put it on her cheek.

Joseph watched while he fed bits of meat to Prophet. He looked in his sack and pulled out a dish covered in waxed paper. "I made these this mornin'. Butter tarts. The flakiest crust you'll find anywhere. You gotta use lard, none of that shortenin'. Lard is what makes a crust that'll melt in your mouth. It's my gift to you, David."

As David bit into the sweetness of the tart, he looked at Joseph, his earrings swinging against his shoulders, his hands making patterns in the air as he described the making of the tarts, and David thought, *He acts like a queen.* He looked harder at Joseph, thinking, if you put him in a city, in a gay bar, the old nelly would fit right in. David laughed out loud.

Grace looked startled, but Joseph grinned and nodded his head. "Catchin' on, my young friend?"

As he helped clear the table, David smiled with his new knowledge. Collapsing into his reclining chair, David swallowed his medicine and laid his head back, closing his eyes. He could hear the murmurs between Joseph and Grace, his mother always a living, vivid presence in his life—his reason for hanging on so long to life. "I love you, Mother," he whispered. He opened his eyes to the dry touch of Joseph's fingers on his face. His mother was bringing out the moccasins she had made from rabbit hide and had beaded the nights they sat and watched TV. She presented them to Joseph. He unlaced his red hightops and slipped the beautiful moccasins on his feet. He put his feet out in front of him in admiration. He got up and walked in them. He jumped and clicked his heels together. "Thank you, Grace. You haven't lost your touch, have you? Now it's time for you to go. Don't come back till the mornin'."

Grace gathered her things together and stood looking at David. Her face shifted with emotions: sorrow, pride, fear, love. She kissed her son and hugged Joseph. They watched her leave.

Joseph turned and asked David, "You tryin' to be brave for your mom? Let me tell you somethin' about mothers. They know everything. She feels what you're goin' through. Can't hide it, even though you try."

"No! I don't want her to know how bad it gets. I can see it in her face, she gets crazy not knowing what to do for me. But this is the real crazy part, I don't want to let go of her. That death . . . that place . . . she won't be there."

The Prophet jumped on Joseph's lap and began washing herself. "That's true. Her time isn't here yet. David, you have lived your life in the way that was best for you. You think Grace didn't know why you left here? Think she didn't know you was gay? You can't tell someone like Grace not to go crazy when her son is dyin'. You can't tell her how to mourn you. And you can't be draggin' her along with you when you leave this place."

"I don't want to do that. I feel like a little kid when I was scared of a nightmare. Mother would make it go away. Death is like that nightmare. I gotta meet it on my own, but I'm scared."

"Yes, I know you are," and Joseph reached for David's hand. David's bony fingers closed over Joseph's.

"When I lived in the city, I used to get so homesick for this place. I'd picture the way it looked—the sky, the trees, my relatives. I'd dream it all up in my mind, but I never thought I would come back. I made my life in the city, thinking that I couldn't come back here. My people don't want queers, faggots living among them. But now, some of us are coming home to die. Where else would we go but back to our homes, our families? What a joke, eh? They couldn't deal with my life, now they gotta deal with my death. God, I think about the guys that really can't go home. They have to die alone in some hospital, or even on the street. There was a guy I knew, Ojibwe, and he died outside his apartment. I heard about it after it happened and I got in this rage! People just walking by him, probably thinking, oh here's another drunk Indian, just walking by him! And him, getting cold and no one would touch him." Tears were moving down David's face. He lifted his hand to wipe his face. "That's when I hated being an Indian. My own people, hateful to that guy. He was scared to go home. Probably thought they'd throw him out again, or stone him or something."

"Well, Indians got no immunity from hatefulness or stupidity, David. Maybe he had made his choice to die alone. Maybe he didn't have a home to go to."

David looked shocked. "No, that can't be true. I know what it's like. I grew up here, remember? It seemed like I had to make a choice, be gay or be an Indian. Some choice, eh? So I moved to the city." David sighed, then began to cough.

Joseph stroked Prophet, whose ears were twitching. "Even a city can't take the Indian part away. Even a virus can't do that, my young friend." He dipped into his sack and held out a piece of metal to David. "Look in this. What do you see?"

David held the piece of metal to his face. He saw a blurred image of himself, tumors covering his face. When he tilted the piece of tin, he saw himself laughing and dressed in his finest clothes, dancing in the bar in the city. He tilted it yet another way and saw himself dancing at a pow wow, his hair fanning out as he twirled and jumped. In another tilt, he saw himself as a child, sitting on Grandmother's lap.

"Which one is you?" Joseph asked.

"All of them."

"When the Prophet was a kitten," Joseph said, petting the now sleeping cat, "she used to keep me awake at night. She'd jump on my head just as I was dozin' off. I'd knock her away and turn over, but just when that sweet moment of sleep was callin' me, she'd jump on my head again. I thought maybe she was hungry and I'd get up to feed her. She'd eat, then start the whole routine all over again. She even got Tecumseh in the act. While she'd jump on my head, he'd get under the covers and bite my feet. I finally gave up and got out of bed and went outside and looked at the sky. About the fifth night of these carryin' ons, I *really* looked at the sky. I saw all the stars as if they was printed on the insides of my eyes. I saw the moon like she really was. And I started to pray to Sky Woman, blinkin' and shinin' up there. She answered me back, too, all because the cats was smarter than me. Nothin' hides in front of old Sky Woman. You might think *she's* hidin' when you can't see her, but she's there checkin' everything out. People can't hide from her. And people can't hide from themselves."

"Is that what I've done?" David asked, his face sad. "I've always been proud of being Mohawk, of being from here. I *am* proud of being gay even though everywhere I turned, someone was telling me not to be either. In the city they didn't want me to be Native. In this place, they don't want me to be gay. It can drive you crazy! *Be this. Be that. Don't be this way.* So you get to be like an actor, changing roles and faces to please somebody out there who hates your guts for what you are." David laughed. "When I was diagnosed I thought, well, now I don't have to pretend anymore. It's all out in the open. I'm going to die, and why did I waste my time and tears worrying about all this other stuff? I got real active in AIDS work. I wanted to reach out to all the Indian gays I knew, form support groups, lean on each other. 'Cause the other guys just didn't understand us. I was a fireball for two years, real busy, but then I got too sick to do much of anything. My friends were good, but they couldn't take care of me anymore. I came home. Here I sit, Grandfather, waiting for death, but scared shitless."

Joseph began to hum and sing, "Crazy . . . I'm crazy for feelin' so lonely." He stuck his hand inside the sack and handed David a piece of paper.

We, as the original inhabitants of this country, and sovereigns of the soil, look upon ourselves as equally independent and free as any other nation or nations. This country was given to us by the Great Spirit above; we wish to enjoy it, and have our passage along the lake, within the line we have pointed out. The great exertions we have made, for this number of years, to accomplish a peace and have not been able to obtain it; our patience, as we have observed, is exhausted. We, therefore, throw ourselves under the protection of the Great Spirit above, who will order all things for the best. We have told you our patience is worn out, but that we wish for peace and whenever we hear that pleasing sound, we shall pay attention to it. Until then, you will pay attention to us.

"My ancestor. Quite a man." David held the paper in his thin hands.

"Yes, he was. Diplomats, they called him and his sister. We call them warriors."

David read the words again. "Grandfather, I would like to be a warrior like this man. I would like to see death coming and run to meet it, not afraid, not hiding behind my mother."

"Who says you ain't a warrior? David, the bravest people I knew were the ones that lived and kept on livin'. Those two, Tyendinaga and Molly, they fought to keep us alive as a people. Looks to me like you're as fine a warrior as they was. David, you lived!"

The Prophet suddenly came awake and stretched to her full length. She sat up and washed her face. She blinked at David, her yellow eyes staring at him until he looked away. She jumped off Joseph's lap and settled herself in front of David's feet.

"Trust the Prophet to interrupt the proceedings. Let's go outside and sit on the porch." Joseph stood up and stretched his arms and shook his legs.

David reached for his cane, his body curved and stooped. Joseph got a blanket to wrap him in against the cool night air. David made his way toward the front door. Joseph went to the kitchen and brought out two mugs of coffee and the rest of the butter tarts. They settled on the porch steps.

"David, look at the moon. When she's a crescent like that, I think Sky Woman's smilin' at us. More than likely, laughin'. She has big jobs to do like pullin' in the tides, and we sit here yappin' about life and death."

"The moon is beautiful. Somehow, it never seemed to shine like that in the city." David began coughing again, his body shaking and throbbing.

Joseph held onto him until the shaking stopped. "David, you're just a rez boy, ain't you? Nothin' looks as good as here, eh? But I think so too. One time, a long time ago, I thought about leavin' here."

"Why didn't you? It can't have been easy for you. Or were things different then? Maybe not so homophobic, not so much hatred?"

"Oh, things was bad. But not in that way. There was hatred, alright. The kind that makes people turn to the bottle or put a gun in their mouth and shoot." David winced, remembering his father's death. Joseph continued. "That kind of hatred, self-hatred. I stayed because I was supposed to. I fought it, but I had to stay. It was my job." He began a song. "*Your cheatin' heart will tell on you. You'll cry and cry, the way I do.* Sing with me, David." And they sang until the last words were finished and Joseph hugged David.

"I thought medicine men were supposed to chant and cast spells, not sing old Hank Williams songs," David teased.

Joseph looked surprised. "Oh, some do. Some do. But how many medicine people you know, David?"

"Only you, Grandfather."

"Well then, there you go. What you see is what you get."

"When my father died, I remember being shut out from what was going on. I know they were all trying to protect me and Sister, but we were scared. One day he was there, the next day he wasn't. He wasn't the greatest dad, but he was ours! You were there, Grandfather. Why did he do it?"

Joseph took a deep breath and let it out. It lingered in the night air like a puff of smoke. "Because he didn't know any other way. Are you judgin' him, David? 'Cause if you are, you can forget it. Too many people made a judgment on your father all his life. He doesn't need yours to add to it." Joseph's face became angry, then softened as he took David's hand again. "Children get scared. We fail you because we fail ourselves. We think *you'll* get over it because you're younger and have fewer memories. Grownups are fools, David. Your father didn't know what else to do with his life, a life he thought was worthless. So he shot it away."

David wept. "I've thought about shooting mine away, like him. Like father, like son, isn't that what the people would say? So, I didn't, all because I didn't want to be mentioned in the same breath with him. Pride, that's all that kept me going. And I couldn't do the same thing to my mother and sister that he did to us."

"You're a lot like your dad. Sweet, like he was. Oh yes," Joseph looked at David's disbelieving face, "a sweet man. When we was at residential school together, he's the one that took me under his wing. He fought the grownups and the other kids that ganged up on me. He was always my friend. He didn't fail me, ever. And I tried not to let him down, but I wasn't enough to keep that gun out of his hand. Nobody was enough, David. Not you, or your mom or your sister. Don't you judge him. He wouldn't have judged you." Joseph raised his face to the crescent moon and closed his eyes.

David felt a small piece of pain dislodge from inside him. It floated away in the night's darkness. "Thank you for telling me that, Grandfather. I always loved him."

Joseph smiled, his crooked teeth shining white in the moon's light. "Love is a funny thing, David. It stays constant, like her," he pointed to the crescent. "When you cut through all the crap, the need and greed part, you got the good, lastin' stuff. She knew that," and he pointed again to the moon. "She put herself up there to remind us of her love, not to admire her pretty shine. Of course, the pretty shine doesn't hurt, does it?" And they laughed together.

David said, "I met my pretty shine in the city. He will always be the love of my life, even though he doesn't feel that way about me. We're still friends. . . . God, the city was so different for me—I loved it! Excitement. All those gorgeous men. If I'd stayed here, I wouldn't have known the world was full of gay people. If I'd stayed here though, maybe I wouldn't have gotten AIDS." David pulled the blanket closer around himself and shivered.

Joseph squeezed David's wasting fingers. "Do you regret any of it?"

"No. I've thought about that a lot. I only wish I could have stayed, but I thought I had to make the choice and don't know what would have happened if I hadn't left."

Joseph rustled in his sack. "Who can read the future? Well, maybe I can, but can you read the past as well? Here, take this."

David held out his hand. A dry snakeskin was deposited into his dry palm. The skin was faded but still showed orange-and-black markings.

"I saw this snake shed her skin. I was walking in the bush and heard a very small noise. I watched her wriggle out of her old life, just like she was removin' an overcoat. It took this snake a long time, but then, there she was in her new overcoat, her old skin just lyin' there waitin' for me to pick it up and give it to you."

"Thank you, Grandfather. It's beautiful." David touched the snakeskin and looked into Joseph's face. "I think it would be wonderful if we could shed ourselves like this and have a brand-new, beautiful skin to face the world. Or maybe, to face death."

"We do, David. A snake doesn't put on a new skin with different colors. She has the same one, just layers of it. She doesn't become a new snake, but older and wiser with each shedding. Humans shed. We don't pay attention to it, though. We get new chances all the time. A snake makes use of her chances; that's why she's a snake and we're not. We never know when we got a good thing goin'."

"That's true! Mother used to tell me I was lucky, I had it good compared to other little boys. She was right, of course." David giggled into his hand. "She is always right. Why is that, Grandfather?"

"Now you got me. That's something I'll never know either!"

They laughed, the sound filling the night air. Prophet scratched at the door to be let out. "The Prophet's afraid she's missin' out on something. Those butter tarts, maybe." Joseph got up to open the door.

The Prophet streaked out the open door and ran to the cluster of apple trees. She climbed one and sat on a branch. David could see the yellow glow of her eyes as she watched the men drink their coffee and bite into the tarts.

Joseph remarked between bites, "Prophet does it every time. I'd sit around all night talkin' if she didn't remind me why I was here."

David started to shake. "I'm afraid, Grandfather."

"Yes, I know, David. We'll go inside, and you can lay down while I make some special tea. I'm here with you, David. I won't leave you."

David clutched the snakeskin in his hand and struggled to his feet. He made his way into the house and to the couch where he started coughing and spitting up blood. Joseph cleaned David's face and wrapped the blanket tightly around his skinny body. He went to the kitchen, and David could hear him singing, "I fall to pieces . . . each time I see you again." David smiled, the voice reassuring to him.

"The Prophet's still in that apple tree, starin' at the house," said Joseph, as he brought a steaming mug of liquid to David.

David sipped the tea and made a face. "What is this stuff? It tastes like wet leaves!"

"It is wet leaves. Drink up. It's good for what ails you."

"Yeah, right," David smiled, "I notice you're not drinking any."

"Well, I'm not the sick one, am I?"

David drank the brew, watching Joseph walk around the room, picking up books and stacking them neatly, straightening a picture hanging on the wall, tidying a lamp table. "There's a dust rag in the broom closet. The rug could use a shake and the windows need a wash," David said teasingly.

"You're a regular Henny Youngman, ain't you?"

"Who?"

"All finished?" Joseph pointed to the mug. "If you want more, you can't have it. I only brought enough for one cup "

David pushed the mug toward Joseph. "Please, no more. I think I'll survive without it."

"Ah, survival. Let me tell you about that one." Joseph sat on the couch at David's feet.

David felt heavy in his body. He tried to lift his hand, but it was too much of an effort. He tried to speak, but his voice wouldn't move out of him. He looked at Joseph who was talking, but his voice was thin and far away. He saw that Prophet had come back into the house and was sitting on Joseph's lap. The Prophet stared at David with her yellow eyes and smiled at him. Was that a smile? What was that tea? Wet leaves ... and David was falling was falling back into wet leaves and it was autumn the air smelled like winter he was a boy a boy who jumped up from wet leaves and ran he ran he was chasing something he felt so good so good this is what childhood is you run you laugh you open your mouth you feel the wind on your tongue the sun on your head the apple trees were giving up their gifts of fruit you picked an apple you feel you taste the juice running down your throat the apple made a loud crunch as you bit and the swallows in the tree were waiting for the core to be thrown down so they could share the fruit of the tree the geese were flying you ran you ran into the cornfield and scared the pheasant who was picking at the seed you laughed you laughed it was a perfect day you picked up a feather and put it in your pocket the day was perfect when you were a child you ran you laughed you played you were loved you loved you were a child it was good so good good to be a child in this place this place this place never changed this place this place.

David opened his eyes. The Prophet was washing her tail. Joseph held a turtle rattle in his left hand. He was talking ... *and then the church people sent their missionaries here to teach us to be christian but we* ...

David was falling he fell into the sound of the turtle's rattle he fell into the turtle's mouth he shook his body shook and ... *fought them* ... he fell into the sound of the rattle he was the rattle's sound the music the music he was dancing dancing with the first man he ever loved they were dancing holding holding the music the music the turtle's music was in them through them in them ... *killed us* ... he went home he went with the first man he ever loved the music was beating was beating their hearts the rattle the music they fell onto the bed the music the music touched them the turtle touched them the rattle touched them they touched they touched the touching was music was music his body singing music his body the rattle of the turtle the first man he loved ... *we fought back* ... their bodies singing shaking joining joining everything was music was music so good so good good the first man he loved Thomas Thomas ... *they kept killing us off* ... Tommy Tommy singing sighing joining ... *but we* ... singing our bodies singing Tommy David Tommy Tommy ... *survived.* ...

David's eyes opened. The room was dark. The Prophet was staring, smiling, her eyes brilliant yellow. Joseph was staring also, his eyes sending out shafts of brilliance, laser beams into his soul.

"Grandfather."

Joseph held up the rattle and sang a song with no words, a song in a high, quivering voice. Joseph's face changed shape. He became a cat. The Prophet sat smiling, her teeth white in the dark room. Joseph sang and became a wolf, lemon-yellow eyes steady on David. Joseph sang and he became a snake hissing his song, his eyes sending out shards of light. Joseph sang and shook the turtle. He sang.

"Grandfather."

David was falling he fell into the song of the cat the song of the wolf the song of the snake the song of the turtle he fell he fell into the turtle's mouth the turtle's

song he was shaking was shaking his grandmother was singing was singing a song
a song in Indian his grandmother was singing singing he was singing with Grandmother he was sitting on Grandma's lap her lap she was holding him close so close
. . . *our people survived* . . . she sang his mother sang his sister sang his father sang
he sang he was singing in Indian Indian the voices the songs in Indian . . . *the sick-
nesses came* . . . singing singing his grandmother holding him his mother his father
singing . . . *measles, smallpox* . . . Grandmother talking singing in Indian the language
the song of Indian the people the song Grandma's hair brushing against his face as
she whispered and told him he . . . *AIDS* . . . was an Indian Indian Mohawk singing
songs Mohawk the voices Kanienka'ha'ka the song the song of this place this Indian
place this place.

The rattle was silent. The Prophet was sitting in a hump, the fur around her neck
electric, like an orange ruff. Joseph sat, his laser eyes bright in the face of an old,
old man. He spoke, his voice not audible, the words not recognizable, and David
heard.

"They took parts of us and cut them up and threw them to the winds. They made
lies we would believe. We look for the parts to put ourselves back together. To put
the earth back together. It is broken. We look for truth to put us all together again.
There is a piece here. A part there. We scavenge and collect. Some pieces are lost.
We will find them. Some parts are found, and we do not see them yet. We gather the
pieces and bring them together. We bring them together. We make the truth about
ourselves. We make the truth."

David was falling was falling he fell he fell into the sound of the ancient voice
the ancient words he was falling into the sounds of screaming screaming in his face
dirty Indian faggot fucking faggot the voices screaming you dirty Indian you the
sound of fists of fists the sound of hate the sound of hate you dirty Indian you dirty
faggot the sound of hate the sound of blood the taste of blood in his mouth the
taste the hate the hate . . . *we collect the parts that have been damaged* . . . the hate
the pain as they raped him you dirty Indian faggot the hate the blood the rape the
sound of rape . . . *we hunt for the pieces* . . . the hate the pain the fear the dirty Indian
faggot . . . *we gather it all together* . . . you filthy Indian scum you dirty you dirty
you dirty . . . *we are resisters, warriors* . . . you dirty Indian you dirty faggot the rape
the sound of you dirty filthy . . . *we do not believe the lies they* . . . the taste the taste
the taste of hate in his mouth.

David cried out. Joseph stroked his thinning hair, the turtle held over his body.
"They hurt us in so many ways. The least of what they did was to kill us. They
turned us into missing parts. Until we find those missing parts we kill ourselves
with shame, with fear, with hate. All those parts just waitin' to be gathered together
to make us. Us. A whole people. The biggest missing piece is love, David. *Love!*"

The Prophet leapt in the air and hissed. She leapt again and knocked the turtle
rattle back into Joseph's lap.

"The Prophet says we are not finished. Who am *I* to argue with *her*?"

David tugged at the man's arm. "Joseph. Grandfather. I am so thirsty, so thirsty."

David was falling was falling into the shake of the rattle he fell he fell into the
turtle's mouth he fell he was flying he flew he was inside the turtle the turtle shook
he fell into voices voices asking him are you ready his heart his heart was beating
are you ready his heart grew larger his heart was beating his heart the turtle asked
him are you ready his grandmother held out her hand and touched him are you
ready are you ready his grandmother touched his heart are you ready his father

touched his heart are you ready the people held out their hands are you ready he reached for their hands his heart was beating inside the turtle a drum a drum are you ready Turtle touched his heart are you ready he fell he put out his arms he held out his arms I am ready they touched him I am ready I am ready I am ready.

David opened his eyes. The taste of tears was in his mouth. "I saw it." Prophet jumped delicately on David's chest and licked the salt tears from his face. She sat back on her haunches and watched David speak. "I saw my grandmother, my father. They touched me." He began coughing again, retching blood.

Joseph held a towel to David's mouth and touched the young man's face. "You found your parts, your pieces." Digging into his sack, he pulled out a white feather. "This is from a whistling swan. They stop here in the spring before goin' on to Alaska. The thing about them—they never know what they'll find when they get there. They just know they got to get there. When our bodies are no longer here, *we are still here*." He stood up, his joints creaking and snapping. "Your mother is comin'. The sun is real bright today. It's a good day to go." He scooped Prophet up from David's lap and draped her across his shoulder.

"Thank you, Grandfather," David whispered, his breath coming in ragged bursts.

David heard him go out the front door. He couldn't see, but he heard Joseph talking to the Prophet. He heard the truck door slam and the engine start its rattling and wheezing. David moved his hands on the blanket to find the tin, the snakeskin, his ancestor's words, the feather. He touched them and felt Joseph's presence. The sound of his mother's car made him struggle to sit up. He heard the door open and the footsteps of his mother coming into the room. He felt her standing by him, her cool fingers touching his face and hands.

He opened his mouth to say good-bye.

—1991

BENJAMIN ALIRE SÁENZ

B. 1954

Benjamin Alire Sáenz was born and raised in the farming village of Old Picacho, New Mexico, an hour's drive from the border city of El Paso, Texas. The fourth of seven children, Sáenz spoke Spanish at home and learned to speak and write English in the public schools. At eighteen, influenced by such Catholic thinkers and activists as Thomas Merton, Dorothy Day, César Chavez, and the Berrigan brothers, he left the borderland to attend a Catholic seminary in Denver. Following studies at the University of Louvain in Belgium, Sáenz was ordained a Catholic priest. Although he left the priesthood after three and a half years, much of his writing displays the same combination of intense spirituality and passionate concern for human rights that initially attracted him to the church.

In 1984, Sáenz entered the graduate program in creative writing at the University of Texas at El Paso. Before completing the program, he received a fellowship to attend the prestigious M.F.A. program at the University of Iowa. Sáenz graduated from Iowa and then moved to Stanford University in 1988 on a Wallace Stegner fellowship in poetry. He returned to the

University of Texas at El Paso in 1993 as a faculty member in the bilingual M.F.A. program. Sáenz's first book, a poetry collection called Calendar of Dust, *appeared in 1991 and won an American Book Award from the Before Columbus Foundation. The following year he published* Flowers for the Broken, *the volume of essays and short stories from which the following piece is taken. Two books—the novel* Carry Me Like Water *and a collection of poetry called* Dark and Perfect Angels—*appeared in 1995 and earned him the Southwest Book Award. A second novel,* The House of Forgetting, *was published in 1997.*

The border between the United States and Mexico raises complex questions about the politics of place. The natural landscapes and human communities virtually mirror each other on either side of the border. Residents of Juárez look at El Paso's Franklin Mountains and high-rise skyline each day, while El Pasoans—as Sáenz shows in this essay—gaze at the Juárez Mountains and the barrios of Ciudad Juárez. In "Exile," Sáenz describes how the U.S. border patrol (La Migra) harasses Mexican-American citizens in the name of rounding up illegal aliens. The effect is to alienate, antagonize, and disorient even lifelong U.S. citizens. "¿De dónde eres? ¿Dónde naciste?" Where are you from? Where were you born? "I no longer know," concludes Sáenz.

EXILE. EL PASO, TEXAS

Do you know what exile is?
I'll tell you,
> *exile*
is a long avenue
where only sadness walks.
—ROQUE DALTON

That morning—when the day was new, when the sun slowly touched the sky, almost afraid to break it—that morning I looked out my window and stared at the Juárez Mountains. Mexican purples—burning. I had always thought of them as sacraments of belonging. That was the first time it happened. It had happened to others, but it had never happened to me. And when it happened, it started a fire, a fire that will burn for a long time.

As I walked to school, I remember thinking what a perfect place Sunset Heights was: turn of the century houses intact; remodeled houses painted pink and turquoise; old homes tastefully gentrified by the aspiring young; the rundown Sunset Grocery store decorated with the protest art of graffiti on one end and a plastic-signed "Circle K" on the other.

This was the edge of the piece of paper that was America, the border that bordered the University—its buildings, its libraries; the border that bordered the freeway—its cars coming and going, coming and going endlessly; the border that bordered downtown—its banks and businesses and bars; the border that bordered the border between two countries.

The unemployed poor from Juárez knocking on doors and asking for jobs—or money—or food. Small parks filled with people whose English did not exist. The upwardly mobile living next to families whose only concern was getting enough money to pay next month's rent. Some had lived here for generations, would continue living here into the next century; others would live here a few days. All this color, all this color, all this color beneath the shadow of the Juárez Mountains. Sunset Heights: a perfect place with a perfect name, and a perfect view of the river.

After class, I went by my office and drank a cup of coffee, sat and read, and did some writing. It was a quiet day on campus, nothing but me and my work—the kind of day the mind needs to catch up with itself, the kind of uneventful day so necessary for living. I started walking home at about three o'clock, after I had put my things together in my torn backpack. I made a mental note to sew the damn thing. *One day everything's gonna come tumbling out—better sew it.* I'd made that mental note before.

Walking down Prospect, I thought maybe I'd go for a jog. I hoped the spring would not bring too much wind this year. The wind, common desert rain; the wind blew too hard and harsh sometimes; the wind unsettled the desert—upset things, ruined the calmness of the spring. My mind wandered, searched the black asphalt littered with torn papers; the chained dogs in the yards who couldn't hurt me; the even bricks of all the houses I passed. I belonged here, yes. I belonged. Thoughts entered like children running through a park. This year, maybe the winds would not come.

I didn't notice the green car drive up and stop right next to me as I walked. The border patrol interrupted my daydreaming: "Where are you from?"

I didn't answer. I wasn't sure who the agent, a woman, was addressing.

She repeated the question in Spanish, *"¿De dónde eres?"*

Without thinking, I almost answered her question—in Spanish. A reflex. I caught myself in midsentence and stuttered in a nonlanguage.

"¿Dónde naciste?" she asked again.

By then my mind had cleared, and quietly I said: "I'm a U.S. citizen."

"Were you born in the United States?"

She was browner than I was. I might have asked her the same question. I looked at her for awhile—searching for something I recognized.

"Yes," I answered.

"Where in the United States were you born?"

"In New Mexico."

"Where in New Mexico?"

"Las Cruces."

"What do you do?"

"I'm a student."

"And are you employed?"

"Sort of."

"Sort of?" She didn't like my answer. Her tone bordered on anger. I looked at her expression and decided it wasn't hurting anyone to answer her questions. It was all very innocent, just a game we were playing.

"I work at the University as a teaching assistant."

She didn't respond. She looked at me as if I were a blank. Her eyes were filling in the empty spaces as she looked at my face. I looked at her for a second and decided she was finished with me. I started walking away. "Are you sure you were born in Las Cruces?" she asked again.

I turned around and smiled, "Yes, I'm sure." She didn't smile back. She and the driver sat there for awhile and watched me as I continued walking. They drove past me slowly and then proceeded down the street.

I didn't much care for the color of their cars.

"Sons of bitches," I whispered, "pretty soon I'll have to carry a passport in my own neighborhood." I said it to be flippant; something in me rebelled against people dressed in uniforms. I wasn't angry—not then, not at first, not really angry. In less than ten minutes I was back in my apartment playing the scene again and again in my mind. It was like a video I played over and over—memorizing the images. Something was wrong. I was embarrassed, ashamed because I'd been so damned compliant like a piece of tin foil in the uniformed woman's hand. Just like a child in the principal's office, in trouble for speaking Spanish. "I should have told that witch exactly what I thought of her and her green car and her green uniform."

I lit a cigarette and told myself I was overreacting. "Breathe in—breathe out—breathe in—breathe out—no big deal—you live on a border. These things happen—just one of those things. Just a game . . ." I changed into my jogging clothes and went for a run. At the top of the hill on Sunbowl Drive, I stopped to stare at the Juárez Mountains. I felt the sweat run down my face. I kept running until I could no longer hear *Are you sure you were born in Las Cruces?* ringing in my ears.

School let out in early May. I spent the last two weeks of that month relaxing and working on some paintings. In June I got back to working on my stories. I had a working title, which I hated, but I hated it less than the actual stories I was writing. It would come to nothing; I knew it would come to nothing.

From my window I could see the freeway. It was then I realized that not a day went by when I didn't see someone running across the freeway or walking down the street looking out for someone. They were people who looked not so different from me—except that they lived their lives looking over their shoulders.

One Thursday, I saw the border patrol throw some men into their van—throw them—as if they were born to be thrown like baseballs, like rings in a carnival ring-toss, easy inanimate objects, dead bucks after a deer hunt. The illegals didn't even put up a fight. They were aliens, from somewhere else, somewhere foreign, and it did not matter that the "somewhere else" was as close as an eyelash to an eye. What mattered was that someone had once drawn a line, and once drawn, that line became indelible and hard and could not be crossed.

The men hung their heads so low that they almost scraped the littered asphalt. Whatever they felt, they did not show; whatever burned did not burn for an audience. I sat at my typewriter and tried to pretend I saw nothing. *What do you think happens when you peer out windows? Buy curtains.*

I didn't write the rest of the day. I kept seeing the border patrol woman against a blue sky turning green. I thought of rearranging my desk so I wouldn't be next to the window, but I thought of the mountains. No, I would keep my desk near the window, but I would look only at the mountains.

Two weeks later, I went for a walk. The stories weren't going well that day; my writing was getting worse instead of better; my characters were getting on my nerves—I didn't like them—no one else would like them either. They did not burn with anything. I hadn't showered, hadn't shaved, hadn't combed my hair. I threw some water on my face and walked out the door. It was summer; it was hot; it was afternoon, the time of day when everything felt as if it were on fire. The worst time of the day to take a walk. I wiped the sweat from my eyelids; it instantly reappeared. I wiped it off again, but the sweat came pouring out—a leak in the dam. Let it leak. I laughed. A hundred degrees in the middle of a desert afternoon. Laughter poured out of me as fast as my sweat. I turned the corner and headed back home. I saw the green van. It was parked right ahead of me.

A man about my height got out of the van and approached me. Another man, taller, followed him. "¿Tienes tus papeles?" he asked. His gringo accent was as thick as the sweat on my skin.

"I can speak English," I said. I started to add: *I can probably speak it better than you,* but I stopped myself. No need to be aggressive, no need to get any hotter.

"Do you live in this neighborhood?"

"Yes."

"Where?"

"Down the street."

"Where down the street?"

"Are you planning on making a social visit?"

He gave me a hard look—cold and blue—then looked at his partner. He didn't like me. I didn't care. I liked that he hated me. It made it easier.

I watched them drive away and felt as hot as the air, felt as hot as the heat that was burning away the blue in the sky.

There were other times when I felt watched. Sometimes, when I jogged, the green vans would slow down, eye me. I felt like prey, like a rabbit who smelled the hunter. I pretended not to notice them. I stopped pretending. I started noting their presence in our neighborhood more and more. I started growing suspicious of my own observations. Of course, they weren't everywhere. But they *were* everywhere. I had just been oblivious to their presence, had been oblivious because they had nothing to do with me; their presence had something to do with someone else. I was not a part of this. I wanted no part of it. The green cars and the green vans clashed with the purples of the Juárez Mountains. Nothing looked the same. I never talked about their presence to other people. Sometimes the topic of the *Migra* would come up in conversations. I felt the burning; I felt the anger, would control it. I casually referred to them as the Gestapo, the traces of rage carefully hidden from the expression on my face—and everyone would laugh. I hated them.

When school started in the fall, I was stopped again. Again I had been walking home from the University. I heard the familiar question: "Where are you from?"

"Leave me alone."

"Are you a citizen of the United States?"

"Yes."

"Can you prove it?"

"No. No, I can't."

He looked at my clothes: jeans, tennis shoes, and a casual California shirt. He noticed my backpack full of books.

"You a student?"

I nodded and stared at him.

"There isn't any need to be unfriendly—"

"I'd like you to leave me alone."

"Just doing my job," he laughed. I didn't smile back. *Terrorists. Nazis did their jobs. Death squads in El Salvador and Guatemala did their jobs, too.* An unfair analogy. An unfair analogy? Yes, unfair. I thought it; I felt it; it was no longer my job to excuse—someone else would have to do that, someone else. The Juárez Mountains did not seem purple that fall. They no longer burned with color.

In early January I went with Michael to Juárez. Michael was from New York, and he had come to work in a home for the homeless in South El Paso. We weren't in Juárez very long—just looking around and getting gas. Gas was cheap in Juárez. On the way back, the customs officer asked us to declare our citizenship. "U.S. citizen," I said. "U.S. citizen," Michael followed. The customs officer lowered his head and poked it in the car. "What are you bringing over?"

"Nothing."

He looked at me. "Where in the United States were you born?"

"In Las Cruces, New Mexico."

He looked at me a while longer. "Go ahead," he signaled.

I noticed that he didn't ask Michael where he was from. But Michael had blue eyes; Michael had white skin. Michael didn't have to tell the man in the uniform where he was from.

That winter, Sunset Heights seemed deserted to me. The streets were empty like the river. One morning, I was driving down Upson Street toward the University, the wind shaking the limbs of the bare trees. Nothing to shield them—unprotected by green leaves. The sun burned a dull yellow. In front of me, I noticed two border patrol officers chasing someone, though that someone was not visible. One of them put his hand out, signaling me to slow down as they ran across the street in front of my car. They were running with their billy clubs in hand. The wind blew at their backs as if to urge them on, as if to carry them.

In late January, Michael and I went to Juárez again. A friend of his was in town, and he wanted to see Juárez. We walked across the bridge, across the river, across the line into another country. It was easy. No one there to stop us. We walked the streets of Juárez, streets that had seen better years, that were tired now from the tired feet that walked them. Michael's friend wanted to know how it was that there were so many beggars. "Were there always so many? Has it always been this way?" I didn't know how it had always been. We sat in the Cathedral and in the old chapel next to it and watched people rubbing the feet of statues; when I touched a statue, it was warmer than my own hand. We walked to the marketplace and inhaled the smells. Grocery stores in the country we knew did not have such smells. On the way back we stopped in a small bar and had a beer. The beer was cold and cheap. Walking back over the bridge, we stopped at the top and looked out at the city of El Paso. "It actually looks pretty from here, doesn't it?" I said. Michael nodded. It did look pretty. We looked off to the side—down the river—and for a long time watched the people trying to get across. Michael's friend said it was like watching *The CBS Evening News.*

As we reached the customs building, we noticed that a border patrol van pulled up behind the building where the other green cars were parked. The officers jumped out of the van and threw a handcuffed man against one of the parked cars. It looked like they were going to beat him. Two more border patrol officers pulled up in a car and jumped out to join them. One of the officers noticed we were watching. They straightened the man out and walked him inside—like gentlemen. They would have beat him. They would have beat him. But we were watching.

My fingers wanted to reach through the wire fence, not to touch it, not to feel it, but to break it down, to melt it down with what I did not understand. The burning was not there to be understood. Something was burning, the side of me that knew I was treated different, would always be treated different because I was born on a particular side of a fence, a fence that separated me from others, that separated me from a past, that separated me from the country of my genesis and glued me to the country I did not love because it demanded something of me I could not give. Something was burning now, and if I could have grasped the source of that rage and held it in my fist, I would have melted that fence. Someone built that fence; someone could tear it down. Maybe I could tear it down; maybe I was the one. Maybe then I would no longer be separated.

The first day in February, I was walking to a downtown Chevron station to pick up my car. On the corner of Prospect and Upson, a green car was parked—just sitting there. A part of my landscape. I was walking on the opposite side of the street. For some reason, I knew they were going to stop me. My heart clenched like a fist; the muscles in my back knotted up. *Maybe they'll leave me alone. I should have taken a shower this morning. I should have worn a nicer sweater. I should have put on a pair of socks, worn a nicer pair of shoes. I should have cut my hair; I should have shaved . . .*

The driver rolled down his window. I saw him from the corner of my eye. He called me over to him—*whistled me over*—much like he'd call a dog. I kept walking. He whistled me over again. *Here, boy.* I stopped for a second. Only a second. I kept walking. The border patrol officer and a policeman rushed out of the car and ran toward me. I was sure they were going to tackle me, drag me to the ground, handcuff me. They stopped in front of me.

"Can I see your driver's license?" the policeman asked.

"Since when do you need a driver's license to walk down the street?" Our eyes met. "Did I do something against the law?"

The policeman was annoyed. He wanted me to be passive, to say: "Yes, sir." He wanted me to approve of his job.

"Don't you know what we do?"

"Yes, I know what you do."

"Don't give me a hard time. I don't want trouble. I just want to see some identification."

I looked at him—looked, and saw what would not go away: neither him, nor his car, nor his job, nor what I knew, nor what I felt. He stared back. He hated me as much as I hated him. He saw the bulge of my cigarettes under my sweater and crumpled them.

I backed away from his touch. "I smoke. It's not good for me, but it's not against the law. Not yet, anyway. Don't touch me. I don't like that. Read me my rights, throw me in the can, or leave me alone." I smiled.

"No one's charging you with anything."

My eyes followed them as they walked back to their car. Now it was war, and *I had won this battle.* Had I won this battle? Had I won?

This spring morning, I sit at my desk, wait for the coffee to brew, and look out my window. This day, like every day, I look out my window. Across the street, a border patrol van stops and an officer gets out. So close I could touch him. On the freeway—this side of the river—a man is running. I put on my glasses. I am afraid he will be run over by the cars. I cheer for him. *Be careful. Don't get run over.* So close to the other side he can touch it. The border patrol officer gets out his walkie-talkie and runs toward the man who has disappeared from my view. I go and get my cup of coffee. I take a drink—slowly, it mixes with yesterday's tastes in my mouth. The officer in the green uniform comes back into view. He has the man with him. He puts him in the van. I can't see the color in their eyes. I see only the green. They drive away. There is no trace that says they've been there. The mountains watch the scene and say nothing. The mountains, ablaze in the spring light, have been watching—and guarding—and keeping silent longer than I have been alive. They will continue their vigil long after I am dead.

The green vans. They are taking someone away. They are taking. Green vans. This is my home, I tell myself. But I am not sure if I want this to be my home anymore. The thought crosses my mind to walk out of my apartment without my wallet. The thought crosses my mind that maybe the *Migra* will stop me again. I will let them arrest me. I will let them warehouse me. I will let them push me in front of a judge who will look at me like he has looked at the millions before me. I will be sent back to Mexico. I will let them treat me like I am illegal. But the thoughts pass. I am not brave enough to let them do that to me.

Today, the spring winds blow outside my window. The reflections in the pane, graffiti burning questions into the glass: *Sure you were born . . . Identification . . . Do you live? . . .* The winds will unsettle the desert—cover Sunset Heights with green dust. The vans will stay in my mind forever. I cannot banish them. I cannot banish their questions: *Where are you from?* I no longer know.

—1992

EVELYN C. WHITE

B. 1954

Evelyn C. White began writing about the concerns of black women after becoming a legal advocate for battered women through Seattle's Family Violence Project. She was asked to write a book about her work that was published as Chain Chain Change: For Black Women in Abusive Relationships *in 1985, the same year she completed a master's degree in journalism from Columbia University. Born and raised the eldest of five children in a working-class family in Gary, Indiana, White earned a B.A. in drama from Wellesley and moved to Seattle to enter the directing program at the University of Washington, but eventually left the theater to work with battered women. She joined the reporting staff of the* San Francisco Chronicle *in 1986 and earned a master's in public administration from Harvard in 1991. She is the editor of* The Black Women's Health Book: Speaking for Ourselves *(1990) and coauthor of the photography book* The African Americans *(1993).*

"Black Women and the Wilderness" appeared in The Stories That Shape Us: Contemporary Women Write About the West, *edited by Teresa Jordan and James Hepworth (1995). It voices a point of view that is startling in its contrast with the idea conveyed in mainstream environmental publications*

*that wilderness is a place to visit for refreshment and rejuvenation, reveal-
ing that idea as very much influenced by race. "I was certain that if I ventured outside to admire a meadow or to feel the cool ripples in a stream, I'd
be taunted, attacked, raped, maybe even murdered because of the color of
my skin," reveals White. "My genetic memory of ancestors hunted down and
preyed upon in rural settings counters my fervent hopes of finding peace in
the wilderness."*

BLACK WOMEN AND THE WILDERNESS

*I wanted to sit outside and listen to the roar of the ocean, but I
was afraid.
I wanted to walk through the redwoods, but I was afraid.
I wanted to glide in a kayak and feel the cool water splash in my
face, but I was afraid.*

For me, the fear is like a heartbeat, always present, while at the same time, intangible, elusive, and difficult to define. So pervasive, so much a part of me, that I
hardly knew it was there.

In fact, I wasn't fully aware of my troubled feelings about nature until I was
invited to teach at a women's writing workshop held each summer on the McKenzie
River in the foothills of Oregon's Cascade Mountains. I was invited to Flight of the
Mind by a Seattle writer and her friend, a poet who had moved from her native
England to Oregon many years before. Both committed feminists, they asked me to
teach because they believe, as I do, that language and literature transcend the man-
made boundaries that are too often placed upon them. I welcomed and appreciated
their interest in me and my work.

Once I got there, I did not welcome the steady stream of invitations to explore
the great outdoors. It seemed like the minute I finished my teaching duties, I'd be
faced with a student or fellow faculty member clamoring for me to trek to the lava
beds, soak in the hot springs, or hike into the mountains that loomed over the site
like white-capped security guards. I claimed fatigue, a backlog of classwork, concern
about "proper" student/teacher relations; whatever the excuse, I always declined to
join the expeditions into the woods. When I wasn't teaching, eating in the dining
hall, or attending our evening readings, I stayed holed up in my riverfront cabin with
all doors locked and windowshades drawn. While the river's roar gave me a certain
comfort and my heart warmed when I gazed at the sun-dappled trees out of a classroom window, I didn't want to get closer. I was certain that if I ventured outside to
admire a meadow or to feel the cool ripples in a stream, I'd be taunted, attacked,
raped, maybe even murdered because of the color of my skin.

I believe the fear I experience in the outdoors is shared by many African-
American women and that it limits the way we move through the world and colors
the decisions we make about our lives. For instance, for several years now, I've been
thinking about moving out of the city to a wooded, vineyard-laden area in Northern
California. It is there, among the birds, creeks, and trees that I long to settle down
and make a home.

Each house-hunting trip I've made to the countryside has been fraught with two emotions: elation at the prospect of living closer to nature and a sense of absolute doom about what might befall me in the backwoods. My genetic memory of ancestors hunted down and preyed upon in rural settings counters my fervent hopes of finding peace in the wilderness. Instead of the solace and comfort I seek, I imagine myself in the country as my forebears were—exposed, vulnerable, and unprotected—a target of cruelty and hate.

I'm certain that the terror I felt in my Oregon cabin is directly linked to my memories of September 15, 1963. On that day, Denise McNair, Addie Mae Collins, Cynthia Wesley, and Carol Robertson were sitting in their Sunday school class at the Sixteenth Street Church in Birmingham, Alabama. Before the bright-eyed black girls could deliver the speeches they'd prepared for the church's annual Youth Day program, a bomb planted by racists flattened the building, killing them all. In black households throughout the nation, families grieved for the martyred children and expressed their outrage at whites who seemed to have no limits on the depths they would sink in their ultimately futile effort to curtail the civil rights movement.

To protest the Birmingham bombing and to show solidarity with the struggles in the South, my mother bought a spool of black cotton ribbon which she fashioned into armbands for me and my siblings to wear to school the next clay. Nine years old at the time, I remember standing in my house in Gary, Indiana, and watching in horror as my mother ironed the black fabric that, in my mind, would align me with the bloody dresses, limbless bodies, and dust-covered patent leather shoes that had been entombed in the blast.

The next morning, I put on my favorite school dress—a V-necked cranberry jumper with a matching cranberry-and-white pin-striped shirt. Motionless, I stared stoically straight ahead, as my mother leaned down and pinned the black ribbon around my right sleeve shortly before I left the house.

As soon as I rounded the corner at the end of our street, I ripped the ribbon off my arm, looking nervously up into the sky for the "evil white people" I'd heard my parents talk about in the aftermath of the bombing. I feared that if I wore the armband, I'd be blown to bits like the black girls who were that moment rotting under the rubble. Thirty years later, I know that another part of my "defense strategy" that day was to wear the outfit that had always garnered me compliments from teachers and friends. "Don't drop a bomb on me," was the message I was desperately trying to convey through my cranberry jumper. "I'm a pretty black girl. Not like the ones at the church."

The sense of vulnerability and exposure that I felt in the wake of the Birmingham bombing was compounded by feelings that I already had about Emmett Till. Emmett was a rambunctious, fourteen-year-old black boy from Chicago, who in 1955 was sent to rural Mississippi to enjoy the pleasures of summer with relatives. Emmett was delivered home in a pine box long before season's end bloated and battered beyond recognition. He had been lynched and dumped in the Tallahatchie River with the rope still dangling around his neck for allegedly whistling at a white woman at a country store.

Those summers in Oregon when I walked past the country store where thick-necked loggers drank beer while leaning on their big rig trucks, it seemed like Emmett's fate had been a part of my identity from birth. Averting my eyes from those of the loggers, I'd remember the ghoulish photos of Emmett I'd seen in *JET* magazine with my childhood friends Tyrone and Lynette Henry. The Henrys subscribed to *JET*, an inexpensive magazine for blacks, and kept each issue neatly filed on the top shelf of a bookcase in their living room. Among black parents, the *JET* with Emmett's story was always carefully handled and treated like one of the most valuable treasures on earth. For within its pages rested an important lesson they felt duty-bound to teach their children: how little white society valued our lives.

Mesmerized by Emmett's monstrous face, Lynette, Tyrone, and I would drag a flower-patterned vinyl chair from the kitchen, take the Emmett *JET* from the bookcase, and spirit it to a back bedroom where we played. Heads together, bellies on the floor as if we were shooting marbles or scribbling in our coloring books, we'd silently gaze at Emmett's photo for what seemed like hours before returning it to its sacred place. As with thousands of black children from that era, Emmett's murder cast a nightmarish pall over my youth. In his pummeled and contorted face, I saw a reflection of myself and the blood-chilling violence that would greet me if I ever dared to venture into the wilderness.

I grew up. I went to college. I traveled abroad. Still, thoughts of Emmett Till could leave me speechless and paralyzed with the heart-stopping fear that swept over me as when I crossed paths with loggers near the McKenzie River or whenever I visited the outdoors. His death seemed to be summed up in the prophetic warning of writer Alice Walker, herself a native of rural Georgia: "Never be the only one, except, possibly, in your own house."

For several Oregon summers, I concealed my pained feelings about the outdoors until I could no longer reconcile my silence with my mandate to my students to face their fears. They found the courage to write openly about incest, poverty, and other ills that had constricted their lives: How could I turn away from my fears about being in nature?

But the one time I'd attempted to be as bold as my students, I'd been faced with an unsettling incident. Legend had it that the source of the McKenzie was a tiny trickle of water that bubbled up from a pocket in a nearby lake. Intrigued by the local lore, two other Flight teachers and a staff person, all white women, invited me to join them on an excursion to the lake. The plan was to rent rowboats and paddle around the lake Sacajawea-style, until we, brave and undaunted women, "discovered the source" of the mighty river. As we approached the lake, we could see dozens of rowboats tied to the dock. We had barely begun our inquiry about renting one when the boathouse man interrupted and tersely announced: "No boats."

We stood shocked and surprised on a sun-drenched dock with a vista of rowboats before us. No matter how much we insisted that our eyes belied his words, the man held fast to his two-note response: "No boats."

Distressed but determined to complete our mission, we set out on foot. As we trampled along the trail that circled the lake we tried to make sense of our "Twilight Zone" encounter. We laughed and joked about the incident and it ultimately drifted out of our thoughts in our jubilation at finding the gurgling bubble that gave birth to the McKenzie. Yet I'd always felt that our triumph was undermined by a searing question that went unvoiced that day: Had we been denied the boat because our group included a black?

In an effort to contain my fears, I forced myself to revisit the encounter and to reexamine my childhood wounds from the Birmingham bombing and the lynching of Emmett Till. I touched the terror of my Ibo and Ashanti ancestors as they were dragged from Africa and enslaved on southern plantations. I conjured bloodhounds, burning crosses, and white-robed Klansmen hunting down people who looked just like me. I imagined myself being captured in a swampy backwater, my back ripped open and bloodied by the whip's lash. I cradled an ancestral mother, broken and keening as her baby was snatched from her arms and sold down the river.

Every year, the Flight of the Mind workshop offers a rafting trip on the McKenzie River. Each day we'd watch as flotillas of rafters, shrieking excitedly and with their oars held aloft, rumbled by the deck where students and teachers routinely gathered. While I always cheered their adventuresome spirit, I never joined the group of Flight women who took the trip. I was always mindful that I had never seen one black person in any of those boats.

Determined to reconnect myself to the comfort my African ancestors felt in the rift valleys of Kenya and on the shores of Sierra Leone, I eventually decided to go on a rafting trip. Familiar with my feelings about nature, Judith, a dear friend and workshop founder, offered to be one of my raftmates.

With her sturdy, gentle and wise body as my anchor, I lowered myself into a raft at the bank of the river. As we pushed off into the current, I felt myself make an unsure but authentic shift from my painful past.

At first the water was calm—nearly hypnotic in its pristine tranquility. Then we met the rapids, sometimes swirling, other times jolting us forward like a runaway roller coaster. The guide roared out commands, "Highside! All forward! All back!" To my amazement, I responded. Periodically, my brown eyes would meet Judith's steady aquamarine gaze and we'd smile at each other as the cool water splashed in our faces and shimmered like diamonds in our hair.

Charging over the river, orange life vest firmly secured, my breathing relaxed and I allowed myself to drink in the stately rocks, soaring birds, towering trees, and affirming anglers who waved their rods as we rushed by in our raft. About an hour into the trip, in a magnificently still moment, I looked up into the heavens and heard the voice of black poet Langston Hughes:

"I've known rivers ancient as the world and older than the flow of human blood in human veins. I bathed in the Euphrates when dawns were young. I built my hut near the Congo and it lulled me to sleep. I looked upon the Nile and raised the pyramids above it. My soul has grown deep like the rivers."

Soaking wet and shivering with emotion, I felt tears welling in my eyes as I stepped out of the raft onto solid ground. Like my African forebears who survived the Middle Passage, I was stronger at journey's end.

Since that voyage, I've stayed at country farms, napped on secluded beaches, and taken wilderness treks all in an effort to find peace in the outdoors. No matter where I travel, I will always carry Emmett Till and the four black girls whose deaths affected me so. But comforted by our tribal ancestors—herders, gatherers, and fishers all—I am less fearful, ready to come home.

—1995

MARGARET WALKER

B. 1915

Margaret Walker vividly captures the lush physical beauty of the South while taking a historical approach to the struggles of African Americans in her poetry, novels, biographies, and essays. In works such as the poetry collections For My People *(1942),* Prophets for a New Day *(1970),* October Journey *(1973), and* This Is My Century, New and Collected Poems *(1989), and the novel* Jubilee *(1966), Walker has consciously attempted to nurture the growth of black culture. Jazz rhythms and blues meters pulse in her writing; she dedicated* For My People *to "my people everywhere singing their slave songs repeatedly: their dirges and their ditties and their blues and jubilees."*

The daughter of a Methodist minister and a musicologist, Walker was born in Birmingham, Alabama, and attended church schools in Mississippi, Alabama, and Louisiana. She received a B.A. from Northwestern University in 1935, and an M.A. and a Ph.D. from the University of Iowa in 1940 and 1965. She worked as a newspaper reporter, magazine editor, and social worker before being appointed professor of English at Jackson State College, Mississippi, in 1949, a position she held for more than three decades, supporting a disabled husband and four children. Walker became director of the Institute for the Study of the History, Life and Culture of Black Peoples in 1968.

"Sorrow Home" is collected in This Is My Century, *whose central theme is the twentieth century as a period of struggle for African Americans. The poem juxtaposes lyrical images of the aching beauty of Walker's homeland with symbols of racial hatred and oppression. Other black writers such as Alice Walker and Toni Morrison have done the same in their work, emphasizing the deep rootedness of their people in the southern landscape and the way cruel treatment has placed layers of painful memories across their recollections of the sweetness of home places.*

SORROW HOME

My roots are deep in southern life; deeper then John Brown or Nat
    Turner or Robert Lee. I was sired and weaned in a tropic world.
    The palm tree and banana leaf, mango and coconut, breadfruit
    and rubber trees know me.

Warm skies and gulf blue streams are in my blood. I belong with the
    smell of fresh pine, with the trail of coon, and the spring growth
    of wild onion.

I am no hothouse bulb to be reared in steam heated flats with the
    music of El and subway in my ears, walled in by steel and wood
    and brick far from the sky.

I want the cotton fields, tobacco and the cane. I want to walk along
with sacks of seed to drop in fallow ground. Restless music is in
my heart and I am eager to be gone.

O Southland, sorrow home, melody beating in my bone and blood!
How long will the Klan of hate, the hounds and the chain gangs
keep me from my own?

—1989

RUNNING-GRASS

B. 1952

*"The absence of positive images of people of color in the natural world was
not an accident but is central to the creation of a worldview called 'environmentalism,'" asserts Running-Grass, a black environmental educator.
Through involvement in the antinuclear movement in New England in the
mid- and late 1970s, Running-Grass came to see the link between social
issues and environmental issues, and the ways in which destruction of the
natural world relates to the oppression of people. He later founded and
became the executive director of the Three Circles Center in Sausalito,
California, which originated the field of multicultural environmental education (the "three circles" are culture, community, and ecology). Having earned
a master's degree in environmental studies from Antioch New England graduate school, Running-Grass is now employed by the U.S. Environmental
Protection Agency (EPA) as an environmental justice specialist.*

*Environmentalism has in recent years been confronted with the charge
that it is "elitist and insulated from the needs, aspirations, and experiences
of most people." Because of its focus on the "natural" environment, the
movement has tended to ignore places inhabited by people and to overlook
the fact that environmental degradation occurs disproportionately on lands
inhabited by minority groups. Examples of such "environmental racism"
abound. A member of the Western Shoshone National Council remarked in
1988, "We have a map of the world showing how all nuclear tests have been
conducted on the territory of Native peoples." In 1996, the EPA granted the
Southern Missouri Waste Management Company a permit to build a toxic
waste dump on the Yankton Sioux reservation in Lake Andes, South Dakota,
and waived the usual requirement of a double liner for the dump's waste
receptacles. The following essay gives the example of an unfenced toxic
waste dump that children walk across every day in the poverty-ridden
Hunters Point area of San Francisco.*

*Involving more people of color in the environmental movement, which will
focus attention on environmental racism, will require the dismantling of long-
held stereotypes about such people and the environment. The following essay,
which appeared in the journal* Whole Terrain: Reflective Environmental
Practice *(1995/1996), explores the power of stereotypes and suggests ways in
which the environmental movement might become more inclusive.*

BUILDING A MORE INCLUSIVE ENVIRONMENTAL MOVEMENT

When I first saw the film *The Color Purple,* I was particularly moved by early scenes of two young black girls running, playing and laughing in the beautiful countryside. It was not until after the film that I realized my emotional response was so strong because I had never seen an aesthetically appealing depiction of black people happy in nature. All the other "pictures" I had seen of Blacks in nature were either naked "savages" as in *National Geographic,* or slaves and destitute sharecroppers engaged in brutal physical labor—hardly happy circumstances.

What I found remarkable was that I had lived for thirty years, been educated and deeply involved in the environmental movement, and had never come across images of African-Americans at home and joyous in their natural surroundings. The more frequent and persistent images of savagery and slavery were counter to my own feelings of connectedness with the natural world, yet those images became the background against which I judged my own "abnormality" of being a person of color and an environmentalist. Encouraged by the culturally homogeneous environmental movement, I accepted this abnormality as a given, until my stereotype was challenged by powerful counter-images in the opening scenes of the film.

The absence of positive images of people of color in the natural world was not an accident but is central to the creation of a worldview called "environmentalism." My internalization of negative images was part of a complex dynamic involving my professional goals and sense of self. My professional encounters with environmentalists reinforced the idea that I was an anomaly, different in some way than "others" of my kind. In addition, the environmental movement had so totalized the definition of the "environment" that there was no room for experiences outside the parameters and norms it had set. There was no validation of African, Chinese or Arab-American traditions or environmental experiences; little representation of urban environmental experiences; and marginal inclusion of low income and female relationships to the environment. All such cultural experiences and relationships, buried beneath the surface of mainstream beliefs and values, were marginalized, discredited and painfully trivialized through the use of stereotypes.

The environmental movement is reminded, often in stereotypic fashion, that its origins can be traced back to the efforts of visionary white men to protect the natural world from the predatory interests of industrialists, and keep it safe for the use and enjoyment of the masses. Such an uncritically accepted, limited, and partial history of the movement has left environmentalism open to the charge that it is elitist and insulated from the needs, aspirations, and experiences of most people. Today, the environmental movement is being confronted with its limited history as people of color discover and assert their cultural ties to the natural world, redefine the notion of "environment" to include the city as a significant environment, and reveal the social justice dimensions of environmental issues.

By defining the environment as exclusively the natural environment (itself not a clear term) environmentalists have structured an environmental agenda that excludes "non-natural" environments. The marginalization and trivialization of those places, and the people who live there, has resulted in the phenomenon known as environmental racism.

Environmental racism is defined as the systematic discrimination, based on race, in the distribution of environmental degradation and amenities. This includes the discriminatory formulation, implementation and enforcement of environmental policy, regulations and laws, and disproportionate compensation and remediation of environmental degradation.[1] In response to environmental racism, the environmental justice movement has challenged the stereotypes of mainstream environmentalism.

During a seminar on multicultural environmental education that I recently gave at the University of Michigan, the topic of the lack of people of color in the environmental movement and professions came up. I critiqued some of the typical answers frequently cited as explanations for the glaring absence of people of color from the ranks of environmentalism: "they" are simply not interested; or (a version of the Maslow hierarchy of needs) "they" are so busy trying to survive and get ahead that "they" don't have time for pursuits such as hiking, enjoying sunsets, and saving rare and endangered species; and (reflecting, perhaps, on the dubious science and reactionary arguments of the Bell Curve) "they" do not have the intelligence to understand the complexity and moral significance of the issues. One of the seminar participants asked me why those explanations sound so good if they are obviously not true.

These appealing explanations are based on widely held stereotypes of who "they" are and function, as stereotypes do, by providing attractive and simple explanations to save us from the complicated task of thinking critically about our experiences. The persistence of such stereotypes is in part due to a history of discrimination and violence against people based on class, race, gender, religion, sexual orientation and other distinctions; but it is also reinforced by our naivete of the power of pictures and media to construct and reinforce particular images that sometimes serve regressive social purposes.

An Etiology of Stereotypes

A stereotype is usually an overly broad, negative and inaccurate generalization attributed to a group or class of people or species. Most people know stereotypes are inaccurate and hurtful, but frequently rely on them as a widely accepted and simplified explanation of reality. The origin and reproduction of stereotypes are frequently disguised and communicated either nonverbally, or by specific words or phrases which depend on the prior understanding and shared background of those in the act of communication. They are often directed towards groups of people (targets) and function to reinforce misinformation about them: "welfare mothers," "bureaucrats," and "elitists" are all code words for target groups which mean to describe young, unwed mothers in poverty; civil servants; and liberal intellectuals, respectively.

Stereotypes have a powerful ability to limit the range of thinking, perception and activity of people in subtle ways. As such, they not only diminish the targeted group but the person who holds and applies the stereotype as well. Stereotypes are also frequently unconsciously held and applied. This means that some people may not know that their "picture" is a biased one or that they are applying false information as though it were true—an action which can have an uncanny ability to create what it assumes.

As important as it is to focus on the individual using stereotypes, and on the specific stereotypes themselves, it is also essential to understand the function of stereotypes in the context of systematic oppression. Ricky Sherover-Marcuse created an analysis called the cycle of oppression in which she reveals the critical role of stereotypes in systems of discrimination and oppression.[2] She defines oppression as the systematic mistreatment of a group of people based on some shared characteristic.[3] This oppression relies on misinformation that becomes institutionalized as popular values, assumptions, and the terms of discourse in society. These in turn become justifications for further oppression and the cycle continues anew.

Stereotypes are that form of misinformation which become ingrained in popular consciousness, and develop into a part of society's "normal" and frequently unquestioned consciousness. Stereotypes thus become structured in the institutions of society and are actualized as policies and practices which regulate the lives of citizens. The often repeated observation that there are so few people of color in the environmental professions and movement—beyond being merely an observation—is really a charge that the field is structured in exclusionary ways, and that there exists institutionalized discrimination. One of the key and electrifying moments in the environmental justice movement occurred when activists charged that the environmental advocacy organizations were practicing discrimination because they employed few people of color in any positions of responsibility, and had a long history of ignoring environmental issues affecting people of color.[4]

Models and solutions seeking to facilitate the entry of people of color into environmental careers do not go far enough in solving the problem if they don't take on the structures and institutionalized practices of discrimination. In fact, they can divert attention from deeper causes and issues, and operate as adjuncts or auxiliaries to the discriminatory structures they purport to change.

Internalized Stereotypes

Stereotypes can also be internalized in a process known as internalized oppression, which causes the target to act as if the misinformation were true, thereby reinforcing its truth and credibility. This particularly destructive form of oppression closes the circle and makes challenging the misinformation all the more difficult.

As a local environmental professional of color, I once participated in a museum program where predominantly African-American 7th and 8th graders attempted to guess my profession. The students were aware that I was involved with the environmental field, but had to discover my specific job by asking one question per round before venturing a guess. After a number of questions and wrong guesses, one girl's face lit up and she raised her hand excitedly: "I know what you are," she exclaimed, "A janitor!" I think it may have been difficult for her to conceive that an African-American male could be professionally involved in an environmental career. After all, images and contact with such professionals for children of color is rare. The lack of such powerful experiences and counter-images can cause stereotypes to have an appealing and seemingly indisputable truth-value, especially for children. These are then internalized and define the parameters of conceivable experience creating a situation where people enforce their own limitations and possibilities.

Internal stereotypes of this kind often function as an excuse for us not to participate in an environmental discourse which intimately involves us as "silent partners" (or silent victims). When environmental issues were raised in Hunters Point, San Francisco, a youth of color said "Ecology? That's the White man's problem!"[5] When he was shown an unfenced toxic waste dump that he and his friends walk across several times a day, he grew significantly more interested in the "White man's problem."[6] He discovered, in this case, that this environmental problem was actually the Black man's burden.

The Environmental Movement as Target

Environmentalism has itself been a target group towards which stereotypes have been leveled. This has been, and continues to be, an effort to marginalize, trivialize and discredit not only environmentalists and our agenda, but the natural world as the subject of our concern.

What are some of the stereotypes or misinformation propagated about environmentalists and about the environment?

- Trees: seen one seen them all; they are renewable; they cause pollution.
- Oceans: the solution to pollution is dilution; limitless resource.
- The West: it's a frontier; we won it; it's a wasteland.
- Environmentalists: tree huggers; Communists; extremists; special interest group.
- Insects: they carry disease; dirty; lower life form; need to be killed.

The truth in each of these situations is more complex than the stereotypes allow.

Building Inclusive Communities Means Challenging Stereotypes

In the mid and late 1970's I worked extensively in the antinuclear movement in New England, particularly on the Seabrook power station. When I heard that the station would be powered by uranium imported from then apartheid South Africa, I immediately understood the relationship between the oppression of people and the destruction of the natural world. When I took this back to our local affinity groups, however, most members saw no connection between the two issues and felt no need to join ranks with the anti-apartheid movement then gathering strength in our region. The stereotype that social issues and environmental issues are not connected was too powerful to overcome. Challenging that stereotype required breaking out of isolated perspectives that pit people and issues against one another.

At a recent conference, an environmental educator demonstrated an activity for children. After he had gone through it, he cautioned the audience of educators that it would be necessary to adapt the activity for "inner city kids" of the same grade level. It would have to be made much simpler, he said, so they could understand it. There were no people of color present to counteract the stereotype. The challenge was provided by a white educator who has done years of work investigating race in the context of her personal life. Environmental educators have a special responsibility to get beyond such stereotypes and prejudices. Such challenges need not be ideological—they can be as simple as noticing and calling attention to the stereotype and challenging its veracity. Yet, without the presence of people of color in the environmental movement and professions, certain stereotypes may not receive the strenuous and vigorous challenge they require. This single fact is one of the best arguments for diversifying the environmental field.

If we don't challenge our values and behavior—permeated by racism, sexism and classism—any discussion of building the coalitions essential to our success will be lip service, and have no substantive value. It is only by confronting ignorance and looking inward at our own prejudices that we can build a more inclusive environmental movement, and turn the tide in favor of what we hold most dear. We truly need one another.

—1995

Notes

1. First National People of Color Environmental Leadership Summit. Conference proceedings, 1991.
2. Ricky Sherover-Marcuse, Ph.D. Materials distributed by "Unlearning Racism Workshops," Oakland, California.
3. See note 2 above.

4. *New York Times*, 1 February 1990, p. 1.
5. Leonard Pitt, founder of *EcoRap*, 1993 conversation.
6. See note 2 above.

JAMAICA KINCAID

B. 1949

Jamaica Kincaid was born Elaine Potter Richardson in St. John's, Antigua, in the British West Indies. Like other ordinary Antiguans, Kincaid is descended from the African slaves whom Europeans brought to the island, but she emigrated to the United States as a young woman and now lives in Vermont with her American husband and their two children. After leaving home in 1965, Kincaid traveled to New York, where she became an au pair and studied photography at the New School for Social Research. She also attended Franconia College in New Hampshire and did secretarial work in New York before becoming a staff writer for Ingenue *magazine. Eventually she began to publish in the* New Yorker. *A keen sense of place and elements of autobiography mark the four works of fiction that Kincaid has written thus far:* At the Bottom of the River *(1983),* Annie John *(1985),* Lucy *(1990), and* The Autobiography of My Mother *(1996). Her memoir* My Brother *(1997) was nominated for the National Book Award.*

Kincaid returned to Antigua after a twenty-year absence in the mid-1980s, and the result was her first book of nonfiction. A Small Place *(1988) is an extended essay that angrily indicts colonialism and its residue of poverty and political corruption. "Alien Soil," originally published in the* New Yorker *(June 21, 1993), continues her protest against the effects of British imperialism on her native land. Kincaid's focus in this piece is specifically on how the landscape of Antigua was reshaped by the English to their own taste so that hardly any native flora or fauna remain. The piece points up some of the ways in which a landscape can be profoundly influenced by the power relations among those who live there.*

ALIEN SOIL

Whatever it is in the character of the English people that leads them to obsessively order and shape their landscape to such a degree that it looks like a painting (tamed, framed, captured, kind, decent, good, pretty), while a painting never looks like the English landscape, unless it is a bad painting—this quality of character is blissfully lacking in the Antiguan people. I make this unfair comparison (unfair to the Antiguan people? unfair to the English people? I cannot tell but there is an unfairness here somewhere) only because so much of the character of the Antiguan people is influenced by and inherited, through conquest, from the English people. The tendency to shower pity and cruelty on the weak is among the traits the

Antiguans inherited, and so is a love of gossip. (The latter, I think, is responsible for the fact that England has produced such great novelists, but it has not yet worked to the literary advantage of the Antiguan people.) When the English were a presence in Antigua—they first came to the island as slaveowners, when a man named Thomas Warner established a settlement there in 1632—the places where they lived were surrounded by severely trimmed hedges of plumbago, topiaries of willow (casuarina), and frangipani and hibiscus; their grass was green (odd, because water was scarce; the proper word for the climate is not "sunny" but "drought-ridden") and freshly cut; they kept trellises covered with roses, and beds of marigolds and cannas and chrysanthemums.

Ordinary Antiguans (and by "ordinary Antiguans" I mean the Antiguan people, who are descended from the African slaves brought to this island by Europeans; this turns out to be a not uncommon way to become ordinary), the ones who had some money and could live in houses of more than one room, had gardens in which only flowers were grown. This made it even more apparent that they had some money, in that all their outside space was devoted not to feeding their families but to the sheer beauty of things. I can remember in particular one such family, who lived in a house with many rooms (four, to be exact). They had an indoor kitchen and a place for bathing (no indoor toilet, though); they had a lawn, always neatly cut, and they had beds of flowers, but I can now remember only roses and marigolds. I can remember those because once I was sent there to get a bouquet of roses for my god-mother on her birthday. The family also had, in the middle of their small lawn, a wil-low tree, pruned so that it had the shape of a pine tree—a conical shape—and at Christmastime this tree was decorated with colored lights (which was so unusual and seemed so luxurious to me that when I passed by this house I would beg to be allowed to stop and stare at it for a while). At Christmas, all willow trees would sud-denly be called Christmas trees, and for a time, when my family must have had a small amount of money, I, too, had a Christmas tree—a lonely, spindly branch of willow sitting in a bucket of water in our very small house. No one in my family and, I am almost certain, no one in the family of the people with the lighted-up willow tree had any idea of the origins of the Christmas tree and the traditions associated with it. When these people (the Antiguans) lived under the influence of these other people (the English), there was naturally an attempt among some of them to imitate their rulers in this particular way—by rearranging the landscape—and they did it without question. They can't be faulted for not asking what it was they were doing; that is the way these things work. The English left, and most of their landscaping influence went with them. The Americans came, but Americans (I am one now) are not interested in influencing people directly; we instinctively understand the child-ish principle of monkey see, monkey do. And at the same time we are divided about how we ought to behave in the world. Half of us believe in and support strongly a bad thing our government is doing, while the other half do not believe in and protest strongly against the bad thing. The bad thing succeeds, and everyone, pro-tester and supporter alike, enjoys immensely the results of the bad thing. This ambiguous approach in the many is always startling to observe in the individual. Just look at Thomas Jefferson, a great American gardener and our country's third President, who owned slaves, and strongly supported the idea of an expanded American border, which meant the extinction of the people who already lived on the land to be taken, while at the same time he was passionately devoted to ideas about freedom—ideas that the descendants of the slaves and the people who were defeated and robbed of their land would have to use in defense of themselves. Jefferson, as President, commissioned the formidable trek his former secretary, the adventurer and botany thief Meriwether Lewis, made through the West, sending plant specimens back to the President along the way. The *Lewisia rediviva*, state flower of Montana, which Lewis found in the Bitterroot River valley, is named after him; the clarkia, not a flower of any state as far as I can tell, is named for his co-adventurer and botany thief, William Clark.

What did the botanical life of Antigua consist of at the time another famous adventurer—Christopher Columbus—first saw it? To see a garden in Antigua now will not supply a clue. I made a visit to Antigua this spring and most of the plants I saw there came from somewhere else. The bougainvillea (named for another rest-less European, the sea adventurer Louis-Antoine de Bougainville, first Frenchman to cross the Pacific) is native to tropical South America; the plumbago is from Southern Africa; the croton (genus *Codiaeum*) is from Malay Peninsula; the *Hibiscus rosa-sinensis* is from Asia and the *Hibiscus schizopetalus* is from East Africa; the allamanda is from Brazil; the poinsettia (named for an American ambassador, Joel Poinsett) is from Mexico; the bird of paradise flower is from Southern Africa; the Bermuda lily is from Japan; the flamboyant tree is from Madagascar; the casuarina is from Australia; the Norfolk pine is from Norfolk Island; the tamarind tree is from Africa; the mango is from Asia. The breadfruit, that most Antiguan (to me) and starchy food, the bane of every Antiguan child's palate, is from the East Indies. This food has been the cause of more disagreement between parents and their children than anything else I can think of. No child has ever liked it. It was sent to the West Indies by Joseph Banks, the English natural-ist and world traveller, and the head of Kew Gardens, which was then a clearing house for all the plants stolen from the various parts of the world where the English had been. (One of the climbing roses, *Rosa banksiae*, from China, was named for Banks' wife.) Banks sent tea to India; to the West Indies he sent the breadfruit. It was meant to be a cheap food for feeding slaves. It was the cargo that Captain Bligh was carrying to the West Indies on the ship *Bounty* when his crew so rightly mutinied. It's as though the Antiguan child senses intuitively the part this food has played in the history of injustice and so will not eat it. But, unfortunately for her, it grows readily, bears fruit abundantly, and is impervious to drought. Soon after the English settled in Antigua, they cleared the land of its hardwood forests to make room for the growing of tobacco, sugar, and cotton, and it is this that makes the island drought-ridden to this day. Antigua is also empty of much wildlife natural to it. When snakes proved a problem for the planters, they imported the mongoose from India. As a result there are no snakes at all on the island—nor other reptiles, other than lizards—though I don't know what damage the absence of snakes causes, if any.

What herb of beauty grew in this place then? What tree? And did the people who lived there grow anything beautiful for its own sake? I do not know, I can only make a straightforward deduction: the frangipani, the mahogany tree, and the cedar tree are all native to the West Indies, so these trees are probably indigenous. And some of the botany of Antigua can be learned from medicinal folklore. My mother and I were sitting on the steps in front of her house one day during my recent visit, and I suddenly focussed on a beautiful bush (beautiful to me now; when I was a child I thought it ugly) whose fruit I remembered playing with when I was little. It is an herbaceous plant that has a red stem covered with red thorns, and emerald-green, simple leaves, with the same red thorns running down the leaf from the leafstalk. I cannot remember what its flowers looked like, and it was not in flower when I saw it while I was there with my mother, but its fruit is a small, almost transparent red berry, and it is this I used to play with. We children sometimes called it "china berry," because of its transparent, glassy look—it reminded us of china dinnerware, though we were only vaguely familiar with such a thing as china, having seen it no more than once or twice—and sometimes "baby tomato," because of its size, and to signify that it was not real; a baby thing was not a real thing. When I pointed the bush out to my mother, she called it something else; she called it cancanberry bush, and said that in the old days, when people could not afford to see doctors, if a child had thrush they would make a paste of this fruit and rub it inside the child's mouth, and this would make the thrush go away. But, she said, people rarely bother with this remedy anymore. The day before, a friend of hers had come to pay a visit, and when my mother offered her something to eat and drink the friend declined, because, she said, she had some six-sixty-six and maiden-blush tea waiting at home for her. This tea is taken on an empty stomach, and it is used for all sorts of ailments, including to help bring on abortions. I have never seen six-sixty-six in flower, but its leaves are a beautiful ovoid shape and a deep green—qualities that are of value in a garden devoted to shape and color of leaf.

People who do not like the idea that there is a relationship between gardening and wealth are quick to remind me of the cottage gardener, that grim-faced English person. Living on land that is not his own, he has put bits and pieces of things together, things from here and there, and it is a beautiful jumble—but just try duplicating it; it isn't cheap to do. And I have never read a book praising the cottage garden written by a cottage gardener. This person—the cottage gardener—does not exist in a place like Antigua. Nor do casual botanical conversation, knowledge of the Latin names for plants, and discussions of the binomial system. If an atmosphere where these things could flourish exists in this place I am not aware of it. I can remember very well the cruel Englishwoman who was my botany teacher, and that, in spite of her cruelty, botany was one of my two favorite subjects in school. (History was the other.) With this in mind I visited a bookstore (the only bookstore I know of in Antigua) to see what texts are now being used in the schools and to see how their content compares with what was taught to me back then; the botany I had studied was a catalogue of the plants of the British Empire, the very same plants that are now widely cultivated in Antigua and are probably assumed by ordinary Antiguans to be native to their landscape—the mango, for example. But it turns out that botany as a subject is no longer taught in Antiguan schools; the study of plants is now called agriculture. Perhaps that is more realistic, since the awe and poetry of botany cannot be eaten, and the mystery and pleasure in the knowledge of botany cannot be taken to market and sold.

And yet the people of Antigua have a relationship to agriculture that does not please them at all. Their very arrival on this island had to do with the forces of agriculture. When they (we) were brought to this island from Africa a few hundred years ago, it was not for their pottery-making skills or for their way with a loom; it was for the free labor they could provide in the fields. Mary Prince, a nineteenth-century African woman, who was born in Bermuda and spent part of her life as a slave in Antigua, writes about this in an autobiographical account, which I found in "The Classic Slave Narratives," edited by Henry Louis Gates, Jr. She says:

My master and mistress went on one occasion into the country, to Date Hill, for change of air, and carried me with them to take charge of the children, and to do the work of the house. While I was in the country, I saw how the field negroes are worked in Antigua. They are worked very hard and fed but scantily. They are called out to work before daybreak, and come home after dark; and then each has to heave his bundle of grass for the cattle in the pen. Then, on Sunday morning, each slave has to go out and gather a large bundle of grass, and when they bring it home, they have all to sit at the manager's door and wait till he come out: often they have to wait there till past eleven o'clock, without any breakfast. After that, those that have yams or potatoes, or fire-wood to sell, hasten to market to buy . . . salt fish, or pork, which is a great treat for them.

Perhaps it makes sense that a group of people with such a wretched historical relationship to growing things would need to describe their current relationship to it as dignified and masterly (agriculture), and would not find it poetic (botany) or pleasurable (gardening).

In a book I am looking at (to read it is to look at it: the type is as tall as a doll's teacup), "The Tropical Garden," by William Warren, with photographs by Luca Invernizzi Tettoni, I find statements like "the concept of a private garden planted purely for aesthetic purposes was generally alien to tropical countries" and "there was no such tradition of ornamental horticulture among the inhabitants of most hot-weather places. Around the average home there might be a few specimens chosen especially because of their scented flowers or because they were believed to bring good fortune. . . . Nor would much, if any, attention be paid to attractive landscape design in such gardens: early accounts by travellers in the tropics abound in enthusiastic descriptions of jungle scenery, but a reader will search in vain for one praising the tasteful arrangement of massed ornamental beds and contrasting lawns of well-trimmed grass around the homes of natives." What can I say to that? No doubt it is true. And no doubt contrasting lawns and massed ornamental beds are a sign of something, and that is that someone—someone other than the owner of the lawns—has been humbled. To give just one example: on page 62 of this book is a photograph of eight men, natives of India, pulling a heavy piece of machinery used in the upkeep of lawns. They are without shoes. They are wearing the clothing of schoolboys—khaki shorts and khaki short-sleeved shirts. There is no look of bliss on their faces. The caption for the photograph reads, "Shortage of labour was never a problem in the maintenance of European features in large colonial gardens; here a team of workers is shown rolling a lawn at the Gymkhana Club in Bombay."

And here are a few questions that occur to me: what if the people living in the tropics, the ones whose history isn't tied up with and contaminated by slavery and indenturedness, are contented with their surroundings, are happy to observe an invisible hand at work and from time to time laugh at some of the ugly choices this hand makes; what if they have more important things to do than make a small tree large, a large tree small, or a tree whose blooms are usually yellow bear black blooms; what if these people are not spiritually feverish, restless, and full of envy?

When I was looking at the book of tropical gardens, I realized that the flowers and the trees so familiar to me from my childhood do not now have a hold on me. I do not long to plant and be surrounded by the bougainvillea; I do not like the tropical hibiscus; the corallita (from Mexico), so beautiful when tended, so ugly when left to itself, which makes everything around it look rusty and shabby, is not a plant I like at all. I returned from my visit to Antigua, the place where I was born, to a small village in Vermont, the place where I choose to live. Spring had arrived. The tulips I had planted last autumn were in bloom, and I liked to sit and caress their petals, which felt disgustingly delicious, like scraps of peau de soie. The dizzy-making yellow of dandelions and cowslips was in the fields and riverbanks and marshes. I like these things. (I do not like daffodils, but that's a legacy of the English approach: I was forced to memorize the poem by William Wordsworth when I was a child.) I transplanted to the edge of a grove of pine trees some foxgloves that I grew from seed in late winter. I found some Virginia bluebells in a spot in the woods where I had not expected to find them, and some larches growing grouped together, also in a place I had not expected. On my calendar I marked the day I would go and dig up all the mulleins I could find and re-plant them in a very sunny spot across from the grove of pine trees. This is to be my forest of mulleins, though in truth it will appear a forest only to an ant. I marked the day I would plant the nasturtiums under the fruit trees. I discovered a clump of Dutchman's-breeches in the wildflower bed that I inherited from the man who built and used to own the house in which I now live, Robert Woodworth, the botanist who invented time-lapse photography. I waited for the things I had ordered in the deep cold of winter to come. They started to come. Mr. Pembroke, who represents our village in the Vermont legislature, came and helped me dig some of the holes where some of the things I wanted to put in were to be planted. Mr. Pembroke is a very nice man. He is never dressed in the clothing of schoolboys. There is not a look of misery on his face; on his face is the complicated look of an ordinary human being. When he works in my garden, we agree on a price; he sends me a bill, and I pay it. The days are growing longer and longer, and then they'll get shorter again. I am now used to that ordered progression, and I love it. But there is no order in my garden. I live in America now. Americans are impatient with memory, which is one of the things order thrives on.

—1993

DAN O'BRIEN

B. 1947

The literary work of Dan O'Brien is intimately associated with the land-scapes of the American West, chiefly with the prairies and the mountains. A native of Ohio who initially moved to South Dakota to attend graduate school, O'Brien readily admits that newcomers often struggle to recognize the beauty of South Dakota's plains and prairies. "You gotta stop and poke around," he says. He admits that his first biology lessons occurred in Ohio junkyards when he was a boy, and he understands the potential attractions of places that other people might disdain.

O'Brien has led an eclectic life. At Michigan Tech and Findlay College (now the University of Findlay) in Ohio, he majored in math and business. He then moved to the University of South Dakota for an M.A. in English, followed by another stint in Ohio as a student in the M.F.A. program in creative writing at Bowling Green State University. In 1976, after completing his M.F.A., he became a raptor biologist for the state of South Dakota, work-

ing to release captive-bred falcons into the wild; he later worked for the Peregrine Fund. He spent a year in the creative writing Ph.D. program at the University of Denver, but left when his first two books—a collection of short stories titled Eminent Domain *and a novel,* Spirit of the Hills— *appeared (a month apart) in 1986.* Rites of Autumn: A Falconer's Journey Across the American West *came out in 1988; O'Brien is currently writing a companion to this book. A second novel,* In the Center of the Nation, *was published in 1991, and a third,* Brendan Prairie, *in 1996. O'Brien and his wife, who is a doctor, currently raise between 100 and 300 cattle on their South Dakota ranch.*

"Eminent Domain," selected to appear in the small South Dakota mag-azine called Sunday Clothes, *was the first of O'Brien's stories to be pub-lished and is based on the actual case of an old man in Yankton, South Dakota. O'Brien chose it as the title piece for his first book because the sce-nario in the story—a man loves a particular place and is forced to leave it—symbolizes what he sees happening throughout the West today. It doesn't matter that in the story the embattled place happens to be a junkyard. Willy Herbeck, the story's crotchety protagonist, loves his junkyard home and is willing to fight for it.*

EMINENT DOMAIN: A LOVE STORY

You can say a lot of things to a woman, but don't ever tell her not to let the door hit her in the ass on the way out, because she won't. She'll be gone before that door has a chance to slam and she won't be back until long after the sound of that slam has stopped ringing in your ears.

Willy Herbeck can be the meanest, most insensitive son of a bitch the world has ever seen. He's dirty, sloppy, unsociable, old-fashioned, moody, bullheaded, and ugly. But he's got class. I guess that's why I married him in the first place, and that's why I moved out on him, too. He's got an independent orneriness and when he takes a liking to something he doesn't care what other people think, he sticks by what he's said come hell or goddamned high water.

That's why when I heard that the state highway department had been out to buy the place and Willy had told them to get out, I knew we were in for trouble. Willy, I said, it's a fair price. You haven't sold fifty dollars worth of parts off this place since spring and here they're offering you ten thousand dollars. He just sat there and read the newspaper. They'll get it, I said, the law says you have to sell. Bullshit, he said.

He hadn't even read the letters we'd sent him. I figured he was confused or maybe couldn't read so I went out and offered him top dollar right off the bat. They said he was a funny, hard-to-deal-with kind of guy, so I thought, hell, give him the ten grand, move those junk cars out of the way, and save everyone a lot of problems. He said that there were one hundred and thirteen of them and they weren't for sale, and I tried to explain that he had to sell, that the highway was coming through and that there really wasn't much choice. Then he grabbed me by the arm and led me back to my car and put me in and said good-bye.

So I was stuck. It's my job to get the land that the department needs and I don't get much time. I went and looked up his wife.

They told me she was young and good-looking and worked in a cafe at the intersection of Route 50 and Route 27. I asked for Shirley and the girl smiles and says she'll send her over. She brings me a cup of coffee and I wait. When Shirley comes I can't believe it's true. She's about thirty-five, blonde, nice body, white teeth. That slob of a junk man must have something going for him. The guy had to be fifteen years older than she was, he was dirty, rotten teeth. I looked her over real good, figured there had to be something wrong with her; but if there was, I didn't see it.

I told her what I wanted. Said that Willy had practically thrown me off the place and she should have a talk with him. It's a good price, I said, and let me give you a little inside scoop, the state ain't going any higher. She said she didn't think Willy would sell and I explained to her that he'd have to eventually. She nodded and asked if I needed anything. I said I was all set and as she walked away I wondered why a gal like her was with a guy like Willy Herbeck.

I did like the state man said, because he was right. I tried to talk Willy into selling the place. He was lying under the '48 Dodge in the front yard and I was trying to talk to him. Willy, I said, you can't fight them. They'll come and take it and put you in jail, that's what will happen. He didn't say a word. Keep it up then, I said, be a pighead. He said nothing. I kicked the Dodge, and that brought him out. You listening to me, I asked. Not much, he said. Well you better start listening to me, you're messing with the state, I said and pointed my finger at him. He looked back at me and said, Shirley, don't kick this car. It's a driver. Driver my ass, I said. They were all drivers; just needs a fan belt, he'd say, or a new wheel. They were all drivers, all precious pieces of junk and the truth is none of them were ever drivers. They all just sat and the people would come with good money and try to buy parts and Willy would just say, no, he didn't have it, and the people can see the thing they came for hanging off one of those junk cars and Willy pretends like he's never seen what they're looking for and tells them to get off the place. Now the state was offering him ten thousand dollars for the whole place and he was acting like they were someone who came looking for a gas cap.

Threatening and puffing up your chest is a waste of time. Nobody ever proved a thing in a pushing match, and nobody ever held onto nothing by talking about it.

After dinner he started going in and out of the house, carrying little boxes of things and kind of keeping them hidden from me. I was watching television and trying to ignore him. Finally he quit coming and going and sat down in his chair to watch television. What was all that about, I asked. Nothing, he said. Come on, Willy, I said, I know you're up to something, what was in those boxes? A little of this, a little of that, he said. I could see that he wasn't going to tell me what he was doing so I just ignored him again. But the longer I sat there the madder I got. I'd been living with him for a long time and I'd been bringing in the money ever since the first and now that he had a chance at ten thousand dollars he wouldn't even talk about it. And then he starts sneaking stuff out of the house. I couldn't stand it.

I screamed. Willy, what are you going to do about the state, and what was in those boxes? I yelled a while longer and finally he says, I guess I'll have to fight. And the second he said that I knew he was serious and I knew that those boxes were filled with supplies. Where'd you take those boxes, I asked, and he answered exactly what I knew he'd answer. I took them up to the '26 Packard, he said.

I've been buying land for the state for a long time and I don't think I ever had one like Willy Herbeck. He must be a mean bastard. He even threw that good-looking gal out of the house for trying to convince him that we were offering him a good deal. I talked to her the day after she got thrown out and she said she didn't care if she ever saw him again.

I went out again, hoping that maybe he'd thought it over and changed his mind. I was kidding myself, he was too mean to give in to anything. I knocked on the door and nobody came. I cleaned the dust off the window and looked in. Didn't look like anyone had ever lived there. I walked around to the back. There were car parts everywhere. Cracked engine blocks, old batteries, differentials, transmissions, fenders, hubcaps, junk scattered everywhere.

Behind the house the land rose to what must have been a little hilltop. You couldn't see any ground, nothing but wrecked cars, and nothing new, all old, rusting, smashed cars. I glanced over them all, then hollered to see if anyone was around. There was no answer. As I turned back toward the house I noticed a license plate leaning up against the house. I could see it was an old one. I reached out to inspect it and inches from my outstretched hand the siding on the house shattered, pieces of wood splintered, and I heard the rifle shot. I hit the ground behind an engine block. A voice boomed out from above, GET OUT. I looked up, and this time saw a person sitting behind the wheel of the Packard at the top of the hill.

They say that stainless steel is the best material to put bodies in for burial. When I die, I want them to cremate me, and put the ashes into a Stanley thermos bottle (they're stainless steel), and put the bottle in the glove compartment of the '26 Packard and not tell anybody where I'm at.

They came to see me at work and I told the sheriff, husband or not, I was staying out of it. The sheriff looked over his shoulder at the state man. He took a shot at this man, Shirley, now that's against the law and you gotta do something, he said. No, sheriff, I don't have to do anything, I said. The sheriff turned and led the state man into the corner of the cafe, I went on cleaning the counter. They were back in a minute. This time the state man was doing the talking.

He started off with, Mrs. Herbeck, I know that you're upset about all this and I know that when the state is forced to take over property that there are often serious adjustments to be made. I folded my arms across my chest and listened to him. You and your husband have had a falling out, he said. That's understandable, it's a trying situation. But, he said, and smiled slyly, this is not the time to alienate your husband. This is when he needs you most. Then he winked, and the time that you need him most.

I thought for a second. Okay, I said, I'll talk to him. He touched me on the shoulder and said, now you're thinking straight. He motioned to the sheriff and the three of us drove out to the place to talk to Willy.

When the sheriff stepped out of the car three shots hit the ground in front of him. He leaped back and said he was going to call the Highway Patrol. I told him not to do anything and got out of the car. They both yelled at me to get back but I didn't pay any attention, I knew Willy wouldn't shoot, and I knew right where to find him.

He was sitting in the driver's side of the Packard, peering out of the side window over his rifle barrel. Hold it right there, he said. Hold it yourself, I said, and walked over to the Packard. I looked into the backseat and could see that it was full of food and ammunition. What the hell do you think you're doing, I asked. I thought you weren't coming back, he said. So I'm back for a minute, I said, what the hell are you doing? Nothing, he said.

I took a good look at him sitting there in that old Packard, the backseat full of food and ammunition and the tires all flat. He was dead serious. You think you're protecting this place, I asked. He wiggled his mouth around under his nose and I knew that meant that he figured he was. Well, you're nuts, I said, you aren't protecting anything. You're just making a fool out of yourself. He rubbed the black stubble on his chin. That don't much matter, he said. I could see that there was no sense in even trying to talk him down from the hill. I kicked the Packard. You're a fool, I said, they'll shoot you dead as hell. He'd been staring down the hill toward the sheriff and the state man but raised his eyes to look at me. Don't kick the '26 he said, she's a driver.

He didn't listen to his wife the first time but I still thought he might. Something had to be done, the superintendent was starting to breathe down my neck. The sheriff said he'd give him a week, then go up and get him. Every day the sheriff and I would spend hours at the junkyard, every evening I'd stop at the cafe and talk to Shirley.

Once or twice a day the sheriff would call up through his megaphone, WILLY, YOU'RE GOING TO HAVE TO COME DOWN HERE AND TALK. THE STATE MAN IS HERE AND HE'S WILLING TO NEGO-TIATE. But Willy would not come down. And every time that Willy didn't answer the sheriff's message the sheriff would say, he left, he must have just deserted the whole thing, and the sheriff would step out from behind his car and smile. Then shots would ring out from the top of the hill of junk and the sheriff would jump back behind his car, grab the megaphone and say, WILLY, YOU SON OF A BITCH.

I kept telling Shirley that the ten thousand would be her ticket out of the junkyard. She's a smart gal, she knew what I was saying but played dumb. She kept talking about what was the best way to handle Willy, but she was smelling her share of the money and what she was thinking was what was the best way to get that in the bank. I told her that if she talked him into the ten thousand that she'd be doing herself a favor, that she'd earned it, and I was telling the truth.

If she could just get him to take the cash, she could get her share and get the hell out of there. I'd seen it work before. A guy like Willy could drink himself to death with five grand and a gal like Shirley could get a fresh start. It's a fact of life and Shirley knew her facts of life.

Somewhere there ought to be a law that says you don't have to sell what you got just because someone offers you a good price for it. There ought to be a law that everything isn't for sale, and people should realize that happy is happy and when you got it you got it. Everybody should think about that, especially women.

I kept thinking about Willy up there in the Packard, fighting his little war for no reason, and all the time I was figuring, ten thousand dollars divided by one hundred and thirteen cars in the lot is eighty-eight dollars and forty cents per car. And that's a lot more than they're worth. At first I just got mad when I thought of it. There he was, king of the mountain. But this wasn't a game, it was for real. The sheriff wasn't kidding and it wasn't right that Willy was playing with my life in his game. After all, there wouldn't be a mountain of junk to fight over if it weren't for me. Willy didn't have the ambition to support himself over the years it took to collect all that. In a way that mountain was half mine. I began to hope that the whole thing would just be over.

On the Wednesday after the Thursday when the sheriff had said he'd give Willy another week, the sheriff and the state man paid me another visit. He's still up there, the sheriff said, he shot at me twice today. Now tomorrow we're going up there and get him out, and we won't be pulling our punches. This is about your last chance to talk him down. He talked like he meant it, and I could see that the state man was serious, too. Will you give it another try, Shirley, the state man said, it's in your best interest. I untied my apron. Yeah, I said, I'll try again.

So five minutes later I was walking up that hill toward Willy and the Packard and I was thinking again about all those years of supporting Willy and I could remember them by the heaps of junk I passed. The '57 Chevy with the mashed-in left side had come in on Christmas Day four years ago. I remembered because Willy left the turkey dinner I'd made to go out and get it. And the '58 Edsel that had been driven off a bridge was there, and the wire-wheeled Hudson from fifteen years before and the blue '62 Ford with the green racing stripe, they were all there. I could see them all and could remember all the screaming and fighting that they had caused, and then I saw Willy sitting in the Packard, his very first car, and before I said anything to him I turned and looked over the junkyard. I saw the view that he had from the Packard. I saw every junker—drivers, he'd call them—and I saw every oily piece of junk that I'd helped him collect. And on the horizon, still miles away, I could see the ink-black exhaust smoke from the bulldozers and earth movers.

When she came down off the hill we asked her what he'd said. She said that he hadn't said anything. Then the sheriff asked her what she'd said and she said, nothing. They hadn't said a word to each other. The sheriff frowned, turned away and kicked at the dirt. Shirley turned to me and asked for a ride back.

In the car, she spoke first. You know, she said, I worked for that business probably more than Willy. I nodded my head, I could see what she was getting at. I figure, she said, that since Willy can't talk to you, that I should. I nodded again. I'd been wondering when she'd get around to dealing, she was a woman, she could get Willy to do like she wanted, no matter what he wanted. I think, she went on, that I can convince him to take your offer. This time I smiled, it had paid off. She'd put the ultimatum to him and they'd take the money and she'd be wearing new clothes in a week. Good, I said, I knew you could convince him once you saw what was best. But what, I said, would happen if he still says no, if the sheriff has to go up. She turned to me and said simply, they'll have to shoot him. Then she asked me to turn down a side street and told me to stop in front of a wrecking service. Let me out here, she said.

When two people agree to spend their lives together it seems to me that they gotta be able to pick up the slack for each other. When you live with someone you gotta be able to know that her little hands will scrub the inside of the pickle jar when it's empty, if you'll unscrew the lid when it's brand new.

The sheriff was there before the state man and me. There were four squad cars and the deputies stood behind them, wearing helmets and checking their guns. Sheriff,

I said, I want to talk to him, I think I can talk him out of a fight. You had your chance yesterday, he said, time for talk is done. But you have to let her try, the state man said, it could save some trouble, maybe even a life. The sheriff frowned. How long, he asked. Ten minutes, I said. Okay.

It was just getting light when I started up. I called out to Willy as I went, to be sure he wouldn't shoot in the half-light. Willy, I yelled, it's Shirley, and my voice bounced in all directions off the gray forms of the junkers. Don't shoot me, I said, and halfway up, beside the '41 Studebaker pickup, I called again. Willy, I said, don't be pointing that gun at me. And this time he called back, shut up, he said. When I came to the Packard I could see him sitting there, his rifle barrel pointing out the window and the bill of his baseball cap pulled down low over his eyes. Hold it, he said, what do you want? They're down there waiting, I said. Yeah, he said, I heard them drive in. They're coming up, I said. It was almost light and I saw him glance in the backseat. Well, he said, I'm almost out of food anyway.

I walked over to the Packard. I got a deal, I said. No, Shirley, he said, I've made up my mind, I'm staying with this junk for the rest of my life, and he smiled and rubbed his nose with a greasy hand. That's the deal, I said. His eyes narrowed and I knew he was listening even though he acted like he wasn't.

I talked to Ray over at Ace Wrecking Service, I said. Willy still wouldn't look toward me. He said he'd move them for us, I said. Willy glanced at me from the corners of his eyes. There are one hundred and thirteen of them, right, I asked. He nodded. At twenty dollars apiece for the move, that's four thousand five hundred and twenty dollars, I said. That leaves us over five thousand dollars to buy another piece of land.

He turned his head and looked at me, then motioned toward the seat beside him. Get in, he said. I climbed over the stack of rusted wheels that lay in front of the Packard and Willy kicked at the passenger's door from the inside until it came open and I sat down. We can pick a new piece of ground, he asked. Sure, I said. He'll move all of them, Willy asked. All of them, I said. And I can supervise, he asked. I don't see why not, I said.

Willy cleared his throat and let the rifle barrel slip onto the floor. It went through a hole in the floorboards. He stretched his oily arm over the back of the front seat and leaned back. A new yard, he said to himself and dangled his left arm over the steering wheel. Maybe somewhere out by the dump, he said, I'd like that. And we looked straight ahead, through the shattered windshield, the sun was coming up bright and we could see the black smoke from the bulldozers just beginning to rise.

—1986

MARGARET L. KNOX

B. 1954

Margaret L. Knox is a journalist who specializes in reporting on environ-mental and wildlife issues. In addition to appearing in the pages of news-papers across the country, her work has been featured in Sierra, Smithsonian, Mother Jones, and many other magazines. Born in

Washington, D.C., Knox grew up in the town of Davis, California. After attending various universities—including Grenoble in France—she graduated from the University of California, Santa Cruz, with a degree in history. She worked for a time at the Atlanta Constitution *before she and her husband decided to leave the newspaper and make a go of a career in freelance journalism, which they have been pursuing for more than a decade now. For two years, the couple lived in the African country of Zimbabwe, where they reported news to American newspapers and wire services. Later, when they returned to the United States, they chose to live in Missoula, Montana, for the same reason they were drawn to Zimbabwe: here was a niche unoccupied by other journalists.*

When asked what brought her to write the following profile of "wise use" advocate Chuck Cushman, Knox explained that when she first arrived in Montana, there was a great deal of tension between loggers and the environmental community. Over the course of doing her reporting, she got to know Cushman and other members of the so-called wise use movement—a movement launched in the late 1980s by conservative farmers, loggers, miners, ranchers, and others to protest the way federal lands were being protected by environmental legislation and thus made unavailable for income-producing activities. When the editors of Wilderness *magazine asked Knox to do a piece on Cushman for its Spring 1993 issue, she was already well prepared. Although Cushman for his part knew Knox did not share his opinions—that she was in fact a regular contributor to environmental magazines and journals—he was pleased to be interviewed for her article. "People in the wise use movement are very happy to see their views put into print," Knox explains. "Many of them are quite articulate and savvy about using the media to convey their message." Cushman himself is very personable, as comes across vividly in Knox's piece. As he said to its author in a good-humored admonition: "If your article is negative, I'll use it in my fundraisers."*

THE WORLD ACCORDING TO CUSHMAN

Big Chuck Cushman paces the stage like the huggable host of a kiddie TV show. "I generally just like to have a good time with people," he booms, spreading his hands and rocking back on his heels with a gravelly laugh. "I'm not trying to *scaaaaare* you." This is the Captain Kangaroo of the movement against public lands: he's having a good time, and wants you to feel good, too! He jokes about how long you'll have to sit on your "fanny" tonight. He cocks his head and glances at you sideways. Then he pushes away the pesky podium, scratches his beard with a hand the size of a catcher's mitt, and leans forward, all 270-jean-clad-towering pounds of him oozing sincerity. "You know what a willing seller is for the U.S. Government?" Cushman puts a finger pistol-fashion to his temple. "Right?" He pauses, smiles. A hush falls over the audience of thirty or so golf-shirted businessmen and Sacramento Delta farmers. This is getting serious now. "A .44 caliber willing seller. Right?"

For nearly twenty years Cushman has made a living putting a name to the vague fears of small-town, recession-bound America. The name is the federal government, whose different land-managing agencies are "all the same." A table-full of fill-in-the-blank bumper stickers and posters at the back of the room make Cushman's favorite point: "If You Like the IRS, You'll Love ___." In this case the blank has been filled in with the U.S. Fish and Wildlife Service, the villain that aims to manage the Stone Lakes National Wildlife Refuge near Walnut Grove, California.

As I punch the remote control and scroll back and forth through the video of this August, 1991, speech in Walnut Grove, it occurs to me how simple is the pitch Cushman throws again and again, from Mentone, Alabama, to Sitka, Alaska. In the world according to Cushman, the federal government is one big land-grabbing, tax-base-eating bogeyman. And the government's henchmen are the "preservationists." That's a word Cushman teaches people to use. "Most of *you* are environmentalists," he tells his rural audiences. The "preservationists," on the other hand, are the sharpster urban attorneys and their bleeding-heart, nature-loving clients, the kind of people Cushman's friends refer to in this post-Cold War era as "watermelons": green on the outside, red on the inside.

Cushman has fanned his brand of anti-government anger into three fiery political organizations, all of which, without non-profit status, are highly personalized and secretive fiefdoms. He founded the National Inholders Association in 1978 to fight the regulation of private land within national parks and other federal preserves. A decade later, he was in on the launching of the so-called Wise Use Movement, and created his own Multiple Use Land Alliance to prod conservative farmers, loggers, miners, ranchers, inholders, and off-road motorists to yelp in chorus for less protection and more access to federal lands. And now when private-property rights is becoming a buzzword phrase, Cushman is on stage again with the League of Private Property Voters—antitrope of the League of Conservation Voters—which he launched in 1991 to keep track of congressional votes on policies the Wise Use Movement abhors, like wetlands conservation, growth management, wilderness designation, and the protection of endangered species. "This issue is not about clean water," Cushman tells the Walnut Grove crowd. "It's not about pollution." He pauses, and his next words ring off the far walls. "This is a LAND USE CONTROL ISSUE!"

Like just about every other star of the Wise Use Movement, Cushman has a story of youthful environmental idealism gone sour. There's the story of Cushman as a young Boy Scout rowing Audubon Society members through the surf to Anacapa Island for bird-watching. There's Cushman as a Student Conservation Corps volunteer and an earnest Sierra Club member. And then there's the turning point, when Cushman, the cabin-owner in Yosemite National Park, is riled by a Park Service that wants to tell him what he can do with his own private property. But none of that explains how he came to be so good—and he is good—at selling the anti-green agenda.

Cushman, 49, grew up in the suburbs of Los Angeles, where as a young man he dogged his way up from peanut vendor at Dodger stadium through a few real estate deals with a fellow peanut vendor to become, by the early 1970s, an award-winning insurance salesman for Mutual of New York. To understand the rest, you have to look at the efforts of the late Congressman Phillip Burton to strengthen national park protection in the late 1970s.

Amendments that Burton offered to the Omnibus National Parks Act of 1978 would have directed the National Park Service to buy, within four years if funds were available, the private inholdings in most of the old wilderness parks, including Yosemite. The idea behind his proposals was that logging, strip-mining, junk yards, and subdivisions—often smack in the middle of prime scenery—were fast undermining the intended purposes of the National Park System.

The amendments were rejected, but Burton's campaign incensed cabin-owner Cushman, who organized a group of neighbors in and around Yosemite to file a lawsuit against the National Park Service. The lawsuit challenged current national park-land acquisitions, defended commercial development inside the parks, and went so far as to suggest that Yosemite should sell off the land it already owned. The lawsuit failed, but Cushman's new career was launched. He left his insurance job, obtained the names of more than 30,000 owners of property and permits within the national parks, and founded what would become the National Inholders Association. He has since been enormously successful at playing the politics of resentment in small-town America, painting the government in Washington as a pawn of entrenched and all-powerful conservation groups. Cushman's lobbying, lawsuits, and rural organizing have reduced and defeated parks and monuments, preserves and wild rivers from Big Sur to the Adirondacks. He doesn't always win, but wherever he shows up, he at least makes it a lot more time-consuming and expensive to protect green space, control growth, stem pollution, restrict logging, or manage grazing. Estimates of how much he has cost the conservation community in recent years range as high as $10 million. He can claim responsibility for lost conservation measures on thousands—some say millions—of acres of public lands.

Cushman is also known for shattering hard-fought compromises at the local level. "We had 90 percent of a good wetlands ordinance agreed upon," says John Karpinski of the Clark County Natural Resources Council in Vancouver, Washington. Karpinski, an attorney, had negotiated for months with real estate developers, county planners, and environmental groups to come up with a draft. "Then Cushman came in and incited people to near riots at all his workshops. The commissioners got scared and what finally passed is an abomination." Karpinski's group is now involved in a costly appeal to the state growth management board.

On his stumping, Cushman generally helps spawn—and often is in turn hired by—a proliferation of short-lived local organizations with such confoundingly green-sounding names as Nebraska's Niobrara Basin Preservation Association, which was supported by water development interests and was vigorous, if ultimately unsuccessful, in its efforts to block scenic status for the Niobrara River. Cushman takes groups that are little more than a name and some letterhead and spins them into regional media stars that wield genuine clout with local officials and sometimes with wavering congressional representatives—such as Oklahoma's Mickey Edwards, who dropped his support of the proposed Tallgrass Prairie National Preserve after Cushman orchestrated a campaign that included calling Sierra Club members "Nazis." Cushman says his fee for a single local organizing effort ranges from nothing to $20,000. What that buys is pamphlets, form letters, bumper stickers, balloons, and rousing Wise Use sermons; Cushman knows how to throw a green-bashing party. He also is a master at demonizing the language of land conservation: buffer zones, view sheds, greenlining—all these terms of public-lands planning take on ominous overtones at Cushman rallies. "DO YOU KNOW WHAT A SOUND SHED IS?" he bellows at the Walnut Grove audience. Then he merely laughs. Sometimes he mumbles a misleading explanation: "There is no such thing as a real boundary in a refuge . . . it never stops." Most often, Cushman's explanatory sentences hang unfinished in the politically ionized air of the gymnasiums and community halls he rents. Conservation activists say they are beginning to recognize the Cushman stamp when inflammatory language shows up in a Farm Bureau or Stockmen's Association publication, on the letterhead of a local group, or on a CBS-TV news clip of anti-spotted-owl pickets in the Pacific Northwest.

"We're no magic bullet," says Cushman modestly. "We sit with a local group. We tell them what they need to be competitive." Cushman is speaking from the old farmhouse he moved to in 1991 on 15 bucolic acres of orchard and cropland near the tiny Washington town of Battleground (he gets a kick out of the name). Just across the Columbia River from the growth-managed metropolis of Portland, Battleground is a good base from which to blitzkrieg the growth-pressured communities of the Columbia River Valley and the Olympic Peninsula. Cushman has been devoting a lot of time in the past year to such skirmishes; he and his Wise Use colleague Ron Arnold, of the Center for the Defense of Free Enterprise, have targeted Washington state as one of the most important anti-green theaters for the 1990s. Battleground is also in Clark County, the scene of the marshland protection ordinance Cushman scuttled so deftly in 1992.

"I'm not saying I don't make mistakes," Cushman replies, when asked about misinformation in the Clark County campaign. "I'm sure I do, but I try really hard to be accurate."

When he isn't out in his hickory shirt and work boots shaking a fist at county planners or national park rangers, Cushman is at home in the office he added on to his farmhouse, running a sophisticated, high-tech fundraising and lobbying operation that would make many an environmental activist feel like a Luddite. He says he monitors both C-Span stations on satellite TV, picks up congressional proceedings 24 hours a day on his computer, stays in touch with his lobbyist in the capital, and mans nine fax machines that can send out 4,000 memos overnight. Those fax machines have helped Cushman become a master of the secondary boycott; his best-known effort pressured the Ford Motor Company to drop television advertising in 1991 for "The New Range Wars," one of the acclaimed National Audubon Society documentaries.

Cushman is touchy about his income, what with widely reported tax-liens and small claims filed against him in California. He says he gets a $35,000 salary from his organizations' 16,000 overlapping memberships; members pay fees of $35 a year. He also mentions the fees—as much as $20,000—for specific organizing efforts. We have to take his word for it, because he doesn't have to reveal his financial picture on a tax form the way a non-profit does. "We don't suck off the government teat," is the way Cushman puts his decision not to seek non-profit status. If his members are worried about where their money goes, he says, "they don't have to support us."

Back in the Sacramento Delta, Cushman mustered plenty of support for his jihad against the Stone Lakes National Wildlife Refuge. His work with a group of locals calling themselves the North Delta Conservancy was classic.

The refuge began as a plan for slightly more than 20,000 acres to be plucked from the development-fever of the Sacramento Valley and saved as a resting place for ruddy ducks, white-fronted geese, and double-crested cormorants along the troubled Pacific Flyway. Until Cushman arrived, there wasn't much opposition to it.

Keeping a spot of green space near the sprawling California capital, whether for the benefit of ducks or people, was generally considered a good idea, even by local Chambers of Commerce and a developer's group called the Building Industry Association. That isn't to say Cushman invented the North Delta Conservancy: this small group of refuge opponents, widely discounted in the local media as being manipulated by real-estate interests, was already presenting substitute plans for a refuge that would be controlled locally—and therefore violated or abolished much more easily than one protected under federal law. But shortly after Cushman arrived with his anti-green alarums, Delta residents received a nine-page packet warning that disease-carrying mosquitoes, bred in the refuge, would fly into neighboring subdivisions and kill children. The woman whose signature appeared at the bottom of the letter denied she'd ever written or signed such a thing, but the denunciations were dwarfed by the hysteria. "REFUGE + MOSQUITOES = DEATH," read one sign carried by a demonstrator who made the Sacramento newspapers and TV news. Business groups dropped their support of the refuge.

Delayed, shrunken, and hampered by prohibitions against re-introducing such endangered species as the tiger salamander, the Stone Lakes National Wildlife Refuge was finally signed into law last July. It faces dwindling prospects for adequate funding from Congress. "To a degree, we were blindsided," says Richard Spotts, California representative of Defenders of Wildlife. "When Cushman came on the scene, the chemistry changed dramatically. I was incredibly heckled and three farmers came close to beating me up. Lots of environmentalists were so intimidated they left hearings without testifying."

Ron Klataske, midwest regional vice president for the National Audubon Society, argues that Cushman's successes demand more serious grassroots organizing by the environmental community. To the extent that conservation organizations focus on the Capitol in Washington, he says, their proposals for preserves, monuments, scenic rivers, national parks, and wilderness areas will remain vulnerable. "Conservation activists in large metropolitan areas often think something should be supported just because it has merit," says Klataske, who grew up on a farm and works out of an office in Manhattan, Kansas. "When local opposition crops up, they never know why."

With their support for such mavericks as Ross Perot in the last election, millions of Americans indicated that they retain a healthy distrust of Uncle Sam. That's true in such eastern states as Maine, where federal ownership accounts for less than one percent of the landbase, as well as Nevada, where the federal government is the biggest landowner. But rural Americans also traditionally mistrust the big out-of-state companies that dominate their lives through timber and mining, ranching and real estate. Cushman and the Wise Use leaders simply nudge small-town folks to forgive big business and blame the federal government instead—for everything from jobs lost to wells gone dry. And Cushman has proven time and again his capacity to knock down conservation proposals at the local level before they can clear the final hurdles in Congress.

Chuck Williams, an Oregonian who outmaneuvered Cushman in clashes during the 1980s over the Columbia River Gorge Act, argues that the Beltway mentality today is girdling the entire green movement. "I'm quite frankly disgusted with the mainstream environmental movement," says Williams, who investigated Cushman and wrote a scathing report for Friends of the Earth in 1982. "Cushman isn't taking away our support, the environmental groups are giving it away." That's a point

Cushman himself loves to make about the environmental movement. "We read their book on organizing," he tells me in a telephone interview. "Now they've become factories, they've lost touch with the folk."

Kathy Kilmer, of The Wilderness Society's "New Voices for the American West" campaign in Denver, says, "Sure, the big national groups have been spending time and energy in Washington over the past twelve years. They had to, really, in order to keep high-level Interior and Forest Service officials—not to mention administration people—from wrecking a generation's worth of environmental progress. And maybe some intimacy between local conservationists and the mainstream organizations was lost along the way. But to claim that there's been some kind of wholesale sellout is ridiculous," she adds. "It's a kind of elitism in reverse. National groups like The Wilderness Society have continued to work closely with lots of local and regional organizations, from the Greater Yellowstone Coalition to the Southern Utah Wilderness Alliance. And we're all doing more and more these days to keep those connections alive and well, as The Wilderness Society is with its 'New Voices' program. Still, you can probably say one thing—we can thank Chuck Cushman and the rest of the anti-green bunch for putting more steam in the effort."

Cushman is fond of calling environmentalists tree-worshipping pagans. But he, too, worships a pagan god: Adam Smith's Invisible Hand, or the almighty force of the so-called free market, which, in Cushman's cosmos, should never be dammed or diverted. Cushman's empire burgeoned during the Reagan-Bush administrations— he got his first national exposure when Interior Secretary James Gaius Watt appointed him to the National Park System Advisory Board—and he is worried about the environmental agenda of the still-forming Clinton-Gore team. I asked him whether he expects a setback. "Scares the hell out of us," he snapped. On the other hand, Cushman believes such conservation groups as The Wilderness Society and the Sierra Club were able to raise a lot of money directly in response to the excesses of the James Watt years, and sees no reason why it shouldn't work both ways. He predicts that the new White House team is "going to scare a lot of people and we'll make lots of money."

"If your article is negative," Cushman adds, "I'll use it in my fundraisers."

—1993

EDWARD ABBEY
1927-1989

Some call Edward Abbey the patron saint of the radical environmental movement. Others call him a pernicious influence and a literary hack. Few of his readers come away neutral from his cranky, incendiary writing. For his own part, Abbey relished his role as author and iconoclast, and—in the last decade of his life—as an environmentalist icon himself. Although the novelist Larry McMurtry called him the Thoreau of the American West, Cactus Ed (as he liked to be known) no doubt would have preferred that Thoreau be called the Edward Abbey of New England, and a kinder, gentler version at that. Abbey's character as a writer was summed up by the renowned naturalist Edwin Way Teale like this: "Abbey writes with a deep undercurrent of bitterness. But as is not infrequently the case, the bitter man may be one who cares enough to be bitter and he often is the one who says things that need to be said."

Abbey and his work are inseparable from the Four Corners region of the American Southwest, but he was born and raised in a small town in Pennsylvania. He came west to attend college. After receiving his master's degree in philosophy from the University of New Mexico, Abbey worked between 1956 and 1971 as a ranger and fire fighter, all the while writing his books, which totaled nearly twenty by the time of his death. Although he was a prolific essayist, his claim to fame rests primarily on Desert Solitaire (1968), a memoir of his days as a park ranger in Arches National Monument, and The Monkey Wrench Gang (1975), a novel perhaps best described as an eco-jeremiad adventure story. The Monkey Wrench Gang bears comparison to the work of the great Irish satirist Jonathan Swift: Abbey's modest proposal is to blow up all the dams and powerlines that collectively take the "wild" out of the American West. The fact that this novel came to serve as inspiration for the founding of the radical environmental group known as Earth First! goes to show that life does indeed imitate art.

The essay "Eco-Defense," from One Life at a Time, Please (1988), is quintessential Abbey. In its tone, the piece is passionate, curmudgeonly, and exaggerated, the work of a man deeply in love and fiercely protective of what he loves but with a sense of humor nonetheless. Abbey's anarchist principles and his characteristic disdain for corporations and politicians are evident in the piece. The assault of the "industrial megamachine" on the American wilderness that is "our true home" is a declaration of war in Abbey's eyes; "Eco-Defense" suggests a means of fighting back that has been tried more than once by those who share Abbey's convictions.

ECO-DEFENSE

If a stranger batters your door down with an axe, threatens your family and yourself with deadly weapons, and proceeds to loot your home of whatever he wants, he is committing what is universally recognized—by law and in common morality—as a crime. In such a situation the householder has both the right and the obligation to defend himself, his family, and his property by whatever means are necessary. This right and this obligation is universally recognized, justified, and praised by all civilized human communities. Self-defense against attack is one of the basic laws not only of human society but of life itself, not only of human life but of all life.

The American wilderness, what little remains, is now undergoing exactly such an assault. With bulldozer, earth mover, chainsaw, and dynamite the international timber, mining, and beef industries are invading our public lands—property of all Americans—bashing their way into our forests, mountains, and rangelands and looting them for everything they can get away with. This for the sake of short-term profits in the corporate sector and multimillion-dollar annual salaries for the three-piece-suited gangsters (MBA—Harvard, Yale, University of Tokyo, et alia) who control and manage these bandit enterprises. Cheered on, naturally, by Time,

Newsweek, and *The Wall Street Journal,* actively encouraged, inevitably, by those jellyfish government agencies that are supposed to *protect* the public lands, and as always aided and abetted in every way possible by the compliant politicians of our Western states, such as Babbitt, DeConcini, Goldwater, McCain, Hatch, Garn, Simms, Hansen, Andrus, Wallop, Domenici and Co. Inc.—who would sell the graves of their mothers if there's a quick buck in the deal, over or under the table, what do they care.

Representative government in the United States has broken down. Our legislators do not represent the public, the voters, or even those who voted for them but rather the commercial industrial interests that finance their political campaigns and control the organs of communication—the TV, the newspapers, the billboards, the radio. Politics is a game for the rich only. Representative government in the USA represents money, not people, and therefore has forfeited our allegiance and moral support. We owe it nothing but the taxation it extorts from us under threats of seizure of property, imprisonment, or in some cases already, when resisted, a violent death by gunfire.

Such is the nature and structure of the industrial megamachine (in Lewis Mumford's term) which is now attacking the American wilderness. That wilderness is our ancestral home, the primordial homeland of all living creatures including the human, and the present final dwelling place of such noble beings as the grizzly bear, the mountain lion, the eagle and the condor, the moose and the elk and the pronghorn antelope, the redwood tree, the yellow pine, the bristlecone pine, and yes, why not say it?—the streams, waterfalls, rivers, the very bedrock itself of our hills, canyons, deserts, mountains. For many of us, perhaps for most of us, the wilderness is more our home than the little stucco boxes, wallboard apartments, plywood trailer-houses, and cinderblock condominiums in which the majority are now confined by the poverty of an overcrowded industrial culture.

And if the wilderness is our true home, and if it is threatened with invasion, pillage, and destruction—as it certainly is—then we have the right to defend that home, as we would our private quarters, by whatever means are necessary. (An Englishman's home is his castle; the American's home is his favorite forest, river, fishing stream, her favorite mountain or desert canyon, his favorite swamp or woods or lake.) We have the right to resist and we have the obligation; not to defend that which we love would be dishonorable. The majority of the American people have demonstrated on every possible occasion that they support the ideal of wilderness preservation; even our politicians are forced by popular opinion to *pretend* to support the idea; as they have learned, a vote against wilderness is a vote against their own reelection. We are justified then in defending our homes—our private home and our public home—not only by common law and common morality but also by common belief. We are the majority; they—the powerful—are in the minority.

How best defend our homes? Well, that is a matter of the strategy, tactics, and technique which eco-defense is all about.

What is eco-defense? Eco-defense means fighting back. Eco-defense means sabotage. Eco-defense is risky but sporting; unauthorized but fun; illegal but ethically imperative. Next time you enter a public forest scheduled for chainsaw massacre by some timber corporation and its flunkies in the US Forest Service, carry a hammer and a few pounds of 60-penny nails in your creel, saddlebag, game bag, backpack, or picnic basket. Spike those trees; you won't hurt them; they'll be grateful for the protection; and you may save the forest. Loggers hate nails. My Aunt Emma back in West Virginia has been enjoying this pleasant exercise for years. She swears by it. It's good for the trees, it's good for the woods, and it's good for the human soul. Spread the word.

—1988

TERRY TEMPEST WILLIAMS

B. 1955

In her 1991 memoir entitled Refuge: An Unnatural History of Family and Place, *Terry Tempest Williams (introduced earlier, in "Our Animal Selves," p. 27) weaves together the narrative threads of two shattering events in her life: her mother's dying of ovarian cancer and the simultaneous flooding of the Bear River Migratory Bird Refuge in the Great Salt Lake during an unusually wet winter. Thus are the landscape of her family and the landscape of her childhood changed beyond recognition as Williams struggles to come to terms with change. In the book's epilogue, reprinted here, she wonders whether her mother and other female relatives claimed by cancer have paid with their lives for their unquestioning obedience to a government that tested nuclear weapons above ground in the Nevada desert from 1951 through 1962.*

The essay points up the fact that when place exists as an abstraction, the potential for abuse is dangerously real. Earlier in the book, Williams writes that "a blank spot on the map translates into empty space, space devoid of people, a wasteland perfect for nerve gas, weteye bombs, and toxic waste," referring to the way the U.S. government regards much of the West. She tells the story of a representative from the Department of Energy who came out to examine such a "blank spot" near Canyonlands National Park in Utah as a possible nuclear-waste repository and stared with amazement at the beautiful wilderness of red cliffs and arches, stating simply, "I had no idea." In "The Clan of One-Breasted Women" she asserts, "When the Atomic Energy Commission described the country north of the Nevada Test Site as 'virtually uninhabited desert terrain,' my family and the birds at Great Salt Lake were some of the 'virtual uninhabitants.'"

THE CLAN OF ONE-BREASTED WOMEN

I belong to a Clan of One-Breasted Women. My mother, my grandmothers, and six aunts have all had mastectomies. Seven are dead. The two who survive have just completed rounds of chemotherapy and radiation.

I've had my own problems: two biopsies for breast cancer and a small tumor between my ribs diagnosed as a "borderline malignancy."

This is my family history.

Most statistics tell us breast cancer is genetic, hereditary, with rising percentages attached to fatty diets, childlessness, or becoming pregnant after thirty. What they don't say is living in Utah may be the greatest hazard of all.

We are a Mormon family with roots in Utah since 1847. The "word of wisdom" in my family aligned us with good foods—no coffee, no tea, tobacco, or alcohol. For the most part, our women were finished having their babies by the time they were thirty. And only one faced breast cancer prior to 1960. Traditionally, as a group of people, Mormons have a low rate of cancer.

Is our family a cultural anomaly? The truth is, we didn't think about it. Those who did, usually the men, simply said, "bad genes." The women's attitude was stoic. Cancer was part of life. On February 16, 1971, the eve of my mother's surgery, I accidently picked up the telephone and overheard her ask my grandmother what she could expect.

"Diane, it is one of the most spiritual experiences you will ever encounter."

I quietly put down the receiver.

Two days later, my father took my brothers and me to the hospital to visit her. She met us in the lobby in a wheelchair. No bandages were visible. I'll never forget her radiance, the way she held herself in a purple velvet robe, and how she gathered us around her.

"Children, I am fine. I want you to know I felt the arms of God around me."

We believed her. My father cried. Our mother, his wife, was thirty-eight years old.

A little over a year after Mother's death, Dad and I were having dinner together. He had just returned from St. George, where the Tempest Company was completing the gas lines that would service southern Utah. He spoke of his love for the country, the sandstoned landscape, bare-boned and beautiful. He had just finished hiking the Kolob trail in Zion National Park. We got caught up in reminiscing, recalling with fondness our walk up Angel's Landing on his fiftieth birthday and the years our family had vacationed there.

Over dessert, I shared a recurring dream of mine. I told my father that for years, as long as I could remember, I saw this flash of light in the night in the desert—that this image had so permeated my being that I could not venture south without seeing it again, on the horizon, illuminating buttes and mesas.

"You did see it," he said.

"Saw what?"

"The bomb. The cloud. We were driving home from Riverside, California. You were sitting on Diane's lap. She was pregnant. In fact, I remember the day, September 7, 1957. We had just gotten out of the Service. We were driving north, past Las Vegas. It was an hour or so before dawn, when this explosion went off. We not only heard it, but felt it. I thought the oil tanker in front of us had blown up. We pulled over and suddenly, rising from the desert floor, we saw it, clearly, this golden-stemmed cloud, the mushroom. The sky seemed to vibrate with an eerie pink glow. Within a few minutes, a light ash was raining on the car."

I stared at my father.

"I thought you knew that," he said. "It was a common occurrence in the fifties."

It was at this moment that I realized the deceit I had been living under. Children growing up in the American Southwest, drinking contaminated milk from contaminated cows, even from the contaminated breasts of their mothers, my mother—members, years later, of the Clan of One-Breasted Women.

It is a well-known story in the Desert West, "The Day We Bombed Utah," or more accurately, the years we bombed Utah: above ground atomic testing in Nevada took place from January 27, 1951, through July 11, 1962. Not only were the winds blowing north covering "low-use segments of the population" with fallout and leaving sheep dead in their tracks, but the climate was right. The United States of the 1950s was red, white, and blue. The Korean War was raging. McCarthyism was rampant. Ike was it, and the cold war was hot. If you were against nuclear testing, you were for a communist regime.

Much has been written about this "American nuclear tragedy." Public health was secondary to national security. The Atomic Energy Commissioner, Thomas Murray, said, "Gentlemen, we must not let anything interfere with this series of tests, nothing."

Again and again, the American public was told by its government, in spite of burns, blisters, and nausea, "It has been found that the tests may be conducted with adequate assurance of safety under conditions prevailing at the bombing reservations." Assuaging public fears was simply a matter of public relations. "Your best action," an Atomic Energy Commission booklet read, "is not to be worried about fallout." A news release typical of the times stated, "We find no basis for concluding that harm to any individual has resulted from radioactive fallout."

On August 30, 1979, during Jimmy Carter's presidency, a suit was filed, *Irene Allen v. The United States of America.* Mrs. Allen's case was the first on an alphabetical list of twenty-four test cases, representative of nearly twelve hundred plaintiffs seeking compensation from the United States government for cancers caused by nuclear testing in Nevada.

Irene Allen lived in Hurricane, Utah. She was the mother of five children and had been widowed twice. Her first husband, with their two oldest boys, had watched the tests from the roof of the local high school. He died of leukemia in 1956. Her second husband died of pancreatic cancer in 1978.

In a town meeting conducted by Utah Senator Orrin Hatch, shortly before the suit was filed, Mrs. Allen said, "I am not blaming the government, I want you to know that, Senator Hatch. But I thought if my testimony could help in any way so this wouldn't happen again to any of the generations coming up after us . . . I am happy to be here this day to bear testimony of this."

God-fearing people. This is just one story in an anthology of thousands.

On May 10, 1984, Judge Bruce S. Jenkins handed down his opinion. Ten of the plaintiffs were awarded damages. It was the first time a federal court had determined that nuclear tests had been the cause of cancers. For the remaining fourteen test cases, the proof of causation was not sufficient. In spite of the split decision, it was considered a landmark ruling. It was not to remain so for long.

In April, 1987, the Tenth Circuit Court of Appeals overturned Judge Jenkins's ruling on the ground that the United States was protected from suit by the legal doctrine of sovereign immunity, a centuries-old idea from England in the days of absolute monarchs.

In January, 1988, the Supreme Court refused to review the Appeals Court decision. To our court system it does not matter whether the United States government was irresponsible, whether it lied to its citizens, or even that citizens died from the fallout of nuclear testing. What matters is that our government is immune: "The King can do no wrong."

In Mormon culture, authority is respected, obedience is revered, and independent thinking is not. I was taught as a young girl not to "make waves" or "rock the boat."

"Just let it go," Mother would say. "You know how you feel, that's what counts."
For many years, I have done just that—listened, observed, and quietly formed my own opinions, in a culture that rarely asks questions because it has all the answers. But one by one, I have watched the women in my family die common, heroic deaths. We sat in waiting rooms hoping for good news, but always receiving the bad. I cared for them, bathed their scarred bodies, and kept their secrets. I watched beautiful women become bald as Cytoxan, cisplatin, and Adriamycin were injected into their veins. I held their foreheads as they vomited green-black bile, and I shot them with morphine when the pain became inhuman. In the end, I witnessed their last peaceful breaths, becoming a midwife to the rebirth of their souls.

The price of obedience has become too high.

The fear and inability to question authority that ultimately killed rural communities in Utah during atmospheric testing of atomic weapons is the same fear I saw in my mother's body. Sheep. Dead sheep. The evidence is buried.

I cannot prove that my mother, Diane Dixon Tempest, or my grandmothers, Lettie Romney Dixon and Kathryn Blackett Tempest, along with my aunts developed cancer from nuclear fallout in Utah. But I can't prove they didn't.

My father's memory was correct. The September blast we drove through in 1957 was part of Operation Plumbbob, one of the most intensive series of bomb tests to be initiated. The flash of light in the night in the desert, which I had always thought was a dream, developed into a family nightmare. It took fourteen years, from 1957 to 1971, for cancer to manifest in my mother—the same time, Howard L. Andrews, an authority in radioactive fallout at the National Institute of Health, says radiation cancer requires to become evident. The more I learn about what it means to be a "downwinder," the more questions I drown in.

What I do know, however, is that as a Mormon woman of the fifth generation of Latter-day Saints, I must question everything, even if it means losing my faith, even if it means becoming a member of a border tribe among my own people. Tolerating blind obedience in the name of patriotism or religion ultimately takes our lives.

When the Atomic Energy Commission described the country north of the Nevada Test Site as "virtually uninhabited desert terrain," my family and the birds at Great Salt Lake were some of the "virtual uninhabitants."

One night, I dreamed women from all over the world circled a blazing fire in the desert. They spoke of change, how they hold the moon in their bellies and wax and wane with its phases. They mocked the presumption of even-tempered beings and made promises that they would never fear the witch inside themselves. The women danced wildly as sparks broke away from the flames and entered the night sky as stars.

And they sang a song given to them by Shoshone grandmothers:

Ah ne nah, nah	Consider the rabbits
nin nah nah—	How gently they walk on the earth—
ah ne nah, nah	Consider the rabbits
nin nah nah—	How gently they walk on the earth—
Nyaga mutzi	We remember them
oh ne nay—	We can walk gently also—
Nyaga mutzi	We remember them
oh ne nay—	We can walk gently also—

The women danced and drummed and sang for weeks, preparing themselves for what was to come. They would reclaim the desert for the sake of their children, for the sake of the land.

A few miles downwind from the fire circle, bombs were being tested. Rabbits felt the tremors. Their soft leather pads on paws and feet recognized the shaking sands, while the roots of mesquite and sage were smoldering. Rocks were hot from the inside out and dust devils hummed unnaturally. And each time there was another nuclear test, ravens watched the desert heave. Stretch marks appeared. The land was losing its muscle.

The women couldn't bear it any longer. They were mothers. They had suffered labor pains but always under the promise of birth. The red hot pains beneath the desert promised death only, as each bomb became a stillborn. A contract had been made and broken between human beings and the land. A new contract was being drawn by the women, who understood the fate of the earth as their own.

Under the cover of darkness, ten women slipped under a barbed-wire fence and entered the contaminated country. They were trespassing. They walked toward the town of Mercury, in moonlight, taking their cues from coyote, kit fox, antelope squirrel, and quail. They moved quietly and deliberately through the maze of Joshua trees. When a hint of daylight appeared they rested, drinking tea and sharing their rations of food. The women closed their eyes. The time had come to protest with the heart, that to deny one's genealogy with the earth was to commit treason against one's soul.

At dawn, the women draped themselves in mylar, wrapping long streamers of silver plastic around their arms to blow in the breeze. They wore clear masks, that became the faces of humanity. And when they arrived at the edge of Mercury, they carried all the butterflies of a summer day in their wombs. They paused to allow their courage to settle.

The town that forbids pregnant women and children to enter because of radiation risks was asleep. The women moved through the streets as winged messengers, twirling around each other in slow motion, peeking inside homes and watching the easy sleep of men and women. They were astonished by such stillness and periodically would utter a shrill note or low cry just to verify life.

The residents finally awoke to these strange apparitions. Some simply stared. Others called authorities, and in time, the women were apprehended by wary soldiers dressed in desert fatigues. They were taken to a white, square building on the other edge of Mercury. When asked who they were and why they were there, the women replied, "We are mothers and we have come to reclaim the desert for our children."

The soldiers arrested them. As the ten women were blindfolded and handcuffed, they began singing:

> You can't forbid us everything
> You can't forbid us to think—
> You can't forbid our tears to flow
> And you can't stop the songs that we sing.

The women continued to sing louder and louder, until they heard the voices of their sisters moving across the mesa:

> Ah ne nah, nah
> nin nah nah—

> *Ah ne nah, nah*
> *nin nah nah—*
> *Nyaga mutzi*
> *oh ne nay—*
> *Nyaga mutzi*
> *oh ne nay—*

"Call for reinforcements," one soldier said.

"We have," interrupted one woman, "we have—and you have no idea of our numbers."

I crossed the line at the Nevada Test Site and was arrested with nine other Utahns for trespassing on military lands. They are still conducting nuclear tests in the desert. Ours was an act of civil disobedience. But as I walked toward the town of Mercury, it was more than a gesture of peace. It was a gesture on behalf of the Clan of One-Breasted Women.

As one officer cinched the handcuffs around my wrists, another frisked my body. She did not find my scars.

We were booked under an afternoon sun and bused to Tonopah, Nevada. It was a two-hour ride. This was familiar country. The Joshua trees standing their ground had been named by my ancestors, who believed they looked like prophets pointing west to the Promised Land. These were the same trees that bloomed each spring, flowers appearing like white flames in the Mojave. And I recalled a full moon in May, when Mother and I had walked among them, flushing out mourning doves and owls.

The bus stopped short of town. We were released.

The officials thought it was a cruel joke to leave us stranded in the desert with no way to get home. What they didn't realize was that we were home, soul-centered and strong, women who recognized the sweet smell of sage as fuel for our spirits.

—1991

Part

III

Our economic ideas and values ultimately have consequences for the planetary ecosystem of which we're a part.

ECONOMY

AND ECOLOGY

Loggers or owls? Cheap electricity or free-flowing rivers? The "smell of a job" or a breath of clean air? In the fractious discourse that characterizes environmental debate in contemporary American culture, there is a remarkable consistency: the issues are inevitably reduced to *economics* versus *ecology*. Although as a culture we perceive economy and ecology as separate and oftentimes conflicting concerns, we need to remind ourselves that both words are derived from the ancient Greek word *oikos*, meaning house. Thus we might speak of economy as the housekeeping of the human family, and of ecology as the housekeeping of the greater family that includes the entire earth and all its living beings, human and otherwise.

In this sense, the human economy is inseparable from the world's ecology. The so-called environmentalist, then, is merely one who is critical of human house-keeping. The ancient Greek philosopher Pythagoras enjoined his students always to make their beds. It was just good manners, he very well could have said. Similarly, we might regard environmental issues as a question of manners. The selections in this part are concerned with the manner in which human beings choose to be in the world. Together they are intended to raise questions about the effects human actions have on other human beings as well as the greater, nonhuman community.

The selections gathered in Chapter 7, "Getting and Spending," are concerned—in various ways—with what might be called the traditional understanding of economy as the management of scarce resources. In the two centuries since the Industrial Revolution and the rise of romanticism, Western literature in general and

American literature in particular have been a source of relentless criticism directed toward the market economy. This comes as little surprise, since literature by its very nature is a moral endeavor, whereas the economy in any free-market system is by definition amoral. Herein may lie the root of the tension between those who champion the "economic" argument and those who go to bat for the "ecological." Each of the pieces in "Getting and Spending" participates in that tension and provides a slightly different perspective on it.

The chapter "Land Use" might very well have been entitled "The Lost Frontier." As the world grows more and more crowded with human beings, we increasingly find ourselves confronted with questions of how best to live in the limited space available. America throughout its history has been fortunate in having vast holdings of land to serve as buffer to its expanding population. But as we approach the end of the millennium, even the United States must now reckon with the problem of dwindling open spaces. This can be an especially vexing issue, since American culture is still haunted by the ghost of the frontier; we seem to believe that if things go bad in our neighborhood or if it becomes too crowded, well, there is always a better place, "open country," just over the next hill to which we can remove at our pleasure. The frontier, however, was declared dead over a hundred years ago. In this case, the tension between economy and ecology is played out in terms of development versus conservation and private property rights versus government control. The selections in "Land Use" arise from these debates and raise questions about the impact our culture has on the land that sustains it.

The third chapter in "Economy and Ecology" and the final one (perhaps ominously) in the book is entitled "Peril and Response." Since the 1960s, environmentalism in American culture has been characterized by jeremiads, dire predictions of doom if we do not mend our ways. Again, one might trace this back to the cultural split between the linguistically related words *economy* and *ecology*. The jeremiad is only issued when there is a perceived decline in morals. The perils of pollution and extinction are the outward and visible signs of a human house that is kept poorly if at all. In recent years there has been some discussion of "acceptable" levels of pollution and, indeed, of "acceptable" losses of species. Some people believe that humans are not to blame for these problems, that nature itself is responsible. President Reagan insisted that trees cause pollution. Others believe that human beings can engineer replacements for any losses nature might incur. President Bush promised that under his administration there would be "no net loss of wetlands." Still others believe that any form of human meddling with nature is unacceptable; these people tend to be skeptical of their government's intentions concerning the natural world. That Americans are divided on this issue is evident in the fierce debate that has attended—and continues to attend—the major pieces of environmental legislation that make their way into Congress. Although some of the selections in "Peril and Response" deny any need for change, most of them urge readers to reflect on the high price American culture is exacting from the environment and to respond with adjustments to our ways of seeing and being.

7

*How do our individual decisions about
how to earn and spend money affect our
own well-being and that of the world?*

GETTING AND SPENDING

WILLIAM WORDSWORTH

1770-1850

*Some say that nature poetry in English, as we now know it, begins with
William Wordsworth. Coupled with his appreciation of nature, Wordsworth
used a diction that is down to earth; he brought the language of poetry
closer to the way in which people ordinarily speak, and his effect on all subsequent poetry—especially American poetry—is unmistakable. One of the
pantheon of romantic writers that included Percy Bysshe Shelley, Lord
Byron, and his good friend Samuel Taylor Coleridge, Wordsworth had a
fire about his character, something visible in his eyes, "half burning, half-
smoldering, with an acrid fixture of regard." In his famous preface to the
second edition of* The Lyrical Ballads *(1802), he pronounced this romantic
creed: "All good poetry is the spontaneous overflow of powerful feelings."*

*Wordsworth was born in England and spent most of his life there. He did
travel to the Continent during his college days to make a walking tour of
the Alps, and then again in 1791—at the height of the French Revolution—
when he went to France, there becoming a proponent of the revolutionary
principles that were sweeping this country as they had America fifteen
years earlier. He had hopes that a similar fervor would take hold in
England. All of these events are rendered in his long autobiographical poem
(which in itself is a poetic innovation) entitled* The Prelude *(1795). Later in
life, Wordsworth grew disillusioned with the revolutionary possibilities of
poetry and politics, and became increasingly conservative, in the end placing his faith in orthodox Christianity.*

*"The World Is Too Much with Us" was written in 1807 and can be read
as a reaction to the rapid and massive change in the English economy
brought about by the introduction of power-driven machinery in the late
eighteenth century. The Industrial Revolution moved people off the farms
and into factory jobs, where they earned wages that could be spent on man-*

ufactured goods, the beginning of consumerism. This poem is a cry from the heart of a man who realizes how easy it is to fritter away our limited stores of creative energy on getting and spending money. To Wordsworth, it would be better to embrace the polytheistic religion of the ancients who experienced a world enlivened by the presence of mythical figures such as Proteus, the "Old Man of the Sea," and Triton, the son of the sea god Neptune, than to remain unmoved by the riches of nature, as his contemporaries seem to be.

THE WORLD IS TOO MUCH WITH US

The world is too much with us; late and soon
Getting and spending, we lay waste our powers;
Little we see in Nature that is ours;
We have given our hearts away, a sordid boon!
This Sea that bares her bosom to the moon,
The winds that will be howling at all hours,
And are up-gathered now like sleeping flowers,
For this, for everything, we are out of tune;
It moves us not.—Great God! I'd rather be
A Pagan suckled in a creed outworn;
So might I, standing on this pleasant lea,
Have glimpses that would make me less forlorn;
Have sight of Proteus rising from the sea;
Or hear old Triton blow his wreathéd horn.

—1807

B. TRAVEN
1882-1969

Who was B. Traven? This is a more difficult question than it might seem, because there is considerable controversy among scholars about the life story of the man (or men) who authored such works as The Cotton Pickers *(1925),* The Treasure of the Sierra Madre *(1927), and* The White Rose *(1929), all of which originally appeared in German. Ernst Schürer and Philip Jenkins, the editors of a 1987 volume entitled* B. Traven: Life and Work, *have argued that Traven deserves recognition as "perhaps the greatest anarchist novelist, the writer who pioneered the modern stereotype of seeking a resolution of Western class conflicts in the struggles of the 'wretched of the earth,'" and that he is worthy of attention for "far more than the lengthy maze that was his life."*

According to the standard (but disputed) biography assembled by Will Wyatt, The Man Who Was B. Traven *(1980), Traven was christened Hermann Albert Otto Maximilian Wienecke at his birth in Pomerania, tak-*

ing his mother's maiden name because he was born out of wedlock. After his parents' subsequent marriage, he was renamed Otto Feige. In 1904 or so, he left his family to make a career for himself as an actor, using the stage name Ret Marut. During World War I, he was a peace activist and published a journal called The Brickburner (Der Ziegelbrenner). *After wandering through Europe and England for several years, he shipped out from London in 1924 to Tampico, Mexico, where he promptly changed his name to B. Traven. During the 1920s and 1930s, he produced an extraordinary series of novels (eleven of them) and short-story collections. In 1926, he became Traven Torsvan; in 1947, Hal Croves. He based himself in Mexico for the rest of his life, living in Mexico City and Acapulco and exploring the jungles of Chiapas.*

The following story appeared in the 1928 collection Der Busch *(translated into English as* The Night Visitor and Other Stories). *"Assembly Line" is the story of an encounter between two utterly clashing economic systems, two opposing worldviews: the industrial "assembly line" mentality of Mr. Winthrop from New York City and the subsistence mentality of the Indian craftsman from Oaxaca, Mexico. Winthrop recognizes the market value of the Indian's baskets if only they could be mass produced and sold as containers to a New York candy maker. What he fails to see is that mass production would entirely upset the social and economic balance of the Mexican village, forcing a radical and violently disruptive shift from the goal of subsistence to the goal of accumulating wealth. The Indian, however, has little use for the thousands of pesos promised by the New York entrepreneur and anticipates the inflation and social collapse that would ensue if he were to accept Winthrop's offer. Rather than cutting the cost of each basket, which would make sense in keeping with the "economies of scale" concept in industrialized economic systems, the Indian raises the price per basket. Winthrop goes wild at the illogic of this negotiation, but the Indian craftsman has successfully defended what Traven presents as a balanced, self-sustaining lifestyle against the dehumanizing incursions of industrial capitalism.*

ASSEMBLY LINE

Mr. E. L. Winthrop of New York was on vacation in the Republic of Mexico. It wasn't long before he realized that this strange and really wild country had not yet been fully and satisfactorily explored by Rotarians and Lions, who are forever conscious of their glorious mission on earth. Therefore, he considered it his duty as a good American citizen to do his part in correcting this oversight.

In search for opportunities to indulge in his new avocation, he left the beaten track and ventured into regions not especially mentioned, and hence not recommended, by travel agents to foreign tourists. So it happened that one day he found himself in a little, quaint Indian village somewhere in the State of Oaxaca.

Walking along the dusty main street of this pueblecito, which knew nothing of pavements, drainage, plumbing, or of any means of artificial light save candles or pine splinters, he met with an Indian squatting on the earthen-floor front porch of a palm hut, a so-called jacalito.

The Indian was busy making little baskets from bast and from all kinds of fibers gathered by him in the immense tropical bush which surrounded the village on all sides. The material used had not only been well prepared for its purpose but was also richly colored with dyes that the basket-maker himself extracted from various native plants, barks, roots and from certain insects by a process known only to him and the members of his family.

His principal business, however, was not producing baskets. He was a peasant who lived on what the small property he possessed—less than fifteen acres of not too fertile soil—would yield, after much sweat and labor and after constantly worrying over the most wanted and best suited distribution of rain, sunshine, and wind and the changing balance of birds and insects beneficial or harmful to his crops. Baskets he made when there was nothing else for him to do in the fields, because he was unable to dawdle. After all, the sale of his baskets, though to a rather limited degree only, added to the small income he received from his little farm.

In spite of being by profession just a plain peasant, it was clearly seen from the small baskets he made that at heart he was an artist, a true and accomplished artist. Each basket looked as if covered all over with the most beautiful sometimes fantastic ornaments, flowers, butterflies, birds, squirrels, antelope, tigers, and a score of other animals of the wilds. Yet, the most amazing thing was that these decorations, all of them symphonies of color, were not painted on the baskets but were instead actually part of the baskets themselves. Bast and fibers dyed in dozens of different colors were so cleverly—one must actually say intrinsically—interwoven that those attractive designs appeared on the inner part of the basket as well as on the outside. Not by painting but by weaving were those highly artistic effects achieved. This performance he accomplished without ever looking at any sketch or pattern. While working on a basket these designs came to light as if by magic, and as long as a basket was not entirely finished one could not perceive what in this case or that the decoration would be like.

People in the market town who bought these baskets would use them for sewing baskets or to decorate tables with or window sills, or to hold little things to keep them from lying around. Women put their jewelry in them or flowers or little dolls. There were in fact a hundred and two ways they might serve certain purposes in a household or in a lady's own room.

Whenever the Indian had finished about twenty of the baskets he took them to town on market day. Sometimes he would already be on his way shortly after midnight because he owned only a burro to ride on, and if the burro had gone astray the day before, as happened frequently, he would have to walk the whole way to town and back again.

At the market he had to pay twenty centavos in taxes to sell his wares. Each basket cost him between twenty and thirty hours of constant work, not counting the time spent gathering bast and fibers, preparing them, making dyes and coloring the bast. All this meant extra time and work. The price he asked for each basket was fifty centavos, the equivalent of about four cents. It seldom happened, however, that a buyer paid outright the full fifty centavos asked—or four reales as the Indian called that money. The prospective buyer started bargaining, telling the Indian that he ought to be ashamed to ask such a sinful price. "Why, the whole dirty thing is nothing but ordinary petate straw which you find in heaps wherever you may look for it; the jungle is packed full of it," the buyer would argue. "Such a little basket, what's it good for anyhow? If I paid you, you thief, ten centavitos for it you should be grateful and kiss my hand. Well, it's your lucky day, I'll be generous this time, I'll pay you twenty, yet not one green centavo more. Take it or run along."

So he sold finally for twenty-five centavos, but then the buyer would say, "Now, what do you think of that? I've got only twenty centavos change on me. What can we do about that? If you can change me a twenty-peso bill, all right, you shall have your twenty-five fierros." Of course, the Indian could not change a twenty-peso bill and so the basket went for twenty centavos.

He had little if any knowledge of the outside world or he would have known that what happened to him was happening every hour of every day to every artist all over the world. That knowledge would perhaps have made him very proud; because he would have realized that he belonged to the little army which is the salt of the earth and which keeps culture, urbanity and beauty for their own sake from passing away.

Often it was not possible for him to sell all the baskets he had brought to market, for people here as elsewhere in the world preferred things made by the millions and each so much like the other that you were unable, even with the help of a magnifying glass, to tell which was which and where was the difference between two of the same kind.

Yet he, this craftsman, had in his life made several hundreds of those exquisite baskets, but so far no two of them had he ever turned out alike in design. Each was an individual piece of art and as different from the other as was a Murillo from a Velásquez.

Naturally he did not want to take those baskets which he could not sell at the market place home with him again if he could help it. In such a case he went peddling his products from door to door where he was treated partly as a beggar and partly as a vagrant apparently looking for an opportunity to steal, and he frequently had to swallow all sorts of insults and nasty remarks.

Then, after a long run, perhaps a woman would finally stop him, take one of the baskets and offer him ten centavos, which price through talks and talks would perhaps go up to fifteen or even to twenty. Nevertheless, in many instances he would actually get no more than just ten centavos, and the buyer, usually a woman, would grasp that little marvel and right before his eyes throw it carelessly upon the nearest table as if to say, "Well, I take that piece of nonsense only for charity's sake. I know my money is wasted. But then, after all, I'm a Christian and I can't see a poor Indian die of hunger since he has come such a long way from his village." This would remind her of something better and she would hold him and say, "Where are you at home anyway, Indito? What's your pueblo? So, from Huehuetonoc? Now, listen here, Indito, can't you bring me next Saturday two or three turkeys from Huehuetonoc? But they must be heavy and fat and very, very cheap or I won't even touch them. If I wish to pay the regular price I don't need you to bring them. Understand? Hop along, now, Indito."

The Indian squatted on the earthen floor in the portico of his hut, attended to his work and showed no special interest in the curiosity of Mr. Winthrop watching him. He acted almost as if he ignored the presence of the American altogether.

"How much that little basket, friend?" Mr. Winthrop asked when he felt that he at least had to say something as not to appear idiotic.

"Fifty centavitos, patroncito, my good little lordy, four reales," the Indian answered politely.

"All right, sold," Mr. Winthrop blurted out in a tone and with a wide gesture as if he had bought a whole railroad. And examining his buy he added, "I know already who I'll give that pretty little thing to. She'll kiss me for it, sure. Wonder what she'll use it for?"

He had expected to hear a price of three or even four pesos. The moment he realized that he had judged the value six times too high, he saw right away what great business possibilities this miserable Indian village might offer to a dynamic promoter like himself. Without further delay he started exploring those possibilities. "Suppose, my good friend, I buy ten of these little baskets of yours which, as I might as well admit right here and now, have practically no real use whatsoever. Well, as I was saying, if I buy ten, how much would you then charge me apiece?"

The Indian hesitated for a few seconds as if making calculations. Finally he said, "If you buy ten I can let you have them for forty-five centavos each, señorito gentleman."

"All right, amigo. And now, let's suppose I buy from you straight away one hundred of these absolutely useless baskets, how much will cost me each?"

The Indian, never fully looking up to the American standing before him and hardly taking his eyes off his work, said politely and without the slightest trace of enthusiasm in his voice, "In such a case I might not be quite unwilling to sell each for forty centavitos."

Mr. Winthrop bought sixteen baskets, which was all the Indian had in stock.

After three weeks' stay in the Republic, Mr. Winthrop was convinced that he knew this country perfectly, that he had seen everything and knew all about the inhabitants, their character and their way of life, and that there was nothing left for him to explore. So he returned to good old Nooyorg and felt happy to be once more in a civilized country, as he expressed it to himself.

One day going out for lunch he passed a confectioner's and, looking at the display in the window, he suddenly remembered the little baskets he had bought in that faraway Indian village.

He hurried home and took all the baskets he still had left to one of the best-known candy-makers in the city.

"I can offer you here," Mr. Winthrop said to the confectioner, "one of the most artistic and at the same time the most original of boxes, if you wish to call them that. These little baskets would be just right for the most expensive chocolates meant for elegant and high-priced gifts. Just have a good look at them, sir, and let me listen."

The confectioner examined the baskets and found them extraordinarily well suited for a certain line in his business. Never before had there been anything like them for originality, prettiness and good taste. He, however, avoided most carefully showing any sign of enthusiasm, for which there would be time enough once he knew the price and whether he could get a whole load exclusively.

He shrugged his shoulders and said, "Well, I don't know. If you asked me I'd say it isn't quite what I'm after. However, we might give it a try. It depends, of course, on the price. In our business the package mustn't cost more than what's in it."

"Do I hear an offer?" Mr. Winthrop asked.

"Why don't you tell me in round figures how much you want for them? I'm not good in guessing."

"Well, I'll tell you, Mr. Kemple: since I'm the smart guy who discovered these baskets and since I'm the only Jack who knows where to lay his hands on more, I'm selling to the highest bidder, on an exclusive basis, of course. I'm positive you can see it my way, Mr. Kemple."

"Quite so, and may the best man win," the confectioner said. "I'll talk the matter over with my partners. See me tomorrow same time, please, and I'll let you know how far we might be willing to go."

Next day when both gentlemen met again Mr. Kemple said: "Now, to be frank with you, I know art on seeing it, no getting around that. And these baskets are little works of art, they surely are. However, we are no art dealers, you realize that of course. We've no other use for these pretty little things except as fancy packing for our French pralines made by us. We can't pay for them what we might pay considering them pieces of art. After all to us they're only wrappings. Fine wrappings, perhaps, but nevertheless wrappings. You'll see it our way I hope, Mr.—— oh yes, Mr. Winthrop. So, here is our offer, take it or leave it: a dollar and a quarter apiece and not one cent more."

Mr. Winthrop made a gesture as if he had been struck over the head.

The confectioner, misunderstanding this involuntary gesture of Mr. Winthrop, added quickly, "All right, all right, no reason to get excited, no reason at all. Perhaps we can do a trifle better. Let's say one-fifty."

"Make it one-seventy-five," Mr. Winthrop snapped, swallowing his breath while wiping his forehead.

"Sold. One-seventy-five apiece free at port of New York. We pay the customs and you pay the shipping. Right?"

"Sold," Mr. Winthrop said also and the deal was closed.

"There is, of course, one condition," the confectioner explained just when Mr. Winthrop was to leave. "One or two hundred won't do for us. It wouldn't pay the trouble and the advertising. I won't consider less than ten thousand, or one thousand dozens if that sounds better in your ears. And they must come in no less than twelve different patterns well assorted. How about that?"

"I can make it sixty different patterns or designs."

"So much the better. And you're sure you can deliver ten thousand let's say early October?"

"Absolutely," Mr. Winthrop avowed and signed the contract.

Practically all the way back to Mexico, Mr. Winthrop had a notebook in his left hand and a pencil in his right and he was writing figures, long rows of them, to find out exactly how much richer he would be when this business had been put through.

"Now, let's sum up the whole goddamn thing," he muttered to himself. "Damn it, where is that cursed pencil again? I had it right between my fingers. Ah, there it is. Ten thousand he ordered. Well, well, there we got a clean-cut profit of fifteen thousand four hundred and forty genuine dollars. Sweet smackers. Fifteen grand right into papa's pocket. Come to think of it, that Republic isn't so backward after all."

"Buenas tardes, mi amigo, how are you?" he greeted the Indian whom he found squatting in the porch of his jacalito as if he had never moved from his place since Mr. Winthrop had left for New York.

The Indian rose, took off his hat, bowed politely and said in his soft voice, "Be welcome, patroncito. Thank you, I feel fine, thank you. Muy buenas tardes. This house and all I have is at your kind disposal." He bowed once more, moved his right hand in a gesture of greeting and sat down again. But he excused himself for doing so by saying, "Perdoneme, patroncito, I have to take advantage of the daylight, soon it will be night."

"I've got big business for you, my friend," Mr. Winthrop began.

"Good to hear that, señor."

Mr. Winthrop said to himself, "Now, he'll jump up and go wild when he learns what I've got for him." And aloud he said: "Do you think you can make me one thousand of these little baskets?"

"Why not, patroncito? If I can make sixteen, I can make one thousand also."

"That's right, my good man. Can you also make five thousand?"

"Of course, señor. I can make five thousand if I can make one thousand."

"Good. Now, if I should ask you to make me ten thousand, what would you say? And what would be the price of each? You can make ten thousand, can't you?"

"Of course, I can, señor. I can make as many as you wish. You see, I am an expert in this sort of work. No one else in the whole state can make them the way I do."

"That's what I thought and that's exactly why I came to you."

"Thank you for the honor, patroncito."

"Suppose I order you to make me ten thousand of these baskets, how much time do you think you would need to deliver them?"

The Indian, without interrupting his work, cocked his head to one side and then to the other as if he were counting the days or weeks it would cost him to make all these baskets.

After a few minutes he said in a slow voice, "It will take a good long time to make so many baskets, patroncito. You see, the bast and the fibers must be very dry before they can be used properly. Then all during the time they are slowly drying, they must be worked and handled in a very special way so that while drying they won't lose their softness and their flexibility and their natural brilliance. Even when dry they must look fresh. They must never lose their natural properties or they will look just as lifeless and dull as straw. Then while they are drying up I got to get the plants and roots and barks and insects from which I brew the dyes. That takes much time also, believe me. The plants must be gathered when the moon is just right or they won't give the right color. The insects I pick from the plants must also be gathered at the right time and under the right conditions or else they produce no rich colors and are just like dust. But, of course, jefecito, I can make as many of these canastitas as you wish, even as many as three dozens if you want them. Only give me time."

"Three dozens? Three dozens?" Mr. Winthrop yelled, and threw up both arms in desperation. "Three dozens!" he repeated as if he had to say it many times in his own voice so as to understand the real meaning of it, because for a while he thought that he was dreaming. He had expected the Indian to go crazy on hearing that he was to sell ten thousand of his baskets without having to peddle them from door to door and be treated like a dog with a skin disease.

So the American took up the question of price again, by which he hoped to activate the Indian's ambition. "You told me that if I take one hundred baskets you will let me have them for forty centavos apiece. Is that right, my friend?"

"Quite right, jefecito."

"Now," Mr. Winthrop took a deep breath, "now, then, if I ask you to make me one thousand, that is, ten times one hundred baskets, how much will they cost me, each basket?"

That figure was too high for the Indian to grasp. He became slightly confused and for the first time since Mr. Winthrop had arrived he interrupted his work and tried to think it out. Several times he shook his head and looked vaguely around as if for help. Finally he said, "Excuse me, jefecito, little chief, that is by far too much for me to count. Tomorrow, if you will do me the honor, come and see me again and I think I shall have my answer ready for you, patroncito."

When on the next morning Mr. Winthrop came to the hut he found the Indian as usual squatting on the floor under the overhanging palm roof working at his baskets.

"Have you got the price for ten thousand?" he asked the Indian the very moment he saw him, without taking the trouble to say "Good morning!"

"Si, patroncito, I have the price ready. You may believe me when I say it has cost me much labor and worry to find out the exact price, because, you see, I do not wish to cheat you out of your honest money."

"Skip that, amigo. Come out with the salad. What's the price?" Mr. Winthrop asked nervously.

"The price is well calculated now without any mistake on my side. If I got to make one thousand canastitas each will be three pesos. If I must make five thousand, each will cost nine pesos. And if I have to make ten thousand, in such a case I can't make them for less than fifteen pesos each." Immediately he returned to his work as if he were afraid of losing too much time with such idle talk.

Mr. Winthrop thought that perhaps it was his faulty knowledge of this foreign language that had played a trick on him.

"Did I hear you say fifteen pesos each if I eventually would buy ten thousand?"

"That's exactly and without any mistake what I've said, patroncito," the Indian answered in his soft courteous voice.

"But now, see here, my good man, you can't do this to me. I'm your friend and I want to help you get on your feet."

"Yes, patroncito, I know this and I don't doubt any of your words."

"Now, let's be patient and talk this over quietly as man to man. Didn't you tell me that if I would buy one hundred you would sell each for forty centavos?"

"Si, jefecito, that's what I said. If you buy one hundred you can have them for forty centavos apiece, provided that I have one hundred, which I don't."

"Yes, yes, I see that." Mr. Winthrop felt as if he would go insane any minute now. "Yes, so you said. Only what I can't comprehend is why you cannot sell at the same price if you make me ten thousand. I certainly don't wish to chisel on the price. I am not that kind. Only, well, let's see now, if you can sell for forty centavos at all, be it for twenty or fifty or a hundred, I can't quite get the idea why the price has to jump that high if I buy more than a hundred."

"Bueno, patroncito, what is there so difficult to understand? It's all very simple. One thousand canastitas cost me a hundred times more work than a dozen. Ten thousand cost me so much time and labor that I could never finish them, not even in a hundred years. For a thousand canastitas I need more bast than for a hundred, and I need more little red beetles and more plants and roots and bark for the dyes. It isn't that you just can walk into the bush and pick all the things you need at your heart's desire. One root with the true violet blue may cost me four or five days until I can find one in the jungle. And have you thought how much time it costs and how much hard work to prepare the bast and fibers? What is more, if I must make so many baskets, who then will look after my corn and my beans and my goats and chase for me occasionally a rabbit for meat on Sunday?

If I have no corn, then I have no tortillas to eat, and if I grow no beans, where do I get my frijoles from?"

"But since you'll get so much money from me for your baskets you can buy all the corn and beans in the world and more than you need."

"That's what you think, señorito, little lordy. But you see, it is only the corn I grow myself that I am sure of. Of the corn which others may or may not grow, I cannot be sure to feast upon."

"Haven't you got some relatives here in this village who might help you to make baskets for me?" Mr. Winthrop asked hopefully.

"Practically the whole village is related to me somehow or other. Fact is, I got lots of close relatives in this here place."

"Why then can't they cultivate your fields and look after your goats while you make baskets for me? Not only this, they might gather for you the fibers and the colors in the bush and lend you a hand here and there in preparing the material you need for the baskets."

"They might, patroncito, yes, they might. Possible. But then you see who would take care of their fields and cattle if they work for me? And if they help me with the baskets it turns out the same. No one would any longer work his fields properly. In such a case corn and beans would get up so high in price that none of us could buy any and we all would starve to death. Besides, as the price of everything would rise and rise higher still how could I make baskets at forty centavos apiece? A pinch of salt or one green chili would set me back more than I'd collect for one single basket. Now you'll understand, highly estimated caballero and jefecito, why I can't make the baskets any cheaper than fifteen pesos each if I got to make that many."

Mr. Winthrop was hard-boiled, no wonder considering the city he came from. He refused to give up the more than fifteen thousand dollars which at that moment seemed to slip through his fingers like nothing. Being really desperate now, he talked and bargained with the Indian for almost two full hours, trying to make him understand how rich he, the Indian, would become if he would take this greatest opportunity of his life.

The Indian never ceased working on his baskets while he explained his points of view.

"You know, my good man," Mr. Winthrop said, "such a wonderful chance might never again knock on your door, do you realize that? Let me explain to you in ice-cold figures what fortune you might miss if you leave me flat on this deal."

He tore out leaf after leaf from his notebook, covered each with figures and still more figures, and while doing so told the peasant he would be the richest man in the whole district.

The Indian without answering watched with a genuine expression of awe as Mr. Winthrop wrote down these long figures, executing complicated multiplications and divisions and subtractions so rapidly that it seemed to him the greatest miracle he had ever seen.

The American, noting this growing interest in the Indian, misjudged the real significance of it. "There you are, my friend," he said. "That's exactly how rich you're going to be. You'll have a bankroll of exactly four thousand pesos. And to show you that I'm a real friend of yours, I'll throw in a bonus. I'll make it a round five thousand pesos, and all in silver."

The Indian, however, had not for one moment thought of four thousand pesos.

Such an amount of money had no meaning to him. He had been interested solely in Mr. Winthrop's ability to write figures so rapidly.

"So, what do you say now? Is it a deal or is it? Say yes and you'll get your advance this very minute."

"As I have explained before, patroncito, the price is fifteen pesos each."

"But, my good man," Mr. Winthrop shouted at the poor Indian in utter despair, "where have you been all this time? On the moon or where? You are still at the same price as before."

"Yes, I know that, jefecito, my little chief," the Indian answered, entirely unconcerned. "It must be the same price because I cannot make any other one. Besides, señor, there's still another thing which perhaps you don't know. You see, my good lordy and caballero, I've to make these canastitas my own way and with my song in them and with bits of my soul woven into them. If I were to make them in great numbers there would no longer be my soul in each, or my songs. Each would look like the other with no difference whatever and such a thing would slowly eat up my heart. Each has to be another song which I hear in the morning when the sun rises and when the birds begin to chirp and the butterflies come and sit down on my baskets so that I may see a new beauty, because, you see, the butterflies like my baskets and the pretty colors on them, that's why they come and sit down, and I can make my canastitas after them. And now, señor jefecito, if you will kindly excuse me, I have wasted much time already, although it was a pleasure and a great honor to hear the talk of such a distinguished caballero like you. But I'm afraid I've to attend to my work now, for day after tomorrow is market day in town and I got to take my baskets there. Thank you, señor, for your visit. Adiós."

And in this way it happened that American garbage cans escaped the fate of being turned into receptacles for empty, torn, and crumpled little multicolored canastitas into which an Indian of Mexico had woven dreams of his soul, throbs of his heart: his unsung poems.

—1928

JIMMY SANTIAGO BACA

B. 1952

Jimmy Santiago Baca survived an extraordinarily difficult childhood to become an important contemporary American poet. His Chicana mother and Apache father divorced when he was two, and Baca was transferred back and forth among various relatives and orphanages. Between ages five and eleven, Baca lived at St. Anthony's Home for Boys in Albuquerque, New Mexico. He spent his teenage years in detention centers and surviving on the streets of Albuquerque's barrios. At the age of twenty, Baca received a five-year federal sentence for possession of a controlled substance with intent to distribute (a charge he disputes); he ended up serving six years at a maximum security state prison in Florence, Arizona. He earned a high school diploma in prison and, at the same time, taught himself to read literature and to write poetry. "When at last I wrote my first words on the page," he explains in an essay called "Lock and Key," "I felt an island rising beneath my feet like the back of a whale. As more and more words emerged, I could finally rest: I had a place to stand for the first time in my life. The island grew, with each page, into a continent inhabited by people I knew and mapped with the life I lived."

Baca published his first volume of poems, a chapbook called Jimmy Santiago Baca *(1978),* in his mid-twenties. Since then he has produced another chapbook, Swords of Darkness *(1981),* and six larger poetry collections: Immigrants in Our Own Land *(1979),* What's Happening *(1982),* Poems Taken from My Yard *(1986),* Martín and Meditations on the South Valley *(1987),* Black Mesa Poems *(1989), and* In the Way of the Sun *(1998).* His play "Los tres hijos de Julia" *was produced at the Los Angeles Theatre Center in 1991, and in 1992 a volume of his essays,* Working in the Dark: Reflections of a Poet in the Barrio, *appeared.* Martín *received an American Book Award from the Before Columbus Foundation. Baca was a poet-in-residence at the University of California, Berkeley, in 1989, and the following year at Yale University. Today, he lives with his wife and young children on a small farm atop Black Mesa, near Albuquerque.*

Baca recognizes that people often submit themselves to jobs in order to survive, and in the process sacrifice their dreams of a meaningful life. The following poem, from Black Mesa Poems, *depicts a Native American protagonist preparing to go to his construction job, while imagining, both mentally and in his very bones, his ancestral existence as a hunter following a herd of bison. Throwing his hammer to the ground and uttering something that we moderns cannot comprehend, the character Meiyo seems to represent an archaic, inaccessible state of mind. But in actuality, his frustration mirrors the common urge of contemporary city dwellers to break free from the daily nine-to-five grind and find a means of living more attuned to their true nature.*

WORK WE HATE AND DREAMS WE LOVE

Every morning
Meiyo revs his truck up
and lets it idle. Inside the small adobe house,
he sips coffee
while his Isleta girlfriend
Cristi
brownbags his lunch.
Life is filled with work
Meiyo hates,
and while he saws, 2 × 4's,
trims lengths of 2 × 10's on table saw,
inside his veins another world
in full color etches
a blue sky on his bones,
a man following a bison herd,
and suddenly his hammer becomes a spear
he tosses to the ground
uttering a sound we do not understand.

—1989

THEODORE ROSZAK

B. 1933

Coiner of the word counterculture, *Theodore Roszak has long been regarded as an authority on the disaffected generation of 1960s youth to which he first applied the term. He is also one of the fiercest and most eloquent critics of our "information society." In books such as* The Making of a Counterculture *(1969),* Where the Wasteland Ends *(1972),* Person/Planet: The Creative Disintegration of Industrial Society *(1978),* The Cult of Information *(1986), and* The Voice of the Earth *(1992), Roszak, who draws his insights from psychology as well as history, has raised his alarm with perseverance and clarity: our culture's addiction to information and our idolatry of science will lead in the end to catastrophe. Our culture, he argues, has squandered its soul, and the various waves of alienation and discontent that have manifested among youth since the end of World War II are merely the outward signs of a humanity hungering for meaning. "What, after all," Roszak asks, "is the ecological crisis that now captures so much belated attention but the inevitable extroversion of a blighted psyche?"*

Born in Chicago, Roszak graduated from UCLA and earned his Ph.D. in history at Princeton. He lives in Berkeley, California, and has for years taught history and general studies at California State University, Hayward. Twice nominated for the National Book Award for The Making of a Counterculture *and* Where the Wasteland Ends, *Roszak has extended his cautionary efforts to the novel form with* The Memoirs of Elizabeth Frankenstein *(1995).*

"'Take This Job and Shove It'" is from Chapter 8 (entitled "Work: The Right to Right Livelihood") of Person/Planet. *Roszak's basic premise in this book is that "the environmental anguish of the Earth has entered our lives as a radical transformation of human identity. The needs of the planet and the needs of the person have become one, and together they have begun to act upon the central institutions of our society with a force that is profoundly subversive, but which carries within it the promise of cultural renewal." Work is one of the central institutions that any serious analysis of ecological imbalance must call into question. Youth in the 1970s, when Roszak was writing this commentary, may have been more willing than today's youth to "take up the quest . . . for a new definition of success in which the emphasis is on self-fulfillment and quality of life, as well as on money and security." But the fact remains that finding one's true vocation, one's "right livelihood," is a worthwhile quest that ultimately benefits both person and planet.*

"TAKE THIS JOB AND SHOVE IT"

Each day I move through a world at work, an ocean of human activity as pervasively and as unobtrusively there as the ocean of air that surrounds me. I breathe in the labor of people around me; I live by it, yet I take it for granted like some free resource. People work, I work. That is what we are here to do; it is how we pass the time.

But our work is more than a pastime. It is our life. It takes up years of the portion we have been allotted on this Earth to work out our salvation. And not many of us work at a true vocation . . . sometimes I think very nearly none. Some, like my father, grind their substance away at hard and dirty work for too little pay and appreciation. Most are toiling at jobs whose worst burden is deadly and impersonal routine: typing, filing, checking groceries, selling across a counter, filling out forms, processing papers.

I have done such jobs myself. I still do them. A deal of what I do as a teacher in a colossal state college system is stale paper work and routine committee assignments that have nothing to do with education or scholarship, little enough to do with simple intelligence. Did any of us really have to read Studs Terkel's report *Working* to know what the daily deadly toll of alienated labor is? "I feel like a machine," "I feel like a robot," Terkel's interviewees complain. As I sit down to the task of revising this chapter, the record at the top of the American charts is Johnny Paycheck singing "Take This Job and Shove It." When we do not hear that lamentation from the people around us, it is only because we are not listening to what they say behind the heroic good humor that is the shield of their self-respect. Only look, and you can see their stifled personhood written in their faces; you can see it in the distraction that carries their thoughts to imaginary pleasures and leads to slip-ups and mistakes each day on the job; it is there in their surliness and bad temper. I have seen it in myself whenever I have felt the vital hours of my life being turned to dust by work that did not use the best I have to offer, whenever I have had to carry out the orders of employers who had no interest in the bright and extraordinary powers I could feel within me yearning to be hard-worked for all they were worth.

All of us have a gift, a calling of our own whose exercise is high delight, even if we must sweat and suffer to meet its demands. That calling reaches out to find a real and useful place in the world, a task that is not waste or pretense. If only that life-giving impulse might be liberated and made the whole energy of our daily work, if only we were given the chance to be *in* our work with the full force of our personality, mind and body, heart and soul . . . what a power would be released into the world! A force more richly transformative than all the might of industrial technology.

But *they*—the company, the system—rarely have any use for that calling. Our bosses do not even look for it in themselves. It makes no difference to the profit and loss, it does not show up (so the experts believe) in the economic indicators. So they sweep it out of sight and continue to work us as personnel, not persons. That is very nearly the prerequisite for being a successful boss in this warped economy: to blind oneself to the personhood of one's workers, to insist that business is business. That is treatment fewer workers will now accept; and the trend is by no means limited - to middle-class, college-educated workers. In a recent statistical study, Daniel Yankelovich concludes that, in growing numbers through the seventies, "noncollege youth . . . take up the quest of their college peers for a new definition of success in which the emphasis is on self-fulfillment and quality of life, as well as on money and security." Thus, the Department of Labor reports that, even in a tight job market, twice as many people quit their jobs in disgust as did a decade ago; the number has gone from 200,000 per year to 400,000 and continues to rise.

Yet somehow we carry on. I am always astonished at how resourcefully most people find ways to stick at their jobs without becoming bitter or corrupt. Not everybody, of course. I meet enough people who abstractly and impersonally hate everyone they must deal with in the course of the working day, and even openly sabotage the job. And I meet those who are always posing like mannequins on display, getting by on a few knee-jerk courtesies the company has made them memorize . . . the telephone operators with their by-the-numbers cheerfulness . . . the airline stewardesses with their plastic smiles and public relations sex appeal. The kids who work for the fast-food chains are the saddest cases. Company policy is for them to make like living TV commercials, clean-cut and grinning for all they're worth, happy-happy-happy to be selling the world a billion bad hamburgers a day. Is somebody watching them all the time, checking their act . . . some Big Brother manager? They are so young, and here they are already faking their lives away to hold a nickel-and-dime job. Probably this is their first paid work, and what is it they are learning? How to be a conscientious stooge for the company.

But there are so many others I meet who miraculously manage to stay human on the job. They invent little strategies of self-encouragement and compensation to get them through the day. They decorate their work space with trinkets and placards of their own choosing. They smuggle a transistor radio into the shop to play "their" kind of music, though most of what they hear is idiotic commercials and payola disk jockeys. They divide the day's work into so many little contests and competitions that will pace them along. They secretly challenge themselves to absurdly high standards of neatness and precision to put some sport in the work. They organize games with workmates, they gossip, they flirt, they kid around, they kibbitz with the customers, they exchange jokes and novelties. Perhaps most of all, they gripe. Mutual griping always helps. It relieves the conscience to let someone know that *you* know this is a bitch of a job. That is a way to remind yourself and the world that you are bigger and smarter and better than this dumb job. And if you had *your* way . . .

When I worked as a teller for the Bank of America, I kept my head busy all day long repeating Greek declensions and memorizing poems. It kept my brain alive—and also made me a miserably bad teller. But even my mistakes were a secret gratification—a tiny way of obstructing B of A's smooth flow of high financial banditry. I imagine strategies like these have sustained people through all the most suffocating kinds of toil since the factory bells pealed in the first dawn of industrialism. They are symptoms of our vocational instinct fighting to survive: little sparks and hashes of our thwarted personhood. The pathos of the matter is that no private strategy of this kind will ever turn an empty or fraudulent job into a vocation—nor, for that matter, will any social reform. And far too many of us are entrammeled by just such work, struggling to avoid the embarrassment of acknowledging our entrapment. A phony job is a phony job; a wicked job is a wicked job. These are not matters of morale or social organization; not even revolutionary workers' control can change them. They are objective moral facts attached to certain forms of employment that have become the only jobs many industrial societies seem able to offer millions of workers.

Work that produces unnecessary consumer junk or weapons of war is wrong and wasteful. Work that is built upon false needs or unbecoming appetites is wrong and wasteful. Work that deceives or manipulates, that exploits or degrades is wrong and wasteful. Work that wounds the environment or makes the world ugly is wrong and wasteful. There is no way to redeem such work by enriching it or restructuring it, by socializing it or nationalizing it, by making it "small" or decentralized or democratic. It is a sow's ear that will yield no silk purses.

Here we have an absolute criterion that must enter any discussion of work. *Is the job honest and useful? Is it a real contribution to human need?* These are questions that can only be answered by a worker's own strong sense of responsibility. That is why the struggle for right livelihood is as important as the struggle for industrial democracy. For it does not matter how democratically controlled our work life is: If a job is inherently worthless, it cannot be a vocation. So, if we encourage people to search for responsible work—for work they can love as an image of their personal destiny—then we must not expect them to continue doing what is stupid or ugly. We must not expect them to go on working for the military-industrial complex or for Madison Avenue, to continue producing "people's bombs" or printing party propaganda. One cannot build a vocation on a lie.

The hard truth is that the world we live in, the high industrial world we presume to hold up as the standard of "development," is immensely committed to proliferating work that is wrong and wasteful. It does this in the name of growth, or the national security, or the standard of living; but at the bottom it all comes down to creating jobs that are unworthy of our best energies:

Huckstering jobs—inventing, advertising, selling expensive trash to gullible customers

Busywork jobs—sorting, recording, filing, computerizing, endless amounts of data, office memos, statistical figments

Mandarin-administrative jobs—co-ordinating, overseeing, supervising clerical battalions and bureaucratic hierarchies, many of which—especially in government operations—exist merely to spin their own wheels

Financial sleight-of-hand jobs—juggling cash and credit, sniffing out tax loopholes and quick speculative windfalls in real estate, arbitrage, stocks and bonds

Compensatory amusements jobs—marketing the vicarious glamour and escapist pleasures whose one use is to relieve the tedium and frustration of workaday life: spectator sports, mass media distractions, superstar entertainments, package tours, the pricey toys and accoutrements of "creative leisure"

Cop jobs—providing security against the theft and violence of society's have-nots, policing the streets, hassling the riffraff through the courts, guarding the prisons, snooping into credit ratings, school records, personnel evaluations

Welfare processing jobs—picking up the economy's casualties, keeping them on the public assistance treadmill, holding the social discontent below the boiling point

And at the dizzy top of the heap, we have the billion-dollar boondoggling—the cartel building, multinational maneuvering, military-industrial back scratching—which is the corrupted soul of our corporate economy. The list could go on indefinitely, a spreading network of waste and corruption that touches very nearly everybody's work life. How many of us could not finally be tied into it in at least some peripheral way—like it or not, know it or not? My own profession of university teaching has fattened enormously over the past generation by educating (or training) the personnel who have become the executive functionaries and white-collar rank and file in this flourishing surplus economy.

Many who are utterly dependent upon this dense congestion of socially useless getting and spending may never see the full context of the work they do. That is the peculiar moral dodge made available by our social complexity. It allows us to work in the blind at little, seemingly innocent fractions of big, dishonorable projects. The full extent of culpability may be nearly impossible to delineate; there are so many degrees and shadings. But the ethical issue is nevertheless there at the heart of our economy, and it must be addressed by any honest discussion of work. There is work that is good and useful; and there is work that is not. Work that is not good and useful is work that wastes the lives of people and the resources of the Earth—and industrial society generates a scandalous amount of that kind of work. Perhaps it is what our society does most. In our search for a true vocation, here is indeed a Himalayan obstacle. For it may mean there is a prodigious amount of work we are involved in which no healthy sense of responsibility should permit us to do at all.

—1978

ALAN THEIN DURNING

B. 1964

Few people have thought as deeply as Alan Thein Durning about what our environmental predicament means for our way of life. Durning has made a career of analyzing the relationship between consumption and environmental degradation, pointing out that both overconsumption and poverty harm the environment and posing the question, How much is enough? As a senior researcher at the Worldwatch Institute, Durning authored numerous Worldwatch papers and articles in World Watch *magazine, as well as contributing articles to a number of national publications. He is now a freelance writer and an environmental activist with Northwest Environmental Watch, an organization he started in Seattle. His most recent book is* This Place on Earth: Home and the Practice of Permanence *(1996).*

"The Conundrum of Consumption" is the first chapter of Durning's book How Much Is Enough? The Consumer Society and the Future of the Earth *(1992). The book asserts that the consumer society born in the United States in the 1920s (with brand-name products, processed foods, and the automobile) has moved far beyond American borders and "has been quite effective in harming the environment, but not in providing people with a fulfilling life." Durning estimates that the one-fifth of the world's population that belongs to the consumer class takes home 64 percent of world income and produces two-thirds of world emissions of carbon dioxide caused by burning fossil fuels. After examining the environmental impact of what we in the consumer class eat and drink, how we get around, and the things we buy and use, Durning argues against the myth that we must consume or decline, and suggests that we can only build a "culture of permanence" if we curb our consumption. Moreover, he suggests that our lives can become richer and more satisfying if we give up our fixation on money and material goods.*

It is interesting to note that as people like Durning have begun to draw attention to the environmental cost of the consumer lifestyle, producers of goods have begun to capitalize on the idea of "green consumption," seeking to convince potential customers that buying their products will somehow do the earth a favor. For example, a marketing letter sent out by a bank in 1995 announced "a revolutionary new credit card that's actually good for the earth"—because a portion of the fee charged to merchants for use of the card would be set aside for environmental causes. Oil companies and automobile manufacturers, among others, are perfecting the art of green-flavored advertising ("If nature had a CEO, this would be the company car," proclaims a 1996 ad for the Toyota Land Cruiser). Not to be left out of the act, many environmental organizations now send out catalogs selling an array of goods to raise money for the cause. Can we consume our way out of our environmental predicament? Those who stand to profit would have us believe so.

THE CONUNDRUM OF CONSUMPTION

For Sidney Quarrier of Essex, Connecticut, Earth Day 1990 was Judgment Day—the day of ecological reckoning. While tens of millions of people around the world were marching and celebrating in the streets, Sidney was sitting at his kitchen table with a yellow legal pad and a pocket calculator. The task he set himself was to tally up the burden he and his family had placed on the planet since Earth Day 1970.[1]

Early that spring morning he began tabulating everything that had gone into their house—oil for heating, nuclear-generated electricity, water for showers and watering the lawn, cans of paint, appliances, square footage of carpet, furniture, clothes, food, and thousands of other things—and everything that had come out—garbage pails of junk mail and packaging, newspapers and magazines by the cubic meter, polluted water, and smoke from the furnace. He listed the resources they had tapped to move them around by car and airplane, from fuel and lubricants to tires and replacement parts. "I worked on that list most of the day," Sid remembers. "I dug out wads of old receipts, weighed trash cans and the daily mail, excavated the basement and shed, and used triangulation techniques I hadn't practiced since graduate school to estimate the materials we used in the roofing job."[2]

Manufacturing and delivering each of the objects on his list, Sid knew, had required additional resources he was unable to count. National statistics suggested, for example, that he should double the energy he used in his house and car to allow for what businesses and government used to provide him with goods and services. He visualized a global industrial network of factories making things for him, freighters and trucks transporting them, stores selling them, and office buildings supervising the process. He wondered how much steel and concrete his state needed for the roads, bridges, and parking garages he used. He wondered about resources used by the hospital that cared for him, the air force jets and police cars that protected him, the television stations that entertained him, and the veterinary office that cured his dog.

As his list grew, Sid was haunted by an imaginary mountain of discarded televisions, car parts, and barrels of oil—all piling up toward the sky on his lot. "It was a sober revisiting of that period. . . . It's only when you put together all the years of incremental consumption that you realize the totality." That totality hit him like the ton of paper packaging he had hauled out with the trash over the years: "The question is," Sid said, "Can the earth survive the impact of Sid, and can the Sids of the future change?"[3]

That *is* the question. Sidney Quarrier and his family are no gluttons. "During those years, we lived in a three-bedroom house on two and a half acres in the country, about 35 miles from my job in Hartford," Sidney recounts. "But we have never been rich," he insists. "What frightened me was that our consumption was typical of the people here in Connecticut."[4]

Sid's class—the American middle class—is the group that, more than any other, defines and embodies the contemporary international vision of the good life. Yet the way the Quarriers lived for those 20 years is among the world's premier environmental problems, and may be the most difficult to solve.

Only population growth rivals high consumption as a cause of ecological decline, and at least population growth is now viewed as a problem by many governments and citizens of the world. Consumption, in contrast, is almost universally seen as good—indeed, increasing it is the primary goal of national economic policy. The consumption levels exemplified in the two decades Sid Quarrier reviewed are the highest achieved by any civilization in human history. They manifest the full flowering of a new form of human society: the consumer society.

This new manner of living was born in the United States, and the words of an American best capture its spirit. In the age of U.S. affluence that began after World War II, retailing analyst Victor Lebow declared: "Our enormously productive economy . . . demands that we make consumption our way of life, that we convert the buying and use of goods into rituals, that we seek our spiritual satisfaction, our ego satisfaction, in consumption. . . . We need things consumed, burned up, worn out, replaced, and discarded at an ever increasing rate." Most citizens of western nations have responded to Lebow's call, and the rest of the world appears intent on following.[5]

In industrial lands, consumption now permeates social values. Opinion surveys in the world's two largest economies—Japan and the United States—show that people increasingly measure success by the amount they consume. The Japanese speak of the "new three sacred treasures": color television, air conditioning, and the automobile. One fourth of Poles deem "Dynasty," which portrays the life-style of the richest Americans, their favorite television program, and villagers in the heart of Africa follow "Dallas," the television series that portrays American oil tycoons. In Taiwan, a billboard demands "Why Aren't You a Millionaire Yet?" A *Business Week* correspondent beams: "The American Dream is alive and well . . . in Mexico." Indeed, the words "consumer" and "person" have become virtual synonyms.[6]

The life-style made in the United States is emulated by those who can afford it around the world, but many cannot. The economic fault lines that fracture the globe defy comprehension. The world has 202 billionaires and more than 3 million millionaires. It also has 100 million homeless people who live on roadsides, in garbage dumps, and under bridges. The value of luxury goods sales worldwide—high-fashion clothing, top-of-the-line autos, and the other trappings of wealth—exceeds the gross national products of two thirds of the world's countries. Indeed, the world's average income, about $5,000 a year, is below the U.S. poverty line.[7]

The gaping divide in material consumption between the fortunate and unfortunate stands out starkly in their impacts on the natural world. The soaring consumption lines that track the rise of the consumer society are, from another perspective, surging indicators of environmental harm. The consumer society's exploitation of resources threatens to exhaust, poison, or unalterably disfigure forests, soils, water, and air. We, its members, are responsible for a disproportionate share of all the global environmental challenges facing humanity.

Ironically, high consumption is a mixed blessing in human terms too. People living in the nineties are on average four-and-a-half times richer than their great-grandparents were at the turn of the century, but they are not four-and-a-half times happier. Psychological evidence shows that the relationship between consumption and personal happiness is weak. Worse, two primary sources of human fulfillment—social relations and leisure—appear to have withered or stagnated in the rush to riches. Thus many of us in the consumer society have a sense that our world of plenty is somehow hollow—that, hoodwinked by a consumerist culture, we have been fruitlessly attempting to satisfy with material things what are essentially social, psychological, and spiritual needs.[8]

Of course, the opposite of overconsumption—destitution—is no solution to either environmental or human problems. It is infinitely worse for people and bad for the natural world too. Dispossessed peasants slash-and-burn their way into the rain forests of Latin America, hungry nomads turn their herds out onto fragile African rangeland, reducing it to desert, and small farmers in India and the Philippines cultivate steep slopes, exposing them to the erosive powers of rain. Perhaps half the world's billion-plus absolute poor are caught in a downward spiral of ecological and economic impoverishment. In desperation, they knowingly abuse the land, salvaging the present by savaging the future.[9]

If environmental destruction results when people have either too little or too much, we are left to wonder, How much is enough? What level of consumption can the earth support? When does having more cease to add appreciably to human satisfaction? Is it possible for all the world's people to live comfortably without bringing on the decline of the planet's natural health? Is there a level of living above poverty and subsistence but below the consumer life-style—a level of sufficiency? Could all the world's people have central heating? Refrigerators? Clothes dryers? Automobiles? Air conditioning? Heated swimming pools? Airplanes? Second homes?

Many of these questions cannot be answered definitively, but for each of us in the consumer society, asking is essential nonetheless. Unless we see that more is not always better, our efforts to forestall ecological decline will be overwhelmed by our appetites. Unless we ask, we will likely fail to see the forces around us that stimulate those appetites, such as relentless advertising, proliferating shopping centers, and social pressures to "keep up with the Joneses." We may overlook forces that make consumption more destructive than it need be, such as subsidies to mines, paper mills, and other industries with high environmental impacts. And we may not act on opportunities to improve our lives while consuming less, such as working fewer hours to spend more time with family and friends.

Still, the difficulty of transforming the consumer society into a sustainable one can scarcely be overestimated. We consumers enjoy a life-style that almost everybody else aspires to, and why shouldn't they? Who would just as soon not have an automobile, a big house on a big lot, and complete control over indoor temperature throughout the year? The momentum of centuries of economic history and the material cravings of 5.5 billion people lie on the side of increasing consumption.

We may be, therefore, in a conundrum—a problem admitting of no satisfactory solution. Limiting the consumer life-style to those who have already attained it is not politically possible, morally defensible, or ecologically sufficient. And extending that life-style to all would simply hasten the ruin of the biosphere. The global environment cannot support 1.1 billion of us living like American consumers, much less 5.5 billion people, or a future population of at least 8 billion. On the other hand, reducing the consumption levels of the consumer society, and tempering material aspirations elsewhere, though morally acceptable, is a quixotic proposal. It bucks the trend of centuries. Yet it may be the only option.

If the life-supporting ecosystems of the planet are to survive for future generations, the consumer society will have to dramatically curtail its use of resources—partly by shifting to high-quality, low-input durable goods and partly by seeking fulfillment through leisure, human relationships, and other nonmaterial avenues. We in the consumer society will have to live a technologically sophisticated version of the life-style currently practiced lower on the economic ladder. Scientific advances, better laws, restructured industries, new treaties, environmental taxes, grassroots campaigns—all can help us get there. But ultimately, sustaining the environment that sustains humanity will require that we change our values.

—1992

Notes

1. Sidney Quarrier, geologist, Connecticut Geological & Natural History Survey, Hartford, Conn., private communication, February 25, 1992.
2. Ibid.
3. Ibid.
4. Ibid.
5. Lebow in *Journal of Retailing,* quoted in Vance Packard, *The Waste Makers* (New York: David Mckay, 1960).
6. Sepp Linhart, "From Industrial to Postindustrial Society: Changes in Japanese Leisure-Related Values and Behavior," *Journal of Japanese Studies,* Summer 1988; Richard A. Easterlin and Eileen M. Crimmins, "Recent Social Trends: Changes in Personal Aspirations of American Youth," *Sociology and Social Research,* July 1988; "Dynasty" from "Harper's Index," *Harper's,* December 1990; "Dallas" from Jerry Mander, *In the Absence of the Sacred* (San Francisco: Sierra Club Books, 1991); Taiwan from "Asian Century," *Newsweek,* February 22, 1988; Stephen Baker and S. Lynne Walker, "The American Dream Is Alive and Well—in Mexico," *Business Week,* September 30, 1991.
7. Billionaires from Jennifer Reese, "The Billionaires: More Than Ever in 1991," *Fortune,* September 9, 1991; millionaires estimated from Kevin R. Phillips, "Reagan's America: A Capital Offense," *New York Times Magazine,* June 18, 1990; homelessness from U.N. Centre for Human Settlements, New York, private communication, November 1, 1989; luxury goods from "The Lapse of Luxury," *Economist,* January 5, 1991; gross national product from United Nations Development Programme, *Human Development Report 1991* (New York: Oxford University Press, 1991); member countries in United Nations from U.N. Information Center, Washington, D.C., private communication, January 14, 1992; world average income from 1987, in 1987 U.S. dollars adjusted for international variations in purchasing power, from Ronald V. A. Sprout and James H. Weaver, "International Distribution of Income: 1960-1987," Working Paper No. 159, Department of Economics, American University, Washington, D.C., May 1991; U.S. 1987 poverty line for an individual from U.S. Bureau of the Census, *Statistical Abstract of the United States: 1990* (Washington, D.C.: U.S. Government Printing Office, 1990).
8. Four-and-a-half times richer from Angus Maddison, *The World Economy in the 20th Century* (Paris: Organisation for Economic Co-operation and Development, 1989).

9. Alan Durning, *Poverty and the Environment: Reversing the Downward Spiral*, Worldwatch Paper 92 (Washington, D.C.: Worldwatch Institute, November 1989).

ALICE WALKER

B. 1944

"I am an earthling, and proud of it," says Alice Walker when asked to describe herself. In poems, short stories, novels, essays, and children's books she has expressed a determined resistance to oppression of any kind and a "growing realization that the sincerest struggle to change the world must start within." "Because I was so often filled with despair over my own and the world's shortcomings, especially during childhood, adolescence, and young adulthood, I assumed I would be a suicide by the age of thirty," she admits in the preface to Her Blue Body Everything We Know: Earthling Poems 1965–1990 Complete. *She says her life has been saved countless times by poetry and by the flowers and the trees she has planted. Through writing and gardening, she seems to have found her way to a deep sense of joy and an appreciation of the redeeming power of love for all that is.*

Walker was born in Eatonton, Georgia, the eighth child of sharecroppers. She attended Spelman College, a black women's college in Atlanta, and earned a B.A. from Sarah Lawrence College in New York. After traveling to Kenya to help build a school and working for the New York City Welfare Department, she returned to the South in 1966 and lived there for seven years, working in the civil rights movement and marrying a Jewish law student who was also active in the movement. In 1978, divorced and with a daughter, she moved from Brooklyn, where she'd lived for four years after leaving Mississippi, to rural northern California. Her best-selling novel The Color Purple *(1982) won the Pulitzer Prize and the American Book Award for fiction in 1983. Her most recent novel,* Possessing the Secret of Joy *(1992), is a protest against female circumcision.* Anything We Love Can Be Saved: A Writer's Activism *(1997) collects her essays, speeches, statements, and letters on various political issues. Walker lives in Berkeley, California.*

"We Alone" was first collected in Horses Make a Landscape Look More Beautiful *(1986). These poems grew out of the northern California soil where Walker gratefully took root, feeling that "my spirit, which had felt so cramped on the East Coast, expanded fully. . . . I could, for the first time, admit and express my grief over the ongoing assassination of the earth, even as I accepted all the parts, good and bad, of my own heritage." "We Alone" reminds us of the power we wield as consumers by virtue of our decisions about what we value. If we value gold, we justify mining the earth, and we just might be supporting an economy in a country that practices racist oppression, as was the case in South Africa when Walker wrote this poem. If we were to love "what is plentiful as much as what is scarce," we could free ourselves of consumerist compulsions and feel truly wealthy in the abundance of nature.*

WE ALONE

We alone can devalue gold
by not caring
if it falls or rises
in the marketplace.
Wherever there is gold
there is a chain, you know,
and if your chain
is gold
so much the worse
for you.

Feathers, shells
and sea-shaped stones
are all as rare.

This could be our revolution:
To love what is plentiful
as much as
what is scarce.

—1986

DONELLA MEADOWS

B. 1941

Donella Meadows and her colleagues Dennis Meadows and Jorgen Randers created shock waves with their 1972 book The Limits to Growth, *a report to the Club of Rome (an international group of businesspeople and academics) based on a computer model of global population and economic growth. Showing twelve different futures, the book contained the unmistakable message that the growth of population and consumption to which the modern world is accustomed cannot go on forever, or even very much longer. Coming at a time when growth had become a guiding principle of most economies, the book provoked powerful controversy and criticism. In their 1992 book* Beyond the Limits: Confronting Global Collapse, Envisioning a Sustainable Future, *Meadows and her colleagues restate their original case with updated figures and information.*

Originally trained as a scientist, Meadows sees herself as "a reformer who wants to show that a better world is both imaginable and feasible." She earned a B.S. in chemistry from Carleton College in 1963 and a Ph.D. in biophysics from Harvard University in 1968 before entering the field of system dynamics, which focuses on understanding complex systems as diverse as the human body and the earth's climate. From 1970 to 1972 Meadows was on the team at MIT that produced the global computer model on which The Limits to Growth *is based. In 1982 she began teaching in the environmental studies program at Dartmouth College. Meadows lives on a small commu-nal organic farm in New Hampshire, where she puts her ideas about sus-tainable resource management to work. In 1994 she was awarded a MacArthur fellowship.*

The following essay is from The Global Citizen *(1991), a collection of newspaper columns written by Meadows between 1985 and 1990 that com-ment on world events from a systems point of view. In the preface to the book, Meadows explains what motivated her to become a columnist: "I was finding the state of the world and the feeble responses of policymakers intol-erable. . . . I wanted to see a system-based, globally oriented, long-term viewpoint on the editorial pages of the newspapers." She writes, "Whatever the weekly topic, my columns have all flowed from a system-trained mind that does its best to operate with a holistic picture of how things are inte-grated."*

LIVING LIGHTLY AND INCONSISTENTLY ON THE LAND

I was raised in Illinois, as a good red-blooded American kid, eating Jello, white bread, canned peas, and Midwestern steaks. I watched Howdy Doody and played softball and canasta. On my sixteenth birthday my father gave me a decrepit old car. I used it to drive to my summer job in a drugstore at a shopping mall. Everyone I knew lived just like me. I didn't know there was such a thing as a lifestyle. I went to college on a scholarship and developed tastes for things that went beyond my fam-ily's ken—artichokes and opera and Shakespeare. As a chemistry major I did a term paper on chemical additives in food, and for the first time I began to make con-sumer decisions that didn't come from habit. I read labels and tried to buy foods that were mainly composed of food.

Getting married and moving east didn't induce many changes until I started studying biochemistry. As I learned more about the body's chemical processes, I started putting more whole wheat flour in things I baked, using less sugar and fat, and serving more green vegetables. I eliminated the Jello and everything in cans and swore off soft drinks and coffee. All this was done for our own health, not from any sense of global responsibility.

The quantum leap in lifestyle came when my husband and I spent a year driving through Turkey, Iran, Afghanistan, Pakistan, and India (in those days Americans were welcome in all those countries). In India we became vegetarians because it was diffi-cult to find meat. In the Muslim countries we couldn't buy alcohol. Our clothing had to be simple and practical. Hot showers became major luxuries. We were cut off from television, radio, and even newspapers for weeks at a time. Mostly we lived as the vil-lagers around us did, and we discovered that we were perfectly happy to do so.

Coming home was a shock. Looking with Asian eyes, we couldn't believe how much *stuff* people had. We saw how little the stuff had to do with happiness. We also had strong memories of the poverty, the erosion, the deforestation, and the hunger we had seen. The world was very real to us. We resolved to live our lives in a way more consistent with the whole of it.

At first we had little desire for material things. That wore off, of course, and we became Americans again. But we kept our life simple. We continued to be vegetarians. We traveled by mass transit. We made our own clothes and bread and even furniture. We asked a long set of questions about everything we bought. Is this spinach organic or raised with pesticides? Were these bananas grown on an exploitive plantation or in a worker-owned cooperative? Is our electricity from a hydro dam or a nuclear power plant? If we buy plastic bags, how many nasty chemicals have we caused to be released somewhere? Can we get along without plastic bags?

We were the best global citizens we knew how to be. And we were a pain in the neck. We regarded most of the people around us as unaware, unconsciously wreaking planetary destruction for short-term gratification. We separated ourselves from them. It didn't occur to us that setting up us/them and right/wrong categories might be the surest way of all to wreak planetary destruction.

We moved to New Hampshire because we wanted to restore a beat-up farm to ecological health and to live more self-sufficiently. We ripped the house apart and put it back together with proper insulation. We added space so six or eight people could share the place without stifling one another, and since then we've lived communally. We heat the house and our water partly with wood, partly with oil. We cut the wood with a chain saw, split it with a hydraulic splitter attached to a tractor. We cook on a woodstove sometimes, but an electric stove mostly. Our electricity comes partially from a nuclear power plant.

We grow nearly all our vegetables, all our eggs, some fruit. We grow organically, of course. We've made the soil much better than it was when we came here. We dry, can, freeze, and pickle enough to get through the winter. We buy milk from another farm, grain from the co-op, and ice cream from the supermarket. We raise sheep for wool, some of which we sell, some of which we spin, dye, and knit ourselves. We sell the meat. We recycle organic garbage to the chickens, cans and bottles to a recycling center. We wash out and reuse plastic bags; we use old newspapers to start fires in the woodstoves. We put tons of junk mail out in the weekly garbage pickup, which goes to a trash-to-energy incinerator.

We bought a television when the Red Sox were in the World Series. It's hardly been on since, but classical music plays all day on a CD player. We have old-fashioned spinning wheels and modern computers, an energy-efficient Honda and a wildly inefficient Dodge pickup truck for farm work. We travel by jet all over the world to do environmental work, probably burning up 100 times as much fuel as any other family in our town.

I assume that the inconsistencies in this "lifestyle" are obvious to you. We try to live lightly on the land in a culture where that's impossible. But we have lightened up about our own compromises and those of others. We do our best, we're always willing to try to do better, and we're still major transgressors on the ecosystems and resources of the planet. We're a lot more tolerant of our fellow transgressors than we used to be.

As a child in the middle-class Midwest, I lived out of a subconscious sense of *abundance*. That sense permits security, innovation, generosity, and joy. But it can also harbor insensitivity, greed, and waste. After returning from India, I lived out of a sense of *scarcity*. That is fine when it fosters stewardship, simplicity, and frugality, but not when it leads to grimness, intolerance, and separation from one's fellows. Now I try to base my life on the idea of *sufficiency*—there is just enough of everything for everyone and not one bit more. There is enough for generosity but not waste, enough for security but not hoarding. Or, as Gandhi said, enough for everyone's need, but not for everyone's greed.

—1991

ALLEN GINSBERG

1926-1997

"I saw the best minds of my generation destroyed by madness. . . ." With these words the twenty-nine-year-old Allen Ginsberg ushered in a new age of poetry in America, as he read his poem "Howl" at the Six Gallery in San Francisco in October 1955. Since then, this "mad-eyed visionary," this "bard of disaffected youth," has been the most famous poet in America. His fame derives not only from the originality and power of his work, but also from his refusal to sit quietly on the contemplative sidelines of American culture. In 1961 he reflected: "That we have begun a revolution of literature in America, again, without meaning to, merely by the actual practice of poetry —this would be inevitable. No doubt we knew what we were doing." Ginsberg reawakened Americans to the sheer entertainment value of the poem as performance. He liberated poetry from the parlor, where it had begun to smell of mothballs, and set it loose in the street.

Born in New Jersey and educated at Columbia University, Ginsberg associated in San Francisco in the 1950s with such Beat Generation writers as Jack Kerouac and Gary Snyder. But his poetry defies categorization as part of this movement or any other. In the early 1970s he founded the Naropa Institute in Boulder, Colorado, an alternative school offering classes and workshops in the arts and spirituality, influenced by Tibetan Buddhism. Ginsberg lived in New York City later in his life.

"A Supermarket in California" is one of Ginsberg's most widely reprinted poems, written in 1956 and collected in Reality Sandwiches (1963). Its long lines are reminiscent of those of Walt Whitman, whose questioning ghost is called up in the "neon fruit supermarket" along with that of the Spanish poet García Lorca. The absurd image of these three unruly poets wandering the aisles of the store among fruits, vegetables, and frozen delicacies illuminates the bourgeois values of the place and its other shoppers. Whitman's imagined query "Who killed the pork chops?" urges a more realistic look at the dependencies that are hidden by the abundantly stocked shelves of that most American of consumer institutions, the supermarket.

A SUPERMARKET IN CALIFORNIA

What thoughts I have of you tonight, Walt Whitman, for I walked down the streets under the trees with a headache self-conscious looking at the full moon.

In my hungry fatigue, and shopping for images, I went into the neon fruit supermarket, dreaming of your enumerations!

What peaches and what penumbras? Whole families shopping at night! Aisles
full of husbands! Wives in the avocados, babies in the tomatoes!—and you, García
Lorca, what were you doing down by the watermelons?

I saw you, Walt Whitman, childless, lonely old grubber, poking among the meats
in the refrigerator and eyeing the grocery boys.
I heard you asking questions of each: Who killed the pork chops? What price
bananas? Are you my Angel?
I wandered in and out of the brilliant stacks of cans following you, and followed
in my imagination by the store detective.
We strode down the open corridors together in our solitary fancy tasting
artichokes, possessing every frozen delicacy, and never passing the cashier.

Where are we going, Walt Whitman? The doors close in an hour. Which way does
your beard point tonight?
(I touch your book and dream of our odyssey in the supermarket and feel
absurd.)
Will we walk all night through solitary streets? The trees add shade to shade,
lights out in the houses, we'll both be lonely.
Will we stroll dreaming of the lost America of love past blue automobiles in
driveways, home to our silent cottage?
Ah, dear father, graybeard, lonely old courage-teacher, what America did you
have when Charon quit poling his ferry and you got out on a smoking bank and
stood watching the boat disappear on the black waters of Lethe?

—1956

MERIDEL LeSUEUR
1900-1996

*With roots in the Midwest, a lineage that included a Native American great-
grandmother along with "dissenters and democrats and radicals through
five generations," and lifelong associations with Marxists and prairie pop-
ulists, Meridel LeSueur was called the Voice of the Prairie. She was also a
voice of the oppressed—farm laborers, factory workers, native peoples,
women—in social writings that began during her teenage years. "I am a
woman speaking for us all . . . a woman come to speak in tongues of dust
and fire," she wrote in one fiercely tender poem. Born in Murray, Iowa, she
was raised by a militantly feminist mother and a stepfather who was a
socialist lawyer. She dropped out of high school and lived in a New York
anarchist commune with Emma Goldman before acting in such early
movies as The Last of the Mohicans and The Perils of Pauline. Later she
married a labor organizer and bore two daughters.
After she had a short story accepted for publication in a literary journal in 1927, a fruitful period followed during which LeSueur published
several collections of short stories and a lyrical history of the northern
Midwest, North Star Country (1945). The popularity of her work waned
when she was informally blacklisted during the McCarthy era, and she*

turned to writing children's stories about American cultural heroes: Johnny Appleseed, Davy Crockett, Abraham Lincoln, and Nancy Hanks Lincoln. Later work—including a volume of poetry entitled Rites of Ancient Ripening *(1975), a novel called* The Girl *(1978), and more collections of short stories—expresses a strong earth-based spirituality and champions the creative power of the common people. In all, LeSueur produced nineteen books and more than 125 volumes of her journal (as yet unpublished).*

Resistance to the forces of domination and control and to forms of "progress" that threaten to destroy the all-important bond between people and land is a persistent theme in LeSueur's work, evident in the short story "Harvest" (collected in Harvest & A Song for My Time, *1977). The questions this story raises about technology were perhaps first raised by the Luddites, organized bands of English handicraftsmen (followers of the probably mythic Ned Ludd) who in the early 1800s smashed the textile machinery that was displacing them. Though the Luddites were vigorously repressed at the time, their sentiments about the price of technogical progress live on in America on Amish farms, where the use of machinery is restricted in an effort to preserve the connection to the land and the working together of communities. In LeSueur's story, the woman who is ripe with child represents an earth-based wisdom deeply suspicious of a machine that might separate her husband from a direct experience of the fertile land.*

HARVEST

It was almost noon and the sun stood hot above the fields. The men would be coming in from the corn for dinner.

Ruth Winji stooped at the bean vines thinking she had not enough yet in her basket for a mess of beans. From the hour's picking of berries and beans she had leaned over in her own heat and the sun's heat driving through her until earth memory and seed memory were in her in the hot air and she was aware of all that stood in the heat around her, the trees in the bright sun, earth-rooted, swaying in sensitive darkness, the wheat like a sea in the slight wind, the cows peering from the caverns of shade of the grove behind the barns with their magic faces and curved horns. Root darkness. Tree darkness. Sun. Earth. Body. She thought: *And my body dark in the sun, root-alive, opening in the sun dark at its deep roots,* and it pained her now that she had quarrelled with her husband.

Anxiously she lifted her large fair torso looking for her young husband as he would come from the corn and wheat, swaying a little as he walked, the sun flashing up the stalk of his body, trying not to show the joy he had walking toward her. By noon she always looked to see him come back, for they had not been separated longer in the six months of their marriage. She shaded her face to see him but she could not tell him at that distance from the other two men that worked in the corn. Still she looked trying to find out what he would be doing for she grieved that a quarrel stood up between them, and now she could not tell him that they would have a child.

It was a quarrel about whether he should buy a threshing machine to harvest the ripening wheat. It wasn't that the money was her dowry money; she dreaded the machine. She knew how men came in from riding that monster all day. She had been hired out before her marriage in the three years since she had come from Bohemia and she knew the cold mindless look of them, not in a column of mounting heat as her husband came now to her, a flame from the earth, broken off as if the quick of it had taken to his very flesh.

Her heart went into a great dismay to think of him riding that machine, and she saw with what a glitter that desire sat upon him and her heart was sick. He had never had a machine and now he wanted one, and it was an encroachment like another woman or war.

She leaned over again thrusting her hand in to the warm vine foliage as the berries hung turning away from the heat upon themselves and she plucked them from the short thick stems and they fell sun-heavy in her hand. Her fingers were stained with berry juice and it had run up the naked belly of her arm and dried there.

She could not keep her mind from thinking how more and more now he looked into that catalogue at night where there were pictures shown of all the parts of a thresher. How he looked into this book all the evening without speaking a word.

Their marriage had been wonderful to her in mid-winter. Coming to his farm, snowed in together in January, and it was as if they themselves brought the spring warming, spreading it from their own bodies until it lifted and mounted from the house to the fields, until the whole earth was jutting in green.

Then she had come with him while he plowed and planted or watched him from the windows of the house as if he stood still in union with her as he strode the sun-scarred earth laying it open, the seed falling in the shadows; then at evening he came from them to her, himself half young, half old in the beginnings of his body, his young brows aslant meeting above his nose, his lips full and red, the sun warming and jutting in him too as the spring advanced, and she was not loath to accept him from the fields smelling of salt sweat, and see all that he had planted ripen and grow from that wild heat into the visible world, bright and green, rising to its flower, and now a child growing unseen but certain.

Still and even now, the knowing and remembering in herself of the way of his walking or the manner of his speech, as if he were out of breath, coming partly from the newness of the language to him and partly from his eagerness to know everything, his terrible cunning to know: That was it, that was what she really feared, his new world cunning to know, that's what made the fear go up her body so she had to lift her heavy shoulders and breathe slowly looking out over the slow sheen of the turning wheat where everything seemed almost dark in the sun. Still she could not see him, only the three tiny figures of the hoeing men far afield in the corn.

Now she felt she was losing him, as if he were falling out of some soft burr, their ancient closed fertile life, being shaken from the old world tree, in ways beyond her, that she would not go.

The days in the early spring had been like great hot needles sewing them close together, in and out, binding them close, piercing through both to the marrow and binding them with the bright day and the dark night. So the earth lay and herself too, marked by the plow. The sun rose molten with intent. The sun went down and the dusk blew scented and low upon them. The light of day spun them together in utter tranquility—until he had to come saying, "What about this machine? They say that the work will be done so quick, you wouldn't believe it. They say it, Ruth. What about it? We have just enough to have it. What about it?"

And it was just as if he were about to betray her and she could say nothing, seeing that look of greed and cunning, and it was no good to argue this or that because everyone threshed his wheat with the big harvester and he would get her to peek into the catalogue and tell her how the thing mowed the wheat in terrible broad swaths and he showed her the picture of the seat where he would sit swaying sensitive in his own rich body from that iron seat and then she wouldn't look. She would turn away in fear and it came to lie heavier in her than her own planting that she bore now to the fourth month.

And he kept saying, "We could get one of those, Ruth. We could save money. We could just get one of those." With his curious way of repeating himself, beginning and ending on the same phrase. "I was over there looking at that machine in town. Pretty good, too. Yah, pretty good. I was over there looking and it was good." At those times she wouldn't know him at all, that sensual light would be gone from his young keen face, the little flicker that came up from his body gone, and he would be smiling, distracted, rubbing his palms together, as if he were falling away from her, out of the column of himself to be lost to her touch.

The salesman had even come and Winji had looked askance, speaking low so the man left quickly and she took it as a good sign.

She saw the sun topping the roof of the barn so she hurried up the lane with her berries and her beans. Then she heard a sound that made her step in fright. She saw that monster coming slowly up the road making a corrugated track. It came as if with no motion of its parts through the heat. Ruth Winji ran into the cooled house, closed the door then stood hearing that beat that was like a heart and yet monstrous. It seemed to be going straight over the house and she didn't look out until it had passed and then she saw the monstrous tracks on the road bed.

She remembered her husband had said they were demonstrating one at Olson's and had wanted her to go with him to see and she had said she would not go.

She put the beans on and sat down to wait at the window where she could first see him come up through the orchard. The sunlight made an under-darkness over the lower world so it was dark as a plum, the trees still black-tipped, a sensitive shimmer of darkness like a convulsion seemed to go over the sun or world beneath the gloom of sun so Ruth went into a swoon of heat between the bright upper sun and the painfully sensitive lower darkness.

She must have dozed because she started aware when her husband stood in the room behind her. She didn't turn from the window but knew him there in the soft heated gloom. He hadn't spoken behind her in the room and her body started alive to him like a blind antenna upreaching. He touched her shoulder coming from behind her and she saw his hands burned rosy. She thrust back against him and he still stood invisible touching her.

There was a drowsiness of noon all about them, the soft throaty cluck of the hens, the padding of the dog across the bare swept ground, the crisp whirr of a bird startled up from noon drowse winging from shadow to shadow.

She looked up, saw his face, young, dark, mounted with blood rosy beneath the burned skin, his brows winged strangely at an angle as she looked up, his full young mouth curved willfully, his eyes glinting above her like the eyes of a hawk looking at her from his narrow spare face coming down on her from above, setting his lips on hers.

"The beans," she cried.

"Never mind," he said enamored, "I turned the fire off. Never mind."

Her springing up as she had lifted his whole height to her instantly like a shaft of shadow against the bright outdoors light. Seeing the straight willful neck, plunging to the close-cropped round head, springing against his hard spare sweating body, she pinned him with her arms where the shirt was set and stuck to his strong back and felt the winging of the ribs' spare flight, spanning from her hands the hard thin breast.

At table Winji talked with the hired help about the thresher that had gone by. Ruth listened with lowered head.

"My wife here," Winji said, "doesn't want me to buy it. She wants to keep the old way, God knows why."

The other two men looked at her, the full confused woman sitting at table with them. They seemed to hardly dare lay eyes upon her.

"Well, it's a good one for getting work done," said one.

And they went on talking about threshers and their good and bad points and their makes like men enamoured until she said, "Don't talk about it please, don't speak."

"But we will," her husband said leaning towards her, his fork upraised. "And you're going down with me after this meal and see how it goes."

She did not dispute with him before the men.

After the dishes were cleared he said in the kitchen, "Listen Ruth. The thresher is just down the bend. That's the one I've been talking about. Listen Ruth. I wish you would go down there with me."

"No," she said, wiping off the dishpan carefully.

"You go down and look at it with me. I think it's the best thing we should do. Get it. Buy it. You go down, just for my sake."

"No," she said. "No, I don't want to see it. I'm afraid."

He laughed sharply, his white teeth frightening in his red mouth. "Oh, you'll think it's wonderful when you get over that. Why, it's wonderful."

"No," she said. "It's not wonderful to me."

"Think of it," he said, his eyes glistening in that way she had seen, beyond desire for her. "It will bind the sheaves after it has cut the wheat. . . ."

"What," she said, "bind the sheaves. . . ."

"Yes," he nodded and she saw that lust for knowing and what she took for cunning. "Bind the sheaves at the same time."

"At the same time," she repeated stupidly, "without going around again."

"Yes," he almost shouted, "without going around again."

"Think, how many men did it take on your father's place in the old country to harvest the wheat. . . ."

"Yes. . . . Yes, I know," she said, wringing her hands. "I used to carry a brown jug to the men full of spring water with a little meal sprinkled in it. . . ."

"You just sit on the machine and pull levers, see. Like this." He sat down and pulled levers with nothing in his hands.

"How do you know how?" she said. "You've been practicing," she cried.

"What of it," he said like a boy, as if he had got hold of something. "What if I have. Come with me, Ruth. It's your money in a way . . ."

"No, no," she said. "It's your money. Do with it as you like. It's yours. You're the master of the house, but don't make me see it. I don't want to see it. I wash my hands. I wash my hands . . ."

He stood grinning, shaking his head, chagrined a little: "But you can't wash your hands of the whole new world . . ."

But nevertheless she cried after him from the kitchen, "No. No, I wash my hands," and he went out slowly from her, bewildered.

In an hour she went with him, prevailed upon by his physical power over her. He took her hand in the road and pulled her along. Her face was partly covered by her blue sun bonnet and she hid the free hand under her apron. When they got there a clot of men gathered over the machine like black bees and she stood back. Winji joined them, hardly concealing his delight, going time and again round and round the machine. It was brand new and glinted monstrously in the light.

"Look Ruth, look," he kept saying to her, running back and pointing things out and then running back to the machine. "Look at this," he would say but she couldn't hear. She watched his face in envy and malice. The other men were laughing at her but she didn't care.

"No, no," she kept saying, half-obscured in her sun bonnet, pulling away as her husband tried to urge her to look closer at the thresher. The other men looked at her full woman's body, awed a little and thinking how the two were so newly married. They stood away from her a little sheep-faced and she stood away from them and the machine.

"Come and touch it," Winji urged.

"No, no," she cried, "I don't want to."

"Why, it won't hurt you," the men said. "Don't be afraid."

She could see her husband was a bit ashamed of her, and chagrined. "You know," he said to the men, apologizing for her, "in the old country we don't have them like this, in the old country . . ."

She saw the men patting him on the back as if he had already bought the thresher, envy showing in their eyes and he grew big from their envy, strutting around the machine, rubbing his palms together, forgetting her for a moment so she went cold with dread, then running to her to propitiate her.

"Come and touch it, isn't it splendid, look at that." She saw the big knives thrusting back movement even in their stillness, and then on driving power and the tiny manseat hidden inside, where the little living man was supposed to sit and pull the levers as her husband had been showing her. She was revolted.

But he came close to her and she was bewitched still of his body so she let herself be led straight to the giant and saw all its shining steel close to her and her husband took her hand, still stained by berries, and put it on the steel rump and it was hot as fire to the touch so she drew back nursing her hand. The men laughed and her eyes dilated holding to her husband's face but drawing away.

The men were uneasy. "Never mind, Winji," they said, "lots of our women folks takes it that way at first. My wife says her house was buried in dust the first year the thresher come." They laughed uneasily, shifting, and looking from under their brows at the woman. They turned with ease back to the machine.

She started away down the road. At the bend she turned and looked back and to her horror she saw her husband caressing the great steel body. He was dancing, a little quick dance full of desire, and with his quick living hands he was caressing the bright steel where the sun struck and flew off shining from the steel rumps into her eyes like steel splinters so she turned back sickened, but not before she saw him wave to her, a shy lifting of the hand.

She hadn't told him she was going to have a child. She thought of the child now as a weapon.

She waited while the tension went tighter between them subtly, unspoken now, with his saying now and then at breakfast, at dinner, "Have you changed? What have you against it? Is it a beast?"

She wouldn't answer, only turned against him. And then he turned against her, chagrined and lost without her, trying to win her back to his way and she wouldn't come.

She would cajole him, sitting on his lap in the evening when it was too hot to sleep. "Don't do it. Don't get it." But he knew she was playing a trick to get him. Once he got up, setting her on her own feet and walking away, and that night he didn't come in until late and didn't speak to her but went soundly to sleep.

He grew subtle against her, his summer face hot and congealed, his straight burned neck a pillar of blood against her, his brooding body hot from labor, a wall to her now that made her blind and angered.

When he came in from the cattle with the beast smell about him and milk on his shoes and the lustre of living things, she tried to pull him to her again.

At last there was enmity between them. He didn't talk any more about the machine. They sat together at table without speaking and went to bed silently in the late dusk and she thought he would never come to her again. She felt he was betraying all that and her grief was bitter against a new way, terrible in her so she didn't tell him about the child.

Then one day she went to town and came back early to be near him and go on with the fight, to bring it to come, and there she saw the salesman and Winji at the table leaning over the catalogue and figures and before they shut the book she could see the knives and parts of the machine in color. The two men looked at her guiltily. Winji got up and walked with his back to her and stood stock still at the window. The salesman left as quickly as possible and the two of them stood in the room.

"So!" she said bitterly. "You are going to get it."

"Yes!" he said and she could see the blood flush up his bared neck. "Yes, I am."

"So you don't care," she said, shaking bitterly, clenching her hands together, for she could have torn him to pieces standing there presenting his back to her. "You don't care," she said.

"I don't know what that means." Still he didn't face her. He seemed a stranger with his back turned. "It's for our good to get the machine. This is just woman's stubbornness. It will get us on. We will be powerful people in this neighborhood. . . ."

"Powerful . . ." she repeated.

"Yes," he said now, turning to her uneasily but against her.

She began to cry, not lifting her hands.

The sight of her exasperated him. "What are you crying for," he said in real anger but his face looked guilty. "What are you crying for," he shouted raising his hand. "Stop that bellowing," he swore and struck her.

She recoiled, her face lifted wide to his. He saw her falling back, her great eyes open upon him in grief. He gave a cry and caught her falling arms, thrust her toward himself. Against her he stood straight and she began to cry from her body shaking, rent by the grief in her. He held her and for a moment seemed to know what she had been feeling but it was only for a moment.

Then it was she told him about the child.

He seemed to forget about the machine those long summer days and everything was as it had been before. She looked at him every day and it seemed that it was over. He was bound to her again and she was content.

The wheat hung heavy on the stalk.

She thought he had arranged to have the old red reaper of Olson's and hire many men and she had already spoken for two of the girls to come in and help feed since she was slower on her feet now too.

One day he came in in the early afternoon and she saw he was excited.

He prowled around the house all afternoon and she was uneasy. "Is anything the matter?" she asked him. "No," he said. But when she wasn't looking she caught him looking at her. At supper he said nervously, as if he had been preparing for it the whole afternoon:

"Tomorrow we begin." He kept looking at his coffee but he kept smiling and looking cunningly at her when she wasn't looking.

"Tomorrow?"

"Huh," he grunted.

She set down her knife and fork, unable to eat. "Well?" she said, a cold fear making her hollow.

"I've got a surprise for you," he said.

"A surprise," she said.

"Don't repeat what I say!" he suddenly shouted, threw down his spoon and left the table.

The next morning she woke sitting bolt upright and saw his place beside her empty. She ran to the window but it was just dawn and she could see nothing. She dressed and put on the coffee. Still he did not come. Suddenly she put on a sweater and went as fast as she could down the lane to the beanfield where she could see the wheat and there in the field she saw it standing new and terrible, gleaming amidst the sea of ripe wheat that crested and foamed gently to its steel prow and receded away in heavy fruition.

It was over. There it was. She couldn't say why she was so afraid but she knew it was against her and against him. It was a new way.

A bevy of men stood around. Then they saw her and Winji left them and came towards her beckoning, but she did not move towards him. He came to her.

"Don't be angry, Ruth," he said gently. "We've got to do it. We can't be behind the times, can we? Now with the child."

"No," she said. They both knew that the clot of men around the machine were half-looking their way, waiting to see what would happen.

"Isn't she a beauty," he said in his broken tongue.

"A beauty," she said.

"For God's sake, do you have to repeat after me for God's sake," he said, then beseeching, he begged of her for the first time. "You say it's all right, darling. Ruth, you say it's all right. We've got to get ahead, you know that. Now more than ever, haven't we?" he said softly, standing only a foot away, but she felt his spell.

"Yes, yes," she said in grief, "yes. . . ."

"Go on," she said. "Go on with it."

"But you come down to the fence and see me go down the field the first time," he begged.

She hated him but she went behind him, seeing his heels flicker up as he went in haste, eager to be with his new "beauty."

The mare in the pasture came up and walked near him and stood sadly with them at the fence whinnying softly as her master went down the field, letting the air tremble through her soft nostrils.

Walking away he heard the soft bleat of the mare, felt the men waiting from the machine and for a moment a kind of fear struck him through the marrow as he saw the glistening thing standing to his hand. Down his soft loins, his vulnerable breast, went a doom of fear and yet an awful pride, but he felt shaking at the bones, for leaving the moistness of sleep, the old world of close dreaming in the thick blossomed surface, and the space of mystery where the seed unfolds to the touch in the cool and thick and heavy sap, the world of close dreaming that is like a woman's hair or the breasts of men.

She saw him turn in the sun—wave to her and mount the machine.

—1977

WENDELL BERRY

B. 1934

Wendell Berry (introduced earlier, in "Visions of Home," p. 222) has concerned himself for many years with trying to understand the troubles of the agricultural economy in America, and he believes that farmers would be better off using fewer chemicals and machines. In a 1985 essay entitled "A Good Farmer of the Old School," collected in Home Economics *(1987), he expresses deep admiration for a farmer who once made the change from horses to tractors but soon went back to using horses for just about everything. "Here was an intelligent man, obviously, who knew the value of doing his own thinking and paying attention," writes Berry.*

"A Good Scythe," from Berry's 1981 essay collection The Gift of Good Land: Further Essays Cultural and Agricultural, *reports on one of Berry's own experiences of doing his own thinking and paying attention, in this case with regard to a "labor-saving" device he was once enticed into buying. The essay raises the question of how much labor is really saved by "labor-saving" devices, and whether the labor that is saved might have some value in and of itself. Berry's suggestion that quite a bit of pleasure and satisfaction can be found in doing physical labor with a finely made tool might seem old-fashioned or even archaic to those who are ready to embrace the latest technology just because it's available. But his description of his process of "enlightenment" has the ring of sanity about it, as does the question he poses toward the end of the essay: What possible sense can there be in using quite a lot of money as a substitute for a little skill?*

A GOOD SCYTHE

When we moved to our little farm in the Kentucky River Valley in 1965, we came with a lot of assumptions that we have abandoned or changed in response to the demands of place and time. We assumed, for example, that there would be good motor-powered solutions for all of our practical problems.

One of the biggest problems from the beginning was that our place was mostly on a hillside and included a good deal of ground near the house and along the road that was too steep to mow with a lawn mower. Also, we were using some electric fence, which needed to be mowed out once or twice a year.

When I saw that Sears Roebuck sold a "power scythe," it seemed the ideal solution, and I bought one. I don't remember what I paid for it, but it was expensive, considering the relatively small amount of work I needed it for. It consisted of a one-cylinder gasoline engine mounted on a frame with a handlebar, a long metal tube enclosing a flexible drive shaft, and a rotary blade. To use it, you hung it from your shoulder by a web strap, and swept the whirling blade over the ground at the desired height.

It did a fairly good job of mowing, cutting the grass and weeds off clean and close to the ground. An added advantage was that it readily whacked off small bushes and tree sprouts. But this solution to the mowing problem involved a whole package of new problems:

1. The power scythe was heavy.
2. It was clumsy to use, and it got clumsier as the ground got steeper and rougher. The tool that was supposed to solve the problem of steep ground worked best on level ground.
3. It was dangerous. As long as the scythe was attached to you by the shoulder strap, you weren't likely to fall onto that naked blade. But it *was* a naked blade, and it did create a constant threat of flying rock chips, pieces of glass, etc.
4. It enveloped you in noise, and in the smudge and stench of exhaust fumes.
5. In rank growth, the blade tended to choke—in which case you had to kill the engine in a hurry or it would twist the drive shaft in two.
6. Like a lot of small gas engines not regularly used, this one was temperamental and undependable. And dependence on an engine that won't run is a plague and a curse.

When I review my own history, I am always amazed at how slow I have been to see the obvious. I don't remember how long I used that "labor-saving" power scythe before I finally donated it to help enlighten one of my friends—but it was too long. Nor do I remember all the stages of my own enlightenment.

The turning point, anyhow, was the day when Harlan Hubbard showed me an old-fashioned, human-powered scythe that was clearly the best that I had ever seen. It was light, comfortable to hold and handle. The blade was very sharp, angled and curved precisely to the path of its stroke. There was an intelligence and refinement in its design that made it a pleasure to handle and look at and think about. I asked where I could get one, and Harlan gave me an address: The Marugg Company, Tracy City, Tennessee 37387.

I wrote for a price list and promptly received a sheet exhibiting the stock in trade of the Marugg Company: grass scythes, bush scythes, snaths, sickles, hoes, stock bells, carrying yokes, whetstones, and the hammers and anvils used in beating out the "dangle" cutting edge that is an essential feature of the grass scythes.

In due time I became the owner of a grass scythe, hammer and anvil, and whetstone. Learning to use the hammer and anvil properly (the Marugg Company provides a sheet of instructions) takes some effort and some considering. And so does learning to use the scythe. It is essential to hold the point so that it won't dig into the ground, for instance; and you must learn to swing so that you slice rather than hack.

Once these fundamentals are mastered, the Marugg grass scythe proves itself an excellent tool. It is the most satisfying hand tool that I have ever used. In tough grass it cuts a little less uniformly than the power scythe. In all other ways, in my opinion it is a better tool:

1. It is light.
2. It handles gracefully and comfortably even on steep ground.
3. It is far less dangerous than the power scythe.
4. It is quiet and makes no fumes.
5. It is much more adaptable to conditions than the power scythe: in ranker growth, narrow the cut and shorten the stroke.
6. It always starts—provided the user will start. Aside from reasonable skill and care in use, there are no maintenance problems.
7. It requires no fuel or oil. It runs on what you ate for breakfast.
8. It is at least as fast as the power scythe. Where the cutting is either light or extra heavy, it can be appreciably faster.
9. It is far cheaper than the power scythe, both to buy and to use.

Since I bought my power scythe, a new version has come on the market, using a short length of nylon string in place of the metal blade. It is undoubtedly safer. But I believe the other drawbacks remain. Though I have not used one of these, I have observed them in use, and they appear to me to be slower than the metal-bladed power scythe, and less effective on large-stemmed plants.

I have noticed two further differences between the power scythe and the Marugg scythe that are not so practical as those listed above, but which I think are just as significant. The first is that I never took the least pleasure in using the power scythe, whereas in using the Marugg scythe, whatever the weather and however difficult the cutting, I always work with the pleasure that one invariably gets from using a good tool. And because it is not motor driven and is quiet and odorless, the Marugg scythe also allows the pleasure of awareness of what is going on around you as you work.

The other difference is between kinds of weariness. Using the Marugg scythe causes the simple bodily weariness that comes with exertion. This is a kind of weariness that, when not extreme, can in itself be one of the pleasures of work. The power scythe, on the other hand, adds to the weariness of exertion the unpleasant and destructive weariness of strain. This is partly because, in addition to carrying and handling it, your attention is necessarily clenched to it; if you are to use it effectively and safely, you *must* not look away. And partly it is because the power scythe, like all motor-driven tools, imposes patterns of endurance that are alien to the body. As long as the motor is running there is a pressure to keep going. You don't stop to consider or rest or look around. You keep on until the motor stops or the job is finished or you have some kind of trouble. (This explains why the tractor soon evolved headlights, and farmers began to do daywork at night.)

These differences have come to have, for me, the force of a parable. Once you have mastered the Marugg scythe, what an absurd thing it makes of the power scythe! What possible sense can there be in carrying a heavy weight on your shoulder in order to reduce by a very little the use of your arms? Or to use quite a lot of money as a substitute for a little skill?

The power scythe—and it is far from being an isolated or unusual example—is *not* a labor saver or a shortcut. It is a labor maker (you have to work to pay for it as well as to use it) and a long cut. Apologists for such expensive technological solutions love to say that "you can't turn back the clock." But when it makes perfect sense to do so—as when the clock is wrong—of *course* you can!

—1981

MARTIN W. LEWIS
B. 1956

Martin W. Lewis is an environmentalist who has startled and offended many other environmentalists by advocating urbanization and advanced technology as essential solutions to contemporary environmental problems. Indeed, in the preface to the paperback edition of his controversial 1992 book, Green Delusions: An Environmentalist Critique of Radical Environmentalism, *he acknowledges that his work is "within the established tradition of pugnacious debate." In the book, Lewis takes issue with what he sees as the radical environmentalist belief that cities and machines tend to dehumanize our species and sunder our relationship with nature. Though he does not dispute the fact that "natural landscapes offer infinite aesthetic and intellectual delights" and that "many of us suffer deeply when we feel cut off from nature," he does seek to illustrate the dangers of "establishing rapport with nature through an immediate physical linkage"—that is, through living close to the land and using natural resources directly to meet subsistence needs.*

Lewis majored in environmental studies at the University of California, Santa Cruz, then went on to complete a Ph.D. in geography at UC Berkeley. He spent 1985-86 as a Fulbright scholar in the Philippines. Since 1988, Lewis has taught at George Washington University, the University of Wisconsin, and Duke University. He and his wife, a scholar of Japanese history and geography, currently live in North Carolina. Spin-offs of Green Delusions, *such as the following essay, have appeared in a number of national periodicals.*

"On Human Connectedness with Nature" was first published in a 1993 issue of the journal New Literary History. *In it, Lewis proposes that we seek to "decouple . . . economic from ecological processes," relying less on natural resources and more on synthetic materials for clothing, communication, and energy. Likewise, he claims that among the other benefits of urbanization, "the more densely crowded human settlement becomes, the more space is made available for other organisms." What follows, then, is an "environmentalist critique" of some of the "delusions" of "radical environmentalism."*

On Human Connectedness with Nature

The central theme of modern environmentalism may be the idea that humanity's separation from nature lies at the root of the ecological crisis. Most self-proclaimed environmental radicals embrace this notion with an almost religious fervor, but even liberal and moderate environmentalists generally concur at some level. Vice President Al Gore, for example, expresses this sentiment cogently in his recent book *Earth in the Balance*:

> Ironically, it is our very separation from the physical world that creates much of this pain, and it is because we are taught to live so separately from nature that we feel so utterly dependent upon our civilization, which has seemingly taken nature's place in meeting all of our needs. Just as the children in a dysfunctional family experience pain when their parents lead them to believe that something important is missing from their psyches, we surely experience a painful loss when we are led to believe that the connection to the natural world . . . is something unnatural, something to be rejected as a rite of passage into the civilized world. As a result, we internalize the pain of our lost sense of connection to the natural world, we consume the earth and its resources as a way to distract ourselves from the pain, and we search insatiably for artificial substitutes to replace the experience of communion with the world that has been taken from us.[1]

The "separation from nature" thesis encompasses linked psychological and economic arguments. The former, clearly evident in Gore's passage, revolve around the idea that human beings become psychologically, if not spiritually, impaired when they are removed from direct, intimate, daily contact with the world of nature. An initial economic linkage is posited in the notion that separation from nature brings addiction to meaningless consumption. Rampant consumerism, in turn, exacerbates the destruction of nature by intensifying resource use and generating pollution—further removing humankind from untarnished natural ecosystems. In the more extreme formulations, human separation from nature is said to be exemplified by the production of substances such as plastics that are not found in the natural world. According to Barry Commoner, the entire petrochemical industry represents an assault on the very fabric of nature and should be dismantled. In its place, he contends, we must substitute an older material infrastructure based on such natural products as paper, wood, and metal.[2]

Different schools of environmentalism have diverse interpretations of the "separation from nature" thesis. They also differ on when the decisive rift between humanity and the natural world actually occurred. The most extreme greens sometimes look to the agricultural revolution of the neolithic period with its invention of the distinctly unnatural process of artificial plant and animal selection; "back to the Pleistocene" is thus one of the favored credos of the Earth First! movement. Others locate the origin of separation in the development of urbanism, or in the promulgation of the Judeo-Christian tradition with its injunction for human beings to multiply and gain dominion over the Earth. More numerous are those who reserve blame for the secular theology of Western rationality, casting René Descartes and Francis Bacon into the roles of the central villains. Those who prefer material to ideological factors, however, most often locate the crucial disjunction at the industrial revolution of the late eighteenth century, or even as late as the development of the modern chemical industry, electrical generation capacity, and internal combustion technology in the late nineteenth and early twentieth centuries. Still others would highlight the post-World War II explosive development of synthetic organic chemicals as well as the creation of nuclear weapons and energy, while looking ahead to biotechnology as the ultimate insult to nature—representing a truly blasphemous usurpation of nature's own reproductive processes.

Regardless of which historical period is emphasized, the broad consensus holds that the human separation from nature is growing more pronounced year by year, leading inexorably to intensified ecological trauma for the planet and psychological degeneration for humanity. Yet the proposed solutions for reconnecting people to nature vary even more significantly from one wing of the environmental movement to another. Many members of the Earth First! fringe call for nothing less than the complete re-immersion of human beings into the intimate settings of natural communities, a move that would require deurbanization, an end to all forms of high technology, and the dissolution of large-scale political and economic organization. Socialist environmentalists, such as Barry Commoner, would require only the dismantling of select modern industries—as well as capitalism—coupled with a substantial lowering of consumer expectations in the United States and other wealthy countries. Most liberal and moderate environmentalists, on the other hand, call simply for an intellectual, aesthetic, or spiritual reconnection with nature; many strongly advocate the continued development of high technologies that the radical greens regard as embodying the destructive rift in the first place. Al Gore, for example, is an enthusiastic proponent of a national information highway based on high-speed computers linked by fiber-optic cables. To a true eco-radical, computerization forces people into a synthetic, artificial environment, thus dehumanizing them while sundering their relationship with the world of nature.

Whatever disparities and contradictions may be encountered at the level of specificities, the general thesis of human separation from nature provides a satisfying *partial* account of both contemporary social malaise and ecological destruction. Distance from nature, which has undoubtedly intensified over the past few centuries, easily leads to an unconscionable denial of the finitude of most natural resources, as well as an inability to grasp the limited capacity of ecosystems to process the waste materials generated by human activities. Moreover, for many if not most human beings, natural landscapes offer infinite aesthetic and intellectual delights. A great many of us suffer deeply when we feel cut off from nature.

But while the notion that humanity ought to seek a deeper connection to the natural world is undoubtedly a powerful thesis, we would be well-advised to examine carefully the concomitant ideas that are so often attached to it. In my view, the liberal/moderate view expressed by Vice President Gore has much to recommend it, but the radical extension, based on the conviction that we must reorient our entire economic base toward "natural" rather than artificial products, simply does not hold up to scrutiny. In fact, when one considers concrete issues regarding the provisioning of our basic material needs, the separation of the human economy from natural systems turns out to offer profound environmental benefits, while the continued immersion of our apparatus of production into the intricate webs of nature is itself highly threatening to the natural world of nonhuman species.

The notion that separating humans more fully from nature could yield distinct ecological benefits is considered by the more ardent environmental radicals to be nothing less than heresy. This view has been amply confirmed by several reviews of my recent work *Green Delusions: An Environmentalist Critique of Radical Environmentalism*.[3] In this book I deliberately took a confrontational pose, hoping to stir up controversy and force the environmental movement to reconsider certain ideas that have heretofore been regarded as unquestionable postulates. I naturally expected negative reactions, but what has surprised me is how fundamentally the thesis of economic disengagement, or decoupling, from the natural world has been misinterpreted. Many readers seem to interpret the text as asserting that nature presents no limits to human endeavors, that human beings need not receive any sustenance, material or intellectual, from nature, and that ultimately human society would be better off if we were fully ignorant of natural processes. As David Rothenberg writes in an otherwise balanced commentary published in *Environmental History Review*: "[Lewis's] vision of humanity decoupled from nature will forget the value of the forces and context that have made us possible on this earth. . . . Love of nature is inspired by a sense of wonder before it turns into naive political points of view. And no argument from the extremes of insensitivity disguised as moderation can hope to change this."[4]

No writer can control interpretations of his or her work. Yet one can restate and reformulate one's ideas in order to reduce the chances that they will be interpreted in a spirit contrary to one's original intentions. I will therefore take this opportunity to reiterate more carefully my thesis regarding the desirability of the further removal of certain human activities from the realm of nature.

First, I by no means wish to imply that people should disdain aesthetic, intellectual, or spiritual connections with nature. Connectedness to the natural world in this sense is in general highly beneficial, especially because it tends to instill a love of nature that engenders political support for environmental protection. Yet we must recognize that establishing rapport with nature through an immediate physical connection does take a certain toll. If, for example, the majority of Americans were to decide that they needed to spend a month every year in a wilderness area in order to commune with nature, the immediate result would be the extinction of almost all true wilderness in this country. To use a common cliché, we must take care not to "love nature to death." Certain forms of technologically mediated interactions with nature can offer a relatively less harmful way of establishing connection, however sullied it may seem to purists. Televised nature shows, for example, teach millions a watered-down, but still educational, ecology; more importantly, they proselytize effectively for nature preservation. Such benefits are gained, moreover, without requiring those millions of viewers to trample about in, and thus disturb, the sensitive natural habitats being viewed. Indeed, PBS documentaries—which rely for their production on innumerable synthetic ("unnatural") products—may well be the most powerful force for environmental preservation in the United States today.

Nor does advocating a decoupling of economic from ecological processes necessarily imply a view of economic activities as unconstrained by the limitations of the natural world. It is my strong conviction that human population growth in particular must be contained and ought to be reversed; global primary productivity (of biomass) is essentially fixed, and human beings already consume far too much of it—simply by eating—than is conscionable. In a great many other contemporary human endeavors, limits are also clearly visible. As the environmental sciences demonstrate, the earth has only so much coal and oil, and fossil-fuel exploitation will eventually mine these stores to exhaustion. Moreover, burning the remaining reserves is likely to undermine our economy more quickly by creating substantial, and largely detrimental, climatic changes. In light of the natural limits on non-renewable energy sources, I certainly advocate a wholesale transformation to a solar-based system. Yet I also contend that generating electricity through photo-voltaic solar panels—a procedure that relies on technologically hypersophisticated manipulations of nature in order to create materials never before seen in the natural world—is an activity far *less* directly connected to the processes of nature than is burning coal, a "natural" product produced by natural forces.

There are many other ways in which substituting synthetic products for natural materials, or effectively decoupling our productive apparatus from ecosystemic processes, can benefit nature. This is especially true in those instances in which the "natural" products endorsed by radical environmentalists are derived directly from living organisms. When biological entities and substances ("renewable resources") are extracted from nature, both matter and energy are channeled away from existing pathways into those of the human community. Nature is necessarily reduced in the process. In the creation of many synthetic materials, on the other hand, inert substances can be extracted from geological formations with relatively little impact on biological systems. While the production of synthetics does entail the generation of toxic wastes and other pollutants, there is no *intrinsic* reason why these cannot be reduced to their harmless, and fully "natural" constituents; with the use of natural organic products, on the other hand, large areas of land by *necessity* must be removed from the realm of biological diversity and instead be dedicated to serving the human community.

The potential advantages of synthetic over natural products are especially clear in the case of textiles. Owing to the popular acceptance of the insufficiently analyzed "separation from nature" theme, "polyester" has come to be a virtual icon for all that is artificial and thereby demeaning to humanity and destructive of nature, whereas cotton is emblematic of all that is natural and wholesome. Yet cotton is remarkably environmentally destructive. First, huge expanses of land must be devoted to cotton production—land that could otherwise support diverse natural communities. Cotton also requires irrigation (when raised, as it often is, in arid areas), diverting precious water from precarious dry-land ecosystems. Perhaps most importantly, cotton is among the most pesticide-demanding of all crops. To supply the world's growing demand for this "natural" fiber, tropical forests are being cleared in Central America, the Aral Sea in Central Asia is being reduced to a salt-encrusted wasteland, the Sudd marshland of southern Sudan is threatened with drainage, and the Ogallala aquifer of the central United States is being steadily sucked dry. Cotton clothes even demand extra energy consumption after they have been purchased, since they usually have to be ironed—unlike many synthetic alternatives.

Synthetic fibers, it must be admitted, require substantial energy to be produced, and they yield noxious by-products in the process. More importantly from the consumers' point of view, they do not feel as good, and may not wear as well, as cotton and other natural textiles. But in the course of both technological and regulatory progress we can expect such problems gradually to abate. Toxic waste decomposition in particular has seen tremendous advances over the past decade. Synthetic fibers also require natural feedstocks, such as petrochemicals, which are necessarily limited in quantity. Yet if we would cease the ecologically insane practice of burning oil and instead dedicate the remaining supplies to the synthetic-organic chemical industry, the remaining reserves would be sufficient for centuries if not millennia. But the principal environmental benefit of synthetic fibers lies in the simple fact that their production requires very little land. A decreased demand for cotton could allow us to "liberate" millions of acres of ecologically barren cotton fields, returning these lands to biologically diverse natural communities.

A number of prominent environmentalists have recognized the destructiveness of cotton for some time. One of my own most virulent critics also concurred on this point, but then suggested that salvation could be achieved if only we would abandon cotton for hempen clothing. Since hemp is more productive than cotton and far more resistant to diseases and insects, a hemp-based textile industry would require less land and fewer biocides. But while hemp may be an environmentally superior source of natural fibers, it by no means presents a panacea. Significant acreage would still have to be devoted to hemp culture rather than to the maintenance of biodiversity. Hemp stems must also be retted to release the fibers, a process that generates a considerable biochemical oxygen demand, and could thus intensify our water pollution problem. Moreover, the main reason people stopped wearing clothing made of hemp generations ago in both Europe and East Asia is because it is highly uncomfortable—not because the plant was declared illegal by drug-enforcement agencies.

The environmental problems associated with "natural" textiles extend beyond the fibers themselves to the dye-stuffs used to color them. In the days of natural dyes, large areas of land had to be monopolized by their production. In India alone, 1,750,000 acres were devoted just to indigo as recently as 1897.[5] If the entire world were to return to such natural color-agents today, an even larger area would have to be given over to the cultivation of indigo and other domesticated plants. From where would this land come? Would Indian wheat and rice fields be transformed into indigo plantations, thereby threatening the country's food balance? Or would more of the subcontinent's few remaining natural areas be cleared away for this wonderfully natural crop?

The antipathy to synthetic fibers and the glorification of natural ones has been reinforced by an American cotton industry only too happy to gear its advertising campaigns to such sentiments. Cotton propagandists have an extra advantage, however, in the seldom-mentioned class distinctions coded by textile-wearing habits. In the contemporary United States, natural fibers signify affluence, education, and "good taste," whereas synthetic fibers supposedly signify a working-class absence of these characteristics; primarily for this reason polyester has become the butt of many a comedian's cheap jibes. The result is that an attitude of environmental "correctness" may be mapped subconsciously onto one of class contempt, allowing an otherwise progressive individual to feel righteous in what is partly an expression of class bigotry.

In the realm of communication no less than that of textiles, the advantages of decoupling production and distribution systems from ecosystemic processes are clearly evident. Although utter eco-extremists envision a utopia of small-scale, self-sufficient communities in which virtually all communication is by word-of-mouth, most radical environmentalists remain committed to a broader communication system based on "natural" paper (unbleached and recycled, of course). But while paper recycling and the avoidance of bleaching are surely environmentally beneficial, one must wonder whether this goes far enough. Since fibers break down in the process, paper recycling cannot be conducted in an endless loop; new wood (or some other biological substitute) must always be introduced. For this, large areas of forest land must be devoted to pulp production. Forestry need not be as ecologically devastating as it usually is today, but the continued removal of massive quantities of wood *necessarily* detracts from natural ecosystems. In part this is simply a matter of subtracting nutrients from the forest system as well as steadily reducing the organic constituent of forest soils. One must also consider the pulping process and the manufacturing of paper, which are themselves horrifically polluting—even in the absence of dioxin-producing bleaching. Nor is ink, natural or otherwise, without its environmental detractions. But perhaps most importantly, a paper-based mass communication system must rely on the physical transportation of bulky objects, which is by necessity energy intensive, and therefore polluting. Fleets of airplanes, trucks, and automobiles—or some other energy-demanding forms of conveyance—must be devoted to moving books, newspapers, magazines, and letters from place to place.

Now consider the environmental effects of a decoupled, high-technology, "unnatural" system of communication based on interconnected computer networks, one in which text is converted to digital code and transferred, by telephone lines or over the air, from terminal to terminal. Here no trees need be sacrificed at all, and huge areas of land now devoted to biologically impoverished pulp plantations could be returned to natural habitat. True, silicon (and a few other inert materials) must be obtained in environmentally disruptive operations, but the overall environmental impact remains minimal when compared to that of pulp-extraction. Similarly, some pollution is generated in the manufacture of computers and communications equipment, but not to the same extent as in paper production. Most importantly, the electronic dissemination of information uses very little energy compared to that entailed by the physical delivery of printed paper. Because of these environmental advantages, I look forward to the day when I can retrieve the morning newspaper simply by flipping on my computer switch and clicking a news-deliverer icon.

Environmental radicals often object to my endorsement of computerized communication by citing statistics indicating that paper use tends to increase with computerization. This point deserves careful consideration. Yet I would argue that the problem largely reflects the difficulties of transition that are encountered whenever a new, superior technology replaces an old, inferior one. Unaccustomed to the electronic and magnetic portrayal and storage of information, and continuing to seek the security of the actual feel of paper, many office managers have simply grafted new systems onto old, duplicating many of their efforts. Similarly, individual writers sometimes have difficulty learning to edit on the computer screen, and print out repeated drafts of their texts. Such obstinacy however, is ultimately as wasteful of time as it is of energy and resources. Gradually, corporate and government bureaucracies are discovering that the continued reliance on paper represents a massive inefficiency that is simply too expensive to persist.[6] The "paperless office" may have been a disappointment in that it did not arrive as quickly as predicted, but much evidence suggests that it is indeed on its way. By denouncing computer technology because of the difficulties encountered in the transition period of the 1980s and 1990s, eco-radicals evince the same kind of short-term thinking that they so quickly (and appropriately) denounce when encountered in corporate and governmental planning. Of course, even in the absence of such considerations many eco-radicals would continue to revile computers simply because they create an "artificial environment" wholly removed from the natural world. Against such sentiments, reasoned arguments are of little avail.

Most environmental radicals believe that healing the rift between humanity and nature will require not only extensive readjustments in *how* we live but also in *where* we live. Specifically, they argue that cities, or at least major metropolitan centers, are unfit sites for human habitation. In urban areas the effluents of human life and livelihood are far too concentrated, and thus tend to overwhelm the absorptive capacities of local ecological systems. As Kirkpatrick Sale argues, the "contemporary high-rise city" is an "ecological parasite [that] extracts its lifeblood from elsewhere and an ecological pathogen [that] sends back its wastes."[7] Beyond their concern for the local environment, eco-radicals also denounce cities for their assault on the human spirit. Cut off from nature's own healing powers, city-dwellers are subject to a host of specifically urban maladies, both physical and psychological. As a result they become profoundly alienated from both their fellow human and their fellow nonhuman beings. In essence, the eco-radical critique holds that the entirely human and all-too-artificial environment of the city is itself dehumanizing. To be whole, people must live in relatively small communities that are locationally as well as economically enmeshed within unblemished natural systems.

If anything, the anti-urban thesis of eco-radicalism receives even less support from the available evidence than do the arguments against either computerized communication or synthetic fibers. In a great many respects, urban living puts far less strain on the environment than does rural existence. In simple terms, the more densely crowded human settlement becomes, the more space is made available for other organisms. When people flee urban areas to seek refuge in the countryside, rural population densities necessarily increase, which, all other things being equal, reduces and impoverishes remaining wildlife habitat, especially that required for large and mobile species. City life in the United States also requires much less energy per capita than does rural life, mainly because public transportation is efficiently conducted only in densely populated areas, whereas in regions of dispersed settlement long journeys are required simply to procure basic goods and services. Indeed, as most of us recognize, one of the main reasons Japan and most Western European countries are so much more energy efficient than the United States and Canada is because they are characterized by a much more intensively urban style of life. Intriguingly, Japan—a country not noted for its wildlife preservation ethic—maintains adequate habitat for the brown or "grizzly" bear; California on the other hand, a state of roughly the same area yet containing only about one quarter the population of Japan, is considered too crowded to support such a wilderness species—even though it is the official state symbol. If the Japanese were to adopt en masse the anti-urban proclivities of American suburbanites, let alone eco-radicals, their country would very quickly become too crowded to support any large wildlife species.

The thesis that large cities create distinctively urban pathologies also fails as soon as one extends one's view beyond the United States. European, Japanese, and Canadian cities are not particularly violent or "asocial" places; large Japanese cities are actually much safer than most small American towns. It is also important to recognize that even those peoples who have lived most fully within the fold of nature often exhibit the same kinds of pathologies now usually identified with an urban existence. Overturning long-held romantic mythologies, recent research shows that many hunter-gather and "tribal" agricultural communities have rates of murder, rape, and other violent crimes similar to those of modern, urban, industrial societies.[8]

The ultimate paradox confronting the anti-urban implications of the eco-radical "separation from nature" thesis is encountered when one examines voting behavior. In the United States the pattern is undeniable: urban voters are far more inclined to vote for environmental protection than are rural voters. In California, for instance, there is a profound correlation between support of environmental protection initiatives and population density aggregated at the county level. The most densely populated counties, in other words, are the "greenest," while the most sparsely populated counties are the "brownest." Contrary to eco-radical expectations, living in the midst of nature does not necessarily make people appreciate it, while being largely disconnected from nature on a daily basis actually seems to make many individuals more concerned about its preservation, and willing to act on those beliefs.

The notion that humanity must reconnect with the fabric of nature in order to find a healthy and harmonious existence is by no means unique to the modern environmental movement. The sentiment is probably as old as civilization itself, as is the longing for a primordial age in which all "modern" cares and evils were absent. Indeed, many of the central tenets of modern eco-radicalism can be found in strikingly similar form in the writings of the stoic philosophers of ancient Greece and Rome. As Clarence Glacken notes, "Seneca's eloquent praise of the wise men who had nothing to do with the inventions, improvements, and gadgets of the day describes vividly in sharp and indignant words the evils of civilization too dependent on its machines, its labor saving devices, and its creature comforts." A less-famous Latin author, Dicaearchus, took an even more radical stance, arguing "that men originally lived in a state of nature, using the products that the earth voluntarily afforded. For them it was a happy state, a golden age."[9]

Again and again, the rustic idyll has reappeared. In the United States, the turn of the century marked an especially strong period of Arcadian recrudescence. As Peter Schmitt explains, "psychologists, sociologists, and educators" of the period "developed insights into urban behavior that suggested society could not survive without nature."[10] Yet the preferred method of reconnecting humanity to nature at the time was nothing less than the development of the commuter suburb—the garden community where the close presence of nature would supposedly foster the growth of serene human spirits. The suburbs, however, have failed rather dismally at this (de)civilizing mission, and many environmentalists recognize the modern urban fringe as the worst of all possible worlds; here human habitation is too sparse to support energy-efficient lifestyles, yet too dense to allow the existence of all but the most adaptable species of wildlife. In all likelihood, the even more radical retreat to nature envisaged by the more extreme eco-prophets of today would, if ever enacted, have similar if not more damaging effects on the global ecosystem.

A tremendous amount of evidence suggests that a material recoupling of human economies and lifeways more deeply into the circuits of nature—unless, of course, the human population were first reduced to a small fraction of its current level—

would result only in accelerated environmental destruction. Yet all such evidence is likely to be ignored, if not bitterly denounced, by the most committed eco-radicals, who uncompromisingly view the world as locked in a Manichaean struggle between the good forces of nature and the evil forces of technology and civilization. Even if it could be demonstrated beyond a doubt that a given synthetic material causes less harm to nature than a "natural" substitute, many would still passionately insist upon the superiority of the latter. In the irony of ironies, the ultimate concern of many eco-radicals, like those of their forebears dating all the way to Seneca and beyond, turns out to be not so much with the health of nature, but rather with the salvation of a human spirit that has supposedly been corrupted by civilization. Extremist antihumanism can thus actually return, by a circuitous route, to a position of anthropocentrism.

−1993

Notes

1. Al Gore, *Earth in the Balance: Ecology and the Human Spirit* (New York, 1992), p. 231.
2. See Barry Commoner, *Making Peace with the Planet* (New York, 1990), p. 53.
3. See Martin W. Lewis, *Green Delusions: An Environmentalist Critique of Radical Environmentalism* (Durham, N.C., 1992).
4. David Rothenberg, Review of *Green Delusions: An Environmentalist Critique of Radical Environmentalism*, in *Environmental History Review*, 17 (1993), 87–88.
5. "Indigo," *Encyclopedia Britannica*, 1963 ed., XII, 256.
6. See William Symonds, "Getting Rid of Paper Is Just the Beginning," *Business Week*, 22 Dec 1992, p. 88. See also Richard Brandt, "Does Adobe Have a Paper Cutter?" *Business Week*, 16 Nov 1992, p. 83.
7. Kirkpatrick Sale, *Dwellers in the Land: The Bioregional Vision* (San Francisco, 1985), p. 65.
8. See Robert B. Edgerton, *Sick Societies: Challenging the Myth of Primitive Harmony* (New York, 1992).
9. Clarence J. Glacken, *Traces on the Rhodian Shore* (Berkeley, 1967), pp. 118 and 140.
10. Peter J. Schmitt, *Back to Nature: The Arcadian Myth in Urban America* (Baltimore, 1990), p. xxi.

What does our use of land say about who we are and what we value and believe?

LAND USE

MARGE PIERCY

B. 1936

In numerous volumes of poetry and novels, Marge Piercy confronts the important social issues of our time, exposing sexual, economic, racial, and political injustices and expressing a fierce loyalty to the earth. While Piercy's novels, such as Small Changes *(1973),* Fly Away Home *(1984), and* Gone to Soldiers *(1987), have sometimes been criticized for sacrificing literary integrity to political convictions, most critics agree she is an important and gifted writer. The anger and intensity characteristic of her novels shows up in some of her poetry as well, but many poems in collections such as* The Moon Is Always Female *(1980) and* Stone, Paper, Knife *(1983) are grounded in a deep honoring of the earth's fecundity and celebrate nature's simple pleasures.*

Born to working-class parents in Detroit during the Depression, Piercy developed a political consciousness at an early age and was taught to love natural beauty by her mother, who always kept a garden. The first member of her family to go to college, Piercy earned a B.A. from the University of Michigan in 1957 and an M.A. from Northwestern University in 1958. Inspired by the poetry of Allen Ginsberg, she began publishing poems in the 1960s during her involvement with the antiwar and civil rights movements as a member of Students for a Democratic Society (SDS). The misogyny of other activists led her to become involved with the growing women's movement, and feminist themes began to appear in her work along with ecological themes. Her novels are characteristically peopled by memorable heroines. Woman on the Edge of Time *(1976), a personal favorite of Piercy's, features an impoverished Chicana as its protagonist; this utopian novel presents a model of a culture attuned to nature, which is also necessarily a deeply egalitarian culture.*

Piercy has lived since 1971 in Wellfleet, Massachusetts, and images of the Cape Cod environment permeate her nature poetry. Since 1982 she has shared a house with her husband, the writer Ira Wood; "The Development" is from an earlier period and is part of a longer poem series entitled "Sand Roads," first published in Living in the Open *(1976). While Piercy clearly detests what the developers are doing to the land around the "box half buried in the sand" where she lives in a communal household, and while she and her housemates compost, plant trees, and plant berries for the birds, she also acknowledges that by living in their habitat she is stealing the home of the grey foxes whose new den she discovers. Thus issues of land use are often more complicated than they initially appear.*

SAND ROADS: THE DEVELOPMENT

The bulldozers come, they rip
a hole in the sand along
the new blacktop road with a tony name
(Trotting Park, Pamet Hills)
and up goes another glass-walled-
split-level-livingroom-vast-as-a-
roller-rink-$100,000
summer home for a psychiatrist
and family.

Nine months vacation homes
stand empty except for mice
and spiders, an occasional
bird with a broken back twitching
on the deck under a gape of glass.

I live in such a development
way at the end of a winding
road where the marsh begins
to close in: two houses,
the one next door a local
fisherman lost to the bank
last winter, ours a box
half buried in the sand.
This land is rendered
too expensive
to live on. We feed
four people off it,
a kind of organic tall corn
ornery joke at road's end.
We planted for the birds cover
and berries, we compost, we set out
trees and at night

the raccoons come shambling.
Yes, the foxes left us,
shrinking into the marsh.
I found their new den.
I don't show it
to anyone.
Forgive us, grey fox, our stealing
your home, our loving
this land carved into lots
over a shrinking watertable
where the long sea wind that blows
the sand whispers to developers
money, money, money.

                                              —1976

LOUISE ERDRICH

B. 1954

"My characters choose me and once they do it's like standing in a field and hearing echoes. . . . All I can do is trace their passage," Louise Erdrich has said. In the tetralogy consisting of Love Medicine (1984), The Beet Queen (1986), Tracks (1988), and The Bingo Palace (1994), Erdrich has created a mythical world centered around four generations of Chippewa Indians in North Dakota. The series of novels evokes, as one critic has written, "a culture in severe social ruin, yet still aglow with the privilege and power of access to the spirit-world." Erdrich started out as a poet (she has written two well-received books of poetry and was one of only three poets under the age of thirty-five included in the Norton Anthology of Poetry) and then expanded into short stories and only later into novels at the suggestion of her husband and close collaborator, the writer Michael Dorris. Virtually every work the two published, separately and as coauthors, bears the imprint of both, and in fact they wrote some stories together under the pen name of Milou North.

Born in Little Falls, Minnesota, Erdrich is the oldest of seven children of a father of German descent and a Chippewa mother. She grew up in the small town of Wahpeton, North Dakota, where her parents worked for the Bureau of Indian Affairs boarding school that Erdrich herself attended. A cheerleader for the wrestling team in high school, she didn't think much about her Native American heritage until she enrolled at Dartmouth College in 1972 as part of its first coeducational class. Michael Dorris was hired that same year to teach anthropology and chair the Native American Studies department, and taking one of his classes during her junior year made a lasting impression on Erdrich. After graduating in 1976, she returned to North Dakota as a "poet in the schools." In 1979 she received an M.A. in creative writing from Johns Hopkins University and went back to Dartmouth as writer-in-residence. She and Dorris were married in 1981. The couple had six children—three daughters of their own and a girl and *two boys originally adopted by Dorris as a single parent. Dorris died in 1997.*

Erdrich's short story "Line of Credit," which appeared in Harper's *magazine (April 1992), takes us inside the mind of a North Dakota land developer and shows us what motivates him. Where the farmer in the story sees good fields with rich dirt, the developer sees "the first open land past the last mall." How many of us in America in the 1990s haven't seen open land turned into housing developments and shopping centers? This type of "progress" is so ubiquitous as to seem inevitable, but Erdrich paints an unflattering picture of the psyche that drives it and the culture that supports it. "Although fiction alone may lack the power to head us off the course of destruction, it affects us as individuals and can spur us to treat the earth, in which we abide and which harbors us, as we would treat our own mothers and fathers," she wrote in an essay entitled "Where I Ought to Be: A Writer's Sense of Place" in the* New York Times Book Review *(July 28, 1985).*

LINE OF CREDIT

It is true that I got crazy the week I drew the first payment on my line of credit, but after all, the amount was large. I accepted the bank check, stiff and clean in its plain white envelope, and instead of depositing it immediately put it to my face, smelled the clean rasp of paper, ink. Then I walked out the door and went to my car. I placed the money on the dashboard, where it could tell me all about itself. God knows, I wanted so bad to hear. A long time back, when land was cheap, I'd bought a quarter section just west of Fargo. I'd leased it to a guy named Moen, who put all that acreage into flowers. Sunflowers. Now they were in bloom. It was August, not the dog days of heat but clear and cool. I drove out to the future site with my check reflected in the windshield. My belief was this: I was the luckiest of lucky sons of bitches. I had formed this idea, this plan, it was going to work, and I was going to put it into operation.

I am Mauser & Mauser, Construction. There is no other Mauser, no partner, just myself. I doubled my name because I thought it looked more stable, as though there were generations involved, although I had built up the cash, crews, and equipment by myself over the years. I had made my own success from nothing, from a secondhand Cat bulldozer and a couple of boys who couldn't get their high school diplomas. I had patched together my own company by scraping money off the cash edifice, the limestone facades of banks. I walked through doors of black glass, through the tinted lobbies, over wheat-rich carpet, over sugar-beet wealth and desks of polished oak bought off the interest on loans to sunflower farmers like Moen. I went in with the grit of digging septic systems under my nails and I came out, time after time, with that dirt turned miraculously to paper, crisp and green. Those were the ground-floor days when the local boom was just beginning, way back when there was interstate to build and local crews got hired on by the government. I didn't bid too high and didn't bid too low, and I held where proper, a knack I'd learned at the keno tables. It worked beautifully.

And now I had this. More zeros in a string than I'd ever seen.

I turned down a dirt road between two of my fields, parked, opened my windows, and let the day in, the day of perfect sunflowers. Their leaves brushed in the still air, dollar bills in a vault of blue sky. Their fat, chock-full faces, surrounded by petals, reminded me of legions of rich women in fancy hats.

I laughed and sank back in the warm seat, let the sun shine hard. Cannons popped, set to go off on small timers so the blackbirds wouldn't land. Moen had tied balloons to his fences too, and painted them with eyes to look like owls. The fields looked jolly, circus bright, and of course the blackbirds weren't the least afraid. You could hear them pecking, flapping, talking, feeding noisily and full of joy.

Moen happened by, stopped his truck. I stepped out into the field and both of us stood there awhile, looking at the crop. I told him my first draw had come through, showed him the check even. He did not look pleased, he did not in fact look at me at all. I hadn't thought exactly what my good fortune meant for Bill Moen, but the truth is he only had those fields on a lease which was up four months ago. He knew what was coming. Naturally, I intended to let him work the fields until I broke ground next month. He had to get his yield in, of course. But those fields were the first open land past the last mall, between the DollarSave and Nowhere. Any fool could have figured.

He looked at me sour, scratched his chin. He had a bad shave, all nicked.

"You're putting in what, a new development?" he asked.

I nodded. He nodded. We stood there nodding at the nodding heads of sunflowers. We stood there in a vast field of serene and unthinking agreement, but we were thinking different things. Moen said: "These are good fields. Rich dirt. Too bad."

I didn't want Moen raining on my party.

"Too bad what?" I said. "You'll get a lot of money from this crop, it's a bumper. You'll buy a big damn house right at the end of this cul-de-sac." I stamped my foot on the ground. "We'll build it here. Every one of your kids will have their own room. Your wife will have a dream kitchen."

"I don't have a wife," said Moen.

"Your kids will cook then," I said. I knew he had kids. "We'll make everything the right height, their bathrooms, the dish sink, whatever, so they won't have to always stand on stools."

"Kids grow," Moen said.

"Bless 'em," I agreed, but there must have been a note in my voice, maybe a little edge. Moen was getting on my nerves.

We stood in silence and then Moen said, real loud: "The more you fill it up the emptier it gets."

I couldn't believe my ears.

"People have to live somewhere," I said, and my voice was mild enough, but inside I was boiling. I was mad. My wife, Ira, had told me a trick to try and keep my temper when I was in that no-man's-land between feeling normal and letting go. She said to just put a cage up, a wire cage, to visualize the chain-link and stay inside the damn thing like an animal. She told me that I could pace inside the cage, I could go wild, I could let off my steam like I had just been captured in a jungle. The only thing was, I had to stay in the cage, not jump the fence, not ever let myself out until I knew I was good and ready.

I was not ready. I got into my car, backed out, and drove away without saying good-bye to Moen. I wanted to celebrate, to raise the roof, not deal with his problems, his mistakes. He probably needed those fields to get himself over the edge, he probably felt like shit when he thought of a new house that he never could afford in this life anyway, in this world, and I'd pushed it in his face. I didn't look back. I drove to town and wished I could get Ira and go to this bar I liked called The Library, but she was in a real library. She was back in school getting her psychology degree, after which I told her I sure hoped she would know what to do with me.

I passed the bar. I doubled back, drove right up. I pulled into the lot, went in and sat down. It was quiet, no music, no noise. It was only eleven o'clock and there was nothing happening.

I had two beers. A hamburger. Two more beers. I didn't know what to do—go back to the office or the current work site or what. There was plenty to do, but I felt like that day should be experienced different, out of time, out of my regular life. Because of all the hard work I'd done and the work that was in store, I should enjoy the zeros on the check I held right in my inside pocket. I should go to the lakes, fish, I should eat out, enjoy the cash, the fat roll I'd taken out of my account against the big deposit I would feed it later on. I should, I should. I have never been good about that word. You can't love who you should love, you can't stop loving who you shouldn't. My problem was always with how I should be versus how I really was.

"I should go back to work," I said, and instead I ordered my fifth beer.

That one's always the one that gets me. I weigh 220. I can handle four and then I skate in the sky. I promised, as I poured the Blue Ribbon, that this was my last little gesture.

I took a sip, a slow one, looked at the door as it opened, and kept on staring as this woman walked in. She was wearing a black shirt with the sleeves sliced off. Her arms were round and smooth, full of silver bracelets set with cool stones, turquoise, agates. She was tall, had a snub nose and a round, full mouth. She didn't take off her sunglasses, though the room was dark. Maybe it was so she could look older than she was.

"Baby, I've been waiting for you," I said loud enough so she could have heard if she wanted to, but I was only kidding. I didn't think she'd take me up on the line or take me serious at all. She turned and did that thing some women do, cocked her hip and looked. Just looked. What she did then was nothing, but it said too much. She began to take off her sunglasses. She shifted them down her nose, real slow, but put them back up before I could see her eyes. Her legs were long, a little full in the hips. She had this big blond hairdo that would smell of chemicals or bubble gum. It curled, stood out in a bush, as though just chopped into this shape with a hatchet or messed up in the backseat of a car.

She sat down and when she did take her glasses off I drank her in. She had the sweet trustworthy face of a baby-sitter, the morals of a ferret. I could see it in her eyes.

"Skipping school?" I asked.

She shrugged. "I'm not in school. I'm twenty-one."

"What do you do," I said, "for work?"

"I'm between jobs," she smiled.

That smile just tore right through me, like I'd been looking for it all my life. In Ira's eyes I had been seeing a reflection of Ira, not of myself. Marlis, that's what her name was, looked at me a different way. I was sure that she saw who I was, a man stuck down at the bottom of a well, a drainage ditch, always looking out from the pit of himself like a man in a grave. Marlis saw me down there but she didn't stay up in the blue sky where it was safe. She climbed right down to be with me, and suddenly I was not shit-faced lonely. I had company. There were two of us getting drunk at noon now. Two. There were two of us to look at the row of zeros. Two of us all day. There would be two of us to go to bed. The room felt warm and close. Marlis looked older, suddenly, yet full of high school charm. I thought her breasts would be heavy, light, delicate, big, I couldn't think. I could feel them in my hands as I sat there looking at her.

"What do you want?" she said, smiling that same smile, but I didn't say what my hands wanted. I said a different thing.

"Another beer," I said.

"You got it."

She went over to the bar and bought and paid for one and carried it over by herself.

"Now you're going to have to buy me one," she said. "Fair is fair."

So we sat there for a while, talking, and the thing is, I stopped thinking of her that way. I mean the way I thought of her at first. This thing happened that I was not sure I wanted to happen. I started thinking of her as someone too young, and looking at her made me sad, reminded me of the fact that I was forty-eight and I missed my stepdaughter.

"What do you really want?" she asked me, a little later, grinning as she said it.

I didn't answer her awhile. I just stared at her, and I guess my face was full of conflict, was not exactly the face of a man about to have a good time.

She leaned over, grabbed my chin in her hand.

"What the fuck, you're here, aren't you?"

"Yeah," I laughed at myself, "I was going to say something strange. You want to hear it anyway? At first, I was going to say that I want you. The thing I want, though, is I want to be real."

"Real rich. What you want is to be real rich," she said. "I know you better than you know yourself. You think if you're rich you're more real. My dad was rich."

"I'm rich, too."

"I'm poor," she said. "My dad kicked me out." She touched the tip of my collar. "Maybe we need each other."

We started laughing, and the hell of it was that we couldn't stop. We just kept on laughing and laughing until we were asked to leave. And I knew the bartender.

"Please," I said, "just let me get my shit together."

"Someplace else," he said, not unkind.

We did go elsewhere. We went down the street, and I stopped drinking as the day wore on. Then started again. I called Ira, left a message on our answering machine, and kept on walking. We started near the bridge and in the warmth of August and the length of light we made every bar in Moorhead once and ended up at The Treetop, where they have a piano player sitting at a grand piano. Roses in small vases on the tables. Big menus with gold tassels.

"Good evening, Mr. Mauser," said our host.

I put my fingers up. "For two."

I could tell by the way he looked at us that he hoped that Marlis was my kid, my niece, something like that. She had started looking even younger than twenty, but somehow she never got carded. The maître d' found us a table by the window where we could look out over the city and see the lights come up softly in the dusk. All day I had been asking Marlis about herself, but not until we were sitting up on top of the twin towns looking down at the river and the Hjemkomst Center did she tell me the details.

"Fresh out of Catholic school," she said. "I went to St. Bennie's for a year."

"Sure you did."

"No shit!"

She laughed a little, and then her mouth sagged down on one side, as I was watching, and it was not as though she'd made a face or was constructing any kind of expression at all. It was involuntary, like a mental patient. It was something that she couldn't help, and she kept doing it. She did it again.

"You're making a face," I told her. "Are you okay?"

She slapped her hand onto the place her mouth fell and kept it there, as though she wore a mask and it was slipping off. I had a straight shot and then I don't remember what we ordered, what I ate. I don't remember anything until I found us both way down the end of Main at last in a motel called The Sunset. I was standing at a pop machine, and it was dark. I fumbled change from my pocket and I bought an orange soda, drank it standing in the cold light. When I had drunk the can dry I took out my pocketknife and I enlarged the pull-top hole until it was big enough for me to stuff in my car keys and what remained of my wad of bills. As for the check, I wrapped that in a piece of plastic from the garbage and put it under a rock in the landscaping.

"Marlis," I said as I walked in the door. "You have to take me as I am. I'm poor. My hands are empty, see?"

She turned to me in the light of the bathroom fixtures. Her shirt was off. Her breasts were different than I'd imagined, narrower, sleek.

"Your hands aren't empty, Jack," she said when I touched her.

You might think this was something cheap, that it was ridiculous, that because we met each other in a bar and there was this age difference, nothing good could come of it. True, but what I knew about Marlis at the time was that she'd go to the bottom with me. And she'd stay there, not drowning, just floating amiably, not bored, like a fish in a tank. Ira was strictly dry. She was that hot summer wind that sucks every drop of juice from the air. She was sane, she was kind, and I hardly ever drank around her. Sure, I loved her, and she knew it. Ira also knew that every so often I would just let go and throw myself to the winds of chance, of fate. She could count on two things only: I would come home when I was sober. I would use a Sheik.

This was different, not more threatening to Ira, just different. The minute I touched Marlis I knew it wasn't right. I was in a little moment of sobriety, the kind of clarity that is a smashed-out window in the long hall you're stumbling down. I held her against me as we lay in this rotten bed. Even half passed out, I could tell how uncomfortable it was.

"Look," I said, "this makes no sense."

"I know."

She lowered herself onto me and then—it is unclear how it started—we were making love. She was moving on top of me, the whole bed shaking on its flimsy metal rig, the nonacoustic ceiling magnifying the sound of our breathing until I was sure everybody on the east side of Moorhead could hear it. I was conscious of everything around me, which is usually not the case. I couldn't forget where I was or who I was or that this girl might be a runaway. I put my hands on her hips and it was a kind gesture, not a sexual one. I was just trying to help her keep her balance. I was just trying not to completely embarrass myself.

She began to move faster, faster, until it felt like we were taking off. I had this strange thought I'd never had before, that only women are supposed to have. I'd fake an orgasm, just to stop her, but then she stopped herself. She lunged forward and slipped right off me and smashed her head against the wall over the pillow. It was one of these cheap Sheetrock walls where the studs are set too far apart, but wouldn't you know, you can never get a stud in the right place to hang a picture, but she found one with her skull. After the fervent crash, she sagged down on me, limp and unaware. I rolled out from under her, panicked. I didn't know what to do—give her mouth-to-mouth, give her oxygen? I laid her down on the bed and propped her head up and sponged her with a handful of ice wrapped in a wet washcloth. After a few minutes, her eyes opened.

"Brother," she said, "what happened?"

"You knocked yourself out."

"Holy shit," she said. "I've never done that before."

She lay there, very solemn. "You're really something," she said at last.

"No," I said when I'd grasped her meaning, "it wasn't me. It wasn't sex. You never came, you just smashed your head into the wall."

"Oh for God's sake!" She sat up, mad or embarrassed, and then she laughed abruptly. Her mouth sagged on one side, the way it had in the restaurant, and her voice hardened. "Did you look through my purse while I was out? Feel free. Here."

She leaned down, wincing, and picked up her shirt and her heavy denim shoulder bag. She reached in and drew out a plump little brown envelope of leather. I waved it away, but she insisted that I had to look because, she said, I had already looked. She opened the wallet. "Well, at least you're honest." She threw it at me. "Open it!"

"Okay," I said, "if that's what you want."

I turned her wallet over and dumped everything in it on the bedspread.

There were six credit cards, three gold, three platinum. There were five crisp one hundred dollar bills and change for a twenty. There was a picture of an elderly woman and a picture of Marlis. There was a lucky four-leaf clover encased in plastic.

I didn't know what to say. I looked at the credit cards, all in different names, male names.

"I didn't steal them, just in case you're wondering."

"I was."

"I'm actually twenty-five," she said. She turned on the light beside the bed and let it shine on her face, but she now looked about fourteen to me. I couldn't figure. I wasn't drunk anymore, and I didn't want to be. I just wanted to get out of the room. I had a feeling that I had stumbled against someone much different than I'd thought at first, I had a feeling that this whole thing was very wrong. I wasn't attracted to it in the least, not at all. I thought of Ira, at home asleep, I thought of Mauser & Mauser, my line of work, my project, my check stowed underneath a rock. I felt like a fool for putting this complication, this girl or woman, into my life. Clearly, she wasn't someone who would just go away.

"We're going to hang out here," she said, "get some sleep. Then you're going with me tomorrow. You're going to be my dad, buy me some clothes and a car."

"No, I'm not."

"Yes, you are."

She unzipped a little pouch in the back of her denim bag and removed a card, a driver's permit, the kind that farm kids can get when they need to drive the equipment. There was her birth date, in black and white. I subtracted. Fifteen years old.

"You just told me you were twenty-five."

"I lied."

"I'm getting out of here."

I grabbed my things and started to walk out of the room.

"Have you ever heard the term 'statutory rape'?" she called after me.

I understood. I slept the night on the bedroom floor. I tried not to wonder what was going to happen in the morning. I couldn't decide whether or not I deserved what was in store.

"I suppose you want a sports car," I said the next day, as we sat in the booth of a sunny diner near Pioneer Mall. It was like having the devil for a daughter all of a sudden, and none of the good parts, none of the sweetness, the growing up. There was suddenly this grasping menace that I had to appease.

"First the school clothes, Dad!"

I nodded and picked up the check, pulling the bills off the roll I'd picked up out of the orange-soda can. They were stuck together from the sweet pop. Across the polished tiles and planters in the lobby there was a long, low teenage kind of store stuffed with clothes, flashing neon, playing loud rock music, trimmed with glass and chrome. We went in. She began to touch things all over the place, to unrack things, to take them off their hangers and pile them in her arms.

"Pretend we had a fire," her mouth was sagging, "I need new things, a whole new wardrobe. Pretend that you and Mom got a divorce and you're trying to win my love back by spoiling me. Pretend we're lovers," she licked her lips, and then her face sagged in that funny way again, "pretend we're insane about each other, really."

I've never seen someone try things on the way she tried things on, the whole store went in and out of her dressing room, along with belts, shoes, clothes pulled off the mannequins, socks, underwear. She had the store manager in there with her, helping her, eyeing a big fat sale. At one point, though, in the frenzy, she forgot herself. She forgot to watch me and she handed me a size eight and said she needed a ten and would I go get it at the last rack on the right. Her mistake. I walked over to the rack and hung up the pants and kept on walking. Out of the mall, down the street, over to the bus, and back to The Sunset. It took me an hour to get there, and I tried not to look suspicious as I kicked over rock after rock trying to remember which one I'd placed on top of the wrapped check. By the time I finally found the one that hid my money, my heart was in my throat. But there it was, still big as life, with all the zeros intact.

I'd had my car keys all along, but I hadn't told Marlis where the car was parked. Now I walked over to The Library lot to get it, and there was Ira, sitting in the front seat, reading a book. I guess she figured I'd have to come back here before I came home.

I leaned over beside her, at the open window.

"I'm sorry," I said.

She waved my breath away.

"Get in."

I did, and she drove us straight to the drive-up window of the bank, where I wrote out a deposit slip. "This is the last nice thing I'm doing for you," she told me, and then said nothing, just looked straight ahead, distracted and calm. I watched her pure, clear profile, Nordic, honed and filed. She tucked the receipt into my pocket and then kept driving.

"Where are you going?" I asked. My voice so small, so unnoticeable, so guilty, that she was able to brush it away the same as she had my apology.

"I'm driving you out to the construction site," she said. "Your stuff is already out there in the accounts trailer."

"Oh come on, Ira." I was hurting. "It was just a onetime thing."

She turned on me, her face fierce.

"So is this," she answered. "This is the one time I'm getting rid of you."

I couldn't believe the timing, couldn't quite understand the reasoning, but her self-assurance suddenly made me desperate.

"I haven't done anything to you!"

For some reason this just made her laugh, and her laugh was surprising, free, as though she enjoyed my wit. She stopped abruptly and drove in silence for a mile before she finally spoke.

"It's just that your capacity for fucking up is far beyond what I can help you with."

That gave me something to think about. She hummed a little tune to herself, and it occurred to me to tell her it bothered me, to stop, but I didn't. I thought maybe if I kept my mouth shut she'd turn the car around and bring me home, make me lunch. She pulled up into the construction yard. Her car was already parked there alongside the bulldozer and a couple of tractors, so I guess she had a friend in on this scheme. I felt it coming on then, as she indicated with a neutral wave that I should go. I had this hot place in my stomach, this empty place that sent the anger up my arms like cold jelly, the rage into my head. The sudden feeling was so blinding and futile that it scared even me. I tried to stop it from happening, and I put myself into the cage like she always advised. As soon as I was in the wire enclosure, in my mind I mean, Ira walked away and got into her car. Before I could jump out and catch her, I was alone in the dirt lot. Her car was already raising dust on the road to town.

And she took my car keys. Maybe by mistake, but they weren't there in the ignition.

I stumbled out of the car, wheeled around, went looking in the windows of the other cars, the equipment, finally climbed up on the bulldozer. I was in luck. The silver key was in the ignition, I turned it, started the thing up and went after Ira at full throttle, thinking I would catch her somehow, cut her off before she took the turn to town. I would yell at her, reason with her, weep, pull my hair and throw myself down at her feet or beneath the cleated treads of the dozer. I'd humble myself and start all over just as soon as I stopped being mad, which I was as I moved, as the thing got going. It was as though the power of the machine, the throb and heft of it, the things I could do with a lever and a switch, were part of my anger then.

It got too big for me, too big for the wire net I put up to contain it, too big for anything. It roared over me and I grappled with it weakly for one moment and then I was out of the cage, bigger than life, stronger than shit, rattling iron on iron down the road with my blade in the air and looking for I didn't know what, until I saw it, until I saw Moen's fields.

My fields. The flowers looked at me, all fat and frowsy, full of light.

"Harvesttime!" I shouted, sweeping in with the blade lowered, and I kept on shouting, I don't know what, as I cleared swath after swath as the air above me filled with swirling petals and excited birds, as the seeds rang down on the hot metal, as the seeds poured down my neck and shirt, as the heads of sunflowers bounced off the sides of the machine and the dust flew everywhere, a great cloud that hung around me in the air of a drying noon.

I'm not a truly destructive man. I've constructed about anything that you could name. You look around Fargo—banks, half the hospital complex, the highway, Vistawood Views, the nursing home, most of the mall, house upon house—you'll see it's set up and hooked in and put there to stay by Jack Mauser. I do things from plans. I make them real. I could build myself if I could get a guy that could design me. But since that's not possible, I've always relied on women. Somewhere inside I think, *They're women, they should know.* Like if they make kids, then by God they should be able to make me too.

And that's how trouble starts—you plant all your hopes in another heart. Then, if you're like me, you just leave them to grow, as if the woman you've married is a hired gardener.

I stripped most of a field down before that cold strength stopped flowing through my arms. I was breathing hard and my eyes were fixed upon the gauges and dials of the machine's control panel. I couldn't hear anything around me, anything outside myself, and then gradually my heart slowed and the adrenaline that had flooded me turned so mellow I lay back in my seat. I surveyed the crushed welter of stalks and plants on which the birds were already lighting with starved cries. In the distance I could see people, Moen, my construction crew, coming at me. Ira's car wasn't in sight.

The heat lifted off the fields like a gleaming veil. I'd always intended to build the best house in the whole development for Ira. She wouldn't want one now. But as I sat there, I saw them rising anyway. I saw stone trim with clerestory windows, the Gothic look, or Colonial Homes with shutters, plantation-like spreads with columns to either side of the front door. I would set the mailboxes into little brick hutches that could not be knocked over by a teenager with a baseball bat. I would sod in big lawns, plant seven-year-old maples. The garages would be double, triple, some with arches, and all would open automatically to accept their owners. Executives would buy these places, school principals, the owners of local businesses, wealthy farmers who wanted a town home in the winter. I would name the place The Crest. Just The Crest. Not Crest Park, Crest Acres, Crest Ridge, Crest Wood, or Crest Go Fuck Yourself. My development would speak class through simplicity, like it just meant the top of something, the place we all want to get.

—1992

WALLACE KAUFMAN

B. 1939

Wallace Kaufman is a free-lance writer with eclectic professional and personal interests. From 1965 to 1974, Kaufman was an assistant professor of English at the University of North Carolina at Chapel Hill, but he left teaching to become an independent writer and a real estate appraiser. In 1993, in addition to his writing, he began working as an international housing and privatization consultant. His avocations include mushroom collecting, experimental housing and homestead communities, woodworking, and travel in Latin America, the former Soviet Union, and the Arctic. As a writer, he has become well known for debunking various sacred cows of the environmental movement, particularly for revealing the movement's scientific and economic naivete.

Born in Astoria, New York, the son of a machinist, Kaufman moved to North Carolina to study at Duke University, graduating in 1961. He then received a Marshall scholarship to attend Oxford University, from which he earned a B.Litt. two years later. Kaufman's first book, Natural History of Long Island, *was published in 1965. As an English professor, he coauthored two writing textbooks; as a free-lance writer, he contributed a column on real estate to the* Carolina Financial Times *in 1975–76 and began writing for other periodicals such as the* Christian Science Monitor, Mademoiselle, National Wildlife, *and* Redbook. *He coauthored* The Beaches Are Moving: The Drowning of America's Shoreline *in 1979, published* Finding Hidden Values in Your Home *in 1987, and produced a coffee-table book called* The Amazon *in 1991. Kaufman's interest in Latin America led him to the work of Guatemalan writer Victor Dionicio Montejo, and he has translated two of Montejo's books into English:* El Kanil: Man of Lightning, A Legend of Jacaltenango *(1984) and* The Bird Who Cleans the World, And Other Mayan Fables *(1991). His most recent book is* No Turning Back: Dismantling the Fantasies of Environmental Thinking *(1994). When not traveling, Kaufman lives in Pittsboro, North Carolina.*

The following essay, first published in Orion *magazine and later collected in* Finding Home *(edited by Peter Sauer, 1992), reveals Kaufman's personal ambivalence about both environmentalism and urban development, an ambivalence shared by many Americans and by inhabitants of most industrialized societies today. "In me parts of humanity are at war with each other," he writes. "I am a developer and a conservationist. I love bulldozers, and I've never met a tree I didn't like. . . . I am not so different from most Americans." Kaufman proceeds to criticize the American tendency to idealize rural living and farming rather than coming to terms with the urban and suburban settings in which most of us live: "Why do we find beauty in the farmscape but not in the well-landscaped shopping mall or subdivision? It's sentimentality." He is fond of turning Thoreau's famous dictum from "Walking" inside out, suggesting that environmentalism itself is, strangely enough, the product of development: "In civilization is the preservation of wildness." By pointing out the artificiality of the division between developers and environmentalists, this essay aims to help us "accept that we are both."*

CONFESSIONS OF A DEVELOPER

I am a member of a persecuted minority. It's one whose story you haven't heard. Nobody has written poignantly about the daily personal abuse, the exile within society, the injustices we suffer. We haven't been eloquent in our own behalf either. A literary tradition has not emerged yet among developers.

I try not to be ashamed of who I am, but that is hard when I go to meetings with my friends in the environmental community. I often feel as if I were Italian and through the whole meeting people have been talking about the Mafia; I feel as if I were black and the talk is about nothing but crime and drugs and Willie Horton. Developers, too, are victims of stereotypes.

Like most minorities I can point to the past and say, "See, I come from a people with a rich history. Look how we raised ancient Sumer in the desert. How about that 'rose-red city half as old as time' in Egypt? What about the road we built over the scenic peaks of the Andes—the Inca trail—and the great market squares and shopping centers our Mayans built in the rain forest of Yucatán?"

People look, but they still don't see. Revisionists have already eliminated my forerunners from history. Sumer, Alexandria, Chichén Itzá, the Inca Trail, Venice— these are celebrated as triumphs in the life of civilization, but no one celebrates their developers. America is awash in monuments to soldiers, politicians, musicians, poets, civil rights leaders, teachers, conservationists, athletes, Indian chiefs, dinosaurs, and dogs, but how many monuments do you see to a real estate developer?

Who has raised a statue to Elmer Harmon, who in 1887 created the first planned suburb, which indeed was "the best chance ever offered in America for a poor man to acquire good property"? Harry Black brought skyscrapers like the Flatiron Building to Manhattan, and millions of Americans send postcards celebrating the skyline he inspired, but not even a stubby obelisk bears his name. Why is there no monument to Bill Levitt, whose housing innovations after World War II provided homes for tens of thousands of struggling veterans?

The truth is Americans associate real estate development more with wealth than courage or genius. Despite a reputation for materialism, Americans keep a cautious distance from people whose fame is inseparable from cutting trees, paving, wrecking, laying sewage discharge pipes, and spending large sums of money. It is not the money that is feared. It is the power. Those large sums endow the user with the power to change the face of the earth, the character of a city.

In the mind of an America that loves convenience, cars, technology, comfort, farms, parks, and wilderness, developers occupy a secure but lonely corner. We are what Jewish moneylenders were in the mind of medieval Europe, which craved and hated interest-bearing loans. Development is to the course of civilization what libido is to courtship.

I understand how people feel about development. Give me five minutes and I'll prove it faster than a bulldozer flattens a dogwood. In me parts of humanity are at war with each other. I am a developer and a conservationist. I love bulldozers, and I've never met a tree I didn't like. I would rather walk around a farm than a shopping center, but I believe that in many communities, shopping centers are a good substitute for a "downtown."

I am not so different from most Americans. All of us are by nature developers. When I visit a day-care center I don't see two kinds of kids—one growing plants and feeding fish while the other piles up blocks and pushes model trucks and bulldozers around the sandbox. (Neither toy manufacturers nor the Sierra Club offers a wilderness kit alternative.) Almost all the kids are making skyscrapers, building railroads, making Lego mansions. There we are, the developer animals.

Most kids never grow up to develop anything beyond the living room rug or the sandbox. Perhaps in some of us the developer perspective becomes dominant, while a nature preference prevails in others. Maybe some day someone will locate the development and nature preferences on opposite sides of the brain. In any case, a few people accept the development imperative and learn to build subdivisions, roads, shopping centers, and cities. Along the way they have to learn to destroy woods and prairies, orchards and farms, marshes and meadows.

I propose that if we understand and accept the development urge, we will come closer to solving our land-use problems. We should no more repress the development part of our psyche because some developers pillage nature than we should repress our sexuality because some men and women are pornographers and prostitutes.

I became a developer because I didn't like developers. I thought I could do it better. In 1966 there were five of us young English professors at the University of North Carolina at Chapel Hill who wanted to live in the country and have a little land. I found an eighty-acre "mountain" overlooking the town water supply. We could have four or five acres each for a grand total of $5,000. For months we talked about what we would do. Finally, time came to buy in or drop out. "Too far out," said the James Joyce scholar. "What about snakes?" asked the man who taught about the courage of hunters in Faulkner's fiction. "Can we get a road in there?" wondered the Dos Passos biographer. The whole thing became an excursion into pastoral fantasy. I even said to myself, "Well, maybe the mountain is better off just the way it is."

I was learning my first important lesson in development: no development in the world can pass all the safety tests that concern even a small number of people. Certainly if we lived on the outskirts of Eden and Moses proposed the modest city of Jerusalem, he could not have written a satisfactory environmental impact statement. We certainly couldn't have done it for the irrigation projects of the Nile, or the Tigris and Euphrates. Most people would rather analyze risks than take them. There is no risk-free development. Development is the process of taking risks—financial, environmental, social, and personal.

As an academic myself, I should have known that scholars are not trained to take risks. I came, though, from a blue-collar family where new ideas were few but firmly attached to action. What I had started to do for myself and my colleagues in the English department, I now decided to do on speculation—for all those people who wanted to live in the country in peace with nature. With the help of a graduate student friend whose only expertise was an exhaustive study of the Icelandic Eddas, I put a small down payment on 330 acres of trees that had taken over abandoned farms or grew in untillable valleys and rocky soil.

I was moving too fast to think about what I was doing and why, but I know now. My idea may have been different from other developments, but my inspiration was all-American. The concept had come in a straight line out of the tin double bed in a poor section of Queens where my brother and I used to lie awake at night telling each other how we would get out of the city and live on a jungle farm where we would tame panthers and boa constrictors and the only domestic animal would be a coal-black stallion. This was a child's version of what we often call "The American Dream," the place where we really want to live. Americans have been searching for it for four hundred years. Some Americans, call them developers, have been building places they hope will satisfy the searchers.

Like every other developer I offered my development as one of those places. I said to myself (and probably to a few others), I can provide homes for people without messing up the landscape the way other developers do. What's more I can do it cheaper and give people several acres where they can really appreciate what goes on in nature. While this wasn't a panther farm in the Colombian jungle, it was to be a Peaceable Kingdom of the Piedmont.

What I planned and began to advertise didn't seem like development but the realization of my environmental and social ideals. The principles were simple: (1) make homesites five acres or larger where one person's way of life wouldn't interfere with a neighbor's; (2) write covenants to prevent people from cutting too many trees, polluting the streams, and leaving junk in the woods; (3) keep costs low by bypassing the realtors and paying for development from sales instead of debt; (4) finance the lots so that anyone with a steady job in the local mill could afford to buy.

Realtors assured me the idea was nice, but people really wouldn't want to live in the woods thirteen miles away from town. My friend who read the Eddas nevertheless believed in me. "Don't pay any attention to them," he said, and went on to finish his thesis on Mohammed in medieval literature. The month after we signed the mortgage, he expressed his regrets and moved to the Bronx to explain the terrible justice of Iceland's Snorri to slum kids.

In a way my critics were right. For a year and a half I guided prospective buyers down the little logging road into the property. I thought people would like the design-your-own-lot approach. They could choose how long and how wide the lot would be and what hills and trees might be on it. But even trail-seasoned country lovers arrived expecting to see some kind of development. All they saw was woods. There were no roads cleared, no lots laid out. Sometimes I would meet people on the public road. If I arrived late, they would be standing by our little wooden sign as if it offered some necessary anchor in the wilderness. Some people showed up in dresses and ties, sandals and shorts; some with babies barely able to walk and too big to carry far. They went back to town and talked about their crazy afternoon in the wilds. They didn't buy anything.

I was learning development lessons two and three. People buy a sense of place. They want a recognizable order, a road that leads somewhere, driveways that tell where a house might go. They want electricity. Perhaps they have their ideas of an ideal lot and home, but most people want developers to go ahead and give them something about which they can say yea or nay.

I also learned that satisfying this desire for a sense of place and security means investing a lot of money before answering the first inquiry. This front money means more risk. That means investors expect more profit. It also means more interest expense. In sum, it means more expensive development.

Developers are willing to take risks, but they don't take many. One of the axioms of real estate economics is that success breeds competition. Developers try to minimize their risks by copying other successful developments. We can call developers timid, but many are risking not only their own money but family money, or their friends' money. If they are risking money put up by stockholders or banks, the law, not to mention a bunch of nervous strangers, is always looking over their shoulder.

I was lucky. America celebrated the first Earth Day in 1970. It reaffirmed the intuition that "out in the country" was a good place to live. In many minds the forest became the place where nature could exert its most healing powers. Thirty-three lots and 330 acres sold out by 1972, and our little company had made enough money to put aside some 45 acres of stream valley as common land.

As I said, my buyers were not ready to blaze any trails. I had to build a road. That was the end of my environmental virginity. I rented a little chain saw from the Rent All. I wasn't going to have any bulldozer pushing over my trees and piling them up. I'd carefully select a road line that avoided the big trees. What I had to cut, I would cut so someone could use the logs.

The rented saw was little because I only wanted to do a little damage. But no matter which way I tried to run the road, big trees stood in my way. There were a lot more than I had imagined. It was like trying to shovel a blizzard with a teaspoon. The next day I took a company check and went to town and bought a big Stihl 041 with a twenty-one-inch bar. I intended to execute each and every oak and hickory, holly, and loblolly pine myself. Why let some anonymous bulldozer be my surrogate? If I were going to build a road, I'd take the emotional responsibility as well as the legal.

I managed to curve the road around a few special trees, but I cut dozens that had been standing in place for 150 or 200 years. I rubbed my nose in the damage. I counted rings, learned the marks left by weather and animals and the fall of other trees. I severed grapevines as thick as my arms, and returning the next day saw their watery sap still bleeding from the stubs. I learned the licorice smell of a pine stump, the acid smell of red oak, and the musky tannin of white oak. It was a little like killing and dressing your own meat.

Within a week I had cleared the first half mile. Not too bad, I told myself. The canopy would soon grow back over the road and it would be a shady country lane. Buddy the bulldozer operator laughed when he came to grub the stumps. "Hell, I can't even turn around in that space."

I learned that a road fit for service according to the state of North Carolina has the following characteristics:

The roadbed must be twenty feet wide and paved.

Then there are shoulders. These may be soft. Add four feet on each side.

The shoulders must not be soggy, however, so they are accompanied by ditches. Add six feet each side.

The slopes on the ditches and the embankments must be gradual enough so grass will not fall off or the soil erode. If you have any embankment beyond the ditch add five or ten more feet.

Accommodating all of this kindness to man and nature requires cutting a swath through the forest that is fifty to sixty feet wide. This was no job for one man and a chain saw.

In one day the D-8 Caterpillar had piled up all the trees I had cut and a lot more in three big mounds that looked as though a giant beaver expected someone to turn a river down that roadway. In three or four places I had left an especially large tree near the edge of the road, something like Frost's "Tuft of Flowers" left by the mower. Life, however, happens differently than poems, and most of the trees had to go or have their roots cut: you can't run a road ditch around a tree. The dozer simply lifted its blade eight or ten feet up the trunk of a two-foot-thick oak and pushed until the tree's own whiplashing top helped break the roots' hold in the earth.

One weekend, while the piles were drying, I climbed over them looking for good logs and crotches to salvage for future woodworking. Everything was pinned at some point under something else. I did find a large hollow gum tree which I sectioned and split, intending to use the curved pieces for benches. When I scraped and pried the rot from inside the log, thousands of carpenter ants, beetles, and millipedes fell out and scattered in chaos on the ground. In that insignificant and dying tree a whole community of life had been carrying on confidently through years of darkness. By comparison the light-drenched roadbed was simple and lifeless.

On Monday Buddy arrived with a pickup load of old tires. We threw them on the piles, and he doused the pyres with gasoline. By evening the charred piles smouldered, not a tree or stump recognizable as oak, hickory, gum, or anything else. The next day the ashes were buried, and the road was clear—a red avenue of clay with big trees seeming to stand at numb attention on both sides. The dozer cut through the tops of hills until the roadbed had an acceptable incline. A pan roared up and down the road carrying the cutout earth to fill the low spots. The hills and valleys were being averaged into conformity.

Two days later, after scraping and graveling and grading, a car could drive from one end to the other at fifty miles per hour. Everything was slick and smooth.

I used to stand in that roadway, looking up and down and thinking, "God help me, did I do this?" I was like a man returning time and again to the scene of a hit-and-run accident. But there was no one to report to and not even a corpse to bury.

About that time Carolina Power and Light came along. They could not put their poles in the road right-of-way, so they cleared another fifteen feet alongside the road, felling trees, hacking away brush, and planting their poles.

Now people drove in with their Volkswagen bugs and Saabs and vans, and they began to buy. Nobody lamented the trees that had been cut and burned any more than cried about the destroyed forests of Manhattan Island.

Although each of them came praising the covenants that promised a peaceable and unpolluted kingdom, they approached their homes in the woods with a variety of styles that matched their paths through life. How did they love nature? Let me count the ways.

A young woman with milk goats and chickens allowed them to roam the woods, tearing up the forest floor and eating gardens as well as wildflowers. An insurance man with two Saint Bernards was happy his dogs had lots of room even though they walked through screen doors and knocked down a neighbor's eighty-year-old mother. Lou and Tammy's pack of hounds kept the ex-Marine next door awake. A dentist started a forest fire throwing out his wood stove ashes. The ex-Marine cherished his privacy so much he wouldn't build a drive to his house and carried all his lumber in by hand; but he cleared part of the wildlife buffer for his garden. A stone mason who laid his stone in imitation of natural deposits drained his bathtub, sink, and washing machine into the woods near the creek. An Episcopal minister who built a log house to blend into the woods objected to the width of our roads that didn't blend in, but he controlled beetles in his natural house by periodically treating it with a toxic preservative.

I, the developer, had made a place bound to attract people who were sentimental about nature. They taught me lesson number four, a lesson that ought to be one of the Ten Commandments of the environmental movement: sentimentality applied is just another form of development.

If I am going to be vilified as a polluter and destroyer, I want the judgment to be applied impartially. I don't want someone spared because he wears hiking boots, reads poetry, or milks cows.

For an example of nature sentimentality at its worst look at our attitudes toward farming. The notion that by preserving farmland we have fortified ourselves against development and struck a blow for nature is nonsense. From nature's point of view most farms are hugely destructive. What other form of development routinely poisons its soils and devastates such vast areas, exclusively to serve people? A farm murders natural diversity and extracts the life force from nature's carcass to sell for profit. Most farming is voodoo ecology that makes a walking zombie out of nature. So why do we celebrate America's farmers with such a soft heart? Why do we find beauty in the farmscape but not in the well-landscaped shopping mall or subdivision? It's sentimentality.

When I did my first development back in 1968 I was fortunate to be free from laws and regulations. I made my own decisions about erosion control, lot size, water, sewers, curbs, gutters, electricity, open space, setbacks, traffic flow, curb cuts, and who could do what on their land. In most high-growth areas, including the Research Triangle area of North Carolina where I operate, all these things are now subject to approval by state, county, and city governments.

As a citizen and conservationist I favor controls. I have stood up in countless hearings and asked the planning board or county commissioners to tighten regulations, to require more open space in a subdivision, or to deny a permit for a shopping center. When Congress first considered a bill that would prohibit development on some of our ocean beaches I went to Washington and sat next to the head of the most powerful Political Action Committee in the country, the Realtors PAC, and testified that my leader's position was short-sighted, uninformed, and motivated by greed.

Developers, however, are just like a lot of writers, teachers, farmers, and dancers. We think we can learn the business on our own, asking for help when we think we need it and from the people who make us comfortable. Although I see a legitimate role for the public in my development plans, I still feel the way you do when someone looks over your shoulder as you write a letter or knocks on your door when you're making love.

The public, of course, thinks developers need more attention than it gives to people who merely create culture. There are several reasons for this. First, development is an assault on our sensibilities. It's noisy and it's dirty, and it changes our surroundings right before our eyes. Second, development destroys things we care about deeply—streams, trees, hills, animals. Finally, and most important, development brings out greed.

My attempt to deal with greed taught me my fifth important lesson as a developer. The public is right that development tempts developers to do things they know are not right. It tempts everyone. Almost everyone has a price. In my first development, I began to see sellers who had gotten a good deal from us charging what the market would bear when they resold their lots. The kind of family I grew up in couldn't afford them anymore.

When I did my second development I wanted to protect everyone from greed. Into the covenants for this 225-acre community I wrote a clause that controlled resales. A seller could get the original purchase price of the land plus an amount equal to general inflation. For the house he could get the cost of replacing it. Half of anything over these figures had to be put in a landowners' trust fund to help lower-income people buy land.

Lawyers who undertook a closing on a resale here would call me up as if they could not read. They could read, but they couldn't believe what they were reading.

Sometimes my covenant worked and owners sold at the formula price. Others got their neighbors to waive the profit restriction.

When it comes to money, I learned, there is no such thing as a liberal or a conservative. At the extremes are a few saints and Midases. Everybody else wants as much as he or she can get. I once designed a small subdivision of a farm bought by a professor who specialized in Latin American land reform, a champion of redistributing wealth. He looked at the lot prices I proposed and said, "Aren't these very low? Can't we get much more than this?" I pointed out that after the road and survey costs, he would be doubling his money. And didn't he want as many people as possible to be able to afford his land? No, he wanted the same kind of money everybody else made on real estate.

When it comes to buying and selling real estate I've decided I too might as well make everything I can. If I forgo some profit someone else will grab it. They could be one of James Watt's Sagebrush Rebels or one of my allies in conservation.

I made enough to free my house and land from mortgages and to devote more time to proving that the pen was mightier than the bulldozer. I dropped out of development for five or six years. Then at a conference on land use I ran into a conservative big-time realtor and developer who had grown wealthy on the Research Triangle's land boom. Some years earlier he and other investors had agreed to sell a seven-hundred-acre tract to a land trust that wanted to build a solar village on its south slopes overlooking the softly muscled waters of the Haw River. I had been president of the trust then, and we had failed to raise the money for a bargain price.

The price was higher now, but still a bargain. I sold new stock in my shrunken but still existing company, and we bought. I was back in business. Here were 720 acres full of beautiful beech and oak forests, silent stone chimneys surrounded by walnut and giant oaks, old fields once worked savagely by desperate family farmers and now lying quiet under a blanket of pine needles in the deep shade of big loblollies. The site was big enough to contain both the source and the mouth of several small creeks that ran clear. Wherever there was a soft stream bank or mud puddle, deer, raccoons, possums left their tracks. Turkeys thrived on the acorns and grubs in the leaf mold. It was a place that should have been preserved as a wilderness.

There was no one to preserve it, however, and the market was full of people more than willing to spoil it. If I had had a million dollars I would have bought it and left it for the animals and trees. It would have been the most natural and best-protected place left in this new Silicon Valley. I didn't have enough money for a new pickup truck, much less the funds to pick up seven hundred acres of land. I knew I was once again going to go to war with myself.

I immediately began to write a peace treaty. Like most, it is full of compromises. I drafted a long set of covenants that reflected my accumulated frustrations with the way people use land as well as everything I know about how to protect wildlife, water, and air from people.

The building boom has begun. People have been moving in. Already I have problems. Owners don't want to keep their dogs and cats under control when the poor things could be enjoying such happy freedom of the woods. So there is now a little pack chasing deer and baying raccoons into the trees. I see an occasional cat prowling the roadside for rabbits, birds, lizards, mice, and voles.

There are days when I am ready to plough up the roads I've built and tear down the houses. I'm not alone in my regrets. In a recent issue of *North Carolina Wildlife*, a local conservationist and hunter lamented the changes development had brought to this place. Yet until I came along no one else had made a move to protect this land from the gathering forces of the market. No environmental group had even explored it, although it was one of the few big tracts left in the river valley.

Antidevelopers are fond of printing on their banners and posters Thoreau's declaration, "In wildness is the preservation of the world." History and my own experience suggest the opposite: "In civilization is the preservation of wildness."

Real estate development doesn't pretend to be natural, but in the big picture it is kinder in quantity and often gentler in quality than other land uses. My road building has contributed its share of sediment to local streams and rivers, but not a fraction as much as the nearby dairy farmer's creekside feedlot. Acre for acre fewer toxic chemicals run into our rivers and streams from a subdivision or even a shopping center than from a farm.

Yet Americans are prejudiced for farmers and against developers. We are prejudiced for furry animals and against machines, for green plants and against concrete. The bias against developers and development finds many worthy targets, but like all prejudice, its driving force is irrational fear. We project onto others what we fear within ourselves.

Developers and environmentalists feel betrayed by each other. Betrayal, however, is possible only among people who share common values and commitments. Our dilemma is that as individuals and collectively as a society we have chosen both nature and development.

Almost anyone who drives a car, goes shopping, uses an airport, attends a school, wears factory-made clothing, or owns a musical instrument supports development somewhere. The real way to combat bad development is the same as the way to combat drugs. The users have got to say NO. I wouldn't have trundled my chain saw out to my first development if I had thought no one wanted to live there. Development is not "unnatural." Nature made us the animal that imagines worlds more enjoyable than the world we were given. Then we develop that world. What human beings do to the planet is as much a part of nature as Yosemite Valley.

Knowing that won't help me the next time I set a bulldozer to work in a forest or channel a sparkling stream into a length of dark culvert. Just as we are the animal that imagines how things might be, we are also the one that remembers how things were. It is embarrassing and frustrating. Writing about it has helped me draw yet one more lesson from my life as a developer: none of us will succeed as either developers or environmentalists until we accept that we are both.

—1992

ROBERT FROST

1874-1963

Robert Frost's reputation as a poet derived largely from the pastoral sensibility of his work, its focus on the rural and the natural (as described in the earlier introduction to the poet in "Visions of Home," p. 295). The poet's career, from high school in the 1880s to his death in 1963, spanned an epoch of unprecedented urbanization in the United States. During this period, Americans in all regions of the country began to abandon rural places and lifestyles, migrating to cities in search of jobs and conveniences. With this process of urbanization came an increasing nostalgia for the countryside—for quiet and space and close, frequent contact with nature. As artists and scholars have long known, the pastoral aesthetic is typically an urban point of view.

The following poem, which was published in Frost's Pulitzer Prize-winning collection New Hampshire (1923), details the phenomenon of urbanization from an unusual perspective, describing what happens when a city expands to encompass what was once farmland rather than the process of human migration from country to metropolis. Only the farmhouse "lingers" visibly to indicate that the city has come to occupy land that was once a place of apple trees, flowers, and running water. The poem creates an implicit opposition between the pleasant, natural qualities of the country and the angularity and dinginess of the city, perhaps romanticizing the lost farmland and exaggerating the city's ills. But what is particularly interesting about this poem is how Frost works toward his concluding speculation concerning the psychological significance of the pastoral landscape to the city people, vaguely haunted by the water that still runs "in a sewer dungeon" beneath modern streets. The question for readers is whether Frost actually means to inspire us to restore the land to its former condition or simply to make us aware of the ecological and psychological costs of urban development.

A BROOK IN THE CITY

The farmhouse lingers, though averse to square
With the new city street it has to wear
A number in. But what about the brook
That held the house as in an elbow-crook?
I ask as one who knew the brook, its strength
And impulse, having dipped a finger length
And made it leap my knuckle, having tossed
A flower to try its currents where they crossed.
The meadow grass could be cemented down
From growing under pavements of a town;
The apple trees be sent to hearthstone flame.
Is water wood to serve a brook the same?
How else dispose of an immortal force
No longer needed? Staunch it at its source
With cinder loads dumped down? The brook was thrown
Deep in a sewer dungeon under stone
In fetid darkness still to live and run—
And all for nothing it had ever done,
Except forget to go in fear perhaps.
No one would know except for ancient maps

That such a brook ran water. But I wonder
If from its being kept forever under,
The thoughts may not have risen that so keep
This new-built city from both work and sleep.

—1923

SALLIE BINGHAM

B. 1937

Sallie Bingham is a playwright and fiction writer with a strong feminist con-
sciousness whose family inheritance has also enabled her to be a generous
supporter of the arts. A graduate of Radcliffe, Bingham has taught writing
at the University of Louisville, had several plays produced, and authored
two short-story collections and a number of novels, the most recent of
which are Upstate *(1993),* Small Victories *(1993),* Matron of Honor *(1994),*
and Straight Man *(1996). Bingham founded the Kentucky Foundation for*
Women, which makes grants to local women artists and publishes the liter-
ary quarterly The American Voice. *She also supports the Women's Project*
and Productions in New York City, and theater productions in Santa Fe and
Kentucky.

Bingham's 1989 memoir, Passion and Prejudice, *gives a provocative*
feminist view of life inside the wealthy and powerful Bingham family of
Louisville, Kentucky. Bingham's father was the publisher of the Louisville
Courier-Journal, *a Pulitzer Prize–winning newspaper known for its coura-*
geous stands against segregation, the war in Vietnam, and strip mining.
Bingham's grandfather founded the newspaper with money inherited from
his second wife (the widow of Standard Oil founder and Florida real estate
developer Henry Flagler), who died under suspicious circumstances when
she was 50; Bingham has written a play about this woman, supposing what
she might have done with the fortune had she survived. In the mid-1980s,
Bingham and other female relatives were forced off the board of directors
of the family's vast communications holdings and Bingham decided to sell
her shares on the open market, a move that culminated in her father's sell-
ing the family business to the Gannett Company. "Women have often been
silenced in history . . . to preserve elements in the hierarchy, political or
social, public or private, institutional or personal. I chose to speak," writes
Bingham in the preface to her memoir. She moved to Santa Fe, New Mexico,
in 1991, planning to devote the rest of her life to writing.

"A Woman's Land" was written when Bingham lived outside Louisville
and was published in the Amicus Journal *(Fall 1990), the quarterly publi-*
cation of the Natural Resources Defense Council. The essay points up the
fact that land use is determined by those who can afford to buy land, still
primarily white males, and poses the question of how a woman's use of
land might differ from a man's. "We are in new territory here because we
have no myths or legends, no sayings or parables to guide us," writes
Bingham, who suggests that the "land-patriarchs" have little to say about
the use of land "that does not offend."

A WOMAN'S LAND

Four years ago I bought a piece of wild land. Parts of it had been farmed in a haphazard sort of way, but most of it was woods, or fields on their way back to being woods. Since moving to this piece of land, which is often called a farm, I have begun to wonder about its appropriate uses and about my relation to it, as one of the very few women who own land.

So few women own land that the phrase, woman landowner, seems curious. At once we wonder how she came to own it, how she afforded it—and that recognition of the financial inequities women face obscures another question—can a woman *own* land?

We are in new territory here because we have no myths or legends, no sayings or parables to guide us. We few who own the half-acre our house stands on, or the several acres left from an old farm, or the piece of property that descended through the family, must weave our own theories; we have nothing to go on except the words of the land-patriarchs, and they have little to offer that does not offend.

Women do not usually exploit, even in situations where exploitation is possible or expected; we do not often sell our children, for example. Where poor women have been brought to barter their unborn babies for money, a concept vital to the community breaks down. The mother's heartbreak reflects the disease of her times.

Generally we are not farmers, but gardeners. We may raise a few flowers or some vegetables for the table. We take from the earth what we can use, or what we can enjoy without depleting the supply. Women are not usually hunters or real-estate developers. We do not always seek to convert gifts into power or cash.

The deer in the woods seems to me to have been placed there not for my purposes or for the purposes of the hunter, but to fulfill the law of her existence: to graze, sleep, procreate, or run away from danger, without reference even to my appreciation of her beauty.

The old fields in front of and behind my house seem to exist without reference to their potential productivity. Once they were treed; now, the trees and brush would return if the farmer who rents them for corn kept his machinery in the barn for one season. The land would be revitalized, no longer scoured and soured by chemical sprays and fertilizers. Perhaps in my lifetime those elements the soil has lost would be restored—if the machinery continued to stay in the barn. But soon the "field" would no longer be a field, but a wild place, accessible only to birds and small animals that can move through briars on their hidden paths.

Yet, this would not seem to me to be the land's intention either, but that cycle of change might, once again, bring beeches into maturity on this stretch. The land is given only to itself—it exists for me as the ground under my feet, but not as a possibility, a future, a hope of gain.

Does my attitude make the land into a luxury, affordable only by the very rich, who do not need to consider productivity? If so, women must find another way, for women are not rich, almost by definition, in a sexist society where we are always in charge of the spiritual and social work that holds the community together and pays poorly.

Perhaps I can form a theory based on the communal use of my land, which recognizes several purposes for this piece of common acreage: relief for my eyes and for my soul, a place for my husband's sheep to graze, a horizon for my sons to escape from and through, a place for the barn cat and her kitten to fatten off grain-fed mice, and for my friends to house and tend their special animals—the llama, the three-legged deer. These two curious animals bear, symbolically, the weight of the whole place: they exist outside of the money exchange. Does that make them the curiosities of the rich? Not quite. Their caretakers are not wealthy, and yet their wealth or lack of it does not enter into the exchange. These animals live outside of the area of commerce, or are excluded from it. They are gifts.

The sheep are not gifts. They were bought with a certain end in view: to be converted into cash. However, the sheep's symbolic meaning has changed as they have begun to share the barn with the llama and the three-legged deer. They have names, or at least some of them do. Their purpose is no longer clear.

Is this sheer sentimentality? Again, a luxury of the rich, who do not toil, nor do they spin? Or is it a recognition of the ultimate independence of the sheep (an odd expression for such dumb and dumbly obedient beasts) from our aims or plans?

What defines the land is what escapes definition: the Canada geese who light on the pond and take off with a wild flurry of wings in the morning, always towards the south; the heron outside my studio window who stood for a short while on a stone in the river. These birds did not arrive here, and pause briefly, for our edification. They exist in their own worlds, which we can barely appreciate, which we cannot penetrate or convert into cash.

But what was the motive that brought a hunter to shoot one of our rare bald eagles, so well-marked with spray paint and electronic devices? Surely the hunter was a boy or a man. Surely he sought in the killing something he could take away with him, a talisman or a boast. The need to "make something out of" the experience perhaps defines the male. A woman might have wanted to make the sighting into a story or a painting. But she would not have figured, necessarily, in that story or painting, as the hunter must figure in the shooting of the eagle. The eagle would have lived to see another day, free of the woman—the artist—and her transitory usage; the eagle did not outlive the man's aim.

I am uncomfortable suggesting that a woman's use of the land might be better than a man's. Notions of women's superiority always have a sting in the tail. We carry enough weight in the world without taking on the weight of being morally superior. Yet, the fact remains that women do not destroy land, either as owners who sell off pastures for shopping centers or as employees who operate bulldozers that push down trees. Is it enough to say that we are powerless to commit this evil? I think not. A woman who is able to buy land probably learned something about its care from the way a woman without financial power tended her African violets.

But perhaps the difference in attitudes towards the land is not gender-related. Perhaps the artist, male or female, is able to see trees and open stretches as gifts, not as possibilities for conversion. Perhaps our addictive needs are satisfied by the manufacturing of words out of the landscape, rather than by the manufacturing of tract houses.

Artists who are men are often perceived as living on the fringes of their gender, stripling lads even in old age, Apollos without followers. Often they lack power and money. To the extent that their androgyny is corrupted by power and money, they become more male-like, more interested in conversion, in "making something out of." The rare successful artist who purchases land is perhaps more likely to sell off parts of it for subdivisions than the equally rare woman who can afford to buy and will preserve it.

If the gift survives the addiction, however, as it seems capable of doing, there will still be a need for a woman or an artist to appreciate it—although to all intents and purposes, that appreciation is inessential. Appreciation, if it is converted into action, can save land.

There will always be a few rich women who will endow a piece of land and will it to perpetuity, although for the land to survive, her heirs must accept that it does not belong to them. In how many cases has a woman been able to surmount her heirs' ideas of their rights and leave the land to continue "undeveloped"?

In the case of my land, the woman landowner's heirs despoiled it with their motorcycles and logged out all the old trees and would have sold it to the highest bidder for any purpose whatsoever if the lack of city water and sewage hadn't hampered their aims. It came to me almost by default.

Now, as I work on my will, I am trying to insure that the land remains open forever. This means that it will not be inherited by my sons, but will remain, as it is now, a gift. This is difficult, if not impossible, to do, first on a personal level. All children long to inherit what is of value to the parent; it is a way of receiving commitment and memories. In the case of my sons, their inevitable immersion in the patriarchy means that they will want to "make something out of" the land, should it pass to them. Leaving it to lie fallow, to grow up again with weeds, would seem an eccentric choice for a male landowner.

On another level, the patriarchy itself is dead set against my decision. The right of sons to inherit is fundamental to capitalism, and to the more secretive continuation of a ruling class. How then can heirs be taught to see the land as a gift? Only by stroking the three-legged deer and looking at the silent llama.

—1990

John McPhee

b. 1931

John McPhee has a passion for facts and for telling a compelling nonfiction story that has made him one of the most reliable and respected of the New Yorker's *staff writers since he signed on there in 1965. A patient and methodical researcher, McPhee has written about an amazingly broad range of topics. Wallace Stegner called him "our best and liveliest writer about the earth and earth sciences," but he has also produced pieces on sports, nuclear physics, oranges, cooking, the Swiss army, medicine, aeronautics, and green beans.* Coming Into the Country *(1977), his most popular book, describes the land battles that took place in Alaska in the late 1970s. "I do sketches of people and the work that they do — real people and real places," explained McPhee in a profile in* Sierra *magazine (May/June 1990).*

Born in Princeton, New Jersey, McPhee attended Princeton University and for more than two decades has taught a course there called "The Literature of Fact." He began his literary career as a writer for the Robert

Montgomery Presents *television show, then spent seven years as an associ-ate editor for* Time *magazine before becoming a staff writer for the* New Yorker. *McPhee has published more than twenty-five books, and one of his most persistent interests has been the geology of the American continent. Three of his geological books, in particular, have been linked under the gen-eral title* Annals of the Former World: Basin and Range *(1981),* In Suspect Terrain *(1983), and* Rising from the Plains *(1986). Many of his other works, including* The Control of Nature *(1989) and* Assembling California *(1993), demonstrate this interest in rocks and geologists as well. McPhee's work has been honored with literary awards such as the John Burroughs Medal for natural history writing and various awards from the Association of Petroleum Geologists, the United States Geological Survey, and the American Geophysical Union.*

McPhee is particularly concerned with structure in his writing, with "the way in which two parts of a piece of writing, merely by lying side-by-side, can comment on each other without a word spoken," as he told Norman Sims, editor of The Literary Journalists *(1984). He initially saw* Encounters with the Archdruid *(1971), from which the following selection is taken, as an exercise in structure—he wanted to profile one person by showing him or her interacting with three other people. Eventually he chose to focus on David Brower, long the executive director of the Sierra Club, and three of his adversaries—a mineral engineer, a land developer, and the head of the Bureau of Reclamation.*

Writes McPhee in the pages leading up to the following passage: "Brower is a visionary. He wants—literally—to save the world. He has been an emotionalist in an age of dangerous reason. He thinks that conservation should be 'an ethic and conscience in everything we do, whatever our field of endeavor'—in a word, a religion." What follows is a section of the long essay called "An Island" in which McPhee travels with Brower and Charles Fraser, a real estate developer from South Carolina, to visit Cumberland Island off the Atlantic Coast. Without casting his vote for either Brower or Fraser, McPhee manages in this narrative to evoke the striking similarities and differences between the worldviews of the two men, illuminating the perspectives of developers and conservationists in general—thus we see his technique of juxtaposition at work.

FROM AN ISLAND

On a cold but sunlit November day, a small airplane, giving up altitude, flew down the west shore of Cumberland, banked left, crossed the island, and moved out to sea. Sitting side by side behind the pilot were Brower and Fraser. The plane turned, still descending, and went in low over the water and low over the wind-pruned live oaks and down into a clearing, where the ground was so rough that the landing gear thumped like drumfire. A man in khaki trousers and a wild-boarskin shirt waited at the edge of the woods. The aircraft wheeled around at the far end of the clearing and taxied back toward him through waist-high fennel.

Fraser and Brower had met only the evening before, at Hilton Head, and Fraser, in his direct way, had begun their relationship by giving Brower a dry Martini and then telling him what a conservationist is. Fraser said, "I call anyone a druid who prefers trees to people. A conservationist too often is just a preservationist, and a preservationist is a druid. I think of land use in terms of people. At Hilton Head, we have proved that you can take any natural area and make it available to people while at the same time preserving its beauty." Brower listened and, for the moment, said nothing. He had not expected so young a man. Fraser's dynamism impressed him, and so did Sea Pines Plantation. Fraser, for his part, was surprised by what he took to be, in Brower, an absence of thorns. Expecting an angry Zeus, he found instead someone who appeared to be "unargumentative, quiet, and shy."

Now, on Cumberland Island, the pilot cut the props, and into the resulting serenity stepped Fraser and Brower. Fraser wore a duck hunter's jacket and twill trousers that were faced with heavy canvas. Brower had on an old blue sweater, gray trousers, and white basketball shoes. The name of the man in the boarskin shirt was Sam Candler. Hands were shaken all around. Brower said it was "nice to be aboard the island." The weather was discussed. Amiability was the keynote.

Candler, who was thirty-eight, had spent much of his life on the island. He grew up on its oysters and shrimp. His children were doing the same. Candler knew where the alligators were, and he had a boxful of diamondback rattles, from snakes he had killed with a hackberry stick. Notches on the stick corresponded to rattles in the box, and Candler would have dearly loved to be able to make an additional notch that corresponded to Charles E. Fraser. There was native gentility in Candler, however, and he did not permit his darker sentiments to surface in the presence of his new neighbor. Candler spoke even more softly than Brower did, and the accents of Atlanta were in his voice. He was a slim man of medium height, with dark hair. He owned, with others in his family, the part of Cumberland Island that Thomas Carnegie did not buy. The Candler property, about twenty-two hundred acres at the north end, was the site of a rambling wooden inn (now Candler's house) in which business flourished around the turn of the century but atrophied after causeways were built to other islands. Candler's great-grandfather was the pharmacist who developed and wholly owned the Coca-Cola Company; his son, Candler's grandfather, bought the Cumberland property in 1928.

The pilot said goodbye. The airplane waddled into position and took off.

"An airport is essential here," Fraser said.

"But it's not a nice neighbor," Brower told him.

"Yes, but ours would be just large enough for small private jets, no more," Fraser said. "Let's go see Cumberland Oaks."

Cumberland Oaks was Fraser's working title for the development he intended to build on Cumberland Island. To get to the site, we drove about ten miles on narrow sandlane roads, Fraser at the wheel of a Land Rover that belonged to his company. Sunlight came down in slivers through the moss in the canopies of huge virgin oaks. We stopped near one, and Brower paced the ground under it. The limbs reached out so far that, bent by their own weight, they plowed into the ground, from which they emerged farther out, leafily. Yucca grew in a crotch twenty feet high. Brower computed that the canopy covered fifteen thousand square feet of ground.

We drove on, through long stretches that were straight to the end of perspective. "This is a vast island," Fraser said. "It can absorb dozens of different kinds of uses. You won't even be able to *find* the uses, it's so vast—if it is handled with discretion." Brower was silent. "By going into islands, I tarnish my shining image, because I irritate so many druids," Fraser said. Brower smiled. The Land Rover raced along at forty miles per hour and occasionally bounced over a corduroy bridge. Eventually Fraser said, with both humor and sarcasm in his voice, "Now we're on my property. Don't it look lovely?" Brower said sincerely that lovely was how it looked, with its palmettos, its live oaks, its slash and longleaf pines. To Fraser, it was obviously raw and incomplete, but even now he could clearly see before his eyes finished villas and finished roads. So complete was this vision, in fact, that Fraser turned off the existing road and began to zip through the trees, rounding imaginary corners and hugging subdivisional curves. Spiky palmettos rattled against the Land Rover's sides like venetian blinds. Pine branches smacked against the windshield, making explosive noises and causing us all, instinctively, to blink and cover our heads with our arms. A buck and two does leaped away from the oncoming vehicle, and Candler, raising his voice above the din, commented pointedly that on an island heavy with deer they were the first we had seen. "Variety of wildlife increases sharply with variety of food," Fraser said, accelerating. "A place like Sea Pines Plantation has more wildlife than an untouched forest—more browsing, more habitat variation."

The western edge of Fraser's property was a high bluff over the Cumberland River, a tidal lagoon separating the island from the broad marsh, and as we stood there looking down at the water and across to the distant mainland Fraser said, "We'll have slides here, so kids can slide down the bluff."

"You could have swings here on these cedars," Brower offered.

Fraser said that some of the cedars on his property had been planted by Scottish soldiers who had built and manned a stockade there in the early eighteenth century. Development was thus nothing new around Cumberland Oaks. Looking west across the water and the marsh, he confided that he was envisioning a seven-hundred-and-fifty-thousand-dollar system of towers, cables, and aerial gondolas to carry people to Cumberland Oaks from the mainland. "Brunswick Pulp & Paper owns those forests over there," Fraser said. "I would describe Brunswick Pulp & Paper as 'friendly.'"

Wild grapevines as thick as hawsers hung from the high limbs of Fraser's pines, and as we moved east through the woods Brower found them irresistible. Fraser stopped the Land Rover so Brower could get out and swing on one—fifty feet in an arc through the air. He crashed into a palmetto.

Between the deep woods and the beach, among the secondary dunes of Cumberland Oaks, was a freshwater lake—Whitney Lake—so clear and lustrous that it gave Fraser's property a slight edge over all other parts of the island. Set in all the whiteness of the big hills of powder sand, the lake was so blue that day it paled the blue sky. Near the north end of the lake, three skeletal trees protruded from the slopes of sand—branches intact, but spare and dead. A buzzard sat in each tree. The trees were dead because the dunes were marching. Slowly, these enormous hills, shaped and reshaped by the wind, were moving south. They had already filled up half of Fraser's lake, and, left alone, they would eventually fill it all. Five buzzards stood at the edge of the water. Fraser stood there, too, with the unconcealed look on his face of a man watching a major asset disappear. "We've got to stabilize these dunes," he said.

Brower, for his part, was moved by the lyricism of the scene. If destruction is natural, Brower is for it. "I think it's just fine to see it happen," he said.

Fraser said, "I've got to restore dune-grass vegetation here. I've got to put the lake back to its original size. I'm an advocate of lakes."

"There's a place for development and there's a place for nature," said Candler.

"What would you move the dunes with?" I asked Fraser.

"Spoons, hoes, shovels—earthmoving equipment. You change natural gradings very cheaply with a bulldozer," he said.

Fraser went on to tell us that the lake had been named for Eli Whitney. Planters on the island had given Whitney financial support toward the development of the cotton gin. "This lake shouldn't be allowed to disappear," Fraser said. "There should be canoes on it for children. Children should be fishing here for bream. There is nothing here now but buzzards and dead trees."

Thinking of his three thousand acres as a whole, I asked him privately what he would like to build there by Whitney Lake.

"Houses!" he whispered.

The northernmost tip of the ocean beach was a long spit owned by Candler. We drove up there, inadvertently filling the sky with sandpipers and gulls. Then we turned and, in the late-afternoon light, went south all the way. The big beach ran on and on before us, white and dazzling in the clear sunlight. No other human beings were there. Of the several houses on Cumberland Island, the one nearest to the beach was a half mile back in the woods. We had been driving for a while when Candler remarked that we were nearing the end of his property. He has two and a half miles of beach. He said, "The only thing wrong with this beach—the traffic's so bad." Shells crunched under the wheels and salt foam flew out behind us. Plastic jugs, light bulbs, bottles, and buoys had drifted up along the scum line, but nowhere near enough of them to defeat the wild beach. I remembered the shoreline of the Hudson River at Barrytown, New York. A photographer from *Sports Illustrated* had caught up with Brower near there, and they had gone to some difficulty to get down to the river's edge, so that Brower could be photographed with the wind tousling his white hair against a background of natural beauty. For the occasion, Brower had changed from a topcoat into a ski parka, and the picture was successful—this ecological Isaiah by the wide water. It was just a head-and-shoulders shot, so it did not include the immediate environment of Brower's feet. The shore of the Hudson River, a hundred miles upstream from Manhattan, was literally obscured by aerosol cans, plastic bottles, boat cushions, sheets of polyethylene, bricks, industrial scum, globs of asphalt, and a tattered yacht flag. Now, on the Cumberland beach, Fraser, for the moment, was sounding much like a hard-line real-estate man. He was saying that we had beside us "the finest, gentlest breakers on the Atlantic coast." Brower said that where he came from such ripples were not called breakers. We got out of the Land Rover and walked for a while. Brower paused and studied the reflection of the falling sun on the surfaces of the breakers. This was what mattered to him—the play of light. He saw a horseshoe crab and had no idea what it was. He picked up a whelk shell and a clamshell and asked the names of the creatures that had lived in them. He wondered what made the holes of fiddler crabs. Shrimp boats were working offshore. Brower said he liked the look of them, bristling with spars. Brower seems to think in scenes. He seems to paint them in his mind's eye, and in these scenes not everything made by man is unacceptable. Shrimp boats on a bobbing sea are O.K. On the waterfront in San Francisco, he and I once drove at dusk past a big schooner that is perennially moored there, and its high rigging was beautiful in the fading light. "There should be more masts against the sky," Brower said. And now, back in the Land Rover, he looked up at high cumulus that was assembling over the ocean and he spoke of "sky mountains," while Fraser looked the other way and said that the primary dunes were in a process of severe disintegration, and the Land Rover

moved on at forty miles per hour, crunching Paisley-spotted shells of the tiger crab.
"Have you ever been on a shrimp boat to see how they work?" Brower said.

"I have—when I was twelve," said Fraser. "I want a shrimp boat out of
Cumberland Oaks, taking four or five kids a day."

The distance was so great across the beach and the dunes to the woods that I
asked Fraser how far back he thought the nearest of his houses ought to be.

"The mainland," said Candler.

"That's a real dilemma here," Fraser said. "If the houses are set back in the trees,
it's bad for recreation. What we need is an extensive tree-planting program to build
up destroyed areas by the shore."

"Destroyed?"

"Destroyed. These dunes are not ordinary."

"They have always looked all right to me," Candler said.

"Pine trees grow exceedingly fast down by the ocean," Fraser went on.

Brower was silent.

"Within thirty years, there need to be fifty thousand more points for a week's
visit on the Georgia coast," Fraser said. "You don't decrease the number of Americans taking a vacation by sealing off a particular land area. Surveys show that seventy-five per cent of Americans prefer beaches to all other places of recreation. I
believe in human enjoyment of beaches, but, of course, the druids think it would be
a shame and a crime to have people on this beach—a shame and a crime."

Acres of ducks darkened the swells of the ocean. A wild brown mare and her
gray colt stood ankle-deep in a tidal pool. "Sam, why didn't you buy the property I
bought?" Fraser said.

"I didn't have enough money," Candler said.

A line of pelicans—nineteen of them—flew south just seaward of the breakers.
Pelicans fly single file, and Candler said he could remember them going by in lines
a hundred pelicans long. That was in an era that seems to be gone. DDT has got into
the bodies of pelicans and eventually into the shells of their eggs, and its effect on
the shells is that they come out so thin they crack before chicks are ready to be
born. Brower remarked that the pelican is one of the earth's oldest species. He
quoted Robinson Jeffers, saying that pelicans "remember the cone that the oldest
redwood dropped from." We were nearing the end of the beach, and we could see
Florida across the mouth of the St. Mary's River. The pelicans kept going, like flying
boxcars, across the river. "They're doomed," Brower said. "Maybe we're lined up
behind those pelicans."

—1971

W. S. MERWIN

B. 1927

*W. S. (William Stanley) Merwin has described the impulse behind his work
as follows: "One really wants, hopelessly, to save the world, and one tries to
say everything that can be said for the things one loves." Merwin has spo-*

ken for the things he loves in a dozen volumes of poetry and in plays, essays, parables, and tales enriched by his many translations of works from other ages and cultures. His earlier poems express a bleak view of the human enterprise, but some of his more mature verse invokes the hope that we can learn to listen to the life surrounding us and thus direct our trajectory away from destruction. Merwin has long coupled his writing with activism. When his book of poems The Carrier of Ladders (1970) was awarded the Pulitzer Prize in 1971, he rejected the prize as a protest against American involvement in Vietnam.

The son of a strict, unemotional Presbyterian minister, Merwin was born in New York City and spent his childhood in Union City, New Jersey, and Scranton, Pennsylvania. In 1947 he graduated from Princeton University, where he was far from an outstanding student, with a B.A. in romance languages and medieval literature, and spent a year in graduate school studying modern languages before traveling to Europe. He lived for a time on the island of Majorca, then later in London, New York City, and on a farm in France. In the early 1970s he moved to the island of Maui and began laboring to turn eighteen acres of wrecked pineapple land into a botanical garden. He lives there with his third wife in a house he designed himself, powered by photovoltaics and without air conditioning. He has been involved in numerous local ecological causes, from attempting to block the expansion of the island's airport to opposing a geothermal project in the sole remaining uninterrupted tract of lowland rain forest.

Throughout Merwin's writing is woven what he has called his "deep historical pessimism" over the destruction of the natural world by "an economy that's really based on war and greed" and by an American "specietal chauvinism." He once described his poetic stance as being in opposition to "the positivism and the American optimism" typified by Walt Whitman. "It makes me extremely uneasy when he talks about the American expansion and the feeling of manifest destiny in a voice of wonder. I keep thinking about the buffalo, about the Indians, and about the species that are being rendered extinct. Whitman's momentary, rather sentimental view just wipes these things out as though they were of no importance." "Rain at Night," from Merwin's 1988 collection The Rain in the Trees, is a lament over the exploitation of land and resources for profit, an extension of the "manifest destiny" mindset.

RAIN AT NIGHT

This is what I have heard

at last the wind in December
lashing the old trees with rain
unseen rain racing along the tiles
under the moon
wind rising and falling
wind with many clouds
trees in the night wind

after an age of leaves and feathers
someone dead
thought of this mountain as money
and cut the trees
that were here in the wind
in the rain at night
it is hard to say it
but they cut the sacred 'ohias then
the sacred koas then
the sandalwood and the halas
holding aloft their green fires
and somebody dead turned cattle loose
among the stumps until killing time

but the trees have risen one more time
and the night wind makes them sound
like the sea that is yet unknown
the black clouds race over the moon
the rain is falling on the last place.

—1988

SHARMAN APT RUSSELL

B. 1954

Sharman Apt Russell writes with the flair of a storyteller about the complex realities of life in a southwestern landscape and about broader cultural concerns as well. In books of fiction and nonfiction, she explores the distant past and the richly textured present of the place where she has deliberately taken root and of the country at large. Though she writes evenhandedly about controversial subjects in Songs of the Fluteplayer: Seasons of Life in the Southwest *(1991) and* Kill the Cowboy: A Battle of Mythology in the New West *(1993), her point of view is clearly that of an environmentalist and a feminist. Her children's fantasy book* The Humpbacked Fluteplayer *(1994) envisions the Sonoran desert without the blight of Phoenix. When the Land Was Young: Reflections on American Archaeology (1996) is an expression of her conviction that to understand who we are and to extend concern to future generations, we must be able to imagine how people once lived. A novel springing from her research for this latter book and a new collection of essays are in the works.*

Born at Edwards Air Force Base, California, Russell was the second of two daughters of a test pilot. When her father was killed in a plane crash in the desert in 1956, her mother moved the family to Phoenix, where Russell grew up. Inspired by reading Aldo Leopold's A Sand County Almanac, *she earned a B.S. in conservation and natural resources from the University of California at Berkeley in 1976, and an M.F.A. in creative writing from the University of Montana in 1980. She and her new husband moved to southwestern New Mexico in 1981 with the goal of creating a self-reliant life close to the land, a dream she explores in* Songs of the Fluteplayer. *The mother of two children born at home, Russell teaches writing at Western New Mexico University.*

In an essay entitled "Range War" in Songs of the Fluteplayer, *Russell explores the differing views of ranchers and environmentalists about how public land in the West should be used. As she points out, 70 percent of the West is grazed; ranchers depend on being able to graze their livestock on public land, while environmentalists protest the serious damage done by overgrazing. The issue is highly charged, and in* Kill the Cowboy, *an amplification on her earlier essay, Russell profiles sincere, articulate people across a whole spectrum of opinions, with the aim of fostering dialogue and understanding. Her own opinion on the matter is elucidated in the following selection from* Kill the Cowboy.

THE PHYSICS OF BEAUTY

From our small adobe house, my husband and I drive a dirt road, across the rising Mimbres River, onto a two-lane state highway. After fifteen miles, we turn east up another dirt road, the very one that in 1930 cut the Gila Wilderness in half. From here, it takes over an hour of twisting, turning and bumping to reach the trailhead that leads into Black Canyon. My children are five and eight now. More frequently we take them on day hikes into the Gila Wilderness, walks that often are shorter than we had planned and longer than they tolerate without complaining.

The first mile of this trip is defined by cows. Their excrement, old and new, litters the trail, with clouds of flies and gnats buzzing up from the new. For now, Black Canyon is grazed every other year, and this is the year. It is spring, a phenomenal spring of more rain than anyone has ever seen before. We scare off group after group of mother cows with calves, and we eye them as warily as they eye us. A few shake their heads in menace and maternal warning. My five-year-old son is fascinated. In the last year, his desire to be a cowboy has only intensified; he is saving up his birthday money to buy a ranch. I cannot explain his obsession, no more than I can dismiss it.

"How much does a cow cost?" he asks, as he has many times before. "Are these wild cows? How many cows should I have on *my* ranch? Why is that cow looking at us? Why can't bulls have babies? Is that a bull? Why do cows have horns? Why can't I get closer?"

We walk by a small inholding of private property. Across a pasture fenced off for horses, over the stream that feeds this canyon, we see the metal roof of the house where the permittees on the Diamond Bar allotment live. Only one couple stays out here now and manages the ranch. I have been to meetings with this man and woman. I have eaten lunch with them and laughed at their jokes. I have watched them grow angry as environmentalists accused them of damaging the public land. These are people who never thought they would be standing up in a crowd to defend their livelihood. They are caught in the middle of something they had not anticipated. They bought a ranch. They signed a permit agreement. Everyone important in our society was there: the government, the bank, the lawyers.

We pass by a messy area littered with downed trees, branches, and wood chips. Beavers have been at work. My daughter explains this to me, and I am impressed. Did I know so much about beavers at her age? We pass through a blowdown, where the big dead cottonwoods are fallen soldiers, angled against each other, bleached gray. Although the grasses here have already been grazed once this season, they are rising again, rich and green. The dainty heads of blue grama knock at our ankles and knees. The stream is fifteen feet wide and tumbles past noisily. We hear the whistle, trill, and caw of blue jays and brown towhees. We start to enter the most beautiful country in the world.

Graciously, my husband allows me to run on ahead. He knows how much I enjoy this. I love to run on trails. I love to run through the forest, jumping over logs, navigating water, brought up suddenly, then bounding downhill. The thick vertical lines of ponderosa pine blur. Yellow and white wildflowers flicker in the grass. Such patterns are a jumble in the uncertainty of my peripheral vision; the ground is what I must concentrate on. Rocks, incline, sticks, holes. I match myself to these.

All my running—and I have been a runner, off and on, for twenty years—is based on this kind of fantasy. I am a deer. I am an animal. I am a wild animal. When I run on trails in the wilderness, I am not suddenly faster or younger or thinner or in better shape. But I am, for some reason, exactly where I should be, doing what I want to do. The adrenaline flows faster, and there is an intensity to the concentration, an excitement in the peripheral vision.

Following behind, my husband may well have a more profound experience. He has been on many long horse rides through the Gila National Forest and Gila Wilderness, and he knows these canyons, valleys, rivers, hills, mountains, mesas, and ridges much better than I. He sinks into places that I run through. He will remember the height of the grass and spacing of the trees and vegetation on the slopes. He will know where this canyon is in relationship to all the other folds of canyons and mountains, and he will add to that memory when he comes here next; he will compare it with what he has seen at Willow Spring or Reeds Meadow; he will nurture the growth of the living map inside him. He will build, as he has for these last twelve years, that internal geography, the imprint of land.

As for my children, who knows what patterns they see, what connections they make. We provide them with the only childhood we can, and we are sure to be surprised at the result. This afternoon, my son and daughter pass by towers of ponderosa pine, the same tree we have used for the vigas of our house, for our ceiling, for the upright beams that frame their bedroom windows. My children know to smell the inner bark of this tree for its hint of vanilla. They know that the ponderosa turns yellow only after hundreds of years. The rest of their knowledge is subterranean. They know, without knowing, the shape of the alligator juniper, the Emory oak, the Douglas fir, the narrow-leafed cottonwood. They see the forest, and they do not see it. They are not particularly quiet or receptive. They chatter, instead, about their friends and desires. They are as irreverent as squirrels.

I run until I reach the first stream crossing. It is so high that I must wade, wet to my knees, my tennis shoes soaked. The meadow starts opening up now, nearly filling the canyon bottom. The pine trees are spaced generously apart. The water courses swift and clear and purposeful, its edges meeting smoothly a thick mat of grass. It is a landscape that beckons. Run! A blue heron flaps its wings and retreats with dignity.

I think of a rancher I once talked to as we drove two hours from Reserve to Silver City. His family has been on the same public-lands ranch for a hundred years, and he feels that they have done a good job. The watershed is healthy. Wildlife is abundant. This man believes that his ranch is not an exception. He could name me "four or five families off the top of his head" who have held tight to their heritage and their love. Like Doc Hatfield, he fears that public-lands ranching may not last much longer. A dramatic increase in the federal grazing fee would drive him out of business. No one, of course, would go hungry if that happened. Both he and his wife have college educations—and he could always subdivide his private land.

Still, he says, something, something *would* go hungry. He is trying to talk about his soul.

"I didn't grow up on that ranch," he says. "It was my grandparents', and I spent my summers there. When I went back to become a rancher, I didn't know, I couldn't guess what it would come to mean to me. That kind of life. I can't describe it. But I just don't know anything that could replace it. I just don't know anything that could mean the same."

I stop for another crossing. There is no one here but me. The trees and grass glisten in the sunlight. The rock faces of the canyon move in a medley of shifting shadows. The air is alive with the constant drift of insects, pollen, and leaves. The sounds are musical: water and birds. The beauty of this place stuns me, and I lift my arms in a gesture that is not entirely conscious. I want to absorb this beauty. I want to embrace this scenery. I think about living in a ranch house at the mouth of Black Canyon—not a visitor, not on a day hike, not here for three or four or five hours. I think about *living* here, fully engaged.

"Imagine," the rancher said as we drove past Mogollon Baldy, Mud Spring Mesa, Greenwood Canyon. "Imagine what it would be like to look up at a mountain or a hill and to know that your great-grandfather also looked at that mountain and worked on it and loved it just like you do. That kind of relationship is special. I don't think our society should just throw that away."

I don't either.

I wade through the water and begin to run again.

I think of Connie Hatfield, who believes without irony that ranchers are like Native Americans, a conquered and indigenous land-based people about to lose their culture and lifestyle. "We're like those Indians now," Connie says.

I can see the irony and still empathize with Connie Hatfield.

At the same time, I will not, I cannot, relinquish my own claim to the public lands. I will not relinquish my own vision of wilderness. I will not place the needs of ranchers above my own—not those of the permittees on the Gila Wilderness, not those of that rancher in the car who spoke to me so openly and whom I liked very much. I will not place their needs above my husband's needs or my children's or my children's children or my children's children's children.

I will not place their needs above the land itself.

"I have two criteria for the solution to any problem," says Ed Chaney, a conservationist in Idaho. "Does it work? And is it honorable?"

These are the questions we must apply to the issues of wilderness preservation—and to the larger issue of grazing on our public land. We must apply them to each ecosystem, each allotment, each creek-bed.

Does grazing 1,188 cows work on the Diamond Bar? Is this a sustainable agriculture? Can this area support that many cattle and still be a healthy ecosystem? Can it support that many cattle and still be considered wilderness, using our flawed definitions of the word?

We must consider the possibility that the answer is yes.

If the answer is no, we must find an honorable solution.

I run for nearly two miles until I reach Aspen Canyon. Then, as agreed, I turn back to find my family. They are not much farther along from the point where I left them. I feel energized. Something green has entered my blood. The children are completely naked and building a dam in the stream. My husband is examining grass on the bank. It's a cool season perennial that is seeding again. This year, the range will recover lushly—if the rancher takes his cows off soon.

On our way out, we go off the trail to find the ruins of a Mogollon pithouse. My son and daughter are puzzled by these circles of stone sunk into the ground. "Children like you played here a thousand years ago," my husband tells them. But a thousand years is beyond their scope.

Nothing is simple.

Two weeks after my family's hike into Black Canyon, the Forest Service range conservationist rode the same trail. He rated the condition of the stream area as poor to very poor. Oh, it was still green and grassy. But, as even ranchers know, ungrazed streams in the Southwest would normally be thick with trees and shrubs. There would be cottonwoods and willows of all age classes, young and middle-aged to replace the older giants. There would be deep, shaded, protected pools where trout could feed, there would be dense thickets of growth supporting a rich diversity of plant life and wildlife. An ungrazed stream area is not a stately parklike meadow punctuated by a single blue heron. I had been running though a garden, not a wilderness.

I knew this, of course.

Over a month later, the cows are still in Black Canyon. This certainly is not a walk I would take now. One man does and describes it in a letter to the local newspaper. "The flats surrounding the creek and canyon sides in this area were heavily grazed. The grass was cropped very short, and there were few weeds, and no shrubs or small trees left by the herd of cattle grazing. No problem, I thought, we'll just head up the canyon and soon we'll be in the 'real wilderness.' Six miles later, far above where Aspen Canyon meets Black Canyon, I was still waiting to get to the 'real wilderness.' . . . The whole canyon smelled of manure. . . . If someone had told me before I left on my hike that I would be walking up six miles of overgrazed, smelly cow pasture, I would have told them, 'Nah, no way!'"

The ranchers believe they have no choice. The cows have to go somewhere. The cows have to drink. The ranchers want stock tanks and a new management plan.

An environmentalist tells me angrily, "That area can't support any deer or wildlife now. There are no places for deer to hide or shelter."

A Forest Service official says, "Next year, when Black Canyon isn't being grazed, it'll look great again. There will be lots of grass."

"Unfortunately," he adds, "it's the trees that we really want."

At the very end of the summer, my husband also rides his horse down Black Canyon. He comes back shaken and depressed. Although this year's spring was wet, the summer rains did not come with any generosity. The cows are still in the canyon, and some areas are now completely denuded—bare, brown, eroding. It's wrong, my husband says. It's very wrong.

Is there an honorable solution? At one public meeting, the rancher on the Diamond Bar was asked if he could be "bought out" by an environmental organization.

"This is America," the man shot back. "I'll sell, if you've got enough money!"

"I don't have to *buy* out ranchers who lease public grazing rights," an environmentalist spoke up with equal heat. "I already own that land!"

Nothing is simple.

We must define our terms. We must sidestep our own prejudices and seek out the illusions wrapped in the shimmering nimbus of our words. We must also retain the power of words and the power of the dream. In the physics of beauty, we are still in the Dark Ages.

What can we do but keep looking for the light?

We tell stories.

It is an odd note, but many people concerned with range issues share the attraction for one particular story: the destruction of Africa. There are those who see its analogy here, our Great Plains its savanna, our mountain lion its tiger. These people look across the ocean to a mystical wilderness once teeming with life, the first home of humans colonized and looted, used up, diseased, racked, suffering, no longer beautiful. The state director of ADC mentions the loss of African wildlife: this is what he fears. Allan Savory laments erosion in his native Zimbabwe. Ranchers—who know in their hearts that they are producing *food*, a gift that is tangible, real, and important—speak of starvation. So do those who compare the cost of raising beef to grain. The woman from the Wilderness Society, sitting in her Denver office, became interested in conservation as a Peace Corps volunteer in Liberia. There, she saw too much wildland disappear for "short-term interests." She "came back wondering, wondering what I could do to be a world citizen."

Fear, anger, grief, love.

These emotions drive us.

—1993

RUSH LIMBAUGH III

B. 1951

Born into a family of lawyers in the southeast corner of Missouri, Rush Limbaugh III soared to fame over the airwaves in the early 1990s. In two decades he went from being a college dropout to an invited guest at the Bush White House. After a lackluster start as a disc jockey, Limbaugh came into his own at a radio station in Sacramento, California, where he hosted a call-in talk show that focused on national political issues. When in 1988 he was tapped to take over a slot on WABC radio in New York City, he made his first broadcast on July 4, the day after the United States had gunned down an Iranian jetliner over the Persian Gulf. "So I had an automatic issue to talk about," Limbaugh recalls. His specialty is "analyzing and commenting on events as they occur and play out." His radio audience numbers in the millions, bearing testimony to his popularity as an entertainer and cultural icon. He is also a fluent and entertaining author, one whose want of logic is compensated for by an abundance of humor.

Limbaugh has an offbeat perspective on nature. When he criticizes "the presumptuous view of man and his works" that would ascribe to human beings the power to alter "Creation," he sounds like Robinson Jeffers promulgating the philosophy of inhumanism. When he rejects the claims of some "arrogant scientists" who believe they can unlock "every secret in the universe," he sounds like William Wordsworth. When he admits, "I am in awe of the perfection of the earth," he sounds like John Muir. But when he ridicules "tree huggers" and "environmentalist wackos," he incurs the wrath of many politicized nature lovers. In pondering his place among the others who have something to say about the relation between human beings and the nonhuman world, perhaps we should begin by taking him at his word: "One of Rush's Unalterable Laws is that man and the environment can live together in harmony."

At the beginning of the chapter in his first book, The Way Things Ought to Be (1992), from which "The Environmental Mindset" is excerpted, Limbaugh questions the view entertained by many Americans that nature is fragile. He goes on to insist in this piece, "We have a right to use the earth to make our lives better." In his view, environmentalists interfere with this right, particularly in their "belief that human beings can't be trusted to own very much of the land." His cry echoes that of a contingent of landowners, many of them in the West, who invoke the "takings" clause of the Fifth Amendment, which states, "nor shall private property be taken for public use, without just compensation." These people reason that when governmental policy, such as the Endangered Species Act or the Clean Water Act, is applied to private property, it infringes on their rights as landowners. The questions they raise and Limbaugh broadcasts will no doubt be debated on both legislative and judicial stages for some time to come.

THE ENVIRONMENTAL MINDSET

I used to think that environmentalists were a bunch of political liberals who were just using a different angle to advance their cause. Some of that goes on, but it goes beyond merely advancing liberalism. There are two groups of people that have made environmentalism their new home: socialists and enviro-religious fanatics. And they have chosen two new constituencies which cannot speak or disagree and therefore cannot refuse their "help and assistance": animals and trees.

With the collapse of Marxism, environmentalism has become the new refuge of socialist thinking. The environment is a great way to advance a political agenda that favors central planning and an intrusive government. What better way to control someone's property than to subordinate one's private property rights to environmental concerns.

The second group that has latched on to the environmental movement are people who believe it is a religion; that God is the earth and that God is nothing more than the earth. Actually, it is a modern form of pantheism, where nature is divine. This group wants to preserve the earth at all costs, even if it means that much of the Third World will be forever condemned to poverty. Rather than elevate the Third World, they want to move us closer to Third World conditions. That's somehow cleaner, and purer. It's the way things were before Western white people came along and terrorized the earth by inventing things. They want to roll us back, maybe not to the Stone Age, but at least to the horse-and-buggy era.

Both of these groups are consumed with egocentricity. They behave as though they believe the world began the day they were born and that it's going to end the day they die.

Now, I've spoken about the leaders of the radical environmental movement. The followers are also interesting. They are the people who just want to feel good; the people who want to receive accolades for their perceived care and concern for the environment. Then we have the media who willingly serve as conduits for all of these predictions, studies, prophecies, and tall tales that the environmentalist wackos disseminate.

But there are also many average Americans who consider themselves environmentalists. It is quite natural to want a clean planet, with clean water and air for ourselves and our children. It is quite commendable to not want to destroy that which enables us to live. So, if some scientist comes along and is given credibility by the media, it is not surprising that a lot of people believe him. That is how hundreds of thousands of people are mobilized for the cause and end up on the Mall in Washington and in Central Park in New York.

What these decent people have to realize is that regardless of what perspective they have—socialist, religious, or whatever—a common characteristic of those in the radical environmental movement is the belief that private property rights will have to be severely curbed in this country. That's what is behind the move to take private land out of circulation to preserve wetlands, and the efforts to save the spotted owl. If it rains in your backyard one day and you have an inch of water there, all of a sudden your yard becomes a wetland and you can't build anything there.

This hostility to private property, my friends, is based on the belief that human beings can't be trusted to own very much of the land; that we are selfish and cursed with the desire to change nature. We are 4 percent of the world's population here in America and we use 25 percent of the world's resources. How dare we be so selfish. Never mind the fact that our country feeds the world. Never mind the fact that our technology has improved life everywhere on this planet.

I believe that many environmental leaders are quite sincere, but that they all operate from a fundamentally different viewpoint than most other people. You and I and the vast majority of other people work for a living. We hold jobs in which we produce something or perform a service. We create commerce.

Most of the people running environmental groups don't work. What they do is persuade other people to donate to their cause. They live well, with a fair amount being siphoned off for expenses, conferences, and high salaries. They've become dependent on the income from donations. These people want to improve their standard of living and so they have to build up their donations. There are only so many people who will give to create bird sanctuaries in this country. That's why some environmentalists have gone into crisis mongering to increase the level of their donations. Their appeals and their scare tactics are designed to transform people into foot soldiers in the army of doomsday environmentalism.

It's interesting to note which environmental hazards these people really worry about. It is those that are caused by business or man-made things. Consider the danger of radon gas. If there is one environmental problem that is real, it is radon. Some Easterners have homes where radon seeps in from under the ground and reaches levels many times beyond what is considered safe. But there is no hysteria over radon. Why? Because it's natural, man didn't put it there. There are no dramatic calls for radon studies, nor any calls for evacuations. Everything that happens in their deified nature is somehow acceptable. Things will work themselves out. Well, man-made disasters can also work themselves out. Take the *Exxon Valdez* spill. We were told that the cleanup would take hundreds of years. Now we see that through natural processes and the incredibly resilient powers of the planet, the tide has taken care of much of the damage that man didn't clean up. And, would you believe that more fish were caught last year than ever before in Prince William Sound.

My friends, the earth is a remarkable creation and is capable of great rejuvenation. We can't destroy it. It can fix itself. We shouldn't go out of our way to do damage, but neither should we buy into the hysteria and monomania which preaches, in essence, that we don't belong here. We have a right to use the earth to make our lives better.

—1993

WALLACE STEGNER

1909-1993

Wallace Stegner wrote to his one-time student Wendell Berry in 1990: "You are a hero among those who have been wounded and offended by industrial living and yearn for a simpler and more natural and more feeling relation to the natural world." These words apply equally well to Stegner himself. In a career of nearly sixty years as a writer and teacher, Stegner stood for "seeing life steadily and seeing it whole." Many of his more than thirty books explore the experience of living in the American West and the social and environmental complexities of the region. Commented the writer James D. Houston, "Stegner is a regional writer in the richest sense of that word, one who manages to dig through the surface and plumb a region's deepest implications, tapping into profound matters of how a place or a piece of territory can shape life, character, actions, dreams." One could argue that the West, or place more generally, as a determinant of human character is the abiding theme of all Stegner's work.

Born in Iowa, Stegner spent the formative years of childhood on the plains of Saskatchewan, as he records in his memoir Wolf Willow *(1962). He earned his B.A. at the University of Utah in 1930 and completed his Ph.D. in English at the University of Iowa in 1935. He taught at Augustana College, the University of Utah, the University of Wisconsin-Madison, Harvard University, and the University of Toronto, but he is most closely associated with Stanford University, where he taught from 1945 to 1971, directing the creative writing program for nearly all of those years. Many important American writers—including such nature writers as Edward Abbey, Wendell Berry, John Daniel, C. L. Rawlins, and Alison Deming—have studied at Stanford since the 1950s as recipients of the Wallace Stegner fellowship in creative writing.*

Stegner's work includes novels (his 1972 novel Angle of Repose *won the Pulitzer Prize), collections of short stories and essays, monographs on teach-*

*ing creative writing, and biographies of explorer John Wesley Powell and
conservationist-historian Bernard DeVoto. In many of his essays, he takes
an overtly political stance, critiquing human shortsightedness and abuse.
The following letter, written to a natural resources manager in the Kennedy
administration and later collected in* The Sound of Mountain Water *(1969),
is representative. Stegner's strenuous message is that with regard to land
use, "We need to put into effect . . . some other principle than the principles
of exploitation or 'usefulness' or even recreation." Wild places, he argues in
one of the most famous passages in American environmental literature, are
necessary because they are "part of the geography of hope."*

WILDERNESS LETTER

Los Altos, Calif.
Dec. 3, 1960

David E. Pesonen
Wildland Research Center
Agricultural Experiment Station
243 Mulford Hall
University of California
Berkeley 4, Calif.

Dear Mr. Pesonen:

I believe that you are working on the wilderness portion of the Outdoor
Recreation Resources Review Commission's report. If I may, I should like to urge
some arguments for wilderness preservation that involve recreation, as it is ordinarily conceived, hardly at all. Hunting, fishing, hiking, mountain-climbing, camping, photography, and the enjoyment of natural scenery will all, surely, figure in
your report. So will the wilderness as a genetic reserve, a scientific yardstick by
which we may measure the world in its natural balance against the world in its
man-made imbalance. What I want to speak for is not so much the wilderness uses,
valuable as those are, but the wilderness *idea*, which is a resource in itself. Being an
intangible and spiritual resource, it will seem mystical to the practical-minded—but
then anything that cannot be moved by a bulldozer is likely to seem mystical to
them.

I want to speak for the wilderness idea as something that has helped form our
character and that has certainly shaped our history as a people. It has no more to
do with recreation than churches have to do with recreation, or than the strenu-
ousness and optimism and expansiveness of what historians call the "American
Dream" have to do with recreation. Nevertheless, since it is only in this recreation
survey that the values of wilderness are being compiled, I hope you will permit me
to insert this idea between the leaves, as it were, of the recreation report.

Something will have gone out of us as a people if we ever let the remaining
wilderness be destroyed; if we permit the last virgin forests to be turned into comic
books and plastic cigarette cases; if we drive the few remaining members of the wild
species into zoos or to extinction; if we pollute the last clear air and dirty the last
clean streams and push our paved roads through the last of the silence, so that

never again will Americans be free in their own country from the noise, the exhausts, the stinks of human and automotive waste. And so that never again can we have the chance to see ourselves single, separate, vertical and individual in the world, part of the environment of trees and rocks and soil, brother to the other animals, part of the natural world and competent to belong in it. Without any remaining wilderness we are committed wholly, without chance for even momentary reflection and rest, to a headlong drive into our technological termite-life, the Brave New World of a completely man-controlled environment. We need wilderness preserved—as much of it as is still left, and as many kinds—because it was the challenge against which our character as a people was formed. The reminder and the reassurance that it is still there is good for our spiritual health even if we never once in ten years set foot in it. It is good for us when we are young, because of the incomparable sanity it can bring briefly, as vacation and rest, into our insane lives. It is important to us when we are old simply because it is there—important, that is, simply as idea.

We are a wild species, as Darwin pointed out. Nobody ever tamed or domesticated or scientifically bred us. But for at least three millennia we have been engaged in a cumulative and ambitious race to modify and gain control of our environment, and in the process we have come close to domesticating ourselves. Not many people are likely, any more, to look upon what we call "progress" as an unmixed blessing. Just as surely as it has brought us increased comfort and more material goods, it has brought us spiritual losses, and it threatens now to become the Frankenstein that will destroy us. One means of sanity is to retain a hold on the natural world, to remain, insofar as we can, good animals. Americans still have that chance, more than many peoples; for while we were demonstrating ourselves the most efficient and ruthless environment busters in history, and slashing and burning and cutting our way through a wilderness continent, the wilderness was working on us. It remains in us as surely as Indian names remain on the land. If the abstract dream of human liberty and human dignity became, in America, something more than an abstract dream, mark it down at least partially to the fact that we were in subtle ways subdued by what we conquered.

The Connecticut Yankee, sending likely candidates from King Arthur's unjust kingdom to his Man Factory for rehabilitation, was over-optimistic, as he later admitted. These things cannot be forced, they have to grow. To make such a man, such a democrat, such a believer in human individual dignity, as Mark Twain himself, the frontier was necessary, Hannibal and the Mississippi and Virginia City, and reaching out from those the wilderness; the wilderness as opportunity and as idea, the thing that has helped to make an American different from and, until we forget it in the roar of our industrial cities, more fortunate than other men. For an American, insofar as he is new and different at all, is a civilized man who has renewed himself in the wild. The American experience has been the confrontation by old peoples and cultures of a world as new as if it had just risen from the sea. That gave us our hope and our excitement, and the hope and excitement can be passed on to newer Americans, Americans who never saw any phase of the frontier. But only so long as we keep the remainder of our wild as a reserve and a promise— a sort of wilderness bank.

As a novelist, I may perhaps be forgiven for taking literature as a reflection, indirect but profoundly true, of our national consciousness. And our literature, as perhaps you are aware, is sick, embittered, losing its mind, losing its faith. Our novelists are the declared enemies of their society. There has hardly been a serious or important novel in this century that did not repudiate in part or in whole American technological culture for its commercialism, its vulgarity, and the way in which it has dirtied a clean continent and a clean dream. I do not expect that the preservation of our remaining wilderness is going to cure this condition. But the mere example that we can as a nation apply some other criteria than commercial and exploitative considerations would be heartening to many Americans, novelists or otherwise. We need to demonstrate our acceptance of the natural world, including ourselves; we need the spiritual refreshment that being natural can produce. And one of the best places for us to get that is in the wilderness where the fun houses, the bulldozers, and the pavements of our civilization are shut out.

Sherwood Anderson, in a letter to Waldo Frank in the 1920's, said it better than I can. "Is it not likely that when the country was new and men were often alone in the fields and the forest they got a sense of bigness outside themselves that has now in some way been lost . . . Mystery whispered in the grass, played in the branches of trees overhead, was caught up and blown across the American line in clouds of dust at evening on the prairies . . . I am old enough to remember tales that strengthen my belief in a deep semi-religious influence that was formerly at work among our people. The flavor of it hangs over the best work of Mark Twain . . . I can remember old fellows in my home town speaking feelingly of an evening spent on the big empty plains. It had taken the shrillness out of them. They had learned the trick of quiet . . ."

We could learn it too, even yet; even our children and grandchildren could learn it. But only if we save, for just such absolutely non-recreational, impractical, and mystical uses as this, all the wild that still remains to us.

It seems to me significant that the distinct downturn in our literature from hope to bitterness took place almost at the precise time when the frontier officially came to an end, in 1890, and when the American way of life had begun to turn strongly urban and industrial. The more urban it has become, and the more frantic with technological change, the sicker and more embittered our literature, and I believe our people, have become. For myself, I grew up on the empty plains of Saskatchewan and Montana and in the mountains of Utah, and I put a very high valuation on what those places gave me. And if I had not been able periodically to renew myself in the mountains and deserts of western America I would be very nearly bughouse. Even when I can't get to the back country, the thought of the colored deserts of southern Utah, or the reassurance that there are still stretches of prairie where the world can be instantaneously perceived as disk and bowl, and where the little but intensely important human being is exposed to the five directions and the thirty-six winds, is a positive consolation. The idea alone can sustain me. But as the wilderness areas are progressively exploited or "improved," as the jeeps and bulldozers of uranium prospectors scar up the deserts and the roads are cut into the alpine timberlands, and as the remnants of the unspoiled and natural world are progressively eroded, every such loss is a little death in me. In us.

I am not moved by the argument that those wilderness areas which have already been exposed to grazing or mining are already deflowered, and so might as well be "harvested." For mining I cannot say much good except that its operations are generally short-lived. The extractable wealth is taken and the shafts, the tailings, and the ruins left, and in a dry country such as the American West the wounds men make in the earth do not quickly heal. Still, they are only wounds; they aren't absolutely mortal. Better a wounded wilderness than none at all. And as for grazing, if it is strictly controlled so that it does not destroy the ground cover, damage the ecology, or compete with the wildlife it is in itself nothing that need conflict with the wilderness feeling or the validity of the wilderness experience. I have known enough range cattle to recognize them as wild animals; and the people who herd them have, in the wilderness context, the dignity of rareness; they belong on the frontier, moreover, and have a look of rightness. The invasion they make on the virgin country is a sort of invasion that is as old as Neolithic man, and they can, in moderation, even emphasize a man's feeling of belonging to the natural world. Under surveillance, they can belong; under control, they need not deface or mar. I do not believe that in wilderness areas where grazing has never been permitted, it should be permitted; but I do not believe either that an otherwise untouched wilderness should be eliminated from the preservation plan because of limited existing uses such as grazing which are in consonance with the frontier condition and image.

Let me say something on the subject of the kinds of wilderness worth preserving. Most of those areas contemplated are in the national forests and in high mountain country. For all the usual recreational purposes, the alpine and forest wildernesses are obviously the most important, both as genetic banks and as beauty spots. But for the spiritual renewal, the recognition of identity, the birth of awe, other kinds will serve every bit as well. Perhaps, because they are less friendly to life, more abstractly nonhuman, they will serve even better. On our Saskatchewan prairie, the nearest neighbor was four miles away, and at night we saw only two lights on all the dark rounding earth. The earth was full of animals—field mice, ground squirrels, weasels, ferrets, badgers, coyotes, burrowing owls, snakes. I knew them as my little brothers, as fellow creatures, and I have never been able to look upon animals in any other way since. The sky in that country came clear down to the ground on every side, and it was full of great weathers, and clouds, and winds, and hawks. I hope I learned something from knowing intimately the creatures of the earth; I hope I learned something from looking a long way, from looking up, from being much alone. A prairie like that, one big enough to carry the eye clear to the sinking, rounding horizon, can be as lonely and grand and simple in its forms as the sea. It is as good a place as any for the wilderness experience to happen; the vanishing prairie is as worth preserving for the wilderness idea as the alpine forests.

So are great reaches of our western deserts, scarred somewhat by prospectors but otherwise open, beautiful, waiting, close to whatever God you want to see in them. Just as a sample, let me suggest the Robbers' Roost country in Wayne County, Utah, near the Capitol Reef National Monument. In the desert climate the dozer and jeep tracks will not soon melt back into the earth, but the country has a way of making the scars insignificant. It is a lovely and terrible wilderness, such a wilderness as Christ and the prophets went out into; harshly and beautifully colored, broken and worn until its bones are exposed, its great sky without a smudge or taint from Technocracy, and in hidden corners and pockets under its cliffs the sudden poetry of springs. Save a piece of country like that intact, and it does not matter in the slightest that only a few people every year will go into it. That is precisely its value. Roads would be a desecration, crowds would ruin it. But those who haven't the strength or youth to go into it and live can simply sit and look. They can look two hundred miles, clear into Colorado; and looking down over the cliffs and canyons of the San Rafael Swell and the Robbers' Roost they can also look as deeply into themselves as anywhere I know. And if they can't even get to the places on the Aquarius Plateau where the present roads will carry them, they can simply contemplate the *idea*, take pleasure in the fact that such a timeless and uncontrolled part of earth is still there.

These are some of the things wilderness can do for us. That is the reason we need to put into effect, for its preservation, some other principle than the principles of exploitation or "usefulness" or even recreation. We simply need that wild country available to us, even if we never do more than drive to its edge and look in. For it can be a means of reassuring ourselves of our sanity as creatures, a part of the geography of hope.

Very sincerely yours,

WALLACE STEGNER
—1960

LOUIS OWENS
B. 1948

Louis Owens is a professor of English at the University of New Mexico and a respected scholar of Native American writing. Since the early 1990s, he has been steadily producing fiction as well. His novel Bone Game *(1994), set on the campus of the University of California, Santa Cruz, is a potent combination of psychothriller, vision quest, and academic satire. Asked about his motivations as an artist, Owens responded: "I write, in part, to explore my own identity as a mixed-blood American of Choctaw, Cherokee, and Irish-American heritage. And I write to explore the dilemmas of all mixed-bloods in America. And I write to illuminate our relationship with the natural world. And I write because it is the greatest pleasure." This indeed is the theme of his 1992 book of scholarship,* Other Destinies: Understanding the American Indian Novel. *Previous to his career as academic and author, Owens served on the public lands in the West as a trail worker, fire fighter, and wilderness ranger.*

What do we mean by the word wilderness? *Owens ponders this question in his essay "The American Indian Wilderness," which appeared in the Fall 1994 issue of the* American Nature Writing Newsletter. *To the U.S. Forest Service, which was Owens's employer at the time of the incident recounted in the piece, the word is precisely understood in the language of the 1964* Wilderness Act: *"A wilderness, in contrast with those areas where man and his own works dominate the landscape, is hereby recognized as an area where the earth itself and its community of life are untrammeled by man, where man himself is a visitor who does not remain." This may be an expedient way for a large government agency to identify some of the lands it is responsible for managing, and it may also be a useful way for weekend recreationists, who live at a distance from those lands, to regard them. But what about peoples who not only live closer to these lands physically but also have a centuries-deep connection to them, who indeed may have lived upon these lands historically but have since been "removed"? The question, Owens concludes, is not one of definition and management but of perception and relationship.*

THE AMERICAN INDIAN WILDERNESS

In the center of the Glacier Peak Wilderness in northern Washington, a magnificent, fully glaciated white volcano rises over a stunningly beautiful region of the North Cascades. On maps, the mountain is called Glacier Peak. To the Salishan people who have always lived in this part of the Cascades, however, the mountain is *Dakobed*, or the Great Mother, the place of emergence. For more than eighty years, a small, three-sided log shelter stood in a place called White Pass just below one shoulder of the great mountain, tucked securely into a meadow between thick stands of mountain hemlock and alpine fir.

In the early fall of seventy-six, while working as a seasonal ranger for the U.S. Forest Service, I drew the task of burning the White Pass shelter. After all those years, the shelter roof had collapsed like a broken bird wing under the weight of winter snow, and the time was right for fire and replanting. It was part of a Forest Service plan to remove all human-made objects from wilderness areas, a plan of which I heartily approved. So I backpacked eleven miles to the pass and set up camp, and for five days, while a bitter early storm sent snow driving horizontally out of the north, I dismantled the shelter and burned the old logs, piling and burning and piling and burning until nothing remained. The antique, hand-forged spikes that had held the shelter together I put into gunny sacks and cached to be packed out later by mule. I spaded up the earth beaten hard for nearly a century by boot and hoof, and transplanted plugs of vegetation from hidden spots on the nearby ridge.

At the end of those five days, not a trace of the shelter remained, and I felt good, very smug in fact, about returning the White Pass meadow to its "original" state. As I packed up my camp, the snowstorm had subsided to a few flurries and a chill that felt bone-deep with the promise of winter. My season was almost over, and as I started the steep hike down to the trailhead my mind was on the winter I was going to spend in sunny Arizona.

A half-mile from the pass I saw the two old women. At first they were dark, hunched forms far down on the last long switchback up the snowy ridge. But as we drew closer to one another, I began to feel a growing amazement that, by the time we were face-to-face, had become awe. Almost swallowed up in their baggy wool pants, heavy sweaters and parkas, silver braids hanging below thick wool caps, they seemed ancient, each weighted with at least seventy years as well as a small backpack. They paused every few steps to lean on their staffs and look out over the North Fork drainage below, a deep, heavily forested river valley that rose on the far side to the glaciers and sawtoothed black granite of the Monte Cristo Range. And they smiled hugely upon seeing me, clearly surprised and delighted to find another person in the mountains at such a time.

We stood and chatted for a moment, and as I did with all backpackers, I reluctantly asked them where they were going. The snow quickened a little, obscuring the view, as they told me that they were going to White Pass.

"Our father built a little house up here," one of them said, "when he worked for the Forest Service like you. Way back before we was born, before this century."

"We been coming up here each year since we was little," the other added. "Except last year when Sarah was not well enough."

"A long time ago, this was all our land," the one called Sarah said. "All Indi'n land everywhere you can see. Our people had houses up in the mountains, for gathering berries every year."

As they took turns speaking, the smiles never leaving their faces, I wanted to excuse myself, to edge around these elders and flee to the trailhead and my car, drive back to the district station and keep going south. I wanted to say, "I'm Indian too. Choctaw from Mississippi; Cherokee from Oklahoma"—as if mixed blood could pardon me for what I had done. Instead, I said, "The shelter is gone." Cravenly I added, "It was crushed by snow, so I was sent up to burn it. It's gone now."

I expected outrage, anger, sadness, but instead the sisters continued to smile at me, their smiles changing only slightly. They had a plastic tarp and would stay dry, they said, because a person always had to be prepared in the mountains. They would put up their tarp inside the hemlock grove above the meadow, and the scaly hemlock branches would turn back the snow. They forgave me without saying it— my ignorance and my part in the long pattern of loss which they knew so well.

Hiking out those eleven miles, as the snow of the high country became a drumming rain in the forests below, I had long hours to ponder my encounter with the sisters. Gradually, almost painfully, I began to understand that what I called "wilderness" was an absurdity, nothing more than a figment of the European imagination. Before the European invasion, there was no wilderness in North America; there was only the fertile continent where people lived in a hard-learned balance with the natural world. In embracing a philosophy that saw the White Pass shelter—and all traces of humanity—as a shameful stain upon the "pure" wilderness, I had succumbed to a five-hundred-year-old pattern of deadly thinking that separates us from the natural world. This is not to say that what we call wilderness today does not need careful safeguarding. I believe that White Pass really is better off now that the shelter doesn't serve as a magnet to backpackers and horsepackers who compact the soil, disturb and kill the wildlife, cut down centuries-old trees for firewood, and leave their litter strewn about. And I believe the man who built the shelter would agree. But despite this unfortunate reality, the global environmental crisis that sends species into extinction daily and threatens to destroy all life surely has its roots in the Western pattern of thought that sees humanity and "wilderness" as mutually exclusive.

In old-growth forests in the North Cascades, deep inside the official Wilderness Area, I have come upon faint traces of log shelters built by Suiattle and Upper Skagit people for berry harvesting a century or more ago—just as the sisters said. Those human-made structures were as natural a part of the Cascade ecosystem as the burrows of marmots in the steep scree slopes. Our Native ancestors all over this continent lived within a complex web of relations with the natural world, and in doing so they assumed a responsibility for their world that contemporary Americans cannot even imagine. Unless Americans, and all human beings, can learn to imagine themselves as intimately and inextricably related to every aspect of the world they inhabit, with the extraordinary responsibilities such relationship entails—unless they can learn what the indigenous peoples of the Americas knew and often still know—the earth simply will not survive. A few square miles of something called wilderness will become the sign of failure everywhere.

—1994

9

What are the prospects for the
human enterprise given our current
ways of thinking about the world?

PERIL AND RESPONSE

C. K. WILLIAMS

B. 1936

*Poet C. K. (Charles Kenneth) Williams is an innovative stylist whose work
renders bleak and realistic descriptions of contemporary American life. His
subject matter is fiercely quotidian. His poems are directed toward releasing the extraordinary from within the ordinary, an approach one might
call the Pandora's Box school of poetics. Anne Sexton's comment on his first
book,* Lies *(1969), was "C. K. Williams is a demon." A reviewer of* A Dream
of the Mind *(1992) advised readers that these poems are "not for the faint
hearted." Williams is a native of Newark, New Jersey, and currently lives in
Philadelphia.*

The title poem of Tar *(1983) was called by one critic "Mr. Williams's
fable for the nuclear age, his statement of faith in perdurable, blundering
humanity." It recalls the morning of March 28, 1979, after the news had
broken that the two nuclear reactors that stood on Three Mile Island in the
middle of Pennsylvania's Susquehanna River had experienced a technical
failure that led to a meltdown of 52 percent of the reactor's core. As it
turned out, very little radioactive material actually escaped into the atmosphere and the effects of the accident upon human physical health were
negligible, but at the time there was understandable panic, especially
among those who lived close to the plant. Williams was just one hundred
miles "downwind" from the accident site. "Tar" captures a phenomenon
recognizable by anyone who has ever heard news of an event whose historical significance is immediately and overwhelmingly apparent: as if to
avoid the intensity of emotions that inevitably attend such news, the mind
suddenly fixes on the immediate environment, and everyday details acquire
an intensity ordinarily lacking.*

TAR

The first morning of Three Mile Island: those first disquieting,
    uncertain, mystifying hours.
All morning a crew of workmen have been tearing the old
    decrepit roof off our building,
and all morning, trying to distract myself, I've been wandering
    out to watch them
as they hack away the leaden layers of asbestos paper and
    disassemble the disintegrating drains.
After half a night of listening to the news, wondering how to
    know a hundred miles downwind
if and when to make a run for it and where, then a coming bolt
    awake at seven
when the roofers we've been waiting for since winter sent
    their ladders shrieking up our wall,
we still know less than nothing: the utility company continues
    making little of the accident,
the slick federal spokesmen still have their evasions in some
    semblance of order.
Surely we suspect now we're being lied to, but in the mean-
    time, there are the roofers,
setting winch-frames, sledging rounds of tar apart, and there
    I am, on the curb across, gawking.

I never realized what brutal work it is, how matter-of-factly
    and harrowingly dangerous.
The ladders flex and quiver, things skid from the edge, the
    materials are bulky and recalcitrant.
When the rusty, antique nails are levered out, their heads pull
    off; the under-roofing crumbles.
Even the battered little furnace, roaring along as patient as a
    donkey, chokes and clogs,
a dense, malignant smoke shoots up, and someone has to
    fiddle with a cock, then hammer it,
before the gush and stench will deintensify, the dark, Dantean
    broth wearily subside.
In its crucible, the stuff looks bland, like licorice, spill it,
    though, on your boots or coveralls,
it sears, and everything is permeated with it, the furnace
    gunked with burst and half-burst bubbles,
the men themselves so completely slashed and mucked they
    seem almost from another realm, like trolls.
When they take their break, they leave their brooms standing
    at attention in the asphalt pails,
work gloves clinging like Brer Rabbit to the bitten shafts, and
    they slouch along the precipitous lip,
the enormous sky behind them, the heavy noontime air alive
    with shimmers and mirages.

Sometime in the afternoon I had to go inside: the advent of
our vigil was upon us.

However much we didn't want to, however little we would do
about it, we'd understood:

we were going to perish of all this, if not now, then soon, if
not soon, then someday.

Someday, some final generation, hysterically aswarm beneath
an atmosphere as unrelenting as rock,

would rue us all, anathematize our earthly comforts, curse
our surfeits and submissions.

I think I know, though I might rather not, why my roofers stay
so clear to me and why the rest,

the terror of that time, the reflexive disbelief and distancing,
all we should hold on to, dims so.

I remember the president in his absurd protective booties,
looking absolutely unafraid, the fool.

I remember a woman on the front page glaring across the
misty Susquehanna at those looming stacks.

But, more vividly, the men, silvered with glitter from the shin-
gles, clinging like starlings beneath the eaves.

Even the leftover carats of tar in the gutter, so black they
seemed to suck the light out of the air.

By nightfall kids had come across them: every sidewalk on the
block was scribbled with obscenities and hearts.

−1983

MARY AUSTIN
1868-1934

"She wanted to write books that you could walk around in." Thus Mary
Hunter Austin describes herself in her autobiography, Earth Horizon
(1932). One of the most sagacious, eccentric, and indomitable figures in
American literature, Austin took as her profound theme a concern for the
lands of the American West and for the indigenous peoples she believed
were its most responsible stewards. Her reward for expressing this concern
in thirty-two published books spanning a range of genres was a half century of neglect by literary historians. Only her first and most celebrated
book, The Land of Little Rain (1903), has remained continuously in print. In
recent years, though, readers have begun to rediscover Mary Austin and
her bold lifetime achievement.

Austin is best remembered for her works set in California and the
Southwest, but she was born in Illinois. She journeyed to California with her
widowed mother at age twenty, then taught school for several years before
marrying Stafford Austin and living with him in the Owens Valley on the
east side of the Sierra Nevada, the setting for much of her early work. Here
she had close, daily interaction with the Paiute and Shoshone peoples,

whose culture had a strong influence on her imagination. After a decade of isolation from the mainstream of American culture, Austin literally wrote her way out of the Owens Valley and an unhappy marriage with the publication of her first book. She settled with her daughter in Carmel and became part of a literary circle that included Jack London. After her daughter died and she divorced her husband, she traveled to Rome, London, and New York, writing and lecturing, advocating unpopular causes from women's suffrage and birth control to Indian and Mexican-American rights. She spent the last ten years of her life in Santa Fe, New Mexico, befriending Willa Cather and collaborating with a then-unknown photographer named Ansel Adams on a book about Taos Pueblo.

"The Last Antelope," from the story collection Lost Borders (1909), confronts readers with the moral question that Austin returns to again and again in her work: What sort of landscape destiny is America shaping for itself? The question springs from Austin's personal experience of watching the once-verdant Owens Valley be sucked dry by a thirsty Los Angeles, a venture she actively opposed. She deplored "that spirit which goes before cities like an exhalation and dries up the gossamer and the dew." "We do not take enough account of the power of our inanimate surroundings to take on the spiritual quality of the life that is lived in them," insists one of the characters in Austin's early novel Santa Lucia (1908). Not unlike Thoreau in Walden, Austin took on the responsibility of awakening her readers to the soul that animates the land.

THE LAST ANTELOPE

There were seven notches in the juniper by the Lone Tree Spring for the seven seasons that Little Pete had summered there, feeding his flocks in the hollow of the Carrizal. The first time of coming he had struck his axe into the trunk, meaning to make firewood, but thought better of it, and thereafter chipped it in sheer friendliness, as one claps an old acquaintance, for, by the time the flock had worked up the treeless windy stretch from the Little Antelope to the Carrizal, even a lone juniper has a friendly look. And Little Pete was a friendly man, though shy of demeanor, so that, with the best will in the world for wagging his tongue, he could scarcely pass the time of day with good countenance; the soul of a jolly companion with the front and bearing of one of his own sheep.

He loved his dogs as brothers; he was near akin to the wild things. He knew his sheep by name, and had respect to signs and seasons; his lips moved softly as he walked, making no sound. Well—what would you?—a man must have fellowship in some sort. Where he went about sheep camps and shearings, there was sly laughter and tappings of foreheads, but those who kept the tale of his flocks spoke well of him and increased his wage.

Little Pete kept to the same round year by year, breaking away from La Liebre after the spring shearing, south around the foot of Piños, swinging out to the desert in the wake of the quick, strong rains, thence to Little Antelope in July to drink a bottle for La Quatorze, and so to the Carrizal by the time the poppy fires were burned quite out and the quail trooped at noon about the tepid pools. The Carrizal is not properly mesa nor valley, but a long-healed crater miles wide, rimmed about with the jagged edge of the old cone. It rises steeply from the tilted mesa, overlooked by Black Mountain, darkly red as the red cattle that graze among the honey-colored hills. These are blunt and rounded, tumbling all down from the great crater and the mesa edge toward the long, dim valley of Little Antelope. Its outward slope is confused with the outlines of the hills, tumult of blind cones, and the old lava flow that breaks away from it by the west gap and the ravine of the spring; within, its walls are deeply guttered by the torrent of winter rains. In its cuplike hollow, the sink of its waters, salt and bitter as all pools without an outlet, waxes and wanes within a wide margin of bleaching reeds. Nothing taller shows in all the Carrizal, and the wind among them fills all the hollow with an eerie whispering. One spring rills down by the gorge of an old flow on the side toward Little Antelope, and, but for the lone juniper that stood by it, there is never a tree until you come to the foot of Black Mountain.

The flock of Little Pete, a maverick strayed from some rodeo, a prospector going up to Black Mountain, and a solitary antelope were all that passed through the Carrizal at any time. The antelope had the best right. He came as of old habit; he had come when the lightfoot herds ranged from here to the sweet, mist-watered cañons of the Coast Range, and the bucks went up to the windy mesas what time the young ran with their mothers nose to flank. They had ceased before the keen edge of slaughter that defines the frontier of men.

All that a tardy law had saved to the district of Little Antelope was the buck that came up the ravine of the Lone Tree Spring at the set time of the year when Little Pete fed his flock in the Carrizal, and Pete averred that they were glad to see one another. True enough, they were the friendliest thing that either found there, for though the law ran as far as the antelope ranged, there were hill dwellers who took no account of it, namely, the coyotes. They hunted the buck in season and out, bayed him down from the feeding-grounds, fended him from the pool, pursued him by relay races, ambushed him in the pitfalls of the black rock.

There were seven coyotes ranging the east side of the Carrizal at the time when Little Pete first struck his axe into the juniper tree, slinking, sly footed, and evil-eyed. Many an evening the shepherd watched them running lightly in the hollow of the crater, the flash-flash of the antelope's white rump signaling the progress of the chase. But always the buck outran or outwitted them, taking to the high broken ridges where no split foot could follow his seven-leagued bounds. Many a morning Little Pete, tending his cooking-pot by a quavering sagebrush fire, saw the antelope feeding down toward the Lone Tree Spring, and looked his sentiments. The coyotes had spoken theirs all in the night with derisive voices; never was there any love lost between a shepherd and a coyote. The pronghorn's chief recommendation to an acquaintance was that he could outdo them.

After the third summer, Pete began to perceive a reciprocal friendliness in the antelope. Early mornings the shepherd saw him rising from his lair, or came often upon the warm pressed hollow where he had lain within cry of his coyote-scaring fire. When it was midday in the misty hollow and the shadows drawn close, stuck tight under the juniper and the sage, they went each to his nooning in his own fashion, but in the half-light they drew near together.

Since the beginning of the law the antelope had half-forgotten his fear of man. He looked upon the shepherd with steadfastness; he smelled the smell of his garments which was the smell of sheep and the unhandled earth, and the smell of wood smoke was in his hair. They had companionship without speech; they conferred favors silently after the manner of those who understand one another. The antelope led to the best feeding-grounds, and Pete kept the sheep from muddying the spring until the buck had drunk. When the coyotes skulked in the scrub by night to deride him, the shepherd mocked them in his own tongue, and promised them the best of his lambs for the killing; but to hear afar off their hunting howl stirred him out of sleep to curse with great heartiness. At such times he thought of the antelope and wished him well.

Beginning with the west gap opposite the Lone Tree Spring about the first of August, Pete would feed all around the broken rim of the crater, up the gullies and down, and clean through the hollow of it in a matter of two months, or, if the winter had been a wet one, a little longer, and in seven years the man and the antelope grew to know each other very well. Where the flock fed, the buck fed, keeping farthest from the dogs, and at last he came to lie down with it.

That was after a season of scant rains, when the food was poor and the antelope's flank grew thin; the rabbits had trooped down to the irrigated lands, and the coyotes, made more keen by hunger, pressed him hard. One of those smoky, yawning days, when the sky hugged the earth, and all sound fell back from a woolly atmosphere and broke dully in the scrub, about the usual hour of their running between twilight and mid-afternoon, the coyotes drove the tall buck, winded, desperate, and foredone, to refuge among the silly sheep, where for fear of the dogs and the man the howlers dared not come. He stood at bay there, fronting the shepherd, brought up against a crisis greatly needing the help of speech.

Well—he had nearly as much gift in that matter as Little Pete. Those two silent ones understood each other; some assurance, the warrant of a free-given faith, passed between them. The buck lowered his head and eased the sharp throbbing of his ribs; the dogs drew in the scattered flocks; they moved, keeping a little cleared space nearest the buck; he moved with them; he began to feed. Thereafter the heart of Little Pete warmed humanly toward the antelope, and the coyotes began to be very personal in their abuse. That same night they drew off the shepherd's dogs by a ruse and stole two of his sheep.

In seven years a coyote may learn somewhat. Those of the Carrizal learned the ways of Little Pete and the antelope. Trust them to have noted, as the years moved, that the buck's flanks were lean and his step less free. Put it that the antelope was old and that he made truce with the shepherd to hide the failing of his powers; then, if he came earlier or stayed later than the flock, it would go hard with him. But as if he knew their mind in the matter, the antelope delayed his coming till the salt pool shrank to its innermost ring of reeds and the sun-cured grasses crisped along the slope. It seemed the brute sense waked between him and the man to make each aware of the other's nearness. Often, as Little Pete drove in by the west gap, he would sight the prongs of the buck rising over the barrier of black rocks at the head of the ravine. Together they passed out of the crater, keeping fellowship as far as the frontier of evergreen oaks. Here Little Pete turned in by the cattle fences to come at La Liebre from the north, and the antelope, avoiding all man-trails, growing daily more remote, passed into the wooded hills on unguessed errands of his own. Twice the solitary homesteader, who had built him a house at the foot of the Carrizal, saw the antelope go up to it at that set time of the year. The third summer, when he sighted him, a whitish speck moving steadily against the fawn-colored background of the hills, the homesteader took down his rifle and made haste into the crater. At that time his cabin stood on the remotest edge of settlement, and the grip of the law was loosened in so long a reach. 'In the end the coyotes will get him. Better that he fall to me,' said the homesteader.

The coyote that kept the watch at the head of the ravine saw him come, and lifted up his voice in the long-drawn, dolorous whine that warned the other watchers in their unseen stations in the scrub. The homesteader heard also, and let a curse softly under his breath, for, besides that they might scare his quarry, he coveted the howlers' ears, in which the law upheld him. Never a tip nor a tail of one showed above the sage when he had come up into the Carrizal.

The afternoon wore on; the homesteader hid in the reeds, and the coyotes had forgotten him. Away to the west in a windless blur of dust the sheep of Little Pete trailed up toward the crater's brim. The leader, watching by the spring, caught a jack-rabbit and was eating it quietly behind the black rock.

In the meantime, the last antelope came lightly and securely by the gully, by the black rock, and the lone juniper into the Carrizal. The friendliness of the antelope for Little Pete betrayed him. He came with some sense of home, expecting the flock and the protection of man-presence. He strayed witlessly into the open, his ears set to catch the jangle of the bells. What he heard was the snick of the breech bolt as the homesteader threw up the sight of his rifle, and a small demoniac cry that ran from gutter to gutter of the crater rim, impossible to gauge for numbers or distance.

At that moment Little Pete worried the flock up the outward slope where the ruin of the old lava flows gave sharply back the wrangle of the bells. Three weeks he had won up from the Little Antelope and three by way of the Sand Flat, where there was a great scarcity of water, and in all of that time none of his kind had hailed him. His heart warmed toward the juniper tree and the antelope whose hoof-prints he found in the white dust of the mesa trail. Men had small respect by Little Pete, women he had no time for: the antelope was the noblest thing he had ever loved. The sheep poured through the gap and spread fanwise down the gully; behind them Little Pete twirled his staff and made merry wordless noises in his throat in anticipation of friendliness. 'Ehu!' he cried when he heard the hunting howl, 'but they are at their tricks again'—and then in English he voiced a volley of broken, inconsequential oaths, for he saw what the howlers were about. It was so they plotted the antelope's last running in the Carrizal: two to start the chase from the black rock toward the red scar of a winter torrent; two to leave the mouth of the wash when the first were winded, one to fend the ravine that led up to the broken ridges, one to start out of the scrub at the base of a smooth upward sweep, and, running parallel to it, keep the buck well into the open; all these, when their first spurt was done, to cross leisurely to new stations to take up another turn. Round they went in the hollow of the crater, velvet-footed and sly even in full chase, and biding their time. It was a good running, but it was almost done when, away by the west gap, the buck heard the voice of Little Pete raised in adjuration and the friendly blether of the sheep. Thin spirals of dust flared upward from the moving flocks and signaled truce to chase. The antelope broke for it with wide, panting bounds and many a missed step picked up with incredible eagerness, the thin rim of his nostrils oozing blood. The coyotes saw and closed in about him, chopping quick and hard. Sharp ears and sharp muzzles cast up at his throat, and were whelmed in a press of gray flanks. One yelped, one went limping from a kick, and one went past him, returning with a spring upon the heaving shoulder, and the man in the reeds beside the bitter water rose up and fired.

All the luck of that day's hunting went to the homesteader, for he had killed an antelope and a coyote with one shot, and, though he had a bad quarter of an hour with a wild and loathly shepherd, who he feared might denounce him to the law, in the end he made off with the last antelope, swung limp and graceless across his shoulder. The coyotes came back to the killing ground when they had watched him safely down the ravine, and were consoled with what they found. As they pulled the body of the dead leader about before they began upon it, they noticed that the homesteader had taken the ears of that also.

Little Pete lay in the grass and wept simply; the tears made pallid traces in the season's grime. He suffered the torture, the question extraordinary of bereavement. If he had not lingered so long in the meadow of Los Robles, if he had moved faster on the Sand Flat trail—but, in fact, he had been breathed upon by that spirit which goes before cities like an exhalation and dries up the gossamer and the dew.

From that day the heart had gone out of the Carrizal. It was a desolate hollow, reddish-hued and dim, with brackish waters, and moreover the feed was poor. His eyes could not forget their trick of roving the valley at all hours; he looked by the rill of the spring for hoof-prints that were not there.

After three weeks he passed out on the other side and came that way no more. The juniper tree stood greenly by the spring until the homesteader cut it down for firewood. Nothing taller than the rattling reeds stirs in all the hollow of the Carrizal.

—1909

UNION OF
CONCERNED SCIENTISTS

The Union of Concerned Scientists (UCS) was founded in 1969 with the mission of "advancing responsible public policies in areas where technology plays a critical role." It represents the effort of some scientists to take greater responsibility for how the products of their research are applied, an issue brought into troubling focus by the unleashing of atomic weapons— the product of intensive scientific research in Los Alamos, New Mexico—on the citizens of Hiroshima and Nagasaki in 1945. The organization in its early years concerned itself with cautioning against the spread of nuclear weapons and power; more recently, it has expanded its concern to the impacts of technology on the global environment. In the words of executive director Howard Ris, "We believe that scientists bear a special responsibility for educating themselves, the public, the media, and policymakers" about these impacts.

Accordingly, in 1992 UCS prepared the warning you're about to read, "outlining the damage already inflicted on the world's life-support systems and the dangers that lie ahead, along with recommendations for action to avert a global catastrophe." More than 1,600 scientists from around the world, including most of the living Nobel laureates in the sciences, signed the warning, which UCS presented at a press conference in Washington, D.C., in November 1992 and sent to more than 160 heads of state around

*the globe. The warning testifies to the growing level of concern within the
international scientific community about the problems we have created for
ourselves with our technology.*

World Scientists'
Warning to Humanity

Introduction

Human beings and the natural world are on a collision course. Human activities
inflict harsh and often irreversible damage on the environment and on critical
resources. If not checked, many of our current practices put at serious risk the
future that we wish for human society and the plant and animal kingdoms, and may
so alter the living world that it will be unable to sustain life in the manner that we
know. Fundamental changes are urgent if we are to avoid the collision our present
course will bring about.

The Environment

The environment is suffering critical stress:

The Atmosphere

Stratospheric ozone depletion threatens us with enhanced ultra-violet radiation
at the earth's surface, which can be damaging or lethal to many life forms. Air
pollution near ground level, and acid precipitation, are already causing widespread injury to humans, forests and crops.

Water Resources

Heedless exploitation of depletable ground water supplies endangers food production and other essential human systems. Heavy demands on the world's surface waters have resulted in serious shortages in some 80 countries, containing
40% of the world's population. Pollution of rivers, lakes and ground water further limits the supply.

Oceans

Destructive pressure on the oceans is severe, particularly in the coastal regions
which produce most of the world's food fish. The total marine catch is now at or
above the estimated maximum sustainable yield. Some fisheries have already
shown signs of collapse. Rivers carrying heavy burdens of eroded soil into the
seas also carry industrial, municipal, agricultural, and livestock waste—some of
it toxic.

Soil

Loss of soil productivity, which is causing extensive land abandonment, is a
widespread byproduct of current practices in agriculture and animal husbandry.
Since 1945, 11% of the earth's vegetated surface has been degraded—an area

larger than India and China combined—and per capita food production in many parts of the world is decreasing.

Forests

Tropical rain forests, as well as tropical and temperate dry forests, are being destroyed rapidly. At present rates, some critical forest types will be gone in a few years and most of the tropical rain forest will be gone before the end of the next century. With them will go large numbers of plant and animal species.

Living Species

The irreversible loss of species, which by 2100 may reach one third of all species now living, is especially serious. We are losing the potential they hold for providing medicinal and other benefits, and the contribution that genetic diversity of life forms gives to the robustness of the world's biological systems and to the astonishing beauty of the earth itself.

Much of this damage is irreversible on a scale of centuries or permanent. Other processes appear to pose additional threats. Increasing levels of gases in the atmosphere from human activities, including carbon dioxide released from fossil fuel burning and from deforestation, may alter climate on a global scale. Predictions of global warming are still uncertain—with projected effects ranging from tolerable to very severe—but the potential risks are very great.

Our massive tampering with the world's interdependent web of life—coupled with the environmental damage inflicted by deforestation, species loss, and climate change—could trigger widespread adverse effects, including unpredictable collapses of critical biological systems whose interactions and dynamics we only imperfectly understand.

Uncertainty over the extent of these effects cannot excuse complacency or delay in facing the threats.

Population

The earth is finite. Its ability to absorb wastes and destructive effluent is finite. Its ability to provide food and energy is finite. Its ability to provide for growing numbers of people is finite. And we are fast approaching many of the earth's limits. Current economic practices which damage the environment, in both developed and underdeveloped nations, cannot be continued without the risk that vital global systems will be damaged beyond repair.

Pressures resulting from unrestrained population growth put demands on the natural world that can overwhelm any efforts to achieve a sustainable future. If we are to halt the destruction of our environment, we must accept limits to that growth. A World Bank estimate indicates that world population will not stabilize at less than 12.4 billion, while the United Nations concludes that the eventual total could reach 14 billion, a near tripling of today's 5.4 billion. But, even at this moment, one person in five lives in absolute poverty without enough to eat, and one in ten suffers serious malnutrition.

No more than one or a few decades remain before the chance to avert the threats we now confront will be lost and the prospects for humanity immeasurably diminished.

WARNING

We the undersigned, senior members of the world's scientific community, hereby warn all humanity of what lies ahead. A great change in our stewardship of the earth and the life on it, is required, if vast human misery is to be avoided and our global home on this planet is not to be irretrievably mutilated.

What We Must Do

Five inextricably linked areas must be addressed simultaneously:

1. *We must bring environmentally damaging activities under control to restore and protect the integrity of the earth's systems we depend on.*

   We must, for example, move away from fossil fuels to more benign, inexhaustible energy sources to cut greenhouse gas emissions and the pollution of our air and water. Priority must be given to the development of energy sources matched to third world needs—small scale and relatively easy to implement.
   We must halt deforestation, injury to and loss of agricultural land, and the loss of terrestrial and marine plant and animal species.

2. *We must manage resources crucial to human welfare more effectively.*

   We must give high priority to efficient use of energy, water, and other materials, including expansion of conservation and recycling.

3. *We must stabilize population. This will be possible only if all nations recognize that it requires improved social and economic conditions, and the adoption of effective, voluntary family planning.*

4. *We must reduce and eventually eliminate poverty.*

5. *We must ensure sexual equality, and guarantee women control over their own reproductive decisions.*

The developed nations are the largest polluters in the world today. They must greatly reduce their overconsumption, if we are to reduce pressures on resources and the global environment. The developed nations have the obligation to provide aid and support to developing nations, because only the developed nations have the financial resources and the technical skills for these tasks.

Acting on this recognition is not altruism, but enlightened self-interest: whether industrialized or not, we all have but one lifeboat. No nation can escape from injury when global biological systems are damaged. No nation can escape from conflicts over increasingly scarce resources. In addition, environmental and economic instabilities will cause mass migrations with incalculable consequences for developed and undeveloped nations alike.

Developing nations must realize that environmental damage is one of the gravest threats they face, and that attempts to blunt it will be overwhelmed if their populations go unchecked. The greatest peril is to become trapped in spirals of environmental decline, poverty, and unrest, leading to social, economic and environmental collapse.

Success in this global endeavor will require a great reduction in violence and war. Resources now devoted to the preparation and conduct of war—amounting to over $1 trillion annually—will be badly needed in the new tasks and should be diverted to the new challenges.

A new ethic is required—a new attitude towards discharging our responsibility for caring for ourselves and for the earth. We must recognize the earth's limited capacity to provide for us. We must recognize its fragility. We must no longer allow it to be ravaged. This ethic must motivate a great movement, convincing reluctant leaders and reluctant governments and reluctant peoples themselves to effect the needed changes.

The scientists issuing this warning hope that our message will reach and affect people everywhere. We need the help of many.

We require the help of the world community of scientists—natural, social, economic, political;

We require the help of the world's business and industrial leaders;

We require the help of the world's religious leaders; and

We require the help of the world's peoples.

We call on all to join us in this task.

—1992

ROBERT J. SAMUELSON

B. 1945

Robert J. Samuelson is one of the most articulate critics of environmental doomsayers, arguing that "environmentalism should hold the hype. It should inform us more and frighten us less." Samuelson, a native of New York City, received an A.B. in government from Harvard in 1967. He worked as a reporter for the Washington Post *for several years (1969-73) and as a free-lance writer before becoming a columnist for the* Washington Post *in 1977 and adding a* Newsweek *column in 1984. He writes on a variety of subjects in his columns, not only the environment.*

Samuelson is one of a number of American journalists who have taken issue during the past decade or so with apocalyptic environmental rhetoric. In 1984, free-lance journalist Edith Efron published The Apocalyptics: How Environmental Politics Controls What We Know about Cancer, *a book that directly attacked Rachel Carson's* Silent Spring *(1962) and its legacy of anti-industrial thinking in the environmental movement. Ronald Bailey, a former science writer for* Forbes *magazine, argued in his 1993 book* Eco-Scam: The False Prophets of Ecological Apocalypse *that environmental crises are "hyped to further the interests of specific agencies and advocacy groups" and that we should not worry about the current crop of ecocrises because "humanity's ever-increasing store of knowledge and technology enables us to adjust to changing circumstances faster and more easily as the years pass." A more recent example of what's sometimes called environmental backlash writing is Gregg Easterbrook's 1995 book* A Moment on the Earth: The Coming Age of Environmental Optimism. *Easterbrook points out that the grim environmental forecasts of the 1960s and 1970s, predictions of "nuclear winter" and exponentially exploding human population, have not come to pass and suggests that the earth is durable enough to withstand the activities of modern industrialism. In 1995 the Mobil Corporation developed an ad with a don't-worry-be-happy message featuring Easterbrook's book. "The sky is not falling," the ad begins. "Good news: The end of the Earth as we know it is not imminent. The cycle of decline in the quality of our environment can be broken and, despite what environmentalists are claiming, great strides have already been taken towards improving our situation" (see* Time *magazine, October 23, 1995).*

In 1995, Robert Samuelson published a book called The Good Life and Its Discontents: The American Dream in the Age of Entitlement, 1945-1995. *An excerpt appeared as a* Newsweek *cover story in January 1996, entitled "It's Not as Bad as You Think." The following article, published in a June 1992 issue of* Newsweek, *presents much the same message but in a specifically environmental context. "Our environmental rhetoric is overblown. The planet will survive," writes Samuelson. In particular, he takes issue with the tendency he detects among environmentalists to "vilify and simplify" and to propagate "doomsday scenarios."*

THE END IS NOT AT HAND

Whoever coined the phrase "save the planet" is a public-relations genius. It conveys the sense of impending catastrophe and high purpose that has wrapped environmentalism in an aura of moral urgency. It also typifies environmentalism's rhetorical excesses, which, in any other context, would be seen as wild exaggeration or simple dishonesty.

Up to a point, our environmental awareness has checked a mindless enthusiasm for unrestrained economic growth. We have sensibly curbed some of growth's harmful side effects. But environmentalism increasingly resembles a holy crusade addicted to hype and ignorant of history. Every environmental ill is depicted as an onrushing calamity that—if not stopped—will end life as we know it.

Take the latest scare: the greenhouse effect. We're presented with the horrifying specter of a world that incinerates itself. Act now, or sizzle later. Food supplies will wither. Glaciers will melt. Coastal areas will flood. In fact, the probable losses from any greenhouse warming are modest: 1 to 2 percent of our economy's output by the year 2050, estimates economist William Cline. The loss seems even smaller compared with the expected growth of the economy (a doubling) over the same period.

No environmental problem threatens the "planet" or rates with the danger of nuclear war. No oil spill ever caused suffering on a par with today's civil war in Yugoslavia, which is a minor episode in human misery. World War II left more than

35 million dead. Cambodia's civil war resulted in 1 million to 3 million deaths. The great scourges of humanity remain what they have always been: war, natural disaster, oppressive government, crushing poverty and hate. On any scale of tragedy, environmental distress is a featherweight.

This is not an argument for indifference or inaction. It is an argument for perspective and balance. You can believe (as I do) that the possibility of greenhouse warming enhances an already strong case for an energy tax. A tax would curb ordinary air pollution, limit oil imports, cut the budget deficit and promote energy-efficient investments that make economic sense.

But it does not follow that anyone who disagrees with me is evil or even wrong. On the greenhouse effect, for instance, there's ample scientific doubt over whether warming will occur and, if so, how much. Moreover, the warming would occur over decades. People and businesses could adjust. To take one example: farmers could shift to more heat-resistant seeds.

Unfortunately, the impulse of many environmentalists is to vilify and simplify. Critics of environmental restrictions are portrayed as selfish and ignorant creeps. Doomsday scenarios are developed to prove the seriousness of environmental dangers. Cline's recent greenhouse study projected warming 250 years into the future. Guess what, it increases sharply. This is an absurd exercise akin to predicting life in 1992 at the time of the French and Indian War (1754-63).

The rhetorical overkill is not just innocent excess. It clouds our understanding. For starters, it minimizes the great progress that has been made, especially in industrialized countries. In the United States, air and water pollution have dropped dramatically. Since 1960, particulate emissions (soot, cinders) are down by 65 percent. Lead emissions have fallen by 97 percent since 1970. Smog has declined in most cities.

What's also lost is the awkward necessity for choices. Your environmental benefit may be my job. Not every benefit is worth having at any cost. Economists estimate that environmental regulations depress the economy's output by 2.6 to 5 percent, or about $150 billion to $290 billion. (Note: this is larger than the estimated impact of global warming.) For that cost, we've lowered health risks and improved our surroundings. But some gains are small compared with the costs. And some costs are needlessly high because regulations are rigid.

The worst sin of environmental excess is its bias against economic growth. The cure for the immense problems of poor countries usually lies with economic growth. A recent report from the World Bank estimates that more than 1 billion people lack healthy water supplies and sanitary facilities. The result is hundreds of millions of cases of diarrhea annually and the deaths of 3 million children (2 million of which the World Bank judges avoidable). Only by becoming wealthier can countries correct these conditions.

Similarly, wealthier societies have both the desire and the income to clean their air and water. Advanced nations have urban-air-pollution levels only a sixth that of the poorest countries. Finally, economic growth tends to reduce high birthrates, as children survive longer and women escape traditional roles.

Yes, we have environmental problems. Reactors in the former Soviet Union pose safety risks. Economic growth and the environment can be at odds. Growth generates carbon dioxide emissions and causes more waste. But these problems are not—as environmental rhetoric implies—the main obstacles to sustained development. The biggest hurdle is inept government. Inept government fostered unsafe Soviet reactors. Inept government hampers food production in poor countries by, say, preventing farmers from earning adequate returns on their crops.

By now, everyone is an environmentalist. But the label is increasingly meaningless, because not all environmental problems are equally serious and even the serious ones need to be balanced against other concerns. Environmentalism should hold the hype. It should inform us more and frighten us less.

—1992

BILL MCKIBBEN

B. 1960

Bill McKibben was twenty-seven years old during the hot summer of 1988 when a U.S. Senate committee heard testimony from scientists that they could discern a global warming trend due to a build-up in the atmosphere of greenhouse gases—gases produced largely by human activity. With the clear vision of youth, McKibben understood the "inertia of affluence" that keeps our culture mired in its environmentally destructive ways, and he decided to write a wake-up call. The End of Nature *(1989) captured so dramatically the environmental anxieties of the time that it was read and reviewed more widely than any other nature book since Rachel Carson's* Silent Spring. *The book is a clear exposition of the global atmospheric changes humankind has wrought, an examination of the possible consequences and methods of coping, and a plea to change our ways. McKibben followed this tocsin by tracing the complicity of television in the environmental crisis in* The Age of Missing Information *(1992); more recently, his book* Hope, Human and Wild *(1995) documents examples from Brazil, India, and the United States of places that give him hope for an environmental recovery.*

McKibben grew up "a child of the suburbs" with "only a tenuous understanding of the natural world." He was born to two journalists in Palo Alto, California, who later moved the family to Toronto, Canada, and then Lexington, Massachusetts. McKibben earned a B.A. in government from Harvard in 1982 and was hired as a staff writer for the New Yorker, *where he wrote hundreds of "Talk of the Town" pieces and served as an editor. In 1987 he became a free-lance writer and moved shortly thereafter with his new wife, the writer Sue Halpern, to the Adirondacks, where the couple are raising a daughter.*

In The Age of Missing Information, *McKibben suggests that the most important question of the late twentieth century is: How much is enough? "Not So Fast," which appeared in the* New York Times Magazine *on July 23, 1995, reiterates this question as it rebuts the claim of the "environmental optimists" that there is a market-oriented technological fix available to us in our environmental predicament. Simply, and radically, people have to change their lives, insists McKibben.*

NOT SO FAST

Here's a short chemistry lesson. Grasp it and you will grasp the reason the environmental era has barely begun; perhaps you will grasp the history of the next 50 years.

Put a gallon of gasoline in the tank of your car and go out for a drive. Assuming your engine's well tuned, burning that gallon of petroleum should put about half a pound of carbon in the form of carbon monoxide—CO—into the air. A generation ago that number was closer to one pound; by decade's end, as new technologies clean the exhaust, it should drop to barely a tenth of a pound. The steady decrease in CO emissions, as well as in those of nitrous oxide and particulates, is the reason the air is clearer and safer now in Los Angeles than it was a generation ago.

On the same drive, however, that gallon of gas will transmute itself into almost five and a half pounds of carbon in the form of carbon dioxide. Long considered proof that gas was burning cleanly, invisible and odorless CO_2 is the inevitable byproduct of fossil fuel consumption. It doesn't matter if your car's old or new; there's no filter you can stick on the exhaust to reduce CO_2 production. And if the wide international consensus of scientists is correct, this carbon dioxide is now warming the planet more quickly and to higher temperatures than ever in human history.

CO versus CO_2. One damn oxygen atom, and all the difference in the world.

If you focus on carbon *monoxide*, then you can count yourself among the currently fashionable environmental optimists. Pollution, from their perspective, is an unfortunate byproduct of an essentially sound system. Since smog and its many analogues (river pollution, acid rain, crowded landfills) are precisely the sorts of things that can be tamed with filters and scrubbers, or with small changes in human behavior like recycling, the optimists are in some ways right. Though Congress is even now gutting the laws that have begun to clean America, and though there are plenty of poor and minority communities that never began to get cleaned in the first place, the technology exists to diminish smog, to purify drinking water. It's merely a matter of finding the will to pay for it—there's no reason for rivers to catch fire. (And every poll suggests that the will is there, that after a quarter-century of hard-fought environmental campaigns the American people are far more convinced than their congressmen that the environment is worth cleaning up.) So if CO turns out to be the real issue, then it's just a systems problem. Environmentalism is a success story, and the world we die in will resemble the one we were born into, albeit with more computers.

That's the conventional wisdom of the moment, best expressed by Gregg Easterbrook in his recent book, "A Moment on the Earth." And yet there are those of us who are not soothed—who grow more worried with each passing month, and not simply by the fact of a Republican Congress. Those in this second camp tend to be focused on problems like widespread extinction, growing populations, dying fisheries and dwindling wilderness—signals, like the ever-expanding cloud of CO_2, indicating that our societies and their appetites have simply grown too large. Signals still all but ignored.

Since the environmental movement began, all these crises have been lumped together. The same people who worried about clean air worried about recycling and species extinction, about dirty rivers and the press of population. All these causes are important—now more than ever as the right attempts to undermine environmental protection—but acting as if they were all essentially the same crisis carries risks as well as benefits. While it's certainly easier to focus on things like smog, which people see around them every day, the logic of focusing on the most visible pollution cuts both ways. Such a narrowly pragmatic vision is potentially paralyzing precisely because you *can* clean urban air, you *can* return fish to the Great Lakes, you *can* recycle enough to keep landfills from overflowing.

Unfortunately, you can do all these quite vital things without having any real effect on the more systematic troubles. The progress we've made in solving environmental problems is deceptive: we're making no progress at all on the deeper problems, *because they do not spring from the same sources.* One set stems from a defect in the car; the other set comes from the very existence of the car. And in an odd way, solving the first kind of problem makes the deeper ones ever more intractable—if visible air pollution starts to decline, then the push for better mass transit dwindles, and with it the chances of cutting the invisible CO_2.

The environmental movement, in other words, has reached a diagnostic crisis. To use a medical analogy: The world has presented itself, complaining of chest pains. After three decades of examination, there are still those who insist it's indigestion and want to prescribe some Bromo. Others say arteriosclerosis, which means our most basic behaviors must change. Most people—not just C.E.O.'s—badly want to find out that our problems are not related to our life styles. Change frightens us: we've come to believe, for instance, that our well-being is lashed to constant economic growth. "It's the economy, stupid."

And yet the basic laws of chemistry may soon demand that we give up such fixations. The Intergovernmental Panel on Climate Change, a group of scientists assembled by the United Nations, has calculated that an immediate *60 percent* reduction in fossil fuel use is necessary to stabilize global climate. This could not happen in a world that closely resembles ours. Addicted to growth, busily spreading our vision of the good life around the globe, we are sprinting in the opposite direction. The growth in our economies and populations wipes out our incremental gains in energy efficiency: from 1983 to 1993, despite a tremendous push toward efficiency by power companies, Americans increased their per capita power usage by more than 22 percent. Electric utilities offered rebates for installing compact fluorescent bulbs, and, indeed, between 1986 and 1991 the typical household added one such light. But as Andrew Rudin pointed out recently in *Public Power* magazine, the typical household also added more than seven incandescent lamps.

Since the greenhouse effect and other consequences of our civilization's basic momentum have yet to hit us full-on, no mass movement has developed to challenge that momentum. "We are in an unusual predicament as a global civilization," Al Gore said when I interviewed him early in his Vice Presidency. "The maximum that is politically feasible, even the maximum that is politically *imaginable* right now, still falls short of the minimum that is scientifically and ecologically necessary." And that was *before* Newt Gingrich.

But this state of affairs may not last. According to the most accurate computer models of global climate, for instance, increased global temperatures may be obvious to the man in the street by decade's end. For all the right-wing bluster about taming the environmental movement, for all the happy-talk books about our ecological triumphs, it will take only a hot summer or two, a string of crop failures or some similar catastrophe to bring these issues center stage once more. A spate of recent studies has begun to make clear that an average temperature increase of only a few degrees hides tremendous heat waves, droughts and storms; the insurance industry has actually begun to worry publicly about the greenhouse effect and the losses it will cause.

If and when such stresses really show themselves, though, we will need an environmental movement that understands what is happening—that understands that more recycling is not the main answer, that is willing to advocate the unpopular and the disturbing. Partly this means a stepped-up political campaign—continual pressure on governments around the world to sign and fulfill treaties, share renewable technologies and pass steep new taxes on the use of fossil fuels and other polluters. Already a small segment of the environmental movement has begun to focus on such issues.

But remember the numbers. A 60 percent reduction in fossil fuel use? Even under the most hopeful technological scenarios, it won't happen if we're simultaneously doubling or tripling our economies. More money makes reducing smog easier, because you can afford to build *better* cars; more money makes dealing with the greenhouse effect harder, because you can afford to buy *more* cars. So the sweet dream that we'll all grow rich enough to turn green is simply that—a dream, and one that will turn into a nightmare if we try to follow it.

We face tough choices. The most pragmatic realism, rooted in the molecular structure of CO_2, demands electric cars. It also demands nothing less than heresy: an all-out drive for deep thrift, for self-restraint, for smaller families. Brute objectivity requires new ideas about what constitutes sufficiency: smaller homes, more food grown locally, repair instead of replacement. Environmental visionaries have always talked about simplicity and community, but now atmospheric chemists are starting to say the same things. Not for esthetic and moral reasons, but for eminently practical ones. The world can't support a population of five and a half billion people living like middle-class Americans, much less the eight or nine billion that will soon share the planet with us. That's the crux of the issue—that and the fact that as long as we go on living the way we do everyone else will want to as well. We need China to stop burning so much fossil fuel—the developing world now produces as much CO_2 as the developed—but China will pay no attention until we start cutting back too.

Clearly, it's as immoral as it is impractical for us to demand that underdeveloped countries remain underdeveloped—those countries passionately want to develop. But it's terrifying to imagine Asians owning cars in the same numbers as we do. The only way out of this dilemma is to rethink what we mean by "development"—and to do it here first. We've exported our passion for democracy, our devotion to human rights. But that's not all we've exported. More than a billion humans, one in five of us, watch "Baywatch" every week. If the good life whose pictures we flash around the world doesn't change, then all the treaties on earth won't do the job. We need bicycles and we need buses, and we need to make them seem as marvelous as Miatas.

Rush Limbaugh has it right when he denounces environmentalists as a threat to current ways of life. The systemic environmentalism he fears has one question to ask: "How much is enough?" How much convenience, how many people, how much money? It's a question that won't go away. It's a question with a time limit, too: either we make these changes soon, or it won't be worth the bother.

JULIAN L. SIMON

B. 1932

Julian L. Simon is a prominent economist and author, and his approach to the issue of pollution is to step back from the environmentalist and anti-environmentalist hype and ask, in a scientific mode, straight questions about the source and solution of this problem. Born in Newark, New Jersey, Simon received his undergraduate degree from Harvard University in 1953 and went on to the University of Chicago for an M.B.A. in 1959 and a Ph.D. in 1961. Since 1963, he has been a professor of economics and marketing at the University of Illinois at Urbana-Champaign, except for several stints as a visiting professor at Hebrew University in Jerusalem (Israel). Simon is the author of many books and dozens of technical articles concerning economics, management, and marketing. Most of his work, such as The Management of Advertising *(1971) and* Applied Managerial Economics *(1975), is not directly applicable to the environment. However, he has demonstrated a consistent interest in the connection between economics and human population, authoring* The Effects of Income on Fertility *(1974) and* The Economics of Population Growth *(1977).*

The following essay appeared as a chapter in Simon's 1981 book, The Ultimate Resource. *It asks the question, "What is the effect of human population growth upon pollution levels?" and comes up with the surprising answer that "in the long run, pollution is likely to be significantly less due to population growth." Actually, Simon admits later in his essay that it is extremely difficult to predict with confidence the long-term effects of a larger population on pollution. If there is enough public outcry, government and industry will probably take dramatic action to reduce pollution, so it is possible, argues Simon, that pollution levels could actually decrease despite population growth. Is Simon merely an apologist for unchecked industrial and population growth? Are his implied criticisms of the "zero population growth" perspective justified? These are difficult questions to answer, but it is certainly worth considering his argument that "there is no prima facie case for ceasing economic or population growth due to fear of pollution." In other words, the verdict is still out.*

ARE PEOPLE AN ENVIRONMENTAL POLLUTION?

Human beings have been getting a bad press from writers on environmental matters. You and I and our neighbors are accused of polluting this world and making it a worse place to live. We have been characterized as emitters of such poisonous substances as lead, sulfur dioxide, and carbon monoxide, and as producers of noise, garbage, and congestion. More people, more pollution, runs the charge. Even more ugly, you and I and our neighbors, together with our children, have been referred to as "people pollution" and the "population plague." That is, our very existence is the core of the problem, in that view.

It has come to seem as if one must be against population growth if one is to be for pollution control. And pollution control in itself appeals to everyone, for good reason. A full-length *New York Times Magazine* piece on pollution ended, "The long-term relief is perfectly obvious. Fewer 'capita'."[1] Clearly we must inquire how various rates of population growth would affect the amount of pollution.

The sober question we wish to answer here is, What is the effect of human population growth upon pollution levels? The general answer this chapter offers is that, although there may be some short-run increase in pollution due to population increases, the additional pollution is relatively small. And in the long run, pollution is likely to be significantly *less* due to population growth.

We shall also analyze how prudent risk-avoidance fits with our conclusions about population growth's effect on pollution. Though values enter strongly into any such analysis, we shall see that, on the basis of most commonly held values, the desire to avoid risk to humanity from a pollution catastrophe does not lead to the conclusion that population growth should be limited by social policy.

Income, Growth, Population, and Pollution

The more developed an economy, the more pollutants it produces; this story has been well and truly told by Barry Commoner in *The Closing Circle*, and elsewhere.[2] The total amounts of most kinds of pollutants depend upon the total scale of industry, and this scale may be roughly gauged by a country's GNP (except that, beyond some per capita income, the proportion of industrial products in the GNP begins to decline as the proportion of services increases). A less-known story is that along with higher income and its consequent greater supply of pollutants comes a greater demand for cleanup, plus an increased capacity to pay for it. The technology for cleaning up exists in virtually every case, and waits only for our will to expend the time and money to put it to work.

For many years governments did not control the flow of industrial pollutants very well. But in recent years there has come a change in the rules of the game due to a combination of rising incomes and consciousness raising by environmentalists. And this has caused favorable trends in air and water quality. The *New York Times* can now headline a story, "Industry is finally cleaning up after itself: with major exceptions, pollution controls are working." Furthermore, before the U.S. Clean Air Act of 1970 and the Water Pollution Control Act of 1972 were passed, there were warnings of catastrophic impacts on business. Yet, "since 1970, the environmental agency has tallied only 81 plant closings attributable to pollution requirements, involving 17,600 jobs."[3] And West Germany's biggest strip-mining firm, Rheinbraun, has moved whole villages so carefully that it was given an international prize because its operations restored the countryside "to greater beauty and usefulness than it had before."[4]

If you have any lingering doubts that increases in income are associated with a decrease in pollution, examine the levels of street cleanliness in the richer versus the poorer countries of the world, the mortality rates of richer versus poorer countries, and the mortality rates of richer versus poorer people within particular countries.[5]

As to population growth and total pollution, some writers have claimed that there is only a slight relationship. They point out that pollution in the U.S. grows at a putative 9 percent a year, while population grows at perhaps 1 percent a year, and they adduce the facts that in Australia's rather affluent cities there is much pollution despite the country's low population, and that the communist countries fall afoul of pollution when industrial production goes up, just as capitalist countries. The slight short-run relationship between population growth and pollution may - be seen in figure A. The solid rectangles show the (very small) differences in emitted-hydrocarbon pollution between the two-child and the three-child average family projections for the year 2000, under both high-economic-growth and low-economic-growth projections. Likewise, the pollution differences between high and low economic growth are small. The largest differences are seen to arise from different social choices among pollution-treatment policies. And the general conclusions of the President's Commission on Population Growth "are similar for other pollutants" to these conclusions about hydrocarbons.[6] In brief, population growth has a relatively unimportant effect on pollution levels in the short run, thirty years or less. And growth in GNP has a greater positive influence on pollution than population growth has negative influence, in the short run—before the additional children under discussion join the labor force.

In the long run, however, the total pollution output will be more or less proportional to the labor force, for a given level of technology. A population twice as big implies twice as much total pollution, all else being equal. If the increased population results in a proportional increase in population density, each person will be exposed to twice as much pollution, again all else being equal.

It is not reasonable, however, to assume that all else is equal. When pollution increases, political forces arise to fight it. Once this process begins, the result may be less pollution than ever—or, of course, nothing may happen except an even worse level of pollution. The outcome simply cannot be known in advance; there seems to be nothing in economic logic or political history that can help us predict with confidence whether the long-run result of the larger population and of the initially higher pollution would be a situation better or worse than if the population had not grown so large. Yet we must keep in mind the empirical fact that over the

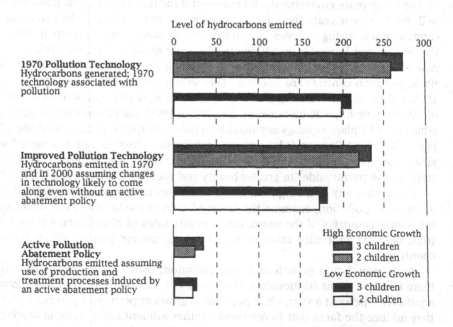

Figure A. Population, Pollution, and Economic Growth

longest sweep of human history, while population has grown enormously, total pollution—as measured by life expectancy, and by the rate of deaths due to socially transmitted and socially caused diseases—has fallen markedly.

Aesthetics, Pollution, and Population Growth

Aesthetics obviously are a matter of taste, and especially here it is not sensible to dispute about tastes. For some people, to be alone in a virgin forest is the ideal, and other visitors would constitute "people pollution"; for others, seeing lots of people at play is the best sight of all.

Of those who praise a reduction of population in the name of making the world more beautiful, I ask these questions: (1) Have you not seen much beauty on this earth that comes from the hand of man—gardens, statues, skyscrapers, graceful bridges? (2) The population of Athens was only 6,000 persons in 1823. Do you think Athens was more beautiful in 1823 or two millennia earlier, when it was more crowded? (3) If the world's population now were a hundredth of what it actually is, would there be a transportation system to get you to Yosemite, the Grand Canyon, the Antarctic, Kenya's wildlife preserves, or Lake Victoria?

Pollution, Population, and Risk of Catastrophe

A safety-minded person might say, "Perhaps the additional risk of the particular pollutant X that is induced by more population is a small one. But would it not be prudent to avoid even this small possibility?" This question is related to the issue of risk aversion. To state the problem at its worst: In an advanced technological society there is always the possibility that a totally new form of pollution will emerge and finish us all before we can do anything about it.

Though the incidence of general catastrophes to the human race has decreased from the time of the Black Death forward, the risk *may* have begun to increase in recent decades—from atomic bombs or from some unknown but powerful pollution. But the present risk of catastrophe will only be known in the future, with hindsight. There is no logical answer to this threat except to note that life with perfect security is not possible—and probably would not be meaningful.

It might make sense to control population growth if the issue were simply the increased risk of catastrophe due to population growth, and if only the number of deaths mattered, rather than the number of healthy lives lived. One flaw in this line of reasoning is revealed, however, by pushing it to its absurd endpoint: One may reduce the risk of pollution catastrophe to zero by reducing to zero the number of persons who are alive. But such a policy obviously is unacceptable to all but a few persons who have values quite different from the rest of us. Therefore we must dig deeper to learn how pollution ought to influence our views about population size and growth.

The argument that population growth is a bad thing because it may bring about new and possibly catastrophic forms of pollution is a special case of a more general argument: Avoid any change because it may bring about some devastating technological destruction as yet unknown. There is an irrefutable logic in this argument. In its own terms, adding a few not-too-unreasonable assumptions, it cannot be proven wrong, as follows. Assume that any alteration in technology may have some unexpected ill effects. Assume also that the system is acceptably safe right now. Additional people increase the need for change, and this makes a prima facie case against population growth. And the same argument can be applied to economic growth: Economic growth brings about change, which can bring dangers. Hence economic growth is to be avoided.

Of course, this sit-tight, leave-well-enough-alone posture is only possible for us 1980s humans, because economic and population growth in the past produced the changes that brought many of us to the "well enough" state that might now be "left alone."[7] That is, the high life expectancy and high living standard of middle-class people in developed countries could not have come about if people in the past had not produced the changes that got the most fortunate of us here—and if they had not suffered some consequences in doing so. We are living off our inheritance from past generations the way children may live off the inheritance of parents who worked hard and saved.

There is nothing logically wrong with living off an inheritance without in turn increasing the heritage of knowledge and high living standards that will be left to subsequent generations. But you should at least be clear that this is what you are doing if you opt for "zero growth"—if zero growth really were possible. (In fact, upon close examination, the concept of zero economic growth, unlike zero population growth, turns out to be either so vague as to be undefinable, or just plain nonsense; and it offers benefits to the well-off that are withheld from the poor.)[8]

Proponents of zero growth argue that future generations will benefit from fewer changes now. That is conceivable, of course. But the historical evidence quite clearly runs the other way: If our ancestors had, at any time in the past, opted for zero population growth or for a frozen economic system, we would certainly be less well-off than we now are. Hence it seems reasonable to project the same trend into the future. Most specifically, a larger economic capability and a larger population of knowledge creators has put into our hands a wider variety of more powerful tools for preventing and controlling threats to our lives and environment—especially communicable diseases and hunger—than society could have bequeathed to us if its size had been frozen at any time in the past.

Furthermore, additional people can also improve the chances of reducing pollution even in their own generation, because additional people create new *solutions* for problems, as well as create new problems. Let's consider a poor-country example: Higher population density may increase the chance of communicable disease. But higher population density also is the only force that really gets rid of malaria, because the swamps that breed malaria-carrying mosquitoes do not co-exist with settled fields and habitation. And of course, if population growth had never occurred, there would not likely have been the growth of civilization and science that led to pharmaceutical weapons against malaria and improved methods of fighting mosquitoes.

On balance, then, we must put onto the scales not only the increased chance of a pollution catastrophe induced by more people; we must also weigh the new knowledge for an increased control of pollutants, and of their ill consequences, that additional people contribute. So it is not at all clear whether the chance of catastrophe (involving 10,000 or 1 million people) is greater with a world population of 4 trillion or of 6 billion, or with a growth rate of 2 percent or 1 percent yearly.

It would be an error to assume that all (or even most) indirect environmental effects of economic and population growth are negative. Happy accidents sometimes arise due to growth. If more genetic changes occur (they occur naturally, or we would not be here at all), some of the mutants will be "undesirable," but others will be "desirable." And some environmental changes also affect species for the good:

SEAFOOD INDUSTRY FINDS FISH THRIVE IN WATER DISCHARGED BY POWER COMPANIES.
The water, used as a coolant in generating plants, is about 20 degrees warmer when it leaves a plant than when it entered. Cultivating catfish, oysters, shrimp, trout and other marine life in this warm water often cuts in half the length of time it takes them to mature. Cultured Catfish Co. of Colorado City, Texas, says its catfish grow to 1½ pounds in three to four months in the warm water flowing from a Texas Electric Service plant. It usually takes catfish, considered a delicacy in some parts of the U.S., 18 months to grow that big in a natural pond.[9]

Still—there is our natural aversion to risk and uncertainty. We should keep in mind, however, that risk and uncertainty are not all in one direction, and that the major social and cultural changes that would be needed to prevent growth are also fraught with uncertainty, and possible catastrophe. For example, what would be the social and political implications of freezing the present pattern of income distribution among the poor and the rich due to reduced economic growth? What would be the effects on incentive if people were told that they could not increase their incomes or have more children? What would be the psychological implications of a stationary economy and society? And which legal sanctions would be imposed to enforce these decisions? Certainly none of these matters is of small importance compared with the likely dangers from catastrophic pollution. Hence there is no prima facie case for ceasing economic or population growth due to fear of pollution.

Summary

More people mean higher total output, and this implies more pollution in the short run, all else being equal. But more people need not imply more pollution, and they may well imply less pollution; this has been the trend in human history as indicated by the most important general index of pollution—increasing life expectancy. Additional people have created new ways of reducing pollution, and contributed additional resources with which to fight pollution. There is no reason to expect a different course of events in the future.

—1981

Notes

1. Edwin L. Dale, Jr., "The Economics of Pollution," *New York Times Magazine*, April 19, 1970, pp. 29 ff.
2. Commoner, 1972.
3. Gladwin Hill in "News of the Week in Review," *New York Times*, October 17, 1974, p. 4.
4. *Newsweek*, December 1, 1975, p. 86.
5. The difference in mortality by income is not merely a matter of higher incomes buying better nutrition. The poorest person in the U.S. can buy a nutritious diet of soybeans, milk, and dog food. The fact that poor people do not eat such diets speaks to the complexity of the income-health relationship.
6. Ridker, 1972, p. 25.
7. An interesting account of the logic of sit-tight is found in Nathan Leopold's description of prison (1958):

Penitentiaries are hidebound institutions, regulated down to their tiniest detail by tradition. There is tremendous inertia to overcome in effecting any change. A compelling reason for doing anything in a given way is that it has always been done that way. Obvious improvements, easier ways of doing something are rejected simply because they are new. In the management of the prison itself, especially with regard to custodial matters, there is a certain amount of justification for this conservatism. The smallest change in routine may involve angles not immediately apparent—not thought of by the administration. But you can bank on it that there are always three thousand active brains engaged in watching attentively for the slightest loophole. And in such matters one mistake is one mistake too many. It is often better, as it is always safer, to stick by the tried and true.

8. For information on that subject, which is beyond our scope here, see *The No-Growth Society*, edited by M. Olson and H. Lansberg (1973).
9. *Wall Street Journal*, December 22, 1977, p. 1.

ROBINSON JEFFERS
1887-1962

When the eminent environmentalist David Brower left the Sierra Club in the late 1960s to found the more politically radical Friends of the Earth, he chose for the new organization's motto some words from a poem by Robinson Jeffers: "Not man apart." Had he still been alive, Jeffers would have been chagrined to find his work appropriated by the cause of environmentalism. Shy, unassuming, and somewhat reclusive, he spent most of his life avoiding the political fray. As if Brower's use of Jeffers's work were not irony enough, in the 1980s the deep ecology branch of the environmental movement also canonized Jeffers, this time for his philosophy of inhumanism, a worldview laid out in dubiously brief terms in the introduction to his book The Double Axe and Other Poems *(1948). Simply stated, inhumanism, according to Jeffers, is the "rejection of human solipsism and recognition of the transhuman magnificence."*

Jeffers's poetry is nearly inseparable from Big Sur, that stretch of the central California coast that provided him with both his inspiration and his home. He came to this stunning jumble of mountain and ocean with his wife, Una, in 1914, and except for short vacations never left. He built a house of stone blocks hewn from the local granite, and it was during this time that he had a spiritual conversion that dissolved the vestiges of the conservative Christianity he had been raised in and awakened him to the fact that humans are not the center of Creation. This insight characterizes the best of his poetry, but it lends an edge of harshness to his vision. Because of the unsavory themes that recur in his poetry—incest, murder, bestiality—many readers, both in his day and ours, interpret his work as sadistic or even misanthropic. Careful reading, however, reveals that Jeffers is not without compassion, that he is in fact pursuing the great religious theme: the nature of suffering. Jeffers's vision can be grasped in the opening line of one of his poems: "To feel and speak the astonishing beauty of things."

When it comes to extinction and what we today call endangered species, how seldom we speak of suffering. Who suffers? The species? Human beings? Something greater? Jeffers's poem "Passenger Pigeons," from The Beginning and the End and Other Poems *(1963), invites the reader to remember one such species that has passed (the last passenger pigeon died in captivity in a Cincinnati zoo in 1914) and to contemplate the fate of our own species.*

PASSENGER PIGEONS

Slowly the passenger pigeons increased, then suddenly
　　their numbers
Became enormous, they would flatten ten miles of forest
When they flew down to roost, and the cloud of their rising
Eclipsed the dawns. They became too many, they are all
　　dead,
Not one remains.
　　　　　　　　And the American bison: their hordes
Would hide a prairie from horizon to horizon, great heads
　　and storm-cloud shoulders, a torrent of life—
How many are left? For a time, for a few years, their bones
Turned the dark prairies white.
　　　　　　　　You, Death, you watch for these things,
These explosions of life, they are your food,
They make your feasts.
　　　　　　　　But turn your great rolling eyes
　　away from humanity,
Those grossly craving black eyes. It is true we increase.
A man from Britain landing in Gaul when Rome had fallen,
He journeyed fourteen days inland through that beautiful
Rich land, the orchards and rivers and the looted villas: he
　　reports that he saw
No living man. But now we fill up the gaps,
In spite of wars, famines and pestilences we are quite
　　suddenly
Three billion people: our bones, ours too, would make
Wide prairies white, a beautiful snow of unburied bones:
Bones that have twitched and quivered in the nights of love,
Bones that have shaken with laughter and hung slack in
　　sorrow, coward bones
Worn out with trembling, strong bones broken on the rack,
　　bones broken in battle,
Broad bones gnarled with hard labor, and the little bones of
　　sweet young children, and the white empty skulls,
Little carved ivory wine-jugs that used to contain
Passion and thought and love and insane delirium, where
　　now

Not even worms live.

        Respect humanity, Death, these
shameless black eyes of yours,
It is not necessary to take all at once—besides that, you
cannot do it, we are too powerful,
We are men, not pigeons; you may take the old, the useless
and helpless, the cancer-bitten and the tender young,
But the human race has still history to make. For look—
look now
At our achievements: we have bridled the cloud-leaper
lightning, a lion whipped by a man, to carry our messages
And work our will, we have snatched the live thunderbolt
Out of God's hands. Ha? That was little and last year—for
now we have taken
The primal powers, creation and annihilation; we make new
elements, such as God never saw,
We can explode atoms and annul the fragments, nothing
left but pure energy, we shall use it
In peace and war—"Very clever," he answered, in his thin
piping voice,
Cruel and a eunuch.

        Roll those idiot black eyes of yours
On the field-beasts, not on intelligent man
We are not in your order. You watched the dinosaurs
Grow into horror: they had been left in the ditches and
presently became enormous, with leaping flanks
And tearing teeth, plated with armor, nothing could stand
against them, nothing but you,
Death, and they died. You watched the sabre-tooth tigers.
Develop those huge fangs, unnecessary as our sciences and
presently they died. You have their bones
In the oil-pits and layer-rock, you will not have ours. With
pain and labor we have bought intelligence.
We have minds like the tusks of those forgotten tigers,
hypertrophied and terrible,
We have counted the stars and half understood them, we
have watched the farther galaxies fleeing away from us,
wild herds
Of panic horses—or a trick of distance deceived the
prism—we outfly falcons and eagles and meteors,
Faster than sound, higher than the nourishing air; we have
enormous privilege, we do not fear you,
We have invented the jet-plane and the death-bomb and the
cross of Christ—"Oh," he said, "surely
You'll live forever"—grinning like a skull, covering his
mouth with his hand—"What could exterminate you?"

                  —1963

Rachel Carson
1907-1964

Rachel Carson was a shy and self-effacing woman who sparked international controversy by challenging the indiscriminate use of pesticides in Silent Spring *(1962), the book that launched the modern environmental movement. A meticulous and thorough researcher and a lyrical writer, Carson was also a philosopher, always seeking the pattern that connects, and a mystic attuned to the "beauty and mystery" of the natural world. Her field was actually marine biology, the topic of her three books preceding* Silent Spring, *and she only undertook the research for the latter book at the prompting of a friend who complained that antimosquito pesticide sprayed on her two-acre nature sanctuary in Massachusetts had destroyed birds as well as mosquitos. The nature writer Ann Zwinger has commented that "the earlier books about the sea came out of a deep and abiding love for her subject," while* Silent Spring *"came out of bitter realization, despair, and fear." Carson was posthumously awarded the Presidential Medal of Freedom in 1980; the citation accompanying the award says that she "created a tide of environmental consciousness that has not ebbed."*

Born in Springdale, Pennsylvania, Carson entered college with the intention of becoming a writer, but studying with a woman biology professor caused her to change her career goal, and she earned a B.A. in science from Pennsylvania College for Women and an M.A. in zoology from Johns Hopkins University. In 1936, Carson took a job with the U.S. Bureau of Fisheries; in 1947 she became the editor-in-chief of publications for the Fish and Wildlife Service and remained employed in this capacity until 1952, when royalties enabled her to write full-time. In 1937, the Atlantic Monthly *published "Undersea," based on a rejected radio script she had written for the Bureau of Fisheries. She expanded this piece into her first book,* Under the Sea-Wind: A Naturalist's Picture of Ocean Life *(1941). Her next book,* The Sea Around Us *(1951), became one of the most popular books ever written about the natural world, winning the National Book Award for nonfiction and the John Burroughs Medal for nature writing and remaining on the best-seller list for eighty-six weeks.* The Edge of the Sea *(1955), a popular guide to seashore life, and* The Sense of Wonder *(1965), which first appeared as a magazine essay entitled "Help Your Child to Wonder," followed.*

Carson was strongly influenced by the philosophy of "reverence for life" articulated by Albert Schweitzer. Indeed, Silent Spring *is dedicated to Schweitzer, "who said, 'Man has lost the capacity to foresee and to forestall. He will end by destroying the earth.'" Carson's deep concern over "the destroying hand of man" permeates the commencement address she delivered on June 12, 1962, at Scripps College in Claremont, California, the text of which follows. Coincidentally, the first installment of* Silent Spring *appeared on the newsstands that day, in the June 16 issue of the* New Yorker.

OF MAN AND THE STREAM OF TIME

As I was carried here so swiftly across the continent by a jet airliner, it occurred to me that I have really been on the way for ten years, for it was that long ago that your President first invited me to come to Scripps College. Through the intervening years, he has renewed that invitation with infinite patience and courtesy. Now at last circumstances have allowed me to accept, and I am very happy to be here.

Had I come ten years ago, I am not certain what I would have talked about. But as I have lived and, I hope, learned, as I have reflected upon the problems that crowd in upon us today, one stands out in my mind as having such vast importance that I want to discuss it with you now.

I wish to speak today of man's relation to nature and more specifically of man's attitude toward nature. A generation ago this would perhaps have been an academic subject of little interest to any but philosophers. Today it is a subject of immediate and sometimes terrifying relevance.

The word *nature* has many and varied connotations, but for the present theme I like this definition: "Nature is the part of the world that man did not make." You who have spent your undergraduate years here at Scripps have been exceptionally fortunate, living in the midst of beauty and comforts and conveniences that *are* creations of man—yet always in the background having the majestic and beautiful mountains to remind you of an older and vaster world—a world that man did not make.

Man has long talked somewhat arrogantly about the conquest of nature; now he has the power to achieve his boast. It is our misfortune—it may well be our final tragedy—that this power has not been tempered with wisdom, but has been marked by irresponsibility; that there is all too little awareness that man is part of nature, and that the price of conquest may well be the destruction of man himself.

Measured against the vast backdrop of geologic time, the whole era of man seems but a moment—but how portentous a moment! It was only within the past million years or so that the race of man arose. Who could have foretold that this being, who walked upright and no longer lived in trees, who lurked in caves, hiding in fear from the great beasts who shared his world—who could have guessed that he would one day have in his hands the power to change the very nature of the earth—the power of life and death over so many of its creatures? Who could have foretold that the brain that was developing behind those heavy brow ridges would allow him to accomplish things no other creature had achieved—but would not at the same time endow him with wisdom so to control his activities that he would not bring destruction upon himself?

I like the way E. B. White has summed it up in his usual inimitable style. "I am pessimistic about the human race," said Mr. White, "because it is too ingenious for its own good. Our approach to nature is to beat it into submission. We would stand a better chance of survival if we accommodated ourselves to this planet and viewed it appreciatively instead of skeptically and dictatorially."

Our attitude toward nature has changed with time, in ways that I can only suggest here. Primitive men, confronted with the awesome forces of nature, reacted in fear of what they did not understand. They peopled the dark and brooding forests with supernatural beings. Looking out on the sea that extended to an unknown horizon, they imagined a dreadful brink lying beneath fog and gathering darkness; they pictured vast abysses waiting to suck the traveler down into a bottomless gulf.

Only a few centuries have passed since those pre-Columbian days, yet today our whole earth has become only another shore from which we look out across the dark ocean of space, uncertain what we shall find when we sail out among the stars, but like the Norsemen and the Polynesians of old, lured by the very challenge of the unknown.

Between the time of those early voyages into unknown seas and the present we can trace an enormous and fateful change. It is good that fear and superstition have largely been replaced by knowledge, but we would be on safer ground today if the knowledge had been accompanied by humility instead of arrogance.

In the western world our thinking has for many centuries been dominated by the Jewish-Christian concept of man's relation to nature, in which man is regarded as the master of all the earth's inhabitants. Out of this there easily grew the thought that everything on earth—animate or inanimate, animal, vegetable, or mineral—and indeed the earth itself—had been created expressly for man.

John Muir, who knew and loved the California mountains, has described this naive view of nature with biting wit: "A numerous class of men are painfully aston-ished whenever they find anything, living or dead, in all God's universe, which they cannot eat or render in some way what they call useful to themselves. . . . Whales are storehouses of oil for us, to help out the stars in lighting our dark ways until the discovery of the Pennsylvania oil wells. Among plants, hemp is a case of evident destination for ships' rigging, wrapping packages, and hanging the wicked."

So Muir, with his pen dipped in acid, many years ago pointed out the incredible absurdity of such views. But I am not certain that in spite of all our modern learn-ing and sophistication, we have actually progressed far beyond the self-oriented philosophy of the Victorians. I fear that these ideas still lurk about, showing them-selves boldly and openly at times, at others skulking about in the shadows of the subconscious.

I have met them frequently, as I have pointed out some exquisite creature of the tide pools to a chance companion. "What is it for?" he may ask, and he is obviously disappointed if I can't assure him that it can be eaten or at least made into some bauble to be sold in a shop.

But how is one to assign a value to the exquisite flower-like hydroids reflected in the still mirror of a tide pool? Who can place in one pan of some cosmic scales the trinkets of modern civilization and in the other the song of a thrush in the wind-less twilight?

Now I have dwelt at some length on the fallacious idea of a world arranged for man's use and convenience, but I have done so because I am convinced that these notions—the legacy of an earlier day—are at the root of some of our most critical problems. We still talk in terms of "conquest"—whether it be of the insect world or of the mysterious world of space. We still have not become mature enough to see our-selves as a very tiny part of a vast and incredible universe, a universe that is distin-guished above all else by a mysterious and wonderful unity that we flout at our peril.

Poets often have a perception that gives their words the validity of science. So the English poet Francis Thompson said nearly a century ago,

Thou canst not stir a flower
Without troubling of a star.

But the poet's insight has not become part of general knowledge.

Man's attitude toward nature is today critically important, simply because of his new-found power to destroy it. For a good many years there has been an excellent organization known as The International Union for the Protection of Nature. I clearly remember that in the days before Hiroshima I used to wonder whether nature—nature in the broadest context of the word—actually needed protection from man. Surely the sea was inviolate and forever beyond man's power to change it. Surely the vast cycles by which water is drawn up into the clouds to return again to the earth could never be touched. And just as surely the vast tides of life—the migrating birds—would continue to ebb and flow over the continents, marking the passage of the seasons.

But I was wrong. Even these things, that seemed to belong to the eternal verities, are not only threatened but have already felt the destroying hand of man.

Today we use the sea as a dumping ground for radioactive wastes, which then enter into the vast and uncontrollable movements of ocean waters through the deep basins, to turn up no one knows where. . . .

The once beneficent rains are now an instrument to bring down from the atmosphere the deadly products of nuclear explosions. Water, perhaps our most precious natural resource, is used and misused at a reckless rate. Our streams are fouled with an incredible assortment of wastes—domestic, chemical, radioactive, so that our planet, though dominated by seas that envelop three-fourths of its surface, is rapidly becoming a thirsty world.

We now wage war on other organisms, turning against them all the terrible armaments of modern chemistry, and we assume a right to push whole species over the brink of extinction. This is a far cry from the philosophy of that man of peace, Albert Schweitzer—the philosophy of "reverence for life." Although all the world honors Dr. Schweitzer, I am afraid we do not follow him.

So nature does indeed need protection from man; but man, too, needs protection from his own acts, for he is part of the living world. His war against nature is inevitably a war against himself. His heedless and destructive acts enter into the vast cycles of the earth, and in time return to him.

Through all this problem there runs a constant theme, and the theme is the flowing stream of time, unhurried, unmindful of man's restless and feverish pace. It is made up of geologic events, that have created mountains and worn them away, that have brought the seas out of their basins, to flood the continents and then retreat. But even more importantly it is made up of biological events, that represent that all-important adjustment of living protoplasm to the conditions of the external world. What we are today represents an adjustment achieved over the millions and hundreds of millions of years. There have always been elements in the environment that were hostile to living things—extremes of temperature, background radiation in rocks and atmosphere, toxic elements in the earth and sea. But over the long ages of time, life has reached an accommodation, a balance.

Now we are far on the way to upsetting this balance by creating an artificial environment—an environment consisting to an ever increasing extent of things that "man has made." The radiation to which we must adjust if we are to survive is no longer simply the natural background radiation of rocks and sunlight, it is the result of our tampering with the atom. In the same way, wholly new chemicals are emerging from the laboratories—an astounding, bewildering array of them. All of these things are being introduced into our environment at a rapid rate. There simply is no time for living protoplasm to adjust to them.

In 1955 a group of 70 scientists met at Princeton University to consider man's role in changing the face of the earth. They produced a volume of nearly 1200 pages devoted to changes that range from the first use of fire to urban sprawl. It is an astounding record. This is not to say, of course, that all the changes have been undesirable. But the distinguishing feature of man's activities is that they have almost always been undertaken from the narrow viewpoint of short-range gain, without considering either their impact on the earth or their long-range effect upon ourselves.

They have been distinguished, also, by a curious unwillingness to be guided by the knowledge that is available in certain areas of science. I mean especially the knowledge of biologists, of ecologists, of geneticists, all of whom have special areas of competence that should allow them to predict the effect of our actions on living creatures, including, of course, man himself.

This is an age that has produced floods of how-to-do-it books, and it is also an age of how-to-do-it science. It is, in other words, the age of technology, in which if we know *how* to do something, we do it without pausing to inquire whether we *should*. We know how to split the atom, and how to use its energy in peace and war, and so we proceed with preparations to do so, as if acting under some blind compulsion; even though the geneticists tell us that by our actions in this atomic age we are endangering not only ourselves but the integrity of the human germ plasm.

Instead of always trying to impose our will on Nature we should sometimes be quiet and listen to what she has to tell us. If we did so I am sure we would gain a new perspective on our own feverish lives. We might even see the folly and the madness of a world in which half of mankind is busily preparing to destroy the other half and to reduce our whole planet to radioactive ashes in the doing. We might gain what the English essayist Tomlinson called "a hint of a reality, hitherto fabulous, of a truth that may be everlasting, yet is contrary to all our experience," for "our earth may be a far better place than we have yet discovered."

I wish I could stand before you and say that my own generation had brought strength and meaning to man's relation to nature, that we had looked upon the majesty and beauty and terror of the earth we inhabit and learned wisdom and humility. Alas, this cannot be said, for it is we who have brought into being a fateful and destructive power.

But the stream of time moves forward and mankind moves with it. Your generation must come to terms with the environment. Your generation must face realities instead of taking refuge in ignorance and evasion of truth. Yours is a grave and a sobering responsibility, but it is also a shining opportunity. You go out into a world where mankind is challenged, as it has never been challenged before, to prove its maturity and its mastery—not of nature, but of itself. Therein lies our hope and our destiny. "In today already walks tomorrow."

—1962

MARILOU AWIAKTA

B. 1936

Marilou Awiakta, a writer of Native American (Cherokee/Appalachian) and Scotch-Irish descent, once stated in an interview that her philosophy "is grounded in the belief that the Creator made everything in the universe as one family—a web of life governed by the law of respect." Awiakta's writing typically addresses such contemporary issues as gender relations, nuclear energy, the environment, and the preservation of native traditions. In her ambitious 1993 book, Selu: Seeking the Corn-Mother's Wisdom, *she aims to reveal the surprising connections between traditional Native American stories and the revelations of late-twentieth-century physics and biology. Ginitsi Selu, the Cherokee "Grandmother Corn," represents the life-sustaining forces of the natural world, forces that will support human beings and other living creatures as long as humans respect nature. Awiakta's book—a combination of personal narrative, poetry, interviews with Cherokee elders, journalistic essays, lengthy quotations from scientists and ethnologists, and modern versions of Cherokee tales—argues that some of the dangerous applications of modern science result from a loss of respect for nature.*

Born in Knoxville, Tennessee, Awiakta was raised in the shadow of Tennessee's Oak Ridge National Laboratory. She graduated from the University of Tennessee in 1958 and worked as a civilian liaison officer and translator for the U.S. Air Force in France from 1964 to 1967, while her husband was stationed overseas. Today she lives with her family in Memphis. Her earlier publications include Abiding Appalachia: Where Mountain and Atom Meet *(1978) and the children's book* Rising Fawn and the Fire Mystery: A Story of Heritage, Family and Courage, 1833 *(1983).*

In the late 1970s, Awiakta became concerned about the Tennessee Valley Authority's plans to build Tellico Dam on the Little Tennessee River in the eastern part of the state, particularly because this dam threatened to inundate sacred Cherokee lands. She threw herself into an article on Tellico for the Houston Chronicle *but gradually grew discouraged about the power of her writing to influence public opinion. In 1981, however, Awiakta began corresponding with the prominent African-American writer Alice Walker (who also has Cherokee blood); the two eventually met at Walker's home in California, and Walker encouraged Awiakta to write about her nuclear experiences. "Baring the Atom's Mother Heart," which appears in* Selu, *was born from that meeting. This piece is not a simple diatribe against nuclear weapons and nuclear energy; instead, Awiakta suggests the need to proceed cautiously with nuclear technology (or with technology in general) and expresses wonderment about the mysteries of the atom.*

BARING THE ATOM'S MOTHER HEART

"What is the atom, Mother? Will it hurt us?"

I was nine years old. It was December 1945. Four months earlier, in the heat of an August morning—Hiroshima. Destruction. Death. Power beyond belief, released from something invisible. Without knowing its name, I'd already felt the atom's power in another form. Since 1943, my father had commuted eighteen miles from our apartment in Knoxville to the plant in Oak Ridge—the atomic frontier where the atom had been split, where it still was splitting. He left before dawn and came home long after dark. "What do you do, Daddy?"—"I can't tell you, Marilou. It's part of something for the war. I don't know what they're making out there or how my job fits into it."

"What's inside the maze?"

"Something important . . . and strange. I see long, heavy trucks coming in. What they're bringing just seems to disappear. Somebody must know what happens to it, but nobody ever talks about it. One thing for sure—the government doesn't spend millions of dollars for nothing. It's something big. I can't imagine what."

I couldn't either. But I could feel its energy like a great hum.

Then, suddenly, it had an image: the mushroom cloud. It had a name: the atom. And our family was then living in Oak Ridge. My father had given me the facts. I also needed an interpreter.

"What is the atom, Mother? Will it hurt us?"

"It can be used to hurt everybody, Marilou. It killed thousands of people in Hiroshima and Nagasaki. But the atom itself . . . ? It's invisible, the smallest bit of matter. And it's in everything. Your hand, my dress, the milk you're drinking—all of it is made with millions and millions of atoms and they're all moving. But what the atom means . . . ? I don't think anyone knows yet. We have to have reverence for its nature and learn to live in harmony with it. Remember the burning man."

"I remember." When I was six years old, his screams had brought my mother and me running to our front porch. Mother was eight months pregnant. What we saw made her hold me tight against her side. Across the street, in the small parking lot of the dry cleaner's, a man in flames ran, waving his arms. Another man chased him, carrying a garden hose turned on full force, and shouting, "Stop, stop!" The burning man stumbled and sank to his knees, shrieking, clawing the air, trying to climb out of his pain. When water hit his arms, flesh fell off in fiery chunks. As the flames went out, his cries ceased. He collapsed slowly into a charred and steaming heap.

Silence. Burned flesh. Water trickling into the gutter . . .

The memory flowed between Mother and me, and she said, as she had said that day, "Never tempt nature, Marilou. It's the nature of fire to burn. And of cleaning fluid to flame near heat. The man had been warned over and over not to work with the fluid, then stoke the furnace. But he kept doing it. Nothing happened. He thought he was in control. Then one day a spark . . . The atom is like the fire."

"So it *will* hurt us."

"That depends on us, Marilou."

I understood. Mother already had taught me that beyond surface differences, everything is in physical and spiritual connection—God, nature, humanity. All are one, a circle. It seemed natural for the atom to be part of this connection. At school, when I was introduced to Einstein's theory of relativity—that energy and matter are one—I accepted the concept easily.

Peacetime brought relaxation of some restrictions in Oak Ridge. I learned that my father was an accountant. The "long, heavy trucks" brought uranium ore to the graphite reactor, which was still guarded by a maze of fences. The reactor reduced the ore to a small amount of radioactive material. Safety required care and caution.

Scientists called the reactor "The lady" and, in moments of high emotion, referred to her as "our beloved reactor."

"What does she look like, Daddy?"

"They tell me she has a seven-foot shield of concrete around a graphite core, where the atom is split." I asked the color of graphite. "Black," he said. And I imagined a great, black queen, standing behind her shield, holding the splitting atom in the shelter of her arms.

I also saw the immense nurturing potential of the atom. There was intensive research into fuels, fertilizers, mechanical and interpretative tools. Crops and animals were studied for the effects of radiation. Terminal cancer patients came from everywhere to the research hospital. I especially remember one newspaper picture of a man with incredibly thin hands reaching for the "atomic cocktail" (a container of radioactive isotopes). His face was lighted with hope.

At school we had disaster drills in case of nuclear attack (or in case someone got careless around the reactor). Scientists explained the effects of an explosion—from "death light" to fallout. They also emphasized the peaceful potential of the atom and the importance of personal commitment in using it. Essentially, their message was the same as my mother's. "If we treat the atom with reverence, all will be well."

But all is not well now with the atom. The arms race, the entry of Big Business into the nuclear industry, and accidents like Three Mile Island cause alarm. Along with me, women protest, organize anti-nuclear groups, speak out. But we must also take time to ponder woman's affinities with the atom and to consider that our responsibilities for its use are more profound than we may have imagined.

We should begin with the atom itself, which is approximately two trillion times smaller than the point of a pin. We will focus on the nature and movement of the atom, not on the intricacies of nuclear physics. To understand the atom, we must flow with its pattern, which is circular.

During the nineteenth and twentieth centuries, scientists theorized about the atom, isolated it, discovered the nucleus, with its neutrons, protons, electrons. The atom appeared to resemble a Chinese nesting ball—a particle within a particle. Scientists believed the descending order would lead to the ultimate particle—the final, tiny bead. Man would penetrate the secret of matter and dominate it. All life could then be controlled, like a machine.

Around the turn of the century, however, a few scientists began to observe the atom asserting its nature, which was more flexible and unpredictable than had been thought. To explain it required a new logic, and, in 1905, Einstein published his theory of relativity. To describe the atom also required new use of language in science because our senses cannot experience the nuclear world except by analogy. The great Danish physicist, Niels Bohr, said, "When it comes to atoms, language can be used only as in poetry. The poet, too, is not nearly so concerned with describing facts as with creating images and mental connections."

As research progressed, the word *mystery* began to appear in scientific writing, along with theories that matter might not end in a particle after all. Perhaps the universe resembled a great thought more than a great machine. The linear path was bending . . . and in the mid-1970s the path ended in an infinitesimal circle: the quark. A particle so small that even with the help of huge machines, humans can see only its trace, as we see the vapor trail of an airplane in the stratosphere. A particle ten to one hundred million times smaller than the atom. Within the quark, scientists now perceive matter refining beyond space-time into a kind of mathematical operation, as nebulous and real as an unspoken thought. It is a mystery that no conceivable research is likely to dispel, the life force in process—nurturing, enabling, enduring, fierce.

I call it the atom's mother heart.

Nuclear energy is the nurturing energy of the universe. Except for stellar explosions, this energy works not by fission (splitting) but by fusion—attraction and melding. With the relational process, the atom creates and transforms life. Women are part of this life force. One of our natural and chosen purposes is to create and sustain life—biological, mental and spiritual.

Women nurture and enable. Our "process" is to perceive relationships among elements, draw their energies to the center and fuse them into a whole. Thought is our essence; it is intrinsic for us, not an aberration of our nature, as Western tradition often asserts.

Another commonality with the atom's mother heart is ferocity. When the atom is split—when her whole is disturbed—a chain reaction begins that will end in an explosion unless the reaction is contained, usually by a nuclear reactor. To be productive and safe, the atom must be restored to its harmonic, natural pattern. It has to be treated with respect. Similarly, to split woman from her thought, sexuality and spirit is unnatural. Explosions are inevitable unless wholeness is restored.

In theory, nature has been linked to woman for centuries—from the cosmic principle of the Great Mother-Goddess to the familiar metaphors of Mother Nature and Mother Earth. But to connect the life force with *living* woman is something only some ancient or so-called "primitive" cultures have been wise enough to do. The linear, Western, masculine mode of thought has been too intent on conquering nature to learn from her a basic truth: *To separate the gender that bears life from the power to sustain it is as destructive as to tempt nature herself.*

This obvious truth is ignored because to accept it would acknowledge woman's power, upset the concept of woman as sentimental—passive, all-giving, all-suffering—and disturb public and private patterns. But the atom's mother heart makes it impossible to ignore this truth any longer. She is the interpreter of new images and mental connections not only for humanity, but most particularly for women, who have profound responsibilities in solving the nuclear dilemma. We can do much to restore harmony. But time is running out. . . .

Shortly after Hiroshima Albert Einstein said, "The unleashed power of the atom has changed everything save our modes of thought, and thus we drift toward unparalleled catastrophe." Now, deployment of nuclear missiles is increasing. A going phrase in Washington is, "When the war starts . . ." Many nuclear power plants are being built and operated with money, not safety, as the bottom line. In spite of repeated warnings from scientists and protests from the public, the linear-thinking people continue to ignore the nature of the atom. They act irreverently. They think they're in control. One day a spark. . . .

I look beyond the spectres of the burning man and the mushroom cloud to a time two hundred years ago, when destruction was bearing down on the Cherokee nation. My foremothers took their places in the circles of power along with the men. Outnumbered and outgunned, the nation could not be saved. But the Cherokee and their culture survived—and women played a strong part in that survival.

Although the American culture is making only slow progress toward empowering women, there is much we can do to restore productive harmony with the atom. Protest and litigation are important in stopping nuclear abuse, but total polarization between pro- and anti-nuclear people is simplistic and dangerous. It is not true that all who believe in nuclear energy are bent on destruction. Neither is it true that all who oppose it are "kooks" or "against progress." Such linear, polar thinking generates so much anger on both sides that there is no consensual climate where reasonable solutions can be found. The center cannot hold. And the beast of catastrophe slouches toward us. We need a network of the committed to ward it off. Women at large can use our traditional intercessory skills to create this network through organizations, through education and through weaving together conscientious protagonists in industry, science and government. Women who are professionals in these fields should share equally in policy making.

Our energies may fuse with energies of others in ways we cannot foresee. I think of two groups of protesters who came to Diablo Canyon, California, in the fall of 1981. Women and men protested the activation of a nuclear power plant so near an earthquake fault. The first group numbered nearly three thousand. The protest was effective, but it says much about the dominant, holistic mode of American thought that an article about the second group was buried in the middle of a San Francisco newspaper.

After the three thousand had left Diablo Canyon to wind and silence, a band of about eighty Chumash Indians came to the site of the power plant. They raised a wood-sculptured totem and sat in a circle around it for a daylong prayer vigil. Jonathan Swift Turtle, a Mewok medicine man, said that the Indians did not oppose nuclear technology but objected to the plant's being built atop a sacred Chumash burial site as well as near an earthquake fault. He said he hoped the vigil would bring about "a moment of harmony between the pro- and anti-nuclear factions."

The Chumash understand that to split the atom from the sacred is a deadly fission that will ultimately destroy nature and humanity. I join this circle of belief with an emblem I created for my life and work—the sacred white deer of the Cherokee leaping in the heart of the atom. My ancestors believed that if a hunter took the life of a deer without asking its spirit for pardon, the immortal Little Deer would track the hunter to his home and cripple him. The reverent hunter evoked the white deer's blessing and guidance.

For me, Little Deer is a symbol of reverence. Of hope. Of belief that if we humans relent our anger and create a listening space, we may attain harmony with the atom in time. If we do not, our world will become a charred and steaming heap. Burned flesh. Silence . . .

There will be no sign of hope except deep in the invisible, where the atom's mother heart—slowly and patiently—bears new life.

—1993

RUDOLFO ANAYA

B. 1937

Rudolfo Anaya is a writer whose voice and vision are profoundly rooted in the land and culture of his native New Mexico. "Sense of place," he has written, "does not merely mean that a writer uses the landscape of the place as background. It means that the spirit of the place affects and influences the characters by shaping their consciousness." This "sense of place" frequently emerges in Anaya's fiction and essays in the form of "cuentos," folktale-like renderings of his own experiences or imagined events that occur in the remembered landscapes of his rural childhood, peopled with farmers, cowboys, curanderas, and hunters.

Anaya was born and raised in the town of Pastura, northeast of Albuquerque. He attended college and graduate school at the University of New Mexico, where he also taught in the English department from 1974 until his retirement twenty years later. His novel Bless Me, Ultima (1971) is regarded as one of the classic works of the Chicano literary renaissance that began in the 1970s and continues today. Anaya's other volumes of fiction include Tortuga (1979), The Silence of the Llano (1982), The Legend of La Llorona (1985), Lord of the Dawn, the Legend of Quetzalcoatl (1987), Alburquerque (1992), and Jalamanta: A Message from the Desert (1996). He has also edited collections of Chicano essays and fiction, and in 1986 he published a travelogue called A Chicano in China.

In recent years, Anaya has become increasingly outspoken about environmental problems, particularly in the American Southwest. He states in his 1995 essay "The Spirit of Place" (published in Writers of the Southwest, edited by David King Dunaway) that "we are beginning to realize that the earth is a fragile planet. . . . One service the writers who are writing the Southwest are performing is alerting people to the destruction of their place, their homes." The following story, "Devil Deer" (collected in The Anaya Reader, 1995), is a grotesque hunting narrative that records a vision of bucolic harmony gone awry. The primary characters in the story, Cruz and Joe, are rural Chicanos who desire merely to participate in the traditional autumn hunting "ritual" of their community, but this activity—and the community itself—is disrupted when Cruz encounters a deformed "devil deer" on the grounds of the top-secret weapons laboratory at Los Alamos. The laboratory, which may represent the nation's military-industrial complex, is blamed for not only contaminating the environment but also breaking the chain of family tradition, the hunting culture that has been passed from generation to generation.

DEVIL DEER

At night, frost settled like glass dust on the peaks of the Jemez Mountains, but when the sun came up the cold dissolved. The falling leaves of the aspen were showers of gold coins. Deer sniffed the air and moved silently along the edges of the meadows in the high country. Clean and sharp and well defined, autumn had come to the mountain.

In the pueblo the red riztras hung against brown adobe walls, and large ears of corn filled kitchen corners. The harvest of the valley had been brought in, and the people rested. A haze of piñon smoke clung like a veil over the valley.

Late at night the men polished their rifles and told hunting stories. Neighbors on the way to work met in front of the post office or in the pueblo center to stop and talk. It was deer season, a ritual shared since immemorial time. Friends made plans to go together, to stay maybe three or four days, to plan supplies. The women kidded the men: "You better bring me a good one this time, a big buck who maybe got a lot of does pregnant in his life. Bring a good one."

Cruz heard the sound of laughter as neighbors talked. In the night he made love to his wife with renewed energy, just as the big buck he was dreaming about. "That was good," his young wife whispered in the dark, under the covers, as she too dreamed of the buck her husband would bring. Deer meat to make jerky, to cook with red chile all winter.

These were the dreams and planning that made the pueblo happy when deer season came. The men were excited. The old men talked of hunts long ago, told stories of the deer they had seen in the high country, sometimes meeting deer with special powers, or remembering an accident that happened long ago. Maybe a friend or brother had been shot. There were many stories to tell, and the old men talked far into the night.

The young men grew eager. They didn't want stories, they wanted the first day of deer season to come quickly so they could get up there and bag a buck. Maybe they had already scouted an area, and they knew some good meadows where a herd of does came down to browse in the evening. Or maybe they had hunted there the year before, and they had seen deer signs.

Everyone knew the deer population was growing scarce. It was harder and harder to get a buck. Too many hunters, maybe. Over the years there were fewer bucks. You had to go deeper into the forest, higher, maybe find new places, maybe have strong medicine.

Cruz thought of this as he planned. This time he and his friend Joe were going up to a place they called Black Ridge. They called it Black Ridge because there the pine trees were thick and dark. Part of the ridge was fenced in by the Los Alamos Laboratory, and few hunters wandered near the chain-link fence.

The place was difficult to get to, hard to hunt, and there were rumors that the fence carried electricity. Or there were electric sensors and if they went off maybe a helicopter would swoop down and the Lab guards would arrest you. Nobody hunted near the fence; the ridge lay silent and ominous on the side of the mountain.

All month Cruz and Joe planned, but a few days before the season started Joe was unloading lumber at work and the pile slipped and crashed down to break his leg.

"Don't go alone," Joe told Cruz. "You don't want to be up there alone. Go with your cousin, they're going up to the brown bear area. . . ."

"There's no deer there," Cruz complained. "Too many hunters." He wanted to go high, up to Black Ridge where few hunters went. Something was telling him that he was going to get a big buck this year.

So on the night before the season opened he drove his truck up to Black Ridge. He found an old road that had been cut when the Los Alamos fence had been put in, and he followed it as high as it went. That night he slept in his truck, not bothering to make a fire or set up camp. He was going to get a buck early, he was sure, maybe be back at the pueblo by afternoon.

Cruz awoke from a dream and clutched the leather bag tied at his belt. The fetish of stone, a black bear, was in the bag. He had talked to the bear before he fell asleep, and the bear had come in his dreams, standing upright like a man, walking towards Cruz, words in its mouth as if it was about to speak.

Cruz stood frozen. The bear was deformed. One paw was twisted like an old tree root, the other was missing. The legs were gnarled, and the huge animal walked like an old man with arthritis. The face was deformed, the mouth dripping with saliva. Only the eyes were clear as it looked at Cruz. Go away, it said, go away from this place. Not even the medicine of your grandfathers can help you here.

What did the dream mean, Cruz wondered and rolled down the truck window. The thick forest around him was dark. A sound came and receded from the trees, like the moaning of wind, like a restless spirit breathing, there just beyond the Tech Area fence of the laboratories. There was a blue glow in the dark forest, but it was too early for it to be the glow of dawn.

Cruz listened intently. Someone or something was dying in the forest, and breathing in agony. The breath of life was going out of the mountain; the mountain was dying. The eerie, blue glow filled the night. In the old stories, when time was new, the earth had opened and bled its red, hot blood. But that was the coming to life of the mountain; now the glow was the emanation of death. The earth was dying, and the black bear had come to warn him.

Cruz slumped against the steering wheel. His body ached; he stretched. It wasn't good to hunt alone, he thought, then instantly tried to erase the thought. He stepped out to urinate, then he turned to pray as the dawn came over the east rim of the ridge. He held the medicine bag which contained his bear. Give me strength, he thought, to take a deer to my family. Let me not be afraid.

It was the first time that he had even thought of being afraid on the mountain, and he found the thought disturbing.

He ate the beef sandwich his wife had packed for him, and drank coffee from the thermos. Then he checked his rifle and began to walk, following the old ruts of the road along the fence, looking for deer sign, looking for movement in thick forest. When the sun came over the volcanic peaks of the Jemez, the frost disappeared. There were no clouds to the west, no sign of storm.

Cruz had walked a short distance; a shadow in the pine trees made him stop and freeze. Something was moving off to his right. He listened intently and heard the wheezing sound he had heard earlier. The sound was a slow inhaling and exhaling of breath. It's a buck, he thought, and drew up his rifle.

As he stood looking for the outline of the buck in the trees he felt a vibration of the earth, as if the entire ridge was moving. The sound and the movement frightened him. He knew the mountain, he had hunted its peaks since he was a boy, and he had never felt anything like this. He saw movement again, and turned to see the huge rack of the deer, dark antlers moving through the trees.

The buck was inside the fence, about fifty yards away. Cruz would have to go in for the deer. The dark pines were too thick to get a clear shot. Cruz walked quietly along the fence. At any moment he expected the buck to startle and run; instead the buck seemed to follow him.

When Cruz stopped, the buck stopped, and it blended into the trees so Cruz wasn't sure if it was a deer or if he only was imagining it. He knew excitement sometimes made the hunter see things. Tree branches became antlers, and hunters sometimes fired at movement in the brush. That's how accidents happened.

Cruz moved again and the shadow of the buck moved with him, still partially hidden by the thick trees. Cruz stopped and lifted his rifle, but the form of the deer was gone. The deer was stalking him, Cruz thought. Well, this happened. A hunter would be following a deer and the buck would circle around and follow the hunter. There were lots of stories. A buck would appear between two hunting parties and the hunters would fire at each other while the buck slipped away.

Cruz sat on a log and looked into the forest. There it was, the outline of the buck in the shadows. Cruz opened his leather bag and took out the small, stone bear. What he saw made him shudder. There was a crack along the length of the bear. A crack in his medicine. He looked up and the blank eyes of the buck in the trees were staring at him.

Cruz fired from the hip, cursing the buck as he did. The report of the rifle echoed down the ridge. Nearby a black crow cried in surprise and rose into the air. The wind moaned in the treetops. The chill in the air made Cruz shiver. Why did I do that, he thought. He looked for the buck; it was still there. It had not moved.

Cruz rose and walked until he came to a place where someone had ripped a large hole in the fence. He stepped through the opening, knowing he shouldn't enter the area, but he wasn't going to lose the buck. The big bucks had been thinned out of the mountain. There weren't many left. This one had probably escaped by living inside the fenced area.

I'm going to get me a pampered Los Alamos buck, Cruz thought. *Sonofabitch* is not going to get away from me. The buck moved and Cruz followed. He knew that he had come a long way from the truck. If he got the buck he would have to quarter it, and it would take two days to get it back. I'll find a way, he thought, not wanting to give up the buck which led him forward. I can drive the truck up close to the fence.

But why didn't the buck spook when he fired at it? And why did he continue to hear the sound in the forest? And the vibration beneath his feet? What kind of devil machines were they running over in the labs that made the earth tremble? Accelerators. Plutonium. Atom smashers. What do I know, Cruz thought. I only know I want my brother to return to the pueblo with me. Feed my family. Venison steaks with fried potatoes and onions.

As he followed the buck, Cruz began to feel better. They had gone up to the top of the ridge and started back down. The buck was heading back toward the truck. Good, Cruz thought.

Now the buck stopped, and Cruz could clearly see the thick antlers for the first time. They were thick with velvet and lichen clinging to them. A pine branch clung to the antlers, Cruz thought, or patches of old velvet. But when he looked close he saw it was patches of hair that grew on the antlers.

"God Almighty," Cruz mumbled. He had never seen anything like that. He said a prayer and fired. The buck gave a grunt, Cruz fired again. The buck fell to its knees.

"Fall you *sonofabitch!*" Cruz cursed and fired again. He knew he had placed three bullets right in the heart.

The buck toppled on its side and Cruz rushed forward to cut its throat and drain its blood. When he knelt down to lift the animal's head he stopped. The deer was deformed. The hide was torn and bleeding in places, and a green bile seeped from the holes the bullets had made. The hair on the antlers looked like mangy, human hair, and the eyes were two white stones mottled with blood. The buck was blind.

Cruz felt his stomach heave. He turned and vomited, the sandwich and coffee of the morning meal splashed at his feet. He turned and looked at the buck again. Its legs were bent and gnarled. That's why it didn't bound away. The tail was long, like a donkey tail.

Cruz stood and looked at the deer, and he looked into the dark pine forest. On the other side of the ridge lay Los Alamos, the laboratories, and nobody knew what in the hell went on there. But whatever it was, it was seeping into the earth, seeping into the animals of the forest. To live within the fence was deadly, and now there were holes in the fence.

Cruz felt no celebration in taking the life of the buck. He could not raise the buck's head and offer the breath of life to his people. He couldn't offer the corn meal. He was afraid to touch the buck, but something told him he couldn't leave the deer on the mountainside. He had to get it back to the pueblo; he had to let the old men see it.

He gathered his resolve and began dragging the buck down the ridge toward the truck. Patches of skin caught in the branches of fallen trees and ripped away. Cruz sweated and cursed. Why did this deer come to haunt me? he thought. The bear in the dream had warned him, and he had not paid attention to the vision. It was not a good sign, but he had to get the deformed deer to the old men.

It was dark when he drove into the pueblo. When he came over the hill and saw the lighted windows, his spirits raised. This was home, a safe circle. But in his soul Cruz didn't feel well. Going into the fenced area for the deer had sapped his strength.

He turned down the dirt road to his home. Dogs came out to bark, people peered from windows. They knew his truck had come in. He parked in front of his home, but he sat in the truck. His wife came out, and sensing his mood, she said nothing. Joe appeared in the dark, a flashlight in his hand.

"What happened?" Joe asked. Cruz motioned to the back of the truck. Joe flashed the light on the buck. It was an ugly sight which made him recoil. "Oh God," he whispered. He whistled, and other shadows appeared in the dark, neighbors who had seen Cruz's truck drive in. The men looked at the buck and shook their heads.

"I got him inside the fence," Cruz said.

"Take Cruz in the house," one of the men told Joe. They would get rid of the animal.

"Come inside," Joe said. His friend had been up on the mountain all day, and he had killed this devil deer. Cruz's voice and vacant stare told the rest.

Cruz followed Joe and his wife into the house. He sat at the kitchen table and his wife poured him a cup of coffee. Cruz drank, thankful that the rich taste washed away the bitterness he felt in his mouth.

Joe said nothing. Outside the men were taking the deformed buck away. Probably burn it, he thought. How in the hell did something like that happen. We've never seen a deer like this, the old men would say later. A new story would grow up around Cruz, the man who killed the devil deer. Even his grandchildren would hear the story in the future.

And Cruz? What was to become of Cruz? He had gone into the forbidden land, into the mountain area surrounded by the laboratory fence. There where the forest glowed at night and the earth vibrated to the hum of atom smashers, lasers, and radioactivity.

The medicine men would perform a cleansing ceremony; they would pray for Cruz. But did they have enough good medicine to wash away the evil the young man had touched?

—1995

JOSEPH BRUCHAC

B. 1942

A prolific poet, fiction writer, and essayist, and a mesmerizing oral story-teller, Joseph Bruchac attributes his literary inspiration chiefly to the natural world and Native American culture. Born of Abenaki, English, and Slovak ancestry in Saratoga Springs, New York, he was raised by his Abenaki grandfather in the Adirondack foothills of upstate New York. He and his wife raised their own two sons in the same house and still live there today. Although he particularly likes to work outside ("in the earth-mother's soil, with my hands") and has supported himself at various times as a laborer, surveyor, and tree surgeon, Bruchac writes and teaches, he says, because "it gives me a chance to share my insights into the beautiful and all too fragile world of men and living things we have been granted."

Bruchac (pronounced "brew-shack") earned his undergraduate degree at Cornell University in 1965 and received an M.A. a year later from Syracuse University. After further graduate study at the State University of New York at Albany, he went on to complete a Ph.D. through the Union Institute in 1975. Bruchac's writing has appeared in hundreds of literary journals and anthologies, and he has written and edited numerous books as well. His books include the poetry collection Near the Mountains *(1987), the novel* Dawn Land *(1993), and* The Man Who Loved Buffalo *(1997). He coedited* Keepers of the Earth *(1988),* Keepers of the Animals *(1991), and* Keepers of the Night *(1994). His own edited collections include* Survival This Way: Interviews with American Indian Poets *(1987),* Native American Animal Stories *(1992), and* Returning the Gift: Poetry and Prose from the First North American Native Writers' Festival *(1994).*

In "The Circle Is the Way to See," which appeared in the 1993 anthology Story Earth: Native Voices on the Environment, *Bruchac retells and then comments on a traditional story about Gluskabe, the trickster figure of many northeastern Native American communities. The story itself emphasizes the danger of overhunting animals, thus exhausting the planet and leaving nothing for future human generations. But Bruchac pushes the meaning even further in his commentary, arguing that we need to look at our current environmental dilemmas from the perspective of the earth: "The sickness is not that of the planet, the sickness is embodied in human beings, and, if carried to its illogical conclusion, the sickness will not kill the earth, it will kill us." He argues that American society as a whole should imitate the Native American tendency to view the world "in terms of circles and cycles," aiming not to promote linear "progress" but to preserve the planet's resources and sustain human culture. This essay is a blueprint for the use of "ancient messages" to help us understand our predicament today.*

THE CIRCLE IS THE WAY TO SEE

*W*audjoset nudatlokugan bizwakamigwi alnabe. My story was out walking around, a wilderness lodge man. *Wawigit nudatlokugan.* Here lives my story. *Nudatlokugan Gluskabe.* It is a story of Gluskabe.

One day, Gluskabe went out to hunt. He tried hunting in the woods, but the game animals were not to be seen. Hunting is slow, he thought, and he returned to the wigwam where he lived with his grandmother, Woodchuck. He lay down on his bed and began to sing:

> *I wish for a game bag*
> *I wish for a game bag*
> *I wish for a game bag*
> *To make it easy to hunt*

He sang and sang until his grandmother could stand it no longer. She made him a game bag of deer hair and tossed it to him. But he did not stop singing:

> *I wish for a game bag*
> *I wish for a game bag*
> *I wish for a game bag*
> *To make it easy to hunt*

So she made him a game bag of caribou hair. She tossed it to him but still he continued to sing:

> *I wish for a game bag*
> *I wish for a game bag*
> *I wish for a game bag*
> *To make it easy to hunt*

She tried making a game bag of moose hair, but Gluskabe ignored that as well. He sang:

> *I wish for a game bag*
> *I wish for a game bag*
> *I wish for a game bag*
> *Of woodchuck hair*

Then Grandmother Woodchuck plucked the hair from her belly and made a game bag. Gluskabe sat up and stopped singing. *"Oleohneh, nohkemes,"* he said. "Thank you, Grandmother."

He went into the forest and called the animals. "Come," he said. "The world is going to end and all of you will die. Get into my game bag and you will not see the end of the world."

Then all of the animals came out of the forest and into his game bag. He carried it back to the wigwam of his grandmother and said, "Grandmother, I have brought game animals. Now we will not have a hard time hunting."

Grandmother Woodchuck saw all the animals in the game bag. "You have not done well, Grandson," she said. "In the future, our small ones, our children's children, will die of hunger. You must not do this. You must do what will help our children's children."

So Gluskabe went back into the forest with his game bag. He opened it. "Go, the danger is past," he said. Then the animals came out of the game bag and scattered throughout the forest. *Nedali medabegazu.*

There my story ends.

The story of Gluskabe's game bag has been told many times. A version much like this one was given to the anthropologist Frank Speck in 1918 by an elderly Penobscot man named Newell Lion. This and other Gluskabe stories that illustrate the relationship of human beings to the natural order are told to this day among the Penobscot and Sokokl, the Passamaquoddy and the Mississquoi, the Micmac and the other Wabanaki peoples whose place on this continent is called Ndakinna in the Abenaki language. Ndakinna—Our Land. A land that owns us and a land we must respect.

Gluskabe's game bag is a story that is central for an understanding of the native view of the place of human beings in the natural order and it is a story with many, many meanings. Gluskabe, the Trickster, is the ultimate human being and also an old one who was here before human beings came. He contains both the Good Mind, which can benefit the people and help the earth, and that other Twisted Mind, a mind governed by selfish thoughts that can destroy the natural balance and bring disaster.

He is greater than we are, but his problems and his powers are those of human beings. Because of our cunning and our power—a magical power—to make things, we can affect the lives of all else that lives around us. Yet when we overuse that power, we do not do well.

We must listen to the older and wiser voices of the earth—like the voice of Grandmother Woodchuck—or our descendants will, quite literally, starve. It is not so much a mystical as a practical relationship. Common sense.

Though my own native ancestry is Abenaki, and I regard the teachings and traditions of my Abenaki friends and elders, like the tales of Gluskabe, as a central part of my existence, I have also spent much of the last thirty-two years of my life learning from the elders of the Haudenosaunee nations, the People of the Longhouse—those nations of the Mohawk, Oneida, Onondaga, Cayuga, Seneca, and Tuscarora—commonly referred to today as the Iroquois.

We share this endangered corner of our continent, the area referred to on European-made maps as New York and New England. In fact, I live within a few hours' drive of the place where a man regarded as a messenger from the Creator and known as the Peacemaker joined with Hiawatha—perhaps a thousand years ago—to bring together five warring tribal nations into a League of Peace and plant a great pine tree as the living symbol of that green and growing union of nations.

That Great League is now recognized by many historians as a direct influence on the formation of modern ideas of democracy and on the Constitution of the United States.

I think it right to recall here some of the environmental prophecies of the Haudenosaunee people, not as an official representative of any native nation, but simply as a humble storyteller. I repeat them not as a chief nor as an elder, but as one who has listened and who hopes to convey the messages he has heard with accuracy and honesty.

According to Iroquois traditions, some of which were voiced by the prophet Ganio-dai-yo in the early 1800s, a time would come when the elm trees would die. And then the maple, the leader of all the trees, would also begin to die, from the top down.

In my own early years, I saw the elms begin to die. I worked as a tree surgeon in my early twenties, cutting those great trees in the Finger Lakes area of New York State, the traditional lands of the Cayuga Nation of the Iroquois.

As I cut them, I remembered how their bark had once been used to cover the old longhouses and how the elm was a central tree for the old-time survival of the Iroquois. But an insect, introduced inadvertently, like the flus and measles and smallpox and the other diseases of humans that killed more than 90 percent of the natives of North America in the sixteenth and seventeenth centuries, brought with it Dutch elm disease and spelled the end of the great trees.

Those trees were so beautiful, their limbs so graceful, their small leaves a green fountain in the springtime, a message that it was time to plant the corn as soon as they were the size of a squirrel's ear. And now they are all gone because of the coming of the Europeans. Now, in the last few years, the maple trees of New York and New England have begun to die, from the top down—weakened, some say, by the acid rain that falls, acid blown into the clouds by the smokestacks of the industries of the Ohio Valley, smoke carried across the land to fall as poison.

Is the earth sick? From a purely human perspective, the answer must certainly be yes. Things that humans count on for survival—basic things such as clean water and clean air—have been affected.

The Iroquois prophecies also said a time would come when the air would be harmful to breathe and the water harmful to drink. That time is now. The waters of the St. Lawrence River are so full of chemicals from industries, like Kaiser and Alcoa, on its shores that the turtles are covered with cancers. (In the story of Creation as told by the Haudenosaunee, it was the Great Turtle that floated up from the depths and offered its back as a place to support the earth.)

Tom Porter, a Bear Clan chief of the Mohawks, used to catch fish from that same river to feed his family. The water that flowed around their island, part of the small piece of land still legally in the hands of the Mohawk people and called the St. Regis Reservation, that water brought them life. But a few years ago, he saw that the fish were no longer safe to eat. They would poison his children. He left his nets by the banks of the river. They are still there, rotting.

If we see "the earth" as the web of life that sustains us, then there is no question that the web is weakened, that the earth is sick. But if we look at it from another side, from the view of the living earth itself, then the sickness is not that of the planet, the sickness is embodied in human beings, and, if carried to its illogical conclusion, the sickness will not kill the earth, it will kill us.

Human self-importance is a big part of the problem. It is because we human beings have one power that no other creatures have—the power to upset the natural balance—that we are so dangerous to ourselves. Because we have that great power, we have been given ceremonies and lesson stories (which in many ways are ceremonies in and of themselves) to remind us of our proper place.

We are not the strongest of all the beings in Creation. In many ways, we are the weakest. We were given original instructions by the Creator. Those instructions, to put them as simply as possible, were to be kind to each other and to respect the earth. It is because we human beings tend to forget those instructions that the Creator gave us stories like the tales of Gluskabe and sends teachers like the Peacemaker and Handsome Lake every now and then to help us remember and return us to the path of the Good Mind.

I am speaking now not of Europeans but of native people themselves. There are many stories in the native traditions of North America—like the Hopi tales of previous worlds being destroyed when human beings forgot those instructions—that explain what can happen when we lose sight of our proper place. Such stories and those teachers exist to keep human beings in balance, to keep our eyes focused, to help us recognize our place as part of the circle of Creation, not above it. When we follow our original instructions, we are equal to the smallest insects and the greatest whales, and if we take the lives of any other being in this circle of Creation it must be for the right reason—to help the survival of our own people, not to threaten the survival of the insect people or the whale people.

If we gather medicinal herbs, we must never take all that we find, only a few. We should give thanks and offer something in exchange, perhaps a bit of tobacco, and we should always loosen the earth and plant seeds so that more will grow.

But we, as humans, are weak and can forget. So the stories and the teachers who have been given the message from Creation come to us and we listen and we find the right path again.

That had been the way on this continent for tens of thousands of years before the coming of the Europeans. Ten thousand years passed after the deaths of the great beasts on this continent—those huge beings like the cave bear and the mammoth and the giant sloth, animals that my Abenaki people remember in some of our stories as monsters that threatened the lives of the people—before another living being on this continent was brought to extinction.

If it was native people who killed off those great animals ten thousand years ago, then it seems they learned something from that experience. The rattlesnake is deadly and dangerous, the grizzly and the polar bear have been known to hunt and kill human beings, but in native traditions those creatures are honored even as they are feared; the great bear is seen as closely related to human beings, and the rattlesnake is sometimes called Grandfather.

Then, with the coming of the Europeans, that changed. In the five hundred years since the arrival of Columbus on the shores of Hispaniola, hundreds of species have been exterminated. It has been done largely for profit, not for survival. And as the count goes higher, not only the survival of other species is in question but also the survival of the human species.

Part of my own blood is European because, like many native Americans today, many of my ancestors liked the new white people and the new black people (some of whom escaped from slavery and formed alliances and even, for a time, African/Indian maroon nations on the soils of the two American continents—such as the republic of Palmares in northeastern Brazil, which lasted most of the seventeenth century). I am not ashamed of any part of my racial ancestry. I was taught that it is not what is in the blood but what is carried in the culture that makes human beings lose their balance and forget their rightful place.

The culture of those human beings from Europe, however, had been at war with nature for a long time. They cut down most of their forests and killed most of the wild animals. For them, wildness was something to be tamed. To the native peoples of North America, wilderness was home, and it was not "wild" until the Europeans made it so. Still, I take heart at the thought that many of those who came to this hemisphere from Europe quickly learned to see with a native eye. So much so that the leaders of the new colonies (which were the first multinational corporations and had the express purpose of making money for the mother country—not seeking true religious freedom, for they forbade any religions but their own) just as quickly passed laws to keep their white colonists from "going native."

If you do not trust my memory, then take a look at the words written by those colonizing Europeans themselves. You will find laws still on the books in

Massachusetts that make it illegal for a man to have long hair. Why? Because it was a sign of sympathy with the Indians who wore their hair long. You will find direct references to colonists "consorting with the devil" by living like the "savages."

The native way of life, the native way of looking at the world and the way we humans live in that world, was attractive and meaningful. It was also more enjoyable. It is simple fact that the native people of New England, for example, were better fed, better clothed, and healthier than the European colonists. They also had more fun. European chroniclers of the time often wrote of the way in which the Indians made even work seem like play. They turned their work, such as planting a field or harvesting, into a communal activity with laughter and song.

Also, the lot of native women was drastically different from that of the colonial women. Native women had control over their own lives. They could decide who they would or would not marry, they owned their own land, they had true reproductive freedom (including herbal methods of birth control), and they had political power. In New England, women chiefs were not uncommon, and throughout the Northeast there were various arrangements giving women direct control in choosing chiefs. (To this day, among the Haudenosaunee, it is the women of each clan who choose the chiefs to represent them in the Grand Council of the League.)

In virtually every aspect of native life in North America—and I realize this is a huge generalization, for there were more than four hundred different cultures in North America alone in the fifteenth century and great differences between them— the idea of the circle, in one form or another, was a guiding principle. There was no clock time, but cyclical time. The seasons completed a circle, and so too did our human lives.

If we gather berries or hunt game in one place this year, then we may return to that place the following year to do the same. We must take care of that place properly—burning off the dry brush and dead berry bushes so that the ashes will fertilize the ground and new canes will grow, while at the same time ensuring that there will still be a clearing there in the forest with new green growth for the deer to eat.

The whole idea of wildlife conservation and ecology, in fact, was common practice among the native peoples of this continent. (There is also very sound documented evidence of the direct influence of native people and native ideas of a "land ethic" on people such as Henry David Thoreau, George Bird Grinnell, Ernest Thompson Seton, and others who were the founders of organizations like the Audubon Society, the Boy Scouts of America, and the whole modern conservation movement itself.) There was not, therefore, the European idea of devastating your own backyard and then moving on to fresh ground—to a new frontier (the backyard of your weaker neighbor).

If you see things in terms of circles and cycles, and if you care about the survival of your children, then you begin to engage in commonsense practices. By trial and error, over thousands of years, perhaps, you learn how to do things right. You learn to live in a way that keeps in mind, as native elders put it, seven generations. You ask yourself—as an individual and as a nation—how will the actions I take affect the seven generations to come? You do not think in terms of a four-year presidency or a yearly national budget, artificial creations that mean nothing positive in terms of the health of the earth and the people. You say to yourself, what will happen if I cut these trees and the birds can no longer nest there? What will happen if I kill the female deer who has a fawn so that no animals survive to bring a new generation into the world? What will happen if I divert the course of this river or build a dam so that the fish and animals and plants downstream are deprived of water? What will happen if I put all the animals in my game bag?

And then, as the cycles of the seasons pass, you explain in the form of lesson stories what will happen when the wrong actions are taken. Then you will remember and your children's children will remember. There are thousands of such lesson stories still being kept by the native people of North America, and it is time for the world as a whole to listen.

The circle is the way to see. The circle is the way to live, always keeping in mind the seven generations to come, always asking: how will my deeds affect the lives of my children's children's children?

This is the message I have heard again and again. I give that message to you. My own "ethnic heritage" is a mixture of European and native, but the messages I have heard best and learned the most from spring from this native soil.

If someone as small and pitiful as I am can learn from those ancient messages and speak well enough to touch the lives of others, then it seems to me that any human being—native or nonnative—has the ability to listen and to learn. It is because of that belief that I share these words, for all the people of the earth.

—1993

U.S. BISHOPS

In a notorious essay entitled "The Historical Roots of Our Ecologic Crisis" that appeared in the March 10, 1967, issue of Science *magazine, historian Lynn White, Jr., assigned a "huge burden of guilt" for humankind's environmental predicament to the Christian tradition. "Christianity, in absolute contrast to ancient paganism and Asia's religions (except, perhaps, Zoroastrianism), not only established a dualism of man and nature but also insisted that it is God's will that man exploit nature for his proper ends," wrote White. "We shall continue to have a worsening ecologic crisis until we reject the Christian axiom that nature has no reason for existence save to serve man," he warned. "Since the roots of our trouble are so largely religious, the remedy must also be essentially religious, whether we call it that or not. We must rethink and refeel our nature and destiny."*

In the past decade many U.S. churches have begun to do just that, and the resulting field of ecotheology boasts a burgeoning literature that includes such works as Creation Spirituality: Liberating Gifts for the Peoples of the Earth *by Matthew Fox (1991),* Ecotheology: Voices from the South and North, *edited by David G. Hallman (1994), and* Is It Too Late? A Theology of Ecology *by John B. Cobb, Jr. (1995). Prompted by a statement issued by Pope John Paul II to commemorate the World Day of Peace on January 1, 1990, entitled "Peace with God the Creator: Peace with All of Creation," the U.S. bishops of the Catholic Church turned their attention to the environment during their November 1991 meeting in Washington, D.C. They formulated their response in a statement entitled "Renewing the Earth: An Invitation to Reflection and Action on the Environment in Light of Catholic Social Teaching." "With these pastoral reflections, we hope to add a distinctive and constructive voice to the ecological dialogue already under way in our nation and in our church," reads part of the statement.*

The statement in its entirety consists of five sections; a portion of the first section and the whole of the last section are reprinted here. The middle sections discuss the biblical vision of the natural world, the perspective on environmental issues offered by the tradition of Catholic social teaching, and areas of potential disagreement (and thus areas where constructive dialogue can take place) between Catholic teachings and tenets of the environmental movement. The last section discusses the need for new attitudes and actions, touched on by Archbishop Daniel Pilarczyk of Cincinnati, president of the bishops' conference, in these comments made at a news conference after "Renewing the Earth" was approved: "Americans are road hogs in the road of life. A lot of us think that the American way is the way it ought to be for everyone, but that ain't necessarily so."

RENEWING THE EARTH

Faced with the widespread destruction of the environment, people everywhere are coming to understand that we cannot continue to use the goods of the earth as we have in the past. . . . A new ecological awareness is beginning to emerge. . . . The ecological crisis is a moral issue.

POPE JOHN PAUL II, JAN. 1, 1990

I. Signs of the Times

At its core the environmental crisis is a moral challenge. It calls us to examine how we use and share the goods of the earth, what we pass on to future generations and how we live in harmony with God's creation.

The effects of environmental degradation surround us: the smog in our cities; chemicals in our water and on our food, eroded topsoil blowing in the wind; the loss of valuable wetlands; radioactive and toxic waste lacking adequate disposal sites; threats to the health of industrial and farm workers. The problems, however, reach far beyond our own neighborhoods and workplaces. Our problems are the world's problems and burdens for generations to come. Poisoned water crosses borders freely. Acid rain pours on countries that do not create it. Greenhouse gases and chlorofluorocarbons affect the earth's atmosphere for many decades regardless of where they are produced or used.

Opinions vary about the causes and the seriousness of environmental problems and their verification. Still we can experience their effects in polluted air and water, in oil and wastes on our beaches, in the loss of farmland, wetlands and forests, and in the decline of rivers and lakes. Scientists identify several other less visible but particularly urgent problems currently being debated by the scientific community, including depletion of the ozone layer, deforestation, the extinction of species, the generation and disposal of toxic and nuclear waste, and global warming. These important issues are being explored by scientists, and they require urgent attention and action. We are not scientists; but as pastors we call on experts, citizens and policy-makers to continue to explore the serious environmental, ethical and human dimensions of these ecological challenges.

Environmental issues are also linked to other basic problems. As eminent scientist Dr. Thomas F. Malone reported, humanity faces problems in five inter-related fields: environment, energy, economics, equity and ethics. To ensure the survival of a healthy planet, then, we must not only establish a sustainable economy, but must also labor for justice both within and among nations. We must seek a society where economic life and environmental commitment work together to protect and enhance life on this planet.

· · ·

V. God's Stewards and Co-Creators

As others have pointed out, we are the first generation to see our planet from space—to see so clearly its beauty, limits and fragility. Modern communication technology helps us to see more clearly than ever the impact of carelessness, ignorance, greed, neglect and war on the earth.

Today humanity is at a crossroads. Having read the signs of the times, we can either ignore the harm we see and witness further damage, or we can take up our responsibilities to the creator and creation with renewed courage and commitment.

The task set before us is unprecedented, intricate, complex. No single solution will be adequate to the task. To live in balance with the finite resources of the planet, we need an unfamiliar blend of restraint and innovation. We shall be required to be genuine stewards of nature and thereby co-creators of a new human world. This will require both new attitudes and new actions.

A. New Attitudes

For believers, our faith is tested by our concern and care for creation. Within our tradition are important resources and values that can help us assess problems and shape constructive solutions. In addition to the themes we have already outlined from our social teaching, the traditional virtues of prudence, humility and temperance are indispensable elements of a new environmental ethic. Recognition of the reality of sin and failure, as well as the opportunity for forgiveness and reconciliation, can help us face up to our environmental responsibilities. A new sense of the limits and risks of fallible human judgments ought to mark the decisions of policy-makers as they act on complicated global issues with necessarily imperfect knowledge. Finally, as we face the challenging years ahead, we must all rely on the preeminent Christian virtues of faith, hope and love to sustain us and direct us.

There are hopeful signs. Public concern is growing. Some public policy is shifting and private behavior is beginning to change. From broader participation in recycling to negotiating international treaties, people are searching for ways to make a difference on behalf of the environment.

More people seem ready to recognize that the industrialized world's over-consumption has contributed the largest share to the degradation of the global environment. Also encouraging is the growing conviction that development is more qualitative than quantitative, that it consists more in improving the quality of life than in increasing consumption. What is now needed is the will to make the changes in public policy, as well as in lifestyle, that will be needed to arrest, reverse and prevent environmental decay and to pursue the goal of sustainable, equitable development for all. The overarching moral issue is to achieve during the 21st century a just and sustainable world. From a scientific point of view this seems possible. But the new order can only be achieved through the persevering exercise of moral responsibility on the part of individuals, voluntary organizations, governments and transnational agencies.

In the Catholic community, as we have pointed out, there are many signs of increased discussion, awareness and action on environment. We have offered these reflections in the hope that they will contribute to a broader dialogue in our church and society about the moral dimensions of ecology and about the links between social justice and ecology, between environment and development. We offer these reflections not to endorse a particular policy agenda, nor to step onto some current bandwagon, but to meet our responsibilities as pastors and teachers who see the terrible consequences of environmental neglect and who believe our faith calls us to help shape a creative and effective response.

B. New Actions

This statement is only a first step in fashioning an ongoing response to this challenge. We invite the Catholic community to join with us and others of good will in a continuing effort to understand and act on the moral and ethical dimensions of the environmental crisis:

—We ask scientists, environmentalists, economists and other experts to continue to help us understand the challenges we face and the steps we need to take. Faith is not a substitute for facts; the more we know about the problems we face, the better we can respond.

—We invite teachers and educators to emphasize, in their classrooms and curricula, a love for God's creation, a respect for nature and a commitment to practices and behavior that bring these attitudes into the daily lives of their students and themselves.

—We remind parents that they are the first and principal teachers of children. It is from parents that children will learn love of the earth and delight in nature. It is at home that they develop the habits of self-control, concern and care which lie at the heart of environmental morality.

—We call on theologians, Scripture scholars and ethicists to help explore, deepen and advance the insights of our Catholic tradition and its relation to environment and other religious perspectives on these matters. We especially call upon Catholic scholars to explore the relationship between this tradition's emphasis upon the dignity of the human person and our responsibility to care for all of God's creation.

—We ask business leaders and representatives of workers to make the protection of our common environment a central concern in their activities and to collaborate for the common good and the protection of the earth. We especially encourage pastors and parish leaders to give greater attention to the extent and urgency of the environmental crisis in preaching, teaching, pastoral outreach and action, at the parish level and through ecumenical cooperation in the local community.

—We ask the members of our church to examine our lifestyles, behaviors and policies, individually and institutionally, to see how we contribute to the destruction or neglect of the environment and how we might assist in its protection and restoration. We also urge celebrants and liturgy committees to incorporate themes into prayer and worship which emphasize our responsibility to protect all of God's creation and to organize prayerful celebrations of creation on feast days honoring St. Francis and St. Isidore.

—We ask environmental advocates to join us in building bridges between the quest for justice and the pursuit of peace and concern for the earth. We ask that the poor and vulnerable at home and abroad be accorded a special and urgent priority in all efforts to care for our environment.

—We urge policy-makers and public officials to focus more directly on the ethical dimensions of environmental policy and on its relation to development, to seek the common good and to resist short-term pressures in order to meet our long-term responsibility to future generations. At the very minimum we need food and energy policies that are socially just, environmentally benign and economically efficient.

—As citizens, each of us needs to participate in this debate over how our nation best protects our ecological heritage, limits pollution, allocates environmental costs and plans for the future. We need to use our voices and votes to shape a nation more committed to the universal common good and an ethic of environmental solidarity.

All of us need both a spiritual and a practical vision of stewardship and co-creation that guides our choices as consumers, citizens and workers. We need, in the now familiar phrase, to "think globally and act locally," finding the ways in our own situation to express a broader ethic of genuine solidarity.

C. Call to Conversion

The environmental crisis of our own day constitutes an exceptional call to conversion. As individuals, as institutions, as a people we need a change of heart to save the planet for our children and generations yet unborn. So vast are the problems, so intertwined with our economy and way of life, that nothing but a wholehearted and ever more profound turning to God the maker of heaven and earth will allow us to carry out our responsibilities as faithful stewards of God's creation.

Only when believers look to values of the Scriptures, honestly admit our limitations and failings, and commit ourselves to common action on behalf of the land and the wretched of the earth will we be ready to participate fully in resolving this crisis.

D. A Word of Hope

A just and sustainable society and world is not an optional ideal, but a moral and practical necessity. Without justice, a sustainable economy will be beyond reach. Without an ecologically responsible world economy, justice will be unachievable. To accomplish either is an enormous task; together they seem overwhelming. But "all things are possible" to those who hope in God. Hope is the virtue at the heart of a Christian environmental ethic. Hope gives us the courage, direction and energy required for this arduous common endeavor.

In the bleak years of Britain's industrial revolution, Gerard Manley Hopkins wrote of the urban decay wrought by industry, and of Christian hope for nature's revival. His words capture the condition of today's world as it awaits redemption from ecological neglect:

> And all is seared with trade;
> bleared, smeared with toil;
> And wears man's smudge
> and shares man's smell:
> the soil
> Is bare now, nor can foot feel,
> being shod.

And for all this, nature is never spent:
There lives the dearest
freshness deep down things; . . .

Because the Holy Ghost over the bent
World broods with warm breast
and with ah!
bright wings.

Saving the planet will demand long and sometimes sacrificial commitment. It will require continual revision of our political habits, restructuring economic institutions, reshaping society and nurturing global community. But we can proceed with hope because, as at the dawn of creation, so today the Holy Spirit breathes new life into all earth's creatures. Today we pray with new conviction and concern for all God's creation:

"Send forth thy Spirit, Lord, and renew the face of the earth."

—1991

Appendix

WRITING ABOUT LITERATURE AND CULTURE

This section of the book focuses on the relationship between critical thinking and effective writing. It provides an important linkage between the kinds of critical reading and interpretation skills and the necessary role that writing plays for thinking about literature and social issues.

It offers ideas, guidelines, strategies, and working principles for writing about literature. This appendix will accompany all the books in the Longman Literature and Culture series (*Literature and the Environment: A Reader on Nature and Culture; Literature, Culture, and Class: A Thematic Anthology; Literature, Race, and Ethnicity: Contested American Identities; Literature and Gender: Thinking Critically Through Fiction, Poetry, and Drama*), a series devoted to reading and thinking critically in ways that promote exploration and discovery. Writing about literature furthers these goals of critical analysis.

What I have attempted to do is focus on innovative approaches that will help you better analyze and understand the exciting and perhaps somewhat unfamiliar territory of writing about literature. I will begin by describing good writing—that is, writing that stays in the mind and positively influences readers. Next, I will offer some principles that underlie successful academic writing generally and critical work in literature classes more specifically. After that, I will discuss what it means to read for meaning, suggest how to get ready for class discussions, and then move to a consideration of the writing process with a particular focus on purpose, audience, drafting, and revising. Since one of the chief difficulties many writers face is "the blank page syndrome," I particularly address the problem of getting started on a writing project. The next section examines the various elements that comprise an essay, its various components. I then move to a brief consideration of the computer, with a particular focus on both word processing and electronic researching. Finally,

I offer a brief guide to research, with a listing of some of the most common bibliographic entries according to the Modern Language Association format.

WHAT IS GOOD WRITING?

Let's begin with some general principles that apply to all good academic writing. Many students equate academic writing with boredom, stuffiness, and abstraction. From their perspective, only academics write—and read—academic writing, which most others find dull, dry, and abstract. Now there is no doubt that writing of this kind exists, but most of it is not good writing, academic or otherwise.

Good writing has energy, clarity, and a liveliness of mind. It creates satisfaction by enlightening and persuading. It asks writers to place themselves at risk since they are making their ideas public. It changes minds because it illuminates its subject in a new light. It explores ideas thoughtfully, drawing upon research and other forms of evidence to persuade the reader.

Good writing has economy: it offers a thoughtful, efficient route toward increased understanding. No reader likes to read an essay that digresses or uses 35 words to state a 15-word idea. You may be assigned an essay with a required length, for example "Write a 2500-word essay that argues for a specific environmental policy to preserve western wilderness." Such essays can be challenging since students sometimes think they have to pad them to get the necessary words. This procedure is ill advised; no essay profits from repetition or flabby style. In this situation, the only choice is to do more reading, researching, and analyzing—subjects I will consider shortly.

Good writing leaves the author with a sense of accomplishment and satisfaction. Writing a passing essay may be easy, but unless writers are engaged in the hard struggle with the text and with their writing process, they are unlikely to experience a meaningful sense of accomplishment. Take your internal pulse after you complete an essay. Do you like it? Do you feel that it succeeds? Are you glad to have written it? Are you aware of your struggles, frustrations, and accomplishments? If you can answer "yes" to these questions, you stand a good chance of success. Good writing reveals insights that are often as surprising to the writer as they are to the reader. Good writing packs a punch. It stays in the memory. It makes a difference.

Although there is no single formula for good writing, certain general truths apply. First, writers need to capture their excitement, passion, and intellectual commitment. If a writer lacks those qualities—that is, writes simply to get done or to fill blank pages—the writing almost always is lackluster. Many times, writers get stuck and cannot complete a good draft, or work for hours and then throw up their hands in despair. If they possess an emotional and intellectual desire to produce a good piece of work, however, half the battle is won. They will try again, revise, seek the help of a teacher or tutor, research the subject more extensively, experiment, and otherwise redouble their effort. Most writers do not produce good first drafts, but if they care about the writing, they find ways to make it into something worth reading.

Good writing thus requires both time and effort. Even a short assignment ("Write a 500-word essay that explores why you think America is—or is not—a classless society") makes significant demands on any writer: time and effort to think, read, reflect, procrastinate, get started and get nowhere, draft, revise, edit, proofread. Few writers, be they students or professionals, can dash off two or three quick pages and achieve satisfying results.

Good writing generally exhibits active and descriptive verbs that perform "work" for the writer. Thus, instead of stating "John McPhee is a good writer and is my favorite author," try "John McPhee writes well and remains my favorite author" or "John McPhee is my favorite author because he writes so well" or "John McPhee, my favorite author, writes so well that reading one of his books is like seeing a movie" or some other version. Note the differences among these sentences: the ways that verbs get changed, altering sentence structure and meaning as well. Lackluster writing can often be traced to overdependence on the verb "to be" in its various forms: "am," "is," "are," "was," "were," "be," "been." If your writing is flat, examine it for overuse of the various "to be" verbs and try to find meaningful, accurate replacements.

Good writing conveys new information to readers. At first glance, this seems to pose a problem: after all, how can you write something "new" about literature when your instructor knows so much more? Although instructors do possess considerable knowledge, they by no means know everything about an essay, story, poem, drama, author, or subject. In fact, their love of literature can make them easy to write for, since they enjoy learning more. The key is to convey new information: an interpretation supported by quotes, analysis, and research; a historical exploration of a work or author; an argument about the meaning or significance of a literary subject; a personal assessment of why or how a literary work affects you; a well-documented research paper; and so on. Instructors respond positively to student work that teaches them something, that changes their interpretations, adds to their knowledge, or improves their appreciation. When students accomplish one or more of those objectives, they produce "good writing."

READING FOR MEANING

To be able to write, you—like any good writer—must find something to say. Too often, students receive an assignment and produce a quick and visceral response (sometimes just before class). One important key to succeeding in a literature class is to learn how to engage in sustained inquiry—that is, learning how to read for meaning and asking questions that lead toward improved understanding. Most literary works are sufficiently complex that at first they often frustrate readers. Success in this class will depend on learning how to read well.

Typically, we read to gain information. That is why we read many textbooks, newspapers, magazines, instructions, and the like. The kind of reading required in an English literature or composition course, however, requires a different set of strategies. Although most of us first read a story, essay, poem, or drama to find out what happens—that is, to gain some information and knowledge of how the "story" will end—the primary intent of literature is not simply to provide readers with information or a plot. Rather, its purpose is to give pleasure, to offer multiple possibilities for interpretation, to surprise, to shock, to amaze, to alter the reader's thinking. Works such as the ones in this book offer *more* than information, and figuring out that "more" takes effort, time, and critical analysis.

Here are some practical strategies and suggestions for how to get the most out of the selections in this anthology:

Sound Reading Strategies

1. Read when your concentration is at its peak. Many people do their reading when they are tired or distracted. They read at work or during television commercials. This is fine if you are skimming for information or pleasure—reading a newspaper, magazine, or the comic page, for example—but the selections in this book demand concentration. You need to read when you are focused and full of energy, alert and clear eyed.

2. Read for pleasure first. During your first time through a text, read for enjoyment. Every author in this book intends to give you pleasure—to make you enjoy exploring and analyzing ideas, language, form, structure, style, arguments.

3. Read actively, not passively. As you read, stop occasionally and imagine what will happen on the next page or in the next section; such a process helps to involve you in the ebb and flow of the text. Stop, occasionally, to write down your prediction, your emerging interpretation, your view of why you think the author wrote this work, what its strengths and weaknesses are. Compare your responses to those of your classmates.

4. Reread. Read the first time for pleasure; read the second time for increased understanding. Most of the selections in this anthology present complicated ideas in complicated ways; the reader's job is to figure out what the selection means beyond the obvious. How does the writer make her/his points? What kinds of similes, metaphors, and other figurative language does the writer use? Are there contradictions and paradoxes? What choices does the writer make—and why? Are the writer's arguments convincing and well supported? These kinds of questions often can only be answered through rereading.

5. Take notes. Underline passages that are memorable, surprising, confusing, provocative—that provoke a personal response. Opposite each underlined passage, write a marginal comment explaining why you underlined the passage, such as:

   "what is she saying here?"
   "why does he stumble—symbolic?"
   "empty purse—are they also empty emotionally?"
   "this desert is real but it is also symbolic of her despair"
   "who benefited from the slave trade?"
   "I can feel the author's love of his family here" etc.

   These comments along with the underlinings point the way toward a good, critical essay. Most importantly, they provide a written record of thoughts and impressions, some of which you may otherwise lose.

6. Discuss. Although reading is a solitary activity, understanding improves when students share interpretations. All readers bring their own experiences to a text, their own strengths, weaknesses, experiences, insights, and blind spots. Perhaps the most important aspect of discussion is learning how to listen, comprehend, and respond thoughtfully. Listening is a parallel activity to reading; it requires us to be attentive and to work hard at understanding someone else's point of view.

GETTING READY FOR CLASS DISCUSSION

Class discussion is almost always a crucial and fundamental element of a literature or composition class. Most of us both enjoy and learn better when we engage in focused, thoughtful discussion with our peers. Aside from reading and rereading the assignment, certain other habits and practices can improve the quality of class conversation. What follows are some suggestions and strategies for preparing yourself to discuss literature in this class and the others you might take.

- Bring your textbook and notes to class. This may seem like obvious common-sense advice, but surprisingly many students do not follow it. It is especially important to have the text handy when enrolled in a class that focuses on literature, because frequently in discussion students need to quote from the assigned text in order to provide support for a comment or clarify an interpretation. Since many students (and faculty, for that matter) write marginal notes in the text as they read, they have an additional reason for wanting the book handy—namely, for ready reference.

- Do not read any out-of-class assignments in class. One of the fastest ways to sour instructors is if they observe you reading the assignment at your desk rather than participating in class activities. Bring your text, have it ready, but use it only for reference or clarification, unless instructed otherwise.

- Take notes. Both lecture and class discussion often produce creative and surprising insights. They trigger important questions that can lead directly to an essay or term paper. When that happens, it is crucial to write them down so that they can be remembered and reconsidered. Some faculty have been known to stop discussion in the middle of class in order to take hurried notes on something that was said. Students should do the same. Aside from having a record of useful comments, taking notes has the added benefit of focusing one's attention more on the discussion, thus keeping the mind from wandering off while others speak.

- Listen carefully. One of the best ways to improve listening is to write down a brief, succinct summary of what someone has said once he or she has finished. This technique is, of course, a form of note-taking. As others in the class speak, good listeners work hard to understand what they are saying and how it improves understanding of the text.

- In a class that centers on literature, discussion usually does not center on factual material ("In what year did Frederick Douglass first publish his autobiography?" "Who was Mother Jones?"). That kind of information, which is very important in terms of knowledge and mastery, is usually presented in a short lecture by the instructor or is something you are expected to learn through reading and outside research. Rather, most class discussions emphasize interpretation, analysis, and argumentation ("Consider the concept of family in Gwendolyn Brooks's poem, 'Mother.'" "What images and associations of the city does Tom Wolfe invoke in 'O Rotten Gotham'—and what effect do they have on you as a reader?"). Meaningful class discussion requires not only offering an interpretation or analysis, but providing support if others in the class disagree. When class discussion goes well, it is usually because reasonable and thoughtful readers express differing interpretations and explanations equally supported by careful textual analysis.

- Be ready to explain yourself. The key to illuminating discussions is not just offering an opinion about a work of literature; it is possessing the knowledge and information to explain it. To do this, a reader should constantly be asking "why?" and then discovering the answer. For example, if a poem makes you feel exalted, it is important to know why and then pinpoint the language, ideas, and arguments that produce this result. Responses to literature are created through a combination of author intent, literary form and structure, social and historical contexts, the reader's personal history, and other factors. Thoughtful class participants learn how to explain themselves and their interpretations.
- Let others speak. When only the instructor or a few students dominate discussion, class soon becomes a bore. Although many instructors like to present short lectures in order to provide information efficiently, class discussion can only succeed if everyone limits his or her time and no one dominates. If you find yourself talking too much or too often, learn to love silence. Quite often, reticent students will begin to speak and participate if the "natural talkers" in the class restrain themselves.
- Be succinct. Students and teachers alike zone out when someone makes the same point repeatedly. Once you say it, don't repeat it. To say the same thing again and again is boring and repetitious—even redundant—even when there is slight variation. Like this paragraph.
- Focus. As you read an assignment, you may discover an interpretation or come up with questions. If so, write them out and bring them with you to class. Many instructors will welcome such written comments and provide class time for discussing them.
- Change the perspective from which you read and interpret the assignment. Put yourself in the place of the author: try to think why she wrote it, what she intended, why she made specific choices. Insert yourself in the role of a character or even that of a reviewer or critic. Write down your comments for use in class.
- Remember that not all interpretations or analyses are equally persuasive or insightful, but that does not mean they lack value, at least to the individual who offers them. This does not mean that anything goes; rather, that interpretation and analysis is a negotiation involving the reader, the author, the text, the class, historical circumstance, and the world of literary criticism. One of the major purposes of class discussion is to provide students and instructors with a rich and reasonable forum in which to test their hypotheses and participate in a collaborative give-and-take about meaning and understanding.

THE WRITING PROCESS

Preliminary Steps

Different writers write differently, and all writers must strive to find the composing process that best suits their needs. Professional writers demonstrate the diversity of composing processes. John McPhee, for example, plans extensively and creates an elaborate structure for his essays and books. This planning process can be extremely laborious, but once he develops the structure (which might take days, weeks, or longer), it provides a framework for the actual writing (and rewriting) that follows. When Jamaica Kincaid writes, she often spends a great deal of time deliberating and choosing. She might write down just one word in an hour, but once that word is on paper she knows it is the right one and seldom if ever changes it. Richard Selzer writes out of a sense almost of compulsion. He pours out many pages of prose every day longhand in his notebooks, only a small fraction of which ever makes its way to print. None of these writers would choose to follow the composing process of any other; what they do works for them.

The pages that follow offer a variety of approaches to writing, not all of which are likely to work for any one student. Even the order is somewhat arbitrary; my "Step One" might be someone else's "Step Four." What all writers must do is experiment, particularly if they are having trouble writing or are not achieving desired results. Although there is no one right way to write, there are wrong ways that can get someone stuck and frustrated. All writers, however, can alter their ways of composing and make the process more efficient and productive; it just takes time, practice, and the will to change.

Step One: Establish a Sense of Purpose

Frequently, instructors establish an outcome for their students in the assignment itself. For example:

> "Analyze the metaphors that Barry Lopez uses to describe wilderness in his essay "The Stone Horse." In your essay, be sure to cite at least three metaphors and discuss their appropriateness to his themes of tenderness and fragility."

This instructor wants students to analyze Lopez's use of metaphors and offer reasons why they are—or are not—appropriate to two major themes in his work. Some students might prefer to write personal responses, but however satisfying to the writer, they are unlikely to fulfill the instructor's purpose (and will probably receive a poor grade).

Some instructors assign essays that allow more individual choice:

> Respond to Tillie Olsen's "I Stand Here Ironing." Can you relate your own experiences as either a parent or a child to this fictional monologue? In your essay, be sure and discuss who this speaker is—that is, describe in your own terms the speaker's values, feelings, and sense of self. Your essay should be at least 600 words, typed, and should include quotations from the story to support your interpretation.

This assignment asks students to present a written response, without specifying content. Students can write a personal reflection or an impersonal analysis, but they must analyze the speaker of the story in an essay of at least 600 typed words and include appropriate supporting quotations.

Whatever the assignment, students need to establish their own sense of purpose and commitment to their readers. Otherwise the writing becomes perfunctory.

Step Two: Analyze Your Audience's Expectations

Although audiences can vary, in most cases you will write essays that will be read by your instructor. My focus will thus be on writing for the teacher. Knowing that an essay is intended for an instructor does not necessarily help you successfully address this audience. What is more important is that your work satisfy the instructor's expectations. How can you accomplish this? Here are some suggestions.

- Study the assignment carefully and make sure that you understand what the instructor is asking you to do. Look for key words and phrases, especially those that are underlined or in boldface. Most assignments clearly state the instructor's expectations.
- Stuck? Then visit your instructor. A short conversation with an instructor can both clarify the situation and bolster confidence.
- Determine whether your instructor wants your essay to be a demonstration of knowledge (a synthesis of class discussion, an informed discussion of the ways a particular theory applies to a particular set of readings); a factual presentation (historical, biographical, a report); an interpretation (what a work means, why a student believes the meaning of the text to be "X"); an appreciation (why this work is so powerful and enduring); or something else. Asking detailed questions about expectations either in class or during an instructor's office hours is essential.
- Consider the assignment a form of conversation, of dialogue with the instructor. An essay offers each student an opportunity to have the instructor's exclusive attention. Successful essays engage readers because they bring a writer and reader together; they are a medium for the exchange of ideas.
- Try to state something new. Think of your audience as someone who is willing to try out your ideas and be surprised and informed by what you have to say. Instructors enjoy having their understanding and appreciation of a literary work enhanced because of something a student has written.
- Avoid plot summary. Because they want to learn something when they read student essays, most instructors do not like plot summary. When writing, assume that the reader already has read the work you are discussing. Plot summary is usually a surefire way to bore a reader—and write a pedestrian essay in the process.

Step Three: Draw On Your Resources

Student Resource List:

- conversations with other students in the class or others who have an interest in the topic
- the local Writing Center, where tutors can help you think through your subject, goals, possibilities, frustrations, structure, focus, and all the other aspects of writing
- the instructor, who is one of the best resources for getting comfortable with a topic and figuring out the best way to proceed
- the library research database, where you can look up primary material (that is, other works that the author has written, historical materials composed at the same time as the subject you are writing about) or secondary sources (books and articles written about your subject)
- electronic conversations over the Internet
- Web pages, which can be particularly helpful if you are researching a contemporary subject

Step Four: Start Early

The time to start writing an essay is immediately after an instructor hands out an assignment. The worst case scenario is to delay the writing until the day before it is due. To put it bluntly, this is a prescription for disaster.

Good ideas need to simmer. They need to be reflected upon, revised, researched, and explored. This takes time. Delay often results in ill-conceived work. Waiting too long to start can create a host of problems for writers, including: disliking what one has written but not having the time to change it; discovering that essential research materials are missing, stolen, or otherwise out of circulation; getting sick or stuck; or even deciding that one's argument no longer makes sense. There is no reason to have to create a panic situation every time a writing assignment is given.

Instead, good writers start early. That way, if something goes wrong, as it inevitably does in some situations, there is time to make adjustments.

Step Five: Share

Most professional writers share their work as they write: they produce a page or two, bring that work home, and read it to someone they trust to give an honest response. Students need to share their writing as well, and many instructors will create that possibility by setting up a rough draft workshop in the classroom or by reading drafts. Many times, an outside reader (not a roommate, spouse, or parent) can best tell a writer when an essay is making sense, where more support is needed, where the work is gaining or losing focus. Such readings can make a huge difference in the success of an essay; almost always, they provide a valuable road map for revision. Take advantage of this opportunity; it can make a world of difference.

Step Six: Revise

Virtually all successful writers spend the great majority of their time not drafting but revising, not writing but rewriting. In general, writing an essay is messy: It demands that writers explore a variety of ideas, go off on various tangents, explore various research sources, find appropriate examples and quotations, etc. As you write at this early stage, it is important not to spend much time editing and revising. Writing at this drafting stage should lead you forward; editing and revising are activities that require you constantly to look backward.

Only after you have finally produced a significant mass of words and ideas is it time to start pulling your essay together. This is revision: refocusing, deleting the unnecessary and repetitious, finding additional examples, cutting and pasting (using the computer, I hope), refining the essay so that it achieves its purpose. Sometimes revision means substantially changing the original; sometimes it means throwing out everything but two or three sentences! Whatever form it takes, revision is almost always the key to producing successful final essays.

Step Seven: Work Appropriately

At different points in the writing process, some kinds of attention are appropriate and others ill-advised. It is important to recognize that a first or second draft of an essay is just that: a draft. It is likely to have a variety of problems with focus, word usage, syntax, support, and other elements. Early in the composing process, writers need to concentrate on global issues: organization, development, finding examples, crafting the overall shape and scope of the essay. There is no sense editing and correcting sentences that may not make it into the final version. It makes no sense spell checking, correcting subject-verb agreement, or clarifying every phrase in the first draft. Instead, experienced writers focus on big ticket items such as building coherence or developing a cogent argument.

Only after a reasonably good draft has been achieved should you edit line by line for usage, correctness, and word choice. Correcting and editing are very important functions, but they should occur only when the writing is close to being finished.

GETTING STARTED

Many writers have trouble getting started; they defer the writing, often until too late. Then they do a poor job, excusing themselves because they ran out of time. Sometimes they sit down to write, but run out of steam after a few paragraphs: the essay lacks focus; everything written down seems dumb or obvious; the essay is too general and vague; the room is too hot; the paper is too white; the pencils are too sharp or not sharp enough. Almost all writers, even professional authors who make their living selling what they produce, have trouble at times getting started. John McPhee, who has written over twenty nonfiction books on sports, geology, wilderness, and many other topics, had so much trouble getting started early in his career that he would go into his office and tie himself into his chair with his bathrobe sash to force himself to get words down on paper. Although tying yourself to your chair may be an excellent technique, here are some less drastic strategies that can help.

Keep a reading log. Marginal notation is an excellent strategy, but many students want their notes and commentary collected in one place rather than distributed in the white space of various textbooks. They use a reading log, which is a written record of their interpretations, questions, and concerns. Your instructor may assign you to keep such a log or journal because it has proven to be so helpful to many students. To be successful, a log must be used consistently, at least three entries per week. When an essay is assigned, a reading log can become a great resource, since it is a repository of ideas and personal responses.

A typical entry might look like the following:

"The Horse"
I loved this poem. The horse is described as being so fluid, so full of power. But I don't understand why its hooves flash "blood red" in the last stanza. Why blood? Nor am I clear as to why it is "eternally riderless." After all, it is the "horseman's desire."
Rhythm. There's a kind of klop/klop rhythm to the lines, especially the last line of each stanza. Or am I imagining it?
Is this in some kind of form—like a sonnet? It isn't 14 lines, so that's not right—but I wonder if this is some form I should know (ask instructor) . . .
I'd love to write about the ways that this horse stands for freedom. Am I reading that into the poem? I don't think so. Freedom is mentioned in line 4 and once again in lines 15 and 26. That has to mean something, I think. . . .

As you can see, this is mostly a response that describes the feelings of the writer—as well as her ideas, confusions, and maybe even a possible essay topic. Even if this student does not choose to write about "The Horse," she is engaging in the kind of close and active reading that will help her throughout this course and beyond.

Write a letter, not an essay. Most writers find it much easier to write a personal letter than an essay. The reasons are fairly obvious: they know and like their audience; the letter is informal; they are used to writing in this format; they can usually find a congenial style for themselves; etc. Some students write their essay as a letter addressed to a friend or close relative, explaining why it is important to write about this story or poem, or why they are uncomfortable and then what it is they would like to say about this topic in an essay. Even though the letter is a fiction, writing it can be a great way to make that initial leap into the topic.

Create writing rituals. Like any sustained activity, writing can be hard to start unless it becomes part of another set of actions. In order to wash the car, for example, a person might gather together clean cloths, fill a pail with soapy water, park the car at the curb, and bring out the garden hose. Washing the car becomes an inevitable result of those preparations.

Writing benefits from the same kinds of ritualized activities. One writer gathers her research materials, reads them over several times, cleans off her desk, turns on her computer, and makes some notes about how she will structure her writing for the day. Other writers have other actions they must perform to write: they make a fresh pot of coffee, put on a certain baseball cap, take a dessert out of the freezer and leave it as a reward for a certain amount of writing (of course, the latter ritual can produce both pages and pounds). A friend of mine takes his laptop every weekday morning to a local coffeehouse, finds a quiet table, and writes for two hours; somehow he finds that ritual more productive than coming into the office where he gets distracted by mail, phone calls, and personal visits from me.

Productive writers discover or create rituals that get them in the mood for writing, that lead them toward pen and paper or the computer. Once you have devised such rituals, they can lead you toward writing.

Use index cards or some easily organizable form of note-taking. Many writers keep track of different ideas, quotations, references, and other pertinent information by listing each as a single entry so that they all can be stored and rearranged. Copying quotations and taping them on cards is one handy technique; another is using the computer to create and organize files, which then can be easily printed out during the drafting process. Each card should include not only a quotation or idea but also source information about where it was found.

Write before writing. Professor Donald Murray, a well-known writer and teacher, advocated that students "write before writing"—and this is excellent advice. How do you do that? One of the best strategies is to purchase a small notebook that fits handily in purse or pocket. As you read, think, and research about your assignments, write down ideas, insights, fragments, potential topics, words, quotations, and snatches of relevant conversations. Use the material in that notebook to jump-start your essay.

Try freewriting. Other writers use the technique of freewriting or quick writing to get started. First, of course, they have to do the necessary reading, rereading, and research. Once they possess some knowledge and ideas, they write nonstop for 10 or more minutes, not worrying about spelling, correctness, transitions, or even coherence. The purpose is to get ideas and sentences on paper; once that is done, the writer organizes, cuts and pastes, develops some ideas and discards others. Freewriting is an excellent way to write before writing, especially since it is low stress and produces a lot of words. Some writers begin their writing process this way, and then use successive and more focused freewritings to create later and longer drafts of an essay. Freewriting usually cannot be used to write a final draft, but with practice, this technique can help a writer get quite far along in the drafting process.

THE ELEMENTS OF A SUCCESSFUL ESSAY

Although there are many different kinds of essays, most of the good ones share certain features.

1. **A main point.** Most successful essays drive toward a central conclusion or major insight. It really does not matter if the essay is an appreciation, a critique, an argument, or a close reading: it collects around a main point like iron filings around a magnet. For example, let's say I am writing about William Stafford's poem "Traveling Through the Dark." After multiple readings, two entries in my reading log, and one freewriting, I begin to glimpse what makes this poem moving and powerful to me. I write a "discovery" draft, toward the end of which I compose the following sentence that defines my main point and thus becomes my thesis:

   "Traveling Through the Dark" is therefore a powerful poem that holds a central contradiction: it is a celebration of life that describes the poet's act of destroying the life of an innocent fawn. I think it reveals the speaker as tender and compassionate, perhaps in contrast to the unnamed, unseen other driver who first hit the doe.

   This is enough of a start for an essay because it is making a significant point that I can now develop over the course of an essay.

   Please note: Not every writer knows the main point when first starting an essay. Oftentimes, writers discover their main point during the composing process. Thus good writers do not worry if they begin to write without a main point; if they are completing the assignment and still do not know their main point, however, that usually means real trouble.

2. **Specificity.** A successful essay examines a work of literature by analyzing a particular theme, meaning, image, use of language, argument, or interpretation. Too often, beginning writers attempt general and grandiose themes or generalized statements; they try to write, for example, about "the genius of Edward Abbey" or "That Perfect Poetic Form: The Ballad." Although there is much that can be said about both topics, they are too vague as stated to be covered in a short essay; indeed, they are more appropriate for entire books. An essay needs to examine more specific topics: *What Edward Abbey means by 'the Hoboken mystique' in his essay* "Manhattan Twilight, Hoboken Night" or *A Bittersweet Play of Voices in Langston Hughes's* "Ballad of the Landlord." An essay on either of these more focused topics is more likely to succeed.

3. **Complexity.** Good essays lock in on a complex subject and develop it thoughtfully. In general, this means that an essay must pursue a subject that is not superficially obvious to the most casual reader. To look for insights

beyond the obvious, a writer must examine a work of literature for contradictions and paradox. Many literary authors use contradiction and paradox to put a spin on their creations. Theodore Roethke's "My Papa's Waltz," for example, is a poem that can be read simultaneously as a loving tribute and as a cry for help. Which interpretation is correct? Most critics would say that the poem can and should be read both ways at once, that it represents the complex and contradictory feelings a young boy has toward his father.

To achieve complexity, then, writers must be willing to explore seeming contradiction and not be afraid to take risks; they must be willing to explore questions that have no right answer. For example, to return to "Traveling Through the Dark," a student might at first compose the following focus sentence:

"Traveling Through the Dark" is a terrific poem because it is about a man in the wilderness.

This statement, though perhaps true, does not offer a writer any real purchase on a topic worth writing about. It is not very specific and does not offer a complex view of the poem. Why is the poem terrific? What is meant by "terrific"? Is every poem about a man and wilderness terrific? Other than finding a lot of different ways to repeat this main point, there is not much that can be said that would fill more than a page or so of text. This topic does not allow a very complicated or insightful essay to be written. After some struggle, this writer reformulates her main point as follows:

"Traveling Through the Dark" is about literal and figurative darkness, about the darkness of night and the darkness of death.

This statement is more specific, and it offers a thoughtful and complex interpretation of "darkness," an important image in this poem. The statement may need to be refined further, but it offers a useful starting point.

4. **Examples and illustrations.** Almost always, successful essays incorporate many examples, illustrative quotations, and statements that prove the point(s) that the writer is making. In English Studies, most successful essays put forward assertions that then have to be proven and supported. They move from the general to the specific and back again, weaving the particular constantly into the fabric of the overall argument. Clearly one of the most important ways to achieve this end is to use quotations, examples, and particular citations for support. Just as an economist uses statistics, a writer of essays about literature must nail down insights with an appropriate use of specific quotation. Quotes from the primary text (the actual work of literature being studied) or from secondary texts (criticism, history, biography, etc.) illustrate the points being made and persuade readers that the author knows what she is talking about. They also can inspire a writer to dig deeper into the meaning of a work of literature.

5. **Coherence.** All readers have formal expectations when they read. Although different in various cultures, these formal expectations guide readers and help them to understand what the writer is doing. They allow readers to anticipate where the writer is headed, a very important dimension to suc-

cessful interaction between readers and writers. Typically, in United States higher education, successful essays have a beginning, middle, and end in some formal sense. They exhibit logical transitions between the various parts of the essay. They provide the reader with a sense of wholeness and completion. Typically, a formal essay will:

- articulate a main point
- illustrate and exemplify that main point through several pages that develop and explore the theme of the essay through the use of analysis, appropriate quotation, assertions, insights
- conclude by offering possibilities for additional exploration, returning to the image or argument presented at the beginning of the essay, summarizing and extending what has already been stated, or otherwise creating a sense of completion

6. **Style.** Instructors generally enjoy reading essays that express the voice, personal commitment, and investment of the writer—what we typically call "style." Style cannot be located in any one element; rather, it consists of a writer's individual perspective, phrasing, word choice, sentence construction, creation of paragraphs, organization, even formatting (font, type size, illustrations, spacing, etc.).

One of the most important aspects of style is word and sentence variety. Successful writing keeps readers interested not just because of ideas, examples, and coherence, but also because of language use that pleases, surprises, and delights. Here is an example of a passage that has a lot of repetition and not much sentence variety:

Theodore Roethke's "My Papa's Waltz" is a powerful poem. It is a poem that draws its power from its theme of love and fear. The poem is written from the point of view of a young boy. The title of the poem . . .

This passage is likely to bore a reader because the sentences all have a similar subject-verb structure, use many of the same words, and express little sense of style. It is acceptable to write such sentences in a first draft, but once a writer starts moving toward the final draft, an improved version that achieves much more sentence variation is needed:

A powerful poem, Theodore Roethke's "My Papa's Waltz" expresses the love— and fear—that a young boy feels for his father. As is made clear from the title of the poem . . .

This revised version consolidates the sentences, cuts out the repetition of words ("is," "power," "of"), and expresses more vividly the stylistic personality of the writer. Successful writers create word and sentence variety in order to enhance their style.

Another key aspect to creating a successful style is not to overreach. That is, one of the worst decisions a writer can make is to refer constantly to a thesaurus while writing or to otherwise insert words and phrases that "sound good" because they are long, Latinate, or unfamiliar. A thesaurus is an excellent tool to rediscover a synonym that has slipped out of memory, but you should not use it to replace a familiar word with one you do not know. For example, a writer might state that he has "a great deal of empathy for a character's situation." But with the help of a thesaurus, he might revise that sentence to read that he has "a surfeit of vicarious emotion for a character's locale." Although brimming with excellent words, the second sentence makes little sense and sounds as though its author is living in the wrong century. It is far better to use words you know and can control.

7. **Correctness.** Correctness is easy to define but difficult to achieve: It consists of getting everything right. English instructors in particular urge their students to aim for correctness as part of what they do; after all, they are the educational caretakers of sentence structure, research format, spelling, grammar, and diction. Many writers have a difficult time achieving correctness on their own; they need the help of an outside reader (such as a tutor) to help them see error patterns or other areas where their essay needs to be edited and refashioned into standard academic English.

One of the best ways to get help with correctness is to go to the course instructor, who can provide professional help. Another good strategy is to buy a good handbook and then use it. Most handbooks have sections on grammar, usage, computers, footnoting, and other writing considerations. If a student possesses the motivation and knowledge to use such a handbook, it can be a great resource.

Here is a brief checklist that can help determine if an essay is ready to be handed in.

THE WRITER'S CHECKLIST

___ Essay has a title.
___ Writer's name is included on all the pages.
___ Spelling has been checked.
___ Footnotes are in proper form as determined by instructor.
___ Sentence structure has been checked, especially for fragments, run-on sentences, and comma splices (to obtain definitions of these terms, consult a handbook, or see instructor or Writing Center tutor).
___ Essay has been typed or completed on a word processor.
___ Pages are numbered.
___ Print is double-spaced with one-inch margins around all four borders.
___ Essay has been read carefully by a Writing Center tutor or some other informed and attentive reader.
___ Essay has been read carefully by the author at least one day after "finishing" it.
___ Quotation marks, semicolons, and colons are used properly and consistently (again, consult a handbook, or see instructor or Writing Center tutor).
___ Essay includes sufficient supporting material, such as quotations, examples, and narrative summaries.

A Note About Using Computers
for Writing and Research

Another important resource is a computer. Students who know keyboarding and are familiar with word processing programs (such as Word or WordPerfect) have a strong advantage over those students who use less versatile technologies. Word processors allow writers to produce words relatively quickly and then revise them more easily. What with the "copy" and "cut and paste" functions on a computer, basic revision becomes easy, as long as the writer has a good sense of the essay's structure, purpose, and overall organization. A good word processing program can make a lot of editing easy, from spell-checking to formatting headers, footnotes, and page numbers.

Any writer who uses a computer to write an essay must *BACK THAT ESSAY UP CONTINUOUSLY* on a floppy disk during the entire writing process; too many tragedies occur when computers stall or otherwise eat up hours of work. Few events are more frustrating to a writer, especially one under deadline, than to write three or four effective paragraphs and then suddenly find that the computer has stalled or that the word processing program has crashed. The only remedy is to SAVE the writing to a floppy disk continuously during composing.

Once an essay is on disk, a good word processing program can make a lot of work easier, such as:

- adding and deleting sentences, paragraphs, ideas
- moving words and whole passages for improved focus and clarity
- revising passages until they are focused and coherent
- checking spelling (but be careful of misused words that are spelled correctly)
- making final copy look more presentable by formatting an essay in terms of margins, spacing, typeface, and related elements.
- printing out rough drafts

Most writers who use computers agree that essays in progress should not just exist in virtual space, on screen. For one thing, a computer screen can hold only a small portion of the essay, even if it is single-spaced, making it hard to see how the different parts of the essay connect with one another. For another, many writers have a difficult time seeing errors or lapses on screen; somehow, the monitor display makes all writing look professionally presentable. Thus most writers find that they have to print out successive drafts of their essays; indeed, some of them revise the essay on paper the old-fashioned way, with pen, pencil, or scissors and paste, and then translate those revisions to the text via computer. Whatever revision method a writer chooses, printing drafts of the essay on paper is almost always a good idea.

Engaging in research on the World Wide Web via computer is much less beneficial, at least as of this writing, but it can be fun and it offers a dazzling array of images, texts, ideas, opinions, and information. To view material on the Web, users have to use a browser, the two chief competitors being Netscape's Navigator and Microsoft's Internet Explorer. The term "browser" is perfect for what these software programs do: They allow users to browse through an extraordinary array of verbal, audio, and visual presentations, from restaurant reviews and music CD catalogs to mapping programs and hobbyist bulletin boards. The materials available through the Web are seemingly infinite, but most of them are aimed toward the casual and commercial user.

The Web is much less useful to the student engaged in specific and narrow research on an author. Few long textual works have been scanned electronically, although there are sites that allow a user to access some classic works of literature, as well as dictionaries, thesauruses, handbooks, and the like. If a reader is looking for scholarly articles, however, the first and best resource is still the library. The library's electronic databases, including the Wilson Periodical Index, the PMLA Index, ERIC, and the Humanities Index, to name just a few, are extraordinarily rich electronic treasure-troves.

Starting one's research with the computer by accessing either library databases, the Internet, or the Web is an excellent way to initiate a project. Using search engines and search commands, a writer can build a useful bibliography of names, articles, and periodicals; the next step is to make use of the library stacks and spend some time reading the scholarship the old-fashioned way, in books, magazines, and journals. The mode of doing scholarship may change, but it is unlikely that the print medium will be replaced by the digitized computer file, if only because it is easier both to read longer texts on paper and to write marginal notes about them. The other great advantage that books have is that they are not battery operated and do not have to be plugged in, a real plus when on the bus or at the beach.

REFERENCE AND CITATION

One of the most frustrating moments in writing a research essay is discovering that you cannot find where a crucial quotation comes from. Almost always, it seems, that quotation is the I-beam on which the entire essay hangs, and no matter where you look, it has totally disappeared from sight. You vaguely remember that it came from an article but that's all, and now you need to know author, title, periodical, year and date of publication, and page number. So you spend an hour searching desperately through books, note cards, legal pads, computer files, bookshelves, desktops, briefcases, and wastebaskets while methodically beating your head against the nearest hard object.

There is no surefire way to prevent this from happening, other than careful researching. Each time you find a quotation or important item of source material, write it down, including essential information such as author, title, and page number; that way, you will almost always be able to find it again if you need to cite it. Thus every note card or piece of paper with a quotation should have a brief reference on it indicating where it came from. In addition, using either a copying machine, a word processor, or the old-fashioned pen and paper method, make sure you have all the necessary bibliographic material that you need to write a "Works Cited" page, something that I will discuss shortly. This means creating a separate file or folder where you keep full bibliographic information on all your sources. Researched essays require students to perform three related actions: to quote sources, to provide appropriate references for those sources, and then to indicate on a Works Cited page where those quotations can be found. Let's take these steps in order.

Quoting Sources

Whenever you are indebted to an author for a specific quotation, specific information, or a particular insight or idea, it is necessary to give that author credit through quotation and citation. This means that you have to know the difference between the knowledge gained through research and "common knowledge," which is what most people are expected to know. For example, if you were writing an essay about Amy Tan and you indicted that she is a popular contemporary author, such a statement would not need to be footnoted since it is common knowledge. If, however, you stated that she was born in 1952 in Oakland, California, and that both her parents are from China, you would need to indicate that you learned that information from, say, *Contemporary Authors*, since it is not general knowledge. Deciding what information you need to reference and what is common knowledge is a judgment call, one that your instructor can help you to determine. Remember, however, that if you are deeply indebted to an author for information or an interpretation, you need to state that in a footnote or a parenthetical citation.

The two primary ways of quoting material are through direct quotation and paraphrase. Direct quotation consists of putting specific words, phrases, or sentences within quotation marks followed by a parenthetical citation. For example:

In her autobiographical talk-story "White Tigers," Maxine Hong Kingston writes:

"My American life has been such a disappointment" (45).

Note that the quotation from Kingston's essay/story appears in quotation marks and that it is followed by a parenthetical page citation so that the reader can turn to p. 45 in the cited book and find the quotation. The particular edition from which this quotation is taken will appear on the Works Cited page that appears at the end of every research essay. Whenever directly quoting an author or work, this kind of format is needed.

Indirect quotation is a bit trickier, in that it requires writers to decide whether the passage or idea that they are using is derived from a specific text or is common knowledge. If the idea or information is derived from a specific text, then it needs to be cited. For example:

Many of us attribute great and even mystical powers to our mothers. This is certainly the case with Maxine Hong Kingston who endows her mother with supernatural powers within a world of ghosts and dark spirits as illustrated in "Shaman" (The Woman Warrior, 57-109).

Even though the writer is not quoting directly from the book, this statement is derived from a reading of Kingston's story "Shaman," and therefore a citation is required. Whether the writer paraphrases an interpretation, summarizes the writer's life, or condenses several articles into a two- or three-sentence review, if the idea derives from a book or article, parenthetical citation is required.

Using Footnotes and Parenthetical Citation

Many of the newer word processors have a footnote feature which will organize, number, and format your footnotes. This is a useful aid, especially since footnotes are often hard to format. Unfortunately, many contemporary research essays (at least in English classes) do not require formal footnoting. About the only occasion when students are required to use them is if they need to comment on a statement or source and do not wish to put that comment in the main body of the essay, or if the essay is quoting from just one source and thus it is easier to cite it in a footnote than an entire page at the end of the essay. Check with your instructor to see if footnoting will be required.

The more common form of citation used today is parenthetical; that is, the citation is inserted between two parentheses as demonstrated in the quotations from *The Woman Warrior*. Parenthetical citation is advocated by the Modern Language Association, since it is efficient for both writers and readers. Footnotes drag a reader's eye down to the bottom of the page and break the flow of the text; parenthetical citations maintain the flow of the essay while providing necessary information about sources, page numbers, and research. Moreover, it is much easier for writers to use parenthetical citation since they do not have to worry about numbering their references in sequence and fitting them onto the page.

Parenthetical citation is formatted in slightly different ways, depending on whether the quotation appears within your sentence or as a block that is separated from your own writing. Note the differences below:

> One of the more important genres that have recently received critical and popular attention are the narratives of slaves. One of the earliest and most influential collections of those narratives is The Classic Slave Narratives edited by Henry Louis Gates. Gates makes a good case for why these texts were created:
>
> > The black slave narrators sought to indict both those who enslaved them and the metaphysical system drawn upon to justify their enslavement. They did so using the most enduring weapon at their disposal, the printing press. (ix)
>
> Thus what we can see in the narratives is an account of the life they led as slaves, an account which by virtue of its own telling condemns the system of values that supports slavery for the sake of economic gain.

Note certain key conventions: Because the quotation is two or more sentences long, it gets set off in a block. Because it is set off, it does not need quotation marks around it. The page from which the quotation is taken appears at the very end within parentheses, after any end punctuation.

Here is a different version of the same student essay. In this case, the author is using only a part of the Gates quotation and is thus using internal parenthetical citation. It is called "internal" because the citation occurs within the student's own sentences:

> One of the more important genres that have recently received critical and popular attention are the narratives of slaves. One of the earliest and most influential

collections of those narratives is <u>The Classic Slave Narratives</u> edited by Henry Louis Gates. Gates makes a good case for why these texts were created, since he believes that the authors "sought to indict both those who enslaved them and the metaphysical system drawn upon to justify their enslavement" (ix). By that Gates means that what we can see in the narratives is an account of the life they led as slaves, an account which by virtue of its own telling condemns the system of values that supports slavery for the sake of economic gain.

Note the differences: Here the quotation is short, being less than a full sentence; thus it can be easily integrated into the student author's own paragraph. The page number still is cited, but now—since the citation occurs within the student's own sentence, it must be followed by a period since it ends a sentence.

Here is one more example of internal parenthetical citation:

In his Introduction to <u>The Classic Slave Narratives</u>, Henry Louis Gates writes that the slaves wanted to be "free and literate" (ix) and that is why they told their powerful and terrible stories. I agree, but only in part: I think we have to be equally aware that the slaves told these stories as a profound way of coming to terms with an experience that virtually defies language.

This internal parenthetical citation immediately follows the quotation it references, and no punctuation marks surround it since they would interfere with the grammar of the sentence.

Internal parenthetical citation provides necessary reference information with as little obstruction as possible. Thus it does not include abbreviations such as "p." for page or "2nd ed." for second edition; all the necessary bibliographic information goes onto the Works Cited page so that the reader can locate your sources. If you are citing a poem, your instructor will likely want your parenthetical reference to include line numbers; if citing a play, you will need to include act, scene, and line so that your instructor can find the quotation easily. Such inclusions follow the rule of thumb for parenthetical references: Include only the information a reader will need to find the quotation easily, neither more nor less.

Providing Full References: The Works Cited Page

Once you have filled in all the appropriate parenthetical citations, it is time to complete the project by writing a "Works Cited" page. Just as its name suggests, the Works Cited page is a bibliographic list that allows the reader to track down the specific books, articles, magazines, films, and other resources you cite in your essay.

No short guide can provide a complete list of proper forms; indeed, the Modern Language Association, to name just one such group, publishes an entire book devoted to forms and formats for references and bibliographies (see Joseph Gibaldi and Walter S. Achtert, *MLA Handbook for Writers of Research Papers*, 4th ed. [New York: MLA, 1995]). What I will include here is a brief listing of the more common forms for books, articles, periodicals, short works of literature, film, TV, and news-papers. These forms should provide proper formatting for most of the research sources that you will use.

Titles on the "Works Cited" page should be arranged alphabetically according to the first initial of the author's or editor's last name. You need only include the texts you actually cite; if for some reason you want to include every book or article that you read while researching your essay, even if you did not use all of them, title your page "List of Works Consulted," but first check with your instructor. You can use the model entries in the pages that follow to put your entries in the correct format. The entries do not correspond to real authors or real books or articles (for the most part), but the form (and explanations) should prove useful.

One last suggestion: even when an essay has proper references and a full "Works Cited" page, it is often helpful to the reader if the author opens with an Acknowledgments page. You can find a model in many scholarly books: the author begins her book by thanking those people who have helped in the formation of ideas, the reading of drafts, the revision of sentences. If your instructor allows it, writing an Acknowledgments page that leads off your essay can help establish the context for the essay that you have produced, and it is an excellent way of saying thank you to those students, staff members, and faculty who have helped you pro-duce it, from conception to final draft.

SAMPLE CITATIONS FOR "WORKS CITED" FROM AN ESSAY ON LITERATURE AND CULTURE

A single book by a single author:

Auteur, Robin. Literature and Culture. New York: Knopf, 1997.

Note the order: author's name (last name first); then the title of the book, under-lined, except for the final period. Then the place of publication, followed by a colon (if the city is not well known, include the state abbreviation as well. If the title page lists several cities, give only the first, as in Portsmouth, N.H. or Fargo, N.D.). Then the name of the publisher, followed by a comma. And then the year of publication.

A single book by two or more authors:

Auteur, Robin, and Chang Lee. Literature and Culture. Columbus, Ohio: Ohio State

UP, 1949.

The first author appears with last name first, then the second author follows with first name first. If the book has more than three authors, give the name of the first author only (last name first) and follow it with "et al." (Latin for "and others"). The phrase "University Press" is abbreviated as "UP" for the sake of efficiency.

A book in several volumes:

Auteur, Robin, et al., eds. Literature and Culture. 4th ed. 3 vols. Chicago: Gilead UP,

1998.

Note that "eds." here means "editors" and not "edited by." The abbreviation "eds." always means "editors," whereas "ed." can mean either "editor" or "edited by," depending on its context.

Auteur, Robin. <u>Literature and Culture</u>. 11 vols. Ed. Chang Lee. Columbia, S.C.:

Wellman, 1955.

You will need to indicate the total number of volumes after the title. If you have used more than one volume, you can indicate which one as follows: (3:30), which means you are referring to page 30 of volume 3. If you have used only one volume of a multivolume work, in your entry in Works Cited indicate the volume number right after the period following the date, i.e., "Wellman, 1955. Vol. 2." You need only include the page reference in your parenthetical citations since readers will know all examples come from volume 2 when they consult the Works Cited page.

A book with a separate title in a set of volumes:

Auteur, Robin. <u>Literature and Culture</u>. Vol. 1 of <u>Encyclopedia of Literature and</u>

<u>Culture</u>. New York: Balloon, 1994.

Auteur, Robin. <u>Literature and Culture</u>. Ed. Chang Lee. Vol. 113 of <u>The Literature and</u>

<u>Culture Reader</u>. Princeton: Princeton UP, 1988.

A revised edition of a book:

Auteur, Robin. <u>Literature and Culture</u>. Rev. ed. Hamburg, Germany: Berlin UP, 1974.

Auteur, Robin. <u>Literature and Culture</u>. Ed. Chang Lee. 5th ed. Norfolk: Harcourt, 1997.

A reprint of an earlier edition:

Auteur, Robin. <u>Literature and Culture</u>. 1911. Ellis, Iowa: Central UP, 1993.

Note that the author is citing the original date (1911) but indicates that the writer is using the Iowa Central University Press reprint published in 1993.

An edited book other than an anthology:

Auteur, Robin. <u>Literature and Culture</u>. Ed. Chang Lee. 4 vols. Cambridge, MA:

Harvard UP, 1969.

An anthology:

<u>Literature and Culture</u>. Ed. Robin Auteur. 12 vols. Monrovia, Louisiana: Literature and

Culture Books, 1918.

Or:

Auteur, Robin, ed. <u>Literature and Culture</u>. 12 vols. Monrovia, Louisiana: Literature and

Culture Books, 1918.

Note that you have two choices: You can list it either by title or by editor.

A work by one author in a multivolume anthology:

Auteur, Robin. "Critical Studies." Literature and Culture. Ed. Chang Lee. 5th ed. 3

vols. New York: Farrar, 1997. 3:145-98.

This entry indicates that you are citing Auteur's essay, entitled "Critical Studies," which appears in volume 3 of a five-volume anthology entitled Literature and Culture, edited by Chang Lee. Note that the page numbers of Auteur's complete essay are cited.

A work in an anthology that includes a number of authors:

Auteur, Robin. "Critical Studies." Literature and Culture. Ed. Chang Lee. Fargo, N.D.:

Houghton, 1888. 243-76.

Start by listing the author and the title of the work you are citing, not the title of the anthology or the name of the editor. The entry ends by citing the pages of the selection you are citing. Note that the title of the short work you are citing is in quotation marks; if it is a long work (book length), the title is underlined. If the work is translated, after the period that follows the title, write "Trans." and give the name of the translator, followed by a period and then the name of the anthology.

Citing other works in the same anthology:

Auteur, Robin. Literature and Culture. Lee 301-46.

To avoid repetition, under each author's name (in the appropriate alphabetical order), list the author, the title of the work, then a period, one space, and the name of the editor of the anthology, followed by the page numbers for the selection.

Two or more works by the same author:

Auteur, Robin. Critical Studies. Boulder, Colo.: U of Harriman P, 1948.

—— Literature and Culture. Seattle: Jacob H. Library, 1955.

Note that the works are given in alphabetical order on the Works Cited page, so that *Critical Studies* comes before *Literature and Culture.* In the second listing, the author's name is represented by three dashes followed by a period. If the author is the translator or editor of a volume, the three dashes are followed by a comma, then a space, then the appropriate abbreviation (trans. or ed.), then (one space after the period) the title.

The Bible:

The HarperCollins Study Bible. Wayne A. Meeks, Gen. ed. New York: HarperCollins,

1989.

Note: If using the King James version, do not list the Bible in your Works Cited page, since it is familiar and available. In your essay, cite chapter and verse parenthetically as follows: (Isaiah 52.7-12 or Gen. 19.1-11).

A translated book:

Auteur, Robin. <u>Literature and Culture</u>. Trans. Chang Lee. New York: Culture Studies
Press, 1990.

Note that "Trans." can mean "translated by" (just as "ed." can mean "edited by"). It
is also the abbreviation for "translator."

An introduction, foreword, afterword, or other editorial apparatus:

Auteur, Robin. Introduction. <u>Literature and Culture</u>. By Chang Lee. New York:
Epicurean, 1990, vii-x.

Use this form if you are specifically referring to the Introduction, Foreword,
Afterword, etc. Otherwise, list the work under the name of the book's author. Words
such as *Preface, Introduction, Afterword,* and *Conclusion* are capitalized in the entry
but are neither enclosed within quotation marks nor underlined.

A book review:

Auteur, Robin. Rev. of <u>Literature and Culture</u>. Ed. Chang Lee. <u>Critical Studies</u> 104
(1991): 1-48.

This is a citation for a review of a book entitled *Literature and Culture.* The review,
which does not have a title, was published in a journal entitled *Critical Studies.*

Auteur, Robin. "One Writer's View." Rev. of <u>Literature and Culture</u>. Ed. Chang Lee.
<u>Critical Studies</u> 104 (1991): 1-48.

This is a citation for a review which has a title.

"One Writer's View." Rev. of <u>Literature and Culture</u>. Ed. Chang Lee. <u>Critical Studies</u>
104 (1991): 1-48.

This is an anonymous review of *Literature and Culture.* Place it on your "Works
Cited" page under the first word of the review's title; if the review lacks a title, begin
your entry with "Rev. of" and then alphabetize it under the title of the work being
reviewed.

An encyclopedia:

Auteur, Robin. "Literature and Culture." <u>Encyclopaedia Britannica</u>. 1984 ed.

This is how you cite a signed article; note that the article is from the 1984 edition
of the *Encyclopaedia.*

"Literature and Culture." <u>Encyclopaedia Britannica</u>. 1984 ed.

This is how you would cite the same article if it were unsigned.

An article in a scholarly journal that numbers its pages consecutively from one issue to the other through the year:

Auteur, Robin. "Literature and Culture." Critical Studies 33 (1992): 231-59.

Auteur's article appeared in the journal, *Critical Studies*, in 1992; the volume number was 33 and it appeared on pages 231 through 259. Even though each of the four volumes of *Critical Studies* published in 1992 has a separate number, you do not need to indicate the volume number since the pages are numbered continuously throughout the year.

An article in a scholarly journal that begins each issue during the year with page one:

Auteur, Robin. "Literature and Culture." Critical Studies 12.2 (1993): 9-21.

Note that you now must provide the volume number followed by a period and then the issue number, with no spaces in between.

An article in a weekly, biweekly, or monthly publication:

Auteur, Robin. "Literature and Culture." Critical Studies 30 Mar. 1945: 1-12.

If you are citing from a very well known weekly, such as *Newsweek* or *The New Yorker*, you can omit the volume and issue numbers.

An article in a newspaper:

Auteur, Robin. "Literature and Culture." Critical Studies Times 17 Mar. 1947, sec. 6:

9+.

Because newspapers often have a number of sections, you should include a section number before the page number so that your reader can find the article easily. Auteur's article begins on page 9 of section 6 and continues on to a later page.

A personal interview:

Lee, Chang. Personal interview. 26 Apr. 1974.

Auteur, Robin. Telephone interview. 14 Feb. 1983.

Note that the interviews are *with* Chang Lee and Robin Auteur, not *by* Chang Lee or Robin Auteur.

A lecture:

Lee, Chang. "Literature and Culture." University of Wisconsin-Milwaukee. 31 Oct.

1995.

A television or radio program:

Literature and Culture. Public Television, Charlotte, N.C. 3 Feb. 1996.

A film or videotape:

<u>Literature and Culture</u>. Dir. Chang Lee. MGM, 1948.

A recording:

Auteur, Robin. "Literature and Culture." <u>Chang Lee Reads Personal Favorites from</u>

<u>Around the World</u>. Harmony, HAR 4853C, 1988.

A performance:

<u>Literature</u>. By Chang Lee. Dir. Robin Auteur. Urban Theatre of the Arts, Urban,

Wisconsin. 4 July 1912.

A file from the World Wide Web:

Auteur, Robin. "Literature and Culture." <u>Critical Studies</u>. http://www.litcult.wor

.vvv.ecp.tlc/text/rmudts/ittip.html (18 May 1995).

Note that the citation includes the author's name (if available), the name of the article, the name (underlined) of the entire text from which the article was taken (if
available), the URL (Uniform Resource Locator), followed immediately by the date
that you visited the site.

At this point, you may have decided that you have had enough of citations. If the
particular form you are looking for does not appear in this list, consult the *MLA
Handbook for Writers of Research Papers* or some other more extensive reference
book. The basic principle of citation is that you should be absolutely clear about
essential research information in the most concise format possible.

FINAL WORDS

Much more could be said about writing essays about literature and culture, but perhaps the most important goal for such essays is that they provide a sense of satisfaction to both the writer and the reader. Writing an essay invites analysis, research,
discovery, and satisfaction. The exciting and provocative reading selections in this
book create many possible topics to engage writers on the voyage ahead.

CHARLES I. SCHUSTER

CREDITS

INDEX OF AUTHORS AND TITLES